WOMEN OF COVENANT

WOMEN OF COVENANT

THE STORY OF
RELIEF SOCIETY

Jill Mulvay Derr
Janath Russell Cannon
Maureen Ursenbach Beecher

Deseret Book Company
Salt Lake City, Utah

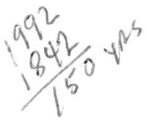

Library of Congress Cataloging-in-Publication Data

Derr, Jill Mulvay.
    Women of covenant : the story of Relief Society / Jill Mulvay
Derr, Janath Russell Cannon, Maureen Ursenbach Beecher.
       p. cm.
    Includes bibliographical references and index.
    ISBN 0-87579-593-5
    1. Relief Society (Church of Jesus Christ of Latter-day Saints)
I. Cannon, Janath Russell. II. Beecher, Maureen Ursenbach.
III. Title.
BX8643.R38D47 1992
267'.449332 – dc20   91-47981
                                                    CIP

Contents

PART TWO: SACRED TRUSTS

FOREWORD

It is fitting that the history of Relief Society is being published during the society's sesquicentennial year. The founding of the women's organization of The Church of Jesus Christ of Latter-day Saints, celebrated by a membership of over three million women in 135 countries and territories, is cause for both rejoicing and reflection. The events of Relief Society's 150 years inspire us and make us aware of the level of faith and accomplishment of our sisters past.

It is through these accomplishments of the pioneers of Relief Society, the founding sisters both in Nauvoo and throughout the world, that we see the embodiment of testimony and fortitude. Surpassing tremendous obstacles, women endured and prospered, sustained by their covenants with the Lord and their unique sisterhood.

The sisters, although imperfect by their own admission, understood much of what it means to be a daughter of God and to work together in his name. Through the works of women, done under the auspices of Relief Society, we learn about the core gospel principles of charity, integrity, hard work, education, loyalty, and sisterhood.

We also learn that the women of Relief Society were intrepid and worthy of emulation. Our sisters made "charity never faileth" more than an organizational motto; they made it the personal motto by which they lived. The charitable works of Latter-day Saint women demonstrate their confidence in the Lord and their sure witness of the promised blessings of eternity. The sisters relished the comfort that came from their eternal vision, even when the comforts of life were denied.

Newly created homes contained essentials only, and often missionary husbands were absent. Women raised children, relying on support from other women. Life for the sisters of Zion brought many problems—personal and organizational. It was, after all, no small task to build a sisterhood or a family. Still, the history of Relief Society is one that testifies that close relationships with the Lord, with family, with sisters, and with priesthood leaders make life worthwhile despite the personal and organizational challenges.

The remarkable stories and accomplishments of Relief Society members benefit from the authors of this work. Excellent historians all, Janath, Jill, and Maureen have lived with this history over years. The authors embody the best of Latter-day Saint womanhood and bring to this work their insights, compassion and skills. This volume, the fruit of long labor, is rich.

As we celebrate the history of Relief Society, we rejoice in a sisterhood with women who love the Lord and show that love through charitable acts toward their brothers and sisters. We reflect upon the goodness of women.

Watching Relief Society grow in new lands, we know that wherever the Church is, Relief Society will be, and our history will be enriched through new generations of righteous women who will join together. Proclaiming their belief through their lives of charity, they will build personal testimony, bless each other, develop and exercise charity, strengthen families, and enjoy sisterhood.

So it is with the daughters of God, and because it is, we celebrate Relief Society.

ELAINE L. JACK

PREFACE

This history is a work of scholarship and love, presented with gladness during the sesquicentennial year of the Relief Society of The Church of Jesus Christ of Latter-day Saints. It is the story of the women of the Church and the sacred promises that bind them to God and to the community of his saints. It is a record of women's unique stewardship within that community as members of Relief Society.

Every Latter-day Saint woman is a woman of covenant. Each at baptism entered into a covenant with Jesus Christ, promising to serve him and keep his commandments, and each subsequently received the gift of the Holy Ghost as companion and guide. An ever-increasing number of sisters have augmented these covenants in holy temples. Latter-day Saints, men and women, enter such vital covenants through divinely revealed ordinances performed by the authority of the holy priesthood of the Lord Jesus Christ. These sacred rituals signal the covenant or "coming together" of God and his daughters and sons, God promising great blessings to those who honor their promises to him.

The story of Relief Society has been shaped by such covenants, promises that not only bind men and women to God but also bring them together as brothers and sisters in "the fold of God," the Church, so they can "look forward with one eye, having one faith and one baptism, having their hearts knit together in unity and in love one towards another." (Mosiah 18:21.) The holy priesthood restored through the Prophet Joseph Smith is the Lord's instrument for bringing his saints into this "unity of the faith," that as they become one, he might claim them as his own and dwell among them. (Ephesians 4:13; D&C 38:27; D&C 104:59.)

The story of the women of Relief Society is tightly interwoven with the story of men called and ordained to offices in the priesthood. Since its founding by the Prophet Joseph Smith in 1842, the Relief Society has been counterpart, companion, and complement to the priesthood quorums. Like the men's quorums, the Relief Society has worked in connection with and under the direction of the presiding authorities of the Melchizedek Priesthood, which "has power and authority over all the offices in the church in all ages of the world, to administer in spiritual things." (D&C 107:8.) United under priesthood direction, Latter-day Saint women and men further the Lord's work of exaltation for all of his children.

The Relief Society has played an essential role in that work; its members have ministered graciously and creatively to the temporal and spiritual welfare of those within and outside the Latter-day Saint fold. Indeed, Relief Society's efforts to forward the kingdom of God on the earth have resulted in significant political, economic, education, and social achievements, an impressive and important part of the society's many-faceted past. Programs and responsibilities in these areas have changed dramatically over time, influenced by changing circumstances in the Church and in the world at large. The remarkable flexibility of the Relief Society in temporal matters and its responsiveness to the needs of a given time have been possible because of firm grounding in its central spiritual purpose, "to save souls."

Holy women aren't perfect

This is not the story of perfect women, but it is nonetheless the story of "holy women," as spoken of by ancient apostles Peter and Paul. Relief Society sisters have tried, erred, repented, rebelled, accepted, adapted, felt pain, and known joy. This is their story, the story of imperfect Saints seeking holiness, changing responsibilities, and eternal covenants, the story of Relief Society, the legacy of sisters worldwide.

This is history written from the inside. All three of its authors freely acknowledge their faith in and adherence to the gospel of Jesus Christ as taught in The Church of Jesus Christ of Latter-day Saints. All three are enthusiastic Relief Society workers; one has been teacher and counselor, one has been ward president, and one has served as counselor to the general president.

The genesis of the book is interwoven into the whole fabric of Church growth and expansion. When in 1978 the revelation making the priesthood available to all worthy male members was received, a barrier to Church growth was removed. The Church, and with it Relief Society, would find place worldwide as never before. It was in Africa, at that auspicious period, that the first discussion of this history took place between Relief Society President Barbara B. Smith and former counselor Janath R. Cannon, both delegates to a 1979 triennial conference of the International Council of Women in Nairobi. Later that year, the Relief Society presidency formally asked Sister Cannon and Jill Mulvay Derr, a published historian, to undertake the research and writing of the history.

During the next decade the work progressed. As the anticipated sesquicentennial of Relief Society approached, both authors were in Europe, Janath as matron of the Frankfurt Temple, Jill with her professor husband in Switzerland. At their request Maureen Ursenbach Beecher, affiliate with the Joseph Fielding Smith Institute for Church History, became the stateside anchor, working near the book's sources to finish the research, draft remaining chapters, and begin weaving the whole into one piece. Jill came back to Utah for the final shaping and revision, and Janath reviewed the whole by mail or fax.

Differences in age, experience, and point of view are reflected in the work of the authors. The initial division of labor according to two historical periods, 1830 to 1921 and 1921 to the present, is reflected in the book's two parts — part one, "Sacred Patterns," and part two, "Charity Never Faileth" — each of which carries the marks of its original author. Janath, from her position of participant observer, saw the twentieth century Relief Society with an understanding that came from her responsibilities on the general board and in the general presidency. The chapters in part two are enhanced in style and content by the immediacy and intimacy of her involvement there. Jill and Maureen, younger to Relief Society work, brought to the study years of research in church and women's history. They wrote part one from a greater distance, albeit with no less affection. At each stage all three reviewed and amended each other's works in the hope that the whole would be greater than the sum of its parts.

In libraries and archives the authors plied the tools of the historian, winnowing through masses of material for the kernels of truth that could best tell the story. What was wheat, and what chaff, was not always apparent nor mutually agreed upon. Rather than erase our occasional variations in interpretation, we have chosen to let them stand witness to changes over time against backdrop of common commitments. Resolving our differences did not mean dissolving them; rather the process led to a cooperative search for the core truths, the deeper verities upon which we all would agree.

This work would not have been possible without the commitment to harmony and unity that has been a significant theme throughout Relief Society's history. As authors we have benefited from the continued support of general Relief Society officers. Since its inception in the mind of President Barbara Smith, the project has been blessed by her successors, Presidents Barbara W. Winder and Elaine L. Jack. Sister Jack has graciously read and insightfully responded to drafts of the manuscript in counsel with the First Presidency through members of the Quorum of Twelve Apostles and the Quorum of Seventy. Final completion of this history at this time and in this form would not have been possible without her loving support and without the assistance of these priesthood leaders. They reviewed the manuscript with care and respect and provided wise counsel, that Relief Society and priesthood leaders might all "speak the same thing . . . [and] be perfectly joined together in the same mind." (1 Corinthians 1:10.)

We appreciate Sister Jack's foreword and are grateful to her administrative assistant, Carol L. Clark, for writing the chapter dealing with 1990 to the present, "Roots and the Vision." Other members of the Relief Society staff, particularly Anna Christensen Cates, Helen Pehrson, and Nadine Knight, have provided hours of assistance.

Colleagues in the Joseph Fielding Smith Institute for Church History at Brigham Young University have proven invaluable. Carol Cornwall Madsen provided trustworthy historical background; her studies have extended our reach as well as our grasp. Friend and mentor Leonard J. Arrington made comments and suggestions on the original outline and the unwieldy first draft; he has supported the project from the outset. Ronald K. Esplin, Richard L. Jensen, and Dean C. Jessee helped with specific sections, and Marilyn Rish Parks was invaluable as typist and editorial assistant.

This work also would not have been possible without the thousands of Relief Society leaders and members who have kept careful personal and official records. Relief Society general officers have likewise written and published histories indispensable to this study: Emmeline B. Wells's historical summaries in the *Woman's Exponent*, Susa Young Gates's lengthy history, published in part in the *Relief Society Magazine* but available to researchers, and the general board's *A Centenary of Relief Society* (1942) and *History of Relief*

Society, 1842–1966. As the chapter notes and bibliography indicate, this history has been enriched immeasurably by recent scholarship in Mormon history and women's history.

The Library and Archives of the Historical Department of The Church of Jesus Christ of Latter-day Saints have been the mother lode, the chief source of this history's raw data. All quotations from materials there have been used with permission. The archives and library staff have been helpful beyond their duty, and encouraging when our spirits flagged. Pauline Musig deserves our special thanks.

The informal network of women has come to our aid: friends, sisters, neighbors, visiting teachers have with patience and forbearing provided services too numerous to specify. From typing manuscripts to preparing meals, they have participated in our labors, and we are grateful. Our husbands and children, too, have served; we appreciate their tolerance of our absence and patience at our other-mindedness.

In the manuscript's final stages, the felicity of its prose and the accuracy of its documentation were enhanced by editor Dawn Hall Anderson and by William B. Quist, who checked references. The Smith Institute and the Center for Religious Studies of Brigham Young University provided supportive funding. Amy Browning-Crompton Rossiter and William Slaughter helped find photographs. The design is by Kent Ware.

From its beginning in 1980, Eleanor Knowles of Deseret Book has taken a personal interest in this book. She has proven a gentle and patient midwife whose experienced editorial hands have delivered this creation forth from the authors' unruly manuscripts into a life of its own. We are grateful for her care.

As women of covenant who have been invited to "acknowledge the hand of the Lord in all things," we affirm that we have witnessed his spirit in the lives of the women we have studied and that we ourselves have felt his grace in this work.

Acknowledging as we do assistance from so many quarters, each individual author accepts full responsibility for what she has written. This book presents our own interpretations and is not an official history, nor is it an official statement of Church doctrine and policy. The authors send it forth trusting its readers will receive it with understanding and love and be blessed thereby.

JILL MULVAY DERR
JANATH RUSSELL CANNON
MAUREEN URSENBACH BEECHER

WOMEN OF THE RESTORATION
1830–1842

Meeting together in the Nauvoo Relief Society in 1842, Latter-day Saint women heard the Prophet Joseph Smith make a statement that they and generations of their daughters would not forget: "This Society is to get instruction thro' the order which God has established — thro' the medium of those appointed to lead — and I now turn the key to you in the name of God and this Society shall rejoice and knowledge and intelligence shall flow down from this time."[1] The Prophet's turning of the key to women opened to them new opportunities for service and learning and granted them authority to carry out new responsibilities within The Church of Jesus Christ of Latter-day Saints. It marked, as he predicted, "the beginning of better days" for them and for their organization. Commissioned to save souls and look to the poor and needy, Relief Society women were set apart and empowered to fill that ministry. Unity furthered their work and made them sisters who would "cherish one another, watch over one another, comfort one another," with the hope that they would one day "sit down in heaven together."[2]

The Relief Society has advanced its work from 1842 to the present not as an independent organization but as an integral part of the Church. Following the Church's organization in 1830, Joseph Smith gradually established the priesthood quorums and offices necessary for carrying forward the work of the kingdom of God on earth. In 1842 he organized the Relief Society, an elect body of women, to serve as counterpart and companion to the men's priesthood quorums. In effecting the organization, he appointed women to their first offices in the Church, emphasizing "the necessity of every individual acting in the sphere allotted him or her."[3] The women understood that their new responsibility was a "high and holy calling," and that the Church "was never perfectly organized until the women were thus organized."[4]

As the church organization was perfected in Nauvoo, so were the Church's highest ordinances perfected. Through revelation, and in anticipation of the completion of the temple then being built in Nauvoo, Joseph Smith introduced sacred temple ordinances that endowed women and men with spiritual power and sealed them together in marriage for time and all eternity. Through this "new and everlasting covenant," parents were bound in eternal union with their children. Thus, before his death in Nauvoo, the Prophet clarified important roles for women in both church organization and divine ordinances.

The Relief Society was not the only female benevolent society at the time of its founding. It shared and continues to share with many other women's organizations a concern for charitable work, community work, education, women and children's health, and opportunities for sisterhood. Later, at various times, Relief Society would join with other women's organizations in unitedly advancing common purposes. Notwithstanding these important connections, Relief Society has maintained a sense of separate identity, uniqueness, and sacred mission to be understood only within the context of the "restoration of all things."

The concept of restoration was central to the beliefs of women who became members of the Female Relief Society of Nauvoo, providing them, and all Latter-day Saints, a unique world view. "The understanding and knowledge we have of the scriptures makes *friends* and everything appear in a very different light to me," wrote Elizabeth Haven in 1839.[5] She and others who joined the first Relief Society had already committed themselves to the "preparatory work for the second coming of the Messiah," the glorious work unfolding under the direction of the Prophet Joseph Smith. They had entered into a covenant to serve Christ and, as his saints in latter days, to forward the final gospel dispensation. The organization of Relief Society in 1842 marked the expansion rather than the commencement of this covenant. The eager search for truth, the enlargement of spiritual gifts received, the willing service and sacrifice that characterized women's early church experience would find new expression in their Relief Society organization. Relief Society in its turn would become part of the "restoration of all things," but only in its turn, after early Latter-day Saint women had, like the early Christian women described by the apostle Paul, served faithfully as "fellow laborers" in the nascent church.

"It is necessary in the ushering in of the dispensation of the fullness of times . . . that a whole and complete and perfect union, and welding together of dispensations, and keys, and powers, and glories should take place and be revealed from the days of Adam even to the present time," Joseph Smith wrote in September 1842.[6] Just six months earlier he had declared the importance of Relief Society to that "perfect union." The women's organization, like the temple ordinances, was part of his final work. An understanding of the cosmic importance and extent of the work in which he was involved had been revealed to him "line upon line, precept upon precept" over a twenty-two–year period. It had begun in 1820 with his personal quest, a quest in which thousands more would participate as the Restoration unfolded.

As a youth of fourteen living in Palmyra, New York, Joseph became sensitive to his frailty and began to "mourn for my own sins and for the sins of the world." Concerned, he said, "for the wellfare of my immortal Soul," he searched the scriptures, but in listening to the claims of the clergy of the day he became utterly confused about "who was right and who was wrong." Prompted by a scripture admonishing men to "ask of God," he "cried unto the Lord for mercy for there was none else to whom I could go and obtain mercy and the Lord heard my cry in the wilderness." Through a glorious visitation of God the Father and His Son, Jesus Christ, Joseph received forgiveness of his sins and came to understand that he must join none of the established churches.[7]

Joseph's confusion in this "war of words, and tumult of opinions" was not unique. His mother, Lucy Mack Smith, understood well her son's search for God's assurance and his inquiries about which church to join, for both were part of her own experience. In her history, dictated in 1853, she recalled a time following her sister's death when, steeped in reflection and "anxiety of mind, I determined to obtain that which I had heard spoken of so much from the pulpit—a change of heart."

Lucy's searching for a "change of heart" was to remain part of her life for some time. After her marriage to Joseph Smith Sr. in 1796, she became concerned about her husband's resistance to established religion and knelt in a grove to plead with the Lord that he would be led to the truth. The answer she received brought her peace, though her husband remained aloof from established churches. Her searching continued, and in 1802, when she contracted consumption, which threatened to prove fatal, she "made a solemn covenant with God," she recalled, promising, "if he would let me live, I would endeavour to serve him according to the best of my abilities. Shortly after this, I heard a voice say to me, 'Seek, and ye shall find; knock, and it shall be opened unto you. Let your heart be comforted.' "[8]

After her recovery, Lucy sought the word of God in various churches and finally determined, she said, "that there was not then upon earth the religion which I sought." She studied the Bible and decided to be baptized without affiliating with a church, although a few years later she and three of her children—Hyrum, Samuel, and Sophronia—became members of a Presbyterian congregation.[9] Her search for truth is indicative not only of the feelings that would prompt her son Joseph, but also of the era of religious turmoil in which the Smiths lived.

Post-revolutionary American women and men pondered and experienced religion with an intensity singular in the nation's history. What Joseph Smith termed "an unusual excitement on the subject of religion" was an indication of the new nation's growing religious pluralism. Even before adoption of the 1787 constitution with its promise of religious freedom, an American Reformation was underway and several distinct new religious communities were formed. Revivalism swept the northeastern United States in a series of waves known as the Second Great Awakening, starting in 1797 and peaking between 1825 and 1837.[10] It affected not only upstate New York, but all of New England, as well as the southern back country where Baptists and Methodists had kept alive the enthusiasm of the earlier Great Awakening (1740–1743).

New emphasis not on doctrine or sacraments but on personal religious experience and renewed consciousness of God's absolute sovereignty and Christ's atoning love compelled large numbers of people, like Lucy Smith, to seek a change of heart. Raising such core Christian concerns as salvation, the millennial reign of Christ, and ongoing revelation from God, at first the Second Great Awakening spurred cooperation and seemed to promise long-awaited Christian harmony. As increasing competitiveness bred intense sectarian conflict, many devout Christians turned away from established churches, seeking instead the primitive Christian church described in the New Testament.[11]

"He Speaks of Things Before Untold"

Many of the first members of Relief Society recalled having asked the same religious questions as Joseph Smith. Born and raised in Pennsylvania, Desdemona Wadsworth Fullmer "praied much in secret alone to Lord" and finally "reseive[d] a change of hart." She wrote that she then "began to read the Bible much and all the difernt creeds of the churches to know what people I shuld joine."[12]

To her pleas for forgiveness, New Englander Sarah Studevant Leavitt received what she termed "an answer of peace and a promise that I should be saved in the kingdom of God." She continued seeking, "looking forward to a time when the knowledge of God would cover the earth."[13]

In Tennessee, fourteen-year-old Drusilla Dorris, a serious student of the Bible, listened to revival teaching and concluded, as had Joseph Smith and his mother, "that none of the Churches had the gospel as taught in the New Testament." It seemed strange to her "that no one was doing as the Bible told them."[14]

Elizabeth Ann Whitney recalled her quest in Ohio as a Campbellite, or Disciple of Christ, "to know how to obtain the spirit and the gifts bestowed upon the ancient saints."[15]

Eliza R. Snow, another Campbellite seeker, remembered having wished to "see, and listen to a true Prophet of God, through whom He communicated His will to the children of men. But, alas!" she recalled, "that day and those blessings had forever gone by! So said the clergy of my own time, and the clergy professed to know."[16] In a poem published in 1829, six years before her conversion, she anticipated a "shining seraph," the "voice of sacred Truth," bringing "immortal triumphs" and unending social joys to replace the transitory pleasures of earth:

> He speaks of things before untold,
> Reveals what men nor angels knew,
> The secret pages now unfold
> To human view.[17]

There is no indication that the young Joseph Smith anticipated the visit of an angel or the unfolding of "secret pages," but he received both. Beginning in 1823, three years after his first vision of the Father and the Son, he was visited on several occasions by Moroni, "a messenger sent from the presence of God." Moroni delivered to the young man a sacred text, the Book of Mormon in its original language. The heavenly guidance Joseph received in translating the book did not eliminate his need for earthly assistance. His immediate family—his mother and father and eight sisters and brothers—readily accepted his prophetic calling and supported him. So did his wife, Emma, and a handful of close friends. Emma Hale Smith, born in 1804 as the seventh of nine children of a Harmony, Pennsylvania, couple, would be at the Prophet's side or attending to his affairs through the rest of his ministry. "I have never seen a woman in my life," her mother-in-law would later write, "who would endure every species of fatigue and hardship, from month to month, and from year to year, with that unflinching courage, zeal, and patience, which she has ever done."[18]

On September 21, 1827, nine months after her marriage, tall, dark-haired, dark-eyed Emma accompanied Joseph to the Hill Cumorah and sat nearby in a borrowed wagon as the Angel Moroni delivered to him the golden plates he would soon begin to translate. Tension in the Palmyra area over Joseph and his "gold bible" made it impossible for him to pursue the work of translation there, so in December 1827 Emma and Joseph moved southeast to Harmony, a three-day journey. There they negotiated to buy a small farm near the home of Emma's parents, Isaac and Elizabeth Hale, and began translating the Book of Mormon. Emma, a former schoolteacher, served as scribe along with her brother Reuben. Joseph "would dictate to me for hour after hour," she later recalled, affirming that "no man could have dictated the writing of the manuscripts unless he was inspired."[19] Though she did not actually see the plates, Emma did not doubt their existence or her husband's divine gift to translate. Her father was skeptical but tolerant, promising to protect his daughter and her husband from slander or violence.

At Harmony during 1828, their second year of marriage, Emma and Joseph suffered two devastating losses. In June their firstborn son died a few hours after he was born, and Emma lay near death for several days. Then, as her health improved after a fortnight, Joseph was informed that Martin Harris, who had lent financial support to the Book of Mormon translation, had lost the first 116 pages of the precious manuscript Joseph had entrusted to him. Though pained beyond any sorrow either had yet known, the young couple endured the losses and Joseph was assured by revelation that the works, designs, and purposes of God "cannot be frustrated, neither can they come to naught."[20] During 1829, with the help of a full-time scribe, Oliver Cowdery, and new quarters for the work of translation at the home of Peter and Mary Whitmer, he completed the Book of Mormon manuscript. In March 1830 some five thousand copies came off the press.

The first edition included testimonies from eleven official witnesses affirming they had seen and some held the plates translated by Joseph Smith. As the newly published book was distributed and read, a larger circle of women and men likewise received their own spiritual confirmation or witness of its divine origin and importance. Mary Musselman Whitmer received her witness prior to the book's publication. At the Whitmer farm near Fayette, New York, while the translation was being completed, she had graciously hosted Joseph and Emma Smith and Oliver Cowdery in addition to caring for her own large family. She did not view the plates in connection with the five official Whitmer witnesses—her husband and four sons—but left to her posterity a personal testimony that an angel had shown her the plates and told her: "You should receive a witness that your faith may be strengthened." She testified that the experience "nerved her up for her increased responsibilities."[21]

When Abigail Leonard heard about the Book of Mormon, she and a group of friends with whom she had gathered asked for a manifestation "of the truth and divine origin of this book," although they had not yet seen it. Having requested such a witness "by the gift and power of the Holy Ghost," Abigail testified, "I immediately felt its presence. Then, when the Book of Mormon came, we were ready to receive it and its truths. The brethren gathered at our house to read it, and such days of rejoicing and thanksgiving I never saw before nor since."[22]

Zina Diantha Huntington, in her early teens, returned from school one day to find the book on the windowsill of the family's sitting room. As she picked it up, she felt the "influence of the Holy Spirit" and pressed the book to her bosom, whispering, "This is the truth, truth, truth!"[23]

Sarah Studevant Leavitt said, after she heard about the visitation of Moroni to Joseph Smith, "It came to my mind in a moment that this was the message . . . for me and not for me only, but for the whole world, and I considered it of more importance than anything I had ever heard before, for it brought back the ancient order of things and laid a foundation that could be built upon that was permanent."[24]

Women and men kneel in prayer at the home of Peter and Mary Whitmer in Fayette, New York, April 6, 1830, date of the formal organization of the Church of Jesus Christ in latter days. (Drawing by William Whittaker, courtesy LDS Church Visual Resources Library)

These women would find their spiritual understanding extended and amplified through the Prophet's teachings to Relief Society and the promises of the temple in Nauvoo.

Women and men who desired to manifest their commitment to the witness they had received were baptized. Joseph Smith affirmed that the ancient authority to baptize had been restored to him and Oliver Cowdery during a visitation of John the Baptist on May 15, 1829. The authority to confer the Holy Ghost and organize the Church was restored later that spring through the ancient apostles Peter, James, and John. On April 6, 1830, more than fifty men and women gathered at the home of Peter and Mary Whitmer. There the sacrament was administered and six men officially organized the Church according to law. Among others, Lucy and Joseph Smith Sr. were baptized that day.

Emma Smith was baptized along with several people from Colesville, New York, on June 28, 1830. Like an increasing number of their antagonistic neighbors in Harmony, Emma's parents, Elizabeth and Isaac Hale, wanted nothing to do with the new church. Threatened with persecution, Joseph and Emma left Harmony to return to friends at Fayette in August 1829. Emma never saw her parents again.

For Emma, as for many other early Latter-day Saints, the church family of which she had become a part took on increasing importance. She was not alone in feeling the sting of separation from her family. Phebe W. Woodruff recalled that when she left the Maine home of her childhood to cast her "life lot among the Mormons," her mother's grief was almost more than she could bear. Three times her mother asked her: "Will you come back to me if you find Mormonism false?" Three times Phebe answered, "Yes, mother, I will." "My answer relieved her trouble," Phebe recalled, "but it cost us all much sorrow to part." At the time of departure Phebe knew the final farewells would be too difficult. She remembered, "I wrote my good-byes to each, and leaving them on my table, ran down stairs and jumped into the carriage."[25]

Caroline Barnes Crosby, who would join Relief Society in July 1842, was a convert of not quite one year when she and her husband left their Massachusetts home to gather in Kirtland with the Saints. En route they went to Canada to see Caroline's family, to say goodbye and bear testimony of the truth of the restored gospel. "We spent a week very agreeably with them," she recalled, "conversed much upon the subject of our religion, found some of them very hard hearted, while others and especially mother was very much inclined to listen to our arguments. . . . The zeal and love for the cause in which I was engaged supported me beyond everything and I only felt to mourn for them because they had not the same consolation that I had."[26]

Special Blessings for Women

In July 1830, before her final departure from Harmony, Emma Smith received through her husband, Joseph, a revelation from God that would find fulfillment in her calling as the first Relief Society president. Later published in the Doctrine and Covenants as section 25, it is the only revelation in the book addressed wholly to a woman. It contains specific admonitions for Emma as well as general counsel, closing with the pronouncement: "This is my voice unto all." The section helps define the gifts and responsibilities of all women of the Restoration.

"Hearken unto the voice of the Lord your God, while I speak unto you, Emma Smith, my daughter," the revelation commenced, affirming that "all those who receive my gospel are sons and daughters in my kingdom." Emma was assured, as Joseph had been, that her sins were forgiven and that she too had been called of God. In the sixteen verses of the revelation, Emma was commanded to be "faithful and walk in the paths of virtue"; to "lay aside the things of this world, and seek for the things of a better"; to "continue in the spirit of meekness"; to "beware of pride"; and to "murmur not because of the things which thou hast not seen." She was also promised blessings for her faithfulness, including preservation of life, "an inheritance in Zion," and "a crown of righteousness."

These aspects of the revelation underscored the importance of Emma's personal relationship with God. Other verses addressed her relationship with others. Through her baptism she had already manifested a willingness to become part of "the fold of God," the community of Saints, "to bear one another's burdens, that they may be light; [and] to mourn with those that mourn . . . and comfort those that stand in need of comfort."[27] Now she was to "cleave unto the covenants" that she had made. Such covenants bound Latter-day Saints together, sanctifying the meaning of socially defined roles both within the family circle and within the larger church family, where people addressed one another as brother and sister.

Emma was to be a comfort to her husband, Joseph, "in his afflictions, with consoling words, in the spirit of meekness." She was to let her soul delight in him "and the glory which shall come upon him." She, in turn, was promised that through the laying on of hands she would receive the Holy Ghost. Promised that her husband would support her in the Church, Emma was instructed in her individual responsibilities, including continued work as a scribe for Joseph and the making of "a selection of sacred hymns." Finally, she was to be ordained, or set apart, "to expound scriptures, and to exhort the church, according as it shall be given thee by my Spirit."

When the Relief Society was organized in Nauvoo in 1842 and Emma was elected as president, Joseph confirmed fulfillment of the promise in section 25 that she was "an elect lady" called of God, declaring that as president of the Female Relief Society of Nauvoo she would expound scriptures and exhort the Church. He added then that "not she alone, but others, may attain to the same blessings."[28]

Section 25 was the only revelation solely to a woman included in the published Doctrine and Covenants, but many other revelations from God to individual Latter-day Saint women were received through men ordained to the Melchizedek Priesthood and specifically designated as patriarchs. The patriarchal blessings they pronounced upon the heads of men and women were written down and became part of the Church's official but unpublished records. These blessings show the variety of spiritual gifts with which women were blessed and indicate that while women were not ordained to offices in the Melchizedek and Aaronic priesthoods, they shared in the gifts, blessings, and responsibilities that came to Latter-day Saints through the restoration of these priesthoods. Most patriarchal blessings declared the recipient's lineage within the house of Israel, exhorted faithfulness through trials and temptations, and identified personal talents and spiritual gifts. Many, like the revelation for Emma, included commandments or prophecies regarding an individual's future opportunities and responsibilities. Almost without exception, the blessings promised eternal or celestial life to the faithful.

"Sister Leonora, I lay my hands upon your head in the name of Jesus of Nazareth, to place & seal a blessing upon you to be written for your future benefit," Joseph Smith's brother Hyrum told Leonora Taylor in 1843. Though her lineage in Israel was not mentioned, she was promised "a Crown Celestial" like Sarah's and like Rachel's. In 1836 Joseph Smith Sr. told Margaret M. Martin, who was of the "lineage of Judah," "In thy days wilt thou be a Sarah. . . . Thy faith shall be made steadfast and unwavering." One woman was pronounced "a daughter of Abraham through the loins of Manasseh"; another, "a daughter of Abraham of the house of Joseph and of the lineage of Ephraim . . . and thereby a legal heiress to the blessings of the celestial world." These definitions were important to those who believed they were assuming leading roles in the modern house of Israel.[29]

Latter-day Saints were called to pass on to their children Israel's priesthood blessings. Promises regarding parenting were often revealed in patriarchal blessings. "Thy children shall stand in the covenant, by the power of God," one woman was told. Fulfillment of all such promises required faith and diligence, and women found joy in teaching their children the principles of the gospel. "We read considerable, mainly the Bible, Book of Mormon and Doctrine and Covenants," Drusilla Dorris Hendricks recalled; "had our children baptized when eight years old, and in fact, could hardly keep them waiting until they were old enough."[30] Nancy Naomi Alexander Tracy and her husband wanted their son "to have a big name out of the Book of Mormon," so they named him after two great men — Lachoneus Moroni. She taught her children "the principles of the gospel and to obey and listen to the council of the Lord's anointed."[31]

Through the organization of Relief Society, women would receive additional support for their efforts to bring to pass promises such as that revealed to one sister: "Thy posterity shall be numerous upon the earth, and thy sons and daughters shall cause you to rejoice in the holy one of Israel."

Patriarchal blessings promised women a diversity of spiritual gifts. "Thou shalt be blessed with spiritual gifts," one was told, "even those of tongues and interpretation." "Thou shalt have . . . power to keep the destroyer from thy household." "The spirit of prophecy and revelation shall rest upon you," another was told, "and the light of the Lord shall dwell within you and wisdom shall be given unto you to enable you to become perfected before the Lord. . . . Thou shall be numbered among the mothers in Israel for thou shall have a knowledge by which thou shall teach the Daughters of Zion how to live." Gifts of prophecy and wisdom were similarly promised another woman: "Thou shalt be a natural Prophetess in the house of Joseph and great shall be thy wisdom which will reach within the vail, and you shall hear the voice of Angels from time to time."

The promise of spiritual gifts and the possibility, through continued faithfulness, of being "sealed up to eternal life" and having one's name "written in the Lamb's book of life" were of great significance to individual women. Caroline Barnes Crosby noted that the blessings she and her husband, Jonathan, received in 1836 "cheered and rejoiced our hearts exceedingly. I truly felt humble before the Lord, and felt like exclaiming like one of old, 'Lord what am I, or what my fathers house, that Thou art thus mindful of us.' " Her blessing, she said, "led me to search into my own heart, to see if there was any sin concealed there, and if so, to repent, and ask God to make me clean, and pure, in very deed."[32]

The Saints saw the promise and realization of spiritual gifts as the fulfillment of ancient prophecy concerning the last days: "It shall come to pass afterward, that I will pour out my spirit upon all flesh; and your sons and your daughters shall prophesy, your old men shall dream dreams, your young men shall see visions."[33] After persecution forced Joseph and Emma to leave Colesville, New York, in July 1830, the Saints there were anxious for their return. During their absence, the Prophet Joseph recalled, Sally Knight "had a dream, which enabled her to say that we would visit them that day, which really came to pass, for a few hours afterwards we arrived; and thus was our faith much strengthened concerning dreams and visions in the last days, foretold by the ancient Prophet Joel."[34]

Sally's parents-in-law, Joseph and Polly Knight, and their children formed the nucleus of the Colesville Branch. They had known Joseph Smith since 1826, when he had worked in their neighborhood and courted Emma at nearby Harmony, and they supported him as both friend and prophet. Newel Knight, Sally's husband, recalled how his sister Polly received the gift of wisdom after she was chosen by a local minister "as a mark for his abuse" against the new church. There was an exchange of letters between Polly and the priest "in which the priest was so decidedly used up, that he was glad to give it up and back out complete whipped." In telling the story, Newel expressed regret that he had not saved the letters "so that my children may see how a weak woman, inspired by the Lord, was enabled to confound and put to confusion the learned of the day."[35]

Zina Diantha Huntington was fourteen years old when she was baptized in New York by Hyrum Smith. "Soon after this," she later recalled, "the gift of tongues rested upon me with overwhelming force." Alarmed at the strange manifestation, she "checked its utterance" and then found to her great dismay that the gift left her entirely. Later, deciding she "had offended the Holy Spirit by whose influence [she] had been so richly blessed," Zina walked to a spring in a meadow. "I offered up a prayer to God and told Him if He could forgive my transgression, and give me back the lost gift, I would promise never to check it again, no matter where or when I felt its promptings."[36]

The Gathering at Kirtland

By the end of 1830 Latter-day Saints were clustered in upstate New York—at Manchester, Fayette, Waterloo, and Colesville—and scattered in various parts of the eastern United States. The Church experienced rapid growth when four missionaries were sent to Ohio's Western Reserve and within a month of their arrival in the fall of 1830 baptized over one hundred settlers. In December the Prophet Joseph received a revelation commanding all members to "assemble together at the Ohio."[37] The gathering at Kirtland, Ohio, would provide a brief refuge from worldly ills and hostility

Lucy Mack Smith, seated
below a framed sheet
from the Book of
Commandments, was painted
by English artist Sutcliff
Maudsley in Nauvoo
sometime before 1844.
(Courtesy LDS Museum of
Church History and Art)

and new opportunities for instruction, unity, and manifestations of the Spirit.

By the spring of 1831, most of Lucy Mack Smith's family had preceded her in the move from New York to Kirtland. She made the journey with her two sons, William and Don Carlos, and eighty Saints from the Waterloo, New York, branch, who agreed by acclamation that "everything should be done just as Mother Smith said." As leader of these traveling Saints, her own account testifies, she was blessed with requisite spiritual gifts of faith and administration. The group arrived at Buffalo to find the harbor at Lake Erie ice-locked. They took deck passage on a boat, even though it seemed certain that with ice piled "up to the height of twenty feet," the boat "would remain in the harbour at least two weeks longer." When the Saints on deck began to complain, Mother Smith fiercely rebuked them: "You profess to put your trust in God, then how can you feel to murmur and complain as you do! You are even more unreasonable than the children of Israel were. . . . Where is your faith? Where is your confidence in God? Can you not realize that . . . he rules over the works of his own hands?" Lucy challenged her brothers and sisters to lift their hearts in prayer to God that the ice might break, freeing the boat. Within minutes they heard a thunderous noise, and the ice parted just long enough for their boat to pass through.[38] Joseph and his brother Samuel greeted their mother and her company upon their arrival in Kirtland.

The gathering of the Saints at Kirtland provided an outpouring of spiritual manifestations, including healings and speaking in tongues. The strength of the Church depended on its members' ability to integrate the outpouring of spiritual gifts with divinely revealed ecclesiastical order. One convert, a Sister Hubble, professed the gift of prophecy, and some new converts began to heed her "revelations and commandments." But the Lord affirmed in a revelation given to Joseph Smith that the Prophet alone had been appointed "to receive commandments and revelations."[39] To differentiate between prophetic utterances and private manifestations became an important lesson for the Saints.

The building of a temple at Kirtland symbolized the integration of organizational form and spiritual content. When church leaders met to consider how to replace the log meetinghouse that the Saints had outgrown, Joseph presented the revelation he had received commanding them to build a temple — "a house of prayer, a house of fasting, a house of faith, a house of learning, a house of glory, a house of order, a house of God."[40] They were commanded "to observe their covenants with sacrifice," for which they would be blessed, for within the house God would endow "with power from on high" those whom he had chosen.[41]

Three years of sacrifice and labor by both men and women followed the laying of the cornerstone on July 23, 1833. In 1836 Eliza R. Snow, recently baptized and moved to Kirtland, proffered a much needed "cash donation," presumably from her inheritance, to the building of the temple.[42] "The brethren were laboring night and day building the house of the Lord," recalled Heber C. Kimball. "Our women were engaged in spinning and knitting in order to clothe those who were laboring at the building, and the Lord only knows the scenes of poverty, tribulation, and distress which we passed through in order to accomplish this thing." Heber's wife,

Vilate, worked with a younger woman to spin a hundred pounds of wool one summer, then "wove and got the cloth dressed, and cut and made up into [clothing], and gave them to those men who labored on the Temple," refusing to reserve for herself "even so much as would make her a pair of stockings."[43] Some women helped with the masonry work and even drove the teams that hauled the rock. Two young women who boarded with Lucy Mack Smith — Mary Bailey and Agnes Coolbrith — made and mended clothes for the temple workmen (and later married Lucy's sons, Samuel and Don Carlos).

It was a time "when the Saints all considered that what they possessed belonged to the work of the Lord," Sarah M. Kimball said, explaining that "the women would churn and cheerfully send their butter to the workmen on the Temple and eat without any on their own tables." As a result, "they were all hopeful and joyous; she had never seen happier days in her life that she knew of."[44]

Women sewed carpets and draperies for the temple interior. One day as Polly Angell and other women were gathered to work on these furnishings, Joseph Smith and Sidney Rigdon stopped by. As Polly recalled, the Prophet commended them, saying, "The sisters are always first and foremost in all good works. Mary was first at the resurrection; and the sisters now are the first to work on the inside of the temple."[45]

Over one thousand Saints assembled in the newly finished temple for the dedication on March 27, 1836. Nearly eight hundred more were turned away with the promise that the service would be repeated four days later. The Saints received spiritual rewards for their temporal sacrifices at the services and in the days, weeks, and months that followed. The two sessions, morning and afternoon, included hymns, addresses, testimonies, and Joseph Smith's special dedicatory prayer asking that "all people who shall enter upon the threshold of the Lord's house may feel thy power, and feel constrained to acknowledge that thou hast sanctified it, and that it is thy house, a place of thy holiness.[46] In his history, the Prophet noted that the Saints "sealed the proceedings of the day by shouting hosanna, hosanna, hosanna to God and the Lamb."[47]

"Blessings were poured out," recalled Nancy Tracy. "It was verily true that the Heavenly Influence rested down upon that house, and the people were glorious and long to be remembered. Heavenly Beings appeared to many. I felt that it was heaven on earth."[48]

Women cherished memories of the monthly fast meetings held in the temple on Thursdays. "Many, many were the pentecostal seasons of the outpouring of the spirit of God on those days," remembered Eliza Snow. Presendia Huntington Buell recalled how once when she was at home during a monthly fast meeting, a little girl bid her to come and look at the temple, and the two of them saw "angels clothed in white walking upon the temple."[49] Mary Fielding [Smith] wrote to her sister July 8, 1837, regarding one fast meeting: "The hearts of the people were melted and the Spirit & power of God rested down upon us in a remarkable manner. Many spake in tongues & others prophesied & interpreted. . . . Such a time of love & refreshing has never been known."[50]

In reflecting upon the spiritual experiences she had in connection with the temple, Nancy Tracy remembered asking: "Shall we always enjoy such blessings? No, this is to prepare us that we shall have strength to endure, for we have the opposing element to contend with and shall be made perfect through suffering."[51] The "opposing element" in and around Kirtland gained momentum as anti-Mormons sought to repudiate the doctrine of the Saints and a number of dissenting members "came out boldly against the prophet, . . . renouncing all their allience with the church." "These were some of our nighest neighbors and friends," mourned Caroline Crosby. "We had taken sweet counsel together, and walked to the house of God as friends."[52]

Hostilities in Missouri

Continued hostility, dissension, and financial distress led to the evacuation of the Saints from Kirtland. By July 1838 the last contingent had left Ohio for newly established Mormon settlements in northern Missouri. Seven years earlier, in July 1831, Joseph Smith had received a revelation designating Missouri as a land "appointed and consecrated for the gathering of the Saints" and Independence in Jackson County as the place for the city of Zion.

Saints who gathered at Independence tried to live the law of consecration and stewardship, a plan revealed to Joseph Smith for the voluntary redistribution of surplus wealth in order to build the Church and help the poor. While collective attempts to live the law were unsuccessful, certain individuals felt blessed for their efforts, among them Vienna Jacques, a forty-six-year-old convert from Massachusetts who had accumulated considerable wealth. In 1833 she consecrated her property to the Church, and by revelation

Joseph Smith affirmed that she should "receive money to bear her expenses, and go up unto the land of Zion," Missouri, where she would "receive an inheritance from the hand of the bishop."[53] In September 1833, the Prophet personally thanked her, writing that a spirit had whispered to him: "Joseph thou art indebted to thy God for the offering of thy Sister Viana which proved a savior of life as pertaining to thy pecunary concern therefor she should not be forgotten of thee for the Lord hath done this and thou shouldst remember her in all thy prayers and also by letter."[54]

Neither Vienna Jacques nor any of the twelve hundred Saints who settled in the Independence area remained there long. Hostile Missourians, who clashed culturally with the predominantly Yankee Mormons and feared their growing numbers and potential political power, drove them out before the end of the year. Holding fast to the belief that Zion would ultimately be established near Independence, Saints settled further north in Missouri's Ray, Caldwell, Daviess, and DeWitt counties. According to Joseph Smith, this was also sacred ground. Due to continuing harassment from local residents, however, the Saints ultimately abandoned these areas as well. Their flight at the end of 1838 marked the height of anti-Mormon persecutions in Missouri.

That fall Patience D. Palmer and her husband were among eight Latter-day Saint families moving from New York to Missouri. Camped about four miles below Haun's Mill on Shoal Creek, she reported that she and other sisters "were washing our clothes in the creek; and the children, with shoes and stockings off, were playing about," when a young boy on horseback "came riding furiously down the creek" to tell them of the massacre of some seventeen men and boys at the mill. While their husbands remained behind, Patience and the other women fled with the barefoot children into the woods. Recalled Patience: "I had six small children at my side and a baby at my breast. We ran over bush, over hills and hollows, and as our children ran over the rough untrodden ground stains of blood were left from their tender feet. When we would stop for a short rest mothers would take their clothes from their own backs to lay on the ground for the children to stand on and warm their cold, raw feet." As the Palmers prepared with other Saints to leave the state of Missouri "or be exterminated," they had almost no food; for three weeks they lived on parched corn that had to be partially chewed by the parents before the younger children could eat and digest it.[55]

Leaving their sacred temple sites at Independence and Far West was the greatest disappointment to the persecuted Saints. Of that sorrow Eliza Snow wrote encouragingly: "What though our rights have been assailed? / What though by foes we've been despoiled? / Jehovah's promise has not failed; / Jehovah's purpose is not foiled."[56]

The conflict in Missouri resulted in the deaths of more than a score of the Saints, the imprisonment of Joseph Smith and other leaders, and substantial losses of members' property. Twenty-eight-year-old Elizabeth Haven wrote in March 1839 to her cousin Elizabeth Bullard in Massachusetts: "Between five and seven thousand men, women and children driven from the places of gathering out of the state from houses and lands, in poverty, to seek for habitations where they can find them."[57] Emma Smith crossed the frozen Missouri River without Joseph—two children in her arms and two more clinging to the skirts that hid the cotton bags carrying part of the manuscript of the Prophet's Bible translation. "No one but God, knows the reflections of my mind and the feelings of my heart when I left our house and home, and allmost all of everything that we possessed excepting our little children, and took my journey out of the State of Missouri, leaving you shut up in that lonesome prisen," Emma wrote to Joseph in Liberty Jail. "If God does not record our sufferings and avenge our wrongs on them that are guilty, I shall be sadly mistaken," she reflected, ending, "But I hope there is better days to come to us yet."[58]

"Better Days to Come"

Not in Missouri, then, but in Nauvoo, Illinois, would the Saints gather and build their temple, continuing the work of the Restoration. Before church organization and ordinances could be perfected, however, the next significant stride in the spread of the gospel was required. Seven members of the Quorum of the Twelve left in late summer 1839 on a mission to England. Their departure from Nauvoo at the end of a summer plagued with fever from the mosquito-infested swamps was a trial for themselves and their families. "Most of them when they left this place . . . were worn down with sickness and disease," the *History of the Church* records.[59] Wives, though sick themselves and scantily provided with shelter and provisions, supported their husbands in the revealed call to "go over the great waters, and there promulgate [the] gospel."[60] Shortly after Heber C. Kimball departed, his wife, Vilate, wrote to him: "As to my feelings I don't know but I am perfectly reconciled to your going, but I must say I have got a trial of my faith if I never had before. The day you left home was as sick a one as I ever experienced."[61]

The success of the apostles in Great Britain was astounding. In Herefordshire Wilford Woodruff baptized a large number of converts from the United Brethren, a group who had been seeking the primitive church. In services of the United Brethren, held in small chapels and members' homes, women had served as lay preachers along with the men. John and Jane Homes Benbow welcomed Elder Woodruff at their Herefordshire farm, and the pond there served as the baptismal font for some six hundred people. Jane Benbow, whose family had provided her with an inheritance, though not wealthy, was financially better off than most. She and her husband presented Brigham Young, president of the Twelve, with 250 pounds to further the latter-day work in England. This contribution, coupled with 100 pounds from Hannah Pitt Kington and her husband and contributions from many other members, enabled the Twelve to forward a comprehensive publishing program in England, including new editions of the Book of Mormon and of Emma Smith's hymnal and the launching of a new monthly magazine for British Saints, the *Millennial Star*.[62]

From England Brigham Young wrote his wife, Mary Ann, expressing his gratitude for her sacrifice, and the sacrifices of other devoted women, in supporting the work of the kingdom. "When I think how diligant you are," he said, "and how faithful to my famely and willing to suffer for the sake of my going to preach the gospel you must be blest and blest you shall be I pray the Lord to Bless you and I Bles you and all the faithful sisters."[63]

Blessings were indeed in store for the faithful women. The truths they had sought would continue to flow down from above; there were, as Emma Smith had hoped, "better days to come."

PART ONE

SACRED PATTERNS

CHAPTER 1

THE TURNING OF THE KEY
1842–1844

To Ellen Douglas, who arrived in Nauvoo, Illinois, in 1842, the new Zion established by the Latter-day Saints on the banks of the upper Mississippi River was indeed a promised land. "I think we are far better here than in old England," she wrote to her parents, adding with regard to work and food, "I wish the people in England could get as much as we can."[1] The first European Saints had sailed from Liverpool to New York in 1840. By 1846, when the main body of the Saints left Nauvoo, 4,733 converts had arrived there from Europe, most of them British like Ellen. She found housing scarce, though "scores of houses" had been built and more were under way. More Saints were arriving daily, and Ellen noted, "there is 3 or 4 families in one room, and many have to pitch their tents in the woods, or anywhere they can."[2]

When Joseph Smith moved his family to the river settlement in May 1839, a small community, optimistically named Commerce, was well under way, with a schoolhouse already built. There were church services, quiltings, fairs, a debating society, and other such amenities of a developing community.[3] Saints continued arriving through the summer, and by August, with optimism of their own, they expanded the town and named it Nauvoo—beautiful place of rest, according to Joseph Smith's translation of the Hebrew. Forced from Missouri by mob pressure and a state-issued "extermination order," the Saints were seeking permanence and peace.

During her first year of marriage, 1841–42, nineteen-year-old Bathsheba Smith set up housekeeping in five successive homes in the Nauvoo area. As newlyweds, she and her husband, George A. Smith—just returned from the mission of the Twelve to England— spent the first month with George A.'s parents across the river at Zarahemla, Iowa. The couple "rented a small log cabin close by."

They had furniture, cooking utensils, and bedding, "but," wrote Bathsheba, "the house leaked and smoked and was otherwise uncomfortable." They next bought a log house and built a brick chimney "and that smoked." George A., then the youngest member of the Quorum of the Twelve Apostles, was counseled by his cousin, the Prophet Joseph Smith, to move to Nauvoo. There the couple rented "an old log house . . . which smoked and was open and coald." Later Joseph gave them a lot with a small log house on it." "It was the worst looking house we had yet lived in," Bathsheba recalled. "It had however the desirable qualities of neither smoking nor leaking."[4]

Finally Bathsheba and George A. set to work building their own home—a one-and-one-half-story frame house with two rooms above and two below. Its completion was left to Bathsheba after George A. left Nauvoo to resume extensive missionary labors. Her frequent letters to him reported progress on their homestead. "Will soon have peas," she wrote to him in June 1844. "A good many of our flowers are in blossom. Our Cow has had the hollow horn. I believe she is well now. I have soald six pounds of butter since you left."[5]

The economic success, if not survival, of most Nauvoo households depended upon the resourcefulness and hard work of women. Many, like Bathsheba Smith, had husbands, brothers, or fathers serving missions. Public works projects, such as the temple, took men away from the household regularly. Frugal housewifery was important, and women frequently took on additional outside work. They comprised half of an active school-teaching force, for example, setting up ad hoc classes whenever suitable space was available. Spinning, weaving, dyeing or coloring, knitting, sewing, quilting, plaiting palm leaf or straw for hats, millinery work, fine tailoring, and fine laundering brought in much-needed income. A single woman as seamstress or "spinster" might find herself in a succession of homes earning her keep by plying her needle or her wheel.

Rapid expansion over a short period of time made Nauvoo something of a boom town, though it lacked a major industry. Construction and anything connected with it—sawmills, brickyards, a lime kiln, a tool factory, and carpenters' and joiners' shops— were the most profitable concerns. Many craftsmen, including women, made matches, leather goods, pottery, jewelry, and combs. The city had gristmills, a bakery, a printing office, a brewery, an iron foundry, and a chinaware factory. Yet Sally Randall, who arrived from New York State in the fall of 1843, observed of the city, "It is a hard place for poor people that have no money to get a living. There is so many poor that depend on their work for a living that they can hardly get enough to be comfortable."[6]

Nauvoo's poverty was often exacerbated by sickness. Swamps in the lowlands near the river made the climate so unhealthy that scores died of malaria-like fevers each summer. Children were particularly vulnerable. When her year-old son, George, became ill, Bathsheba feared, "he was a going to have the feavor."[7]

While building the "city beautiful" involved hard work and even some suffering, life in Nauvoo rose above mere subsistence. There were lyceums and institutes and an embryonic university with secondary-level offerings in sciences, philosophy, literature, history, music, and languages. Private and public lectures, concerts, debates, and dramas were popular. The establishment of the Masonic lodges involved the men, almost all of whom were ultimately members.[8]

Most of these activities paralleled trends in contemporary America, where women were also working at new patterns of organization. During the eighteenth-century Great Awakening, tens of thousands had converted to various religions, and in many instances women took a more active part than did their husbands and fathers. Women brought together by shared religious faith organized into praying societies, and other societies with moral, educational, missionary, and charitable aims.

In the nineteenth century, benevolence, which had once consisted of individual neighborly aid, became, as historian Keith Melder wrote, "a collective process, encouraging bonds of sisterhood at all levels of organized operations, in local, regional, state, and national activities."[9] Female benevolent societies usually met weekly and collected donations. Many had programs for missionary work, the distribution of tracts and Bibles, and charitable work. Some cities had so many organizations that they formed large unions under centralized leadership. As Americans migrated westward, so did the benevolent movement. Inland towns settled by New Englanders generally supported such women's associations. According to Melder, "Between 1800 and 1840 the women's benevolent movement had evolved from minute beginnings in a few American cities and towns into a great body of organizations numbering well into the thousands."[10]

The Nauvoo Relief Society Is Organized

Many Latter-day Saint women were undoubtedly aware of the benevolent movement, and some perhaps had been involved in it before coming to Nauvoo. Besides, the organization of priesthood quorums, Masonic lodges, and the Nauvoo Legion strengthened brotherhood among Latter-day Saint men, and women may well have felt the need for a sisterly counterpart.

One such woman, Sarah Melissa Granger, came from Phelps, New York, a town near both Palmyra, where Joseph Smith had experienced his early visions, and Utica, one center of the American benevolent movement. Twenty-one-year-old Sarah moved to Commerce with her parents and siblings in 1839 and soon became acquainted with one of the town's prominent land agents and merchants, Hiram Kimball. They were married, and their elegantly furnished home became the center for various social activities for church and community leaders. It also figured in the beginnings of an organization for women. Sarah later recalled that in the spring of 1842, "a maiden lady (Miss Cooke) was seamstress for me, and the subject of combining our efforts for assisting the Temple hands came up in conversation. She desired to be helpful, but had no means to furnish. I told her I would furnish material if she would make some shirts for the workmen." The project soon expanded in scope when it occurred to them, as Sarah wrote, "that some of our neighbors might wish to combine means and efforts with ours, and we decided to invite a few to come and consult with us on the subject of forming a Ladies' Society. The neighboring sisters met in my parlor and decided to organize."[11]

These women organized themselves according to the pattern prevailing in contemporary women's societies. By making constitutions and electing officers, they functioned as "miniature democratic laboratories," teaching their members self-government.[12] It is not surprising that at the meeting of the Cook-Kimball group on March 4, 1842, the members decided to draft a set of rules and delegated Sarah Kimball to ask Eliza R. Snow to write a constitution and bylaws for the fledgling organization.

Eliza Snow presented the resulting documents to the Prophet Joseph Smith for approval. At this juncture the Latter-day Saint organization departed from other benevolent societies of the time. Joseph observed that the constitution and bylaws were "the best he had ever seen," reported Sarah Kimball, but they were not

Parlor of the Hiram and Sarah Kimball home in Nauvoo, Illinois, restored in 1982, recreates setting for March 4, 1842, gathering that was precursor for Female Relief Society of Nauvoo, organized two weeks later by Joseph Smith. (Photo by Craig Dimond, courtesy LDS Church Visual Resources Library)

appropriate to the purposes of the Church as a whole. He asked Sister Snow to invite the women to meet on the following Thursday, saying that he would provide "something better for them than a written Constitution." "I will organize the women," he promised, "under the priesthood after the pattern of the priesthood."[13]

Convinced that they were to have a unique women's organization, one organized according to God's plan, the sisters gathered with Joseph Smith in the upstairs room of his red brick store on March 17, 1842. At that meeting several women remarked that the new institution should differ from other benevolent societies, Eliza R. Snow declaring "that the popular Institutions of the day should not be our guide—that as daughters of Zion, we should set an example for all the world, rather than confine ourselves to the course which had been heretofore pursued."[14]

The names of the women who gathered in the lodge room above Joseph Smith's store on Thursday, March 17, 1842, are listed in the record as follows: "Mrs. Emma Smith, Mrs. Sarah M. Cleveland, Phebe Ann Hawkes, Elizabeth Jones, Sophia Packard, Philindia Merrick [Myrick], Martha Knights [Knight], Desdemona Fulmer [Fullmer], Elizabeth Ann Whitney, Leonora Taylor, Bathsheba W. Smith, Phebe M. Wheeler, Elvira A. Coles [Cowles],

Margaret A Cook, Athalia Robinson, Sarah M. Kimball, Eliza R. Snow, Sophia Robinson, Nancy Rigdon, and Sophia R. Marks."[15]

The youngest were three teenagers, and the oldest, a woman in her fifties. Eleven of the women were married, two were widows, six were unmarried, and the marital status of one is unknown. Their education and backgrounds varied greatly, as did their economic circumstances. Their diversity would be magnified many times as the organization's membership continued to grow, but they were and would continue to be one in anticipating that a women's organization formed under the direction of men called of God would be crucial to their individual and communal lives as Latter-day Saints.[16]

Joseph Smith directed the first meeting, assisted by John Taylor and Willard Richards, members of the Quorum of Twelve Apostles. Elder Richards, a personal scribe for Joseph Smith, served as record-keeper at this meeting, during which the nature, leadership, and purposes of the new society were established.

The women voted to acknowledge those present plus seven others as members "in full fellowship, and admit them to the privileges of the Institution about to be formed." Then Joseph Smith set forth an organization to show the sisters "how to go to work. . . . He propos'd that the Sisters elect a presiding officer to preside over them, and let that presiding officer choose two Counsellors to assist in the duties of her Office."[17]

Elizabeth Ann Whitney nominated Emma Smith, wife of Joseph Smith, as president, and she was elected by those present. She immediately chose as her counselors Sarah M. Cleveland and Elizabeth Whitney. Joseph, undoubtedly pleased with the choice of Emma as president, spoke with pride of her unique standing among the women of the Church. He read from the Doctrine and Covenants the revelation (now section 25) proclaiming her "an elect lady, whom I [the Lord] have called" and stated that "she was ordain'd at the time the Revelation was given, to expound the scriptures to all; and to teach the female part of [the] community." He also read to the sisters from the first chapter of Second John, an epistle from the apostle John to "the elect lady," to show "that respect was there had to the same thing," suggesting, as Eliza Snow later taught, that a similar organization for women existed in New Testament times. Emma "was called an Elect lady," he said, "because [she was] elected to preside."[18] Her new calling was, therefore, a fulfillment of the revelation given twelve years earlier.

Emma, thirty-eight years old, with four living children, could easily have been consumed in other responsibilities at the time of this meeting. "The Homestead," where she and Joseph lived, consisted of a parlor and two sleeping rooms and, according to the census taker, had been stretched to accommodate eleven others early that year. Emma once told Joseph that she desired to be "a blessing to all who may in any wise need aught at my hands," and she was known for her ministrations to the needs of her neighbors as well as for her personal warmth and quick wit.[19] As the Prophet's wife, she had long been the Church's able and gracious First Lady, and her new calling was an appropriate affirmation of her unique position. She would "teach the female part of the community" and "expound the scriptures to all," Joseph declared, observing that these gifts were not for Emma alone, "but others, may attain to the same blessings."[20]

Because Emma had already been "ordain'd [set apart] at the time the Revelation was given," she was not set apart at this time with her counselors. Rather, John Taylor "confirm'd upon her all the blessings which had been confer'd on her," blessing her to be "a mother in Israel and look to the wants of the needy, and be a pattern of virtue; and possess all the qualifications necessary for her to stand and preside and dignify her Office, to teach females those principles requisite for their future usefulness."[21]

Elder Taylor also blessed the two counselors, Sarah M. Cleveland and Elizabeth Ann Whitney, in connection with their ordination. He later explained that theirs was not an ordination to the priesthood, but rather a blessing that set them apart for their new positions.[22]

Elizabeth Whitney, who was forty-one years old with seven children ranging in age from new babe to nineteen, was loved for her spiritual strength, often manifest through her exercise of the gift of tongues, a gift promised her in Kirtland by the Prophet Joseph. Known affectionately as "Mother Whitney," she would strengthen the women's organizations of the Church from this first calling in Nauvoo until her death in 1882.

Sarah Cleveland, the oldest woman at the meeting, was the wife of one of Nauvoo's non-Mormon merchants. The Clevelands would leave the city a year later, but Sarah emerges from the minutes of the first year's eighteen meetings as an intelligent leader. Emma Smith had witnessed Sarah's generosity and compassion firsthand when she and her children, retreating across the river from Missouri, had taken refuge with the Clevelands in Quincy. Joseph found them there on his return from prison. Eliza R. Snow, a boarder in Sarah's home the spring the Relief Society was organized, wrote of her as "my excellent friend."[23] The leadership of women of such spirituality and charity augured well for the new society.

At its first meeting the Nauvoo group voted to appoint three other officers: Phebe J. Wheeler, a widow, assistant secretary; Elvira A. Cowles (later Holmes) and Eliza R. Snow, both single women, treasurer and secretary, respectively. Eliza was an obvious choice for secretary. Her poetry, published in Illinois papers in Quincy and Nauvoo, had already earned her the title of "Zion's poetess." But her unwavering allegiance to the society would prove most important. She would later bring her carefully kept "Record of the Organization, and Proceedings of The Female Relief Society of Nauvoo" to Utah, where it would provide indispensable precedents when, under the direction of Brigham Young, she worked with local bishops in establishing ward Relief Societies.

At the first meeting in Nauvoo, Joseph Smith painstakingly instructed the women in parliamentary procedure, a mechanism practiced as the sisters (and the brethren) present debated various names for the new organization. Perhaps the orderly nature of their discussion prompted John Taylor to observe in the next issue of *Times and Seasons* that he and others "were much pleased with [the Society's] *modus operandi* . . . they are strictly parliamentary in their proceedings; and we believe that they will make pretty good democrats."[24]

The process of choosing a name reflects the group's own hopes for their society's future. Joseph Smith had begun the meeting by declaring the purpose of the organization: "that the Society of Sisters might provoke the brethren to good works in looking to the wants of the poor—searching after objects of charity, and in administering to their wants to assist; by correcting the morals and strengthening the virtues of the female community, and save the Elders the trouble of rebuking; that they may give their time to other duties, &c. in their public teaching."[25]

Sarah Cleveland suggested that the organization be called "The Nauvoo Female Relief Society." Discussion centered around the word *relief*. John Taylor felt *benevolent* would be a better term, but the women objected because of its current popularity. Emma Smith was emphatic about not wishing to have the new organization "call'd after other Societies in the world," some of which were infamously corrupt. Eliza Snow agreed that *benevolent* was in that regard a tainted term, but also wondered about use of the word *relief* since it might convey "that we intend appropriating on some extraordinary occasions instead of meeting the common occurences."

At this point Emma poured forth her own enthusiasm for the possibilities of the new society. "We are going to do something *extraordinary*," she declared. "When a boat is stuck on the rapids, with a multitude of Mormons on board, we shall consider that a loud call for relief—we expect extraordinary occasions and pressing calls." The debate was closed, and the name "The Nauvoo Female Relief Society" was put forward for vote. Poet Eliza R. Snow suggested that "The Female Relief Society of Nauvoo" had a better ring, and that title carried unanimously. That done, Joseph Smith proclaimed: "I now declare this society organiz'd with President and Counsellors &c. according to Parliamentary usages—and all who shall hereafter be admitted into this Society must be free from censure and receiv'd by vote."[26]

"Relief" was a defining purpose of the group, and before this first meeting closed the Prophet declared, "All I shall have to give to the poor, I shall give to this Society," and he offered five dollars in gold "to commence the funds of the Institution."[27] The other two brethren present also made donations that day, as did each member of the presidency and Sarah Kimball, setting a pattern that would continue over the next two years. Setting another precedent for the society, Emma Smith observed that one of the sisters among them was in need, noting that Philindia Myrick, a widow whose husband had been killed at Haun's Mill, "is industrious—performs her work well, therefore recommend her to the patronage of such as wish to hire needlework." Emma must have understood that with three children to rear and provide for, Philindia could use the support of the sisters. This pattern of observant concern was one that Emma and her counselors would reiterate: members of the society would watch over one another.

Defining the Responsibilities of Relief Society

The minutes of the Female Relief Society of Nauvoo provide insight into the workings of the organization, which met weekly. At the sixth meeting, on April 28, 1842, the Prophet instructed the women regarding their "charitable society," saying, "This is according to your natures—it is natural for females to have feelings of charity—you are now plac'd in a situation where you can act according to those sympathies which God has planted in your bosoms. If you live up to these principles how great and glorious!"[28] The women themselves rejoiced in the opportunity of being organized for the most basic of gospel imperatives. At the twenty-third meeting, July 28, 1843, Elizabeth Ann Whitney quoted John 13:35, "By this shall all men know that ye are my disciples, if ye have love one to another," saying, "The Lord confirms it again & again he is delighted with our acts of charity &c."[29]

In July 1843, to facilitate the society's work amid Nauvoo's expanding population, a visiting committee of four, prototype of present-day visiting teachers, was appointed within each of the four wards to assess needs and collect donations.[30] There was no precedent for Relief Society women working at the ward level, and in August 1843, Catharine Spencer of the second ward's visiting committee expressed concern that "we were taking the Bishops place in looking after the poor & solicitting donations." Reynolds Cahoon, president of the Zarahemla Stake visiting by invitation, spoke to Sister Spencer's question. He "said they were not acting in the Bishop's place nor intruding upon them in their calling." He offered his insights on church government, affirming that all had been done in the true order. As Joseph Smith had appointed Emma Smith Relief Society president, she had covenanted to follow him, he said; she had appointed the visiting committee, and "they had nothing to do but to move forward." He assured the women that "they were in their place And those who would act perseveringly *in their* place—Should be bless'd with great blessings more than they could conceive."[31]

The weekly routine for the society's charitable work consisted of sisters reporting those in need, the treasurer accepting donations, and occasionally a vote on apportionment of the donations, which consisted of money, goods, and services. Typically, the money contributions weekly totaled from twenty-five cents to $1.00, but sometimes substantially larger sums were donated, such as the $20.87 contributed April 19, 1842, and the $71.00 contributed June 23, 1842. At a time when a dozen eggs could be purchased for a nickel and a restaurant meal for twenty-five cents, these were considerable sums. The cash was used for various purposes, such as the purchase of food or bedding, schooling for needy children, and, in one case, a destitute sister's fare to New Orleans.

Many of the goods donated were articles of clothing, especially clothing for women and children. In addition, flax, wool, yarn, and cloth were often recorded as donations. Shingles, soap, candles, tinware, jewelry, baskets, quilts, blankets, and other bedding all found their way into the register at one time or another, as did food: onions, apples, meat, flour, bread, butter, sugar, crackers, and tea. At one point Joseph Smith proposed to donate a plot of land to be deeded to the society's treasurer, "that the Society may build houses for the poor."[32] Though the proposal did not materialize, it indicates the Prophet's eagerness to assist in expanding the scope of the society's relief work.

Like Miss Cook, the young woman who had first approached Sarah Kimball offering to provide sewing but who had no cloth, many women could donate only service to the society. Visiting neighbors to ascertain who was in need was a service that was essential to the work. The ward visiting committees of four were "to search out the poor and suffering — To call on the rich for aid and thus as far as possible relieve the wants of all."[33] In that effort, some women were assigned beyond their own borders. Sarah D. Rich, for example, was issued a certificate in 1843 authorizing her to receive any donations "as friends abroad shall feel disposed to put into her hands" for the benefit of the poor.[34]

In addition to visiting and soliciting aid, women performed other services, many of them reflecting the peculiar skills of the women themselves. Donated wool and flax had to be spun and colored, cloth had to be sewn into clothing, sick Saints had to be nursed. In fact, women not only offered their work as a donation, but also sought work for needy persons whom the society might be able to pay for their services. In May 1842 Emma Smith told the group she had "hired a poor man to plough and fence father Knights lot at $22.60, and solicited the Society in behalf of the payment which might be made in provision, clothing, and furniture."[35] The emphasis was then, as it continued to be, on working for one's benefits.

Relief Society minutes reflect the eagerness with which the women took up the charitable work. The meeting of July 7, 1843, is a good example. Following Counselor Whitney's request that the sisters "speak and express to each other their feelings as the members of one family," several voiced their concern for the welfare of others. There were general needs: Sister Pratt mentioned a Brother Henderson, "an industrious, and worthy person," a widower with nine children in need. There were spiritual needs: Sister Durfee asked the sisters to "unite like the ancient saints in faith & pray'r" for Porter Rockwell's deliverance—he was then imprisoned in Missouri under suspicion for an assassination attempt. And there were specific needs, even for those about whom nothing was known: Sister Sessions, concerned about a man whose appearance "bespoke deep poverty," offered to donate two pairs of "pantaloons" and a shirt. Materials and skills combined to meet a variety of needs. Sister Farr offered flax and tow to spin, and Sister Kelsey offered to do the spinning. Sister Geene had some coarse linen to donate for pantaloons and thread to make them, and Sister Woolley would take the red yarn she had intended for a carpet and instead offer it for mittens for the temple builders. Sister Downey, Sister Snow, and Sister Abbott would sew and knit. Sister Granger would do anything that was needed.

Foreshadowing the employment exchange of later Relief Society work, Sister Markham acted as agent in offering a place for a young girl "with a suitable person" in LaHarpe, and Sister Allen recommended Brother Parks's daughters, both in need of work. Counselor Whitney reported her care over the past year for a sickly young English convert for whom Brother Ivans was providing sustenance, and wondered, considering the size of her family, if someone else might take over his care now. Sister Jones was willing, even though her house might not be quiet enough. The needs were many, but the women took on what they could in the service of all.

In concluding her minutes of the meeting, secretary Snow recorded: "A union of feeling prevail'd through the meeting. All present manifested a disposition to do all in their power towards assisting the poor and in forwarding the building of the Temple."[36]

At the end of the society's first year of operation, from March 17, 1842, to March 16, 1843, the treasurer reported that the organization had received "in donations of money, clothing, provisions &c. &c" $507.00, and had "expended in appropriations for the relief of the poor" $306.48.[37] As a Sister Peck observed at the thirty-second meeting, October 14, 1843, "this society had done a great good in relieving the distressed. [W]e have not said 'be ye warmed and cloathed' without trying to do it."[38]

An English immigrant who was both a society member and a recipient of the group's aid was Ellen Douglas, whose optimistic observations about Nauvoo began this chapter. By April 1844 her husband had died and both she and her children had contracted a long-term illness. In a letter written to her family that month, she recounted the society's recent ministrations to her and her children. Though she was a member, she had at first resisted aid. "After I begun to get well I went down into the city on a visit to where Ann lived, and I stayed two nights and I had a horse to ride home on," she wrote. "The woman where Ann lived would have me make application to the Female Relief Society for some clothing which I needed for myself and family. I refused to do so, but she said I needed something and that I had been so long sick and if I would not do it myself she would do it for me." Succumbing to this no-nonsense encouragement, Ellen relented. "We went to one of the sisters and she asked me what I needed most. I told her that I needed many things. While I was sick my children were [wore] out their clothes because I could not men[d] them, so she said she would do the best she could for me. Ann came over in a few days and they brought the wagon and fetched me such a present as I never received before from no place in the world. I suppose the things they sent were worth as much as 30 shillings."[39]

Ellen had become a member of the society at its tenth meeting, May 27, 1842. She was one of the 186 women admitted at that meeting, an influx that brought the membership to 661. The number had expanded so rapidly that this tenth meeting was held in the "Grove" rather than in the room above Joseph Smith's store where the women had gathered previously. A little over a year later, in July 1843, with 1,179 members recorded on the rolls, the group was divided into fourths, according to the geographic areas (wards) where the women lived. They were to meet subsequently one ward at a time, "that all might have equal privileges."[40]

On July 7, 1843, the society inaugurated its new meeting plan, with the original presidency presiding over all four groups. The change had perhaps been premature, since attendance dwindled; by the end of the summer the ward groups were so depleted that it was decided to reincorporate the body as a whole. By the society's last recorded meeting, March 16, 1844, the record that began with twenty names concluded as a register of 1,341. In addition, there are indications of Relief Societies functioning outside of Nauvoo, at least in Macedonia and probably in LaHarpe and Lima, where collections were taken up among the sisters.

Sisterhood and Gifts of the Spirit

Clearly the Relief Society had tremendous appeal to women. Comparing the content of each meeting's minutes with the enrollment suggests that the first appeal of the society was spiritual: the women came to be taught the gospel as Joseph Smith presented it to them, to women. It was his message, and Emma Smith's encouragement, that tasted sweet to them and brought them in such numbers to feast together. Their acts of charity followed inevitably as an outgrowth of the light of Christ that the gospel ignited in their souls. They began to minister temporally and spiritually to one another, gradually building the sisterhood that would draw others into the organization.

At the society's twenty-first meeting, July 15, 1843, the minutes record that after ten sisters donated money and goods, "Sister Husted rose wept said She had nothing to give. Spoke of her trouble in Mo [Missouri] the Death of her Husband &c. Counsellor Whitney said it was not her duty to give not even her mite but rather — She should be helped then recommended her to the charity."[41]

At the fifth meeting of the Relief Society, on April 19, 1842, Counselor Sarah Cleveland expressed "the happiness she felt in the present associations of females." At that meeting sisters nurtured one another spiritually, exercising the gifts of the spirit spoken of in the New Testament and the Doctrine and Covenants. Some bore testimony, others spoke in tongues and interpreted tongues, and, following the closing prayer and song, the sisters exercised the gift of healing on behalf of an ailing sister. The secretary commented that "nearly all present arose & spoke, and the spirit of the Lord like a purifying stream, refreshed every heart."[42] Not only did these gifts remain with the women, but even more frequently, the sisters enjoyed the gifts spoken of in the New Testament as the "word of wisdom" and the "word of knowledge": that all-important gift to *know* by the power of the Holy Ghost that Jesus is the Christ.

The society was not only to perform charitable work, but also to acquire and exercise the gift of charity, beginning within the group itself. Emma Smith admonished her sisters to "divest themselves of every jealousy and evil feeling toward each other."[43] "Let your hearts expand," the Prophet exhorted; "let them be enlarged towards others — you must be long-suff'ring and bear with the faults and errors of mankind. How precious are the souls of men! — The female part of the community are apt to be contracted in their views. You must not be contracted, but you must be liberal in your feelings."

He admonished the sisters to apply these principles in their families. "Let this Society teach how to act towards husbands to treat them with mildness and affection," he said. "When a man is borne down with trouble—when he is perplex'd, if he can meet a smile, not an argument—if he can meet with mildness, it will calm down his soul and soothe his feelings. . . . When you go home never give a cross word, but let kindness, charity and love, crown your works henceforward."[44]

Originally new members were admitted by a simple vote, but by June 1842, as membership expanded beyond the circle of women who were already acquainted, Joseph suggested that "henceforth no person shall be admitted but by presenting regular petitions signed by two or three members in good standing in the Society."[45]

From time to time objections were made to those applying for membership. On one such occasion, after previous objections to an applicant, a "Sister O.," had been removed, Joseph said that he was "going to preach mercy." "Christ was condemn'd by the righteous Jews because he took sinners into his society—he took them upon the principle that they repented of their sins," he reminded the sisters, then specified the application to their situation. "It is the object of this Society to reform persons, not to take those that are corrupt, but if they repent we are bound to take them and by kindness sanctify and cleanse from all unrighteousness, by our influence in watching over them." Joseph Smith felt that "so goodly a Society as this . . . [should] take Sis. O. as Jesus received sinners into his bosom" and by kindness encourage her reform.

Enlarging the example into a lesson for all, the Prophet observed: "Nothing is so much calculated to lead people to forsake sin as to take them by the hand and watch over them with tenderness." He also noted that individuals who are "unacquainted with the principle of godliness" display a "contraction of feeling and lack of charity." In contrast, "the pow'r and glory of Godliness is spread out on a broad principle to throw out the mantle of charity. God does not look on sin with allowance, but when men hav sin'd there must be allowance made for them."[46]

As far as the Prophet was concerned, the society had been organized for spiritual as well as temporal aid. "The Society is not only to relieve the poor but to save souls," he told them.[47] Such is the end point of charity, "the pure love of Christ."[48]

The sisters extended spiritual aid by remembering those in need through collective and individual prayers. Their concern is recorded often. At one meeting counselors Whitney and Cleveland asked sisters to pray on behalf of children. One woman asked the sisters to pray for her paralytic daughter. A Sister Jones, anticipating a journey to Ohio, where she would "visit friends who were moving in the higher classes of Society . . . requested the prayers of this Society that her testimony may be instrumental of good."[49] The Prophet had admonished the sisters as early as the first meeting to be aware of women who were having difficulty abiding by Church teachings; the society's prayers were often requested on behalf of such transgressors.

Finally, the society prayed for its leaders, particularly for Emma Smith during her long months of absence in 1843, due in part to illness. Joseph Smith had exhorted the sisters "always to concentrate their faith" in their leaders. "We should arm them with our prayers," he said.[50] He appreciated such prayers, affirming in August 1842 that they "avail much," and entreating the sisters: "Let them not cease to ascend to God in my behalf."[51]

Not prayers alone were brought to the Prophet's aid. In late July 1842, Missouri officials sought him with renewed vigor, armed with writs for his arrest and extradition on charges of complicity in the attempted murder of ex-governor Lilburn Boggs. The Nauvoo city council and the Female Relief Society both prepared petitions requesting Joseph's protection at the hands of Thomas Carlin, governor of Illinois. The first bore some eight hundred signatures; the second, about a thousand.

Eliza Snow, amanuensis to Emma Smith in the drafting of the Relief Society petition, accompanied Emma to Quincy, as did Amanda Smith, whose husband and son had been killed at Haun's Mill in Missouri. They had reason to expect a friendly reception. From his first meeting in 1839 with Sidney Rigdon, who had been sent to represent the Latter-day Saints, the governor had publicly taken their part. "The Gov. received us with cordiality," Eliza wrote in her diary, "assuring us of his protection." Even then, however, she sensed some lack of conviction, for she added, "it remains for time and circumstance to prove the sincerity of his professions." Her doubts were well founded. She later wrote, "But alas! soon after our return, we learned that at the time of our visit, and while making protestations of friendship, the wily Governor was secretly conniving with the basest of men to destroy our leaders."[52] The petition and Emma Smith's subsequent letter to the governor, pleading with him "to lighten the hand of oppression and persecution which is laid upon me and my family, which materially affect

Emma Hale Smith, first president of the Relief Society, as she appeared in 1845. The baby is David Hiram, born November 17, 1844. (Courtesy LDS Church Archives)

the peace and welfare of this whole community," proved of no avail.[53]

"The Order of the Priesthood"

As it collectively joined to raise funds for the new temple, to relieve the poor, to petition, and to pray, the Female Relief Society of Nauvoo resembled on the surface its contemporaries in the eastern United States. Yet Latter-day Saint women regarded their society as very different from these popular institutions of the day: "There are many Benevolent Societies abroad designd to do good but not as this," said Reynolds Cahoon, one of Joseph's close associates and president of the stake at Zarahemla, Iowa, visiting members of the Relief Society in 1843. "Ours is according to the order of God, connected with the priesthood according to the same good principals."[54]

The order of the priesthood—"which encompasses powers, keys, ordinances, offices, duties, organizations, and attitudes"—

had been unfolding for thirteen years, from 1829 to 1842, when the Relief Society was organized.[55] The restoration process began in 1829, when heavenly messengers bestowed upon Joseph Smith and Oliver Cowdery the authority to baptize, to lay on hands for the gift of the Holy Ghost, to preach, and to ordain other elders. After the Church was formally organized in 1830, other priesthood offices were added during 1830 and 1831, including deacons, teachers, priests, bishops, and high priests. In 1832 the order of the priesthood was more clearly defined when Joseph Smith received a revelation, Doctrine and Covenants 84, that distinguished the Melchizedek (Higher) Priesthood from the Aaronic (Lesser) Priesthood and affirmed that "the body hath need of every member, that all may be edified together, that the system may be kept perfect."[56] The First Presidency was organized in 1832, the first stake high council in 1834, and the Quorum of the Twelve and a quorum of the seventy in 1835. On March 28, 1835, Joseph presented another major revelation on priesthood, Doctrine and Covenants 107, which explained the history, power, and preeminent authority of the Melchizedek Priesthood, its relationship to the Aaronic Priesthood, and the duties incumbent upon various offices of, or "appendages" to, the Melchizedek Priesthood.

Restoration of the full order of the priesthood would not be complete until, as Moroni had promised Joseph Smith in 1823, God further revealed "the Priesthood, by the hand of Elijah the prophet."[57] In April 1836, as Joseph and Oliver Cowdery knelt in prayer in the Kirtland Temple, "the eyes of [their] understanding were opened" and they saw Moses, Elias, and Elijah, and the Lord Jesus Christ, each of whom conveyed a message or authority. Elijah committed to the Prophet "the keys of this dispensation," keys that the Prophet came to understand could be used only in connection with the sacred ordinances of the temple. These keys of redemption and sealing would, as foretold by the ancient prophet Malachi, "turn the heart of the fathers to the children, and the heart of the children to their fathers."[58]

The bestowal of these keys commenced, but did not complete, the restoration of the fullness of the priesthood. Historian Ronald K. Esplin observed: "Joseph Smith only gradually comprehended what God required of him, and more gradually still, found means to do it. . . . Learning and then implementing all essential aspects of his temple-related responsibilities became for Joseph Smith a central concern the entire last decade of his life."[59] This concern impelled the doctrinal and organizational innovations the Prophet made in Nauvoo and resulted in profound blessings for women. In Nauvoo, as the full order of the priesthood was taught and implemented, women assumed a new and significant place within church ordinances and organization.

A revelation received by Joseph Smith January 19, 1841, commanded the Saints to build a temple at Nauvoo, declaring that "there is not a place found on earth that [the Lord] may come to and restore again that which was lost unto [them], or which he hath taken away, even the fulness of the priesthood." As God's covenant people and church sacrificed to build a temple unto his name, he would reveal to them his ordinances and "things which have been kept hid from before the foundation of the world, things that pertain to the dispensation of the fulness of times." He promised to "show unto [his] servant Joseph all things pertaining to this house, and the priesthood thereof."[60]

The women who gathered in 1842 to sew shirts for temple workmen and in other ways contribute to the work may or may not have been pondering this revelation, but they answered inward stirrings that prompted them to join together in a more formal organization. A history written by Sarah M. Kimball in 1882, in her capacity as general secretary of the Relief Society, recounts how Joseph Smith seized the occasion of reviewing the drafted constitution for this "Ladies' Society" to organize women as only a prophet of God could, according to priesthood patterns God had revealed to him. She adds to the account in the minutes her own experience and understanding that after Joseph Smith had seen the bylaws and offered the "something better" to the sisters, he added, significantly, "I have desired to organize the Sisters in the order of the Priesthood. I now have the key by which I can do it. The organization of the Church of Christ was never perfect until the women were organized." He wanted Sister Snow "to tell the sisters who delegated you that their offering is accepted of the Lord, and will result in blessing to them." Setting the time and place for the meeting, he promised: "I will organize you in the order of the Priesthood after the pattern of the Church."[61]

Sarah Kimball's retrospective account succinctly conveys her understanding of the Prophet's intentions for the Relief Society and points to the truths he taught women at this founding meeting concerning their place in "the restoration of all things." With regard to these concepts, three words in the account are of capital and interrelated importance: pattern, priesthood, and keys.

These words are further clarified by the Prophet's teachings in subsequent visits to the Relief Society, as recorded in the organization's official minutes. In them, he makes clear (1) that he organized the Relief Society according to the same pattern as he did the priesthood quorums, (2) that he taught Relief Society members the same "doctrine of the priesthood" he had taught the priesthood quorums, (3) that he delegated to the Relief Society certain "keys," or authority, and (4) that the inclusion of women within the structure of the church organization reflected the divine pattern of the perfect union of man and woman, a pattern emphasized in the highest priesthood ordinances administered in the temple and essential to the restoration of the fullness of the priesthood. These seminal concepts are worth examining in detail.

The Relief Society, organized "after the pattern of the Church," closely resembled the priesthood quorums in organizational structure and procedures. At the founding meeting, Joseph Smith "propos'd that the Sisters elect a presiding officer to preside over them, and let that presiding officer choose two Counsellors to assist in the duties of her Office."⁶² Thus the Relief Society presidency, like stake presidencies, bishoprics, and quorum presidencies, would be patterned after the First Presidency with a president and two counselors. The presidency of the Relief Society, "like the first Presidency of the church," would be elected "to continue in office during good behavior, or so long as they shall continue to fill the office with dignity."⁶³

By 1842 the pattern of church organization required the keeping of a record. The Prophet Joseph had lamented in 1835, as he established the Quorum of the Twelve, that he lacked written accounts of "every decision which has been had, upon important items of doctrine and duties . . . which, had we now, would decide almost any point of doctrine which might be agitated." By his request, at the Relief Society's founding meeting Willard Richards acted as scribe, keeping careful minutes of the proceedings until Eliza R. Snow was chosen as secretary. "The minutes of your meetings will be precedents for you to act upon—your Constitution and law," the Prophet explained. The Relief Society presidency was also to "serve as a constitution—all their decisions be considered law; and acted upon as such." Like the priesthood quorums, then, the Relief Society actually had two constitutions, its minutes and its presidency, a "living constitution."

In a church that emphasized continuing revelation, precedents were important but not sufficient in and of themselves. Built into the Prophet's dual use of the term "constitution" to apply to both the living presidency and the preserved minutes was a healthy tension: a thrust to conservative behavior, to cling to what went before as recorded in the minutes, countered by an expectation that the current presidency would respond to changing needs by overriding precedents and initiating new policies.[64]

For one thing, the Relief Society presidency would determine to what extent additional officers might be necessary. "If any Officers are wanted to carry out the designs of the Institution, let them be appointed and set apart," the Prophet suggested.[65] This the women did, as in the calling in July 1843 of a committee of teachers in each of Nauvoo's four wards to visit the sisters to assess needs and collect contributions. Visiting teachers have remained a permanent part of Relief Society, although their functions have changed over the years. Other officers have also been appointed and set apart as needs have arisen.

With its own presidency, records, and officers, the Relief Society was a self-governing entity, distinct but not independent. Rather, it was interdependent with other "necessary appendages belonging unto the high priesthood."[66] As described in Paul's analogy of the body of Christ, these were many members "fitly joined together and compacted by that which every joint supplieth," with Christ as the head.[67] Joseph Smith confirmed that "the body hath need of every member, that all may be edified together, that the system may be kept perfect."[68] He instructed members of the Relief Society that "all must act in concert or nothing can be done."[69]

Joseph Smith's April 28, 1842, Discourse

The sixth meeting of the Relief Society, April 28, 1842, was the occasion for an important discourse from the Prophet, in which he would "make observations respecting the Priesthood, and give instructions for the benefit of the Society." A few weeks before, he had expressed his hope that the society "might be built up to the Most High in an acceptable manner," declaring "that the Society should move according to the ancient Priesthood."[70] His lengthy and significant discourse to the women schooled them in doctrines revealed and taught earlier. At this meeting, however, the Prophet applied them directly to women and their callings within the Church.

"Let every man stand in his own office, and labor in his own calling," Joseph had recorded in September 1832.[71] In April 1842 he gave the women "instructions respecting the different offices, and the necessity of every individual acting in the sphere allotted him or her; and filling the several offices to which they were appointed." He further "spoke of the disposition of man, to consider the lower offices in the Church dishonorable and to look with jealous eyes upon the standing of others — that it was the nonsense of the human heart, for a person to be aspiring to other stations than appointed of God — that it was better for individuals to magnify their respective callings, and wait patiently till God shall say to them — come up higher." The injunction applied to women as well as to men.

The Prophet explained that "the reason of these remarks being made, was, that some little thing was circulating in this Society, that some persons were not doing right in laying hands on the sick &c."[72] Rejoicing "that the sick could be heal'd," he referred "to the commission given to the ancient apostles 'Go ye into all the world' &c. — no matter who believeth; these signs, such as healing the sick, casting out devils &c. should follow all that believe." In Doctrine and Covenants 84:64–66, he had already clarified the familiar verses from the Gospel of Mark, emphasizing that "*every soul* who believeth upon your words, and is baptized by water for the remission of sins, shall receive the Holy Ghost," with signs and "many wonderful works" following "them that believe." "No matter who believeth," Joseph now added, "whether male or female."

He then "ask'd this Society if they could not see by this sweeping stroke, that wherein they are ordained, it is the privilege of those set apart to administer in that authority which is conferr'd on them — and if the sisters should have faith to heal the sick let all hold their tongues, and let every thing roll on." He continued to reason that "there could be no devils in it if God gave his sanction by healing — that there could be no more sin in any female laying hands on the sick than in wetting the face with water — that it is no sin for any body to do it that has faith or if the sick has faith to be heal'd by the administration." He returned to this subject several times during his discourse and concluded by offering "instruction respecting the propriety of females administering to the sick by the laying on of hands — said it was according to revelation

&c. said he never was placed in similar circumstances, and never had given the same instruction."

Elder Franklin D. Richards reflected years later on the importance of the Prophet's sermon, still fresh in the minds, he observed, of those who had heard the Prophet's words, "as did also myself." It was, explained Elder Richards, "just before he (Joseph Smith) commenced giving endowments," and he was "hastening the work of the Temple to get ready for it."[73] In September 1843 the first women, prepared by the instructions Joseph Smith gave to the Relief Society, were endowed. Their anointing and blessing of one another would then find enduring expression as they ministered in the ordinances of the holy endowment.

Joseph Smith was more reserved in encouraging women to exercise the gift of tongues. "If any have a matter to reveal, let it be in your own tongue," he advised. "Do not indulge too much in the gift of tongues, or the devil will take advantage of the innocent. You may speak in tongues for your comfort but I lay this down for a rule that if any thing is taught by this gift of tongues, it is not to be received for doctrine." The same warning against abuse of the gift had been enunciated in Kirtland in 1836.[74]

The Prophet had opened with a warning to those who aspired to higher offices and whose jealousy had, he implied, led some to question other sisters' rights to exercise spiritual gifts. He returned to the theme of pride, cautioning the Relief Society to guard against it. Those with spiritual gifts should "not boast themselves of these things, neither speak them before the world," he had taught in 1832.[75] Referring to men with significant callings within the Church, "aspiring men, 'great big Elders' as he called them, who had caused him much trouble," he expressed his concern to the sisters that "the same aspiring disposition will be in this Society, and must be guarded against.... He said we had a subtle devil to deal with, and could only curb him by being humble." The counsel echoed the Prophet's March 1839 letter from Liberty Jail, warning those in church callings who "aspire to the honors of men" or "to gratify our pride, our vain ambition" that the "heavens [will] withdraw themselves" because "the rights of the priesthood are inseparably connected with the powers of heaven, and . . . the powers of heaven cannot be controlled nor handled only upon the principles of righteousness." That is, "by persuasion, by long-suffering, by gentleness and meekness, and by love unfeigned."[76]

In offering the Relief Society "observations respecting the

priesthood," Joseph reiterated the same principles. "Not war, not jangle, not contradiction, but meekness, love, purity, these are the things that should magnify us," he said. He promised great blessings to souls thus enlarged: "If you live up to these principles how great and glorious. – if you live up to your privileges, the angels cannot be restrain'd from being your associates."

The Prophet Joseph, like the ancient prophet Moses, "sought diligently to sanctify his people that they might behold the face of God."[77] The emerging order of the priesthood was a means to this end. In both ancient and modern times, sanctification was to be accomplished through the authority and ordinances of the Melchizedek Priesthood, particularly temple ordinances. "The Church is not now organiz'd in its proper order, and cannot be until the Temple is completed," he explained. That promise was, as yet, for most members, a future blessing. In the meantime, Relief Society would serve as schoolmaster in preparing women toward the great end of sanctification and eternal life in God's presence. "Every person should stand and act in the place appointed," the Prophet instructed the women, "and thus sanctify the Society and get it pure."

The doctrine of the priesthood, taught personally by the Prophet to women, was precious to them. One member of the Female Relief Society of Nauvoo, Mercy Fielding Thompson, later testified: "I have been present at meetings of the Relief Society and heard him give directions and counsels to the sisters, calculated to inspire them to efforts which would lead to celestial glory and exaltation, and oh! how my heart rejoiced."[78]

With knowledge came responsibility. Toward the end of his long discourse, the Prophet Joseph observed: "After this instruction, you will be responsible for your own sins. It is an honor to save yourselves – all are responsible to save themselves." Indeed, because the Relief Society was "not only to relieve the poor but to save souls,"[79] he delegated to the women special keys or authority to minister to the spiritual welfare and salvation of the female members of the Church.

Three times during his April 28, 1842, discourse the Prophet spoke of "keys." First, with plain and poignant foreboding of his imminent death, he said that "as he had this opportunity, he was going to instruct the Society and point out the way for them to conduct, that they might act according to the will of God – that he did not know as he should have many opportunities of teaching

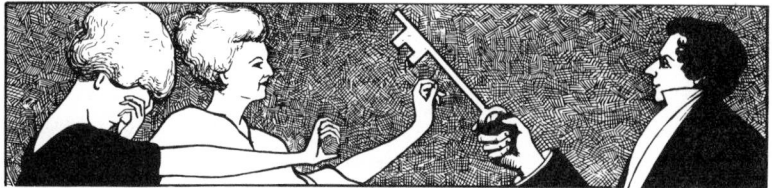

Women move from darkness into light, receiving new knowledge and authority as Joseph Smith turns the key to them. Illustration by Joseph A. F. Everett for the March 1936 cover of *Relief Society Magazine.*

them—that they were going to be left to themselves,—they would not long have him to instruct them—that the church would not have his instruction long, and the world would not be troubled with him a great while, and would not have his teachings—He spoke of delivering the keys to this Society—and to the Church—that according to his prayers God had appointed him elsewhere."

Second, the Prophet spoke of the "keys of the kingdom." While several revelations in the Doctrine and Covenants affirm that the governing and sealing "keys of the kingdom" belong to the apostles, on this occasion he seemed to use the term in a broader sense to indicate endowments of knowledge and discernment. He promised that such keys would be given to "those whom God has appointed to honor, whom God has placed at the head to lead . . . that they may be able to detect everything false."[80]

Finally, he declared: "This Society is to get instruction thro' the order which God has established—thro' the medium of those appointed to lead—and I now turn the key to you in the name of God and this Society shall rejoice and knowledge and intelligence shall flow down from this time—this is the beginning of better days to this Society."

The Prophet's April 28 declaration that he was turning the key to women is of singular importance to Latter-day Saints because it opened to women channels for service and learning hitherto closed to them. Prior to the organization of the Relief Society, women had not acted in any official capacity within the latter-day church organization, nor had they participated in sacred temple ordinances.

A careful consideration of Joseph Smith's use of the term "keys" in connection with Relief Society is critical to understanding the important new stewardships women received in Nauvoo. Keys, essential instruments for unlocking, carry now, as they did in 1842, two important meanings for Latter-day Saints. First, keys imply authority. Second, keys are a means of obtaining, in the Prophet's words, "knowledge and intelligence" from God. The turning of the key, the creation of the society itself, opened to women their place and responsibility in the organization of the Church. It also, as Joseph foresaw, created for women a place by the side of their brethren in receiving the blessings of the temple, where they together would be endowed with light and knowledge from above.

No other authority than that of the Prophet could have brought Relief Society into being. He held the keys of the kingdom of God on earth, the directive power, the right of presidency. Only he was legally entitled to make the Relief Society an official part of the kingdom and to bind it to the whole in heaven as on earth. Only through his authority, and by power of his priesthood, could he grant Relief Society the authority to act in all things within the scope of its commission.[81]

The temporal commission or duties of Relief Society would change as contemporary circumstances required, but its spiritual commission was a permanent mandate: to "teach the female part of the community," and to "save souls," as Joseph Smith declared, or, as restated by President Joseph F. Smith in 1906, "to look after the spiritual welfare and salvation of the mothers and daughters of Zion; and to see that none is neglected, but that all are guarded against misfortune, calamity, the powers of darkness, and the evils that threaten them in the world."[82]

Under the presiding authority of the Melchizedek Priesthood, the Relief Society officers appointed and set apart in Nauvoo "were now authorized to direct, control, and govern the affairs of the society," observed Elder Bruce R. McConkie, explaining that "under this appointment their lawful acts would be recognized by the Lord and he would work with them in the rolling forth of the kingdom in the sphere assigned them."[83]

The Relief Society organization was to be self-governing; but, like the priesthood quorums, it was to operate within the order of church government, that is, under the direction of the Melchizedek Priesthood, which as Joseph Smith taught by revelation "has power and authority over all the offices in the church in all ages of the world." (D&C 107:8.) This priesthood, named after a great high priest but signifying the Holy Order of the Son of God, Jesus Christ, who is the true King of Righteousness, is honored by all Latter-day Saints, male and female. Women and men both submit themselves unto the Melchizedek Priesthood and receive instruction, as

Joseph told the sisters, "thro' the order which God has established — thro' the medium of those appointed to lead."[84] With the Prophet's turning of the key, Relief Society, like the priesthood quorums, became an official part of the order of church government, each individual member adding a new dimension to her relationship of honor and obedience to priesthood truths and doctrines.

"While the sisters have not been given the priesthood, it has not been conferred upon them," explained Joseph Fielding Smith, president of the Council of the Twelve in 1958, "that does not mean the Lord has not given unto them authority. Authority and priesthood are two different things."[85] Historically, other leaders have made a similar distinction, clearly differentiating between the authority women receive and priesthood offices to which men are ordained. At various times Relief Society history actually has been revised with this distinction in mind. Thus, in preparing the official history of the Church in 1855, the Quorum of the Twelve edited the wording in the original minutes, "I now turn the key to you," to read "I now turn the key in your behalf."[86]

In 1880, commenting on the actions of the Female Relief Society of Nauvoo, John Taylor explained that when members of the Relief Society presidency in Nauvoo were "ordained," they were not ordained to priesthood offices, but received blessings that set them apart for their sacred callings. Eliza R. Snow and Bathsheba Smith, who had been present at the Nauvoo meeting, nodded agreement.[87] In 1906 Relief Society president Bathsheba Smith and secretary Emmeline Wells corrected a published historical account of the first Relief Society meeting that included Sarah M. Kimball's recollection that the Prophet had desired to organize women "in the order of the priesthood." Almost certainly at the request of the priesthood leaders concerned about misunderstanding, they searched for the phrase in the original Relief Society minutes and confirmed that "no such statement was made" there.[88]

More recently, during the last half of the twentieth century, the word *keys* itself has come to be more precisely defined by Latter-day Saints, and is now exclusively associated with the right to direct the exercise of priesthood authority. Those who hold the keys of the priesthood, wrote Elder Bruce R. McConkie in 1984, "are empowered to direct the manner in which others use their priesthood."[89] The "keys of the kingdom," in keeping with scriptural precedent, are now understood to be the entire quantity of governing and sealing keys held by the First Presidency and Council of the Twelve.[90] These recent refinements in usage, like earlier revisions and clarifying comments, illustrate church leaders' efforts over the past one hundred and fifty years to define and strengthen administrative channels of priesthood authority.

Whether Latter-day Saint women were "ordained" or "set apart," whether the key was turned to them or in their behalf, whether they were organized "in the order of the priesthood," "after the pattern of the priesthood," or "under the priesthood," seems to have been less important to them than the fact that they were organized by a prophet of God "according to the order of God." Their society was different from contemporary female benevolent societies because it was "connected with the priesthood," a connection that was neither tentative nor tangential. In 1964 Joseph Fielding Smith confirmed that "the Relief Society was revealed to the Prophet Joseph Smith as a fundamental part of the gospel," that "in this the greatest dispensation of all, because it is the last, the women are given some measure of divine authority particularly in the direction of government and instruction in behalf of the women of the church."[91]

Reynolds Cahoon, one of the first church leaders to receive his temple endowment, had earlier stressed the fundamental importance of the Relief Society to the Church, asserting in August 1843 that "the Order of the Priesthood is not complete without it." Through his close association with the Prophet, he had come to understand that the inclusion of women within the structure of the church organization reflected the divine pattern of the perfect union of man and woman. This pattern, emphasized in the highest priesthood ordinances administered in the temple, was essential to the restoration of the fullness of the priesthood. Anticipating the day, soon to come, when women would be endowed, stake president Cahoon told the women, "You knew not doubt but this Society is rais[e]d by the Lord to prepare us for the great blessings which are for us in the House of the Lord in the Temple." "The Church is not now organiz'd in its proper order," the Prophet Joseph had said, "and cannot be until the Temple is completed."[92]

Blessings of the Temple

Women would both work to contribute to the temple's completion and rejoice as partakers of its blessings. Mercy Fielding Thompson prayerfully considered how to assist with the building of the temple and received "what seemed to be the whispering of the still small voice" prompting her to "try to get the Sisters to subscribe one Cent per Week for the purpose of buying glass and nails for the Temple." With the blessing of Joseph Smith, she followed the inspiration she had received, involving her sister Mary Fielding Smith in the penny-fund effort and drawing much-appreciated support from Mary's husband, Hyrum, the Prophet's brother. In response to a notice placed in the *Millennial Star* in June 1844, twenty English pounds came from Latter-day Saint women in England. Mercy and Mary eventually collected one thousand dollars.[93]

Interest in forwarding work on the temple had been the impetus for the spring 1842 gathering at Sarah Kimball's home, though the first-year efforts of the subsequently formed Female Relief Society of Nauvoo were directed primarily toward relieving the poor. In June 1843, however, as the group began its second year of meetings, counselor Elizabeth Ann Whitney announced that "she had received instructions [from Emma Smith] that we might not only relieve the wants of the poor but also cast in our mites to assist the brethren in building the Lord's House."[94] The secretary recorded how "the sisters express'd their feelings one by one," manifesting a unanimous "desire to assist in forwarding the Temple and in aiding the cause of Zion." Sister Jones offered to board one of the temple workmen. Mrs. Durfee said she would "go abroad with a wagon & collect wool." Mrs. Felshaw wanted to donate soap. Mrs. Smith, resubmitting the original scheme proposed the year before by Margaret Cook and Sarah Kimball, "suggested that merchant's wives donate material that others may be employ'd." Mrs. Granger said she would knit or sew, and Mrs. Angell was willing "to repair old clothes if necessary when new material cannot be obtain'd." Dolly Meekum "had giv'n all her Jewelry for the Temple [and] was willing to do anything she could." Miss Wheeler volunteered "any portion, or all of her time."[95] Similar sentiments prevailed through the summer and fall, with Sister J. Smith expressing in October the women's continuing sense of urgency: "O that we might rouse to action and thus call down the blessings of God upon us."[96]

Women tasted some of the blessings promised in connection with the temple when they began performing baptisms for the dead in the Mississippi River in September 1840. A revelation to Joseph Smith in January 1841, however, stressed that "this ordinance belongeth to [the Lord's] house."[97] The involvement of living persons in performing essential ordinances on behalf of the dead would form a fundamental part of temple worship. In restoring such ordinances, the Prophet "opened doors for the spiritual reunion of families that had lost members to death, or, as was common among early converts, had been estranged when loved ones joined the church, never to meet again in life," observed Carol Cornwall Madsen in her comprehensive study of Latter-day Saint women and the temple.[98]

Sally Randall was one of many who took profound comfort in this promise. Her fourteen-year-old son George died less than a month after she moved from New York to Nauvoo with her husband and two sons. "With a trembling hand and a heart full of grief and sorrow," she sent news of the death to the non-Mormon family members she had left behind. Then, five months later, she assured them of newly discovered peace and hope, writing: "[George's] father has been baptized for him and what a glorious thing it is that we believe and receive the fulness of the gospel as it is preached now and can be baptized for all of our dead friends and save them as far back as we can get any knowledge of them. I want you should write me the given names of all of our connections that are dead as far back as grandfather's and grandmother's at any rate. I intend to do what I can to save my friends. . . . I expect you will think this is strange doctrine but you will find it to be true." To her mother, who had also lost a child to death, she testified, "Oh, mother, if we are so happy as to have a part in the first resurrection, we shall have our children just as we laid them down in their graves."[99]

Sally Randall's letter is dated April 21, 1844, just two weeks after Joseph Smith's King Follett funeral sermon, wherein he addressed several thousand Saints "on the subject of the dead" and promised, "Yes! Yes! Mothers, you will have your children [in eternity]." Commenting on the keys he had received from Elijah eight years earlier in the Kirtland Temple, the Prophet affirmed: "It is necessary that the seals be in our hands, to seal our children and our dead for the dispensation of the fulness of times."[100]

Promises concerning the salvation of the dead acquired even deeper meaning after the Prophet Joseph introduced the temple endowment in 1842. Ten years earlier, in 1832, it had been revealed to him that the highest ordinances of the Melchizedek Priesthood "holdeth the key of the mysteries of the kingdom, even the key of the knowledge of God," and that in these ordinances, "the power of godliness is manifest."[101] Such ordinances would prepare men and women to "see the face of God, even the Father," to "dwell in the presence of God and his Christ forever."[102] Those worthy to inherit this celestial glory would indeed become "partakers of the divine nature," "heirs of God, and joint-heirs with Christ."[103] The preparation of the Saints for celestial exaltation required the fullness of the priesthood as endowed through the ordinances of the temple.

In January 1842, with the Nauvoo Temple well under way, Joseph Smith wrote of its anticipated completion "as an event of the greatest importance to the Church and the world." God "has begun to restore the ancient order of His kingdom unto His servants and His people," the Prophet testified, and "all things are concurring to bring about the completion of the fullness of the Gospel, a fullness of the dispensation of dispensations, even the fullness of times . . . to prepare the earth for the return of His glory, even a celestial glory, and a kingdom of Priests and kings to God and the Lamb, forever, on Mount Zion."[104]

Two months later, on March 30, 1842, he instructed members of the newly organized Relief Society regarding their important role in the "kingdom of Priests and kings," the "holy nation" which would be established as the Saints were endowed through temple ordinances.[105] Since he was "deeply interested that [the Relief Society] might be built up to the Most High in an acceptable manner," he cautioned them against adding members too quickly without "a close examination of every candidate." According to Relief Society minutes, he said that "the Society should grow up by degrees — should commence with a few individuals — thus have a select Society of the virtuous and those who will walk circumspectly. . . . The Society should move according to the ancient Priesthood, hence there should be a select Society separate from all the evils of the world, choice, virtuous and holy — Said he was going to make of this Society a kingdom of priests as in Enoch's day — as in Pauls day."[106]

Bathsheba W. Smith, present at the Nauvoo meetings, reviewed the original minutes in 1905 while serving as Relief Society general president and presiding over women's work in the temples and commented on the Prophet's teachings. "He said . . . he wanted to make us, as the women were in Paul's day, 'A kingdom of priestesses.' We have the ceremony in our endowments as Joseph taught."[107]

The sacred ritual of the temple endowment was initiated May 4, 1842, as nine men met with the Prophet in the upper room of his store, the same room in which the Relief Society was holding its weekly meetings. "In this council," wrote Joseph Smith, "was instituted the ancient order of things for the first time in these last days," including "washings, anointings, endowments and the communication of keys pertaining to the Aaronic Priesthood, and so on to the highest order of the Melchisedek Priesthood . . . and all those plans and principles by which any one is enabled to secure the fullness of those blessings which have been prepared for the Church of the First Born, and come up and abide in the presence of the Eloheim in the eternal worlds."[108] He explained that the new "knowledge and intelligence" communicated through the endowment ceremony was intended only for the spiritually minded and that all the Saints would receive it once a proper place for sacred instruction had been established.[109]

Bishop Newel K. Whitney, husband of Relief Society counselor Elizabeth Ann and a participant in the first endowment session, attended the May 27, 1842, meeting of the Relief Society to testify of "great blessings [that lie] before, that would astonish you if you could behold them." As recorded in the minutes, he rejoiced in the formation of the Relief Society, which enabled women to "improve upon our talents and to prepare for those blessings which God is soon to bestow upon us." Regarding those blessings, he continued, "In the beginning God created man male and female and bestow'd upon man certain blessings peculiar to a man of God, of which woman partook, so that without the female all things cannot be restor'd to the earth—it takes all to restore the Priesthood. It is the intent of the Society, by humility and faithfulness, [to receive such blessings] in connexion with those husbands that are found worthy." Bishop Whitney promised the sisters, "God has many precious things to bestow, even to our astonishment if we are faithful. . . . I rejoice that God has given us means whereby we may get intelligence and instruction. . . . It is as much our privilege as that of the ancient saints." His comments encouraged the sisters to prepare "to receive grace for grace, light and intelligence—if we have intelligence we have pow'r—knowledge is power."[110]

Joseph Smith's promise, upon turning the key to women, that

"knowledge and intelligence shall flow down" was fulfilled as women of this dispensation began to receive the blessings of the temple endowment. Emma Smith received her endowment September 28, 1843, the first of a small group of women who were endowed before the Nauvoo Temple was completed.[111] Before the Saints left Nauvoo, some three thousand women would be endowed with sacred knowledge through participation in temple ordinances. It was for many as the Prophet Joseph promised Mercy Fielding Thompson it would be for her: the endowment "will bring you out of darkness into marvelous light."[112]

In addition to the endowment, Joseph Smith received and established by revelation temple ordinances that sealed husband and wife together in marriage "for time and for all eternity." Latter-day Saints learned that unless a marriage were performed "through him whom [God] anointed and appointed unto this power," it would not be "valid neither of force" when a husband and wife died.[113] "Acting with the sealing powers conferred upon him in the Kirtland Temple, Joseph Smith both performed sealings and delegated the sealing power to others before the completion of the Nauvoo Temple," explains historian Carol Cornwall Madsen.[114]

The revelation on eternal marriage, Doctrine and Covenants 132, taught that marriage in the "new and everlasting covenant" brought the same promise that Abraham and Sarah had received concerning their seed or posterity, that "both in the world and out of the world should they continue as innumerable as the stars."[115] Men and women sealed though priesthood power in the new and everlasting covenant could, if they remained worthy, receive "an exceeding, and an eternal weight of glory," "thrones, kingdoms, principalities, and powers," "a fulness and a continuation of the seeds forever and ever."[116] By pursuing the narrow way to "exaltation and continuation of the lives," they would become involved in "the continuation of the works of [the] Father, wherein he glorifieth himself." Ultimately, they would "be gods, because they have no end; therefore shall they be from everlasting to everlasting, because they continue."[117] Such promises are given in full measure to both marriage partners.

Indeed, fulfillment of the promise of eternal godhood or parenthood in the highest degree of celestial glory requires both man and woman. Scripture shows that through celestial marriage, a man and a woman enter into an "order of the priesthood,"[118] and Joseph Smith made clear that in connection with the temple, men and women together would ultimately receive a "fulness of priesthood" unavailable to either of them alone. Eliza R. Snow relied on this understanding in summarizing the unique status of Latter-day Saint women and the spiritual blessings available to them: They "occupy a more important position than is occupied by any other women on the earth. Associated, as they are, with apostles and prophets inspired by the living God—with them sharing in the gifts and powers of the holy Priesthood . . . participating in those sacred ordinances, without which, we could never be prepared to dwell in the presence of the Holy Ones."[119] A "kingdom of priestesses" had indeed been established as Joseph had prophesied, not so much as an organization, but by virtue of the numbers of women so anointed in the early days of the church.[120] As the ancient apostle Paul had preached: "Neither is the man without the woman, neither the woman without the man, in the Lord."[121] As the work of the priesthood quorums was to prepare men for the highest order, so was Relief Society to school women for that same glory.

In immediate terms, Joseph Smith spoke to the Saints about the reverence owing to their spouses. Wrote Lucy Walker Kimball, "He often refered to the feelings that should exist between husband and wives, that they . . . should be his bosom companions, the nearest and dearest Objects on earth in every sense of the word." "Men," he said, "must beware how they treat their wives. They were given them for a holy purpose."[122]

The revelation on the new and everlasting covenant of marriage, Doctrine and Covenants 132, also contained instructions regarding plurality of wives. It affirmed that Abraham, Isaac, and Jacob, in taking additional wives, "did none other than that which they were commanded," and appointed Joseph Smith to restore the ancient practice.[123] Under his direction a small group of men and women contracted plural marriages in Nauvoo. Lucy Walker, Eliza R. Snow, and Emily and Eliza Partridge, among others, became plural wives of Joseph Smith. These marriages, too, were performed and sanctified in connection with temple ordinances.[124]

Urgently, with premonition of his imminent death, two to three years before the Nauvoo Temple was completed and dedicated the Prophet introduced ordinances to seal together husbands and wives, parents and children, brothers and sisters, living and dead. Sacred covenants, endowments, and sealings bound God's people to Him and to one another so that they might become, like the Zion of Enoch's day, "of one heart and one mind."[125]

Saints had learned by revelation that such union is "required by the law of the celestial kingdom," that life in that realm is characterized by perfect unity.[126] In latter days as in ancient times, Jesus Christ invited Saints to believe on his name so that "they may become the sons [and daughters] of God, even one in me even as I am one in the Father, as the Father is one in me."[127] The belief of Latter-day Saints that we are children of a Mother in Heaven as well as our Father in Heaven, Christ being our Elder Brother, deepens mortal understanding of divine oneness, fullness, perfect unity. Though no extant recorded sermon of Joseph Smith discusses the nature of a heavenly mother, Zina D. H. Young, for one, witnessed that the Prophet personally had taught her the doctrine as she mourned the death of her own mother. Certainly the concept comes as a logical extension of his teaching that godhood is eternal parenthood, "a fulness and a continuation of the seeds forever and ever."[128] Significantly, however, Eliza R. Snow's Nauvoo poem known and sung for 150 years as "O My Father" is the earliest recorded expression of Latter-day Saint belief in a heavenly mother. Eliza Snow confirmed, "I got my inspiration from the Prophet's teaching[.] All that I was required to do was use my Poetical gift and give that Eternal principal in Poetry."[129] Published in the *Times and Seasons* in November 1845, sixteen months after the Prophet's martyrdom and three months before Saints began leaving Nauvoo, the poem's eight simple quatrains lent a sense of intimacy to the sweeping vision of eternity the Saints had recently received. Lines over which Eliza Snow later acknowledged she had labored articulated longing for and connection to the Mother who is in heaven.

MY FATHER IN HEAVEN

O my Father, thou that dwellest
  In the high and glorious place;
When shall I regain thy presence,
  And again behold thy face?
In thy holy habitation,
  Did my spirit once reside?
In my *first* primeval childhood
  Was I nurtur'd near thy side?

For a wise and glorious purpose,
  Thou has plac'd me here on earth,

And withheld the recollection
　　Of my former friends and birth:
Yet oft times a secret something
　　Whispered, you're a stranger here;
And I felt that I had wander'd
　　From a more exalted sphere.

I had learn'd to call thee Father,
　　Through thy spirit from on high;
But, until the key of knowledge
　　Was restor'd, I knew not why.
In the heav'ns are parents single?
　　No, the thought makes reason stare;
Truth is reason—truth eternal,
　　Tells me I've a mother there.

When I leave this frail existence—
　　When I lay this mortal by;
Father, mother, may I meet you
　　In your royal court on high?
Then, at length, when I've completed
　　All you sent me forth to do;
With your mutual approbation,
　　Let me come and dwell with you.[130]

Thus the crowning doctrine concerning woman, pronounced by the Prophet, was published by the poet. There could have been no more fitting epilogue to women's experience in Nauvoo. There they had learned a new pattern of responsibility and blessing and experienced a new order. They had received in their organization keys, or authority, and through the ordinances of the temple new knowledge and intelligence. They and their brethren realized together that the Church of Jesus Christ could not be complete without the women, nor indeed, the women without the Church. Fullness of the priesthood encircled and included them. Here was harmony and balance in astounding clarity—a sacred pattern from beginning to end, from time to eternity. Through his prophet, God had revealed the doctrine, extended the keys, and restored the vision. Nauvoo would not realize the fullness, nor yet perhaps would Deseret. But the principles were in place; the daughters, like the sons, would search out the way in years to come.

CHAPTER 2

"TRIBULATION WORKETH
PATIENCE"
1844–1866

"Then came the awful tragedy—the assassination of the Prophet Joseph and his brother Hyrum in Carthage jail," remembered Mary Ann Phelps Rich, the fifteen-year-old daughter of Mormon converts. "The Saints were all plunged in grief, not knowing what to do."[1] Women were helpless observers of what preceded the shooting of the two men on that "ever to be r[em]embered awful day of the 27 of June 1844."[2]

Tension had been building over the past weeks. Zina Jacobs noted in her diary on June 17, "The Bretheren are halving to prepare to defend them selves again," following the court hearing of the *Expositor* affair, the destruction of an anti-Mormon press, which escalated action against the Mormons. The Nauvoo Legion was preparing to defend the city: "3 compan[i]es arived, t[w]o from over the river," she noted. "The bretheren are still in town tra[i]ning." She added three days later, "Joseph and the bretheren are in councel supplicating the throne of grace for His divine direction." "O God save thy people," she pleaded.[3]

"Hundreds have left the city since the fuss commenced," wrote Vilate Kimball to her husband, Heber. "Joseph went over the river," she added. Joseph's departure caused her no concern until she heard that he had "sent word back for his family to follow him." Then "my heart sunk within me. . . . For a little while I felt bad enough, but did not let any body know it, neither did I shed any tears. I felt a confidence in the Lord, that he would presurve us from the ravages of our enemies." Even as she wrote, however, the Prophet, having "composed his mind, and got the will of the Lord concerning him," was returning to Nauvoo, intending to go on to Carthage to face charges.

"They have just passed by here, on their way thare," Vilate

continued in her letter. "My heart said Lord bless those Dear men, and presurve them from those that thirst for their blood. Their giveing themselves up, is all that will save our city from destruction."[4] Three days later the bodies of Joseph and his brother Hyrum were returned to Nauvoo "in a new wagon which had no cover other than green bushes which had been laid over the top of the box."[5]

The women, however grieved, were not without warning of the impending tragedy. As early as April 28, 1842, Joseph had told them in a Relief Society meeting that they "would not have his instruction long . . . that according to his prayers God had appointed him elsewhere."[6] Organizing and authorizing the Relief Society had been one of several significant actions of the spring of 1842, tasks that he seemed impelled to perform as the temple approached completion and his own mission neared its end.

Other developments were also part of the winding-up of the Prophet's ministry: the introduction of temple blessings to men and women; the imparting of keys to the Twelve, and the bestowing upon Brigham Young of "the keys of the sealing power, . . . this last key, . . . most sacred of all."[7] In all of these developments women would be partakers; part of the purpose of Relief Society from the beginning had been to prepare them for those soul-saving responsibilities.

One of the final developments in doctrine and practice, however, created more discord than rejoicing among the Saints; misunderstood, it eventually led to the suspension of the Nauvoo Relief Society. Celestial or plural marriage was already in limited practice before the Relief Society was organized in 1842; at least nine of the twenty women at the first meeting were already, or soon would be, partakers in the newly reinstituted Old Testament practice, five of them as plural wives of the Prophet Joseph himself.[8] Others would become participants during the two years of the Nauvoo Relief Society. Yet their president, Emma Smith, found the principle untenable. Faithful to her husband through the persecutions of New York, Ohio, and Missouri, supportive of him in his administrative duties, homemaker to him and hostess to his guests, mother to his children, she could follow him anywhere but into polygamy.

Emma Smith had passed through her own "winter of discontent" in the year prior to the 1844 season's Relief Society meetings. Hesitantly she had permitted her husband to marry other wives in the new order; more recently she had disavowed that action and refused to participate further. Part of her private agenda for the Relief Society had been if not to abolish, at least to retard the practice, not only in its corrupted form of "spiritual wifery," as promoted by apostates, but also in its pure form as advocated among the Prophet's closest associates.

Emma Smith began each of the March 9 and 16, 1844, meetings with the reading of a W. W. Phelps text, "The Voice of Innocence," which pleaded protection for the "virtuous mothers, wives and daughters of Nauvoo" against "debauchees, vagabonds, and rakes." It specified the persecutions through which many Nauvoo women had passed, then affirmed that none of these pierced so deeply as the boast of one Orsimus Bostwick that he could "take half a bushel of meal and get what accommodation he wanted with almost any woman in the City." The "Voice of Innocence" text closed with the resolution that Joseph Smith be tendered thanks for his action against Bostwick, and with a disavowal of the "spiritual wife system" of John C. Bennett as publicized two years earlier.[9]

The document could be read aloud in less than ten minutes. The meetings, begun at ten o'clock and one o'clock each Saturday, lasted two hours each, indicating that much more was said than the minute taker recorded.

The second Saturday another document was read alongside the "Voice of Innocence." This open letter had first been read to the women two years earlier, at the second meeting of the new society. An epistle signed by Joseph Smith, Brigham Young, and others of the Quorum of the Twelve, this earlier document, in terms so general as to be easily misconstrued, had impugned those who pretended to priesthood authority to persuade the sisters into evildoing. In hindsight it is not difficult to recognize John C. Bennett and his associates as the men "aspiring after power and authority, and yet without principle," and "spiritual wifery," their counterfeit of celestial marriage, as the threat to women's virtue. "We do not want any one to believe any thing as coming from us contrary to the old established morals & virtues & scriptural laws," the letter states, seeming to confirm monogamy as the order of the kingdom. But, it continues, "we wish to keep the commandments of God in all things, as given directly from heav'n to us, living by every word that proceeded out of the mouth of the Lord," suggesting that the Saints should not reject polygamy when the Prophet had received it as revelation.[10]

The immediate difficulty was Emma's own, the climax to years of her struggle against the principle. But she enlisted her sisters in her battle, using the most powerful weapon she had: her position as president of the Relief Society. Applying her own interpretation to the 1842 epistle against spiritual wifery, she opposed the practice her prophet-husband was promoting, thus bringing dissent into the inner circles of the Church. With each successive meeting that March, she became more vehement in her demand for reformation, even requiring that the women "examin[e] the conduct of their leaders of this Society—that you may sit in judgment on their heads." In her strongest claim to validation, referencing the powers conferred on her in the organizational meeting two years earlier, she ended by claiming, as the minute taker wrote, "if their ever was any Authourity on the Earth she had it—and had yet."[11] Seeds of discord were sown, tares among the gospel's greening wheat.

Emma's actions, like the highly publicized dissent of other prominent Saints in Nauvoo, threatened the essential order and unity without which the Church could not survive. Following the Prophet's martyrdom in June 1844 and the subsequent contention regarding the succession of church leadership, Zina Jacobs would painstakingly transcribe into her journal the words of Brigham Young: "He spoke of Union and said that it must be by this principle we are saved, by this the Saviour would come and reign, by union the authority of the Priesthood stands, and holds its Dominion."[12]

In pitting her authority against that of the prophet through whom her authority had come, and in planting disorder and disunity among the sisters, Emma Smith had erred egregiously. Joseph had warned that "all must work in concert or nothing can be done"; Emma's actions were out of harmony. Though she closed the March 16, 1844, meeting by announcing her intent to call another when a "suitable place can be obtained," no further meetings of the Female Relief Society of Nauvoo are recorded.

The women who stood to be most anguished by Emma Smith's opposition to plural marriage, those who were or would be participants in the new order, understood and forgave her. Eliza Snow, who "dearly loved 'Sister Emma,'"[13] later credited her with noble motives, suggesting that it was Emma herself who disbanded the Nauvoo Relief Society: "Emma Smith gave it up so as not to lead the society in erro[r]," she told a new Relief Society group in Utah in 1868.[14] In 1880 John Taylor, remembering Emma Smith's attitudes and actions, concurred only that it was because of Emma's opposition to polygamy that the society had to be discontinued: "Sister Emma got severely tried in her mind about the doctrine of Plural Marriage and she made use of the position she held to try to pervert the minds of the sisters in relation to that doctrine."[15]

The Relief Society as an organization, for the time being, ceased to be. Groups of women still met for other purposes, mostly in communities away from Nauvoo. A Penny and Sewing Society met in Boston, and a Benevolent Sewing Society, formed in Lowell, Massachusetts, in July 1844, was still receiving enquiries in September.[16] A ladies' handwork society was organized by Charles C. Rich in one of Nauvoo's satellite towns,[17] and groups of women converts met in Britain, either as Relief Societies or in response to Mary and Mercy Fielding's penny drive. However, in Nauvoo feelings were so high that Brigham Young, successor to Joseph Smith in church leadership, was quoted as saying in a meeting of the Seventy, "When I want Sisters or the Wives of the members of the church to get up Relief Society I will summon them to my aid but until that time let them stay at home."[18] He would call Relief Society into activity again, but not until years had passed and the women's proven faithfulness had restored his confidence.

The Nauvoo generation of Relief Society members would for many years remember the disruption of their organization. When in the late 1860s President Brigham Young commissioned Eliza R. Snow to reestablish the society churchwide, she would find it necessary to correct a prevailing belief. "It has been said that the Society in Nauvoo did more harm than good," she acknowledged, "but it was not so." She reminded the women that "the society did a great deal of good, saved a great many lives &c."[19] And in 1873 Mary Isabella Horne, at the institution of the women's organization in Utah, would express gratitude that "it is now 3 years since our [Relief] Society was organized and we have not had cause to suspend our meetings as in the days of the beginning."[20]

By the time of Eliza Snow's call to revive the society in Utah, the lesson would have been well learned. "Without order we have no claim to the Spirit; we must have the spirit or we cannot remain organized," she would tell her sisters.[21] For the time being, Hannah Ells, who took the minutes in Eliza's absence, returned the precious record book to Sister Snow, who had been visiting some miles away and so was not at any of the March meetings. Eliza packed it away, not knowing when or how its sacred words would again be available to her sisters. Decades later and a thousand miles away, Emmeline Wells would reason that "Sister Eliza R. Snow brought with her the records from Nauvoo which proves that this association was never discontinued since its first organization."[22] Certainly in hindsight there seems to have been no cessation of women uniting to serve in the kingdom.

However bereft of their organization, Nauvoo women were not without involvement in ecclesiastical matters. The Second Quorum of Seventy, for example, opened its meetings to its members' wives in February 1845, with the stipulation that when there was priesthood business to transact, the women were to remain at home.[23] Even then, Brigham Young had to admit that the women "have a right to meddle because many of them are more sagacious & shrewd & more competent to attend to things of the financial affairs." Nevertheless, he excluded them from meetings in which temporal matters were discussed.[24]

More important than temporal affairs, however, were the spiritual matters to be attended to. The temple, in support of which the women had assembled in Sarah Kimball's parlor two years earlier, was still of prime importance. There were over twelve thousand Saints in Nauvoo; nearly half would receive their endowment before leaving.[25]

As the building progressed, several of the women already endowed in the Prophet Joseph's makeshift endowment room in the red brick store—Vilate Kimball, Elizabeth Ann Whitney, Mary Ann Young, and Bathsheba Smith—helped to prepare rooms in the Nauvoo Temple for the ceremonies. Others, such as Clarissa and Emily Cutler and Julia Durphy, sewed the veils that would furnish the interior. Sylvia Lyons brought pictures for the walls and a rocking chair and comforter.[26]

"The Wilderness of Our Affliction"

Through the fearsome last days of Nauvoo, while the temple formed the Saints' chief joy, preparing for the move west became their major activity. All Nauvoo was "one vast machanic shop," remembered Bathsheba Smith of the frenetic preparations for the trek. "Our parlor was used as a paint shop in which to paint wagons."[27] The order and unity that Zina Jacobs had found so satisfying soon gave way in these last weeks to confusion and disorganization. As the Saints began their westward trek in 1846, the wards and stakes into which the Nauvoo area had been organized became

"Madonna at Dawn," painted in 1936 by Minerva Teichert, depicts a weary pioneer mother in the tradition of Mary, mother of Christ, as long-suffering woman and deliverer. (Courtesy LDS Museum of Church History and Art)

meaningless. Not only was there no longer a Relief Society as such, but the networks of women who had been each other's strength were also torn asunder. Priesthood quorums were separated geographically, no longer able to meet together. Crossing Iowa in the mud and muck of early spring, the Saints fell into groupings according to circumstance more than by design.

Family ties provided the operative organization for the trek. The metaphor expanded to include large companies connected into family-like bodies, each headed by a patriarchal leader. Overall, a new tribal identity, a sense of divine familial relationship, grew, as the westering Saints saw themselves as the children of Israel in the wilderness.[28]

For the women, the family connection was a comforting concept, as is suggested in the trail diary of Eliza R. Snow. Her mother dead, her father estranged from the Church, Eliza found herself tied to the group through her plural marriage to Brigham Young. He had arranged for her care in the family of Stephen Markham, traveling in the company of Heber C. Kimball, to whom she looked as a father.

But Eliza felt her strongest connection with the sisters in this extended family. In Winter Quarters, where they camped over the winter of 1846–47, they discovered new bonds of sisterhood. At the conclusion of her first visit with the other wives of Brigham

Young, Eliza wrote warmly of her sister wives "for whom my love seem'd to increase with every day's aquaintance." No mere social visit, this had been a time of communion in which "the spirit of the Lord was pour'd out."[29]

In Winter Quarters and the other layover places along the trail west, other aspects of Relief Society, temporal and spiritual, were still functioning among the women. Seldom had the ministrations of women, organized or individual, been more needed. Sickness and death stalked the Saints as they struggled through the exposure and lack of nourishment of early spring and the ever-present disease-bearing mosquitoes of summer, only to find they must wait out the winter on Indian lands in Iowa or Nebraska, less than halfway to Zion. Exiled in what one person called the "wilderness of our affliction," the Saints had only each other, and God, to turn to.

"There was not a wagon in the whole camp, but what had sickness in it," wrote Drusilla Dorris Hendricks, but "we bore it with the patience of Job."[30] Accustomed to serving their families as doctor and nurse, women individually extended their care to one another and to their children and husbands, fathers and brothers, as they had through the Relief Society in Nauvoo. Louisa Barnes Pratt, whose husband was serving a mission in Tahiti and who was, therefore, the sole caregiver for their four daughters as they journeyed west, was stricken with severe dysentery as they approached Winter Quarters. "We were all admitted into a sister Henderson's house, a kind lady she was," she wrote. The next day Louisa and the girls continued on. Louisa "was conveyed to camp half dead with cholera morbus," as she called the disease. "The sisters thronged about my wagon. One proposed brandy and loaf sugar. I told her if she would bring it in a glass tumbler with a silver teaspoon I would take it, but would not drink it from a tin cup. She made haste to bring the medicine according to directions. It had the desired effect, and I was better."[31]

A disproportionate number of women to men in the Winter Quarters population presaged the difficulties of survival in a land where hunting and farming were essential. By late spring 1847, 500 men had gone with the Mormon Battalion, another 150 with the pioneer company. "Thus were left the aged, the feeble, the women and the children," Presendia Kimball recalled. "Only a few men were left to raise grain and vegetables, and protect the women and children."[32] Women did what they could to prepare and preserve what the men could provide and to supply themselves as they were able. Leonora Taylor recorded taking her sister wives berrying; Mary Richards wrote of gathering grapes; and several diarists spoke of braiding straw and making hats and baskets to barter for food. They furnished their tents, wagon boxes, dugouts, and cabins for greater comfort. Two sisters even built their own house.

Despite all their efforts to make homes in the wilderness, the women could not create normalcy out of the chaos of that winter. Not only was the death rate astronomical, but the infant mortality was intolerable. Jane S. Richards, who later became Weber Stake Relief Society president, suffered the deaths of two children before her husband returned from his mission to England. Of the 338 whose deaths are recorded in the sexton's record that year, 135, or more than one-third, were under age two. Of the 62 babies listed by midwife Patty Sessions in one year's record of deliveries, 22 died before they were six months old.[33] Women thus bereaved were supported by others who had known the same loss. "Sister Elvira Holmes' babe died," wrote Eliza Partridge Lyman, who had herself lost her baby boy five months earlier. "Received an invitation . . . to spend the day with her which I accepted. Visited with her the grave of her child."[34]

With understanding expanded through the sermons of Joseph Smith to the Nauvoo Relief Society and reinforced by their own experiences, the women found themselves open to their own power and potential for service.[35] With or without an organization, they recognized obligations of service and gave heed to such messages from their prophet and their temple experiences.

Healing was among the promised gifts. Indicative of their faith was the administration of Sister Persis Young to nineteen-year-old Helen Mar Kimball Whitney. The young woman had recently lost her first child in death, and the birthing had left her weak with infection, complicated by scurvy, or "blackleg," as it was called. Fasting, several of the sisters had met at Helen's mother's house to pray for her return to health, but the meeting had ended abruptly. Helen remembered: "I, being very weary and sad in spirit at the close of the day, had lain down, and I fell asleep. . . . I was quite young, and not having been healed as I had been told I should be, my faith was considerably shaken." Morning came, and with it, Persis Young. "She had been impressed by the Spirit to come and administer to me," wrote Helen, "and I would be healed; that she could not sleep, and she had come there in obedience to that

Spirit. She had been so long under its influence that she shook as though palsied when she laid her hands upon my head with my mother. She rebuked my weakness, and every disease that had been, or was then, afflicting me, and commanded me to be made whole, pronouncing health and many other blessings upon me. ... From that morning I went about to work as though nothing had been the matter. Thus did the Lord remember one of His unworthy handmaidens and fulfill the promise that had been given by the gift and power of the Holy Ghost."[36] In no way did Persis Young claim priesthood power, nor was this a priesthood administration. The blessing of healing came in divine response, Helen affirms, to the prayer of faith offered by one woman in behalf of another.

In accounts of "little meetings" recorded by several women are reports of other manifestations: "The gift of tongues and interpretation, and the gift of prophecy" were given them for their "comfort and consolation in this trying time." Such spiritual affirmation had supported and given Presendia Buell [Kimball] "courage in the darkest hours of her lonel[iness]." When "her cup seemed to be running over with bitterness, she could recall to mind what had been shown her in vision, and the promises made to her if she proved faithful and true."[37] Helen Mar Whitney recorded, "The love of God flowed from heart to heart, till the wicked one seemed powerless in his efforts to get between us and the Lord, and his cruel darts, in some instances, were shorn of their sting."[38]

In all this—in doctrine, in ministrations, in endowments from on high—the spirit of the Nauvoo Relief Society lingered. Emmeline Wells reflected that "the sisters never lost sight of this institution as it had been established, nor the promises made to them of its future greatness, by the Prophet Joseph Smith."[39] Though the organizational structure had been dissolved, the sisterhood remained even more firmly cemented by the bonding of necessity. Years later, when the women's organization as envisioned by Joseph Smith would be reinstated by Brigham Young, it would be those women who had passed together through the learning of Nauvoo and the testing of Winter Quarters who would rebuild the Relief Society in the mountain of the Lord's house.

A New Life in the Salt Lake Valley

For most women, crossing the plains from Winter Quarters to the Valley of the Great Salt Lake was easier than the first winter's stay in Nebraska. After the pioneer company led out along the trail, the move became an organized migration. The lessons of the previous year's confusion had been learned, and following the "Word and the Will of the Lord" provided the needed organizational structure for the trek.[40] The details of that trek are readily available in numerous individual accounts; to generalize them would be to distort each woman's reality. Suffice it to say, wagon by wagon, the Saints entered the Salt Lake Valley, a society transplanted whole into a pristine desert.

The Church itself also stood in need of further organization. Joseph Smith's death had dissolved the First Presidency, leaving the Quorum of the Twelve as the presiding body, Brigham Young its president. Returning from the valley, President Young was sustained president of the Church in Kanesville December 27, 1847, and in 1849 men were called to fill existing vacancies in the Twelve and to preside over the Salt Lake Stake and its nineteen wards.

Maintaining life and then alleviating physical discomfort were the priorities of the women entering the valley in the early years. Improving their rude cabins and providing sufficient food for themselves and the thousands who arrived season after season required ingenuity and hard work. Most of the women could supply both.

Women sometimes sowed, tended, and harvested crops, but these were unusual tasks for women, even in the starvation years. More often they performed the traditional woman's work, in the house or only as far outside as a kitchen garden.[41] Even that was not light work in frontier Utah: in order to tend her vegetable garden, Relief Cram Atwood "carried water from City Creek," a particularly strenuous task since, she added, "the ground was as dry as an ash heap to the depth of a foot or more."[42]

Mary Jane Lambson wrote to her sister Bathsheba Smith the first fall in the valley, "I have done my warshing the two last times though I am quite lame in my back yet at times. I have made Alford a shirt and knit him a pare of socks, made the babe a dress, a bonnet [and] knit her a pare of stockings and a blue linsey dress made myself a garment and apron so besides many other little things."[43]

Supporting a missionary husband made a woman's work heavier on two counts: she must sustain herself and her children without his help, and often she would be required to send money to him as well. Jane Snyder Richards remembered October 1849 for two reasons: her husband went on a second mission to England, to be gone three years, and her mother arrived from Council Bluffs. "We had a hard time in getting along," she wrote. "My sickly baby was a great anxiety. I had to earn what I could. For what had we to live on. In the spring I saved straw and from it braided forty hats for men and boys." By this time the California gold rush was drawing emigrants through Utah, a ready market for the women's goods. "I remember an emigrant coming along and wanted to buy [a hat]," continued Jane. She made one to order, and sold it for a dollar. "He was supprised at its cheapness." Jane, and many others, took in boarders, charging five or six dollars a week. Through it all, she counted her blessings: "We always had plenty of fresh meat, and eggs."[44]

Not all were so blessed. Eliza Lyman recorded in her diary that spring that when her own larder was empty, "Jane James, a colored woman, let me have about two pounds of flour, it being about half she had." That same Jane Manning James remembered not so much the starvation winters as the work she and her husband Isaac did, accumulating farm animals, "horses, cows, oxen, sheep, and chickens in abundance." Even so, she wrote, "I spun all the cloth for my family."[45]

Despite the demands of subsistence, the women found time to fill their spiritual needs. Attendance at the Bowery was uplifting when President Brigham Young and others of the General Authorities spoke. When several of the leading men returned to Winter Quarters, however, their wives turned again to their practice of holding blessing meetings to buoy up their spirits through the long and frightening winter. Fearful that they might be out of order if they met without priesthood leadership, they would invite John Smith or some other man to conduct for them.

When there were physical as well as spiritual needs beyond those they could meet through their own immediate families, the Saints found cooperative means to meet them. A number of associations would emerge in the 1850s—the Universal Scientific Society, the Polysophical Society, various dramatic societies, and the Deseret Theological Institute among them.

Predating these was the Council of Health, established in 1848 under direction of Thomsonian (herbalist) doctor Willard Richards. An offshoot group of women emerged who met to discuss women's particular health needs. Richards's wife, Susannah Lippincott, a nurse from England, taught classes in midwifery, child care, and diseases of children. Foreshadowing lessons the Relief

Society would offer a half-century later, Zina D. H. Young, Emmeline B. Wells, Patty Sessions, Presendia Kimball, and others faithfully attended the classes. In 1851 the Female Council of Health was formalized under the direction of Phoebe Angell, and by 1852 the organization had representatives in all but two of Salt Lake City's nineteen wards, again prefiguring the outreach that would come with the reorganization of Relief Society in 1867.[46]

Concern for their sisters' health led the Female Council of Health to design a dress style more practical and less constricting than the current tightly corseted fashion. In September 1852, about the time the famous "Bloomer" costume was being promoted by radical eastern women, Patty Sessions noted in her diary, "I went to Sister Smiths to help form a fashion for the females that will be more conducive to health than the long tight waisted dress filed with whale bone and hickery that they ware now."[47] The "Deseret costume," then publicly modeled by Eliza R. Snow, consisted of a loose-fitting, high-collared blouse, full skirt about mid-calf in length, and full pantaloons to the ankle. In deference to Brigham Young's plea that the women not drain the economy by ordering eastern fabrics, the costume was to be made of homespun.

Both style and fabric were singularly unpopular with most women. Those few who adopted the costume formed a group that met periodically to reinforce one another.[48] Nevertheless, even Eliza ultimately remained unconverted: an 1856 daguerrotype shows her still as tightly boned as her slim figure would allow. For all their spinning and weaving of homegrown fibers, the wearing of eastern goods and styles, at least for Sunday best, was a statement of gentility that women of the Mormon frontier made, and would continue to make, despite the difficulty of their wilderness lives.[49]

Effects of the Women's Movement

The Female Council of Health and Latter-day Saint women's eagerness to organize for the study of women's hygiene and dress reform paralleled similar trends among contemporary British and American women. The "Ladies Physiological Reform Societies," founded in the United States upon the model of female benevolent societies, pointed to the need for the education of women physicians and to the need for women's medical colleges, since orthodox medical colleges generally excluded women. The Boston Female Medical College and the Female Medical College of Philadelphia, both founded in 1850, would graduate hundreds of female physicians, including Latter-day Saints Romania B. Pratt, Ellis Reynolds Shipp, and others in the 1870s.

Women's medical colleges were one manifestation of the new woman's movement stirring in Great Britain and America. The famous 1848 convention at Seneca Falls, New York, provided focus and leadership for the small but vocal group of American women who since the 1830s had been articulating discontent with woman's position in contemporary society. The convention saw as its far-reaching purpose the initiation of a broad movement for the emancipation of women from all the forces that held them bound—legal, economic, political, educational, and psychological.

Since many of the women who gathered at Seneca Falls had been active abolitionists, their rhetoric often compared women in their limited sphere with slaves. Elizabeth Cady Stanton wrote in 1856: "Her [woman's] bondage, though it differs from that of the negro slave, frets and chafes her just the same."[50] Legally, nineteenth-century American women were fettered by gender-biased laws that declared them so subject to their husbands that at marriage they lost many of the legal rights they had held as single women: the right to hold and control property, even that which they brought with them into the marriage; the right to their own earnings; and the right to guardianship of their children in case of divorce. "Civilly dead," they lost their individuality as entities under the law; their rights were subsumed into those of their husbands.

In the larger society, American women had little opportunity for education, little access to the public ear, and not even a silent vote in public affairs. Traditionally women had made significant economic contributions to their households, as has been shown in the case of Latter-day Saint women living in frontier communities through the 1840s. But, as the United States underwent rapid industrialization, the number of women factory workers steadily increased and their labor for long hours and low pay was undervalued.

Industrialization had a different impact on middle-class women, pulling their husbands daily to a distant workplace while they stayed home. Though technology gradually reduced women's traditional domestic labor, a new cult of domesticity evolved. Home, which had once been the workplace for both men and women, became "woman's sphere," housekeeping her major occupation. Pulpit and press enunciated a new ideal of "true womanhood," defining the primary female virtues as piety, purity, domesticity, and submissiveness. Some middle-class women began lacing around themselves a dream of ladylike uselessness, a cult of delicacy that, like their taut corsets, restricted their activities to a narrow range.

Women's advocates of this era usually regarded religion, as interpreted by its contemporary practitioners, lay and clergy, as a cornerstone of male-female inequality. Sarah Grimké addressed her 1838 *Letters on the Equality of the Sexes and the Condition of Women* against those clergymen who preached that God had ordained women's inferior state; and Stanton composed a two-volume *Woman's Bible*, a feminist reinterpretation so embarrassing to her more orthodox colleagues that her own suffrage association disowned it.

The Latter-day Saints who were building a new Zion in the Great Basin were not isolated from these issues and addressed them from a perspective informed by the covenants they had made. Eastern woman's rights advocates pledged to break down the existing societal order, but Latter-day Saints had dedicated themselves to establishing a new order—the kingdom of God. This kingdom, Brigham Young testified, was ruled by "the Government of the Son of God"—the priesthood restored through Joseph Smith.[51] According to President Young, men and women who subjected themselves to the priesthood's "beautiful order" would "live strictly according to its pure system of laws and ordinances" until they were unified as one, all working "for the good of the whole more than for individual aggrandizement."[52]

Even in the temporary absence of the Relief Society, which Joseph Smith had taught was essential to the completeness of this "beautiful order," Latter-day Saint women felt connected to and supportive of priesthood government. Eliza R. Snow responded to the national clamor for equal rights in an 1852 poem inviting "those fair champions of 'female rights,' " to come to Deseret and see "a perfect form of government" established by men "clothed with the everlasting Priesthood."[53] The Eastern activists, she observed in 1856, "seek with noble, yet with fruitless aim, / Corruptions and abuses to reclaim." Their efforts to remove the "curse of Eve," as the age described and explained woman's subservient position, were as useless as trying to "unlock without a key." "Without the Holy Priesthood," she declared, "'tis at most / Like reck'ning bills in absence of the host." Only by means of the priesthood could women and men truly reform and "renovate the earth."[54]

The importance Latter-day Saints attached to the order of priesthood government in the 1850s is reflected in the editing members of the Quorum of the Twelve performed as they compiled the *History of the Church.* The documents that were their sources came from Nauvoo in the 1840s, but the interpretations placed upon them reflected their experience during the decade following the death of the Prophet Joseph Smith. The unwillingness of Emma Smith and others to sustain the Twelve, the complicated move to and colonization of the Great Basin, the challenge of assimilating the flood of arriving immigrants all pointed to the overriding importance of order and unity.

Thus it was that the 1855 editorial changes rendered Joseph Smith's Nauvoo declaration to the Relief Society, "I now turn the key to you," as "I now turn the key in your behalf." His stated intention of "delivering the keys to this society and to the church" was revised to read "He spoke of delivering the keys of the Priesthood to the Church." These alterations unmistakably clarified the presiding authority of priesthood leaders.

Latter-day Saints believed that the principles of righteous priesthood governance differentiated their sacred order from the male-dominated secular society that feminists blamed for woman's oppression. On more than one occasion Brigham Young clarified Paul's statement that "the husband is the head of the wife." He instructed the men to "show the women by their superior ability that God gives husbands wisdom and ability to lead their wives into his presence,"[55] and insisted that the husband/father must earn the respect of his family. They were not expected to follow him in unrighteousness.[56]

For women and men, the "beautiful order" held both challenge and promise. Though woman "feels at times, neglected now—/ Misjudged and unappreciated too," Eliza R. Snow affirmed, "Hers is a holy calling." The poet testified that "through submission, faith and constancy," with "noble independence in her heart," woman would fulfill her "present and eternal destiny."[57] In submitting their will, personally or collectively, to that of a righteous priesthood leader, women would not only preserve the kingdom, but would also gain experience in a well-ordered earthly school. There "the ruled will be prepared to rule," until "By weight of character—by strength of worth; / And thro' obedience, Woman will obtain / The *power of reigning, and the right to reign.*"[58]

Women's responsibility for their personal progress to salvation continued as a theme in gospel discourse, as reflected in the apostles' editing of Joseph Smith's April 28, 1842, sermon to the Relief Society. Women were to continue in their exercise of spiritual gifts; and of their healing powers the editors added, "Who are better qualified to administer [to the sick] than our faithful and zealous sisters, whose hearts are full of faith, tenderness, sympathy and compassion. No one." The keys promised to women were generally interpreted by the editors to be those powers granted husband and wife in their temple sealing and other temple ordinances; thus the editors noted that "faithful members of the Relief Society should receive them [the keys] in connection with their husbands, that the Saints whose integrity has been tried and proved faithful, might know how to ask the Lord and receive an answer."[59] The redaction of the minutes in no way diminished the importance of individual women to the kingdom of God or depleted their right to act under direction of the Spirit. After the edited sermons of Joseph Smith to the Relief Society were read to Brigham Young, he "was much pleased with them."[60]

"Resurrected" Relief Societies

That women could act upon their individual inspiration and initiative and at the same time within the parameters of priesthood leadership, they themselves demonstrated in the 1850s. Prompted by their desire to help neighboring Native Americans, a circle of faithful sisters revived Relief Society. Their example, with subsequent priesthood approval, rippled outward and onward, following and confirming the pattern of partnership established in Nauvoo.

As when Sarah Kimball first organized her neighbors to sew shirts for the temple workmen, Matilda Dudley established a charitable "Indian Relief Society." As Richard L. Jensen recounts in his thorough study of "Forgotten Relief Societies, 1844–67," she and her sisters Mary Hawkins, Amanda Smith, and Mary Bird, most of whom had attended Relief Society in Nauvoo, met on January 24, 1854, to organize "a socity of females for the purpose of makeing clothing for Indian women and children."[61] Sister Dudley, a thirty-five-year-old convert from Pennsylvania, invited others to join with them, and two weeks later the charter group, augmented by twelve, decided to make a rag rug to sell for fabric from

Minutes of the first
"Indian Relief Society,"
organized in 1854.
(Courtesy Special Collections, Brigham Young University)

which to sew for the natives. They agreed to pay a membership fee of twenty-five cents and to meet weekly at various homes to work from nine to four each day, both requirements entailing sacrifice for most of the members.

Whether he was aware of it or not, these Salt Lake women had been meeting for four months when Brigham Young toured the southern settlements to ratify a then uneasy peace with the Utes. At Fillmore and at Parowan in central Utah, he challenged the caucasian Saints to befriend the Indians, to overcome their aversion to them, to mingle with them, and to teach them. He addressed the women in particular: "I am sure there [are] women present who have spoken in tongues that they would have to go among the Lamanites & instruct them to sew to knit to wash & perform all domestic works. . . . Now I tell you the time has come that you will have to carry out that which you have seen years &

76

years ago." He also announced, "We are going to propose to the sisters when we get home to make clothes, &c for the Indians & I give you the privilege to make clothing for those little children & the women."[62]

The women of Parowan took the challenge. By 1855 "Aunt Mary Smith, sisters Meeks, West, and Fish were set apart as nurses and teachers to the [Paiute] females, to teach them their organization, the taking care of children, &c., and to nurse according to revelation."[63]

Meanwhile, back in Salt Lake City Brigham Young reinforced Matilda Dudley and her sisters in their special Indian Relief Society. "I propose to the sisters in this congregation," he told one group, "to form themselves into societys . . . to clothe the Lamanite children and women and cover their nakedness. All the Lamanites will be numbered within this Kingdom in a very few years and they would be as zealous as any other." He added two further instructions: the new Indian societies should clothe not only the Indians but also "the poor brethren"; and a society should be established in each ward. Though bishops were to initiate the organizations, they seldom participated directly in their operation.

Sister Dudley had already organized a society in her own Thirteenth Ward and become its president. Now, following the new policy, she disbanded the original group to their own wards. Over the next months, under direction from their bishops, at least twenty-two Indian Relief Societies were formed, primarily in Salt Lake City. As visitors spread the word to outlying wards, those wards also organized and contributed to the store of clothing amassed for the Indians. In 1854 items of clothing and bedding valued at $1,540 were contributed, including nearly nine hundred items sewn specifically for the Indian women and children.

Soon the labors of the women expanded to meet needs in their own community. Lucy Meserve Smith, writing of her Provo Relief Society, told of their collections in behalf of the handcart pioneers caught by early snows in the mountains near South Pass in 1856. As soon as the freezing Saints' dilemma was announced in general conference, she wrote, "The sisters stripped of their Peticoats stockings and every thing they could spare, right there in the Tabernacle, and piled [them] into the wagons to send to the Saints in the mountains." Returning to Provo, she added, "My counselors and I wallowed through the snow until our clothes were wet a foot high to get things together," collecting goods in such volume that "the four bishops could hardly carry the bedding and other clothing we got."

The labor continued beyond the handcart emergency, remembered Lucy. "We peaced blocks carded bats quilted and got together I think 27 Quilts, besides a great amount of other clothing, in one winter for the needy." Of her Relief Society work she later wrote, "I never took more satisfaction and I might say pleasure in any labour I ever performed in my life."[64]

Priscilla Merriman Evans was one of those women who, with her young baby, came into the valley with a handcart company. She affiliated with the Relief Society after she settled in Spanish Fork, Utah. The women there met in a private home, where Bishop John L. Butler instructed them "in regard to moving out as a Female Relief Society," she recorded. "Mrs. Beck was nominated first as secretary, but as she could neither read nor write, they sent for me. I was sustained as secretary." Copying from the minute book into her own diary, she records some of their activities. "President Lucretia Gay," she wrote, "worked ten days cording and spinning wool for shirts. She furnished 1/2 pound of wool, worked four days cording and spinning hair for lariats for the brethren. . . . She also helped to make a pair of pants and she made one pair of mittens." Others of the presidency—Armelia Berry and Ruth Davis—and members Lydia Markham, Martha Davis, and Harriet Simmonds similarly contributed.[65] The project this time was to support the men assigned to protect the settlements from the anticipated attack of Johnston's army, at that time camped in the mountains east of the valley.

A succinct, if casual, description of the Salt Lake City meetings of the Relief Society comes from Wilford Woodruff, the inveterate diarist of early Mormonism. He wrote on June 17, 1857: "In the afternoon I attended the 14 ward female relief society at my House with Robert Campbell. We both addressed the meeting. There were about 50 present, sewing, knitting, sewing carpet rags, making quilts, &c. It is a laudable undertaking. All the females in the ward meet at my house each wednesday afternoon. They open & close with prayer. Mrs Phebe W. Woodruff is President & Mrs. Pratt Secretary. They Clothe all the poor in the ward & during the last Quarter they made a Donation to the prepetual Emigrating fund of $126." Then, as though he remembered his apostolic calling and responsibility, Elder Woodruff added, "I wish all go & do likewise."[66] The records of that particular ward society show its having been organized September 17, 1856, "in a time of scarcity and under trying circumstances," and functioning until March 28, 1858, when it was disrupted by the Saints' move south occasioned by the threat of war.[67]

Not all the societies thus organized remained active even that long. Yet, however briefly they functioned, their meetings re-affirmed the sisters' sense of united purpose and continuity with their Nauvoo roots. The bishopric of the Salt Lake Seventh Ward, for instance, called a meeting on March 21, 1857, to "resurrect the Female Relief Society." The bishop, himself newly called, "knew nothing of its former operations, but this did not much concern him. The question was what can be done in future." The sisters, however, remembered: harking back to the Nauvoo society, Sister Leonard "testified to the immense good which those societies had already accomplished & felt this could again be done."[68] Continuity, as well as "unity of action and purpose," were important compo-nents of these "resurrected" Relief Societies.

Activities of the 1850s Relief Societies varied from ward to ward, settlement to settlement, according to local needs. Their bishop asked the Seventh Ward women to add to their ongoing aid to the poor such occupations as basket making and sewing clothing, and requested that they "have the seat in the Stand cush-ioned." Women in Spanish Fork made hair ropes, quilts out of scraps, and clothing out of wagon covers and sacks. "Spinning and weaving our scanty supply of wool, gathering up old tin and making it into cups" were ways of contributing. Women in Salt Lake Stake's Thirteenth Ward collected contributions from members and held a ball "for the purpose of procuring money for weaving and other expenses." In addition, Bishop Edwin Woolley asked them to make rag carpets for the tabernacle, and they made at least seven quilts, wove twenty-nine yards of cloth from donated material, sewed seven garments, and braided straw hats for the poor.[69]

The movement referred to as the "Mormon reformation," a time of rebaptisms, renewed commitment, and heightened spiri-tuality, influenced the direction of the Relief Societies, infusing a spiritual component into the task orientation already established. The same thrust toward recommitment may well have inspired their very organization, as suggested in the minutes of an 1855 fast meeting in Salt Lake's Eighteenth Ward. Although Eliza R. Snow, a member of that ward, had not been active in the movement to restore the society, at that fast meeting she gave "an Exho[r]tation to the Sisters," which was followed immediately by "remarks by the Bishop in regard to organizing a society to make up clothing for the Poor." She and several other women were then confirmed to the work during the same meeting. Such fervor translated into immediate action indicates that the rebaptism by which the Saints were symbolizing their renewed faith was infusing all their activities with a spiritual center.[70]

In typical Latter-day Saint fashion, even the very practical work meetings had a religious content. Susa Young Gates described "the cessation of all labor just an hour before supper to permit a little 'experience' or testimony meeting to lift the overburdened spirits of the women into a rarified spiritual atmosphere."[71] It is unlikely that every group followed that pattern; for most there are insufficient records to be sure. What is certain is that the memory of Nauvoo was very much in the minds of those who had been part of that first Relief Society, for the Nauvoo blend of spiritual and temporal clearly resurfaced in the activities of the nascent Utah societies.

In the summer of 1857 the Relief Societies were scarcely well begun in their works of charity when word came to Brigham Young that the 2,500-man battalion known as Johnston's army was en route to Utah. Erroneously led to believe that the Mormons were in rebellion against the United States, President James Buchanan had ordered the army to accompany Albert Cumming, designated to replace Brigham Young as governor of Utah. By fall 1857 the army had reached the Rocky Mountains; Mormon harassment kept them there, awaiting spring thaws before they could enter the settlements in the valleys to the west. President Young then announced a "scorched earth" policy of defense: the Saints would move, destroying everything behind them, rather than tolerate once again the depredations of a mob, official or vigilante. "There shall not be one building, nor one foot of lumber, nor a stick, nor a tree, nor a particle of grass and hay, that will burn, left in reach of our enemies," he proclaimed.[72] By March 1858 the Big Move was on, as thirty thousand Latter-day Saints left their homes in Salt Lake City and northern settlements for Provo and points south, or from outlying colonies to the central regions of concentration.

What this move meant to the women can be conjectured from the accounts of a few who recorded it. Mary Ann Weston Maughan, for example, who had driven the first settler's wagon into Cache Valley, eighty miles north of Salt Lake, not two years earlier, loaded her wagon in March to leave "for some place in the South." Of their first year's harvest, the Maughans left 15,000 bushels of wheat in their house. The wheat was gone on their return. "We left our crops in the ground; these they could not steal," she added.

On the move, Mary Ann, her husband, Peter, and their five children first camped a week at Box Elder (Brigham City), over the mountain from their home. Then they stayed for a few days in Salt Lake City, in a room in Willard Richards's now vacant house. Finally they moved on to Pond Town (present-day Salem), seventy miles south of Salt Lake City. Living there in wagon boxes and tents, the family survived the spring and early summer much as they had lived through the primitive conditions of Kanesville and the trail west ten years earlier.

By the end of June, the threat seemed to have dissipated. Governor Cumming would govern fairly, it appeared, and the army would pass peacefully through deserted Salt Lake City to camp fifteen miles away. "When we git the news good & solid we will go home," President Young told the Saints in Provo who had been hosting the refugees all spring.[73] Presumably their lives could return to normal.

Not Mary Ann Maughan's life, however. Indian threats kept her family away from Cache Valley, except for Peter and the other men of the settlement, who went to harvest their crops. Mary Ann was given use of a home near Willard, just north of Ogden, where she stayed with her children until the following spring. And since she was the Relief Society mainspring in her Cache Valley settlement, in the light of long absences such as hers, one can understand how the societies fell apart under the strain.

Organized though it was, the move south so disrupted the life of the Saints that what was expected to be an orderly displacement dissipated into ad hoc groupings. Ward Relief Society networks pulled asunder as families, rather than staying in assigned settlements with their wards, located either with kin or friends or where opportunities for work or housing might be found. Only the host wards in existing southern communities remained intact. There the Relief Societies continued to fulfill their roles of succor and solace to their fleeing co-religionists. The humble phrase "helping them locate and seeing they were taken care of," with which Spanish Fork Relief Society president Rhoda B. Snell described her group's service, grossly understates the countless deeds of charity performed for the refugees by the women.[74]

To many, the return to their homes was heartbreaking. Mary Ann Maughan found not only the grain stolen, but also that "travelers and their horses had camped in my house, and it took some time to shovel out the dryed mud and hay and other rubbish." With admirable humor she added, "Some of our goods were burned, and our chairs and other effects were visiting all over the fort and Indians camps."[75]

She was not alone in that situation. When Martin Luther Ensign and his family returned to their Brigham City home, they found that "all was desolate, the doors & floors overhead & board fences were all taken to make boxes to hold flowr & other things in the move." People had not been malicious or thieving, but as Ensign explained, "Meny [were] not expecting to return so all was free to all."[76]

The massive disruption of the move and the challenges the women returned to afterwards explain why those infant Relief Societies, for the most part, did not survive. Except that there were indeed houses, the women sank back to their beginnings in the Salt Lake Valley. Putting their homes to rights took all their effort and energy. Chronicler Andrew Jenson noted from various ward histories that Relief Societies discontinued in the Salt Lake First, Third, Sixth, Eleventh, Thirteenth, Fifteenth, and Sixteenth wards.[77] His count is a conservative estimate; it is unlikely that more than three or four Relief Societies survived the move south and the nine years that followed until 1867, when Eliza R. Snow, under Brigham Young's direction, would again build on the foundation laid in Nauvoo. The central leadership she provided would prove the key to future success.

Twice the pattern had been repeated: women gathering to perform acts of charity; their work acknowledged by their priesthood leaders; their incorporation into the general organization of the Church; then their disruption in a time of major upheaval. Yet a third time would the phoenix arise from its own ashes, this time to last a hundred years and more.

CHAPTER 3

WISE STEWARDS
1866–1887

"In Union Is Strength," embroidered in white on a large blue banner, caught the eye of a journalist visiting Utah for the first time in 1877. Mrs. Frank Leslie, wife of the publisher of *Leslie's Illustrated*, a national magazine, came across the banner amid the many examples of Mormon women's handwork offered for sale in the Women's Commission House in the Old Constitution Building on Salt Lake City's Main Street. It hung among the braided straw bonnets and flowers, laces and quilts, skeins of yarn and rag carpet, shoes, yard goods, and even some locally cultured silk. With her beginner's glimpse of the Mormons, Mrs. Leslie could not have understood the importance of the motto to the Relief Society women in whose display it hung. In retrospect, however, that principle clearly undergirded the women's work of the most formative decades of Relief Society development, 1866–1887.

Presently, Mrs. Leslie would later write, "Miss Snow," proprietor of the store, entered. "She is a lady considerably past middle age," the writer noted of the seventy-three-year-old woman. She had "a good and pleasing face, a quiet, refined manner, although cold and reserved, and a very precise and deliberate mode of speech." To her gentile visitor, Eliza R. Snow, "with a smile of conscious strength and power," told the story behind the commission store, a history indicative of the kind of flexible initiative practiced by Relief Societies as by women's organizations elsewhere.[1]

The previous year, 1876, had marked the centennial of the founding of the United States of America. At Philadelphia there were to be grand displays honoring the occasion, and space was to be provided in the main building to illustrate "a sphere for woman's action and space for her work." Women had raised over $100,000 for their display when organizers informed their committee that there would not be any space for them there. Their response surprised the managers: they raised even more money and built a separate building. From May to October the Woman's Pavilion displayed achievements in journalism, medicine, science, art, literature, invention, education, commerce, and social work.[2]

Resolved to participate with their eastern sisters in celebrating women's accomplishments, Utah women responded quickly—they had just six weeks' lead time—to Sister Snow's invitation to submit examples of their work to be sent to Philadelphia. So numerous were the submissions that Eliza appealed to the territorial legislature for funds to ship the display to the exposition and care for it there. The request was denied.

"Notwithstanding this disappointment," Eliza Snow counseled her sisters, "we need not regret the efforts that have been made, but let us turn them to good account, and do the next best thing, by uniting our energies in getting up a Centennial Territorial Exhibition at home."[3] So they sent to Philadelphia a modest collection of the smallest items and, from the impressive collection remaining, set up an exhibit as their own centennial celebration fair.

On July 4, 1876, the Women's Centennial Territorial Fair opened. For two months visitors paid ten cents each to view table after table filled with laces, collars, and handkerchiefs of Utah-grown silk; crochet work, embroidery, and patchwork; flowers in wool and wax; wreaths of hair; straw hats, frames, and baskets; and a gallery of fine art. The *Deseret News* reported, "This fair is by far the best ever presented in Utah,"[4] despite the fact that the Deseret Agricultural and Manufacturing Society had been sponsoring similar events in Utah since 1856.[5]

When the fair closed two months later, far from merely "avoiding bankruptsy," as Sister Snow had feared, it had not only cleared expenses but also made a profit to devote to charitable purposes.[6] President Brigham Young saw in the enterprise the possibility of an ongoing venture that would serve well the goal of Utah's economic self-sufficiency. In a letter addressed "to the President and Members of the Relief Societies," he requested that they turn the fair into a commission store where home manufactured goods could be purchased.[7] The idea was not new to Sister Snow, who, in organizing ward Relief Societies in 1868, had proclaimed that "the time would come when the Female Relief Societies in Utah would establish stores, to sell things that they would manufacture."[8] Soon even more diversified stock filled the shelves, ads appeared in local newspapers, and President Young was holding up the enterprise as an example "to the sterner sex."

Not that all went entirely according to his wishes. "Well I told Sis[ter] Eliza Snow," he said later, "that I did [not] want one person to work in that store and get wages. Now then they have not been working a week there before they get some one in there that wants wages. I told Sis[ter] Eliza they could not get wages and if they did not understand it, I would understand it for them." Anticipating her reply he added, "Well, but they can't live."[9] Thereafter Eliza, in no need of wages, managed the store herself, assisted by volunteers.

Eliza R. Snow, general president of the Relief Societies of the Church, had long prided herself on possessing "a disposition to conform to circumstances."[10] That flexibility was just one of the attributes that contributed to her usefulness in a cooperative society such as nineteenth-century Mormonism. Joining with the Saints at Kirtland, she suffered with them the internal dissension there, and traveled with her family and that of Zina Huntington, who would become her successor in the Relief Society, to Missouri. There she experienced the violence that drove them to Illinois, where she participated in the work of the Relief Society of Nauvoo, serving as secretary. She became a plural wife to Joseph Smith just ten weeks after the founding of Relief Society, and on his death was married for time to his successor, Brigham Young.

However intense her admiration for her prophet-husbands, being connected by marriage to the leaders of the Church proved of little material benefit to Eliza in her early years. Necessity, her own tenacity, and her developing self-confidence brought her through the sickliness of Winter Quarters and the dreariness of the Great Plains. In the Salt Lake Valley she grew slowly but persistently in those skills of leadership for which she is now recognized: she wrote prolifically and prepared two volumes of poetry for publication; she assisted in the founding of a literary society; she became a magnet for women of intellectual bent as well as those who recognized her spiritual sensitivity. Although she applauded the rebirth of the Relief Society in the 1850s, she did not promote it beyond her own ward. By the 1860s, however, her health had improved; her place in Brigham Young's Lion House family was established; her communication with her prophet-husband was practiced; and her commitment to the building of the kingdom was beyond question. By 1866 Eliza was able to write an absent friend, "My health has been good during the winter. I have been to the house of the Lord from two to five days in a week, I think without exception."[11] While her ordinance work in the endowment house was satisfying, she had more energy than that required, and the kingdom would soon demand it of her.

"Let Them Organize Female Relief Societies"

Other forces were at work in the late 1860s. The end of the Civil War freed the United States government to pay attention to its western territories. Gentile incursion into the Great Basin would increase. Soon the railroad would link his people with the Babylon from which they had escaped, and much as Brigham Young appreciated the ease with which immigrants would now come to Zion, he knew the dangers of too-ready access to "the States." His economy of self-sufficiency was threatened unless the Saints could pull together better than they were doing. Unity was the cry, cooperation the desperate need.

As 1866 drew to a close, President Young was meeting with the Twelve when the issue of the temporal kingdom was raised. As Wilford Woodruff recorded in his journal, "President Young said if we could get up Female Relief Societies and they would use their influence to get the sisters to make their own bonnets and make and wear their own home made clothing it would do much good."[12] The idea was not long in germinating; by the end of December Brigham had called Eliza R. Snow to head up the work. She was ready, and he would support her.

At first it seemed that the major thrust of the work was temporal. President Young's instruction at the April 1868 conference was for the women, under direction of bishops, "to establish your relief societies, . . . and establish yourselves for doing business."[13] He had earlier given them the responsibility of providing for the poor: "let a sister appeal for the relief of suffering and poverty, and she is almost sure to be successful, especially if she appeals to those of her own sex," he told the Saints. "We recommend these Female Relief Societies to be organized immediately."[14]

"Now, Bishops, you have smart women for wives, many of you," the president continued. "Let them organize Female Relief Societies in the various wards. We have many talented women among us. . . . You will find that the sisters will be the mainspring of the movement."[15] On a later occasion he expressed even more strongly

Eliza R. Snow (right), Emmeline B. Wells, and Elizabeth Ann Whitney, longtime friends, directed the work of Relief Society during the enterprising 1870s and 1880s. (Photograph by Charles R. Savage, courtesy LDS Church Archives)

his confidence in the abilities of women: "There is an immense amount of talent, and I may say of real sound statesmanship within a community of ladies; and if they would only train their minds, and exercise the rights and privileges that are legitimately theirs, and would contemplate subjects that they now pass over and never think about, they would find that they have an immense amount of influence in guiding, directing and controling human affairs."[16]

At the same time Relief Society was being restored, Sunday Schools were being reinstituted, Schools of the Prophets were being created for the instruction of the men and to coordinate temporal affairs, and temple ordinances for the dead were again being performed in the endowment house. It was, as historian Richard Cowan termed it, "a remarkable period of ecclesiastical expansion."[17]

Eliza Snow was not hasty in pushing the program. "It is not a thing of the moment," she would write to the Fillmore, Utah, Relief Society; "it need not be rushed forward."[18] Beginning in the late summer of 1867, Sister Snow went, at the invitations of bishops, from ward to ward in her mission of organizing or reorganizing ward Relief Societies. "To me it was quite a mission," she later wrote, "and I took much pleasure in its performance. I felt quite honored and much at home in my associations with the Bishops, and they appreciated my assistance."[19]

In the Salt Lake City First Ward, for example, Bishop Henry Moon called the sisters to a meeting in the ward schoolroom "to be instructed and organized into a Female Relief Society according to the true order . . . as instituted by Joseph Smith the Prophet." "As he was not well acquainted with that order himself," the minute-taker recorded, "he requested Eliza R. Snow who did understand the order, to take hold and assist in organizing the Society in a propper manner." As she had done many times in the previous three years, Sister Snow "made some preliminary remarks and then moved that Sister Miriam G. Chase be the President" of the First Ward Relief Society. "Seconded and carried unanimously," record the minutes. She then proposed Julia A. Adams and Sidney Thayne as counselors, and a secretary and an assistant secretary. All were "carried by a clear vote." That done, Sister Chase and her counselors came forward to be set apart and blessed by Bishop Moon "to the office whereunto they had been appointed." The visiting teachers who had served in the formerly organized society, presumably one remaining from the 1850s, were reinstated in their callings, and new ones were nominated. The women "being known by their Friends and Neighbors around them they were all recommended as being worthy."[20]

The "preliminary remarks" made by Sister Snow but not recorded here can be deduced from reports by secretaries in other wards on similar occasions. To the Salt Lake City Eighth Ward sisters, she said that "the time had come for the Sisters to act in a wider sphere than they had previously done." She had been present, she reminded them, "when Joseph Smith first spoke of organizing such a Society . . . according to the order of God."[21] In the Salt Lake City Third Ward she told the women, "It is no ordinary thing, to meet in an organization of this nature. This organization belongs to the organization of the Church of Christ, in all dispensations when it is in perfection." Always Sister Snow carried with her the precious minute book, the "Record of the Female Relief Society of Nauvoo," from which she would often read. Her intimate knowledge of that organization and its history, and her guardianship of the volume itself, dictated to her the pattern after which the society must again be established in Utah. There were to be a president and two counselors, and other officers "to carry out the designs of the institution," she told the Third Ward women. The Prophet Joseph, she remembered, "was very particular to have the Sisters transact their buisness in a buisiness like manner. He attached great importance to this Society."[22]

At the conclusion of an organization meeting in the West Jordan Ward in the southwestern part of the Salt Lake Valley, Bishop Archibald Gardner testified to the significance of what had transpired. "I have believed a long time that the Sisters have been curtailed," he said. "We know that there is a high calling for the sisters. Then why not let them be expanding. . . . I do rejoyce to have heard read the minutes of the first organization of this society. Any one could see that it was from a right source, from God."[23]

Always it was made clear that the pattern established in Nauvoo was to be followed explicitly again. The sisters of St. George, Utah, having established their society without the aid of Sister Snow, addressed their questions to her by letter. "We desire to be equal and side by side with our Sister Societies, in the correctness and excellence of our regulations, as well as in the spirit of charity, progress, and union in our sacred Faith," wrote secretary Augusta Jackson.[24] Five weeks later Sister Snow's reply was read to the sisters there, much as other letters were read in outlying stakes throughout Zion.

The Relief Society in Fillmore, Utah, had been organized for some time when on June 16, 1868, having received Eliza Snow's detailed letter of instructions, they met to reorganize the society "more properly than it had at first been done." Their first question had been an obvious one: should the bishopric or other priesthood leaders attend the meetings? In reply, Sister Snow clarified a basic concept of the organization. No, she replied, they should not. "The object of the Society is to RELIEVE THE BRETHREN," not to create more duties for them. The bishop, she explained, or whomever he might appoint (allowing for those occasions when he might appoint Eliza Snow herself), would organize the sisters by suggesting whom to choose for president and counselors, "although it is the privilege of the president to choose her own counselors, or at least they must be those that she has confidence in; but of course, the bishop has more wisdom in selecting them than she can have." That having been decided by nomination and vote, "the president and counselors are to be ordained and set apart, just as the Brethren are set apart for offices."[25]

Sister Snow then described the other officers—secretary and treasurer—and the visiting teachers and their duties and outlined the order of business in the meetings. "Observe order so that the Spirit of God will be with you," she explained, "and learn to do business as orderly and as dignified as men."[26]

The male model, however, was not to stultify the spirit of the meetings. After the business was done, Sister Snow told the women, "arise and express your feelings," a very female prescription in a male-oriented organizational world. "Call on your counselors to speak, and if possible get all to speak, if it is no more than five words." That the sisters should thus "overcome embarrassment and learn to speak words of wisdom and comfort" was a message Sister Snow frequently wrote or spoke to the women. The promise that the Holy Spirit would rest upon them was accompanied by the warning that the presidency should "discourage all enthusiasm," by which she meant that the Pentecostal gifts of speaking in tongues, prophesying, and interpreting tongues were not to be encouraged in the meetings.[27]

The pattern thus outlined was mere skeleton. On the bare bones of the recommended organization, the women were now to put the meat of their industry, to "act according to circumstances from time to time." Local needs would determine what they were to do. Beyond the officers suggested, wrote Sister Snow, "the Presidency, with the vote of the House, can appoint any officer or committee that may be needed." Meetings for work and for business could be interspersed, or work could be done at home and meetings be devoted more to spiritual exercises. Most important, the responsibility for the success of the society rested not only on the presidency: each sister "should strive to make the meetings useful, interesting and attractive, and so manage that it will be an honor to anyone to become a member."

Overall, Sister Snow reiterated one lasting message. Order in the kingdom must be maintained. "Without order we have no claim to the Spirit," she emphasized. "We must have the spirit or we cannot remain organized." The order in which the local societies found their place was the order of the priesthood. "Each society is under the controle of the Bishop and could not exist without his counsel," she told one group. "The Pres. of the society should be subject to the Bishop as he is subject to his Superior or file leader; the members follow out this order being subject to the President and so on."[28]

Not that the working out of that order would always be simple. Advice to Willmirth East, a Relief Society president in Arizona, suggests how differences arising between levels of authority could be resolved. Sister East's bishop apparently objected to the recommended frequency of the visiting teachers' visits. "Perhaps the B[isho]p has not been properly informed," suggested Sister Eliza. Inferring that the problem might have become an issue between her friend and the bishop, she recommended that perhaps "you or some other judicious sister" should explain the program to him. But, she stressed, they must "not oppose his wishes. There is no virtue in breaking one law to keep another. *We will do as we are directed by the Priesthood.*"[29]

It was important that the program be made clear: the visiting teachers were a key part of the charitable purpose of the society in that as they called from house to house they would solicit contributions. But that was not their main purpose. "I hope the sisters do not think that [visiting teaching] consists merely in begging for the poor," Sister Snow told the members of one Relief Society. "I consider the office of a Teacher a high & holy office. . . . You want to be filled with the spirit of God, of wisdom, of humility, of love, that in case they have nothing to give they may not dread your coming." Rather, she hoped, the women would "perceive a difference in their houses after you have visited them."[30]

Early in this incarnation of Relief Society, the visiting teachers saw themselves as modeled on the priesthood quorum of teachers, at that time an adult office and calling. They held their own report meetings, and in some cases they had a president or a presiding teacher. That office was later deemed unnecessary, and responsibility reverted directly to the Relief Society president. Seldom were the teachers set apart as were the president and counselors. Eliza Snow reminded her friend Mary Elizabeth Lightner in Minersville, Utah, that under the original pattern established "in this Dispensation," only the president and counselors were set apart. "The time probably will be when the society will set apart its different officers," she added, "but, as yet, we have to work with much crude material, and it seems wisdom to merely appoint by vote." Then, recognizing her sisters' divine potential at the same time she acknowledged their human frailties, she instructed, "Tell the sisters to go forth and discharge their duties, in humility and faithfulness and the Spirit of God will rest upon them. . . . Let them seek for wisdom instead of power and they will have all the power they have wisdom to exercise."[31]

Sister Eliza's challenge to the teachers had more to do with spirituality than with temporal well-being. "As she enters a house," she told one group, the teacher "should surely have so much of the spirit of the Lord . . . to know what spirit she meets in there." That spirit lacking, the teacher should retire to pray and "plead before God and the Holy Ghost to get it." Then, Sister Snow promised, "you will be able to meet that Spirit that prevails in that house . . . and you may feel to talk words of peace and comfort." Should the spirit be lacking, or should the teacher "find a sister feeling cold," she advised, "take her to your heart as you would a child to your bosom and warm it up."[32]

As the societies matured, each found its own routines within the general pattern. The Salt Lake City Third Ward found quilting appropriate. "We spent our time very agreeably and finished the quilt," wrote the secretary. "Those that could not get around the quilt spent their time in sewing carpet rags." But then the Martha tasks gave way each meeting day to the Mary needs of the women. "At half past 3 o clock," reads the record, "the work was put up [and] the minutes of the last meeting were read and accepted Presidentess Weiler then requested the Sisters to Speak their feelings."[33]

For women accustomed to quieter roles, speaking in public was more threatening than the needle pricks of quilting. A sister in this same society confessed later that "if she could talk about House Cleaning she might talk."[34] "Do not let your Pres. have to say all," pleaded Sister Snow. "Has not God endowed you with the gift of speach?" Then to the fainthearted she reminded, "if you are endowed with the spirit of God, no matter how simple your thoughts may be, they will be edifying to those who hear you."[35]

Sister Eliza knew whereof she spoke. When Brigham Young had asked her to organize the women into Relief Societies, she had felt confident of her abilities. Her later reminiscence, however, recognizes a second layer to her assignment, one that moved her beyond the talents she recognized in herself. "Not long after the re-organization of the Relief Society," she wrote, "Pres. Young told me he was going to give me another mission. . . . I replied, 'I shall endeavor to fulfil it.' He said, 'I want you to instruct the sisters.' " This requirement had been a part of Emma Smith's calling, but in the Nauvoo prototype, it had been Joseph Smith who had done most of the teaching. Now Eliza must apply to herself the requirement of the revelation to Emma, "to expound scriptures, and to exhort the church, according as it shall be given thee by my Spirit." The blessing was, however, to follow: "thou shalt receive the Holy Ghost, . . . and thou needest not fear."[36]

Years later, as a young married woman, Emily S. Richards recalled Eliza's empathy as she experienced it: "The first time Aunt Eliza asked me to speak in a meeting, I could not. . . . She said, 'Never mind, but when you are asked to speak again, try and have something to say,' and I did." Under such encouragement, Emily Richards improved until in 1889 she could address the annual convention of the National Woman Suffrage Association in Washington, D.C., to the praises of a surprised journalist there. Her account described the delicate, refined Latter-day Saint woman as "trembling slightly under the gaze of the multitude, yet reserved, self-possessed, dignified, and as pure and sweet as an angel. . . . It was not the words themselves but the gentle spirit [that] went with the words and carried winning grace to every heart."[37]

The two decades 1866 to 1887 are so full of women's achievements that a volume could easily be dedicated to those years alone. It was not just a matter of leadership, although a factor was certainly the bringing together of Eliza R. Snow, a woman of vision, understanding, industry, and spirituality, with Brigham Young, a divinely guided entrepreneur with expansive dreams and kingdom-centered ambitions. "President Young has turned the key to a wide and extensive sphere of action and usefulness," wrote Sister Snow in an early treatise. "If any of the daughters and mothers in Israel are feeling in the least circumscribed in their present spheres, they will now find ample scope for every power and capability for doing good with which they are most liberally endowed."[38]

The 1860s Relief Societies for the most part began where they were most comfortable and where the need was greatest: with works of charity. In the little town of Rockville, in southern Utah, the society was barely four months old before the presidency called a special meeting to consider "how to raise means to send to St. Joseph in Arizona to relieve the needs of families whose property had been destroyed by fire."[39]

Local needs generally received the societies' first attentions, however, as their records show. A sample from the Salt Lake City Third Ward is that for June 29, 1870:

Donations Received

Emily Weiler	2 lbs. wool	$1.00
Zarviah G. Eardley	calico 3 yds.	.45
Janet Moffat	knitting 1 pr socks	.75

A quilt had been sold, bringing $7.00 into the treasury, which money was then "put out to usury," a way of saying it was deposited in an interest-earning account.[40] The goods would then be dispersed among the needy. Typically, while donors and their contributions are meticulously recorded and moneys carefully annotated, no name of any recipient of Relief Society charity is to be found. Rather, there will be entered a simple notation: "Paid to poor, $14.90," or "cash to Welsh aid fund, $20.00."[41] When an aggregate record of such distribution was collected in 1876, with only 110 of 300 wards reporting, $60,292.91 had been disbursed "for the relief and support of the poor"; $5,981.20 "for the emigration of the poor"; and $1,917.63 "for sundry charities."[42]

That Brigham Young recognized the compassionate role of the Relief Society is indicated in a letter he wrote in 1869, addressed not to the bishop but to "Pres. Female Relief Society, 17th Ward." The letter reads, "Sister P . . . & child are in needy circumstances; she has complained to me & I have referred her to your Society for assistance, feeling assured that you will do what is in your power to make them comfortable." Another account is written in Emmeline B. Wells's diary: "towards evening Mrs. M . . . D . . . came here and said she was destitute of a home, I told her to stay until I could see what could be done for her in our Society."[43]

Although most such needy people would be cared for in private homes of members, with support from the Relief Society, the bishop, and the county, at least one ward founded a home for their care. On a three-acre plot that they purchased, the Relief Society of West Jordan, Utah, erected "a neat brick house" in which "the poor people of the Ward are comfortably cared for."[44]

An Emphasis on Self-sufficiency

Compassionate service was traditionally the work of women, and organization in a Relief Society made the work more efficient, the possibilities for outreach wider. For the Relief Societies in the 1870s there were new temporal stewardships waiting, however. Deseret would need all hands on deck as it moved through economic revolution from isolated agrarian community life toward the full commercial cooperation of statehood. And to be useful in the kingdom was to be faithful to the religion; church and community were one in the minds of nineteenth-century Saints. As Daniel H. Wells, counselor in the First Presidency, observed in 1876, "Building, manufacturing, agriculture etc. are just as much needed in [the kingdom of God] as in any other kingdom, and any man or woman who is engaged in any of these callings with pure motives, is just as much on a mission as if preaching the gospel."[45]

From their arrival in Utah, the Mormons had clung with determination to an economy based on self-sufficiency. Brigham Young had said in 1858 that while armies could not destroy the people, trade with the Gentiles could. And despite several commercial windfalls — the built-in market offered by the presence of a federal army, the opening of mines and markets in neighboring territories, and contracts to construct transcontinental telegraph and railroad systems — the leaders held to self-sufficiency as the official church policy. They did not expect absolute economic independence, of course, but they did seek sufficient autonomy to prevent closer ties with the outside world from producing changes in the essential character of their economy.[46]

The two organizations brought simultaneously into service, the Relief Society and the Schools of the Prophets, were assigned responsibilities for preservation of the economic status quo. The latter, taking its name from the 1833 Kirtland organization established by Joseph Smith, was not so much a school as an invitational forum or town meeting of priesthood holders in a given community. Members raised and resolved issues of theology, church governance, and community development. That these schools, not only in Salt Lake City but also in several outlying communities, were called into being in 1868 and dissolved in 1872 suggests that their overriding purpose was to face the crisis of the coming of the railroad. That the Relief Societies continued after that crisis passed indicates the larger scope of their purposes.

The two did overlap for the short period, however, mainly in the promotion of cooperative merchandising. Brigham Young had long recognized that in American domestic commerce women are the chief consumers; now he perceived that they could be the means to market as well as manufacture and consume home goods. In order to keep retail profits in Utah, church leaders established cooperatives under the wholesale umbrella of Zion's Cooperative Mercantile Institution, and urged the Saints, often under threat of discipline, to deal there exclusively. Each ward was to create an outlet, and members were to subscribe the initial capital. Relief Societies in several wards bought shares, and some established their own branches, such as the 1869 "Female Relief Society's Cooperative Mercantile and Millinery Institution of Weber County."[47]

The entrance of women into commerce caused some consternation among male leaders. Minutes of one meeting of the Salt Lake Stake bishops provide a telling reflection both of the process of ecclesiastical involvement in commerce and of prevailing attitudes toward women. Bishop Hunter, presiding over the February 18, 1869, meeting, "called upon the Bishops to report who had commenced in the cooperative movement." Nine reported progress. The Eighth Ward explained that "under the auspices of the F[emale] R[elief] Society," it had subscribed about one thousand dollars and was ready to commence shortly. Mention of the women's involvement prompted counselor L. W. Hardy to clarify: "he considered that they [the women] would act in union with the Bishops in this cooperative movement, and females to manage the store, but not to dictate." George B. Wallace, spelling out the order of accountability, affirmed that the stores "would be altogether under the direction of the priesthood of the different wards, and they under the direction of the first presidency, though the stores would be managed by the sisters of the F. R. Society." Bishop E. F. Sheets remembered that "the president distinctly stated at Provo that he wished the sisters of the relief society to open two stores there, and manage them, an[d] on that principle he himself had commenced in the 8th ward in establishing a co operative store." Bishop Edwin Woolley, whose obstinacy was legend, responded to his colleagues with typical sarcasm: "said he had attended the Bishops meetings for fifteen years, and yet knew nothing after all, but would have to appeal to the Sisters of the relief society to know how and what to do."

Then President Young himself arrived, and the bishops turned

The main floor of this Relief Society hall built in 1869 by Salt Lake City Fifteenth Ward housed its cooperative store. Upstairs, society members worked on goods sold in the store and held their meetings. (Courtesy LDS Church Archives)

to him for clarification, "whether the relief societies were intended to control and carry on the cooperative stores of each ward, or simply to aid and assist in these stores." His reply was gently chiding: "He had asked his brethren to open cooperative stores in their wards, and as they did not do it, he turned around and asked the sisters knowing that they would do it." The principle to be retained was, as always, that the work be carried out in unity of purpose. He "had counselled the brethren to cease trading with our enemies and he was thankful to know that they had carried it out."[48]

While women cooperated with men in ventures that basically the men directed, the men assisted the sisters in projects of their own as well. Eliza R. Snow, encouraging the Relief Societies in Weber County to build their own hall, assured them that if they, "with the sanction of the brethren, undertake to build a house, the brethren will help them." That was the rule she had observed in other wards as they embarked on such projects, and she had every reason to presume it would continue in Ogden as well.[49]

The scope of the temporal ventures of Utah women in the period of Eliza Snow's presidency has been widely published.[50] The commission store described in the introduction to this chapter, the cooperative stores, Relief Society halls, the silk industry, the grain saving, the health-care provision—each has been described from the general level, as though all Latter-day Saint women had participated in all the ventures as prescribed from headquarters. Such was not the case. Each ward Relief Society selected the nature and degree of its participation in the general projects, and each woman determined her role within her ward organization. In order to look more closely at each of the major projects of the LDS women, let us consider one ward and how the particular activities were conducted there.

One Relief Society's Experience

The Salt Lake Stake Fifteenth Ward was located in what is now downtown Salt Lake City. Three blocks wide by nine blocks long, it ran from South Temple Street to Third South, and from Third West to the Jordan River. Originally agricultural in purpose, the neighborhood had become increasingly urbanized, and by the 1870s it had a combination of residential and light commercial buildings. Farmers may have resided in the ward, but their farms were now further from the city center.

Sarah M. Kimball had been called to preside over the ward Relief Society in 1857. In January 1868, when many ward reorganizations were taking place, Bishop Robert T. Burton reinstated her in that position. Unlike other new presidents, Sister Kimball had little need of assistance from Eliza R. Snow; in fact, Sister Snow took the organization chart Sister Kimball drew up and used it, with a few modifications, as a model for other wards. Presidency, secretary, and treasurer were familiar offices. But Sister Kimball also added "deaconesses" to prepare the meeting rooms, and a quorum of teachers "to inquire after the prosperity and happiness of the members . . . to speak words of wisdom, of consolation and peace . . . to know that the sick are properly taken care of, and if any are in need of assistance from the society." As the society expanded, Sister Kimball added, as needed, messengers, superintendents of work, a board of "apprizers," and a "commission merchantess."[51]

Some ward Relief Societies at the time were meeting in ward schoolhouses or meetinghouses; most gathered weekly in the homes of individual sisters. Sarah Kimball was not long in realizing that a permanent home was essential. By November 1868 the Fifteenth Ward Relief Society had raised enough funds to lay the cornerstone for their own Society Hall, the first in the Church. With appropriate decorum, the members paraded from their meetinghouse to their property and waited while her counselors ceremoniously escorted their presidentess to her place. There, silver trowel in hand, Sister Kimball set in place the "consecrated rock," then mounted it to make her remarks. Describing the "unpretending edifice" the sisters had planned on their forty-by-fifty-foot lot, she spoke of an upper story where the society meetings would be held, to be "dedicated to art and science," and a lower floor where the store would be devoted "to commerce and trade." "I view this as a stepping-stone to similar enterprises on a grander scale," she added.[52]

Sister Kimball herself let the contracts for the sixteen-by-thirty-foot building, hiring contractors to design and frame out the building and build inside fittings for an agreed price of $805.00 less donated labor. The property itself had cost $100.00. The lath and plaster cost $160.56. Other paid workmen painted, grained and varnished the benches, and built the cellar. Bishop Burton countersigned the society's $2,500.00 bank loan, all of which was repaid within five years.

Aware of the progress of the Fifteenth Ward building, a woman in a neighboring ward was reported to have asked the reason for their success. Replied Sister Kimball, it was because "we had acted in unison" and had "kept in motion that which we received." As the walls rose, Eliza Snow addressed her Fifteenth Ward sisters. Picking up Sister Kimball's stepping-stone metaphor, she recounted her own vision: that the sisters eventually, "instead of going forth to lay the foundation for a store . . . would go as Adam and Eve went to lay the foundation of Worlds."[53] A spiritual core lay at the center of even the most physical enterprise.

Their hall completed, the women ordered their meetings accordingly. While relieving the wants of the poor was a sacred mission, Eliza Snow had said, it "was secondary to the spiritual and moral influence that should be exercised by the sisters." Their meetings focused on that purpose. While they picked wool or

Shredding and sewing rags to be braided or woven into carpets was a prominent part of many Relief Society meetings through 1890s. Women in Springville, Utah, demonstrate the process in this 1898 photo by George E. Anderson. (Courtesy LDS Church Archives)

quilted, they visited "without the merits or demerits of neighbors being discussed," and Bishop Burton praised them for their "testimony of good will."

Even so, there were times when the spirit faltered. At one meeting Sarah Kimball lamented the lack of energy on the part of the sisters. Sister Duncanson "felt grieved to see the backward feeling manifest." Week after week, as "the ever faithful basket of carpet rags was brought forth," the sisters were losing interest. Prescribed Relief Society lessons as such were nearly forty years away, but these sisters determined they would not spend time mindlessly. They agreed to come to meeting prepared to instruct and entertain each other with reading, speaking, and singing. In the months that followed they sewed their carpet rags and stitched their quilts to readings from scripture, from Parley P. Pratt's *Key to the Science of Theology*, and from contemporary periodicals such as *Woman and Her Era* and the *Phrenological Journal*.[54]

The interworking of the bishop and the Relief Society president of any ward was, as it still is, a crucial factor in the success of ward operations. One bishop, in his inaugural address to his ward Relief Society, confessed to "the opposition that societies met from some of the brethren. Said he had no fears of the sisters transcending the bounds of the Priesthood. Felt to render them support and faith."[55] In the face of such possibilities, Bishop Burton and Sister Kimball created a winning symbiosis. A Canadian-born convert, he had joined the body of the Saints in Nauvoo and, like Sister Kimball, had shared with them the westward migration. Where Sarah's secular service to the Salt Lake community had been through her teaching, his had been military and political. Both carried heavy family responsibilities, Bishop Burton for his three wives and twenty-six children, widow Kimball for her three sons and two adopted daughters. They shared a compassion for all humanity. The bishop praised the president for her "motherly attention to all who needed assistance, whether of the household of faith or not."[56] Each valued in the other that certain independence of spirit which combined a willing cooperation with inspired ingenuity. As Sarah expressed it, "the legitimate exercise of spiritual power" is possible only under divine direction.[57] Eight years into their work together, she affirmed that as long as they had labored together there "had not been the least jar," and that Bishop Burton had always spoken "in the most fatherly manner," an interesting observation, since he was three years her junior.[58]

It was well they held such complementary values, for twice during his administration Bishop Burton would serve missions of about two years each, leaving the welfare of the ward in the hands of his counselors and the Relief Society president, and for the last two years he coupled his ward responsibilities with a new calling as counselor to the Presiding Bishop. From a reading of the ward Relief Society minutes, however, it is evident that his confidence in the women's organization was well placed.

Throughout the minutes there is a sense of the ongoing care of the poor, the sick, and the elderly of the ward, both male and female, and of immigrant families. The "poor funds" were consistently maintained by collections at meetings and by visiting teachers on their blocks. Beyond the usual food and clothing distributions, quilts for the poor were a staple, and soap was donated to the needy. One desire of the society, to build and operate a home for the homeless, never came to fruition, though later minutes mention support of an orphans' home.

That there was money and energy left over when the poor were provided for is indicated in cash contributions made to the temple, to the new meetinghouse, and to the Perpetual Emigrating Fund, and in the work expended in carpeting the wardhouse and putting on "soshables," dinners and entertainments for the elderly.

The largess of the Fifteenth Ward Relief Society extended beyond its boundaries: the great Chicago fire of 1871 spurred Sister Kimball to an ambitious suggestion: would it not be appropriate for the Relief Societies throughout the Church to concentrate their means in relief of the fifty thousand homeless there? she wrote to Eliza R. Snow. "If our Hall can be rendered servicable," presumably as a gathering place for goods contributed, "we shall feel blessed in having it thus appropriated." Declining Sister Kimball's veiled suggestion that the societies mount a general campaign, Sister Snow nevertheless encouraged the Fifteenth Ward to stretch to its own limits: while she had "nothing particular to suggest," she assured the ward that "our merciful religion will prompt in every direction that wisdom and compassion shall demand." Within a month, groups and individuals in Utah had sent fourteen thousand dollars in goods and cash to the Chicago relief effort.[59]

Probably the greatest expenditure of the energies of the Fifteenth Ward's Relief Society came in response to the home industries and self-sufficiency pleas of church leaders. Beginning with the building of the Society Hall, with its cooperative store on ground level and work space above, the commercial ventures expanded to the limits of the women's ingenuity and skill. A store inventory from 1871 includes such disparate items, made either by or for consumption by ward members, as woolen cloth, carpet rags, spools of cotton, crewel and braid, quilts, shoes, valentines, straw for braiding, hickory shirts, school books, garden seeds, and salt. Particular officers in the society were set in charge of manufacture of shirts, temple clothing, braided straw hats, feather brushes, carpets, and clothing. The latter led to the creation of a tailoring establishment; the demand for knitted items led to the importing of knitting machines for use by the society and for sale at twenty-five dollars. Need for space required an addition to the original Society Hall, and eventually a new and enlarged building.

Sarah Kimball used her ingenuity and expansive conception of women's abilities to create opportunities for them: the Society Hall first, then readings during work meetings; singing lessons for a poor but gifted sister; classes in physiology for the women; an embroidery class for girls; a kindergarten, for which the society offered to pay tuition for needy children and training costs for teachers; and education in political processes to encourage the sisters in "intelligent and conscientious voting." Her unique vision of women's world was diverse and inclusive: "Sew carpet rags and talk on Suffrage" typifies the blend of activities in her Relief Society.[60]

Storing Wheat for Times of Need

The Fifteenth Ward's response to Brigham Young's call for a grain-saving program was an example followed by sister wards. In 1876 he asked Emmeline B. Wells to lead the women in storing grain against a time of famine. "The men have been tried for years" in the attempt, said her husband, Daniel H. Wells, "but they have continued to let the grain go; now we want to see if the sisters will be more successful."[61] At the November inaugural meeting, Eliza R. Snow supported Sister Wells in her assignment. "The Lord, through his prophet, has called on the mothers in Israel to prepare for a famine . . . , to purchase and take care of wheat," she said.[62]

The need was dramatized in the report of Elvira Barney that in three counties, Morgan, Summit, and Wasatch, an early frost had destroyed most of the wheat, so there was none there to be purchased. Representatives from other ward Relief Societies reported the project already under way. Sisters in Manti, Utah, had already stored sixty or seventy bushels. In Salt Lake City, the Twentieth Ward Relief Society and Retrenchment Society was beginning a fund to buy grain, while Sister Chase of the First Ward offered her own bin to her society, but warned of the possibility of weevils in the wheat. Sister Hyde of the Seventeenth Ward reassured the women that in the dry atmosphere of Utah, she expected the wheat "would keep good for some time."[63]

"We have the faith, nerve, and land to build upon," wrote Sarah Kimball to Brigham Young, inviting him to be the first to donate to the fund. Confident of their cooperation, Sister Kimball arranged to meet with Bishop Burton and his counselors. She went to the meeting well prepared. There were three options for providing storage, she said. First, President Wells had offered use of space in his building. Second, through selling stock subscriptions the Relief Society could purchase the vacant land behind their store to build on. Third, and obviously her personal choice, she would donate some of her own land if the ward would help in constructing a fireproof granary and filling it with 350 bushels of wheat. One of the counselors said he was "always pleased with a plain statement of facts such as had been presented by Sister Kimball." Over the next weeks the matter was settled, and by October

1877 the Fifteenth Ward Relief Society had completed a fireproof granary built of rock. Its capacity was about one thousand bushels.[64]

"We brethren, you know, should assist our 'female brethren' " in the work, said President John Taylor in a sermon in Kaysville, Utah. He told a modern parable of a woman who over the years had slipped occasional bills from her household money into the family Bible. Hard times came, and she encouraged her husband to "have faith in God," and read "the good, old Book," wherein he, of course, found the cache of money. "Now we may find a time when we may need this wheat that our sisters are storing up," President Taylor concluded. "Let us not be too confident about our affairs, and do what we can by way of helping them."[65]

Throughout the settlements of the Great Basin, Relief Societies repeated the pattern of collecting and storing grain. Their methods varied from gleaning the wheat themselves to investing money and purchasing grain from the dividends. Beaver Relief Society president Lucinda Houd responded by gathering "a few kindred spirits, eight of them in all." Taking their lunch with them, "they went into the fields to glean," reads an account in the *Woman's Exponent*. "All through the heat and dust of that weary day they continued their labors until at nightfall, tired and footsore, but happy, they returned with their treasure, five grain sacks closely packed with heads of the precious wheat."[66]

Sarah Petersen of Sanpete County, Utah, suggested the dedication of the "Sunday eggs," by tradition a woman's "pin money," for Relief Society projects. The idea spread like wildfire, "and certainly the faithful female of the hen species arose to the occasion."[67] Years later, societies with cash on hand were encouraged to watch the wheat market and buy when prices were low. Advised the *Woman's Exponent* in September 1893, "If the crickets and grasshoppers should destroy the crop next year as now seems probable . . . it would be a source of satisfaction to have wheat in the bins instead of cash in the coffers."[68]

The women had sole jurisdiction over their wheat. An 1883 letter over the signatures of the First Presidency left no doubt: "No Bishop has any right, because of his authority as a presiding officer in the ward, to take possession of this grain. It belongs to the societies who have collected it, and it is their province to dispose of it for the purpose for which it has been collected."[69]

The women's autonomy over the wheat project is further revealed in a letter of stake Relief Society president Mary Ann Hyde concerning a ward's desire to use its grain money to build a hall. "I cannot take the responsibility of allowing stored wheat to be diverted from the legitimate object of gathering for a time of need," she wrote. "We are not sure of the coming harvest, and we already know Sister E. R. S[now']s instructions." "I suppose it would be well for them to build a hall," she added, "but not at the expense of their little store of grain."[70] The incident illustrates not only the relative importance of the grain storage and the society hall, but the chain of consent the women followed in such questions, from ward to stake to general Relief Society officers.[71]

Sericulture and Medical Services

Two other major projects of the Relief Societies during Eliza R. Snow's presidency were significant: silk manufacture and the Deseret Hospital and related medical services. In anticipation of a vigorous sericulture in Utah, Brigham Young had from the first encouraged immigrating European Saints to bring with them silk-worm eggs and seeds for the mulberry trees on which silkworms feed. From 1855 to 1876 various individuals had succeeded in limited production; the first dress produced from Utah silk, however, did not come until spring 1877. The "mission was given to all Branches of the Relief Society" by President Young in the last general conference over which he presided.[72] A "Deseret Silk Association" had been organized two years earlier, with Zina D. H. Young as its president. The overlap of the two organizations was a comfortable one: Eliza Snow was on the silk association's board and Zina Young would soon officially be Eliza's counselor in Relief Society. Besides, they were sister wives living under the same roof, with all the ease of interaction that such proximity allows.

However much support the sericulture received from church and later from government subsidy, the industry was never very profitable either to individuals or to the state. As a showpiece, however, and a symbol of the sisters' ability to adorn their homes and dress themselves beautifully in the workmanship of their own hands, the silk production was significant. The industry survived just past the turn of the century, when it dwindled to oblivion, leaving only occasional rows of mulberry trees to shade the streets and stain the sidewalks with their falling berries.[73]

More durable among the 1870s and 1880s Relief Societies was the continuation of their work to provide medical services. The same railroad that threatened Deseret with the costly importing

of "States goods" also blessed the Saints with access to medical
education, advances, and supplies. By the 1870s the corps of mid-
wives/physicians and the sporadic classes that trained them were
no longer sufficient to the needs of an increasingly urban and
industrial society. The Thomsonian doctors with their herbal remedies had run their course, and the well-intentioned but apprentice-
trained midwives were hard-pressed to deal with the usual mala-
dies, let alone cases of lead poisoning from the mines or typhoid
carried in water supplied by open ditches through now heavily
populated cities and towns. Even birthings called for more knowledge than those good women possessed. Mary Ann Weston
Maughan, for example, midwife and Relief Society president in
Cache Valley, Utah, tells in her diary of having a Dr. Ormsby
administer chloroform to deliver a Sister Goodwin after Sister
Maughan had done what she could. The next entry has Sister
Maughan "out with a subscription list to gather some money to
pay Dr. Ormsby for attending Sister McNeal who has lain in bed
five years and now wishes to be placed under the doctor's care."
She received $5.50.[74] However loath the women were to be attended
by male physicians, midwives lacked the expertise of the eastern-
trained doctors.

Brigham Young heard the pleas of such women as Nicoline
Olsen, who wrote in 1867 to suggest the "fitting up" of a maternity
hospital and obstetrical training center, and Martha Jane Coray,
who in 1872 requested that he reestablish the Council of Health
to educate obstetrical practitioners.[75] In 1873, just two weeks after
a meeting in which Amanda Smith "regretted that . . . sending for
doctors had become so prevalent" among the Saints, seeing such
action as a lack of faith, Bathsheba W. Smith announced to a
congregation of women that "the President had suggested to her
that three women from each Ward in the city be chosen to form
a class for studying physiology and obstetrics."[76] The next decade
would create of the two seemingly opposite thrusts a typically Mormon blend of faith and works in the treatment of injury and disease.

"President Young is requiring the sisters to get students of
Medicine," announced Eliza R. Snow to a Relief Society conference in Ogden in 1873, adding that a Mrs. Barker would be holding
classes in Salt Lake City for young women who would prepare
themselves ahead in physiology, anatomy, and other branches. "If
they cannot meet their own expenses, we have means of doing so."
Her sense of the importance of the work set it ahead of even the

gathering itself: "Instead of expending means to emigrate foreign Saints," she counseled, "spend that means in educating young women."[77]

But home-taught practitioners could not meet the needs of the growing population. Under Relief Society encouragement and occasional subsidy, Romania B. Pratt (Penrose), sister wives Ellis Shipp and Margaret Shipp (Roberts), and Martha Hughes (Cannon), among others, went to eastern colleges to receive degrees in medicine. Not only did the women doctors establish practices in Utah on their return, but for years afterward they taught classes in midwifery and home nursing, though the Female Medical College for which Sister Snow had solicited support never materialized.[78]

One course offered by Dr. Pratt and Elvira S. Barney in 1878 invited students to attend for six months. "By bringing bedding and boarding themselves," the announcement sheet suggested, women could expect expenses of fifty dollars for "tuition, fire, lights and partially furnished rooms." Textbooks, ordered from New York, would cost another twenty. Ten students could board at Dr. Barney's house, where the "recitations" would be held.[79] There is no way to ascertain how many women were actually trained under such programs; however, the programs continued successfully into the twentieth century.

By the 1880s it was apparent that home care of the sick and injured was no longer adequate. In 1874 Salt Lake City Episcopalians established St. Mark's Hospital, and in 1876 the Roman Catholic Sisters of the Holy Cross founded Holy Cross Hospital. By the time the nuns' operation outgrew its space on Salt Lake City's Fifth East and they moved to a larger facility, the Relief Society was looking to rent a building to begin its own hospital, in the planning since 1877. The vacated space was good enough for a start.

In July 1882 the Relief Society opened the Deseret Hospital, with Dr. Ellen B. Ferguson as house physician and Dr. Romania B. Pratt as eye and ear consultant. Two male physicians were also on staff. The facility boasted "a full equipment of instruments and appliances" purchased from eastern suppliers. Eventually there would be thirty to forty beds, though there were seldom more than sixteen patients at a time, either in the Fifth East location or later when the women took over the old Deseret University building in the Seventeenth Ward.[80]

Among the reasons they gave for opening their own hospital, Mormon women stressed their desire to provide care in an environment where physical treatments could be accompanied by spiritual ministrations. From the handwritten autobiography of Hannah Adeline Hatch Savage comes an account of the care she received there after the birth of her second child in 1887. She described the facility as "a poor excuse for a hospital," but testified to the healing that followed her blessing at the hands of Lucy Bigelow Young.[81] The threads of healing the sick by faith and treating disease with informed skill were coming together as never before among the Saints.

Funding was always a problem for the hospital, and a general misunderstanding that care was provided free of cost created ill will among Saints unwilling to pay. Subscriptions from wards and stakes and pleas for donations, generously heeded at first, did not keep up with costs, and the hospital ceased operation in the early 1890s. It would be a decade before the Groves LDS Hospital would be in operation, but the point had been made. Once again the Relief Society had filled the role of change agent, recognizing a need and demonstrating how it could be met by the Church at large.

Expanding "Woman's Sphere"

Necessity in every case was the mother of the Mormon women's invention, as their involvement in welfare, grain storage, home industry, and medical care attest. Responding to need and to President Young's call, they readily performed for the community at large an expanded version of the kind of service they had been giving their families. "My sphere of usefulness is being enlarged," wrote Susa Young in 1879, suggesting the pride felt by the generation of Latter-day Saint women who expanded "woman's sphere" — traditionally private and domestic — into the public domain.[82]

The sisters' enlarged interests, capabilities, and responsibilities are reflected in bright detail in the *Woman's Exponent,* a tabloid-sized newspaper established in 1872 and published semimonthly by and for women. In the forty-two-year history of the *Exponent,* it served as unofficial organ of the Relief Society, carrying notices of activities of local groups as well as stake and general conferences. Amid a miscellany of notes on fashion, foods, and family, the most conscientious columns of the paper dealt with women's rights and

WOMAN'S EXPONENT.

The Rights of the Women of Zion, and the Rights of the Women of all Nations.

VOL. 9.	SALT LAKE CITY, UTAH, NOVEMBER 15. 1880	No. 12.

A DAY OF MOTHER-LIFE.

This day has been so full of cares,
Of accidents and plans astray;
Of dust and sultry, fainting air,
And even danger and dismay,
I gladly saw the curtain close
About the gorgeous bed of Day;
And Night approach and bring repose
To call me from my toil away.

To-day my busy hands and feet
Would need be faster though they flew—
Breakfast to set and rooms make neat.
And washing over-see or do.
Children to dress and husband aid
In weighty things which may not wait—
This done, one hasty kiss he gave
And vanished through the arbor gate.

The steep and oft forbidden stairs
The baby climbs to very top,
And twenty other mischief's dares,
And mother's work as often stops,
And now he bumps his precious nose
And must be petted and caressed;
His brother now has hurt his toes
Which must be gently bathed and dressed.

The yeast thrice spilled, no bread is made,
The fat is scorching in the pot—
The dinner very late is laid
And then baked apples there forgot.
We linger some for pleasant talk—
But oh! what means that brazen glare?
That volume high of flame and smoke?
Ah' fly! the woodyard is on fire!

Then husband, I and washmaid too,
With tubs and buckets swiftly run;
Two neighbor sisters also flew
To help us do what could be done.
Husband pulled the cordwood down
And flung huge blazing brands about,
While we the crackling cinders drowned
With careful search till all were "out."

The battle won, with panting breath
We sought again the portal shade;
But there, the dining table left,
A housewife's heart might sore dismayed—
Baby, left king of all the feast,

And fainter grow in distance blue
The outlines of my favorite schemes
Obscured by clouds of household care
So dull and irksome—Nay, I dream!
'Tis for these babies pure and fair.

With brighter thoughts and lighter heart,
I list my darlings' evening prayer;
I think, and tears unbidden start,
Of when death claimed one jewel rare.
I kiss and bless and lay them down—
In innocence and peace to sleep;
If they remain I'll never frown
Though household cares roll fathoms deep.

I'm glad and more than satisfied
While they are happy, hale and sweet,
Though to their wants my hands are tied
And busy serving them my feet.
Leave wider fields for those whose homes
Are not with household jewels set;
While I before the Heavenly Throne
Give thanks that mine are spared me yet.

St. George, Aug. 1880.   LU DALTON.

REPROOF.

BY HANNAH T. KING.

To reprove well and wisely has ever seemed to me one of the most desirable attainments. It is a most disagreeable office, and yet at times a most necessary one; it is desirable to use language that shall soften instead of hardening the offender; it is also good to command the voice, that its tones may be persuasive rather than severe; the countenance also should denote sorrow more than anger. The reproof of a wise and virtuous person is ever a token of love and care for our welfare, whether it comes from relative, friend or employer, and should be received with silent dignity. Some are apt to look upon a reprover as an enemy, or as unkindness, but this is for want of due consideration, for if they speak for our good it must benefit us; and all have the power to make good come out of reproof. A candid, noble mind will bear it without one feeling of

angel in the way!" If ever I have envied, it has been called out by such women; their dignity of character, their self-controling power, their abnegation of self. Oh, let us imitate such models, for they are worthy. A passive spirit is a sweet one, let it be embodied in whom it may; not passive when it is our duty to be energetic, but where we should honor and obey. Not passive when our child is insolent and disobedient; firmness then must be aroused to put down rebellion and restore order. But if children are taught from babyhood to be obedient to legal authority, they will rarely rebel, and will not oblige a parent to speak many times before they will obey. When I see a disobedient child, I blush and mourn for the mother, for I know there lies the mischief. The Savior's description of one in authority should be the model for the head of a family: "I say to this one, come, and he cometh, and to another, go, and he goeth, and to my servant, do this, and he doeth it."

The fundamental principle of a well ordered family is obedience to the laws of that house; and where this is in full force, little reproof will be needed; and when it is given it will be but the echo of our own heart and conscience, and we at once bow beneath the rod and kiss the hand that wields it. Oh, how mighty is that being who walks in innocency before God! Who, though conscious of many imperfections, can say, with hand on heart and looking upward, "I desire, my Father, to be thine, only thine; I desire to be pure even in Thy sight. Excelsior! is my motto, my war cry in the battle of life."

Let us then be humble, not servile; meek, but not abject; passive, but not inert; self-reliant, yet thankful for assistance when needed. Let us reprove as we would desire to be reproved, remembering ever that "the wounds of a friend are better than the kisses of an enemy;" and many a one has been made a firm friend by the sweet way in which their reproof has been received, and the reprover has at once merged into the consoler, the adviser, the benefactor and the friend for life.

Front page of November 15, 1880, issue of *Woman's Exponent,* a semimonthly tabloid-size newspaper published from 1872 to 1914.

woman suffrage, the necessity of education for women, home industries, the on-going debate on women's proper place in the world, and, until the 1890 Manifesto discontinued church approval of the practice, plural marriage. The editors, contributors, and readers of the *Exponent* were firmly rooted in Latter-day Saint belief and community, but they eagerly reached outward to connect with other women in America and abroad who were also forging new roles for themselves in medicine, journalism, and other trades and professions, and in politics.

Begun by Edward Sloan, an editor of the Salt Lake *Herald,* the *Exponent* was first edited by Louisa Lula Greene (Richards), then for nearly thirty-five years by Emmeline B. Wells. At the outset considered unimportant, if not merely whimsical, the *Exponent* grew with the women in influence and responsibility until in 1881 Edward Tullidge considered that it "now wields more real power in our politics than all of the newspapers in Utah put together."[83]

The praise is certainly exaggeration, since subscriptions to the paper never rose above a thousand; its readership and influence, however, far exceeded what might be suggested by the paucity of its press run. It continued its role as an unofficial organ of the Relief Society until 1914, when the *Relief Society Magazine* began. That magazine was published until 1970.

The *Exponent* both signaled and supported the entry of Mormon women into the wider world of commerce, education, professional life, and political involvement that exploded with the decade of the 1870s.[84] It was not without precedent, however; the political action of Latter-day Saint women had its roots in the Nauvoo Relief Society, when Emma Smith, Eliza R. Snow, and Amanda Smith delivered to Governor Carlin their petition for guarantees of safety to Joseph Smith and the Saints. Now again they would enter public affairs, and this time their success would reach far beyond their immediate purpose. Mormon women's response to federal challenges to their practice of plural marriage brought with it, almost as a by-product, the right of suffrage.[85]

Within a decade of the announcement of the Saints' practice of plural marriage, federal injunctions against polygamy had begun, increasing in effectiveness as they progressed. The women reacted with escalating activity, writing letters and sending memorials to Congress. The 1870 Cullom Bill, yet another attempt to quell the practice, raised their resentment to fever pitch. When the sisters heard on January 4 that the bill had passed in the House of Representatives, they organized for action. Through Relief Society channels, they announced a planning meeting in the Fifteenth Ward Society Hall two days later.

Latter-day Saint women, said Sarah Kimball in her introduction to the meeting, would be "unworthy of the names we bear and of the blood in our veins, should we longer remain silent." If the bill became law, it would make "menial serfs" of LDS men, and "if they make serfs of them, what do they make of us?" A committee of Fifteenth Ward Relief Society members and their secretary was appointed to draft a resolution while the women present voiced their indignation. Said Eliza R. Snow, it was "high time" to "rise up in the Dignity of our calling and speak for ourselves." "The world does not know us," she said, "and truth and justice to our brethren and to ourselves demands us to speak. . . . We are not inferior to the Ladies of the World, and we do not want to appear so," she added. She represented Brigham Young as saying that women should "take a wide sphere of action," which she and her sisters interpreted as official sanction of their efforts.

Toward the end of the meeting, two proposals were made that, however appropriate they seem now, were quite radical in their time: Bathsheba Smith moved "that we demand of the Gov[ernor] the right of Franchise," and Lucy Kimball asked that the women "be represented at Washington." Both motions passed in that unofficial forum, and Eliza Snow and Sarah Kimball were "elected as representatives."[86]

Had the meeting been covered by an alert reporter, suggests historian Lola Van Wagenen, headlines the next day might have read "Utah Women Seek Franchise," followed by "Snow and Kimball Elected to Represent Mormon Women in Washington." Instead, five days later a mildly worded account of the event published the resolutions as drafted and a vague summary of "a few very appropriate remarks" made by the leading sisters.[87] The women were obviously more interested in being effective than demanding, and the matter at hand was the Cullom Bill, not woman suffrage itself.

On January 13, 1870, a stormy Thursday just one week after the planning meeting, over three thousand women gathered in the old tabernacle on Temple Square in a "Great Indignation Meeting." Thirteen thoughtful and articulate women addressed the assembly, their speeches obviously directed not so much at their sisters but at the press representatives, the only men present. Their efforts were not amiss: newspapers across the United States picked up the story and ran it with accompanying editorial comment. The New York *Times* called it "A Remarkable Meeting." The New York *Herald* said that "in logic and in rhetoric the so called degraded ladies of Mormondom are quite equal to the woman's rights women of the East," while the *Journal of Commerce* compared the Mormon speakers with the most articulate suffragists of the day: they were "fully up to the mark of the best efforts of [Lucretia] Mott, [Elizabeth Cady] Stanton, [Susan B.] Anthony or any other of the female suffrage women . . . while in respect of good temper, and the absence of bitter personal allusions, the Tabernacle gathering will certainly carry off the palm" of victory. The complimentary press coverage not only enhanced the public view of the women themselves, but also reflected well on the entire LDS community.[88]

The pattern of that meeting was repeated in outlying settlements throughout Mormondom, until by March 9 at least fifty-six such indignation meetings had been held and countless LDS women had had opportunity of publicly defending the principle and their right to practice their religion.

The effect was immediate: not three weeks after the tabernacle meeting, the territorial legislature, having debated the issue of woman suffrage in the territory, passed a bill in the house. The territorial council followed suit on February 9, and acting governor S. A. Mann, albeit with some trepidation, signed it into law three days later.[89] The following week, Eliza Snow led her sisters of the Relief Society in a memorial to Mann, thanking him for his action. His reply concluded with the "confident hope that the ladies . . . will so exercise the right conferred as to approve the wisdom of the legislation."[90]

The women met to approve the memorial in a meeting in the Fifteenth Ward Society Hall. Their sentiments were frankly spoken and carefully recorded. With remarkable freedom they expressed diverse opinions, ranging from Sarah Kimball's exultant assertion that she would now "openly declare herself a womans rights woman," to Margaret Smoot's disavowal that "I have never had any desire for more rights than I have," and her stated concern: "I consider the path [of political involvement] frought with great difficulties." Nevertheless, even she signed the memorial. "Great and blessed things are ahead," affirmed Phebe Woodruff, warning the women not to "run headlong and abuse the privilege. . . . May God grant us strength to do right in his sight," she concluded. "I feel comforted and blessed this day," said Presendia Kimball. "I am glad to see our daughters elevated with man and the time come when our votes will assist our leaders and redeem ourselves. . . . The day is approaching when woman shall be redeemed from the curse placed upon Eve." "The yoke on women is removed," rejoiced Sister Woodruff. "God has opened the way for us."[91]

There were cautions as well as exultation. Sister Kimball remembered that a Brother Rockwell had predicted that "women would have as much prejudice to overcome in occupying certain positions as the men would in letting them," to which Bathsheba Smith responded confidently, "there is nothing required of us that we cannot perform."[92] As Brother Rockwell predicted, however, the challenge was long-lived and complex. As Sister Russell, the secretary, articulated a year later, "we had always been counciled to leave public matters with the men, that we had obeyed this council so perfectly, we were in extreme ignorance concerning our own government. . . . Now in this condition," she continued, when "the right of the Ballot had been conferred upon us, [we] hoped we would prepare ourselves to honor the confidence that was placed in us." Then, simply and succinctly, she stressed once again the importance of the unity that underlay the entire program: "that our united strength joined with the Brethren would result in good to the people."[93] On election day, February 14, 1870, twenty-five women voted, about 1 percent of the total electorate, a meager beginning to what would become for Relief Society women a right worth defending.[94]

A Time to Retrench

Hardly a year into the 1860s reorganization, Brigham Young expressed satisfaction with the burgeoning work of the Relief Society. "The sisters have already done much good," he told an audience in the old tabernacle, "and I wish them to continue and go ahead." One of his purposes in reestablishing the society, however, seemed not to be moving forward. His tour to the southern settlements in 1869 again called attention to the extravagance with which the women entertained him and his entourage. A note in the diary of John D. Lee, at whose Washington, Utah, home the president's party stayed overnight, tells the tale: President Young, "being weary, . . . retired to rest. The women were cooking all Night."[95] From town to town it was the same: huge meals laid on the best linens and served on the finest china available for the visitors. If there was no fine table service available in one town, dishes used in the settlement before would be washed and sent ahead by wagon for use the next day. "I will come back & take a Bowl of Milk & mush with you," President Young had said to his host, but the request for simplicity went unheard. The sisters continued to absent themselves from meetings in order to prepare meals.[96]

Brigham Young understood the reasoning of the Saints. "Brother Brigham, let us manifest our feelings towards you and your company," he reported their protestations. "I tell them to do so," he explained, "but give me a piece of johnnycake; I would rather have it than their pies and tarts and sweetmeats."[97]

President Young must have eaten yet another feast at Gunnison, Utah, when he spotted Mary Isabella Horne, visiting from Salt Lake City with her son, who was bishop in Gunnison. "I invited her when she returned, to call the sisters of the Relief Society together, and ask them to begin a reform in eating and housekeeping," he announced in the tabernacle the following week. He wanted the members to "agree to have a light, nice breakfast in the morning, for themselves and children, without cooking something less than forty different kinds of food, making slaves of themselves and requiring three or four hired girls to wash dishes."[98]

As usual, there were spiritual laws behind President Young's temporal instruction; In this case one such purpose had to do with sisters' spirituality. They were entrusted with the care of their children and so should be prepared to "live so as to rebuke disease." "It is the privilege of a mother to have faith and to administer to her child; this she can do herself, as well as sending for the Elders to have the benefit of their faith," he concluded.[99] In the same vein, a century later President Gordon B. Hinckley also saw women's exercise of the gift of prayer in connection with the healing of the sick. Citing James's instruction "to call for the elders of the church" to anoint with oil "in the name of the Lord," Elder Hinckley emphasized James's conclusion that "the prayer of faith shall save the sick." Addressing the women, he affirmed that it is women's "privilege to pray, with the full expectation that your Father in Heaven will hear that prayer when it is offered in faith."[100] Nurturing her own mind and spirit was more important to a mother's responsibilities than the meals she prepared for her family.

When she arrived home, Sister Horne, who was president of the Fourteenth Ward Relief Society, called on Eliza Snow. Together they met with Brigham Young, and they came away with a clearer sense of the assignment and with their own vision of its possibilities. Inviting to her home the presidents of several adjoining ward Relief Societies, Sister Horne made her point quickly: the table was set simply and with plain food. "Retrenchment" was a concept easily demonstrated.[101] President Young's suggestion spawned a reform movement that gained momentum as meetings fell into a semimonthly pattern and moved from private residences to the spacious and centrally located Fourteenth Ward meetinghouse. Twice monthly, sisters from wards across the valley, and even from beyond, met at what became the "Junior and Senior Cooperative Retrenchment Association."

For most of the women who attended, the meetings met spiritual needs and strengthened relationships. The sisterhood crossed ward boundaries, providing continuation of bonds formed in earlier times. Testimony bearing, the most frequent exercise of the group, built faith and continuity of spiritual well-being.

Rather than conflict with Relief Society, the biweekly meetings provided Relief Society leaders an essential locus of administrative networking. Isabella Horne's six counselors were Relief Society workers, one of them Sister Snow herself, which meant that the two organizations overlapped to the point that their functions merged. Often Sister Snow would announce her need to speak to presidents or ward representatives "following this meeting." The sisters who carried Relief Society messages to outlying wards consulted first and reported later at the semimonthly meetings. In this regard the meetings became prototypes of subsequent central committees, later general boards, of the women's organizations. Assignments from President Young and projects initiated by the women were first announced and discussed there, and expressions of support and cooperation from sisters attending became the commitments of the wards they represented. Sericulture, cooperative stores, grain storage, the *Exponent*, home industry, medical classes, the Deseret Hospital, and eventually the united order: all were fostered through the Retrenchment network.

At the same time the women's group was taking shape, the needs of his young daughters and their contemporaries pressed on Brigham Young's mind. After consultation with Sister Snow, he called his wives and daughters to a meeting in the parlor of the Lion House on November 18, 1869, and what was eventually to become the Young Women's Mutual Improvement Association was born.[102]

The first matter of business was the drafting of resolutions of retrenchment in dress and behavior to which the young ladies, both single and married, subscribed. To them the matter simplified initially to the sacrifice of ruffles, frills, and furbelows, of "frivolous conversation" and "evil society." "We do not want to look like Quakers but we want to look neat and respectable, and not appear as dowdie," proclaimed one president, remembering perhaps the Deseret costume of the 1850s.[103] The term "a good Retrenchment girl" became standard parlance.

Spurred on by the Young daughters, and fostered by the older women's group, "Junior Retrenchment" spread to wards throughout Deseret. Older teenaged girls and young married women met, with the retrenchment ideals common to their commitment, and agendas centered on gospel understanding and the religious life. At the Cooperative Retrenchment semimonthly meetings the president of any of the Salt Lake organized groups, or one of her six counselors, might report, to the approbation of her seniors.

Like Topsy, the movement "just growed," with little imposed structure, and activities varying from ward to ward. The overlap with Relief Society caused concern for at least one bishop who feared competition between the programs, but the sisters themselves found the symbiosis comfortable, and the movements spread simultaneously.

Reports of Eliza Snow's trips were a highlight of any meeting. "In compliance with the request made by Mrs. Horne," she prefaced her remarks in a July 1875 meeting, "I will give a synopsis of our visit South." The two women, along with Elizabeth Howard and Elvira Barney, had accompanied President Young and several members of the Quorum of the Twelve to Sanpete County in central Utah. Compared with today's elaborately planned General Authority visits, this was extemporaneous in the extreme, especially for the women. Eliza Snow reported, "Tuesday [we] went to Moroni. President Young told me to make arrangements for a meeting for the sisters and as many of the brethren as wished to attend." The local Relief Society president asked Sister Horne to preside, and Sister Horne then called on President Young to speak. "He spoke to considerable length as it was the first time he had preached since leaving home."[104]

Current local issues formed the substance of the talks: a Presbyterian minister had been engaged to teach school, to President Young's consternation; several Protestant missionaries had at the time been dispatched to Utah for the purpose, as they saw it, of Christianizing the Mormons, so his concern was not unfounded. Sister Snow hit the subject even more firmly in a subsequent address to the sisters: "I told them I would rather a child of mine should never know its alphabet than to attend the school of those who were not Latter-day Saints." Her concern for the children of Zion had been gnawing at Sister Snow's awareness for some years, and would continue to bother her a year or so yet.[105]

Meanwhile, having met with Saints in most of the towns in the county, the brethren completed their business and returned home, while the sisters went on to Gunnison, Levan, Nephi, Santaquin, Payson, Spanish Fork, Springville, and Provo, "holding sweet communion" with the Relief Societies as they went. In Nephi they organized the young women. "There was over one hundred," Eliza reported. "It was a beautiful sight to see." In two weeks the traveling sisters had restored bonds among the Saints, men as well as women, in eleven communities. Visiting in homes as well as meeting in public, they carried personal news, encouragement, and instruction, keeping strong the ties of sisterhood.[106]

In the 1870s the "leading sisters" paid as much attention to the young women as to the already formed Relief Societies. "It is the young that are particularly subjected to the snares that are now in our midst," Sister Snow warned. "Those who have been organized into Retrenchment Societies are now in the safe path."[107] As early as 1872 she suggested to one concerned bishop that the young men also be organized, "but of course we women cannot dictate," she noted. At the Lehi (Utah) Ward, however, Sister Snow, aware of some local problems among the youth, asked the girls to bring their beaux to the evening's meeting. "[I] told them I wanted them to sustain the young ladies in their positions," she reported. If the youths, she continued, would not "leave off their drinking and tobacco where were the young girls to get husbands? The young men did not wish the girls to be in advance of them. I heard the next morning that the young men had been after the Bishop to organize them before night."[108]

Sister Snow's influence spread even further. While on tour in England in 1872, she met with Junius Wells, "a humble young man" serving as a missionary. When she told him of the young ladies' retrenchment organization, she reported, he "wished something similar could be done with the young men." On his return home, Elder Wells observed the retrenchment groups in operation and met again with Sister Snow, whom he called "the genius" of the organization. It is not surprising that soon after, in June 1874, he was called by Brigham Young to organize the Young Men's Mutual Improvement Association.[109] By 1878 the name of the Junior Retrenchment Association had been changed to the Young Ladies' Mutual Improvement Association, reflecting even more clearly the parallels in purpose and activities of the two groups. Even so, the Relief Society remained the umbrella organization for the YLMIA, and the visitors continued to include them in joint and separate meetings.

The ideal of retrenchment was soon overshadowed by the larger purposes of gospel living. The specific aims of simplicity of table and fashion gave way to a more general self-improvement agenda. "What do I want to retrench from?" asked Eliza Snow. "It is my ignorance and every thing that is not of God."[110] But that had always been the intent of Brigham Young: "Retrench in every-thing that is bad and worthless, and improve in everything that is good and beautiful," he had said to his daughters at the outset.[111]

As the separate identities of the junior and senior organizations became more pronounced, local branches of the senior groups, where they existed, were subsumed in the Relief Society. Only the general retrenchment meetings continued, identified regularly in the *Woman's Exponent* as "The Ladies Semi-Monthly Meeting." Their quasi–general-board function diminished with the sustaining in 1880 of the three presidencies of women's organizations and the creation of boards for each; even so, it was not until 1904 that the retrenchment meetings finally dissolved. Of the original presidency, only Mary Isabella Horne and Bathsheba W. Smith were still alive, and Sister Horne was in poor health.[112]

Yet one more permanent organization was to grow in the fertile soil of the Relief Society. At dinner with the Farmington Ward Relief Society president following a Relief Society conference there in July 1878, Sister Snow and her companions listened to the con-cerns of another Farmington woman, Aurelia Spencer Rogers. Emmeline B. Wells wrote in her diary that Sister Rogers "talked to us about an Association for little boys; she has been much exercised" about their lack of training. The idea of organizing for the children found immediate response in the visitors' minds. "We all spoke to Bishop Hess and he approved & on the way home on the train we decided to go to [President John] Taylor and take the matter before him."[113] President Taylor responded enthusiastically and subscribed in behalf of the entire church. Within a month there was a Primary Association in Farmington, and a month after that, one in the Eleventh Ward of Salt Lake Stake. In between, in one flurry of organization, Sister Snow and her companions or-ganized a Primary presidency in each of the fifteen wards of Box Elder Stake, and "the Elders set them apart." Two days later 250 children attended an inaugural meeting there. Announcing their progress to her sisters in a Retrenchment Association meeting, Sister Snow asked for a vote of confidence in the idea: "On motion the entire assembly rose to their feet."[114] The sisters were eager to take on the task of collective motherhood and to extend their nurturing outside the home into the church community.[115]

"I feel assured that the inspiration of heaven is directing you," Eliza Snow wrote to Sister Rogers, "and that a great and very important movement is being inaugurated for the future of Zion."

Sister Rogers concurred: "While thinking over what has to be done for the best good of the children," she later wrote, "I seemed to be carried away in the spirit, or at least I experienced a feeling of untold happiness which lasted three days and nights. During that time nothing could worry or irritate me; if my little ones were fretful, or the work went wrong, I had patience, could control in kindness, and manage my household affairs easily. This was a testimony to me that what was being done was of God."[116]

Relief Society Is Formally Reorganized

Meanwhile, by the mid-1870s it was becoming apparent to President Brigham Young that the administrative organization of the kingdom as it had come with the Saints from Nauvoo was no longer adequate. From ten thousand Saints in Nauvoo in the 1840s, the Church had grown to over a hundred thousand in 1877. What had been one center community with a few scattered settlements of the 1850s was now one Salt Lake stake of nearly twenty thousand people and nineteen additional stakes spread along a north-south axis over four hundred miles long. In one personally taxing summer season, his last, President Young totally reorganized the Church, stake by stake, until a workable order was achieved. No longer would apostles preside directly over stakes, nor would bishops, traveling bishops, and presidents share ward governance. Each stake now had its own local presidency, each ward its own resident bishopric. Quorums of priesthood were set in their places, and order prevailed churchwide.[117]

For the women's work, the implications of the general reorganization were obvious. Relief Society was organized in most wards, but word-of-mouth instructions from Eliza R. Snow, even with help from her Retrenchment Association colleagues, could hardly carry messages to and relay reports from the 240 wards now functioning. As she observed, "there was a body but no head."[118] Following the pattern of the priesthood organization, the women of Weber Stake in the Ogden area were the first to adopt a stake Relief Society organization; others would follow.

Six months later, the usual general retrenchment meeting in the Fourteenth Ward was preempted by a special meeting. President John Taylor and several other members of the Twelve had been invited, said Eliza R. Snow in opening the meeting, but pressing business kept them away. Presiding Bishop Edward Hunter and Elder A. M. Musser attended, to the gratification of the sisters.

As President Young had inaugurated the stake organization in Ogden, so Sister Snow "considered [it] proper to carry out" the same pattern throughout the Church. That said, she nominated Mary Isabella Horne as president of the Salt Lake Stake Relief Society, a role that Sister Horne filled, simultaneously with her presidency of the Retrenchment Association, to her death. She and her counselors, Elmina S. Taylor and Sarepta Haywood, were sustained, and ward presidents were instructed, as in the Weber Stake pattern, to prepare reports for a quarterly meeting three months hence. A pattern was emerging that would outlast the century.

For all the forming officialdom, however, the warmth of sisterly relations was not endangered. Sister Taylor, hesitant to accept that responsibility and others that would follow, recorded in her diary how "Sr. Snow clasped me in her arms and said she always felt like blessing me all over because I am such a faithful worker in the Kingdom." And in a too-frequent form of female self-effacement, she added, "I fear I do not merit it but will strive to in the future."[119]

By the end of the decade, then, the "leading sisters," as they were called, or "home missionaries" in the cause of the women's work, had traveled through most of Zion adding to the core Relief Societies the two auxiliaries, Primary and Young Ladies' Mutual Improvement Association. Stake Relief Society presidencies were being organized. Every program, however, and each adaptation, each change, had to be approved ward by ward or stake by stake. The Salt Lake Stake Thirteenth Ward, for example, noted a meeting of its Junior Retrenchment Association at which the name was changed to Mutual Improvement. The importance granted the consent process is indicated in the fact that Eliza Snow herself attended to propose the change, and members of the Twelve were present "by special invitation." "Much wise counsel" was given that evening, says the report, including that of Joseph F. Smith, then junior among the apostles but a former member of the First Presidency. He spoke of "the importance of the higher education and superior knowledge women should attain" and challenged the daughters of Zion to know for themselves of the truth of the gospel. He "alluded to Woman's voice in the Church, and the privileges she had of voting, etc. which were equal to the brethren in strength and power and influence."[120] There was no question that in his view the women's work of the Church was of similar significance to that of the men.

Local activities of all three women's organizations were in full swing. At the head, however, only Eliza R. Snow had been formally called by priesthood authority. On June 18 and 19, 1880, a conference of the Salt Lake Stake organizations had been planned, with Relief Society to meet on Friday, and Primary and Young Ladies' to gather on Saturday. On the agenda, however, were motions of importance to the whole church. With little fanfare, in the Primary meeting, with the entire middle section of the Tabernacle filled with children, Ellen Clawson was called as stake president of the Primary, with two counselors. Just as quietly, Sister Snow proposed that Louie B. Felt be selected as a "general superintendent" of all the Primary Associations in all the stakes of Zion. She also was given two counselors.

The children present expressing a desire to hear from him, President John Taylor spoke. His address, however, strayed from admonitions to the children and turned to the concerns of the women. He asked secretary L. John Nuttall to read from the minutes of the first Nauvoo Relief Society and explained Emma Smith's ordination to expound scriptures. He told of his having been called upon to ordain her counselors at that first meeting. It was as though the moment were being relived, as though there were some continuity to be established. After much instruction to the sisters, President Taylor concluded and Sister Horne, who was conducting the meeting, arose. Whether it had been so planned or came by impromptu inspiration is unclear, but she moved, and Sarah Kimball seconded, that President Taylor publicly appoint Eliza Snow as president of all the Relief Societies. He did so, and the children and women present sustained her appointment. Sister Snow chose as counselors Zina D. H. Young and Elizabeth Ann Whitney; President Taylor proposed them, and the conference sustained them. "These sisters form a central organization for all the Relief Societies of all the stakes of Zion," read the minutes. The children sang "Lord, Dismiss Us with Thy Blessing," and the meeting adjourned.[121]

The Nauvoo pattern was reestablished, as the Prophet Joseph had instructed: "that the Sisters elect a presiding officer to preside over them, and let that presiding officer choose two Counsellors to assist in the duties of her Office — that he would ordain them to preside over the Society — and let them preside just as the Presidency preside over the church." The organization was again complete, "after the pattern of the priesthood."[122]

That afternoon the Young Ladies' MIA repeated the pattern one more time, approving President Snow's nomination of Elmina S. Taylor and two counselors as presidency of the central committee of that organization. It was not until a month later, however, that the final blessing fell upon the chosen leaders, and again it was an ad hoc addition to another meeting, this time the general retrenchment meeting. "I was not aware till last evening of this meeting," said President John Taylor by way of introduction. "At least I had forgotten it, and had arranged to leave this city this afternoon." However, he remained and fulfilled the remaining office of organization in the Lord's name: the setting apart of the new presidency. In so doing, he reviewed the Nauvoo precedent, clarifying as he did the meaning of the term "ordination" as it applied to the sisters. The ordination then given, he explained, "did not mean the conferring of the Priesthood upon those sisters." Sister Snow and Bathsheba Smith, who had been present at the first Relief Society meeting, nodded their agreement. He then set apart the new presidency of the Relief Society: to Eliza R. Snow, conferring "power and authority . . . to bless, elevate and strengthen thy sisters"; to Zina Diantha Young, "to be a wise counselor" and to "have joy in thy labors"; and to Elizabeth Ann Whitney, "to be esteemed as a Mother in Israel," to be "blessed in thine old age" and to "have a place in the Celestial Kingdom of God with thine husband." Sister Whitney served just three years before she died.[123] That the blessings found fulfillment is suggested in one woman's response. Mary Ann Burnham Freeze, called as stake president of the Young Ladies' Mutual Improvement Association, recorded her response to a Relief Society conference in March 1883. "I enjoyed myself exceedingly," she wrote. "[I] felt like shouting hallelujah while listening to Sister E. R. Snow, H. M. Whitney. I never heard the sisters speak with such power as they did that afternoon."[124]

The prodigious productivity of the 1870s had been brought into a workable order. As president over the women's work, President Snow now had the means whereby to correlate activities, regulate procedures, and keep abreast of local accomplishments of the three organizations. From stake to stake the three presidents or their representatives traveled by spring wagon or by train — "on the cars," was their term — holding conferences for women, young women, and children as they went. "A stake officer in one town . . . might drive the team herself, or press into service her boy or a neighbor's son," wrote Susa Young Gates, "and around that stake the Salt

Lake party would go, sending word ahead by the prized local tele-graph."[125] Or Eliza herself would drive, her companions building their confidence by reminding themselves that she had, after all, driven teams much of the way across the plains.

By 1880, the twenty stakes in Utah and one in Arizona were all fully organized with stake Relief Society officers presiding over from four to thirty-six ward societies each.[126] During the same dec-ade that stake organization was proceeding in the western United States, branch Relief Societies were being organized in mission fields around the world. Soon after Sarah Kimball's Bishop Burton, now a mission president, had organized the sisters in White Chapel, England, and other branches in the London district in 1874, a Relief Society existed in Nottingham and another in Glasgow, Scotland.

In 1873 a small Relief Society was organized among the native Hawaiian women at Laie, the Latter-day Saint colony on the wind-ward side of Oahu. Wives of missionaries organized a group of mainland and native sisters in a Relief Society, which several times between 1874 and 1877 entertained King Kalakaua and Queen Kapiolani, rulers of the islands. The concept of women organized in such aid societies had caught the interest of the king, and he traveled the islands organizing Hui Hoola Lahui (Relief Society) in all the churches there. Among the Latter-day Saints themselves, by 1879, reported Margaret Cluff, she, two mainland sisters, and two native sisters, Kaahamie and Kealohamie, formed a superin-tendency that functioned much as a stake Relief Society presidency, visiting Relief Societies on the various Hawaiian Islands. For the mainland missionary wives, the auxiliaries were a particular boon, offering them administrative and teaching opportunities among the natives in a mission in which the roles of the wives were undefined, dependent mainly on the women's own initiative.[127]

The work was proceeding apace among the people of Lamanite extraction on the mainland. Branches formed under missionary leadership often, as in the case of Thistle Valley, had Relief So-cieties led by the president's wife. On an 1880 visit to the Sanpete County societies, Eliza Snow and Zina Young met with the Thistle group. "The log meetinghouse was much too small," read the report in *Woman's Exponent*, "so the meeting convened, forenoon and afternoon, in the bowery outside." Brother Spencer, the presiding officer of the branch, introduced Sister Eliza; the converts were most interested in her relationship to the Prophet Joseph. On her part, as she began speaking, Sister Snow was "deeply affected" in the realization of prophecies concerning the Native Americans. Presumably through a translator—Brother Spencer himself knew the language—she spoke for an hour; her words "flowed forth, as it were, fresh from the fountains of her soul." In the afternoon Sister Spencer was named president of the newly formed society, with the native Sister Susan, wife of Nephi, as a counselor, the first Lamanite so chosen.[128]

Of the two-week Sanpete County visit, the Lamanite meeting was the highlight. Stake Relief Society president Mary Ann Hyde, reporting to her own ward, remarked on the interest of the Indian women in Sister Eliza, whom, she said, they addressed as "Mother," adding that it had been "prophesied in the days of Nauvoo that the Lamanites will call her Mother."[129] The title would again be implemented in the childless Sister Snow's honor; at her funeral she would be designated a "mother in Israel."

In continental Europe, Relief Societies in Scandinavia, where missionary work had long been established, were soon to follow the British example. By 1880 sisters were organized in thriving branches from Fredrikstad, Norway (1877), to Copenhagen, Denmark (1879), to Stockholm, Sweden (1880). The greatest trial to the European societies was the obedience of the sisters to the doctrine of gathering: by the time the *Relief Society Magazine* published a photograph of the first officers of the Copenhagen group, at least five or six had emigrated to the United States.[130] Within the next decade, sisters in Germany, Switzerland, and the Netherlands were also organized. When the Church celebrated its Jubilee Year in 1880, the white silk banner prepared for the Relief Society represented three hundred societies worldwide.

As though reliving the Nauvoo pattern, though, once the organizations were running on well-oiled wheels, the leading sisters turned again to what was then and would always be of highest priority: the saving work of the temple. It was as Presiding Bishop Edward Hunter said in an 1877 meeting. Claiming to have "a better opportunity than any of the brethren to understand the great good the sisters were accomplishing," he praised their work "in caring for the poor and sick, and in helping to build Temples."[131] Eliza Snow and her sisters had been faithful workers in the old "Temple pro tem," the endowment house on Temple Square, from its construction in 1855 to its demolition in 1889. After the St. George Temple was dedicated in 1877, the Logan Temple in 1884, and the Manti Temple in 1888, the Salt Lake sisters made frequent trips

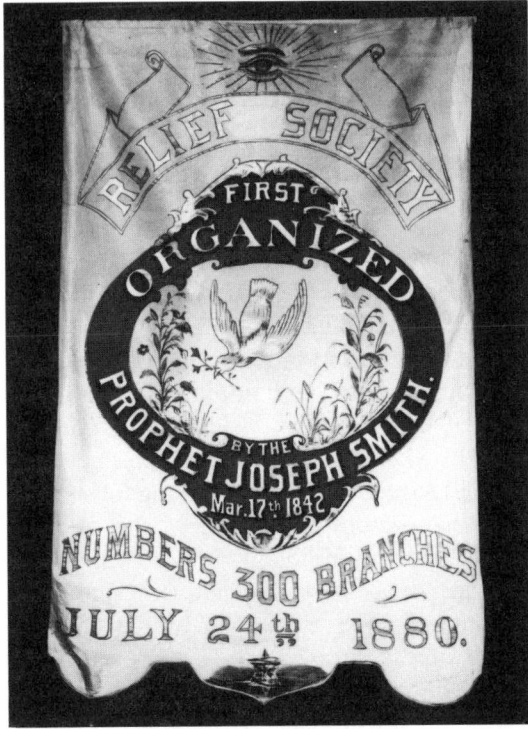

A banner made of Utah silk was the Relief Society entry for Church's fifty-year Jubilee parade. The all-seeing eye at the top represented sisters' conviction that Relief Society was organized by divine revelation and that God continued to watch over their work. A dove with an olive branch suggested the peaceable spirit of the society and the healing balm of its charitable works. The banner is now preserved in LDS Museum of Church History and Art.

to those temples also. To perform ordinance work for the dead was the first cause of Eliza R. Snow and Zina D. Young's 1880–81 tour to St. George; during that winter they also organized some thirty Primaries and addressed many more meetings. The two traveled over a thousand miles by wagon, Eliza figured, and occasionally slept along the trail overnight between settlements.[132]

The temple work and the temporal work merged in the minds of the women of Zion. That their leading sisters figured so prominently in both gave them even greater stature in women's eyes. Especially did the combined roles add to the position of their beloved "Aunt Eliza": as well as Relief Society presidentess, they regarded her as their priestess. And in consideration of the blessings she would give the sisters both in the holy house and in their own homes, they added the title of prophetess to her honor. Many of the more than fifty thousand Saints endowed in the endowment house during its thirty-four years, men and women both, would have seen her there. The next two of her successors as Relief Society general president would be called ex officio to preside over the women's work in the Salt Lake Temple after its 1893 dedication, continuing the link between the two forms of service until 1910. In Sister Eliza, her sisters saw embodied the organizational authority and the prophetic gifts, two important manifestations of religious power.

As the sisters saw in Eliza Snow the many facets of her being, so she recognized in their lives a similar complexity. To those gathered in a Relief Society meeting in Ogden in 1873, she spoke of "a great many things." She talked of their freedom as women, of their trials, of the work of the kingdom. She addressed the young sisters, encouraging them to heed the "monitor" within them, to "get the Holy Ghost." "You are living to be Saints," she admonished.

To the mature sisters, President Snow spoke of their need for a Relief Society hall, of the request of Brigham Young for women to get a classical education, to study medicine; of the plea for nurses; of the opportunities to study physiology, anatomy, and such. "Don't you see," she urged, "that our sphere is increasing? Our sphere of action will continually widen, and no woman in Zion need to mourn because her sphere is too narrow." Then, as though she recognized the burden she was placing on her already encumbered sisters, she paused. "God bless you, my sisters, and encourage you, that you may be filled with light," she prayed.

In recognition of their many responsibilities, she continued: "Let your first business be to perform your duties at home. But inasmuch as you are wise stewards, you will find time for social duties" — the schooling, the doctoring, the building of a hall — "because these are incumbent upon us as daughters and mothers in Zion." Then came the promise: "By seeking to perform every duty you will find that your capacity will increase, and you will be astonished at what you can accomplish."

She concluded with her blessing. "The Lord help us. The Lord is with His Saints . . . and he watches over them by night and by day. Inasmuch as we continue faithful, we shall be those that will be crowned in the presence of God and the lamb. You, my sisters, if you are faithful will become Queens of Queens, and Priestesses unto the Most High God."[133]

CHAPTER 4

IN BONDS OF SISTERHOOD
1888–1901

"We welcome Sisters Eliza and Zina as our Elect Lady and her counselor," wrote the Kanab Relief Society minute taker in 1881, "and as Presidents of all the feminine portion of the human race."[1] As inflated as the claim seems in this century, to the women of nineteenth-century Mormondom it bespoke an eternal perspective with which they were comfortable.

Eliza R. Snow and Zina D. H. Young were linked not only as presidency members but also as "the honored wives of our revered and martyred Prophet Joseph Smith," both having been sealed to him in Nauvoo.[2] That they were also sister wives to Brigham Young cemented even firmer their bond, especially during the years that both lived in the Lion House, his family residence in Salt Lake City.

In another sense, however, the two were the yin and yang of nineteenth-century Relief Society: where Sister Eliza was the head of the women's work, Aunt Zina was often said to be its heart. They complemented each other: where Aunt Eliza could see her sisters' circumstances with a clarity born of her own disciplined self-containment, Zina, the "great mother-heart," took them in her spiritual arms and blessed them by her unconditional acceptance. Eliza taught doctrines of exaltation, created organizations to address the sisters' needs, and prayed blessings on their heads; Zina bore spiritual witness, applied the balm of gospel principles, and spoke peace to her sisters' souls. Where Eliza challenged, Zina comforted; where Eliza anticipated divine perfection, Zina understood human imperfection. Their talents overlapped; each valued the other's gifts and built upon them, to the good of the work.

When on December 5, 1887, Eliza Snow departed this life, the loss to Zina Young was as the loss of her own sister. Eliza's funeral was to be a state occasion, with services in the Assembly Hall on Temple Square. The day before the funeral, Emmeline B. Wells and Dr. Romania Pratt went wearily "from place to place to notify presidents of Relief Society to march in the procession."[3] The phalanxes of women leaders were to be official representatives of mourning women churchwide.

The Assembly Hall was draped in cream white mull, with white roses and green sprays, in accordance with Eliza's own request. "No black for me, dear love, when I am dead," had suggested a verse in the *Woman's Exponent*, initiating a practice that continued among the Saints for many years.[4] The white bunting "looked pure and lovely as her whole life had been," reported an observer.[5]

For several weeks following Eliza's death, Zina had no heart to carry on her Relief Society work; even when she resumed, there was an emptiness. "Aunt Zina was lonely as usual," remarked Emmeline Wells following Sister Young's return from meetings in Nephi, Utah.[6] But the work must continue, and, as President John Taylor decreed in general conference the following April, Zina was to head it.

The mantle of leadership fell uneasily on sixty-seven-year-old Sister Zina. Although she was sustained in general conference in April 1888, it was not until October that she settled on her counselors, Ogden Stake Relief Society president Jane S. Richards and Bathsheba W. Smith. The correspondence secretary, with duties more like those of a managing director, was Emmeline B. Wells. "See dear aunt Em, she can help you," wrote Zina's daughter in encouraging her mother. "She is a natural made General, and can assist you by a few judicious letters and appointments, and give yourself a chance to do your best that you do."[7] The efficient Emmeline was to remain secretary through two more administrations, to her own presidency in 1910.

Zina Huntington Young had little reason for self-doubt, although she did serve more comfortably in individual ministrations to the women than in public office. She had mothered her own three children and, at the death of their mother, four more of Brigham Young's children. Trained as a midwife, she had delivered babies for most of her sister wives in the Lion House. Bearing the homely remedies of her Thomsonian practice—both herbal and other concoctions, such as the concentrate of water in which two toads were boiled—she also ministered to women and men outside Lion House gates as well. One such visit is recorded: The patient

Zina D. H. Young
with her daughter
Zina Young Card,
who lived in Alberta,
Canada. Though they lived
800 miles apart, they
managed long and frequent
visits, mother to deliver
daughter's babies, and
daughter to assist mother in
Relief Society work.
(Courtesy Mary Brown
Firmage Woodward and
Brigham Young University
Photo Archives)

was apparently near death, her daughters weeping in the room and the spiritually gifted Elizabeth Ann Whitney kneeling in prayer at her bedside. "Into the house, and up stairs and to the sick room, walked Aunt Zina, not knowing why she had come so late in the evening. Mother Whitney . . . arose and exclaimed, 'The Lord has sent you, Sister Zina, you can surely do something to save her.' Calmly, and without losing any time, she prepared restoratives, and soon there was rejoicing instead of grief."[8] Lines in Aunt Zina's honor praise her ability "To soothe the heart, the swollen eye, / When none but she and God were nigh."[9] Such was her gift, pronounced upon her by Patriarch John Smith in 1850.

But in administrative office, Zina never felt fully confident. "I always feel like a babe in the hands of my Father in Heaven," she said in the last general Relief Society conference over which she presided.[10] Her doubts were unfounded: if she had not the administrative genius of Eliza Snow, still she could move her sisters with her "few words, which were full of power and rich with wisdom," as one secretary recorded.[11] Zina's quiet strength corresponded to the solidity of Relief Society itself following two decades of fruitful development. The steady maturity of the women would serve the Church well through the dramatic political and social changes of the 1890s.

The day after she was set apart as president, Zina left for Canada, where her namesake daughter was about to give birth. Secretary Emmeline Wells was left in charge. "Evidently my work will be more extensive in the future than it has been," she observed. "Responsibilities come thick and fast upon the women of Zion. Those who will must take up the burdens and carry them."[12] A decade earlier, Relief Society affairs were insufficiently settled to permit the president's departure; now things could comfortably rest *in status quo*, as Emmeline observed, until Aunt Zina's return. Not only were there now established policies in the general presidency and office, but since the organization of stake Relief Societies after 1877, local presidencies also had gained experience and confidence.

The calling of Relief Society stake officers had begun as part of the churchwide reorganization in 1877 with a general meeting of the Weber Stake women convened under the direction of President Young. Jane S. Richards's call as president of the Weber Stake Relief Societies was formalized then, and quarterly stake Relief Society conferences initiated.[13] Subsequently Eliza Snow assisted Sister Richards in choosing counselors and accompanied her to conferences in each ward of her stake to ratify by common consent the action of the stake conference. Eliza then participated throughout the Church in the calling of similar officers in each of the twenty stakes then organized. A new level of female administration had been established, and in the decade following, a corps of local "leading sisters" had assumed their mantles.

The general presidency and other experienced Relief Society workers nurtured those stake administrators with care. Even before April 1889, when general Relief Society conferences began in Salt Lake City, but especially afterwards, the Salt Lake sisters would invite their stake counterparts for visits, offering meals and overnight accommodations during which the talk would invariably be of Relief Society affairs. Sister Wells's diary illustrates: "I had today after the Relief Society Conference in the big Tabernacle Dr. Pratt [Relief Society assistant general secretary], Sister Standring, Pulsipher, Harrison, Mitchell, Smallberg & Madsen also Hayen [visiting ward and stake leaders] to lunch with me. Then Aunt Zina

& Sister Richards came home with me and talked over some matters." It is no wonder that her entry for the day concludes: "It has been a tiresome day for me very indeed and I am glad it is over."[14] However stressful such long days must have been, they provided intimate moments in which nascent leadership skills could be nurtured and directed. That the Relief Society general offices were in the *Woman's Exponent* office, where editor Emmeline spent her days, made her the indispensable disseminator of ideas, information, and instruction to the women at other times when they were in the city. It would be difficult to overestimate her importance to the Relief Society during Zina Young's presidency. That the two were next-door neighbors and had known each other since Nauvoo days also facilitated communication and cooperation. Friendships between women were the heart of the expanding Relief Society network.

Overall, the Relief Society, claiming an 1888 membership of 22,000 in more than 400 wards and branches, had impressive holdings and responsibilities. Their properties, halls and granaries, and cash were valued in excess of 95,000 dollars. They held 32,000 bushels of grain in storage. Some local groups had stores selling merchandise and home manufactures, and all had responsibilities in caring for the sick and the distressed and in preparing the dead for burial. At headquarters, the *Woman's Exponent*, though independent, remained closely linked to Relief Society support; and the Deseret Hospital, under general Relief Society direction, still operated.[15] More than ever, though, the real work of the society took place at the local levels.

After the organization of stake Relief Society leadership, the major responsibilities slid easily and appropriately to local officers who were as tried in the gospel as any of the "leading sisters" who directed the society from Salt Lake City. Mary Pitchforth, Relief Society president in Juab (Utah) Stake, for example, had been with the group of United Brethren converted by Wilford Woodruff in England in the 1840s. Despite her family's opposition—she was just fifteen years old—she had "offered herself for baptism." After years of service to her family and the Saints in Juab Stake, she still "offered herself."[16] Utah Stake Relief Society president Mary John had been born, converted, and married in Wales before emigrating to Utah in 1861. In Provo, where she and her husband settled, she had been secretary of the Third Ward Relief Society for ten years, counselor in the stake organization, and then president herself for twenty-one years.[17] Farther from the center stakes, Willmirth East presided in St. Joseph Stake in Arizona. She addressed her sisters in the accent of the American South, having been born in Georgia. She married there at age fifteen and was converted with her husband fifteen years later. As a pioneer in Arizona with her husband, she completed the rearing of her eleven children and, in addition to being Relief Society president, took active part in community affairs, serving at least once as district school trustee.[18]

Another remarkable local Relief Society leader, Julia Lindsay of the Bear Lake Stake in Idaho, had unknowingly followed the path of the Church from New York, settling in Ohio just after the Saints established a center place in Kirtland. Her father, responding to local bias, forbade mention of Mormonism. Then he himself attended a meeting, and his conversion followed. Thirteen-year-old Julia was baptized in 1837. Of that time she later wrote, "In answer to my prayer for a testimony I received the gift of tongues." In her subsequent pioneering, Julia Lindsay watched while cholera, scarlet fever, and typhoid fever diminished her family. "God sustained me and helped me to bear it," she later wrote. She served in the Bear Lake Stake Relief Society for thirty-five years, with "fortitude and great determination," visiting each society in her widespread stake at least annually, through "many storms, bad roads and inconveniences of travel."[19]

Acknowledging both the growth of the Church and the competence of stake leaders such as these, President Zina Young announced in the Relief Society conference of October 19, 1893, that she would "increase the sphere of usefulness" of stake sisters by calling them as "aids" to the general presidency. Their added responsibility was to "visit among the adjacent stakes," by assignment or by invitation, when the Salt Lake sisters could not. Sister Young anticipated that "much good might be effected by the interchange of ideas and thoughts," and that "greater union and love" would be promoted by the sisters becoming familiar with each other's labors. The new program "had come to her like a power and a glow and joy," Sister Young explained. The first general board, formed in October 1892, was, simply enough, the combined stake Relief Society presidents. Elder Franklin D. Richards, present at the 1893 conference, confirmed the appropriateness of the "timely" change.[20] Designed after the pattern of priesthood organization, Relief Society was running smoothly and serving Latter-day Saint women well, both in Utah and abroad.

Building Bridges with Gentile Women

Among and around the homes of Mormons in the Great Basin, as well as in the missions, lived a number of non-Mormons. Surrounded by industrious, well-organized Saints, these "gentiles," as the Mormons called them, felt excluded from the tightly knit LDS community. Mormon interests had from the 1850s created a political and economic structure that, despite the incursions of gentile businessmen and their families, still controlled Utah. Although by the 1890s the power centers were diversifying, gentiles had long felt themselves a disadvantaged minority. Women were affected to the core by the separation. Such everyday activities as visiting, shopping, and the care of their children divided them along religious lines. They were seldom involved in the same community activities, the LDS women's lives centering as they did in the Church and its ready-made ward society. The self-sufficiency policies of the Church discouraged the Saints from shopping in mercantiles established by gentile businessmen, whose goods came mainly from the eastern states. Mormon outlets, carrying a greater proportion of "home industry" goods, clearly identified themselves by a logo of an all-seeing eye and the inscription "Holiness to the Lord" over the lintel.

Education and welfare, long the province of women, also divided Mormon from gentile. Schools had long been maintained by the various LDS wards, and instructors taught without apology from Mormon texts. Gentile parents were even more loath to send their children to these schools than were Mormons to patronize the later Protestant mission schools. And Latter-day Saints, with their as yet unspoken but much practiced intent to "take care of our own," provided welfare services to which others had, or felt they had, no access. Even without polygamy, Mormon women and gentile women had little common ground on which to meet. With so little opportunity for connecting, there was much occasion for misunderstanding between the two groups. Add polygamy, and the chasm between Latter-day Saint women and their American contemporaries could not be bridged.

The 1880s had seen congressional antipolygamy legislation honed to the point of effective prosecution. The 1882 Edmunds Act had facilitated the arrest and imprisonment of men married plurally. Both men and women were forced into hiding to avoid arrest or subpoenaed testimony. Some women whose husbands had been arrested were themselves imprisoned on contempt charges for refusing to name the father of their children. Plural wives were often exiled to out-of-state "safety zones" beyond the reach of marshals, or provided sanctuary in settlements far from their homes. It was not unusual for Relief Society representatives to a remote stake to be invited to visit an unnamed "underground girl," a woman in hiding lest she be forced to witness in court against her polygamous husband.[21]

The same Senator Edmunds who had sponsored the 1882 act was by 1886 gathering support for yet another attempt to quash polygamy. He was not insensible to the pleas of the women, having received their representatives in his office as much as seven years earlier. Emmeline B. Wells had then been assigned to attend the 1879 meetings of the National Woman Suffrage Association in Washington, D.C., the first official representation of Mormon women in such a forum. President Zina Young's widowed daughter, Zina Y. Williams, accompanied Emmeline by assignment. Both were neophytes to political action on the national stage, but moved through the machinations of participation in the conference with a confidence born of faith in their cause. Besides attending the conference, together and apart they kept a steady schedule of lobbying visits to senators, congressmen, and even to President and Mrs. Rutherford B. Hayes. Finally, after several tries, they approached Senator George F. Edmunds, even then preparing his first antipolygamy bill. None of their petitions bore the desired fruit of lessening congressional opposition to church practices.[22] Now Senator Edmunds was building support for yet another bill, this time to break the control of the Church as well as halt the practice of plural marriage.

In 1886, women on each side of the Utah Mormon-gentile fence made presentations to Congress indicative of their divided interests. The first came in March, when a mass meeting of over two thousand Latter-day Saint women produced a statement of grievances, hoping to promote the defeat of the latest Edmunds bill. Emmeline B. Wells and Dr. Ellen B. Ferguson together carried the resolutions to Congress and to President Grover Cleveland.[23]

Meanwhile, gentile women, who saw in plural marriage an insidious threat to the sanctity of home and family, were preparing a counter memorial to Congress and the president. Their crusade against the practice resulted in the 1878 founding of a Utah-based Anti-Polygamy Society. Matching size and format with the *Wom-*

an's Exponent, Jennie Anderson Froiseth published the *Anti-Polygamy Standard* between 1880 and 1883; and paralleling Tullidge's *Women of Mormondom*, the poignant accounts of faithful Latter-day Saint women, she edited and published *Women of Mormonism, or the Story of Polygamy as Told by the Victims Themselves*. The movement spread across Protestant America; Harriet Beecher Stowe, for example, wrote the foreword to Froiseth's book. Anti-polygamy rhetoric reached newspapers and lecture halls, much of it from women's voices.

By 1886 the Utah antipolygamy campaign had found a focus — the establishment of a refuge for polygamous women — and a champion, Angie Newman, a Nebraska-based social issues activist. With support from the Methodist Episcopal Home Missionary Society and the core members of the Anti-Polygamy Society, she set out to finance "a good home" guaranteeing protection to "women who would renounce polygamy and church rule." In Washington she pleaded convincingly for a shelter for such "victimized" Mormon women.

The Mormon women's memorial represented one meeting of 2,000 women; Newman accompanied her plea with endorsements of organizations representing 300,000 women. And she promoted a cause Congress wanted to support. Congress, now in the throes of debate on the Edmunds bill, agreed to underwrite her project. At a cost of $50,000, a stately, three-story stone building in downtown Salt Lake City opened its doors in 1889 to disenchanted plural wives and their children. The number of applicants for its protection seldom reached twenty in any given year, however, and by 1893 the refuge was pronounced a failure.[24]

Such anti-polygamy sentiment only stiffened Mormon resolve and allegiance to the principle. The real blow to the Saints was the passage in 1887 of the Edmunds-Tucker Act, which nullified already operative civil rights and duties, including woman suffrage, which had been granted in 1870. In its campaign, the federal government finally held a trump card: the new legislation allowed the Church to be escheated of its properties, including its temples. It became increasingly evident to church leaders that if the saving ordinances of the temples were to be preserved, plural marriage must be sacrificed.[25] On September 24, 1890, President Wilford Woodruff published the results of his prayerful deliberations: the Manifesto, which officially abolished further plural marriages.

The general conference two weeks later was electric with tension. "I knew the manifesto was to be read and a vote taken on it," noted Emmeline Wells. "A great crowd was attracted thither." In the session Orson F. Whitney, noted for his skill as an orator, read the Articles of Faith, emphasizing the Saints' belief in subjecting themselves to "kings, presidents, rulers and magistrates," and in "obeying, honoring and sustaining the law." He then read the press release that had been signed by President Woodruff. Lorenzo Snow, president of the Quorum of the Twelve, called for a sustaining vote. No dissenting vote was noted. "Many testified of its truth and the inspiration that prompted from the spirit of the meeting," observed Sister Wells.[26] "Today the harts of all ware tried but looked to God and submitted," Zina Young wrote in her diary. "We are the same Latterday Saints, [but] they will not allow us to keep sacred our covenants," she added.[27]

Not all the women of the Church would feel their "harts ware tried" at the official cessation of polygamy. For some there were tears of relief. "The principle" had been variously experienced by plural wives as a blessing and as a curse; as a hindrance to self-development and as an opportunity for self-expression; as a begrudged sharing of a husband's affection and as an enriched opportunity for personal growth and a closer sisterhood. "The plural wife," wrote second wife Annie Clark Tanner, who spent most of her married life apart from her husband, "in time becomes conscious of her own power to make decisions." Another plural wife described her sister wives, "those two dear women with whom I served through hard work and poverty through so many years," as "more beloved of me than is any of my natural sisters." Yet another admitted her ambivalence: "I have taken pleasure in practicing this pure principle although I have been tried in it."[28] Daughters would now be freed of the obligations their mothers had accepted; on the other hand, they might not find in monogamy husbands as proven in worthiness as those they might have preferred in polygamy.

For the next several years there would be no clear interpretation of the injunction that there were to be no new plural marriages in the United States. Did that mean also in Canada, or Mexico, or on the high seas? And what of marriages already contracted—must they be abandoned? What responsibilities had polygamous husbands to their existing plural families? "May we be faithful and true," prayed Sister Young of the difficult choices facing the Saints.[29]

Whatever its costs, the principle of plural marriage had had some unexpected benefits in politicizing Mormon women. Not only had it required of individual women that they act as heads of households, that some among them pursue professional careers, and that they cooperate economically and personally, but its defense also gave them impetus for public action. Whether plural wives or not, happy or unhappy, Latter-day Saint women had found common cause and gained political experience in supporting their husbands, their church, and their way of life against the antipolygamy forces. As Lawrence Foster summarized, "indirectly and almost in spite of itself, Mormon polygamy in the late nineteenth century contributed to a greater degree of autonomy and political activism among the women of the church."[30]

"The Rights of the Women of Zion, and the Rights of the Women of All Nations," read the masthead of the *Woman's Exponent* from 1879 to 1896, an indication that Mormon women's political action moved them beyond their own circle. The question of woman suffrage would involve Relief Society organizationally as well as women individually. From 1871, when Susan B. Anthony and Elizabeth Cady Stanton had visited Utah to address the largest body of enfranchised women in the United States, the Mormon women had joined arms with the Eastern suffragists in their crusade. The connections made then endured: Utah sisters collected a 13,000-name petition for suffrage, they continued correspondence, and Utah representatives were sent to national conventions. From 1879, when Emmeline B. Wells and Zina Young Williams attended their first meeting of the National Woman Suffrage Association in Washington, D.C., Mormon women committed themselves to association with what was then the radical fringe of American feminism.[31]

When the NWSA sponsored a meeting in Washington, D.C., for the purpose of forming an international alliance for woman suffrage, Relief Society and Young Ladies Mutual Improvement Association representatives attended. Both groups became charter members of the International Council of Women in 1888, and of its United States affiliate, the National Council of Women, in 1891. The NCW's avowed purpose, to foster "better understanding among organized women of varying interests and beliefs," was in harmony with the needs and aims of Latter-day Saints. Elder Franklin D. Richards applauded the women's affiliation. "In the great world there are many Societies of worldwide importance," he said in Relief Society conference in April 1894. "Ours is one with them now, and is of like importance in a national and international sense. . . . The sisters when they go down to Washington to these great Councils will have influence and power there, and they have had."[32] The Relief Society and the YLMIA maintained membership in the NCW and ICW until 1987.

With enthusiasm, Relief Society women organized themselves into chapters of the Woman Suffrage Association in both Utah and Idaho. Official church sponsorship came about when Sister Young and her counselors met with President Wilford Woodruff and several of the Twelve January 2, 1889. There was reason for haste—the annual suffrage meeting was to be held in Washington in less than three weeks, and Utah women hoped before then to organize the territorial association recently authorized by the NWSA. Priesthood leaders' support forwarded the effort.

A week later, in an effort to bring together a coalition of Mormon and gentile women, Emmeline B. Wells called on Jennie Froiseth, who was ideologically in favor of woman suffrage but opposed to the enfranchisement of Utah women. Mrs. Froiseth declined to attend an organizational meeting for the Woman Suffrage Association, perhaps because it was to be held in the Assembly Hall on Temple Square, with Mormon women who "believed in the rightfulness . . . of polygamy" taking the lead.[33]

At the meeting, which took place January 10, 1889, Emily Richards and Margaret N. Caine, both monogamous wives, were elected representatives to the NWSA. Eleven days later they were able to report to their national colleagues a thriving Utah organization with two hundred paid members. The society flourished. Soon the regular Salt Lake City Retrenchment meeting was given over to suffrage business, and local wards were appending suffrage meetings to their regular Relief Society meetings. Campaigns, rallies, and conventions overlapped the usual Relief Society activities and enjoyed wide coverage in the *Exponent*.

Many Utah gentile women, however, saw the alliance of their Mormon neighbors with the radical suffragists as unwomanly. Typical of the conservative, genteel matrons who formed the American mainstream, they espoused traditional values of home and family. Despite their practice of polygamy and their support for suffrage, so did the Mormon women. The closer the two groups came in their individual celebration of the Victorian values, the greater the antipathy between them. Historian Kathleen Marquis aptly described the competition between these two groups of such similar substance as "diamond cut diamond."[34]

The publication of the Manifesto in 1890 let the air out of gentile opposition to the Saints, though the balloon was slow to deflate. For Mormon women, the Manifesto led to a reshaping of network alliances. Long the rallying cry of the first-generation converts, defense of the right to marry plurally had held them in a tightly bound camaraderie. By 1890, however, a new generation of leaders had arisen. Over the old retrenchment web of shared defense against incursions from Babylon, the young leaders laid a new fabric based on the organizational patterns of Relief Society, Young Ladies, and Primary. The defensive alliance that had held the first generation connections taut could now relax, even disappear, while the new sisterhood strengthened and extended. Stake Relief Society organizations became their own networks, as dependence on the leaders in Salt Lake diminished. And as they found mutual causes, Mormon and gentile women learned to cooperate. Public welfare work, kindergarten, state-sponsored education, and now suffrage brought them into contact. Clubs in which women organized themselves — the Woman's Press Club and the Reapers among the Mormons, and the Blue Tea and the Ladies' Literary Club among gentiles — gradually crossed religious lines, their cooperation encouraged by the founding in 1892 of the Utah Federation of Women's Clubs.

A public event that climaxed Utah women's initial foray into public life was the 1892–93 Columbia Exposition at Chicago, a world's fair for which two hundred buildings were constructed on more than five hundred acres of Lake Michigan waterfront. For Utah, the opportunity was significant, since groundwork was being laid for the territory's admission as a state. For women generally, the opportunity presented itself as yet another forum for suffrage petitioning; and for Utah Mormon women, it was a chance to present themselves and their religion to the world in a positive light. Relief Society and the YLMIA would co-sponsor a day's program on May 19, 1893, as part of the world "Congress of Representative Women."

The overall effort brought Mormon and gentile women into cooperation: Margaret Blaine Salisbury, wife of a gentile miner and capitalist, was named to represent Utah on the Board of Lady Managers; her equivalent on the territorial level was Relief Society board member Emily Richards. At the planning meeting, presentations were heard from Alice Merrill Horne, the granddaughter of Bathsheba Smith, and from gentiles Corinne Allen and Mrs. J. B. Thrall. Emmeline Wells's diary charts the close friendship that took root and grew between herself and Mrs. Salisbury. Of such timbers bridges would be built.

An incident at the Congress itself marked another step toward tolerance. In 1883 Rosetta Luce Gilchrist had published "Apples of Sodom: A Story of Mormon Life," a fiction piece defaming the Latter-day Saints. Now at the Exposition she played a prominent role. As a correspondent she also wrote pieces for several newspapers. From the Ashtabula *News Journal,* the *Woman's Exponent* copied one of her reports, containing the following account of the Relief Society's presentation: "Before the session closed Mrs. Wells called me to the platform and I went and sat by Brigham Young's wife [Zina D. Young] and took by the hand each of those women with whom my sympathy has been so long, they knowing ... that I had written a book against their institutions."[35] Aunt Zina had already learned the lesson of forgiveness, as she expressed to her sisters after her 1886 experience: "[I] felt to carry no malice in [my] heart towards those who were against us."[36] The *Exponent* editorialized of the fair, "This work is bringing women into a nearness of contact that will increase confidence, and a more universal sisterhood will be established by the association and relation of this vast army of workers."[37] That "more universal sisterhood" would nevertheless be slow in coming. Two years after the fair, when the question of woman suffrage as a clause in Utah's proposed constitution arose, there was still a marked Mormon-gentile rift, though some individual women would cross religious lines in their political efforts.

Meanwhile, the Relief Society was strengthening its own firm foundation.

The Jubilee: Reflecting Backward and Inward

As the national congresses had been occasions for Relief Society sisters' taking tentative steps forward and outward, so the celebration of their Jubilee in 1892 was a time of reflecting backward and inward. The approaching fiftieth anniversary, wrote Zina Young, "causes us to view with wonder the past, with gratitude the present."[38] All year the central board discussed the celebration, often, as Emmeline Wells noted, in her parlor. Not always was there agreement—one counselor "did not coincide" with the pres-

Members of the Birkenshaw Branch in England sat for photograph in 1896. President Emma Hustler, seated in the middle row, fifth from left, brought the photo to Utah when she emigrated. It was published in *Relief Society Magazine* in August 1947. (Courtesy LDS Church Archives)

ident in some matters; nor did all the formulated plans come to fruition—the intended history, for example. But what did come of the planning meetings was appropriate to the occasion and bonding for the women.

On the day of the anniversary, coincidentally a Thursday, as was the 1842 organization meeting day, Relief Society women throughout the Church met as stakes or as wards to celebrate. Priesthood leaders were to be invited to attend and participate. A ten o'clock meeting, suggested instructions from the presidency, should include music, refreshments, and conviviality and feature the recitation of the Relief Society story from its Nauvoo beginning to its present in the local ward or stake. As minutes of local units reveal, the retelling of the founding story had already become a yearly ritual that included personal reflections and testimonies. In the observance in her Almo, Idaho, ward, president Jane Durfee said, "with peculiar feelings," that "this was a great work the Sisters were engaged in and that Joseph Smith was inspired by God to organize it." Dorcas G. King, treasurer of the group, infused her history of the society with her own testimony of its importance. Relief Society was, she said, the "best organized in the Land for the benefit of Humanity. And especially for the Elevation of women." She closed by exhorting her sisters "to find out the true position that woman was Ordained of God to fulfill & to lift ourselves out of the life of inertia . . . to one of intelegent usefulness the equal of our brother Man."[39]

A larger observance was held at the Weber Stake tabernacle in Ogden, Utah. Sisters from various wards "brot their Pic Nic & spent the day delightfully," recorded one diarist.[40] President Jane S. Richards was in charge, aided by her counselors, and—in a growing tradition among Relief Society presidents—her husband. "Assisting to get up arrangements & material for Jubilee celebrations on the 17th," Brother Richards had recorded in his diary two days earlier. He delivered a major address in the tabernacle, and counselor Hattie C. Brown wrote and read the history of the Weber County Relief Society.[41]

"Prayer at high Noon was offered by M. A. Wake," noted the Almo Ward minute taker, recalling the most unusual and significant feature of the occasion. Each group had been instructed to "join in a universal prayer of praise and thanksgiving." Through a simultaneous offering of prayers, the women in remote wards and branches had connected in a worldwide circle of faith with their sisters in the various stakes and in the "Big Tabernacle" in Salt Lake City. There Joseph F. Smith represented the First Presidency in voicing the noon prayer of praise and thanksgiving. "Thou hast preserved us from the designs of the destroyer, and from the powers of darkness," he said. "Thou hast given unto us a degree of light which has made our hearts to rejoice. . . . Thou hast given us a desire to establish righteousness in the midst of the people." And in conclusion, "Fill [our] hearts with thy peace."[42]

The past was very much present throughout the celebration, as women related personal memories of their Nauvoo and early Utah Relief Society experiences, many in homely detail. "The President, Emma Smith," remembered Mary Isabella Horne, "exhorted us to faithfulness in the discharge of our duties, and especially to humble ourselves and not ask God to humble us, as He might do it in a way that would not be very pleasant to us."[43] Sweet content prevailed, and worthy pride in a history of achievement. "The sick and destitute have been blessed, the cast down have been comforted, and the Lord has filled our hearts with joy and peace," said Bathsheba Smith.[44]

For all the backward reflection, the Jubilee also viewed the future. Particularly significant in the light of events yet to be was the remark in President Smith's talk that "it would be an excellent thing to erect a building, . . . a hall for the Society to meet, and which would be in a measure self-sustaining."[45] Sister Bathsheba remembered well his words and reiterated them in the Relief So-

ciety conference three weeks later, nurturing a seed whose interrupted growth would eventually yield the sweet fruit of the present
Relief Society Building. "We have helped the brethren," she told
the sisters, "and now think it only fair for them to help us build a
hall for ourselves."[46]

More pressing now, however, to the sisters as to the brethren,
was the completion of the Salt Lake Temple. On April 6, 1892,
following the Jubilee, some forty thousand Saints gathered on the
grounds to observe the laying of the capstone on the temple, already
thirty-nine years in the building. It seems in retrospect a fitting
culmination of the Jubilee, that Relief Society sisters should celebrate the building of another temple, more permanent than the
one that had precipitated the organization in the first place. A year
of contributions in kind, labor, and cash remained before the
temple would be dedicated, but the women joined with their brethren in completing the work on time. The dedication, conducted by
President Woodruff, took place on the Tuesday of April conference, 1893. "President [Zina] Young expressed her feelings in rap-
turous terms," the secretary recorded that evening at Relief Society
board meeting. Mary Ann Freeze expressed similar jubilation. "It
was glorious beyond description," she wrote. "I never experienced
such feelings before, being compelled to weep with perfect joy."
She had, however, experienced more dramatic if not more intense
manifestations of the Spirit on another temple occasion. In May
1888 she attended three dedicatory sessions at the Manti Temple,
which she recorded in her diary.

"We arose all excitement and preparing for the Temple," her
account begins. "Started up the hill at 9 a.m., which was unnecessary but we were so anxious to be on hand." The services began
two hours later and continued another four and a half hours. Mary
Ann wrote, "Soon after I was seated I heard soft strains of music
that appeared to be instrumental." The organist played a selection,
then the other music began again. "It was clear & penetrating &
yet soft & subdued. I involuntarily looked around to see from
whence it proceeded, but not seeing anything, concluded it must
be the choir practicing in an adjoining room, being anxious to
render their singing in a perfect manner. I momentarily expected
to see some door open & they come walking in." It was not until
Lorenzo Snow, one of the Twelve, called the meeting to order,
Mary Ann wrote, "& the Choir arose immediately before me, that
I sensed the divine source from whence [the music] proceeded."

She added her interpretation of the meaning of the experience: "My gratitude was unbounded that the Lord had by such a heavenly manifestation showed me that I was accepted of him."[47]

That Mary Ann's priesthood leaders recognized her worthiness as well is indicated in a later entry: "Apostle Lorenzo Snow & wife Minnie called to see me and brought the joyful tidings that I had been selected to be a worker in our holy Temple." She was confined to bed at the time, and added, "Brother Snow said, 'you haven't got time to lie there in bed; we want you in the Temple.' I have longed & prayed for this for months & years."[48] A year after the Salt Lake Temple dedication, Elder Franklin D. Richards "rejoiced in the growth of the society that the work and power of the sisters had increased and become more potential [potent] since the dedication of the Temple."[49]

Legally Incorporating Relief Society

At the Jubilee celebration in the Salt Lake Tabernacle, Emmeline Wells spoke of the Relief Society as being "perfectly organized." The principles of governance Joseph Smith taught to the women in Nauvoo informed the minutes that had become their constitution and their law. To deviate from that organization, it seemed to many, would be to deny the inspiration on which the society was based. Yet not a week following the Jubilee, Relief Society president Zina Young, counselors Jane Richards and Bathsheba Smith, and sisters Sarah Kimball, Isabella Horne, and Emmeline Wells sat in conference with President Wilford Woodruff, Joseph F. Smith, and Franklin D. Richards while attorney Franklin S. Richards presented to them the concept of incorporation of the Relief Society as a legal entity under 1888 Utah law, after the pattern of a private corporation or association. "After the reading of one of two [articles] Aunt Zina saw some objections and the reading was discontinued," wrote Emmeline Wells in her diary. In the light of the dissent that was to accompany the debate, it seems, in retrospect, appropriate that Emmeline's entry for the day describes the weather as "stormy."[50]

The reasons for legal incorporation of Relief Society were irresistible to those who had seen the Church escheated of all its properties as a result of the Edmunds-Tucker Act and who recognized the vulnerability of its fiscal position. Its holdings, scattered through the various units, were subject to dispute, its moneys inconsistently managed. On the general level, Relief Society's lack of registered title and secular status jeopardized its continuing membership with national associations. As the National Council of Women was then incorporating, so, it advised, should its affiliates, in order to take their place in the complex world of business and government.

Discussion of the proposal continued through the summer, but by October conference time, the decision to incorporate had been made. "It does bother Aunt Zina so much," observed Sister Wells. "She fears it will take from its spiritual character and make it only temporal." Sister Young was not alone in her concern, continued Emmeline: "the Relief Society incorporation will be accomplished, although there is an under current against its being done."[51] The articles were drawn up; the bonds for the directors were signed the day after the semiannual conference; and the National Woman's Relief Society was born.

Incorporation required some notable changes. There were to be a president, three vice presidents, a secretary, and a treasurer, all chosen from among the required twenty-three directors. Business meetings were to be formalized and prescheduled, and, in direct contradiction of Joseph Smith's injunction, there was to be a written constitution. While Zina Young publicly said little of the matter, her counselor Jane Richards, Jane's husband Franklin D. and son Franklin S. Richards, and Emmeline Wells spoke in defense of the change, while L. John Nuttall, secretary to the First Presidency, incorporated the various branch societies. Emmeline saw the move as "progressive," and for nearly a decade of uncertainty, she assumed the task of interpretation, explanation, and reassurance.[52]

Personnel changed little. Zina Young remained president; Jane Richards and Bathsheba Smith, counselors, became vice presidents, with Sarah Kimball added to their number. Emmeline Wells was general secretary, and Isabella Horne continued as treasurer. The stake presidents completed the board of directors, expanding the old seven-member central board to twenty-three. The official letterhead now read "Organized March 4, 1842," reflecting the date of the meeting in Sarah Kimball's parlor and suggesting that the corporate history would now interpret the organization as having begun with the women themselves. "Incorporated Oct. 10, 1892," confirmed the new status.

Sarah Kimball's Fifteenth Ward record provides an example of the local pattern. A board of five directors—designated as president, two vice presidents, a secretary, and a treasurer—was to be elected to serve for two-year terms. Failure to hold elections at the end of the term, their bylaws stated, "shall only result in the old officers holding over." Three trustees were to hold legal title to all real estate.[53]

In fact, if not on paper, the workings of the Relief Society changed very little. Semiannual directors' meetings were *pro forma;* the minutes of the April 1895 meeting conclude with the comment that "after some . . . talk about equal suffrage and the coming Conference of the Relief Society, the meeting of the Directors adjourned for six months without really enacting any business."[54] The general business of the society was conducted, as before, in informal gatherings at the *Exponent* office and at the conferences. In the wards and stakes, aside from the tightening of fiscal matters, the work proceeded as before. By 1902, the bylaws had been almost totally revised or ignored, but not until 1945 were the words "National" and "Woman's" deleted from the title.

Fighting for the Right to Vote

Meanwhile the great cause among Relief Society women in Utah had become the regaining of their lost right to vote. The same 1887 Edmunds-Tucker Act that had confiscated Church properties had withdrawn from women the electoral franchise they had enjoyed since 1870. "The franchise so gloriously given us and enjoyed so long," said Sister Zina at the Jubilee celebration, "has been taken from us without cause. It may be restored to us again; let us hope for this."[55] There was more to repossessing the pilfered privilege than simply hoping for it, however, and the women organized suffrage associations in all the counties of Utah.

Passage of the Edmunds-Tucker Act seriously compromised whatever allegiance women had felt to the federal government. "As the government has now disfranchised us we can speak with perfect freedom on the pure and holy principles of the Gospel," Sister Zina had said at the Weber Stake Relief Society conference. There was a new, defiant freedom in the air; "these days are the best we have yet seen on earth," she affirmed,[56] in much the same paradox with which Dickens began his novel of the French Revolution. For the Saints, the worst of times could as readily prove the best of times.

Their disfranchisement won for the women of Utah even more support from their Eastern sisters in the cause of suffrage than had their initial enfranchisement in 1870. Belva Lockwood, a national woman suffrage leader who had long defended the Mormons, now published a broadside of her presentation at an 1888 suffrage convention. "No absolute despotism could have more fully infringed upon the rights of American citizens than did the Government upon these Mormon women," she summed up. Romanticising their response for her Eastern audience, she continued: "But they bore it all uncomplainingly; took up their own burden of work, banded themselves together for protection, sang and prayed together, believing that out of trials would come blessings, even as blessings had come in the early days of their tribulations."[57]

Lockwood's view was only partly true, and only briefly. If the women were not heard to complain, under the surface they were biding their time; their voices would yet be heard. If the women prayed, they accompanied their prayers with works. And if they sang, they sang from the *Utah Woman Suffrage Song Book*, to the chorus of "Hope of Israel":

> Woman, 'rise! thy penance o'er,
> Sit thou in the dust no more;
> Seize the scepter, hold the van,
> Equal with thy brother, man.[58]

Band together they did. The Utah Territory Woman Suffrage Association had been organized in 1889 in determined response to the federal edict. Within a few months there would be fourteen auxiliary chapters throughout the territory, all of them under LDS church sponsorship. Relief Society meetings, their spiritual and charitable business completed, would dismiss into suffrage meetings in which the women addressed their political concerns and planned their campaigns. Relief Societies in Utah were united on issues of suffrage and the repeated question of statehood.[59]

With the discontinuation of polygamy, the territory's chances for statehood and the autonomy which that guaranteed increased. An appeal to Congress secured passage of an enabling act that authorized and funded a constitutional convention. In November 1894 delegates were elected to begin the process in spring 1895. Early to respond with congratulations and advice was Susan B. Anthony, long a defender of Mormon women, as of all women, in the fight for equal rights. "Now in the formative period of your constitution is the time to establish justice and equality to all the people," she wrote. Do not allow the state's constitution "to be

Susan B. Anthony, seated center, and Anna Howard Shaw, seated second from left, visited a woman suffrage convention in Salt Lake City May 13–15, 1895. Emmeline B. Wells, standing third from right, presided at the convention, and Zina D. H. Young, seated left, and Sarah M. Kimball, seated second from right, gave addresses. (Courtesy LDS Church Archives)

framed on the barbarism that makes women the political slaves of men," she added.[60]

Initially the battle seemed half won, however; both major parties had included a woman suffrage plank in their platforms. Still the women did not assume an easy victory. Ellen B. Ferguson urged Woman Suffrage Association members to canvas delegates in support of the clause, warning that "many are inclined to hang back, saying wait till we are a State then we will give to women Suffrage." The women responded with well-directed activity. "Went to suffrage meeting," wrote Ruth May Fox in February. "We decided to interview the delegates to the Constitutional Convention. . . . Mr Hill was favorable. Mr Vanhorn did not think the constitution was the place for suffrage to come up."[61] The warnings were timely; hardly had talks begun when the political rights of women became the most bitterly fought issue of the convention.

Church and civic leaders were involved in the fray. Thirty-eight-year-old Brigham H. Roberts, a Democrat from Davis County and a president of the Quorum of Seventy, argued with flamboyant oratory against inclusion of woman suffrage. Men and women filled the gallery for his speeches. Ruth May Fox recorded in her diary her disappointment at having stood or sat on a table all day only to learn that he would not speak until the next day. "What a shame," she added, "he does not use his eloquence in a better cause."[62] Elder Roberts's speeches were met with equivalent skill by Bishop Orson F. Whitney, author and publisher, whose short-lived feminist newspaper *Men and Women* made its appearance in the midst of the convention. Others of the delegates continued in less effusive but equally effective support of the suffrage clause.

In hindsight, the inclusion of suffrage may seem a foregone conclusion, but the opposition was heated and fueled by old Mormon/gentile antipathies. The majority of gentile women, underestimating LDS women's independence despite their patriarchal ecclesiastical system, assumed that a Mormon woman's vote would, in effect, simply double her husband's. They campaigned against including woman suffrage in the Utah constitution, finally circulating a petition so widely that they obtained 15,366 signatures opposing inclusion. Latter-day Saint women responded with a petition of their own, with 24,801 signatures in favor of inclusion. In the end the delegates voted overwhelmingly for a constitution containing provision for universal suffrage, and on November 5, 1895, the people accepted the constitution and the vote for women. Refuting in part the accusation that LDS women would not vote independently, in the first election following statehood plural wife Martha Hughes Cannon, a Democrat, won a seat in the state senate, outrunning her husband Angus, a Republican, in the same race.

The issue of suffrage in the Utah state constitution found Mormon women well prepared for political action. Their long battle to defend polygamy had left them skilled in leadership and strategy in a democratic setting; winning the suffrage war proved of lasting importance and left them in the forefront of the national struggle for women's rights under the law. The inclusion of the clause that "both male and female citizens of this state shall enjoy equally all civil, political, and religious privileges" was their secular adaptation of the Savior's statement, "all are alike unto me."

While during the nineteenth century Latter-day Saint women had merged their various cultural identities into a distinctively Mormon culture, now, at the cusp of the century, they were looking outward from their solid stance, seeking to connect with, not separate from, American female culture. Torn between their need for separation as part of a covenant people and the potential for good implied by association with their sisters not of the fold, collectively and individually they sought the golden mean, the happy equilibrium.

For women of the Relief Society, the term "gay nineties" seems a singularly inappropriate designation for that decade of the thirteen years of Zina Young's presidency. In the Mormons' interface with the world at large, it was a time of fluctuation, of outreach and retreat, of invitation and rebuff, of acceptance and rejection, of battles lost and battles won. It presaged a period of adaptation and adjustment as Utah entered the United States of America as a state equal with its sister states, and Latter-day Saints left their position as peculiar sect and moved toward the Church's place as an acknowledged world religion. Gradually the fortresslike mountains that had protected the Saints were surmounted and Zion was finding herself wherever the pure in heart were.

Internally, for the Relief Society, it was a time of consolidation, of adjustment, of extending a central vision into local action. Like the tranquil Mississippi on whose banks it had begun, Relief Society had survived the rocks and rapids of its beginnings, had been augmented by tributaries from the mountains and plains, and now, deep and steady, was beginning to extend its life-giving nutrients to the dry and thirsty land. The eddies and currents concealed beneath its placid surface would continue to energize the organization; the growth-generating tensions between Mormon women and their gentile sisters, between Relief Society mothers and their maturing daughters, between priesthood leaders and their Relief Society partners, all were beneficial. The sweet uses of adversity were generating a strong and stable sisterhood.

CHAPTER 5

PEACEABLE MOTHERS IN ZION
1901–1910

"Our 'Mother' is at rest," wrote Zina Card, informing the women of the Church that "Aunt Zina" Young, their Relief Society president of thirteen years, had passed away.[1] Ten weeks later, in October 1901, Lorenzo Snow, president of the Church, would also die, without having reorganized the Relief Society. Counselor Jane S. Richards, mourning the dual loss, said she "felt that we were motherless and fatherless." Bathsheba Smith, the other counselor, shared Jane's sense of indirection, she related later, but had been comforted by a dream concerning the Relief Society. In it she saw "the Prophet Joseph watching over them." The Prophet, she felt reassured, "would look after the Relief Society."[2]

In a solemn assembly on November 10, presidencies were sustained in the Salt Lake Tabernacle to preside over both the Church and the Relief Society. Joseph F. Smith became sixth president of the Church, and Bathsheba Wilson Bigler Smith was sustained as president of Relief Society. "It was a very grand and imposing spectacle to witness," wrote Emmeline B. Wells, "to see quorum after quorum of the holy priesthood and finally the whole congregation rise to their feet and raise the right hand" in support of each person in his or her position.[3] It was the first time a Relief Society presidency had been so sustained.

The occasion conveyed an important message to the new presidency, who recognized the Relief Society's need for priesthood support. "We have not taken these responsibilities upon ourselves, but have been called in the order of the holy Priesthood," they clarified. "We humbly desire to magnify the callings given to us of the Lord, and in order to do so acceptably, we shall need the faith and support of the First Presidency of the Church, the Apostles, presidents of Stakes and Bishops, whom we ever feel to uphold, and with whom we desire to work in harmony."[4]

At age seventy-nine, Bathsheba Smith was a generation older than her priesthood leaders in years and experience. At fifteen, in 1837, she had been baptized with her family in what is now West Virginia. "I felt to rejoice and firmly believed that I was accepted as a member of Christ's kingdom," she wrote. She married George A. Smith, the missionary who had brought them the gospel, and became thereby the wife of the Church's youngest apostle. Later, in Nauvoo, she was the youngest of the married women at the founding of Relief Society. Endowed in Nauvoo before the death of Joseph Smith, she officiated in the temple there until the expulsion of the Saints from Illinois. In the Salt Lake Valley she divided her attention among her family, the work of the endowment house and later the temple, and the Relief Society. She had served in the presidency of Relief Society during the whole of Zina Young's term. A widow for a quarter century, she now lived near the temple in a white cottage with green shutters, where she tended the lilacs, roses, trailing myrtle, hollyhocks, and larkspur in her garden. Emmeline B. Wells's description of her as "always stately and somewhat majestic, a woman one would be sure to notice more than casually," is enlarged by accounts of her self-sufficiency, her approachable mien, and her often unintentional humor. She was an exemplary wife and mother in the polygamous Smith family; her grandchildren, one or another of whom often lived with her in her widowhood, adored her.

Rooted in the early restoration and the Nauvoo revelation of Relief Society, Bathsheba Smith was pulled inexorably into a new century where the women were experiencing Mormonism differently. Relief Society as she knew and loved it was not appealing to many of her sisters, especially the younger women. Declining enrollment, and poor attendance of those enrolled, spoke undeniably of the need for innovation. Yet she knew the society was grounded in revelation. She would need to look back to its origin and history for knowledge, example, vision, and achievements. Facing ahead, she would need imagination, insight, and a willingness to adjust to circumstances and to accept alteration in church affairs. Balancing continuity with change would require a steadying hand.

The Relief Society was not alone in its struggle with change. American life itself, and Mormon life with it, was changing, permanently altered by rapid industrialization and urbanization. Added to this, for Latter-day Saints, was the unique transformation taking place in the Mormon community. The 1890 Manifesto announcing the discontinuance of plural marriage had signaled church leaders' recognition that the Church could not survive, let alone expand, if it retained its identity as a kingdom separate from the world. The Church of Jesus Christ of Latter-day Saints entered the twentieth century with a membership that, though still striving toward a more perfect unity in spiritual matters and missionary responsibilities, was no longer united regarding political and economic matters.[5]

The Mormons had dissolved their own political party, the People's Party, in May 1891, but non-Mormon concern with the Church's political influence continued, climaxing with the 1903–1907 Smoot hearings. In the process of determining whether or not to seat Reed Smoot, newly elected Republican senator from Utah and a member of the Quorum of the Twelve, a senatorial investigation publicly scrutinized church doctrine and practice. Not only did the Church's political power come into question, but fresh attacks on Mormon women and the old practice of plural marriage also came from national women's organizations, while muckrakers dragged Latter-day Saint men and women through renewed defamation in the media at large.[6]

Concerned about being understood by nonmembers, the Church initiated new public relations efforts, such as the Bureau of Information established on Salt Lake City's Temple Square in 1902, while individually and collectively Latter-day Saint women continued to strengthen their connections to non-Mormon women. Nineteenth-century Mormon thought had emphasized the differences between "Zion" and "Babylon"; the twentieth-century attitude was one of accentuating the similarities. This profound shift in emphasis not only affected Latter-day Saints' relationships with nonmembers but also required adjustments within the church organization. From 1901 to 1921, Relief Society under the direction of two tradition-oriented presidents, Bathsheba W. Smith and Emmeline B. Wells, would wrestle with changes necessitated by this disruptive, but creative, transitional period.

By 1900 conversions and natural increase had raised Church membership to 268,331 men, women, and children in forty-three stakes and twenty missions. The pattern of frequent visits from central leaders to each settlement, and the personal involvement that had been feasible in the Utah stakes, was now impractical. By 1900 the Church's extensive colonization effort had ended and the focus had shifted from establishing settlements to strengthening wards and stakes, the primary community for most Latter-day Saints. Church leaders had decided that smaller stakes would bring about "an increased growth spiritually."[7] The unwieldy Salt Lake Stake, first divided into three stakes in 1899, had become seven stakes by 1904.

Members' lives were most directly affected at the ward level, where Relief Society carried out virtually all its functions, as did the Young Ladies' and Young Men's Mutual Improvement Associations, the Primary Association, and the Sunday School. A new priesthood movement, carried forward between 1902 and 1910 under the direction of President Joseph F. Smith, provided uniform courses of study for the priesthood quorums and regularized their meetings and procedures, significant changes that increased members' activity. The revitalization of priesthood work likewise tied priesthood quorums more closely to ward and stake organizations and, at the same time, emphasized the primary importance of the priesthood quorums over the other church organizations, which were now collectively termed "auxiliaries." A correlation committee was appointed in 1907 to coordinate priesthood and auxiliary programs and responsibilities and eliminate overlap. Continuing correlation and systematization streamlined church administration, facilitating membership growth during the period of transition.

The division of the church organization into priesthood quorums and auxiliaries gradually decreased auxiliary autonomy and posed a particular challenge to Relief Society sisters, who would struggle to mesh two different but not necessarily contradictory self-definitions. The original definition of the Relief Society as a complement or partner to priesthood quorums, established in Nauvoo and essentially carried out in the nineteenth century in the West, gave the women important charitable, political, and economic responsibilities, among them the mothering of the Primary and Young Women's associations. The new definition of Relief Society as one of five auxiliaries functioning under priesthood direction would influence many of the changes implemented during the next two transitional decades, 1901–1921.

A Time for New Ideas and Methods

"Now you have your house," invited Jane S. Richards, president of the Weber Stake Relief Society, "come and see what the mothers and grandmothers have to tell you." The occasion was the 1902 dedication of Huntsville Ward's Relief Society hall, and the address was directed to the young women. Jane, who as a young mother had carried her baby girl to meetings of the Nauvoo Relief Society, found it hard to understand why the granddaughters seemed unwilling to receive what the grandmothers had to give.[8] Dwindling involvement was a concern everywhere. Mary J. R. West, counselor in the Snowflake (Arizona) Stake Relief Society, encouraged the young girls to "join the Relief Society, so they can grow up with the work." Her plea was especially poignant, since the stake's recent quarantine for diphtheria had stretched their society's charitable assets to their limits.[9]

Nor was the problem limited to young women; general board members traveling in Bannock and Fremont stakes in Idaho found that "wherever they went the average attendance was about one third of the number of sisters enrolled,"[10] at a time when enrollment itself was not automatic with church membership.

The lack of interest noted in rural areas was even more pronounced in urban centers. Mary Isabella Horne reported the women were even "more indifferent in attending our conferences in the city than elsewhere." Well might she know, for she was president not only of the Salt Lake Stake Relief Society, but also of the Salt Lake General Cooperative Retrenchment Society. Women from various wards were still attending the semimonthly retrenchment meetings in the Fourteenth Ward, where they reported not only their own activities but also those they observed in visits to outlying areas.

The Relief Society was not the only group calling to women for their commitment and loyalty. The women's club movement, which had gained momentum in the United States since 1868, had reached Utah. Daughters and granddaughters of the pre-Utah converts were prime movers in such groups as the Utah Woman's Press Club, the Reapers Club, and the Authors' Club, all organized in the 1890s. With the turn of the century, fifty-four descendants of pre-1869 pioneers, most of them LDS, organized the Daughters of Utah Pioneers. A Utah chapter of Daughters of the American Revolution was also formed. Relief Society general secretary Emmeline B. Wells was herself founder of the Press Club, and counselor Annie T. Hyde was president of the first Daughters of Utah Pioneers. Their example gave tacit approval to their sisters' involvement in such groups. Nevertheless, divided loyalties and diminished available time were obviously eating into Relief Society activity.[11]

Relief Society leaders in most general and stake positions were undeniably older women. Many of them were of the Nauvoo generation, charismatic in their leadership style and accustomed to the informality that had typified their networking of the past half century. Beginning with birthday parties honoring Eliza R. Snow, a practice had grown of recognizing individual women, especially Relief Society officers. In Montpelier, Idaho, for example, a celebration in January 1902 surprised three women. Retiring president Petria Hogansen had served since 1879; counselor Elizabeth Bridges, since the 1869 organization of the ward society; and treasurer Ann Bunney, since 1874. All three had crossed the plains with handcarts, and in total, they had spent eighty years in Relief Society service. The celebration began at two o'clock and extended through an outdoor supper, "a real feast . . . of the bounties of the earth," into the evening, with speeches, music, and other entertainments. Two hundred people attended, according to a report in the *Exponent*, "mostly aged and middle-aged people who seemed to appreciate the company of each other, even more than ever before."[12]

Nor was Montpelier unique. Similar testimonials to Rachel Ivins Grant of Salt Lake City; Emma S. Smith of Snowflake, Arizona; Agnes Cross Douglas of Payson, Utah; Rebecca Atwood Wareham of Manti; and Susan Grant of Davis County, all reported in the *Woman's Exponent,* suggest how widespread was the practice.[13] Capping such honors was the celebration of President Bathsheba Smith's eighty-fourth birthday at the general Relief Society conference in October 1906. "A Swarm of B's Bringing Blessings," a collection of epigrams prepared for that event, was later published as a commemorative booklet.

The tradition was fading, however, along with the pioneer sisters and the personal bonding they had established. A new order, businesslike and impersonal, was taking its place. Changes at the general level are indicative. Board meetings under Zina Young's direction had been fairly casual, the main business having been conducted semiannually at the corporate meetings. With Bathsheba Smith's presidency came a more structured style: the monthly gatherings accelerated to weekly board meetings; the visits to stakes were set up in more orderly fashion. Even the Relief Society president's relations with President Joseph F. Smith were formal, ironic considering that he was married to "Aunt Bathsheba's" niece Julina.

Increasing church membership demanded the more formal operation, yet loss of the old intimacy, the personal concern, the long-established sisterhood was costing the society dearly, both in membership and in activity. Change was imperative.

The first change came in a direction predictable in hindsight: mother education courses in Relief Society meetings. "The dear old ladies who study the Bible, the Book of Mormon and the standard church works" might still, as the *Woman's Exponent* editorialized, be "able to tell our young mothers many things for their edification and benefit in rearing their families." But folk wisdom, or "what the grandmothers had to tell," was being replaced in the twentieth century by scientifically based studies of human growth and development. "The tendency of the age is for new ideas and methods," observed the *Exponent* writer.[14]

The general board responded. Not over-eagerly, of course — President Bathsheba Smith declined one professor's offer of his book as a guide for the courses, explaining that the Relief Society "should go slow, and not go in at the big end of the ham, and be careful in accepting new things."[15] Her counselors, however, were less hesitant. Ida Dusenberry, a leader in the kindergarten movement, was already well versed in early childhood training. Her enthusiasm provided momentum; President Smith's conservatism, and stability.

As a beginning, each stake was instructed to develop its own course of study, to meet its own needs. Although sharing course outlines and lesson materials across ward boundaries was initially discouraged, the general board invited the presidents to submit their plans for approval, after which they would be sent to the *Exponent* for publication.

The general rubric for the classes was "the mothers' work," but what emerged was as varied as the makeup of the local Relief Society populations. Some, like the Parowan (Utah) Stake, began with cosmic principles, rarely getting to any practical considerations before the course was over. "Pre-existence of Spirits," "Object of Existence," and "What Manner of Women Shall We Be?" formed the basis for subsequent lessons on infant care and child development. Sisters in the Alpine (Utah) Stake saw the whole as a series of passages in women's lives, beginning their course with "Whom Shall Our Daughters Marry?" and progressing through

OUTLINES FOR

Mothers' Work

IN THE

Jordan Stake Relief
Societies

Arranged by

CHRISTEN F. MILLER
SLORENE EWMAN
ELEANOR ENSEN
FIDELIA E NELSON

Jordan Stake Board

HILDA H. H. LARSON, President
MARIA T. GOFF, First Counselor
ZINA BECKSTEAD, Second Counselor
ELIZABETH GARDNER, Secretary
ELIZABETH MONSON, Asst. Secretary
AGGIE CUSHION, Treasurer

Commercially typeset and printed, this Jordan (Utah) Stake syllabus was one of many locally generated lesson outlines published between 1902 and 1913. (LDS Church Visual Resources Library)

"The Young Wife," "Pre-existence of Spirits," and "Pre-natal Culture" to practical lessons in infant care. Woodruff (Utah) Stake prefigured late twentieth-century thought about child development by focusing its first four lessons on the quality of the marriage into which the young are born.[16]

Enhancing the program to attract younger women was not the sole purpose for the mothers' work courses, however. The need was real; President Joseph F. Smith told the Relief Society leadership at their conference April 3, 1903, that "it is your duty to assist all you can in giving to the daughters of Zion a proper education, to assist the mothers to perform wisely their duties in that capacity."[17]

Moral, spiritual, and physical needs of children and their mothers were to be addressed in the new classes to be taught either by Relief Society members or by guest instructors who had studied in these fields. The expectation was that the classes be brought "up to the standard of excellence . . . and be progressive."[18]

"Progressive" was one of the buzzwords of the period. It connoted not only moving forward or advancing, but specifically implied advances in the application of science to everyday life. Progressive education, for example, meant education based on new methods resulting from experimentation and research into psychology and pedagogy. The progressive approach had earlier spread to other areas of women's work: "domestic science" was firmly established as the prevailing approach to housework, and "social work" would soon be the professional equivalent for such charitable services as the society had always performed. Simply understood, the message would be translated "Mothers must be progressive. Plan our work and do it systematically, then we will have time to study and attend to our duties."[19]

That these waves of professionalism would also be incorporated into the work approach of Relief Society was a function partly of awareness at the grass-roots membership level, and partly of the preparation of their leadership. Ida Smoot Dusenberry, second counselor to Sister Smith in the presidency, had since 1899 been principal of the Kindergarten Normal Training School at Brigham Young Academy. A woman of great energy, she graduated from BYA and attended Boston's Chauncey Hall College after the birth of her two children and the death of her husband. Throughout her tenure as counselor, she continued as principal and also represented Relief Society at various councils in the United States and abroad.

Annie Taylor Hyde, President Smith's first counselor, was, like Sister Dusenberry, college educated and public spirited. Schooled at home and at Deseret University, she had taught children privately and, after her marriage in 1870, mothered eight children of her own. In 1902, just prior to her calling to the general presidency, she had founded the Daughters of Utah Pioneers. She, too, traveled widely.

These two broadly educated women formed a strong lobby for the new approaches to home and family education. General board minutes reveal their support of the mothers' work, promoting the preparation of lesson materials at the general level. Even so, the preparation of outlines for the whole Relief Society did not begin until 1913,[20] after the mothers' work courses had already been part of the curriculum for ten years.

Nor had the Relief Society been alone in fostering mother education. President Theodore Roosevelt spoke in 1905 to a Congress of Mothers advocating values familiar to Latter-day Saint women. His remarks were reported at length in the *Woman's Exponent*. "Yours is the work which is never ended," he said, defending the separation of spheres by gender, husband as breadwinner, wife as housewife and mother. Children were to be valued and taught a strict work ethic, and were expected to "wrest success from labor and adversity." He abhorred restrictions on family size, considering even two-children families to be indications of "race suicide." The mother's reward for her "loving unselfishness and self-abnegation," he concluded, would be "the highest and holiest joy known to mankind."[21]

The instigation of formal instruction programs in parenting had a natural carryover. By 1905 Parowan (Utah) Stake was offering a course more broadly based in personal and family relations, under the title "Our Home." Included were topics such as self-control, hospitality, amusements, sympathy, and the evils of backbiting. Role orientation is suggested in the paired consideration of "the father, his authority, position and rights" and "the mother, her authority, position and rights."[22] At the same time, the St. Johns (Arizona) Stake was offering a program in community-wide social awareness, with topics such as visiting the sick, assisting the poor, reverence for the aged, proper care of the dead, and intellectual, moral, and religious culture of women. The course concluded closer to home, as the women were led in discussion of children's behavior in church meetings. The list of topics instantly bridges the years between mothers of small children then and now: "whispering; laughing; eating; throwing things on the floor, such as paper, flowers, nutshells, fruit peelings, etc."[23] Overall, precedent was being set for course work that blended the practical and the ethereal, the mundane and the ideal, earthly problems and divine aspirations.

The notion that Relief Society meetings could provide a place of instruction in areas other than mother education gradually spread through various local units. Salt Lake City's Pioneer Stake, for instance, established a library from which teachers could prepare lessons dealing with the "lives and histories of great women who had done philanthropic and charitable organized work" and "the noted women of our day." Their outline, which eventually included such exemplary women as Emma Hale Smith and Lucretia

Mott, was heartily approved by the general board. Other stakes returned to studying the scriptures as had been recommended during Zina Young's administration. Sisters in Juab (Utah) Stake reported that they "had taken up the Book of Mormon since they got through the mother's work." In Vernal the sisters "were reading chapters from the Bible, . . . the sisters asking questions." Maricopa (Arizona) Stake Relief Societies had begun the Doctrine and Covenants.[24]

In the Relief Society conference of 1907, President Bathsheba Smith expressed her vision of the new direction: "There is nothing good, which is suitable for woman's work, that cannot be properly brought in the Relief Society. The study of the best literature, sciences, nature, cooking, in fact the whole field of domestic science, child study, nursing, home making, house furnishing," she began. Then, as though her vision suddenly expanded beyond the traditional boundaries demarcating woman's sphere, she continued: "Ethics, Civics, Patriotism, Morals, Manners, the Gospel, the Virtues, — all, all, and kindred subjects are within scope of the Relief Society."[25]

The mothers' work had catapulted the Relief Society into a program that would seem for women of later generations its chief purpose: education. Joseph Smith's injunction that the society "save souls," coupled with the clarifying doctrine that "ye cannot be saved in ignorance," infused the Relief Society's educational thrust for the twentieth century.

New Ways to Contact the Sisters

As the society was reformulating its purposes, the creativity of local workers was being matched by the energy of the general board members. By 1903 there were fifty-five stakes but only five general presidency officers and twenty-three board members. Tasks such as reviewing courses of study and gathering reports could be turned over to committees or paid staff. But the personal visits, the life-blood of Relief Society since its 1867 rebirth, were threatened by the mounting numbers of local units and the distances involved. Sister Dusenberry's visit to California in 1902, for example, not only cost the board seventy-five dollars, but also took her from her family and Brigham Young Academy responsibilities long enough to travel to Sacramento, San Francisco, Los Angeles, and San Diego. Not all the board members could endure so long a trip. Wrote Emmeline B. Wells in 1906, "Since Sister Zina's death I have not traveled so much among the sisters and Sister [Bathsheba] Smith cannot travel far from home."[26]

The general board's goal was to visit each stake twice yearly. Rather than abandon the ideal, the board adopted two stratagems: they enlarged their corps of "missionaries," women assigned to accompany general board members on their visits, or to represent the board on their own;[27] and they arranged geographically adjacent local units into quasi regions so that several groups could be visited at once.

Board members and missionaries, Phebe Young Beattie reported to the National Council of Women in 1904, had attended more than sixty Relief Society conferences in the year previous, traveling "long distances and often by team over rough country roads through mountain passes or canyons" to deliver their messages.[28]

Scheduling several conferences together was another partial solution to the logistical problems of official visits. Letting local convenience govern conference dates was no longer an available luxury. Even then, visits were not assured. Secretary Wells had apologized to an Arizona Relief Society president in 1906, "I have made up my mind that your appointment is going to be kept; that even if they have to go back or round about, they must come to you and to Maricopa as you were both left out last year."[29]

Despite the difficulty and expense, general board and missionary visits to outlying wards were more important than ever as the Church grew. In a poignant reminiscence published in the *Relief Society Magazine*, Fay Ollerton Tarlock recalled the impact of a week-long visit from Susa Young Gates and Elizabeth McCune—"the daughter of Brigham Young and the wife of a millionaire"—at her parents' home during a visit of the two sisters to the Parowan (Utah) Stake. "High Church people had been in our home before," she remembered, "but none so eminent as Mrs. Gates.... She fairly scintillated as she talked. The week became a veritable *Arabian Night's* entertainment, with two gifted Scheherazades to make each minute seem a second. No two women could have been more charming or gracious guests. Totally unlike, they had a genuine love for each other, and they gave generously from the rich store of their past." Some time later Fay saw Sister Gates again in a Salt Lake City restaurant. The older woman recognized the girl, despite her more mature appearance. "She looked up from her table and stood up, saying, 'You are one of the Ollerton girls!' "[30] The kind

of lasting loyalty that such incidents create had long proven powerful in the organizational and the personal lives of LDS women. Both at the center and in the outposts of Mormondom, increasingly it was difficult to find an equally effective bonding mechanism when the numbers grew too large, the faces too many.

The semiannual Relief Society conferences in Salt Lake City, day-long affairs where instructions were given and reports received, provided another occasion for contact. Typically the sessions, held in the Assembly Hall at 10:00 A.M. and 2:00 and 7:30 P.M., were open not only to officers but all members of the society. Primary and YLMIA workers were welcome, as were bishops and other priesthood leaders. The morning session consisted mostly of reports from the various stakes. Each stake and ward Relief Society president was asked to attend or to send a proxy, and of those, several would be invited to report. In the afternoon, general board members and priesthood leaders would speak. At the close of the evening session, the board would invite the ward and stake officers to remain to ask questions.

The leaders attempted to foster sisterhood and facilitate communication in a number of ways. Sister Hyde announced at the 1904 April conference that the women were "trying to get a little closer together this time, by giving a luncheon today," and Sister Dusenberry echoed "her desire to get nearer to the sisters."[31] Even though many stakes were represented at the semiannual conferences, distances and the press of family responsibilities kept many Relief Society workers at home.

The old and intimate ways of providing leadership and receiving feedback were obviously faltering. The *Woman's Exponent*, now more than ever a Relief Society organ, partially alleviated the problem of communicating, as did the 1902 publication of *The General Relief Society: Officers, Objects and Status*, the prototype Relief Society handbook. Originally intended to answer questions addressed to the general president, the final product went beyond any immediate practical need, relating the history of the society, listing its current officers, and recording speeches of President Lorenzo Snow and members of the Relief Society presidency. Finally, in the last eleven pages of the ninety-seven-page booklet, came the instructions to local Relief Societies. It sold for twenty-five cents a copy.

More than a manual of instructions, the publication was a symbol of the society's strength, a statement of its coming of age.

It was the first of a series of histories that tied the women's organization back to its Nauvoo roots as it defined its present and looked ahead to its future. Subsequent histories would be published in 1931, 1942, and 1966, each commemorating a milestone in the organization's development.

The *Woman's Exponent* remained the most eloquent written voice of Mormon women, though it frequently reminded its readers of its financial difficulties. In a poignant note, editor Emmeline B. Wells, whose subsistence came largely from subscriptions, reminded her sisters that printing is not done without money, and "although writers, poets, etc. may go hungry, machinery does not run itself."[32] The official importance of the tabloid is illustrated in the August 1909 conference of the Sevier (Utah) Stake Relief Society. Several speakers referred to the paper, and the secretary read two excerpts from its pages, one on the Nurse School, one reporting to the National Council of Women. However, when Brother Martin Jensen asked how many in the congregation actually subscribed, only nine raised their hands. "Let us double it," he challenged, offering his own dollar. Nine more subscriptions followed.[33] However encouraging that modest success, if there were but nineteen subscriptions from each stake, that was not enough to keep the paper solvent; the *Exponent*'s difficulties continued, and in four years it would publish its last issue.

Not just the *Exponent* experienced financial difficulties. Although ward Relief Societies could raise their own funds, the general board had no available revenues. While local units had traditionally reimbursed visiting sisters their travel costs, office expenses remained to be covered: rent due to the *Exponent* for use of its office space, a ten dollar monthly stipend to Sister Wells for secretarial services, printing, postage, and other costs. The Relief Society had decided in 1898 to collect ten cents a year annual dues from each member and had set March 17 as its collection day. A yearly dues campaign ran through Bathsheba Smith's administration as well, with suggestions of how and when to collect the money. However, no one was to be excluded from membership. "If any are not able to pay, the society will make up the deficiency," reported the Salt Lake Stake.[34] Occasionally a benefactor would assist the general office with finances, as when the sisters in Fremont (Idaho) Stake, hearing that the board was short of funds, sent one hundred dollars out of their treasury; and when one T. H. Morrison presented fifty dollars in gold to Bathsheba Smith "because of favors bestowed upon himself and family when they came to Salt Lake City, strangers in a strange land without home, and in time of sickness and death."[35] For the most part, however, the board was consistently hard-pressed to meet its expenses, and its attempts to systematize the work of the organization were hampered for lack of funds.

Sericulture, Grain, and Medical Care

Long-standing programs of the Relief Society were in flux at the turn of the century. For instance, the silk industry—for which Utah women had planted mulberry trees, preempted bedrooms, endured the hated worms, and learned reeling and weaving skills—was losing ground. The bounty money paid by the state from 1897 to 1904 to those who raised the cocoons brought a sevenfold increase in production, but as soon as that support ceased, so did interest in the industry. A few dedicated sericulturists held on. In 1904 a Rockville, Utah, woman threatened road builders with a rifle to prevent their cutting down her eight mulberry trees to widen the road fronting her property. In Utah County, official encouragement ceased in 1906 when stake president David John proposed the dissolution of the Silk Association "as silk could be more reasonably purchased from China and Japan and from the East."[36] Yet in 1908 the *Woman's Exponent* was still expressing hope in the face of discouragement, believing that interest could be revived, even though the trees were being cut down.[37]

The silk industry proved a mixed blessing for LDS women, observed historian Chris Arrington. "They made little money at it and were burdened with . . . the menial work." Still they persisted for forty-five years with resourcefulness and determination. "They used their own organization, the Relief Society, effectively, and they found a strengthened sisterhood in their effort," she concluded.[38]

If the silk culture was foundering, grain-saving was still a viable enterprise during this period. The various stakes were dealing with such difficulties as weevils, mice, and appropriate storage facilities. The great San Francisco earthquake of April 18, 1906, however, gave the women a dramatic object lesson in the purpose for which they were so diligent. Immediately after news of the disaster came over the telegraph, Bathsheba Smith and others met in the offices of the *Exponent*, which served then as general board headquarters. Knowing they had milled flour ready to ship, they dispatched one delegation to arrange for a railroad car while others purchased clothing and bedding from the ZCMI department store to send. Emmeline B. Wells reported that "the first car load of flour that reached the sufferers was from the Relief Society sisters." Nearby stakes and wards gathered goods and money, which the general officers collected in donated space near their Templeton Building offices. At least sixteen carloads of wheat from fourteen Utah communities were dispatched to San Francisco, much of it presumably from Relief Society stores.[39]

Other opportunities arose to use the Relief Society grain for charitable purposes. The women responded to a 1907 famine in China by sending a carload of wheat, and, closer to home, Uintah (Utah) Stake Relief Society loaned grain "to the people on the reservation" where "it surely relieved the suffering of many people." During another year, the delegate sisters reported to the National Council of Women, the Relief Society had "donated two thirds of the grain that had been stored" for seed to the farmers.[40]

The charity work of the society in wards and stakes continued unabated. At a December 21, 1901, conference, leaders encouraged Salt Lake Stake wards to "look after the poor and make their hearts rejoice during the cold weather." American Fork First Ward of the Alpine (Utah) Stake bought five tons of coal to distribute among the poor that winter, and "helped the missionaries some." Snowflake (Arizona) Stake combined efforts to provide a cow for a poor family. Women in Nebo (Utah) Stake aimed their largess not only to feed and clothe the poor, but also to "help them to take care of themselves by furnishing them work." Some wards reported they "had no poor," but Bear Lake (Idaho) Stake reminded the sisters of other needs: "the money you collect is nothing in comparison to the comfort you may be." Providing and supporting medical care, still essentially women's work, was particularly important in rural areas. Cedar (Utah) Ward, where the only physician in the stake resided, received frequent calls to aid the needy, "of which there is quite a percent," who came to the doctor for medical care. And in Parowan, Utah, a 1902 report noted "unusually heavy duty in caring for the sick and aged for the past six months."[41]

Relief Society's concern for the medical needs of the indigent had already engendered one of the most successful programs of Sister Smith's administration: the nursing classes.

Since 1896, when the Deseret Hospital closed its doors, the

Relief Society had had no formal program for providing medical care. In 1898, Margaret C. Roberts began offering an annual course in nursing through the auspices of the Salt Lake Stake Relief Society. The course was so successful that in 1902 the general board agreed to sponsor it for "bright and energetic young women, of good moral character" from other stakes. Students came from Utah, Idaho, Arizona, Colorado, Wyoming, Mexico, and Canada. The rules remained the same: since the purpose was to provide nurses for charity cases, students would be trained free of charge, or for a nominal ten dollars, in exchange for contracting to perform a given amount of charity nursing at little or no charge. Students who were unwilling to agree to these terms were required to pay the full $50.00 fee.

The program was not without problems. Other equally competent female physicians were also conducting classes in nursing and obstetrics and competing for the pool of trainees. Some stakes conducted their own classes; Margaret Salmon in Summit, Utah, for one, reported "a number of very efficient nurses" having been trained there.[42] While the 1903 Relief Society class had eighty-six enrolled, of whom seventy-five graduated with certificates from the State Medical Board, by 1907 enrollment had dwindled to nine, and even finding a room in which to hold classes had become a problem.[43]

With the opening of the Groves LDS Hospital in 1905, yet another competitive nursing course soon became available. Since the hospital course was three years in duration, ill feelings arose, the hospital-trained nurses resenting being classed with Relief Society nurses whose course was a mere eight months long. Sister Dusenberry addressed the issue in a general board meeting, proposing that either the standards of the Relief Society class should be raised or the class should be suspended. The latter course was followed, with the Salt Lake stakes filling the need for training until the class was reinstated in 1913. It then continued until 1920.[44]

The opening of the LDS Hospital afforded another avenue of service: the Relief Society was asked to provide hospital linens. The board purchased a thousand dollars' worth of linen and implements, and the women of various Salt Lake stakes undertook the sewing. The request was recorded in the minutes of September 4, 1908; one week later the goods were "all ready for delivery" from Grant, Liberty, Pioneer, Salt Lake, and Ensign stakes.[45]

Reaching Out Abroad and at Home

While the Relief Society work in wards in the Great Basin region was largely on a fairly mature level, young new societies were sprouting in mission field branches all over the world. Emmeline B. Wells was fond of applying to the Relief Society the phrase more commonly applied to the British Empire: "the sun never sets" on Relief Societies throughout the world, she would boast.[46] By 1909 the official report would list branches of the society in Mexico, Canada, England, Scotland, Ireland, Wales, Norway, Sweden, Denmark, Germany, Switzerland, Greece, Turkey, Holland, Belgium, Australia, Tasmania, New Zealand, South Africa, Hawaii, and Samoa.

In Europe, as elsewhere, it was the wives of missionaries and mission presidents who overcame the difficulties of language to promote the work among the women. No accurate count exists of the numbers of missionary wives who carried the Relief Society message abroad, but one woman is credited with having organized at least nineteen branches in Europe: Romania B. Pratt Penrose, a physician who had been fully involved in Relief Society projects in Utah, including the nurse work. The wife of Elder Charles W. Penrose, an apostle, she had been a member of the organizing board and staff of Deseret Hospital. In 1909 she accompanied her husband on his mission to Europe. To her dear friend Emmeline Wells, she wrote of the more than forty active societies there. Her advice to the Utah sisterhood was to instruct their sons in the work of Relief Society so they would be able to organize societies in the branches over which they might preside as missionaries.[47]

Not just in non-English-speaking missions were language barriers a challenge. In the settlements of Utah, immigrant women with little opportunity to learn English would cling to their native tongue. Some language groups in this period had full ward organizations, and some, such as Germans in Logan and Richmond and Scandinavians in Spring City, built their own meetinghouses.[48]

In Hawaii, Sister Wells reported in conference in 1902, "the energy of the Relief Society sisters" was commendable. "The sisters take great interest in their meetings and their work," returned missionary Alice R. Woolley reported. Native home missionaries "spend almost their entire time visiting in different districts," successfully bringing many otherwise indifferent sisters to meetings. Many had been converted through their efforts. "Our white sisters," she added, referring to the mainland missionaries, "visit all the Islands at least once a year."[49]

Not all the mission societies could report such success. Hattie Blair of New York City reported in 1906 that her Relief Society was "not very flourishing." Members lived far apart, she said, and it was difficult and expensive for them to gather often. She ended her report with the plea that "visitors from Utah" be sent to them.[50]

Such would be the desire of most of the 35,000 Relief Society members worldwide. The challenge was staggering, for not only did Relief Society leaders minister to their sisters in the gospel, but they must also represent them in various arenas where women's voices were raised in worthwhile causes. The cause of peace, for instance. In 1898, four LDS women attended the American Mothers Congress in Washington, D.C., where they heard addresses on peace and sang peace songs. They returned to Salt Lake City committed to furthering this cause: the end of war. On May 18, 1899, peace demonstrations were held in eighteen countries. In the United States, 163 meetings were held, attended by nearly seventy-five thousand women. Utah women joined ranks with "an enthusiastic demonstration in favor of peace and arbitration."[51]

Two years later, in 1902, the visit to Utah of May Wright Sewall, president of the International Council of Women, rallied even more support for peace. She was royally feted by Relief Society leaders, addressing an "enormous" crowd in the Assembly Hall. At her request, the women sponsored another demonstration for peace the following May, a tradition that not only continued but gained momentum in subsequent years. In 1903, for example, Mormons and other Utahns joined in 138 meetings in schools and wards, churches and tabernacles, almost as many as in the entire United States three years earlier. Relief Society sponsorship of peace movement events was felt to be appropriate and "in unison with the mission of . . . Relief Society work."[52] "Instead of encouraging war and bloodshed," Emmeline B. Wells observed, the "best elements" of society were "waging moral and spiritual warfare against taking up arms and fighting for commercial interests or 'right of way.' "[53]

While peace demonstrations were essentially an undertaking in which the Mormon women were supported by men, another great social movement, prohibition, was, among the Latter-day Saints, the men's undertaking in which they received support from women. A long and complex issue in Mormon country, as well as in the United States generally, the politics of enforced temperance differed measurably from the principles announced in the Word of Wisdom. As the Church's support for the peace movement would ultimately face resistance from avowed patriotism and American nationalism, so official support for prohibition would be tempered by political, economic, and social factors mediating against it. Ellis Shipp's poem "Prohibition" in the March 1909 *Exponent* reveals the motives that kept the movement alive for many women, the hope that there would come an end to "the midnight vigils anxious wives and mothers keep," but the conjectured result of prohibition was never realized.[54]

Despite causes they held in common, for Mormon women, ties with women of similar intent but differing creed were never easy to establish and maintain. President Bathsheba Smith was more focused on matters at home than connections abroad, so when continued affiliation with the National and International Councils of Women was questioned, it was her counselors and secretary who supported the cause. Rapport with women of influence was sufficiently important that the Relief Society continued to send representatives whenever feasible. When antipolygamists lobbied to exclude Utah women from these councils, Susan B. Anthony and May Wright Sewall, both of whom knew Sister Wells and others personally, spoke effectively in their defense.

Three Utah women—Ida Smoot Dusenberry, Alice Merrill Horne, and Emily S. Richards—were specially assigned to attend the 1904 Berlin meetings of the International Council. There Susan B. Anthony, now eighty-four years old, offered prayer in a German Protestant church, the first woman to do so, and was received with especial honor by the German empress. The American women, who were overwhelmed by the elaborate arrangements made for the comfort of the delegates, learned some lessons about European customs. Arriving at one reception "fashionably late," they "were ushered into a great banquet hall, the tables still weighted with the remains of an elaborate feast, the toasts all finished, and the receiving party bidding adieu to the guests." Since then, wrote the embarrassed delegate, "we have driven up to the door 'when the clock was striking the hour.' "[55]

The connections Mormon women made with their national and international counterparts at such conferences remained strong through the twentieth century. Unfortunately, however, the rift between Mormon women and their gentile sisters in Utah widened when they had occasion to join hands in committee work during this same decade. The Mormons were often less than considerate of the feelings of their gentile co-workers. When a group of mostly European delegates from the International Council meetings were traveling through Utah in 1909, a committee, chaired by Emmeline B. Wells, formed to arrange their reception in Salt Lake City. Corrine M. Allen, one of the committee members and the non-Mormon wife of a Utah congressman, objected to the proposed presence on the stand of President Joseph F. Smith, a polygamist, but Sister Wells insisted on his right, as husband of one of the committee, to be there.

A rift seemed inevitable, and a second incident cemented hard feelings: Ida Dusenberry, who knew the European delegates from meetings she had attended in Toronto, boarded their train in Ogden. When it arrived in Salt Lake City an hour early, she informed the Mormon members of the committee but not the gentiles. By the time the non-Mormon committee members caught up with the party, the program was already in progress. From the point of view of the visitors, the reception was splendid; the Utah women, however, experienced a setback disappointing to those "who have labored for years to reconcile matters of religion in Utah."[56] Experience would later prove disaster and hard times to be more conducive to uniting Mormon and gentile in the valleys of the Rocky Mountains than were world affairs and high society.

Building Relationships in the Church

Within the Church itself, organizational streamlining was occurring. The old retrenchment meetings in the Fourteenth Ward dwindled and died, their purpose having been preempted by the effectiveness of the central boards of Relief Society, YLMIA, and Primary. The YLMIA and the Primary Association, both offspring of Relief Society, were maturing into independence, each having come of age with the introduction of its own organ, the *Young Woman's Journal* and the *Children's Friend*. In 1902, when the general boards of all three organizations discussed the feasibility of traveling together and conducting their stake auxiliary meetings simultaneously, each favored having separate schedules.[57]

Ties became more casual than formal. Gatherings such as a mothers and daughters meeting in the Cedar Valley (Utah) Ward encouraged the passage of young women out of YLMIA and into Relief Society and were "for the benefit of the young women," that they "will be prepared to take the places of their mothers."[58] Yet the passage was sometimes blocked by mothers who were more interested in chastising than welcoming the daughters. The *Exponent*, for instance, published an article pointing out the "extravagance of dress" and "all sorts of luxuries and recreation" that were, "to the serious-minded and thoughtful, simply appalling."[59] Such divisive attitudes may partly explain Relief Society's continuing difficulty in attracting young women into its program. At a joint Relief Society–YLMIA board meeting, both bemoaned "sisters who were old enough to be grandmothers remaining in the ranks of the Young Ladies."[60]

With increasing independence from each other, then, the women's boards each continued to work out their relationship to priesthood leadership. Shortly after his calling as president of the Church, Joseph F. Smith clarified for the Relief Society leaders his expectations of them: "You were appointed by the Lord and should take the lead and supervision of all questions coming within the sphere of your calling."[61] Elder Orson F. Whitney of the Quorum of the Twelve reiterated to this new century's women the message of the Prophet Joseph Smith: "He taught that the sisters were to act with the brethren, to stand side by side with them, and to enjoy the benefits and blessings of the priesthood, the delegated authority of God."[62] Relief Society, said President Joseph F. Smith on another occasion, "is instituted and intended for the correction of all these imperfections, lacks and needs and the filling up of all the vacancies that may exist with perfect knowledge, perfect understanding, perfect fidelity to duty, and to the performance of those great and good works that are necessary."[63]

Throughout the Church men and women were learning practical ways of complementing each other's abilities. On the ward level, for example, patriarch George Mumford of the Beaver (Utah) Stake would accompany the Relief Society members every Sunday morning as they visited the aged and infirm sisters, and administer the sacrament to them.[64] William Southwick of the Alpine (Utah) Stake reported, "These sisters have more faith, are more devoted and accomplish more than the brethren in this line. . . . The Lord made no mistake when he organized this society; what would we have done without it?"[65]

Practical considerations made it convenient for the Summit (Utah) Stake to schedule meetings of the Relief Society stake board and officers in different parts of the stake "in connection with

Priesthood meetings," an early local attempt at correlation. President Andrew Kimball of the St. Joseph (Arizona) Stake had found the same sort of cooperation useful. He reported in the general Relief Society conference, "We have invited the sisters to join us on priesthood day . . . [A]t 2 o'clock we have the sisters meet with us, and there they have the key to the work of the Lord." The combined opening meeting set the stage for individual sessions when "the sisters [would] retire to other rooms and the brethren go on with their detail work."66 Thus, steps were again being made toward cooperative effort, toward working "side by side."

From cooperation sprang appreciation. In the Snowflake (Arizona) Stake Relief Society conference in 1905, President Emma S. Smith sisters told her: "We need the instructions given by the brethren." She added, "I am thankful for the confidence they repose in us and hope we may be worthy of it."67 Secretary Nellie Beecroft reported priesthood visitors at the Weber Stake Relief Society conference in Ogden, Utah: "The brethren came freighted with blessings for the Relief Society workers; their counsels were wise and fatherly and their words of appreciation and commendation will be a stimulus to all."68

"Our husbands are the best husbands in the world," noted Richfield (Utah) Relief Society president Minnie Nebeker, as she described the help the women there had received in replacing their old Relief Society hall with a newer, larger one. After raising money from their own efforts, the sisters "met with the Bishopric, counseled with them," and with their further contributions "raised between $500 and $600." "It is the nicest Relief Society Building I have seen," commented visiting general board member Julina L. Smith. Cooperation was a two-way street, and both lanes were open.

Sister Smith noted the importance to the women of their halls. Although the trend toward having a Relief Society room in the ward building rather than their own halls had commenced, most Relief Societies still sought to maintain their own buildings. Granaries, as well, were still being built, and stake officers reflected pride in reporting their holdings: in Wayne (Utah) Stake, four halls, five granaries; Nebo, Utah, district, nine granaries, four halls; Millard, Utah, five halls, five granaries; and Cassia, Idaho, ten wards, "nearly all had granaries," was the partial tally at the June 1906 Relief Society conference.69

Emmeline B. Wells, in an editorial in the *Woman's Exponent*, pointed out the importance to the women of their property hold-ings. The Relief Society holds property, she said, "not for specu-lation, but for permanency." Referring to the land Joseph Smith had given to the Nauvoo society as a beginning, she reflected that "an institution that holds in trust real estate, houses and lands, wheat and merchandise ... cannot be considered as occupying an inferior place in the community." Reflecting on the history of the society, she reminded readers, "there have been many enterprises and home industries started and managed by women under the auspices of this society, not all successful, but in the majority of cases they have flourished."[70]

"We Want to Have a House"

While women in wards and even some stakes had their own halls, the general officers of the three women's organizations were still meeting in rented rooms. The Relief Society was headquar-tered in the *Woman's Exponent* offices, which the society rented from editor Emmeline B. Wells. By 1900, while Zina D. H. Young was still president, the general presidencies of the Relief Society, the Young Ladies' Mutual Improvement Association, and the Pri-mary Association had made plans for a shared "woman's building" to house their general offices. "We want to have a house and we want land to build it on and it should be in the shadow of the temple," Sarah M. Kimball, Relief Society vice president/counse-lor, had told the sisters in 1896.[71] The women had considered buying land, but were elated when the First Presidency offered them a lot directly across the street east of the temple. President Lorenzo Snow told them that when they had $20,000 raised toward the building, he would give them the deed. They could be as sure of it, the secretary noted his words, "as you will be of happiness when you get to heaven."[72]

In a meeting with stake Relief Society presidents at the October 1900 general conference, the general officers launched the fund-raising program. Letters went out to all stake Relief Societies. Ward societies were asked to appropriate one-third of their cash on hand as a beginning; women would be asked for personal contributions later.[73]

By the October conference in 1901, stake representatives were reporting enthusiasm for the building. "The sisters were liberal in contributing towards the Woman's Building," said Eliza M. Oram, of Pocatello, Idaho. Adelia Crosby, of Panguitch, Utah, noted that "the sisters seem very willing to assist."[74] It mattered little that the sisters might never themselves see the building. "The Relief Society Central Building will reflect credit on the daughters of Zion," said Lydia D. Alder to the South Sanpete (Utah) Stake Relief Society conference. Her counselor, Abagail Shoemaker, "exhorted all present to not fail in contributing."[75]

And contribute they did. Records show amounts from stakes in such sums as $33.90 from St. George, Utah, and $38.15 from Bear Lake on the Utah-Idaho border. Individual women gave— some fifty cents, some a dollar—the amounts in a steady stream to be recorded in the cash book of the building fund. Minutes of the general board for April 9, 1903, note cryptically that "the great need we had of a hall of our own to meet in was talked about for the hundredth time."

For the next three years the contributions continued, until $14,005 had been raised by the three women's organizations. Then disturbing rumors reached the ears of President Bathsheba Smith that their plans had been shelved. A letter to the First Presidency asked if it were true, that they were not to have their building. Word came back: the rumors were true. A Presiding Bishop's building was to be built on the lot they had been promised and would incorporate within it the women's offices.[76] An associate reported that Sister Smith was "overcome with grief."

Subsequent general board meetings were filled with heated responses, modestly expressed in the minutes as "some members felt very much grieved over the way matters stood." "We felt pledged to those who had contributed the money for a building that was to be their own," explained Sister Hyde. Talk of "changes for which the board were not accountable" expressed the helplessness the women felt. The following week's minutes included the revealing comment that "some unnecessary paragraphs [have been] expunged from previous minutes."[77]

A month later the general officers were still unwilling to accept the finality of the decision. Had not Joseph Smith himself introduced the idea of a house for them, back in Nauvoo? Had not President Snow promised them one in Salt Lake City? Were they not well on the way to their required $20,000?

However, had not the Prophet Joseph also taught them to be united with their brethren? "Not war, not jangle, not contradiction," he had said, "but meekness, love, purity, these are the things that should magnify us." Even more to the point, "You need not

Bathsheba W. Smith, in wicker chair, is flanked by counselors Annie Taylor Hyde, left, and Ida S. Dusenberry. Standing are Emmeline B. Wells, right, who will succeed "Aunt Bathsheba" as president in 1910, and Clarissa S. Williams, who will become president in 1921. (Courtesy Evalyn Darger Bennett and Utah State Historical Society)

be tearing men for their deeds, but let the weight of innocence be felt; which is more mighty than a millstone hung about the neck." And again from the Nauvoo society's minutes, "All must act in concert or nothing can be done—that the Society should move according to the ancient Priesthood."[78] So they reconsidered objecting and chose rather to acquiesce and begin making plans for the space they would occupy in the new Bishop's Building. It was not what they had expected, but the Prophet Joseph, as well as their own experience, had also taught them that God reveals things differently from what mortals expect. It would fall to a later generation to see the fulfillment of the promises made to their mothers.

To their sisters, by way of explanation, Annie T. Hyde in conference in the Bannock (Idaho) Stake "spoke of the woman's building; said they were going to join with the brethren in building the house"; and Julia Farnsworth told the sisters in Sevier, Utah, that "the brethren had agreed to take the care of the building upon themselves."[79]

In January 1910 the Bishop's Building, "in the shadow of the temple" at 40 North Main Street, was completed. The Relief Society had a second floor suite consisting of a large reception room with a president's office adjoining, an office for the secretary, and a committee room, adequate for their needs then, but a far cry from the four-story Relief Society Building that would eventually be built when the Bishop's Building was demolished.

When that time came, memories long retained would haunt the planners. Belle S. Spafford, ninth president of the Relief Society, under whose direction the present building would be constructed, told of an unusual visit to her office. A woman in her eighties had traveled from Southern Utah, walked up the stairs of the Bishop's Building because she was afraid of elevators, and approached President Spafford with her five-dollar contribution to the new building. "Although we're glad to meet you," quizzed Sister Spafford, "it was not necessary. . . . Why didn't you give it to your ward Relief Society?"

"I have another little matter that I need to take up with you," the woman countered. "Several years ago one of the Relief Society presidents raised money for a Relief Society building, and I paid five dollars then. And I want to know what became of my other five dollars." Sister Spafford explained how the Relief Society had contributed to the Bishop's Building, had been housed there rent-free, and would now receive back the money they had contributed in the first place.

"Do you mean that the Brethren are going to give us back our money?" the woman sputtered, incredulous.

"Yes, exactly," returned Sister Spafford. "You have contributed ten dollars to this building."

"You know, I'm glad I came!" responded the woman as she left. "I'm glad to know the Brethren are honorable men."[80]

For 1910, despite disappointment, the new accommodations were adequate, "appropriately and tastefully furnished." "It is the first time in all its history," editorialized the *Woman's Exponent,* "where the General Society has had rooms for the transaction of business pertaining to the great work of this, the first and largest organization of women in the Church."[81]

On January 21, 1910, six days before the building was to be dedicated, the sisters held the first celebratory event there. The day was auspicious and the theme consistent: it was the 106th anniversary of Eliza R. Snow's birth, and the women spent the evening discoursing in her memory. The tribute to "her implicit faith in the Gospel, endurance and fortitude under trials," by Sarah

Jenne Cannon, must have struck home to the women assembled. "It is no trifling thing to be a Saint," Carrie S. Thomas quoted from Sister Eliza's first volume of poems.[82]

If the loss of their building had been a disappointment, there was still much to be pleased with in the work of Relief Society in this first decade of the twentieth century. In their own organization, they had inaugurated a program of prepared lessons that would continue and expand; they had maintained their connections with their sisters nationally and internationally; they had seen sister missionaries called two by two, just as the elders were; they had continued the useful grain-storage program and discontinued the unsuccessful silk culture; they had seen the nurse classes faithfully taught and attended; and they counted societies meeting in twenty-two countries.

Latter-day Saint women, having witnessed the end of the nineteenth century, now looked into the twentieth with optimism and enthusiasm. The opening of the heavens—the restoration of priesthood power and the truths of the gospel—meant for them also the end of woman's enslavement. Wrote Lydia D. Alder in 1901, "The close of the Nineteenth Century, that had seen so much advancement, both in science and education, showed also to the world the great progress made by woman. . . . From being either the plaything or the slave of man, not thought worthy of the higher education, if of any at all, see her side by side with him, in the schools or the colleges, oftimes carrying off the laurels, or standing at the head of the class." To the unasked question, "What has brought it about?" she answered, "Believers in the divine mission of the Prophet Joseph Smith know and bear witness in all the world of the reason." Speaking of the organization of the Relief Society, she marvels that he gave the women "instructions so far in advance of his day that they are not all carried out even now."[83]

For what women now were, and could become, Latter-day Saint women credited the restoration of the gospel. They reflected on their Nauvoo beginnings, "believing that the Prophet Joseph Smith had conferred upon the sisterhood great blessings, that were to be unfolding from time to time, and that were in the process of development of great intellectual and spiritual progress."[84]

So they looked to the new century for continuation of these openings and unfoldings in their lives. To their daughters the *Young Woman's Journal* reinforced the message: "To women there belongs a right which lies deeper than suffrage, higher than education, and sweeter than enforced virtue. It is the right of choice; the right to choose what she shall be."[85]

Fruit of that choice, reasoned Emmeline Wells in two separate speeches, including one to the National Council of Women, would be the redemption of women from the curse placed upon them in Eden. "As woman took the lead in the great drama in the Garden of Eden and the curse followed, and she suffered the consequences; the daughters of Eve will, we think, be instrumental in a great measure through the Gospel in effecting the redemption of woman from the curse."

That release would restore women to a position of equality with the sons of Adam. "The man and the woman will be equal," she wrote, foreseeing the *"awakening* of woman and her cooperation with man in the world's great work."[86] The lessons learned in interacting with priesthood leaders in corporate operation of church programs would be a schoolmaster toward that end.

A Last Blessing

When she was not in the temple or presiding over board meetings, President Bathsheba Smith was often to be found in her garden, planting, cultivating, and pruning her flowers. To the Relief Society, as to the flowerbed, all three operations were essential: new programs must be initiated; the soil must be maintained, loose and moist; and the perennials, those faithful vines which grew year after year, must be pruned. The cutting back, however painful it might be to the gardener, or, metaphorically, to the vine, was essential. It would provide opportunity for new growth without destroying the stock or root. The true vine, renewed and invigorated, would continue to grow and bear fruit, and sweet would be the taste thereof.

In one of her last messages to the Relief Society, Sister Smith offered her benediction on the work: "I bless you with the blessing of a mother in Israel; and I pray that your work may seem light and not burdensome, and that the rich outpourings of the Holy Spirit may buoy you up."[87] She died in office September 20, 1910.

CHAPTER 6

HOLDING FAST THE COVENANT
1910–1921

Relief Society officers of the Willard (Utah) Ward met together in June 1911 to discuss the "bad condition" of their society's weevil-infested wheat. Clearly "it would have to be seen to at once" and every effort made to sell what could be salvaged. Then the more difficult question of whether or not to buy more wheat must be answered. The women could not reinvest in grain until they paid to repair the granary, and some of the sisters had heard rumors from their northern Utah neighbors that Relief Societies were being counseled to stop the thirty-five-year-old practice of storing grain.

The sisters must have been pleased to receive a clarifying letter from the society's general president Emmeline B. Wells.[1] Acknowledging that wheat storage had long been a "vexed problem" for many local societies, she affirmed that grain storage should continue, but old methods had "not proved satisfactory and should be changed." The cost of local granaries had been out of proportion to their effectiveness, and many societies had suffered considerable loss from spoilage.[2] The general presidency had consulted with the First Presidency and the Presiding Bishopric and now wanted sisters to follow the leaders' counsel to store wheat in "elevators owned and conducted by responsible parties," such as the elevator erected by the Church in Richfield in central Utah. This method, already in use by many societies, was "found better than depositing wheat in local grist mills, and far more satisfactory than that of each Relief Society building a separate granary."[3] Uneasily the women in Willard decided to embrace the new method, one sister affirming that "it was a good thing" and assuring the wary: "We should not let it try us."[4]

Perhaps no one felt more tried in the question of grain storage than Emmeline B. Wells herself. In 1876 Brigham Young had given her the mission of leading sisters in a churchwide effort to save grain, and she had chaired the Central Grain Committee until 1880, when the Relief Society assumed exclusive management of the project. After that, in her travels with the society's central board and her work as general secretary, she continued to protect this "sacred trust" of Relief Society.[5] Nevertheless, during her eleven-year tenure as Relief Society general president, the society would not only change its storage methods but would also sell all its wheat and suspend the practice of storing grain.

The presidency of Sister Wells was characterized by breaks with long-standing traditions she had worked to maintain. Eighty-two years old at the time she was called as general president, she had already served for more than two decades as the general secretary. Like her immediate predecessors and beloved friends Zina D. H. Young and Bathsheba W. Smith, she not only cherished but also embodied Relief Society's past. She had spent her adolescent years in Nauvoo, known the Prophet Joseph Smith, made the westward trek, assisted Eliza R. Snow, edited the *Woman's Exponent*, and represented Relief Society in national gatherings of women.

Small, attractive, strong-willed, and invariably dressed in pastel colors with lace or a flowing scarf about her neck, "Aunt Em" was an institution in herself. "She's the girl without rubbers, stays out until two," wrote Heber M. Wells, quipping about her habit of working at the *Exponent* office late into the night.[6] Acquainted with the first five presidents of the Church, Aunt Em would serve as Relief Society general president under two more, Presidents Joseph F. Smith and Heber J. Grant. She would be the society's last president from the Nauvoo generation, "a loving link . . . between the heroic beginnings and the glorious present of this latter-day dispensation," or, as she once observed, "the 'last leaf upon the tree.'"[7]

The early life of Emmeline Blanche Woodward Harris Whitney Wells schooled her in reverses. In the two years following her baptism in Massachusetts at age fourteen, she graduated from a girls' school, became a teacher, married, moved to Nauvoo, bore and lost a son, and was abandoned by her husband. She found comfort in her second marriage as a plural wife of Newel K. Whitney and was devastated by his death in 1850. Her last marriage, to Daniel H. Wells, provided the stability necessary for bringing up two Whitney daughters and three Wells daughters and then engaging in nearly full-time Relief Society work. Experienced in making difficult personal transitions, Sister Wells presided over Relief Society through many institutional transitions. Despite her age, or perhaps because of it, she was, according to one board member, a "sturdy and wise president" who was "glad to permit old truths to be dressed up in new phraseology, and old forms modified to meet changing condition[s]," but steadfastly "refused to permit changes which would disintegrate and finally, perhaps, destroy the institution itself."[8] How to preserve the essence of Relief Society while relinquishing cherished traditions would be the central challenge during her eleven-year presidency.

Sustained with President Wells at the October 6, 1910, meeting of the Church's semiannual conference were her counselors, Clarissa S. Williams and Julina Lambson Smith, women of her daughters' generation and well experienced in Relief Society work.[9] Clarissa Williams, a stepdaughter of Bathsheba W. Smith, had served since 1901 as Relief Society's general treasurer and continued in that capacity until June 1911, when she turned the accounts over to the new treasurer, Emma A. Empey. The mother of eleven children, a gracious and gifted executive, Sister Williams would provide skillful and supportive leadership through an era of significant administrative change. Julina Lambson Smith, wife of President Joseph F. Smith and niece of Bathsheba W. Smith, had also served as a member of her aunt's board. A midwife with seven children of her own, Sister Smith had a propensity for peacemaking that would ease the board through some difficult and potentially divisive decisions.[10]

Campaigning for Moral and Social Reform

The year 1910, when this presidency was sustained, marked the deaths of Twain and Tolstoy, Florence Nightingale, Mary Baker Eddy, and Julia Ward Howe. The nineteenth century receded further into the past as science and discovery propelled the twentieth century forward. In 1910 Marie Curie published her "Treatise on Radiography" and the following year she won the Nobel Prize for chemistry. During the next decade Amundsen and Scott reached the South Pole, Einstein postulated the general theory of relativity, and Freud published his *Introduction to Psychoanalysis*. Motorized taxis, airmail postage, and transcontinental phone calls bespoke the ever-quickening pace.[11] Virtually no aspect of Relief Society— meetings, records, grain storage, nurses training, visiting teaching, charity work — remained untouched by what its leaders termed "the great progress being made in the world today."

Enthusiasm for progress, both scientific and spiritual, swept the United States as the Progressive movement, an impulse for moral and social reform that began before 1900 and continued through Emmeline B. Wells's administration.[12] The movement probably influenced certain changes in Relief Society organizations and programs; its support for legislation for women and children, its cooperation with community agencies in charity work and in campaigns for public health and community betterment, and its administrative refinements and new educational program were similar to activities usually labeled Progressive.

American women played a critical role in the campaign for moral and social reform. They moved beyond their homes into the public sphere in part because their traditional home concerns — children's health and education, the production of food and clothing — had become public and commercial enterprises, political issues. Women "assumed that their training as cooks, seamstresses, house cleaners, and mothers qualified them to help in legislation concerned with food inspection, sweatshop sanitation, street-cleaning, and public schools," observed historian Aileen S. Kraditor.[13] Relief Society women enthusiastically participated in this "social housekeeping" or, as one sister termed it, "social motherhood."[14] They were committed to "strengthening the virtues of the . . . community." In this spirit, at the October 1911 Relief Society conference "the entire congregation arose to their feet to express their approval of the stand for a clean, moral government."[15]

In April 1913 Annie Wells Cannon, president of Salt Lake City's Pioneer Stake Relief Society, a daughter of President Wells, and a member of the Utah State Legislature, placed within the context of Relief Society history her sisters' efforts at social reform, affirming: "After the key was turned for woman by the Prophet Joseph Smith she began to look around and to think . . . she would not be out of her sphere in public life; so she turned her eyes to education and to general development, and little by little, step by step, she has gained a prominent place in the world's work."[16] Sister Cannon was proud that members of the Relief Society had united with other Utah women to sustain the juvenile court and to secure a minimum-wage law for women, the appointment of a woman to the minimum-wage commission, a widowed mothers' pension law, and legal provisions for equal guardianship of children.

Women of the Portland (Oregon) Branch worked in 1911 to improve the home conditions of women laboring in stores and factories. That year Relief Society representatives from each of the Salt Lake City stakes waited through an entire city council meeting, "being thoroughly fumigated with cigar smoke" and enduring "a postgraduate course in city gravel beds," to successfully oppose the granting of a license for a bar to the city's popular Salt Palace resort.[17] Most of Relief Society's efforts for social reform were centered in Salt Lake City, where in 1912 the general board appointed its own legislative committee to evaluate such local social legislation as race-track gambling, Sunday closing, and dormitories for the state university.[18]

Women's traditional concerns with family health drew them into community efforts to protect food and water, improve sanitation, and guard the health of infants and children. In 1912 social worker Jane Addams was appointed head of a new Children's Bureau in the United States Department of Commerce and Labor. As it gathered, analyzed, and published statistics, the bureau helped mobilize women in a long-term campaign to reduce infant mortality. Many communities set up milk depots or stations where needy families could get nutritional information and fresh milk at whatever price they could afford. Relief Society's general board and Salt Lake City stakes helped sustain such a program in Salt Lake City by contributing funds and the services of nurses and volunteers during 1913 and 1914.[19] Utilizing the new information available on infant and child health, Relief Society sponsored a special "Baby Day" throughout the Church in 1916 and helped to forward the 1918–1919 "Children's Year" campaign for child health.[20]

In 1912 Emmeline B. Wells asked the First Presidency to help Relief Society establish a home in Salt Lake City to temporarily house immigrants, to accommodate out-of-town sisters coming to attend conference or work in the temple, and to provide housing for younger working women.[21] Women arriving in the city needed reasonably priced lodging where they would have "security, friendship, and association with our people," noted an article in the *Relief Society Bulletin*.[22] The First Presidency granted the board the use of the "spacious house" at 36 West North Temple Street. The Presiding Bishopric donated a double gas range; the Grantsville

Relief Society, ninety yards of homemade carpet; and the Primary and YLMIA general boards, fifty dollars each. The home was dedicated on December 19, 1913.

Cornelia H. Clayton, matron of the home, collected rents and arranged free lodging for charity cases, including a number of homeless, unemployed, handicapped, and immigrant women. The home, which also included an employment bureau, was too small to fill such a range of needs, and many out-of-town sisters "found it almost impossible to ever get rooms" there.[23] In 1920 the YLMIA general board opened a larger boarding home for young women in the Beehive House, and the following year the Relief Society home was closed.

The eagerness of the general presidency and board to maintain a home and employment bureau and later a department for social services reflected their desire to address the multiplying social problems that accompanied American urbanization and modernization. To their efforts at social reform, they added new emphasis on moral reform. In October 1912 Relief Society general officers, upholding recent counsel from President Joseph F. Smith, formally resolved to show reverence for sacred places, keep the Sabbath day holy, denounce card playing, observe the Word of Wisdom, and "show our reverence for the sacred garment of the holy Priesthood by refusing to wear short sleeves or low-necked dresses."[24]

Four years later, in September 1916, President Smith and his counselors issued a letter to the general boards of the Relief Society, YLMIA, and Primary Association denouncing continuing immodesty and indecency in the attire of the "daughters of Zion" and calling for prompt action spearheaded by a committee of representatives from the general boards.[25] Publishing the First Presidency's letter as "A Call to the Women of the Church," the women's new nine-member Social Advisory Committee suggested that local leaders of the three organizations begin to "teach by example and precept a proper modesty of dress," hoping the sisters would "be tactful and prayerful, and avoid giving offense."[26]

Relief Society was to head the campaign, President Smith said, because it could "bring about reforms by having the mothers make the effort in the homes of the Saints."[27] A February 1917 editorial in the *Relief Society Magazine* suggested that mothers begin by wisely choosing their own books, magazines, films, and dress. Each woman was to ask herself, "Am I measuring up, in this respect, to the highest standards of modesty and to my professions as a member of the Church of Christ?"[28]

Emphasizing motherhood as a sacred and eternal calling, Relief Society leaders also warned women against the contemporary movement for birth control. Margaret Sanger's book *Family Limitation* appeared in 1915, and the first American birth control clinic opened in 1916. Church leaders, both men and women, condemned the new movement as "race suicide . . . one of the great curses of the age."[29] For the most part the Relief Society took an affirmative approach, praising and supporting mothers in their responsibilities.

By request of the First Presidency, the sisters' Social Advisory Committee was expanded to include representatives from the general boards of the Sunday School, the Young Men's Mutual Improvement Association, and Religion Class. Stephen L. Richards of the Council of the Twelve was appointed committee chairman.[30] Elder Richards affirmed that he had "heard many eminent men and women analyze social problems and suggest remedies," and while he felt that the Church "may need some of the methods of the social organizations of the world," he was convinced that "the great need in society today is individual righteousness." Accordingly, he stressed the importance of "home-building and home-making" among the Latter-day Saints.[31] The efforts of the committee both to work within the Church and to promote cooperation with government and community agencies exemplified the inclination of the Saints to connect moral and social reform, individual and community improvement.[32]

Developing and Unifying the Curriculum

Formation of the Social Advisory Committee also indicated continuing concern with correlating the work of the various arms of the Church organization and administrative procedures to meet the needs of expanding membership. During the presidency of President Joseph F. Smith, from 1901 to 1918, membership nearly doubled. "Administrative modernization," as one historian termed it, involved increased central planning, improved financial management and record keeping, and coordination of auxiliary programs. The Church's push for systematization, reinforced by the Progressive Era's emphasis on efficiency and scientific management, precipitated changes in Relief Society conferences, curriculum, meetings, records, and accounts.

During 1913 and 1914, the Correlation Committee, chaired by

David O. McKay of the Council of Twelve and composed of representatives from priesthood quorums and church auxiliaries, worked to coordinate conferences and correlate gospel studies. Counselor Clarissa S. Williams and Amy Brown Lyman, the board's newly appointed general secretary, represented Relief Society. The committee decided in 1913 that in order to save time and money, each stake Relief Society was to hold its annual conference "in connection with and as part of the Stake Quarterly Conference," to be attended by a visiting general board member during May, June, July, or November.[33] Even under this plan, however, not every stake received a general board visit at its annual conference.[34]

While the Correlation Committee was unable to fully correlate the gospel study of the different auxiliary organizations, it successfully prodded the Relief Society general board to change its educational program and implement a unified course of study. Longer than any other auxiliary, Relief Society had resisted "a blanket program" of study. Since the introduction of mothers' classes in 1902, each stake had been responsible for developing its own lesson outlines. The "advisability of adopting uniform plans for the use of the Relief Society in all the stakes" was discussed as early as 1903 and repeatedly thereafter, but the general board remained divided on the issue.[35] Some board members, Emmeline B. Wells foremost among them, believed that allowing stakes to prepare their own outlines helped "educate and develop the sisters in their own locality" because they did "the thinking and studying of the subject required, which is all helpful to the mind and heart."[36]

Outlines prepared by various stakes, initially published in the *Woman's Exponent* and later appearing as pamphlets, featured an impressive variety of topics in varying degrees of detail, often with individual authors listed by name.[37] Many stakes developed Relief Society libraries to provide for teachers in the wards resources such as the Sunday School's *Juvenile Instructor*, James E. Talmage's *Articles of Faith*, Ritchie's *Primer of Sanitation* (for health topics), and genealogical magazines and circulars. Observed board member Alice Merrill Horne: "Leadership developed, originality cropped out and intense individuality appeared in the stakes because of their own planned programs . . . and a splendid enthusiasm . . . permeated the whole Relief Society structure."[38]

Another board member, Susa Young Gates, assessed the situation differently. Having completed a round of stake visits, she reported in 1911 that "many stakes had asked that uniform plans

187

be adopted."[39] The board's standing committee for reviewing stake outlines published an optional outline for stakes in the April 1912 *Woman's Exponent*, listing ten possible topics for lectures to be based on the research of local talent, including, among others, active use of the franchise, the teaching of foreign language in grade schools, faith and integrity in families, and tree planting.[40]

Some board members continued to press for a uniform "line of study" while others defended the "diversity of interests" in the stakes. President Wells herself "did not feel to exercise too much authority over the stakes" since "they knew their own conditions best."[41] The board, like the Church as a whole, was struggling to find a new balance between central planning and local initiative.

In March 1913, Sisters Williams and Lyman joined the rest of the Correlation Committee in recommending that Relief Society members study "Principles of the Gospel," a course that might "correspond with that given to the Melchesedic [sic] Priesthood Quorums, *and should be uniform throughout the Church*."[42] The board could determine the amount of time to be given to this gospel study and recommend additional topics, such as charity work, home economics, or public health. This authoritative nudge settled the board's lingering differences, and by November 1913 Relief Society's first "unified plan for work" was complete.

Thirteen thousand copies of the new *Relief Society Guide*, edited by Susa Young Gates, were ready for distribution in January 1914. The *Guide*, which the board hoped would be "broad enough and of sufficient scope for all needs and desires," included lesson outlines for four meetings a month.[43] One of the meetings would focus on charity work and business; another, the study of genealogy and the bearing of testimony; a third, home ethics and gardening; and a fourth, literature, art, and architecture. During July and August, societies that did not adjourn for the summer could hold work and business meetings and discuss various health topics. The *Guide* also recommended an order of business for meetings and suggested that all lessons except the genealogy lesson be preceded by a ten-minute talk on current events. During the first year all lessons were optional except the genealogy lessons, which corresponded with the theological lessons of the priesthood quorums. Hoping to introduce the work "as easily and successfully as possible," the board distributed the *Guide* through stake boards free of charge, also providing at no cost during 1914 a monthly sixteen-page *Bulletin* with supplementary lesson material.[44]

In their choice of topics Relief Society women paralleled the popular secular interests of other American women who, in their women's club work, addressed similar themes. The January 1914 *Bulletin* explained that the new emphasis on "the temporal things of the Kingdom" reflected the board's desire to attract to Relief Society "younger women who will be the future leaders."[45] Pleased with the plan, Emmeline B. Wells was nevertheless concerned. As the new guide went to press, she "expressed the fear that in these outlines we are getting too far away from the spiritual side of our great work, and from the thought that inspired the first organization of the Relief Society. The Society stands first for spirituality, and then for charity and mercy."[46] Her vision and emphasis on tradition and spiritual values, echoed by others, would remain an important counterpoint to the era's preoccupation with efficiency, rationality, and professionalism.

The decision to establish a uniform course of study was validated by the overwhelmingly positive response of Relief Society women to the new lesson plans. As members of the general board visited outlying stakes, "in every instance," they reported, the societies were "delighted with the new outlines furnished by the board." Sister Wells herself, upon visiting the Benson (Utah) Stake, found that the membership had "increased double in number since the new work began."[47] By September 1914, after assessing their experiment in uniform study a success, the board had begun planning the next year's course work and had agreed that all optional work would be discontinued at the end of the year. Furthermore, they decided that the 1915 courses would be presented in a new monthly medium: the *Relief Society Magazine*.

At the beginning of 1914, as the board moved forward with the *Guide* and the *Bulletin*, President Wells decided to terminate publication of the *Woman's Exponent*. The decision seemed inevitable, since declining subscriptions had gradually impeded regular publication of the paper. Personal pain to Emmeline was also inevitable. She had been the paper's editor for thirty-nine of its forty-two years, and it had become, as Julina Smith observed, "like her own child." Recognizing that Relief Society must have its own publication, she had hoped the *Woman's Exponent* might continue to play that role, proclaiming on the masthead of each of the fourteen issues of its last volume: "The Organ of the Latter-day Saints' Woman's Relief Society."[48] In reality, however, as Carol Cornwall Madsen has observed, "it was Emmeline's paper, her source of livelihood, and her public voice."[49] A new generation of Relief Society women were attracted neither by its content nor by its outdated format. Sister Wells had considered presenting it in the form of a magazine and even giving it to the board, provided she could remain editor and her daughter Annie Wells Cannon assistant editor. But when the *Bulletin* became a reality, she announced her decision to "[give] up the paper, the name of the paper, and the idea of having her name used as editor."[50] The February 1914 issue of the *Woman's Exponent* was the last. The old tabloid, which seemed so out of date in that self-consciously "modern" age, was not doomed to oblivion. The next generation, searching for its past, would welcome the *Woman's Exponent,* discovering there, just as Emmeline had predicted, "a fountain of material on the lives of the veterans of Mormonism."[51]

The new *Relief Society Magazine,* which appeared in January 1915, was published in the same six-by-nine-inch format as the *Bulletin* and designated as "Volume 2." While the *Bulletin* had proven a "tremendous financial undertaking," subscriptions and advertising provided firm financial footing for the forty-eight-page *Relief Society Magazine.*[52] In fact, by the end of 1915 the magazine had paid its own way and earned a surplus, which justified further increasing its size the following year and paying contributors a small honorarium.[53] Editor Susa Young Gates, business manager Janette A. Hyde, and assistant manager Amy Brown Lyman, the trio who had piloted the *Bulletin* before launching the magazine, were delighted.

The enthusiasm with which subscribers and readers greeted the *Relief Society Magazine* suggested that it filled a long-felt need. A conduit for official directives and messages, the magazine compensated, in part, for less frequent stake visits from the general board. It reported Relief Society general conferences, furnished lesson material and articles of interest to society members, and featured news from local units, fiction, poetry, and and occasional recipes. In the first number President Joseph F. Smith expressed his hope that the new publication would "be made an instrument which will reach the hearts and the understandings of all the sisters."[54] His hope was a benediction: the *Relief Society Magazine* was a magnet that drew women together, "uniting them all in a strong bond of common interest," as one stake Relief Society president observed, and helping them forge the renewed sense of collective identity necessary for a new age. By 1917 the magazine had 12,190

In the art-deco style of the period, designers of the *Relief Society Magazine* wove into its borders the sego lily, recently adopted as an official symbol, and sheaves of wheat. (Courtesy LDS Church Archives)

subscribers, over one-fourth of the society's worldwide membership.[55]

From its first issue in 1915 until its last in 1970 the *Relief Society Magazine* featured the weekly lessons for use in local wards. Topics changed from year to year, but the broad categories—theology, art and literature, homemaking and family life, and, after 1919, social science—remained constant for more than half a century. Relief Society lessons gave women whose primary efforts had been or were centered in family life a "continuing education" that required only as much time as they had to give. Some were interested listeners, others dedicated students, and, as the quality of the instruction gradually improved, many became committed teachers who learned much from their month-long lesson preparation.[56]

The lessons had demonstrable applications. Home ethics and gardening lessons in 1914 spawned an interest in beautification, generating, for example, a campaign by Eagar Ward of the St. Johns (Arizona) Stake "to improve our village and home surroundings." The sisters urged the cleaning of outbuildings and corrals, repair of irrigation ditches and headgates, and even "opening up our main street to the County bridge across the river thereby beautifying our street, and saving so much travel in going to the lower country."[57] Lessons in home economics or domestic science taught women how to "save steps, to lessen the friction everywhere in the domestic machinery." Such endeavors, declared Susa Young Gates in 1916, "are the order of the day."[58] Alice Merrill Horne credited the 1914–16 art and architecture lessons with change wrought among women in Idaho: "When we used to travel to conferences," she quoted a stake president as saying, "the coaches would be filled with nodding passengers. But now, as we travel, the women are all alert to the landscape, craning their necks to discover the color of a cloud shadow in a grain field or an alfalfa patch. . . . And they have the men interested, too, Mrs. Horne!"[59]

In its health education curriculum, the general board provided source material, in Utah often in cooperation with the Utah State Board of Health: 15,000 pamphlets on various health topics were mailed in July 1915. Abroad, however, there was the obstacle of language. Rose Ellen Valentine, president of the German-Austrian Mission Relief Societies, wanted material on nutrition for her sisters and went to see a renowned hygiene specialist in Dresden. She was at first refused admittance, until she explained that she was trying to help two thousand German-speaking women to take better care of their families' health. "I told [the doctor] frankly who I was and the purpose of my visit," she recalled. He promised her a copy of his own forthcoming short text on nutrition and invited her to write an article on the Word of Wisdom for publication in *Hygiene Wegweiser*, a German scientific periodical.[60]

Literature lessons, ranging from Benjamin Franklin's *Autobiography* to the hymns of Eliza Snow, were particularly loved by women. But the theological studies proved even more lasting in the Relief Society curriculum. From 1914 to 1921 genealogy formed a prominent part of the theology course work. Susa Young Gates, who since 1907 had been teaching genealogy in connection with the Church-sponsored Genealogical Society of Utah, adapted the lessons for Relief Society use.[61] In the Northern and Central States missions these lessons proved, one correspondent claimed, "the best material ever used . . . to attract and hold the interest of strangers as well as new converts." But the work did not have the same immediate appeal everywhere. When Salt Lake City's Ninth Ward had difficulty interesting sisters in the lessons, its officers interspersed life stories and autobiographies of the members "in order to stir up interest"—a modification that gradually won support.[62]

Other theological lesson topics emphasized scripture study. The promise to Emma Smith, and to her successors, that they would "expound scriptures" and teach the women, was and is still fulfilled in the course work. Appropriately, the sharing of testimonies, moved temporarily to the work and business meeting, was returned to the theology (spiritual living) meeting, where it remains. "This phase of our work," observed President Wells, "brings a peace and comfort that can come to us no other way."[63]

The new Relief Society curriculum presented some challenges. What was to be done about members' "habit of bringing their sewing to meeting"? the Sanpete (Utah) Stake asked in 1915. Deeming sewing and knitting during lessons "undesirable," the board recommended that it be "reserved for the regular work meeting."[64] However, in Salt Lake City's Forest Dale Ward, where "much sewing [had] been done in the past," work meetings continued to be the best attended.[65]

Some wards found it difficult to "secure efficient class teachers," reporting that in many instances lessons were "merely read from the Magazine." Since 1902, when the mothers' classes had begun, only a small number of women had felt comfortable assuming the position of "instructor," the title suggested by the general board. The Relief Society, spurred by the Correlation Committee's suggestion that each general board make teacher training part of its program, began providing help for instructors in connection with its general conferences, in stake meetings, and through the *Relief Society Magazine*.

The general board also placed new emphasis on the educational role of the Relief Society block or district teachers, later known as visiting teachers. Like the priesthood-directed block or ward teachers, these Relief Society teachers were to make monthly visits to the homes of members. Traditionally their calling had been a key aspect of the society's charity work. The teachers, Weber Stake Relief Society president Jane Richards had observed in 1907, were "not only to gather means but to teach and expound the principles of the gospel."[66] In 1916 the general board formalized this aspect of teachers' duties by asking them to discuss a gospel topic during each visit. The board would not introduce uniform monthly messages until 1923, though a number of stakes outlined messages for the teachers before that time.

Susa Young Gates, editorializing in the 1915 *Relief Society Magazine*, expressed her hope for sisters engaged in the Relief Society's new educational program: "This Society possesses the principles of light, hope, and education for women — let us go to, and develop those powers into a perfected and divinely appointed whole — a Society which will be an auxiliary indeed to the priesthood of the Church of Christ."[67]

Challenges for a New Age in Administration

The new educational program and magazine exemplified Relief Society's creative adjustment to the demands of a new age. In making these adaptations and others, Relief Society leaders struggled to preserve the essence of the society "organized by revelation." In October 1913, the general presidency and board, after counsel from President Joseph F. Smith, had formally resolved: "That we do declare it our purpose to keep intact the original name and initial spirit and purpose of this great organization, holding fast to the inspired teachings of the Prophet Joseph Smith when he revealed the plan by which women were to be empowered through the calling of the priesthood to be grouped into suitable organizations for the purpose of ministering to the sick, assisting the needy, comforting the aged, warning the unwary, and succoring the orphans."[68] Earlier that year the board adopted an organizational motto and emblem, both of which underscored these basic purposes. The new motto, "Charity Never Faileth," hearkened back to Joseph Smith's original directives to the society to "have feelings of charity" and to minister to those in temporal and spiritual need. The sego lily, the strong and beautiful wildflower selected as the society's official emblem, had with its bulb nourished starving Saints when they first settled in Utah. The emblem and particularly the motto became enduring symbols of Relief Society, quickly identifying for an ever-expanding membership the society's key purposes.

In addition to defining essentials, the general presidency and board increasingly provided direction in specifics. A comprehensive thirty-two-page circular published in the March 1915 issue of the *Relief Society Magazine*, "in response to a very extended call for such help," affirmed that the board "would not wish to lay down fast rules," but nevertheless clearly pressed for systematic procedures. Ward Relief Society meetings were to be held weekly on Tuesdays at 2:00 P.M. Ward officers were to meet weekly, stake officers biweekly, and there was to be a "union" (or leadership) meeting of stake and ward officers once a month. Visiting teachers were to collect dues the second week in January and send them through stake treasurers to the general board. The work of secretaries was to be characterized by "system, order, and regular methods."[69]

As general secretary from 1913 to 1921, efficiency-conscious Amy Brown Lyman worked energetically with her assistants to standardize the board's record-keeping procedures. Susa Young Gates, named corresponding secretary in 1913, helped generate the multiplying directives and circular letters sent to wards and stakes. Relief Society headquarters purchased a one-third interest in the YLMIA's rotary mimeograph machine, a dictaphone, an adding machine, and a new typewriter. Beginning in January 1914 the minutes of the general board and other Relief Society records from 1842 forward were assembled, edited, typewritten, and bound.[70]

This effort was expanded to help secretaries and treasurers in the wards and stakes become more thorough and efficient in their duties. Accurate bookkeeping had become a problem as old forms became outdated—"antiquated," the Utah Stake complained in March 1914, "not in keeping with the present day activities of the Society." The same month the secretary of the Yellowstone Stake wrote "asking that a uniform set of books for secretaries and treasurers be adopted by Relief Society." The board began an extensive revision of record books, worked out in part with the Presiding Bishopric, who had asked that Relief Society reports conform with its own.[71] In January 1916 new record materials were distributed: secretaries' books that included forms for rolls and business minutes, treasurers' books, and, for the first time, standardized forms for recording the visits of and contributions received by Relief Society teachers.

Visiting teachers originally had made their visits with baskets in hand to collect contributions "in kind," appearing at the next work meeting, Sister Lyman remembered, "with this basket with a package of rice and a package of soda and a few bottles of fruit and a few boxes of matches and things of that sort." The items were then appraised by the secretary and entered in the ledger. But accounting could be troublesome. Sister Lyman illustrated this by sharing a letter she had received from a bewildered stake president, who reported that among the contributions for a ward bazaar "was a beautiful pair of ducks given by a very poor lady." The Relief Society president "tried every way to dispose of them, but could not, so she took them home and had them about a week when the hawks killed one and the other one swam down the river. Now she feels that this woman and the books should have credit but she doesn't feel that she could dig up the $3 or whatever it is to pay for the ducks. Hard to fix this on the books, both for the credit of the ducks and then the money received in the disposal of them."[72] The trend churchwide was toward cash contributions, which made accounting simpler, just as filling in blanks to report on meetings was more efficient than the old word-for-word recording of sisters' comments. But Sister Lyman's story hints at the humanness sometimes lost between standardized lines.

The operating expenses of the Relief Society general board gradually increased, and during 1912 the board spent more than it received, saving itself from indebtedness only by drawing from a fund reserved for a history of Relief Society. The board's decision to raise annual dues from ten to twenty-five cents as of January 1914 was sustained by stake presidents in April 1913, but they predicted local opposition.[73] As board members traveled to conferences during the summer of 1913, they encountered more than one stake where the announcement "had met with a rather cold response," though the visits provided a chance to explain the need and thereby develop "a little better feeling." Distribution of the *Bulletin* free of charge during 1914 assuaged some opposition, but even a year later one stake asked to be excused from paying full dues since its members were not "converted" to the increase, and another wanted to retain its dues to contribute to the stake tabernacle. The First Presidency fully supported the general board, declaring that "in no case are membership dues to be used for any other purpose . . . also that any money collected for a special purpose should not be diverted into other channels."[74] Accordingly, the 1916 treasurers' books recommended that ward officers place moneys received into one of four funds—charity, general, annual dues, or wheat—and maintain the integrity of each fund. The general board, under the direction of the Council of the Twelve, consolidated its accounts and set up a system of bookkeeping in 1919.[75]

Relief Society's financial strength lay not with the general board but in the wards, which held and controlled all the funds and property of the society except the membership dues. Annual statistical reports from 1914 to 1920 reveal the collective strength of these funds. At the end of 1917, for example, after $53,883 had been spent for charitable purposes and $123,078 for general purposes, the balance on hand totaled $151,129. In addition, the society valued its wheat on hand at $308,462; its real estate, buildings, and furniture at $238,932; its invested funds at $24,767; and other resources at $16,956 — all of which combined to make the society's total assets worth $740,246. At the end of 1914, net resources were valued at $510,536; at the end of 1920, at $848,784.[76]

While the Relief Society program would remain anchored in the wards, the general board continued to develop a strong identity of its own. The board's multiplying enterprises required that its members become skillful administrators. They managed the home in Salt Lake City for women and girls, administered the Relief Society nurse class, and set up a department for the distribution of temple and burial clothing, in addition to directing the society's semiannual conferences and overseeing the work in the wards, stakes, and missions.

The suite of offices on the second floor of the Bishop's Building, which had served as Relief Society headquarters since 1909, would house the general board until the Relief Society Building was dedicated in 1956. The women guarded their distinct identity as far as the building was concerned, using their own entrance on the building's north side and placing there a large stone plaque identifying the offices of the three women's organizations. Being housed just steps away from the Presiding Bishopric had distinct advantages, facilitating coordination of such matters as grain storage and charity work. As the work at headquarters expanded, however, so did the staff, and the suite became inadequate.[77] Forced to consider placing *Relief Society Magazine* advertising and publishing in the same room with temple clothing, the board feared "the situation will not only become an exceedingly embarrassing one, but at the same time, one of great inefficiency."[78] In 1920 the Relief Society was given the entire second floor of the building.

At the request of the First Presidency, the Temple and Burial Clothing Department of the general board had been established in 1912. The unauthorized publication of pictures of the Salt Lake Temple interior in *Leslie's Weekly* in 1911 and the flooding of Salt

Lake City with "cheap, gaudy postcards" containing similar pictures during 1912 may have made the First Presidency wary of possible desecration of temple clothing sold publicly. In November 1912 they sent a letter to stake presidents and Relief Society presidents informing them that the general board had been instructed "to take charge of the business of supplying temple clothing to all members of the Church," thus placing a "safeguard" around the sacred clothing and "preventing it from being loosely handled or unnecessarily exposed."[79]

Originally housed in offices located between the Lion House and the Beehive House in Salt Lake City, the department moved to Relief Society headquarters in 1920. Julina L. Smith, chairman of the board's temple clothing committee, launched the department with an appropriation from the general board and contributions of clothing from several board members. A capable manager of the enterprise, she was most appreciated for her ability to gather about her work a "sacred atmosphere." The clothing prepared by the Relief Society served as "models for all Israel."[80]

The Bishop's Building also served as the site of the nurse class, supervised since 1902 by Emma A. Empey. Concern over whether or not the class could meet rising standards of professional nursing led the board to suspend it in 1910. But, convinced of the need for nurses trained for the simpler cases of home nursing and district visiting, troubled by the large number of people in moderate circumstances who could not pay for the services of a hospital-trained nurse, and aware that some women had resorted to taking obstetrics courses by correspondence, the board decided in 1913 to revive the class as the Relief Society School of Obstetrics and Nursing.[81] Following a tradition that had its roots in the setting apart of midwives in Nauvoo, Relief Society nurses were "set apart by the brethren holding the Priesthood." When they returned to their home communities, they were to give thirty days' service in charity nursing as well as maintain a spiritual component in their practical work.[82]

As medical knowledge expanded and techniques changed, emphasis on the practical component increased. Beginning in 1917–18 the Relief Society course required twenty hours of actual practical nursing, and the next year registered nurses experienced in hospital training were appointed as class instructors. In the spring of 1920, however, realizing that the class had been "inadequate for the training of practical nurses, because of the lack of opportunity to give to students experience in bedside nursing, under supervision," the general board disbanded the program. By summer's end a long-anticipated cooperative arrangement with LDS Hospital had been worked out for the training of nurses' aides.[83]

Adaptations in Missions and Branches

The headquarters-centered enterprises and the energetic board members who administered them occasionally overshadowed the aging Emmeline B. Wells, though she remained an important factor in board decisions. At Relief Society's semiannual general conference, however, she continued to shine as the era's presiding Elect Lady. A Canadian sister, Maydell Cazier Palmer, recalled seeing her "standing in the pulpit of the Salt Lake Tabernacle in a beautiful blue dress with a filmy rush [ruche] around the collar." She weighed only ninety pounds, "but her voice reached out as if coming from delicate organ music. There was power in that small frame."[84]

The April and October conference gatherings were a time to reunite scattered officers and members, to inquire, instruct, and inspire, to build and celebrate sisterhood.[85] The general presidency and board used the occasion to announce or explain new programs, such as the *Guide* lessons, for which special sessions were initiated to provide instruction and enrichment materials for teachers. As Relief Society became involved in social issues, experts from the community, such as juvenile court judges and health officials, became featured speakers, in addition to Relief Society officers and General Authorities. In 1914 Lizzie Thomas Edward, an outstanding soprano, was invited to assemble and direct a choir for the conference and to plan the conference musical program, working closely with Relief Society organist Edna Coray. The new accent on music led the board to publish in 1919 the *Relief Society Song Book,* which included favorite hymns "transposed to suit the voices of mature women" and new songs about Relief Society. Lucy A. R. Clark's "New Freedom Song," for example, featured a rousing chorus to be sung in march time:

> We come, we come in mighty throngs
> To do the Christian's part:
> The hungry feed, the naked clothe,
> Bind up the broken heart.[86]

Sisters far removed from the Mountain West neither attended

conference nor received visits from the general board as often as those located nearer. Conscious of the need to communicate clearly with branches in the mission field but unable to maintain individual contact with each one, the Relief Society general presidency decided in 1912 to unite "the several branches of the Relief Society in the mission fields under a central head similar to the stake organizations," effecting such organizations immediately in the Central States and Northwestern States missions. In December 1914 the presidency sent letters to wives of mission presidents throughout the Church, requesting that they "have charge of the Relief Society" in their missions. After 1914 "all dues and collections" taken in the missions were retained for use there, with itemized accounting sent annually to the general secretary.[87] Improved reporting enabled the general secretary to tally the 1916 membership in mission Relief Societies in the United States, Hawaii, and Europe at 4,335 members.[88]

Lady missionaries and wives of mission presidents had already launched the organization in many areas. Missionary sisters first set up Relief Society in Australia, for example, but "as the president and elders did not have much understanding of the work . . . the societies did not grow and prosper as they should have done."[89] In Tahiti, where the work had been introduced in the 1850s by missionary wives, sisters continued to meet in four Relief Societies. Their membership totaled eighty-five women, Sister Venus R. Rossiter reported in 1917, but in some instances their island homes were so irregularly serviced by boat that missionaries like herself had never visited them, though she tried to meet as many sisters as possible during the mission's conferences and to instruct them in the work.[90]

During 1915 Ida B. Smith reported recent progress and the modified program of branches in Great Britain. The Relief Society held evening meetings because most sisters worked during the day. Typically, each member responded to the roll call with a sentiment drawn from the scriptures or personal reading, one means by which they could become "acquainted with their own voices in public." Following reports of visits, the prearranged sewing was distributed, and during the work the sisters, "without any confusion or talking," listened to a gospel message from one of the missionaries, a local member, or one of the sisters. "In this way we are leading the sisters out of the rut of gossiping while they sew," Sister Smith confided.[91]

In the mission branches and districts, in the wards and stakes, Relief Society came alive. If the administration of Emmeline B. Wells witnessed a new emphasis on centralization and the evolution of a powerful general board, it also saw the steady strength, integrity, and creativity of the local units she so loved. There women assembled, sometimes with great difficulty. There they struggled to build halls, to store grain, to implement new lesson materials, to raise funds, and to forward the society's charitable work. Though the board pressed increasingly for standardization, the local sisters continued to manifest an enthusiastic diversity.

Sister Bertha E. Wright, reporting in October 1917 her experience as Relief Society president in New York City, lamented that "the cramped flat life of the big Eastern cities keeps the women from a practical knowledge of real home life." Travel to and from meetings cost New York members time and money, so Relief Society was held only once every two weeks. In contrast to the relatively stable population of Mormon communities in the Mountain West, New York members were "largely transient."[92]

The "very scattered condition of the Church members" in South Africa made "almost impossible" the organization of regular Relief Societies there, though President Nicholas G. Smith reported in 1918 that his wife had made a beginning there by organizing a sewing class.[93] On the other hand, in Texas, part of the Central States Mission in 1914, one branch consisted of three hundred members, "probably the largest single Relief Society in the world" at that time, with an average attendance of 85 percent of the membership.[94]

Some members pressed the board for "a special course of study for the missions," since "conditions are very different in the mission field from what they are at home."[95] The new standardized lessons were "not altogether adapted to the Hawaiian sisters," for example, who said they preferred "studies which are of a spiritual nature."[96] Samoan sisters studied the Book of Mormon, and in the Northern States Mission home economics lessons were replaced by lessons on prayer.[97] Women of the Maricopa Stake in Arizona were proud of the "practical work" of the Papago Indian Ward Relief Society, where the emphasis was on teaching cooking, sewing, quilting, and darning. The president, working with her counselor, a graduate of the Indian school at Phoenix, was "making an effort to teach the members to speak English."[98]

Local Innovations, Fund-raising, and Charity

Relief Society remained committed to drawing young mothers into its ranks, but lesson presentations did not accommodate young children as readily as had quilting and sewing. In 1911 Davis (Utah) Stake set up a system for caring for children so that mothers could attend Relief Society meetings, and the next year North Weber (Utah) Stake began using one room as a nursery for babies.[99] In 1917 the *Relief Society Magazine* featured photos of the nursery room one Salt Lake City ward Sunday School had equipped with beds, chairs, and toys, and noted that "two [Relief Society] members could easily attend to a dozen or more children and leave the rest of the members free to enjoy the meeting."[100] In this as in other instances, the initiative of local units led to widespread innovation.

The genealogy lessons and the Temple and Burial Clothing Department were complemented by the genealogical research and temple work performed by Relief Society members. The Relief Society general board suggested that each member spend at least one day each year in the temple or arrange for someone else to do so. Some sisters with access to genealogical libraries in the eastern United States helped sisters further west research their ancestors, and their western counterparts with easier access to temples helped them with work there. During 1917 Relief Society women spent a total of 23,863 days in temple work.

When church leaders announced that two new temples — in Cardston, Alberta, Canada, and on the island of Oahu, Hawaii — were to be constructed, Susa Young Gates spearheaded Relief Society support by recommending that each member subscribe one penny per week. By the end of 1917 the temple fund had brought in the "astounding total" of $13,589, which was received by the First Presidency "with more than ordinary pleasure," since Joseph F. Smith's mother, Mary Fielding Smith, had helped direct the women's original penny temple fund in Nauvoo.[101] Relief Society branches in the Hawaiian Mission worked devotedly to support the projected temple there, contributing over $1,000 in 1914 and 1915 and $2,675 in 1916.[102] In 1918 Tahitian sisters reported that "from their extensive cocoanut plantations each sister donates weekly an allotted number of cocoanuts by which she pays the society dues and Temple Penny Fund dues."[103] When the Hawaiian Temple was dedicated in November 1919, general board member Sarah Jenne

Cannon, the widow of former Hawaiian missionary George Q. Cannon, was invited to speak at the dedication services, the first time a woman had been so honored. The Alberta Temple was dedicated in 1923.

Fund-raising for various projects remained an important aspect of Relief Society until 1970. Sisters continued to build their own halls and granaries and to help finance and furnish ward and stake buildings. In 1911 the Milwaukee (Wisconsin) Relief Society held a Valentine's Day chicken supper in order "to purchase a carpet for the rostrum of their church," although they remarked that "a greater good was done in meeting strangers and talking to them on the restored gospel."[104] In 1917 Tahitian sisters not only made quilts and wove hats but also kept enthusiastically busy "diving for pearls to increase their funds."[105] The Centerville (Utah) Second Ward Relief Society raised $200 for the ward meetinghouse with its December 1920 bazaar, which included "a splendid program" and the sale of refreshments, "quilts, homemade rugs, children's underwear, aprons, [and] dresses."[106]

As Relief Society's new motto affirmed, charity work was still the primary imperative for local branches, and they responded vigorously. When Lamanite sisters in the Catauba Indian Nation in South Carolina were organized into a Relief Society in 1917, they became known for their diligence "in visiting the sick and caring for the poor."[107] Duchesne (Utah) Stake reported in 1911 that it had an emergency closet "from which the poor can be accommodated with bedding, clothing, and medicine." Similarly, in 1914 the branch in Flint, Michigan, had on hand sixty quarts of fruit.[108] Many local Relief Societies reached beyond immediate relief. Women in Spokane, Washington, in 1912 worked a day with the city's home for orphans.[109] In 1916 Salt Lake City's Forest Dale Ward attempted to provide material and emotional support for the children of the "many deserted wives and widows" in the ward, determining that none would be "handicapped."[110]

In 1912 Elizabeth Layton reported that the St. Joseph (Arizona) Stake Relief Society had assisted "from three to four hundred families of Mexican refugees"[111]—Latter-day Saint colonists who had settled in Mexico in the 1880s and '90s and had been forced out in the wake of the revolution begun in 1910. Relief Society remained operative in Mexico through seven years of political instability. "The old money is practically valueless," Lillie Romney observed in 1916, noting that the society was still able to

help the needy with gifts of flour, potatoes, butter, cheese, secondhand quilts, and secondhand clothing for children and infants.[112] Rey L. Pratt, president of the Mexican Mission, testified
in 1918 that through revolution, famine, and disease, "sisters of
the Relief Societies have been as ministering angels to those in
want and in distress, both among those who are members of the
Church, and those who are not."[113]

As other charitable organizations began publishing statistics
regarding their public work, Emmeline B. Wells announced that
"she would like to have an estimate of the work done" by the Salt
Lake City Relief Societies.[114] During 1913 stakes were requested
to quantify certain accomplishments: number of quilts and yards
of carpet made, bushels of wheat stored, books in stake libraries,
halls built, and days spent by sisters in temples.[115] Previously only
the money and provisions collected for and distributed to the needy
had been recorded, but now sisters were asked to tally the number
of days spent with the sick, the number of families helped, and the
number of bodies prepared for burial. Perplexed by this new emphasis on statistics, Norena B. Robbins of the Bannock (Idaho)
Stake observed in November 1915 that in her stake there had been
"hundreds of quilts made but no record kept." Though they had
not enumerated their efforts, she reported, "the Relief Societies
sisters always take care of the sick and care for the dead as we
haven't any undertakers and but a few Drs."[116]

Other sisters were likewise confused. Should they report to
their Relief Society presidents their visits to sick neighbors or days
spent caring for aged parents so these hours could become part of
the record? The board determined that individual acts of service
and compassion would not be counted, but only the work "done
by and through the officers and members of the organization in
their official capacity."[117] The cumulative effort of Relief Society
women in this respect was impressive. During 1917, for example,
the 45,339 members of Relief Society spent a total of 36,581 days
with the sick; made 78,066 visits to the sick; helped 5,868 families;
and prepared 2,311 bodies for burial. In addition, they paid out
$53,883.37 for charitable purposes.[118]

Relief Efforts during World War I

While Relief Societies worldwide were expanding their possibilities and streamlining their programs, the new century's implicit faith that such scientific and spiritual progress would benignly

During World War I
Chicago Relief Society
sisters, organized as
Auxiliary 615 of Red Cross,
posed with Relief Society
banner and U.S. flag in front
of General John B. Logan
monument in Chicago's
Grant Park. (Courtesy LDS
Visual Resources Library)

lead to a more abundant civilization was shattered in June 1914 when Archduke Francis Ferdinand, heir to the Austrian throne, and his wife were assassinated at Sarajevo. The incident ignited nationalistic tensions long smouldering in Europe, and one by one nations—Austria, Serbia, Germany, Russia, France, Belgium, Great Britain, Turkey—entered a war of unprecedented proportion.

At the October 1914 general conference, President Joseph F. Smith announced that missionaries had been evacuated from most of central and western Europe. Local members assumed responsibility for leadership and missionary work, and in both England and Germany church membership actually increased. In November 1914 Ida B. Smith reported "that a great many of the Relief Society sisters in England had volunteered to sew and knit for the soldiers at the front; but that all available funds for buying materials had been exhausted."[119] Eager to help, American and Canadian Relief Societies contributed to an emergency war fund to aid European sisters' relief efforts.

When in 1915 each branch in Great Britain received about fifteen dollars from the fund, the women were delighted and eagerly bought material for making sheets, pillowcases, nightdresses, and underclothing for poor children.[120] Rose Ellen B. Valentine, who presided over Relief Society work in the Swiss-German Mission from 1913 to 1916, reported "the humble beginnings of the charity work of these women" with their contributions of eight and ten cents per month and "their great joy on receiving from Utah $20 for each Society for relief work." Most of the women, she said, were careful planners who had sufficient clothing and bed and table linen, but they worked evenings to patch and knit for "those more needy than themselves." Their thrift was exemplary, Sister Valentine observed in the April 1917 Relief Society conference, deploring by comparison "American waste and extravagance."[121]

It was difficult to accurately record the growth or attrition of Relief Society organizations in Europe following the outbreak of the war. Reports varied, but in 1915, when all of the European Relief Societies were grouped under the charge of Ida B. Smith, there were forty-two branches in Great Britain, nine in the Netherlands, twelve in Sweden, and eighteen elsewhere in Scandinavia, in addition to twelve Swiss and German branches. Sister Valentine had been unable to visit German branches after the war began, but before leaving Europe she received word that the sisters there were "more earnest than ever before in their Relief Society work," that many of them had "sustained severe losses," but that "their tender and aching hearts are filled with only one desire—that of doing good."[122]

The United States joined the Allies by declaring war on Germany on April 6, 1917, mobilizing troops, ships, and supplies with astonishing speed. Within eleven weeks Americans raised over three billion dollars, registered ten and one-half million men, and penetrated the submarine-infested Atlantic to land General Pershing and his troops in France. With everyone in rapid motion, the Relief Society general presidency advised Latter-day Saint sisters to remain "patient and calm." In a wartime epistle that appeared in the July 1917 *Relief Society Magazine*, the presidency, Sisters Wells, Williams, and Smith, urgently advised sisters: "Administer in the spirit of love and patience to your husbands and to your children; guard the little ones; do not permit them to imbibe the spirit of intolerance or hatred to any nation or to any people; keep firearms out of their hands; do not allow them to play at war nor to find amusement in imitating death in battle; inculcate the spirit of loyalty to country and flag, but help them to feel that they are soldiers of the Cross and that if they must needs take up arms in the defense of liberty, of country and homes they shall do so without rancor or bitterness." The sisters were to avoid discussing politics and war in their meetings and visits, to "look after the needy more diligently than ever," and to "teach the peaceable things of the kingdom."[123]

American Relief Societies responded wholeheartedly when President Woodrow Wilson called upon women, men, and children to enlist in the "great civilian army without whose backing mere fighting would be useless."[124] "We want to move as a solid unit," the society's presidency affirmed, "to keep closely together, under the banner of the Relief Society, not diverting our resources or scattering our energies."[125] Since both the National Council of Defense and the American Red Cross worked "through societies already organized," the general board advised ward and stake Relief Societies in the United States to cooperate fully with these organizations in the war effort. Clarissa S. Williams, invited to head the Utah Council of National Defense Women's Committee, rallied Relief Society sisters and other Utah women in a variety of defense efforts: food production and conservation, loan campaigns, fund drives, Americanization programs for foreign-born immigrants, sanitation, and child welfare work.

A new Federal Food Administration with Herbert C. Hoover at its head attempted to curb waste and stimulate food production and conservation. Hoover asked housewives to give daily service to the war effort by preparing wheatless and meatless meals and carefully using milk, fats, sugar, and perishable foods.[126] Local Relief Societies sponsored "Hoover luncheons" and published government recipes. In 1917 the *Relief Society Magazine* posed such questions as "Do I waste flour or bread?" "Do I waste money on finery?" and even "Do I waste time in gossip?" Expanding the theme, editor Susa Young Gates rather pointedly asked, "Are you conserving yourself, the nation's most valuable asset?" With some authority, since she herself had suffered from overwork and nervous exhaustion, she wrote: "No woman will be justified before God, angels, or men, who crowds herself daily to the breaking point and beyond it, no matter how good her motive, nor how unselfish the labor she may be engaged in."[127]

Becoming part of the great "land army of the Republic," many American women filled in for husbands, fathers, and brothers, continuing the agricultural work necessary to feed the nation and its soldiers. The *Relief Society Magazine* praised these workers by featuring photos of them hoeing and hunting. Everyone was encouraged to plant a vegetable garden or somehow engage in food production. When the First Presidency sponsored a potato competition, the five-hundred-dollar second prize for the largest yield of potatoes on one acre of ground went to the Roosevelt (Utah) Ward Relief Society for their production of 39,173 pounds.[128] During one afternoon in October 1917 sisters from small Utah communities of Pleasant Grove, Manila, and Lindon put up 1,100 quarts of tomatoes, peaches, pears, and apricots to store in the Relief Society emergency cupboard.[129]

The First Presidency advised church organizations, including Relief Society, to encourage their members to subscribe to the Liberty Loan campaign, which helped the government finance the war. When asked to subscribe, women in the Alpine (Utah) Ward "gladly gave their mite and within a few hours the amount of $50.00 was raised."[130] The loan campaign provided Latter-day Saints, whose loyalty to the United States government had been questioned even after Utah obtained statehood in 1896, an opportunity to display their patriotism. Relief Societies responded enthusiastically and during 1917 invested $24,686 in Liberty bonds.

As part of its sanitation and health campaign for home defense, the National Council of Defense designated April 1918–April 1919 as "Children's Year," with the goal of saving the lives of 100,000 American children through preventive health measures. The council's Child Welfare Department and the U.S. Children's Bureau carried the campaign into communities nationwide by working through local women's groups, such as Relief Society, to educate women in prenatal care and the importance of proper nourishment for children, and to weigh and measure children under five years of age. In the wake of the terrible conflict depopulating the world, Clarissa S. Williams admonished every man and woman to consider it a duty "to promote the health and happiness of the rising generation."[131]

Following entry of the United States into the war, the general board was "beseiged with letters and inquiries" regarding the involvement of local societies in Red Cross work.[132] A July 7, 1917, letter to stake Relief Society presidents explained that wards and stakes who chose to be involved should be known as "Relief Society Red Cross workers," thus maintaining the identity of the Relief Society organization. Each stake was to form an auxiliary that would work directly with the Red Cross chapter in the county where it was located.[133] The general board advised that Red Cross work be done only during the regular work and business meeting, but the Portland Central Relief Society in Oregon reported that during

1917 Red Cross work "took up many months." The small group made 464 hospital garments, 177 knitted articles, and 24 refugee garments.[134] Many societies rolled bandages and prepared surgical dressings, sponsored "linen showers" in order to gather sheets and towels, or campaigned for funds. Women worked in their own meeting rooms or in special work rooms arranged by the Red Cross. At the request of the Salt Lake County Red Cross, the large kitchen on the fourth floor of the Bishop's Building became a center for preparing surgical dressings.

Collectively, these small local efforts at relief for the war's wounded made a considerable difference to the Allied war effort, particularly to those on the receiving end. One family in England received in 1917 a Relief Society quilt that had originally been donated at the time of the San Francisco earthquake in 1906, but was not needed then and so was forwarded to the Red Cross. Because the Tooele, Utah, sister who sent the quilt had tucked a note inside it, she received personal thanks from the London woman who received it. "It came in very useful, as I lost my husband at the front in March, 1916," the recipient wrote, noting that with eight children and no possibility of working, "it is as much as I can do to keep going."[135]

Outside the United States, Relief Societies were eagerly engaged in war-relief work. In Glasgow, Scotland, women made clothing for soldiers, teaching their young children to work with them in making mittens and wristlets. They also sent "messages of sympathy and good cheer" and their names and addresses, and received "touching replies . . . from the grateful soldiers at the front."[136] Sisters in Winnipeg, Canada, felt the urgency of war work so keenly that "they dropped all work and study and devoted one-half day each week [to] making hospital shirts for the wounded soldiers; also knitting armlets and socks."[137] In Tahiti, women sewed for the local Croix Rouge (Red Cross) and "dried fish and fruit for the Tahitian boys in the army."[138]

"Oh, this cruel war has made such inroads on the homes of the majority of the people!" wrote Mary J. Miller from the Australian Mission in 1918.[139] Hundreds of Latter-day Saint families lost brothers and sons. Relief Society women mourned with one another over the losses. "Touch with healing balm our maternal terrors," was the prayer in one *Relief Society Magazine* editorial.[140] Ten months later prayers around the world were answered; on November 11, 1918, firing ceased on the Western Front. Despite health officials' injunction against public assemblies during the raging influenza epidemic, there was dancing in the streets. The "war to end all wars" was over.

Relief Society Wheat: A Time of Need Arrives

During the war's final months, Relief Society sisters in the United States made their crowning contribution to the war effort by selling the wheat they had stored against a time of disaster. "In all these years we have not had much need to use the grain stored away for the purpose it was designed," Emmeline Wells noted in September 1914, "but with the dark cloud hovering over the world as it now does, we can see the prophetic wisdom of President Young in calling upon the sisters to save grain against a time of need."[141] Quoting Brigham Young's 1876 invitation to the women, she reminded them: "The brethren are to assist the sisters in this work, both in gathering and preserving the grain."[142]

In October 1911, after extended consultation between the general presidency and the Presiding Bishopric, Sister Wells had announced to her board that the sisters' perennial problem of inadequate storage granaries "had been solved by the Presiding Brethren."[143] She elaborated on the solution in a November 1911 letter to Relief Society presidents. The sisters could either deposit their wheat in commercial grain elevators or in the church-owned 60,000-bushel elevator at Richfield, Utah, or funds could be sent to the Presiding Bishopric, who would buy and deposit wheat at Richfield. The women would be required to pay a 5 percent storage charge, but the modern facility preserved the grain and allowed it "to be sold from time to time, with a view to purchasing new wheat, and in this way derive a profit rather than a loss in storing it."[144] The letter advised that decisions regarding wheat should be made in consultation with the bishopric of the ward, the stake Relief Society officers, and the stake presidency. Fully evolved, this policy was emphasized by Emmeline B. Wells in 1915 when she "explained that wheat is stored under the direction of the Presiding Authority of the Church, and everything connected with its distribution is to be done under his direction."[145]

By the time the United States entered the war in April 1917, the worldwide shortage of grain was acute. Some societies, fearing that owners of commercial elevators might speculate with their wheat, withdrew it and redeposited it in their own local granaries or even in their own homes.[146] Other societies postponed pur-

Women of the Moulton Ward in Idaho pose in a Relief Society wheat field at harvest time. (Courtesy LDS Church Archives)

chasing new wheat, some of them redirecting wheat funds into general expenses or charity work, an action that met with strong disapproval from the Relief Society general presidency and the First Presidency. Wheat funds were to be reserved for wheat. The government began controlling the U.S. price and distribution of wheat products and gathered surplus grain for shipment to Europe's starving citizens and soldiers. Early in 1918 food administration representatives in Utah approached a local Relief Society regarding its grain. Local priesthood officials and the general board referred the request to the Presiding Bishop Charles W. Nibley, who explained to government officials that the Relief Society stored grain for charitable rather than commercial purposes. A second government request for Relief Society wheat was urgent — "a matter of the loyalty of the Relief Society to the government" — and the First Presidency and Presiding Bishopric advised immediate release of the wheat.

On Monday morning, May 20, 1918, Bishop Nibley announced to the press the government's request for "all the Relief Society wheat for use in the present war." Accordingly, over the weekend his office had sent out "letters to all ward Relief Societies asking that the societies comply with the government's request." The letter, dated May 18 and sent out over the names of the Presiding Bishopric and Relief Society general presidency, was addressed to bishops and asked them to confer with their societies and report by return mail the amount of wheat on hand for immediate shipment. The price had been fixed by the government, and the money received was to be put in banks and reinvested in wheat after the harvest. By June 24, the Relief Societies in Utah and Idaho had sold about 200,000 bushels to the United States government for $1.20 a bushel.[147] For leaders of the Box Elder (Utah) Relief Society, among others, the sale of the grain was "a most wonderful thing for the world to know . . . and it would preach the gospel more than words."[148]

While the government had guaranteed that Relief Society wheat could be replaced in the fall, that proved impossible. In August 1918 the First Presidency and Presiding Bishopric told stake presidents that societies should postpone purchase of wheat until the government relinquished control of the wheat market. In October bishops and stake presidents were advised that since the wheat market was still unsettled, Relief Societies should consider sending all wheat monies to the Presiding Bishop's Office; the General Authorities not only felt the funds "perfectly safe in the custody of the Presiding Bishopric," but preferred that "they be so held." They would be invested in wheat "as soon as the Government will permit"; in the meantime they would receive 4 percent interest per annum, the same interest rate offered by savings banks, to be paid commencing October 1, 1918.[149]

Relief Society grain storage came to an end for the time being, and wheat funds remained deposited in banks or with the Presiding Bishopric. The general presidency announced in mid-October that they had decided to suspend further gathering of wheat funds for the present and encourage instead the "build up of a substantial charity fund in each ward."[150] The ever-enterprising women, beginning in 1922, would decide to use interest paid on the wheat fund to finance an extensive program of maternity and child welfare work.

The manner in which sale of the wheat came about pointed to the challenge of maintaining a working partnership between Relief Society and priesthood leaders. The Relief Society general presidency had not been included in the decision to sell the wheat to the government. After having themselves sent out the initial letter to bishops announcing the sale, the Presiding Bishopric with great difficulty tried to explain to the Relief Society general board "why the women were not informed but letters sent out under their name."[151] Though she fully supported the sale of the wheat to the government, Emmeline Wells expressed her dismay "that such an important action had been taken without consulting the General Board." Bishop Nibley went to a board meeting and personally apologized on behalf of the bishopric, admitting the mistake and accepting blame. "Wish you would give me 'Thunder,' " he said, adding that the bishopric all agreed that the board should have been consulted "before anything definite was done." Asking the board's "forgiveness for our oversight," Bishop Nibley assured them that the bishopric would see that nothing like it happened again.[152]

Five weeks later the Presiding Bishopric sent a letter to bishops and stake presidents regarding deposit of money received for wheat.[153] Concerned that they had been excluded from yet another decision about Relief Society wheat, and smarting a bit from having learned that the government's letter of thanks had been sent to priesthood leaders rather than to the Relief Society, the general presidency and board decided to write a letter to the First Presidency "asking for information with regard to the exact relationship between the Presiding Bishop's Office and the Relief Society in the matter of directing the storage and sale of grain."[154]

In time, of course, Relief Society received not only thanks but also special recognition for its grain storage mission. During a 1919 visit to Salt Lake City, President and Mrs. Woodrow Wilson called upon Emmeline B. Wells in her apartment in the Hotel Utah and "heartily thanked her for the part played by the Relief Society during the war," particularly the release of the wheat, and expressed appreciation for her work in philanthropy and suffrage.[155] Wheat became an enduring symbol of Relief Society commitment and accomplishment, one of its official emblems.

The question of the "exact relationship" between priesthood and Relief Society leaders was just as enduring. The order and system were clear. The society's March 1915 "Circular of Instructions" confirmed that society officers and members at the general, stake, and ward levels, "while acting independently in their own sphere of activity, are under the controlling power of the priesthood, vested in the Presidency of the Church, the Presidency of the Stake, and the Bishopric of the Ward." Order was indeed a critical element in priesthood leadership. But the power and influence of the priesthood could be maintained only by relationship: by persuasion, not dictum; by long-suffering and kindness, not efficiency.[156] "All must act in concert or nothing can be done," Joseph

Smith had taught the first Relief Society. The statement had new relevance in the twentieth century as men and women who had previously administered church programs somewhat independently of one another were called upon to correlate their efforts, to give up a measure of independence in order to work interdependently. Both women and men occasionally fell back into older patterns of unilateral decision-making, and discord followed. One stake Relief Society president, for example, disregarded her stake president's advice not to hold the society's conference on Sunday. When only twenty women attended, she became "depressed and weighed down with . . . her own inability to fill her position," and her personal distress clouded the whole conference.[157] The partnership with priesthood leaders to which Relief Society women had remained committed since Nauvoo was a compelling ideal, and they believed themselves to be moving steadily toward it when they worked together successfully with priesthood counterparts.

Significantly, the Presiding Bishopric and the Relief Society general presidency successfully strengthened their own relationship and thereby established a pattern for strengthening the partnership between ward Relief Society presidents and bishops. The question provoking increased collaboration was not wheat, but charity work. Close cooperation between the Relief Society general presidency and the Presiding Bishopric would facilitate establishment of the Relief Society Social Service Department and gradually lead to a correlated and comprehensive charity or welfare program.

New Emphasis on Social Welfare

The distribution of charity funds and commodities occurred at the ward level, where both the bishop and the Relief Society were charged with care of the poor. The system paralleled the old decentralized system in the United States in which public charity had traditionally been the responsibility of local officials. Turn-of-the-century concern with efficiency and systematization had prompted efforts to coordinate the multiplying agencies and organizations for public and private charity. Charity Organization Societies, social service exchanges, councils of social agencies, and Community Chests were established to eliminate duplication of effort. During World War I, as these efforts increased, the Church was faced with a dual challenge: how to better correlate charity work within the Church and at the same time coordinate the Church's relief efforts with those of the broader community.

In 1916 George Albert Smith of the Quorum of the Twelve and Relief Society representative Amy Brown Lyman began working with Salt Lake City's Charity Organization Society, which had many Mormon families among its clientele. In June 1917, just after the United States' entry into war, Amy Lyman represented the Church at the National Conference of Charities and Corrections, the forerunner of the National Conference of Social Work, in Pittsburgh. Her previous exposure to social work methods at Hull House in Chicago, the information and insights she received at this conference, and her close connection with the Red Cross all convinced her that Relief Society workers should be specifically trained to carry on welfare work "intelligently" and according to new methods of "scientific charity" or social work. Rational, individualized care, based on investigations and case conferences, looked beyond immediate material relief to the long-term goal of restoring recipients of charity to dignity and as much self-sufficiency as possible.

With the support of the First Presidency and the general board, Sister Lyman and three other delegates, representing stake Relief Society organizations in Ogden, Logan, and Provo, attended a six-week Home Service Institute in Denver, Colorado, in November 1917 to receive Red Cross training in the new social work principles. President Smith "was intensely interested" in Sister Lyman's report of the Denver training. He expressed to her his concern for the Church's own charity work where "there is duplication of effort in which money is wasted, and in many instances, relief funds are not adequate." He encouraged her continued study of family welfare work "with a view of improving the LDS charity work." The next fall she returned to Denver for more course work. President Smith died in November 1918, before she returned, but with the approval of President Heber J. Grant and the support of the Presiding Bishopric, she set up the Relief Society Social Service Department at Relief Society headquarters in January 1919. The new department was to serve as a liaison with community agencies and use new social work methods to help bishops and Relief Society presidents.[158]

The attempt of the Utah Stake Relief Society, with the support of the general board, to modernize its charity work showed the difficulty of implementing the new methods at the local level. When the Red Cross considered extending its postwar home-service work to the civilian population of Utah County, stake Relief Society president Inez Knight Allen and her counselor Annie Palmer, who with Amy Brown Lyman had attended the 1917 Red Cross Home Service Institute in Denver, proposed that the Relief Society assume that responsibility instead. They consulted with the Utah Stake presidency and high council, who gave them "a blessing and encouragement" and "tendered the use of the [stake] Administration Building for an office, or headquarters, agreeing to pay for the heat and light." The women then sponsored a one-month institute to train sixty Relief Society workers in family casework and held meetings with bishops and Relief Society presidents, offering to help investigate families and design constructive family relief plans. Some bishops who initially opposed the work gradually embraced it, explained Sister Allen, noting that "one bishop has turned over all of his charity work to the Relief Society while the others are cooperating with the Relief Society Agency in making family plans." The stake replaced monthly Relief Society donations with an annual stakewide drive for charity funds.[159] Lena Andreason reported that the small Vineyard Ward contributed every six months to Utah Stake Relief Society's Community Welfare Collection: $125.00 in November 1919, $87.25 in May 1920, $125.00 in November 1920, and $80.50 in May 1921.[160]

Impressed by the efforts of the Utah Stake Relief Society, the general board expressed approval but not unreserved praise. "Let us not make fundamental changes nor alter the perfect and wise adjustment of our religious organization to match the world's spectacular methods lest we fall into their mistakes and partake of their errors," wrote Susa Young Gates in a lengthy letter to the general presidency, dissenting from their endorsement of the Utah Stake program. She objected to exclusive use of trained social workers rather than Relief Society visiting teachers, criticized the tendency to shift responsibility and money to a central office or figure and use funds for salaries and overhead, and predicted that individuals receiving "regular financial help" from institutions would find their self-respect stifled.[161]

While charity work previously had been left almost entirely to the wards, the question of how to incorporate modern methods into local Relief Society work became, in the wake of the Utah Stake experiment, a question of general policy. Aware that duplication of effort wasted resources and could potentially harm those in need, the Relief Society general presidency and the Presiding Bishopric, taking their direction from the First Presidency, unitedly decided not to rely on outside agencies to administer charity to

Latter-day Saints. Bishops were to be responsible for the welfare of their ward members, and Relief Society sisters were to labor under their bishops' direction. However, charity was not to be disbursed without careful investigations, as had too often been the case in the past. Starting in the summer of 1920 with a special course taught by Amy Brown Lyman at BYU, Relief Society women were to learn new scientific methods for investigating families, evaluating their needs, and working with the bishop to determine the plan that would best encourage the family toward self-sufficiency. The new social services department run by Sister Lyman under the direction of the general board would serve as a liaison with community agencies and as a training center for special social service aids and Relief Society presidents. Relief Society members at large would become acquainted with principles of social work and sociology through a series of social service lessons. Cooperatively, priesthood and Relief Society leaders were moving Latter-day Saint charity work in important new directions.

"It Is for You to Lead the Women of the World"

As Relief Society women forged a closer working relationship with priesthood leaders, they reexamined their connections with other women's groups. For more than two decades, individual Relief Society members had freely affiliated with various women's clubs and organizations, though they were "advised against joining fraternal societies" and admonished that their first duty was to attend Relief Society.[162] Trying to maintain the loyalty of members by addressing needs they might be tempted to fill in other organizations, the general board updated curriculum, offered life and burial insurance, arranged for stake organizations to serve as Red Cross auxiliaries, and incorporated into Relief Society lessons home science, art, and gardening materials from Utah State Agricultural College so that the college would not be obliged to form separate clubs that might draw Relief Society members.[163] These measures helped keep the identity and membership of Relief Society intact.

The general presidency and board declined numerous invitations to affiliate Relief Society with national leagues and federations of women. It was already "organized enough" and "national enough," the First Presidency once explained.[164] Relief Society had become a charter member of the National Council of Women in 1891 and had incorporated as the National Woman's Relief Society in 1892. In 1913, however, council president May Wright Sewall both visited and wrote to President Joseph F. Smith to ask him why the Relief Society and YLMIA "had latterly withdrawn themselves" from participation in the council, their representation having become "smaller and less certain." She felt that the relationship had been "equally beneficial to both parties," and he confirmed "that the friendship that had existed should continue."[165]

Relief Society could not easily finance the travel of its officers to council meetings, and many of its longtime council participants were aging or occupied by the board's increased duties, so members living in the vicinity of the meeting sites had been appointed to attend and report to the board by mail. In February 1914 the general board considered dropping its corporate status as the National Woman's Relief Society, a name that did not identify it as part of the church organization, and, at the same time, cutting its ties with the National Council of Women. When the board consulted the First Presidency on the matter, they were told that Relief Society did not necessarily need to change its corporate status or its affiliation, but it must remember that its membership in the National Council was in any case temporary, that "the Society must be regarded as paramount in importance to everything else now connected with it, or which may hereafter be connected with it."[166] A month later, President Smith elaborated, affirming that worldly organizations "are men-made, or women-made," while the Relief Society "is divinely made, divinely authorized, divinely instituted, divinely ordained of God to minister for the salvation of the souls of women and men." He did not want "to see the time when our Relief Societies will follow, or commingle and lose their own identity by mixing up with these woman-made organizations that are coming to pass. . . . It is for you to lead the world and to lead especially the women of the world, in everything that is praiseworthy, everything that is God-like. . . . You are the head, not the tail."[167] Relief Society could cooperate with other organizations, but it would always be required to differentiate itself as well. The society tried to achieve this difficult balance with the National and International Councils of Women, continuing over the years to send representatives, several of whom were honored with leadership positions. During World War I, the society achieved similar success in cooperating with the National Council of Defense and the Red Cross.

Upon final ratification of the suffrage amendment to the

United States Constitution in August 1920, Emmeline B. Wells sent congratulations to national suffrage leader Carrie Chapman Catt, affirming that Relief Society suffrage workers joined "in the song of victory which rises from every franchised woman in these United States of America today."[168] The nation's new female citizens would wage subsequent campaigns in their local communities, and Relief Society women would join them.

Cooperating with others in the public arena while maintaining the society's identity and autonomy was not easy. One frustrated Rexburg, Idaho, sister wrote to the general board in 1920 for clarification. The Relief Society in Rexburg, she explained, "is opposed to having the Mormon women cooperate in this way. Since the Mormon women are in the majority, and unwilling to cooperate with the civic body, Rexburg has been prevented from securing a county nurse and high school, and it seems now that the Relief Society there is thwarting the plans for a public library." Seriously concerned by the report, the board immediately responded that "the Relief Society stands for cooperation at all times with movements for advancement."[169]

Charity and Gifts of the Spirit

Preserving its identity was the single most important issue for Relief Society during the administration of Emmeline B. Wells. How could the society work cooperatively with organizations outside the Church and still maintain its unique identity as part of a covenant people? How could it be fully integrated into the larger church organization and still be distinguished as an organization of and for women? How could it modify and improve without losing its essence? Joseph Smith had required of Relief Society sisters a double mission: to relieve the poor and to save souls. How, in the course of their temporal work, could they maintain their devotion to their spiritual goals? Their motto, "Charity Never Faileth," embraced both missions. Lessons, health clinics, and war work would come and go, but charity, "the true love of Christ," would endure.

As a gift of the spirit, charity encompassed and surpassed all other gifts, which, in the course of the development of the Church from an intimate, family-like organization to a major world faith, were in process of reinterpretation. Through an era of unprecedented secular progress, President Wells consistently "urged the members to remember their spiritual duties," to hold fast to their covenants.[170] The temporal manifestations were not to be allowed to replace the spiritual concerns. And yet certain cherished expressions of spirit seemed to be in decline.

The manifestation of the charismatic gifts, particularly speaking in tongues and healing, continued into the 1920s, though with less frequency than in earlier periods. When women of the Alberta Stake in Canada gathered in Relief Society conference in November 1910, the president of the society's Woodruff Branch bore testimony and "then blessed the sisters present through the gift of tongues," another sister interpreting the blessing.[171] In 1913 Emmeline B. Wells noted with concern that though some brethren did not approve of the women administering to the sick, "it is to be hoped the blessing will not be taken from us."[172]

The next year, as though to assuage Aunt Em's fears, in October 1914 the First Presidency sent bishops and stake presidents a letter confirming that "any good sister, full of faith in God and in the efficacy of prayer," could administer to the sick. Sisters, the First Presidency wrote in response to questions, "have the same right to administer to sick children as to adults, and may anoint and lay hands upon them in faith."[173] Although it had long been established that these administrations were not priesthood ordinances, nor were they really Relief Society functions, women continued to look to Relief Society leaders for counsel, particularly with regard to the washing and anointing of women before childbirth. Prior to the First Presidency statement, an official letter from President Bathsheba W. Smith had required that "no sister who is out of harmony with the Presiding Officers of her Relief Society or with the Presiding Priesthood of her ward should be called upon to administer to the sick. A lack of harmony prevents the full flow of the good spirit."[174] Expanding Sister Smith's concern for unity, the First President emphasized that "in all sacred functions performed by our sisters there should be perfect harmony between them and the Bishop, who has the direction of all matters pertaining to the Church in his ward." "The Lord has heard and answered the prayers of sisters in these administrations many times," the First Presidency affirmed, but they gently counseled sisters, referencing Doctrine and Covenants 42:44, to remember "that the command of the Lord is to call in the elders to administer to the sick, and when they can be called in, they should be asked to anoint the sick or seal the anointing."[175] That that policy was to eventually replace the earlier flexibility is indicated in the relative firmness of Joseph Fielding Smith's 1946 statement "that it is far better for us to follow the plan the Lord has given us and send for the Elders of the Church to come and administer to the sick and afflicted."[176]

Washing and anointing prior to confinement or childbirth, however, was the "blessing of one sister to another," intended to provide comfort and reassurance in ways inappropriate to priesthood administration. "Washing of the parts of the body to be affected, and anointing them with sacred oil, then pronouncing a mother's blessing," as general Relief Society president Louise Y. Robison would explain in 1936, was to be "very quietly performed." This was not a priesthood ordinance; sisters were not specifically set apart to perform this office and there was no set form for the service.[177]

As the practice diminished, at least one ward recorded the essential elements of the blessing in its Relief Society minutes book, and one stake, with the best of intentions, tried to facilitate the practice by making mimeograph copies of suggested wording. In some cases, Sister Robison wrote, women "have been over-zealous, or made too much publicity, then the Priesthood authorities have refused to sanction it." The blessing bore apparent similarity to the initiatory ordinances of the temple, and by the 1930s women were able to attend there with increasing ease and greater frequency. In the holy house, women having authority could wash and anoint their sisters, blessing them with spiritual as well as physical health.

The movement toward a more manageable order in the spiritual ministrations of the Saints was not limited to the women's practices. In the process of systematizing an increasingly complex organization, many duties and responsibilities previously carried by individuals were apportioned to holders of specific offices. The prayer circles, for example, that some priesthood leaders had conducted in their homes or ward buildings were first reorganized to restrict membership according to priesthood calling, and in 1929 totally discontinued.[178] The gradual change eliminating from Latter-day Saint practice most public expression of the charismatic gifts churchwide is described by historian Thomas G. Alexander as largely complete by the end of the 1920s: "Except for personal religious experiences, the church leadership clearly wanted religious manifestations to come within recognized lines of priesthood authority and within doctrinally defensible limits."[179]

A gradual transition, then, as much as the gentle direction of the presiding authorities, brought the sacred work so important to sisters under the formal direction of the administrative line of the priesthood rather than the watchcare of Relief Society. While the exercise of the gifts of healing and tongues declined as the new century progressed, women turned with increasing frequency to more approved practices. As individual attendance at scheduled temple sessions replaced for priesthood leaders the prayer circles of the past, so did women's participation in the work of the holy house assume increasing importance to the sisters.

The deviation from one expression of spirituality to another did not portend for the women a cessation of spiritual manifestations. Cautioning members about an overenthusiastic attention to the temporal causes Relief Society was espousing, Susa Young Gates pled in 1918 for increased attention to "spiritual build-up." Rational testimony-bearing, she counseled, was more desirable than excitement and spiritual frenzy. "Tears may spring, hearts may melt," she encouraged, but all in "the calm, sweet spirit of hope, faith and peace."[180]

Individually and collectively, Latter-day Saint women would continue to draw upon other gifts of the Spirit—faith, hope, wisdom, knowledge—to provide in another form the same "blessing of one sister to another" and to extend that blessing to men, women, and children outside their sisterhood. The greatest of these gifts, charity, would endure as the essence of Relief Society.[181]

"Nothing Has Been Irretrievably Lost"

Indomitable little Emmeline B. Wells weathered the eleven years of change that marked her presidency and capped her long years of Relief Society service. "She was to meeting yesterday looking very frail and without much pep, however she is still a miracle," Susa Young Gates wrote to board member Elizabeth Claridge McCune on October 18, 1919.[182] During 1920, at age ninety-two, Aunt Em missed only four board meetings. She presided over her last board meeting March 23, 1921. A few days later, failing in health, she moved into the home of her daughter Annie. There she faced one final, painful break with tradition. President Heber J. Grant came, with the approval of the Council of the Twelve, to release her as general president of the Relief Society.

She was astonished and hurt, knowing that Joseph Smith had declared that "like the first Presidency of the church," the Relief Society presidency was "to continue in office during good behavior, or so long as they shall continue to fill the office with dignity."[183]

Counselors Clarissa S. Williams and Julina L. Smith support aging President Emmeline B. Wells as they lead general board to entrance of Relief Society offices in the Bishop's Building. (Courtesy LDS Church Archives)

It was not a question of worthiness, President Grant clarified. The complex worldwide Relief Society simply needed "a person of greater strength of body than our dear 'Aunt Em' can possibly have at her advanced age."[184] Despite their age and ill health, however, none of her predecessors had been released.

Already ill, and wounded by this final change, Emmeline failed rapidly. She died April 25, 1921.

Emmeline B. Wells had with difficulty relinquished cherished traditions during her presidency, but she had helped Relief Society hold fast to its initial inspired purposes. She merited and received an abundance of honors and accolades for her lifetime of service and achievement, but perhaps she herself wrote in 1902 the most fitting epitaph for her eleven-year presidency: "History may not have preserved it all, there may be no tangible record of what has been gained, but sometime we shall know that nothing has been irretrievably lost."[185]

PART TWO

CHARITY NEVER FAILETH

CHAPTER 7

"RELIEF" BECOMES
"SOCIAL SERVICES"
1921–1928

When Amanda Bagley, Cottonwood Stake Relief Society president, attended Relief Society general conference in the fall of 1921, her heart resonated to a challenge from the new general president to provide better care for babies and their mothers. Amanda had lost her first baby at birth; two women in her neighborhood had died in childbirth. Now President Clarissa Williams was announcing a plan "to establish a maternity home in Salt Lake as a sort of experiment, and later, if this is successful, to extend the work by establishing similar homes in various centers."[1] President Williams noted that the plan, though approved by the First Presidency, was "premature and indefinite at present"; Amanda, however, was galvanized to immediate action.

With President Williams's approval, Amanda Bagley proposed to her stake president, Uriah G. Miller, that the Church purchase a home and convert it into a maternity hospital to be operated by the Cottonwood Stake Relief Society. The proposal was a bold one—it was just twenty-seven years since the Deseret Hospital (1882–1895), operated by Relief Society, had closed for lack of funding.

The prayers and enthusiasm of the women prevailed. The Presiding Bishopric and the First Presidency authorized purchase of the Neil McMillan home and property—a "cool, quiet, restful location"—at Fourth East and Fifty-sixth South in Murray, Utah.[2] Cottonwood Stake Relief Society sisters rallied to provide funds, furnishings, and supplies for the new hospital, and by December 10, 1924, it was ready for the formal dedication by Elder Melvin J. Ballard of the Council of Twelve Apostles.

Since there were no funds for salaries at first, Mary F. Greaves and Agnes M. Merrill volunteered free nursing service. Amanda and her counselor did the washing until a laundress could be found. Some board members worked at the hospital without pay for weeks at a time. By modern standards the ten-bed hospital was unimpressive and patients were slow in coming, but after the initial struggle for acceptance, it was well patronized. President Clarissa Williams's original intentions "to encourage motherhood and to make it possible for women in child-birth to have good care at reasonable rates" were fulfilled. The hospital charge for the standard two-weeks' stay was forty dollars; the doctor's fee was thirty-five dollars, five dollars less than for a home delivery.

In 1926 Sister Bagley, in an eloquent plea, asked the Presiding Bishopric to approve an extension to the south of the residence, which had proven to be inadequate. Babies had to be bathed in the kitchen, she pointed out, and the cook objected. Her request was granted, and the $7,500 addition included a new delivery room, nursery, isolation room, and wards. After Sister Bagley's release, other stake Relief Society presidents managed the hospital, and thousands of mothers and babies benefited.[3]

Amanda Bagley and her sisters represented the best of the 1920s "new woman": capable, concerned, willing, and able to use political and institutional means — as well as do a hospital's laundry — for the community's benefit. They were the steady undercurrent of a decade more often remembered for its superficial froth.

Concern for Children and Their Mothers

Clarissa Smith Williams was herself in the twentieth-century mode, capable and knowledgeable. Her executive ability had complemented the literary and spiritual qualities of President Emmeline B. Wells for over eleven years in the Relief Society general presidency; before that, she served nine years as general treasurer. She was the first general Relief Society president born in Utah, and was called to her position by Heber J. Grant, the first church president born in Utah. They represented a new generation of leaders, businesslike and innovative, willing to adapt old programs and introduce new ones to fit new needs.

Clarissa graduated in the first class of the University of Deseret (later renamed the University of Utah). She supported her missionary husband, William Nugent Williams, by teaching school in Parowan. He later became a successful businessman and political leader in Salt Lake City, and she managed their eleven children

Relief Society general president Clarissa S. Williams, photographed with her own children and grandchildren, admires one of the infants whose health she worked to assure. (Courtesy Eva Darger Bennett)

and hospitable home with the same gracious efficiency she would show as president of the Relief Society.

A step-granddaughter of Bathsheba W. Smith, Clarissa had begun working as treasurer in Aunt Bathsheba's presidency when she still had school-age children. Upon receiving the call, she firmly told her sister and the presiding priesthood authorities, "You might call me to have a conference with you in the late afternoon, and I want you to know that during school days I intend to leave my office just before 3:30 p.m. I have three children yet in school and I want to be home when they arrive."[4] Her continuing concern for children and their mothers would lead her to direct that the interest accrued from the Relief Society wheat fund be used for maternal and child-welfare projects, including the Cottonwood Maternity Hospital. Wheat that had once fed disaster victims was now sprouting in a more versatile form — money. The new president was quick to see its potential: ward and stake societies would receive the means, as well as directives, to take part in the proliferation of social service activities that characterized the Williams administration. These innovations took root in the prewar years and held steady against a drastic change in the general temper of the times.

World War I had interrupted the so-called Progressive Era and introduced a conflict almost as disruptive as the war itself: old values versus a new cynicism. Prewar idealism gave way to disillusioned isolationism, get-rich-quick schemes, and finally a financial crash in 1929 that heralded the beginning of the Great Depression. Material prosperity did not last; neither did such apparent moral victories as the prohibition of liquor, for which Relief Society and other women's organizations earnestly campaigned. "Modern" young women wore short skirts, bobbed their hair, and asserted their right, like men, to drink, smoke, and sow wild oats, as well as to vote. In the Church, the Social Advisory Committee of the General Boards redoubled its efforts to protect young Latter-day Saints from the evils of the day, encouraging wards to promote recreational activities for youth and cooperating with community agencies in anti-tobacco campaigns and measures toward motion picture censorship.

After the passage of the Nineteenth Amendment to the U. S. Constitution in 1920, women who had concentrated on its passage found themselves with a right to vote but bereft of a unifying cause. A small activist group, the National Women's Party, tried to mobilize feminist interest by persistently introducing in Congress an equal rights amendment to the Constitution, but it won little support. Other women's groups, more interested in protective laws for women in industry, opposed the amendment vigorously. The conflict contributed to a general disenchantment with grand solutions to society's ills. By and large, activist women turned their attention to improving their own communities with the help of their newly won vote—not simply in isolated volunteer efforts, but also in connected and cooperative ways. The same would be true of Relief Society.

Due in part to the energy of the nation's new female voters, the Progressive Era's vision of poverty slain by science made headway despite the frivolity and corruption of "the roaring Twenties." The professionalization of social services nationwide, new networks of cooperation among voluntary organizations, and such federal laws as the Sheppard-Towner Maternity and Infancy Protection Act encouraged community health-care projects in which women took particular interest. As one of three women in the Utah House of Representatives and chairman of the public health committee, Amy Brown Lyman, then general secretary of Relief Society, sponsored the bill by which Utah became eligible for the Sheppard-

Towner monies.[5] Part of her motivation may have come from her memory of her older sister Laura and five other young mothers in Pleasant Grove, all of whom died of "childbed fever" within two months in 1882. Her own mother had been an invalid for years following childbirth.

Relief Society involvement in maternity care was traditional. Midwifery and nursing classes in the nineteenth century and the 1916 "Baby Day" and the 1918–19 "Children's Day" anticipated the more extensive activity sparked by the sale of the wheat in 1918. The centralized wheat trust fund of $412,000 was earning interest in a general fund at the Presiding Bishop's office. At the Relief Society general conference of April 1922, President Clarissa Williams proposed that the interest be turned over to the general board for financing "a movement in the interest of maternity and motherhood throughout the Church."[6] She expressed dismay that Church vital statistics showed 58 deaths of mothers and 751 deaths of babies in 1922.

Although she was later disappointed that the Presiding Bishop was sending the wheat fund interest directly to ward Relief Societies instead of to the general board, and that the money was not earmarked for maternal and child health care, President Williams remained undaunted. In the October 1923 Relief Society conference, she reminded the sisters, "it is the advice and counsel of the General Board that this [wheat] money be reserved for maternity and health work." She "regretted" that some wards had used the wheat interest for meetinghouse repairs. Instructions to the stakes clearly admonished use of the wheat fund interest for health and maternity purposes.[7]

Many stakes and wards accepted the general board's challenge. They prepared maternity loan chests (bedding and other necessaries for home delivery), maternity "bundles," layettes, and other items for needy mothers or for home deliveries. Relief Societies in Utah, Idaho, and Arizona cooperated with state boards of health, helping with "clinic and health conferences, follow-up work, and the purchase of equipment."[8] By 1924 John Wells of the Presiding Bishopric could credit Relief Society for a decreased death rate among Latter-day Saint children under age five — five hundred lives saved in one year.[9]

In the fall 1921 Relief Society conference, Lucy Woodruff Smith reported that in the European missions almost every branch had a "maternity chest," adding, "the need of it is very great there."

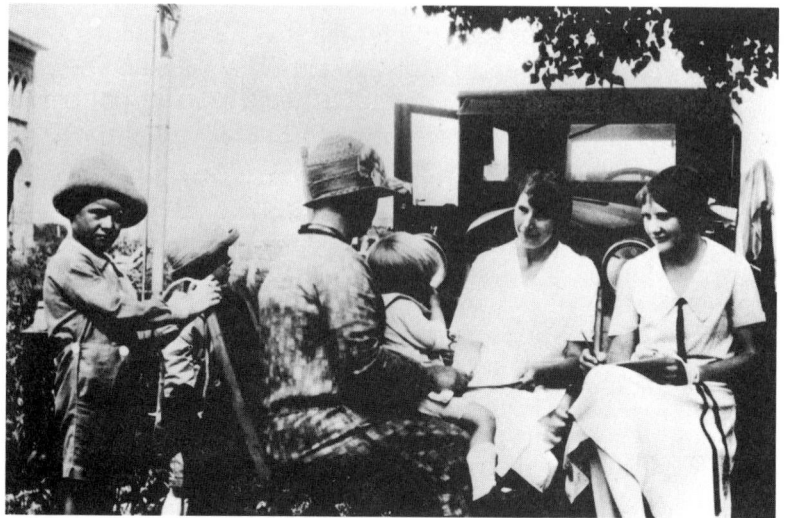

Relief Society nurses or assistants interview a mother while her children wait for examinations at one of many day-long health-care clinics sponsored by local Relief Societies. (Courtesy LDS Church Archives)

Relief Societies were extending help to war-torn Europe as late as 1923, when "five sacks, representing 141 pounds of clothing and $9.30 were given by the [Burton, Idaho] ward to be sent to the German saints."[10]

Stakes also held health clinics for babies and preschool children, often in cooperation with local health agencies. The 1925 Tintic (Utah) Stake report was typical, describing two "child welfare conferences" held in Eureka and Goshen with the Red Cross and other organizations. Children had their teeth examined and were weighed, "then turned over to a nurse and physician where a thorough examination was made along the most approved lines. In Eureka 112 children were examined and but 25 of that number were free from defects." The examining physicians then talked with parents about needed treatment.[11] Some stakes assisted in paying for hospital or nursing care, arranged for weekly health lectures, and provided clothing and equipment for children's hospitals.

With or without wheat interest, and without funds from the Sheppard-Towner Act after its expiration in 1929, health projects moved forward with enthusiasm, both in Relief Society and among other women. They were part of an era of cooperation among welfare agencies, of hope that the social evils of the day, like the enemy in the Great War, could be overcome by allied forces and with the help of God.

Giving Service in Communities

In some ways the decade of the 1920s was a high point of Relief Society involvement in the community. True to Relief Society's charitable commitment, its officers, both general and local, were greatly concerned about community economic problems. Despite a burgeoning national prosperity, farm income in Utah was depressed during the early 1920s. Over 50,000 people left the state, and one-third of the rural population quit their farms. The smaller the town, the greater the proportion of young people who left. Populations shifted from farms to cities. "Transients," those looking for work, often lost and lonely, burdening relief agencies, were considered "a very pressing social problem everywhere."[12] The Relief Society Social Services Department employment bureau, established in 1922, helped some, but in general, the society advocated prevention, careful casework, and, if possible, the return of transients to their home county welfare agency.

"When communities become stricter in these matters," explained the general board, "the transient problem will not be so tense."[13] Casework and thorough inquiry into the relief applicant's background were hallmarks of the society's Social Service Department, which had been working with public and other private welfare agencies since 1919. Most of its work was limited to investigating cases of Latter-day Saints, but the department's interaction with community agencies spread its influence much farther. For example, it provided lectures on social welfare to public health trainees at both the Latter-day Saint Hospital and the University of Utah Medical School.

Training programs also increased the ability of Relief Society workers to give community service. So great was respect for the competency of the caseworkers that in Garfield, Utah, the Smelter Relief Company, the Utah Copper Company, the Utah Copper Bank Club, and the Bingham and Garfield Boarding House all put their relief work under the administration of Relief Society in preference to other agencies.[14]

Addressing needs farther from home, the Relief Society, Young Women's Mutual Improvement Association, and Primary joined in 1921 to help fill a Red Cross request for 15,000 children's garments for Herbert Hoover's European Relief Fund. The Utah chairman—the only female state chairman in the United States—was Annie Wells Cannon. She and Louise Y. Robison, who chaired the work in Salt Lake County, drew sister Relief Society members into the project. One can only guess at the number of articles of clothing they made for children they would never see. In addition, Utahns contributed $91,000 "for the relief of the starving children of central Europe."[15]

Local Relief Societies also sponsored such endeavors as free Red Cross home nursing courses, Red Cross and Christmas Seal charity drives, Red Cross clothing drives for Armenia and for the needy in the Far East. The Lost River Stake reported cooperating with the American Legion and the Ladies Aid of the Baptist Church in conducting "a charity organization whereby people in need will be helped."[16]

Other stakes reached out with neighborly gestures of relief. A 1921 report from Liberty (Salt Lake City) Stake notes "Cash Disbursed" to the Jewish Relief Fund and to the County Infirmary for holiday gifts of "120 bags each containing a glass of jelly, an orange, an apple, cake and candy." Both the general board and local stakes contributed Christmas gifts for the Goshute Indians in 1925. The Relief Society in Parowan, for instance, gave toys to children and gifts to older Indians, with eight "comfy layettes for the prospective mothers."[17]

In supporting community service and cooperating with other relief agencies, the Relief Society was following President Heber J. Grant's lead. When a controversy arose over contributions to a Young Women's Christian Association fund drive from the general board or its members, President Grant expressed his opinion plainly. According to the Relief Society minutes, "While President Grant does not approve of the attitude of the YWCA and YMCA toward our Church, still he feels that since we are all living and working in the same community and will all be benefited by the general and special welfare work that is being done, it is only natural that the people of the Mormon Church should contribute to outside organizations." Not only had the Church then made a contribution, President Grant had also made one personally.[18]

Support for "outside organizations," however, had some limits. A Presiding Bishopric letter dated May 5, 1922, informed church leaders that the First Presidency had decided "the Church machinery or organizations shall not be used for the purpose of collecting money by what is usually known as drives, unless consent is first obtained from the Presiding Bishopric." Accordingly, President Williams declined Relief Society responsibility for a drive for

Armenian Relief Society sisters pose in front of the Hill Cumorah backdrop with mission president Joseph Wilford Booth and his wife, Rebecca. The Booths helped refugee members organize a Relief Society in Aleppo, Syria, in 1922. (Courtesy LDS Church Archives)

old clothes to be sent to the Near East. "This has been a great disappointment to Mrs. Cohen, who had planned to turn the work over to the Relief Society entirely," was the sympathetic comment in the general board minutes.[19]

The headquarters' decision did not prevent charitable outreach, however. The plight of Armenian refugees, victims of genocide in the Turkish Empire, was much in the news in 1921. Relief Society sisters in Idaho supported Near East relief in their stakes, gathering clothing for Armenian refugees in Constantinople. When Joseph W. Booth was called in 1921 to reopen the Palestine-Syrian Mission, he found the Armenian Saints in Aintab, Turkey, "so destitute that one branch had been wiped out. The Saints were eating grass and leaves." After evacuating the Saints to Aleppo, Syria, he reorganized the branch, with a Relief Socity of about thirty members. He noted the charitable work of these sisters, even in their poverty: that at the Relief Society meeting "all present except eight were barefooted. Yet they had come as relief workers, to help others less fortunate than themselves." Inspired by President Booth, these sisters put on a feast for their undernourished fellow refugees and sewed clothing from the hundred yards of cloth purchased by the mission president.[20]

Relief Society and Social Services

The most active Relief Society program of the 1920s was the Social Service Department. Amy Brown Lyman remembered that "as the work of the welfare department grew, and additional workers were employed, it was moved from the general secretary's office and given a separate department" in 1921.[21] Sister Lyman, supervisor of the department, had high professional standards and did much of the work herself, keeping a pencil and pad of paper beside her bed for midnight writing. Her helpers were few but well trained for that day when social services and welfare were comparatively new fields. From 1921 to 1924 they reviewed Latter-day Saint families applying in Salt Lake County for mothers' pensions. Between 1921 and 1928 they also investigated Latter-day Saint families for the Salt Lake County Charity Office (about 330 in 1928 alone), and from 1919 to 1928, for the Community Clinic (7,300 in all).[22]

In wards and branches, welfare still focused on the traditional good works of caring for the sick, sewing for the poor, collecting donations, and other charitable Relief Society activities. The Relief Society Social Service Department, however, was "not a relief-giving agency," according to Sister Lyman, but "primarily a service department." Its emphasis was on "the study of family situations, the making of plans and budgets, the organizing of relief where LDS families were concerned, and the training of workers."[23]

The Relief Society general board conducted its first training course in charities and relief work at the 1920 Brigham Young University summer session. The six-week family welfare institute was taught by Amy Brown Lyman. Follow-up local courses taught by members of the Social Service Department varied from two days to several weeks. In 1925 the general board conducted an even more ambitious twelve-week institute in its offices in the Bishop's Building, with thirty-seven persons registered. Amy Brown Lyman, assisted by Cora Kasius, Lydia Alder, and other board and staff members, supervised field trips to public facilities dealing with problems of health, crime, and dependency, and studies of books by national authorities on social problems. Speakers came from agencies concerned with social work, such as the Utah State Board of Health, the U.S. Veterans Bureau, the Metropolitan Life Nursing Association, the New York Psychological Corporation, and the American Smelting and Refining Company. Elder Stephen L. Richards of the Quorum of the Twelve and Bishop David A. Smith of the Presiding Bishopric also addressed the group.[24]

Further training of Relief Society workers continued in institutes held in various localities. By October 1925, some 1,880 persons, representing one-third of the Church's ninety-four stakes, had participated in courses ranging in length from a few days to six weeks. Priesthood leaders came too; bishoprics and the presidency of the Palmyra (Utah) Stake, for example, "all entered enthusiastically into the proposition of a course in charity and relief work," and the bishops voted to take Sister Lyman's six-session, twelve-hour course along with Relief Society workers.[25]

Relief Society sponsorship of this semiprofessional training demonstrated its organizational vigor. Amy Lyman was determined to carry out her mandate from President Joseph F. Smith, to "adapt modern methods to Church charity work."[26] A total of 126 institutes were held, the last being a special wartime session in 1942. In all, over four thousand Relief Society women participated.[27] These trainees, social service aides, were to assist ward Relief Society presidents in dealing with actual cases. This assistance would involve detailed investigation of family situations. Such work was extremely sensitive, so it is not surprising that at first some presidents hesitated to use aides, a situation that Amy Lyman deplored.[28]

Unlike the aides, the Relief Society Social Service Department had a solidly established status. In addition to organizing relief for LDS families and sponsoring training institutes, the department provided such services as finding employment for girls and women, a service it had offered through its employment bureau since 1922. The purpose was "to place L.D.S. girls in suitable L.D.S. homes and in other reputable places of employment." By 1930 nearly 12,000 women and girls had been placed, mostly in domestic service.[29]

The department also provided adoption services. On April 26, 1922, Relief Society was designated as the church agency for child placement.[30] After a child-placing statute was enacted in Utah in 1923, the department was licensed regularly by the State Board of Health.[31] It would be the official adoption agency of the Church for forty-seven years.

Amy Lyman was determined to professionalize the department's services. The appointment of Genevieve Thornton as supervisor of casework in 1927 boosted this effort. Her qualifications were impressive for this early period—a master's degree in social service administration from the University of Chicago, a residency at Hull House, and job experience at the United Charities of Chicago. The Relief Society general board and the Presiding Bishopric covered one department's administrative expenses, which included a small emergency fund and the modest salaries of ten or twelve staff members. In 1929 such expenses were less than seventeen thousand dollars.[32] The department operated on a frugal budget and the dedication of its determined workers. But they showed the same devotion to caring for the needy as the early Nauvoo sisters had done by succoring the poor with food and blankets.

At a local level, the neighborly Nauvoo methods of giving aid also continued to flourish. The flavor of regular Relief Society work in a small rural ward is well preserved in a 1952 description recorded in the Gooding (Idaho) Ward history. "The work of Relief Society was the same then as it is today," the chronicler wrote, referring to the 1920s. "We made comforters, canned vegetables and fruits, helped the needy. . . . At the time of a death in the ward, the presidency would make the temple clothes, help prepare the body, and dress it, as well as doing all they could to bring comfort to the bereaved family. Many emergencies, small and large, for which we can call a doctor today, often had to be taken care of by those faithful Relief Society sisters."[33]

Not all activities were solemn, however. The Gooding Ward recorder also described a Relief Society anniversary celebration: "The 17th of March was an outstanding day of the year; a dinner was served to all married couples of the ward; we had a program, and the balance of the evening was spent in dancing." The term "married couples" was undoubtedly casual, for Esther Williams Anderson, ward Relief Society president in Gooding about 1927, was herself a widow with four children, twelve registered Jersey cows, a flock of chickens, a cat, and a horse named Monte. She wrote cheerfully of her Relief Society activities: "Our ward was very scattered and our sisters had quite a little difficulty in getting to meetings, but neighbors were good in bringing each other, so we had a very good attendance generally, everyone interested and lessons always given very good and discussions were interesting, reports satisfactory, and socials well attended."[34]

Esther Anderson also contended with transportation difficulties. Her travel to town, about eight miles, was first by surrey or buggy, then by automobile. Her daughter Mildred described the old car as a "Model T Ford with the side curtains, poor headlights, no heater, hand-operated windshield wipers," certainly a far cry from the car of today. "The radiator," she went on, "was frozen up most of the time in cold weather and so were the occupants of the car. When it snowed, we had to hang our heads out of each side of the car to even find the road."[35]

A cheerful independence often characterizes reports from the stakes and missions. Josephine C. Kimball, president of the St. Joseph Stake Relief Society in southeastern Arizona, reported in a general Relief Society conference, "In some instances we have had charity and social service rendered, but we do not need a great deal down there where we are all poor alike."[36]

Good cheer in abundance likewise radiates from a report of a Relief Society fund-raising "Annual Day" in "far-away Tonga," which began at nine in the morning with "a very spirited meeting of all the Relief Societies of Vava'u conference," and ended at midnight. The daytime activities included talks on "topics of vital interest, such as the responsibility of motherhood, the value of child training, etc." Evening festivities featured dancing, a band concert, an auction of "useful articles," more dancing, and then a gargantuan feast of twelve hogs, four or five dozen fowls, "a motley collection of yams, taro, breadfruit, kape, sweet potatoes, steam cooked on hot coals, covered with banana leaves and earth," followed by "cakes, puddings, pies, tarts, scones, and whatnot."[37]

Relief Society members promoted scientific methods in humble but effective ways. Some local societies, for instance, enlisted in the cause of preventive medicine and launched "Swat the Fly" campaigns. "Insist also on the cleaning up of corrals and other breeding places for flies," President Clarissa Williams advised. "Flies could be absolutely eliminated if all members of every community would unite in their destruction." "Each president worked diligently along this line soliciting help from the schools and other public institutions, all of which cooperated willingly in the undertaking," reported the South Sevier (Utah) Stake. In Minneapolis a pageant featured "an act in which two Relief Society teachers visited a home and led a discussion on the importance of the extermination of the house fly."[38]

Nor did the general board give up all of its direct relief projects.

Aid to malnourished children included sponsoring summer trips to the country and taking over the Salt Lake Civic Center milk fund project, with the approval and financial help of the Presiding Bishopric.[39]

From 1923 to 1934 the board operated a storehouse in the Bishop's Building for the renovation and distribution of used clothes and household furnishings. The 1930 annual report listed thirty-seven types of items, ranging from shoes to stoves, with a total of 2,320 items dispensed and a cash balance of thirty-two cents. The storehouse, which had first been opened on Richards Street by the five Salt Lake City stakes in January 1922, might be considered a forerunner of Deseret Industries, established in 1938 as part of the Church welfare program.

Another type of help to individuals began in 1923 when the general board established loan funds and memorial grants honoring past Relief Society general presidents. Amy Lyman enumerated their purposes: "for the encouragement of the art of writing, for salvation for the dead, for assisting in educational work, in nursing and in public health nursing." Each grant was appropriate to the accomplishments of the president being honored: Emmeline B. Wells Fund, for upper division women at Brigham Young University; Zina D. H. Young Nurse Fund, for undergraduate nurses; Clarissa Williams Public Health Nurse Fund; Bathsheba Smith Temple Grant; Amy Brown Lyman Social Service Loan and Scholarship Fund; and Louise Y. Robison Loan and Scholarship Fund.[40] The board also sponsored the Amy Whipple Evans Women's Fellowship in social work.

These funds, which encouraged scholarship and professional training among LDS women, were terminated in 1966 because of "the inadequacy of some of them to meet the needs for which they were established, . . . lack of use of others, and lack of control on still others due to their having been transferred by the General Board to other institutions for administration."[41]

Efforts in Correlation

The 1920s were dynamic years in the entire church. The moral fabric of the western world may have been unraveling, but the Church was led by a president who set the tone of hardworking, practical optimism. Under the leadership of President Heber J. Grant, the Church moved carefully into the mainstream of national and international activity.

The emphasis had already shifted from "gathering the Saints" to "strengthening the stakes of Zion" abroad. On October 18, 1921, the First Presidency announced yet again that missionaries were no longer to encourage immigration to Utah, where work opportunities were scarce. Elder David O. McKay, accompanied by Hugh J. Cannon, circled the globe that year, visiting the Saints and gaining a worldwide perspective. Three new temples were completed between 1919 and 1927: in Mesa, Arizona; Laie, Hawaii; and Cardston, Alberta, Canada. Relief Society women, true to their initial purpose of fostering temple building, raised twelve thousand dollars in a "penny fund" drive for the Hawaiian and Canadian temples.

Internally, the relationships of the auxiliaries and the priesthood quorums were under close scrutiny, as efforts to correlate their diverse but often overlapping programs continued. The First Presidency requested a year-long study of the situation by the combined Church Correlation Committee and the Social Advisory Committee of the General Boards, and in April 1921 they submitted their report. Several changes were recommended: the Sunday School was to be in charge of gospel teaching; Primary and the MIAs, to be in charge of recreation; Relief Society, to assist the bishop in welfare matters; and correlation committees in wards, stakes, and at the general level, to coordinate all programs.

Apparently the recommendations were premature and too drastic, for the committees were released in 1922 with commendation for their efforts and the First Presidency's concluding comment: "We feel . . . that the existing quorums and associations are competent to plan for and execute the activities of each."[42] Not until the end of the 1960s would correlation councils become standard and the auxiliaries be firmly encompassed by the priesthood structure.

One recommendation stuck, perhaps because it was basically in effect already: welfare was the business of Relief Society, although in each ward, the bishop headed the enterprise. The Presiding Bishopric elaborated on the relationship in a 1921 circular letter issued to bishops and stake presidents and reprinted in the *Relief Society Magazine*. The letter recommended that each bishop "should be personally acquainted with the conditions of the poor in his ward, and the Relief Society should cooperate with the Bishop and act under his direction in caring for them." To facilitate cooperation, bishoprics should "invite the Relief Society officers to meet with them monthly, or oftener if necessary, to consider general relief work."[43] While responses to a questionaire sent by the general board to local units at the end of 1921 "showed a great lack of cooperation" in holding these meetings, the trend toward closer collaboration had clearly been set.[44]

At the general level, amiable cooperation flourished between the Presiding Bishopric and the Relief Society officers, no doubt strengthened by the proximity of their offices in the same building. The bishopric's circular encouraged that cooperation, as did the correlation movement toward strengthening the priesthood line of authority and meshing it with the work of the auxiliaries. When the letter was reprinted in the *Relief Society Magazine*, an introduction to it asserted, "It is comforting to the faithful officers and teachers of the Relief Society to find their position and relationship to the bishops clearly and generously recognized."[45]

Opportunity for enhancing the working relationship of Relief Society to bishops was created in 1921 when the Presiding Bishopric encouraged societies to cease building their own halls and move into the ward meetinghouses, where a Relief Society room would be provided for them. Speaking in a 1924 Relief Society conference, President Williams added a caution: the sisters "should not be contented with the darkest room in the basement."[46] Leaving behind both the burden and the independence of maintaining their own meeting places, the sisters gradually accepted the opportunity for ward unity. A historian of the Vernal (Utah) Second Ward mused upon her ward's move from their own hall into the ward meetinghouse: "And now we are established in our apartments it is light & airy the sunny part of the house, we do not have to worry about the coal bill, or the light statements & we can work early or late, but we feel like a girl living with her Mother-in-law."[47]

The change did not come overnight; some of the halls continued to be used for many years. The Washington (Utah) Ward Relief Society renovated its hall in 1924, adding electric lights, an organ, "sixteen chairs, a rocker, six hymn books, and a white stand for use in laying out the dead." And as late as 1941 the Santa Clara (Utah) Ward reported, "The Relief Society house is being renovated. So far it has been reshingled, painted and a cupboard built in the northwest corner. . . . We have bought new curtains and when all is complete we will have a nice home-like place in which to meet." The women also gave the bishop forty-five dollars toward remodeling the chapel, although they did not choose to hold their meetings in the new Relief Society room there until 1949.[48] In Manassa, Colorado, where payments were completed on a new Relief Society building in 1926,[49] the sturdy brick building was still occupied in 1982—by Bishop Larry Smith and his family. As late as 1990 some Relief Society halls were still in use, but not by Relief Societies. The sisters had built well and had moved when they were ready. The fact that at least some could do so on their own timetable is evidence of good relationships with priesthood leaders.

Changes in Visiting Teaching and Curriculum

During the 1920s the general board modified the visiting teaching program to reflect a more professional approach to the charitable work of Relief Society. Traditionally, visiting teachers had both collected donations for the poor and divided and delivered to needy families the money and commodities collected. This method of delivery, functioning outside priesthood channels, was discontinued in 1921 upon the recommendation of correlation-conscious Amy Brown Lyman. The Presiding Bishopric's 1921 circular had defined the relief channels thus: "The ward Relief Society will labor under the direction of the Bishop and will be his chief aid in caring for the poor and unfortunate. The Relief Society teachers should visit every family once a month, or oftener if necessary, and report immediately to the President of the Society cases of need, poverty, distress or sickness. The President, under the direction of the Bishop, will see that relief is promptly given."[50]

However, the same letter reminded visiting teachers that their basic responsibility to render compassionate service was unchanged: they were to continue "visiting the sick, comforting the poor and those who are in distress, praying with them and administering such spiritual comfort as the Gospel of Jesus Christ alone provides." The introduction to the letter in the *Relief Society Magazine* emphasized Relief Society's traditional values and methods: "We may learn some things from modern efficiency experts; but we will never improve on the faithful and gentle sympathy extended regularly from neighbor to neighbor by the unselfish women of the Relief Society System."[51]

Visiting teachers continued to collect donations for the ward Relief Society charity fund, from which Relief Society officers drew money for emergency relief and other purposes. But more attention was now given to reporting such activities to bishops and working under their direction. Closer cooperation between Relief Society and the bishops led to a more unified welfare program in the wards and paved the way for the shift to a church welfare program in 1936.

At the general level, the Presiding Bishopric often stood as an advocate for Relief Society against encroachments on its charity funds. On one occasion, the Benson (Utah) Stake Relief Society was "assessed" twenty-five hundred dollars for a high-school seminary building. The Relief Society president referred the problem to the Presiding Bishopric, who took it to the First Presidency, who responded that "the duties of the Relief Society were to care for the poor, and all other similar beneficent work, and not to pay assessments for building schools, and similar purposes."[52]

Though they might occasionally balk at assessments, Relief Society sisters seemed happy to help furnish and maintain church buildings through voluntary donations. For example, sisters of the Rexburg (Idaho) Stake donated ten cents each to help pay for the pipe organ in the stake tabernacle; two years later they gave forty dollars to pay off the balance owing on the tabernacle's grand piano.[53] Yellowstone (Idaho) Stake Relief Society members raised a thousand dollars for their stake tabernacle and twelve hundred dollars to furnish six rooms at the Idaho Falls LDS Hospital.[54]

Promoting greater unity and professionalism, the general board began in 1921 to provide a uniform message for each pair of visiting teachers to take into the homes they visited. The teachers' stewardship had subtly shifted to a role more in keeping with social service principles: providing education as well as aid. Beginning in the November 1921 issue, the *Relief Society Magazine* included a "Teacher's Topic" each month. The topics were identified as optional until 1923, when they became required. Such topics as "Subjects Vital to Home and Community" and "Fundamental Traits of Character That Secure Real and Lasting Happiness" pointed a new direction for visiting teaching. By 1928 the need to help visiting teachers be more effective brought about the inauguration of a monthly training meeting.

After the introduction of the uniform course of study in 1914, production of Relief Society lessons for many years would be a general board responsibility, as it was in other auxiliaries. Under the direction of the general presidency counselor in charge of education, general board committees (or specialists chosen by them) prepared the lessons, which were published as "Lesson Guides" in the *Relief Society Magazine*. Not until 1944 would lessons have to be cleared by another church agency. Thus, in the 1920s lessons could directly support the general board's current interests, limited only by general guidelines from such agencies as the Committee on Priesthood Outlines and Courses of Study. The most fruitful field for Relief Society at that time was clearly social welfare; even the literature courses reflected that concern. In 1928 the course consisted of six modern plays, "each emphasizing a social problem of a nature that we trust will be interesting to Relief Society members." Included were Henrik Ibsen's *The Doll's House* and George Bernard Shaw's *The Devil's Disciple.* [55]

The 1920 White House Conference on Children, as well as Relief Society's child welfare work under the Sheppard-Towner Act, profoundly influenced the content of the social service lessons. Over half of the courses during the 1920s dealt with children and their problems from a social science perspective. "While the home economics lessons of 1915–1919 had emphasized the culinary aspects of homemaking," comments Carol Clark, "the 1919–1929 lessons discussed child rearing and how mothers could more effectively deal with the issues of human relations specifically in their homes." [56]

Without the resources of professional church writers, Relief Society often relied on respected non-Latter-day Saint professionals for curriculum content. In the 1920s this was particularly true of the social service course. However, even when an entire non-Mormon textbook was recommended for course study, the "Lesson Guides" in the magazine contained only carefully selected portions. Sometimes original material was rewritten, as was the textbook for 1927, *The Challenge of Childhood*, by Ira S. Wile. In any case, curriculum decisions rested with the Relief Society general board.

Teacher training, however, was centrally administered for all auxiliaries from 1919 to 1928, first by the Correlation Committee, then by the Church Board of Education. "Fathers, mothers of children, grandparents, guardians, men in active priesthood quorums, women in auxiliary official positions . . . in short the whole membership of the Church need to teach," encouraged the Relief Society in promoting the general course in 1919. [57] After 1928, as the correlation movement declined, the auxiliaries assumed responsibility for training their own teachers.

In 1921 the need of women to be educated beyond the boundaries of church and home also began to appear in Relief Society lesson materials. A social service lesson for June 1921 declared firmly that "every girl should have ambition to qualify in two vocations — that of home making, and that of earning a living by other means whenever occasion requires." Justifying its position, the lesson continued: "An unmarried woman is always happier when following a vocation in which she can be socially serviceable and financially independent. In no case should she be constrained to accept an unworthy companion as a means of support. Any married woman may become a widow at any time; property may vanish as readily as husbands may die. Thus any woman may be under the necessity of earning her own living and helping to support dependents. Why should not she be trained for the duties and the emergencies of life?"[58]

Official Relief Society sponsorship of careers for women centered on training in health and public welfare, a traditional Relief Society stewardship. After the Relief Society Nurse School was discontinued in 1920, a one-year course for nurses' aides was offered at the LDS Hospital in Salt Lake City.[59] Students, recruited by local Relief Societies, paid no tuition and received a small monthly wage for their services. After eleven months, they returned home, where they had to give one month (or 124 hours) of charity nursing service, usually under the direction of the local Relief Society president, to complete the one-year course.

In May 1922 the Primary general presidency asked if nurse's aides "might spend a portion of their time in training at the [Primary children's] convalescent homes," to eliminate the expense of hiring nurses to assist the home's supervising nurse. They also asked for help from the Relief Society Social Service Department, as "many social problems have already arisen in connection with the home." The requests were granted.[60]

Forty-six nurses' aides graduated from the course over four years before the program was discontinued February 1, 1924, because of objections from the National Hospital Training School Rating Bureau. The one remaining tie was a lecture course in social welfare, inaugurated by Amy Brown Lyman, for graduate nurses at the LDS Hospital and for nurse trainees at other hospitals. The series continued until 1940. After a graduate school of social work was established at the University of Utah, the Relief Society Social Service Department became an in-service training center for the students.[61] Support for Red Cross home-nursing courses and encouragement to women to seek professional training in nursing skills continued to be voiced by Relief Society leaders.

Thus ended official Relief Society sponsorship of training for health-care professionals, which had lasted nearly a quarter of a century. Once again, a need had been perceived and met; then the means were relinquished to other agencies which benefited from Relief Society's pioneering efforts and continuing support. In the stakes and wards, however, maternal and child welfare clinics continued to spring up, with the help of wheat-fund interest.

"Positions of This Kind Should Rotate"

When President Williams's health began to fail in 1928, she recognized the problem her inactivity created for the society. "I wish I felt better," she wrote to Amy Brown Lyman from her summer home in Emigration Canyon east of Salt Lake City. "I am not worrying about Relief Society matters. I can't, and I am trying not to worry about myself."[62] When her health continued to decline, she became the first general president to ask for her release. Her attitude toward release was a courageous break with the tradition of lifelong presidency to which her predecessor, Emmeline B. Wells, had clung so tenaciously. Speaking to the last general conference of Relief Society over which she would preside, Sister Williams said, "You will recollect that it has always been my policy to advocate to you that we do not retain our positions too long, that there are many capable women and that such honor and dignity as comes with positions of this kind, should rotate."[63]

In her short seven years as general president, and in spite of her own ill health, Clarissa Williams led her Relief Society sisters in efforts to make life safer and more healthful for thousands of mothers and children. In Utah alone the society's cooperation with public agencies brought the greatest reduction in maternal and infant mortality rates in the nation; statistics show Utah among the five lowest states in 1931.[64]

During those years, the Social Service Department established its professional credentials. To the credit of inspired leaders, Relief Society carried on a program of intensive training in modern methods of social work, and so prepared a seedbed of trained personnel for the larger church effort to come. In retrospect, this contribution may be as important as the direct relief-giving for which the society is justly honored. In the next decade the society would have not only formidable new challenges but also tempered tools with which to deal with them.

CHAPTER 8

Dark Days – The Great Depression
1928–1940

When Louise Yates Robison was called to be the seventh general president of the Relief Society in October 1928, the Great Depression was only a small cloud on the horizon. The society was, in general, well settled in its social work, comfortable in its community service, and satisfied with the lesson departments. The new executive officers—counselors Amy Brown Lyman and Julia A. Child and secretary Julia A. F. Lund—were all veterans of years of general board service. An era of steady, uneventful progress seemed assured.

The assurance was deceptive, but Louise Robison was remarkably well suited to preside in the hard times ahead. Growing up in a log house in rural Scipio, Utah, she had learned the survival skills of pioneer life; she based on experience her advice to homemakers struggling with meager budgets. Her empathy was practical. When a young, distraught, pregnant, and unmarried woman came to her office for help, the president not only dealt sympathetically and efficiently with her problem but also mended the young woman's torn jacket as they talked. Then she arranged job interviews and gave her money for a hairdo and suitable clothes as well.[1]

"Sister Robison was a humanitarian," recalled her longtime friend and co-worker Belle S. Spafford in later years. "[She] stressed the volunteer compassionate services. 'Go where you're needed; do what you can,' that was her theme."[2] It set the tone for an era marked by Relief Society's responsiveness to community relief efforts, to the Church's new welfare plan, and to the needs of Latter-day Saint women to reaffirm their roots and strengthen their sisterhood.

Sister Robison was an excellent seamstress, having taken a six-month course in dressmaking at the age of fifteen. The Temple and Burial Clothing Department of Relief Society and the welfare sewing programs benefited from her expert interest. Adelia Busch, "ladies supervisor" of the first bishop's storehouse, wrote of President Robison's helpfulness: "Many times when she came to the sewing center, she'd say to me 'You look so tired, come sit down and lets talk it over and see if I can help in some way.' That was heaven to my ears. I always felt a lot better after one of her visits, and a lot wiser, the load on my shoulders didn't seem so heavy."[3]

Both the home-beautification project she instituted in Relief Society and her Red Cross and Travelers Aid Society work expressed Louise Y. Robison's humanitarian convictions. The brief prayer she once introduced as "always kept in my heart" describes well her attitude toward trouble:

> God, give me sympathy and sense
> And help me keep my courage high.
> God, give me calm and confidence
> And please—a twinkle in my eye.[4]

In the quiet first year of her presidency, Sister Robison could hardly have foreseen how much she would need those gifts of sympathy, courage, and good cheer in the decade to come. During the summer of 1929, for example, an editorial in the *Relief Society Magazine* described American society as "this ever-growing, ever-blossoming, surging civilization."[5] Apparently no premonition warned that this thriving economy was about to surge over a cliff.

In the last week of October 1929, western nations plunged into the Great Depression. In the United States, a shaky prosperity built on speculation, a weak banking system, overextended credit, and paper profits collapsed in a stock market crash that would become legendary as "Black Friday." Less than a month later the total loss for the New York Stock Exchange alone was thirty billion dollars; fortunes were wiped out overnight. Bank failures across the country rocketed from 642 in 1929 to 2,298 in 1931.

Small investors suffered with the large, and the Saints were not spared. Family savings disappeared along with big business capital. When the bank in Sugar City, Idaho, failed, the local Relief Society lost all its operating funds. The elderly living on savings were often left with nothing.

Many optimists expected the economy to recover in a traditional cycle, but as factories and businesses cut back or shut down, unemployment spread like a plague. Many women felt lucky to get even a part-time menial job, not only to put food on the table but also to escape from the demoralizing presence of an unemployed husband at home. "The old agitation over a 'career' dies away," pointed out one woman editor, "in a world that is seeking no longer cake and trimmings but the good bread of a daily job."[6]

Utah, already lagging behind the general prosperity of the 1920s, quickly experienced severe repercussions from the crash. Vulnerable exports (agriculture and mining), high freight rates, a high birth rate, and a severe drought in 1931 all took their toll as the economy plummeted. When the depression hit bottom, 35.8 percent of Utah's work force was unemployed.[7] In one Salt Lake City stake more than half of the men were out of work in 1936.[8]

The president of the United States during the early years of the decline was Herbert Hoover. He underestimated the magnitude of the Great Depression and viewed growing unemployment as a temporary emergency that required short-term relief administered through the same private and volunteer organizations that had cooperated so effectively during the postwar decade. But the challenge was massive, the impact worldwide. As historian Arnold Toynbee described the threat, "In 1931, men and women all over the world were seriously contemplating and frankly discussing the possibility that the Western system of Society might break down and cease to work."[9]

Others — Relief Society officers among them — were too busy keeping the system working to speculate about its total breakdown. Almira Rich, the president of the Mount Ogden Stake Relief Society, was the wife of a doctor, mother of seven grown children, clubwoman, and church and civic leader. Herself in secure circumstances, she was increasingly involved in joint Relief Society and community efforts to aid depression victims. In 1931 she was president of the Ogden Central Committee, which distributed food and clothing. By January 13, 1932, she recorded, "the community service had helped 1800 families."[10]

The work took tremendous effort and cooperation, as Sister Rich's journal indicates. On March 7, 1932, she "went down to Community Service to receive clothing gathered by Scout boys . . . called 15 charities to meet Tuesday at 4 o'clock p.m. on planning distribution of clothing." Three weeks later she notes: "flour for unemployed given out through Red Cross for the Government. Mt. Ogden Stake had a list of 125 families." And on April 2, "Have spent most of today on Social Welfare work. Had a dray take the flour allotted to each ward in Mt. Ogden Stake to the house of the Ward Relief Society President. Later came home and did up Saturday cleaning etc. Am very tired tonight."[11]

Relief Society social service aides were available to help busy stake and ward presidents during this stressful time, though Almira Rich does not mention them. She may be typical of overworked Relief Society presidents who either preferred personal effort to delegation or had not learned how to incorporate the available help. At the request of the Presiding Bishopric, in 1930 the general board recommended social service institutes for training local Relief Society workers or aides to assist ward presidents with analyzing needs and resources of specific families and giving general instructions at union (leadership) meetings on "family case work methods." The aides might also assist in contacting county officials and other social agencies.[12] Amy Brown Lyman, counselor in charge of training social service aides, noted that "in some instances, where the Relief Society stake presidency and board have not used the social service aid[e], the Red Cross, and other organizations, have been glad to use her."[13] In the Granite (Utah) Stake, the social service aide helped train priesthood leaders as well as Relief Society presidents, who were encouraged to discuss individual family case problems with her.[14] By September 1932 Dr. T. B. Beatty of the Utah State Board of Health was cited in board minutes as "enthusiastic in reference to the service these women render in the communities where they live."[15]

Relief Society also cooperated closely with local government relief agencies through its Family Welfare (Social Service) Department, which had already served for more than a decade as the connecting link between the Church and community social agencies.[16] Volunteer agencies and government welfare departments struggled together to maintain order against a rising tide of need. Cooperation is evident in the 1931 joint funding by the county charity department, the Church, and the Community Chest of a Salt Lake City warehouse stocked with food, clothing, and coal. The Relief Society Social Service Department investigated needy LDS families and issued warehouse orders for their commodities. The caseload of one worker in the department escalated from seventy-eight families in 1929 to over seven hundred in 1934.[17] Another overloaded worker expressed her frustration with being unable to give more than minimal time to individual cases: "While humanity cries for bread [the social worker] must give emergency orders or even reorders after only a hurried office interview or a volunteer's visit to the home." This was true even though everyone gave "hours of overtime in a determined effort to keep pace with the increasingly heavy load."[18]

That load included psychological stress. Applicants for aid were often pitiful, sometimes angry, desperate, demanding. "It was just a terrible time," remembered Vera W. Pohlman, later general secretary of the Relief Society, as she recalled a crowd entering the state welfare office where she was employed. "They jumped over the railing and tried to upset the files and pushed people around and smashed chairs over desks."[19]

But even in the darkest days of the Great Depression, counselor Amy Brown Lyman retained her faith in scientific social work. Prevention was better than cure, she insisted, and orderly procedure was important. At the October 1932 Relief Society conference she clearly stated the sequence of "responsibility for the care of the poor" established by the Church: first, relatives; second, the county government "which is legally responsible"; third, churches and fraternal groups. Recommending kindness and tact, she nonetheless firmly directed Relief Society presidents to contact the first two groups before dispensing relief. She was equally firm about personal interviews and follow-up, and without complaint worked extra hours herself, often into the night, in order to maintain her professional standards.

Her standards represented the Relief Society style of service: individual, not institutional. Commenting in 1931 on the society's modern methods of welfare work, Sister Lyman explained that it "has no blanket plan of caring for the needy, but aims to treat individuals according to the individual needs, aiming as far as possible to meet the requirements set by standardized social case-working agencies."[20]

The inauguration of President Franklin Delano Roosevelt in 1933 moved the United States toward a "blanket plan" for relief nationwide, realized with the passage of the 1935 Social Security Act. Under Roosevelt, the federal government commandeered the money and the will to mobilize the entire country's resources against the depression.

FDR had pledged "a new deal for the American people," temporary relief on a scale that quickly eclipsed Hoover's one-year appropriation, which had loaned relief funds to states through the Reconstruction Finance Corporation. Soon alphabetical agencies sprang up at the federal level to deal with every twist of the economic tangle. At first the Federal Emergency Relief Administration funded some direct relief as well as offered state governments one dollar for every three they raised for local employment projects. The Roosevelt administration also established the Public Works Administration, the Civilian Conservation Corps, the National Youth Administration, and the Civil Works Administration, succeeded in 1935 by the longer-lived Works Progress Administration (WPA). The agencies invented jobs for millions of Americans, building schools, hospitals, playgrounds, airports, and other public facilities across the country.

WPA funds also subsidized writers, painters, and musicians. A stake Relief Society president in St. George, Utah, Juanita Brooks, recognized the applicability of such funds: she directed the compilation of personal histories of southern Utah pioneers. The resourceful president converted a room in her home to an office and hired women who could type to transcribe the handwritten accounts. Although the monthly wage for the typing was a meager thirty dollars, the money was "a literal godsend" to many, according to Sister Brooks.[21]

The editorial proclamation "1933 a Record Year for Women" was not hyperbolic. Eleanor Roosevelt's gracious and capable example encouraged women's participation in national concerns. In 1933, the *Relief Society Magazine* proudly reported achievements such as Ruth Bryan Owen's appointment as Minister to Denmark, the first woman diplomatic envoy to a foreign government, and Frances Perkins's appointment as Secretary of Labor, the first woman in a U.S. cabinet. That year a Utahn, Dr. Sadie Myers Shelton, was also one of the few women listed in *American Men of Science*. Yet, on the whole, the depression muted women's demand for careers. A Gallup opinion poll asked if wives whose husbands had jobs should work; 82 percent said no—including 75 percent of the women polled. Looking back, one writer summarized: "Although the Depression encouraged innovations in politics and social welfare policy, it also seemed to have a chastening effect on cultural values, calling people back to the tried and true verities of family, hearth, and home."[22]

Because extensive temporary relief measures required the continued cooperation of government and private charitable organizations, Relief Society officers often found themselves involved in the new government programs. In 1934, for instance, Almira Rich,

active since 1931 on the Ogden Central Committee and still stake
Relief Society president, started the new year with a meeting in
her home of the Women's Project Committee of the Civil Works
Administration, which she chaired. She recorded that paying jobs
had been created for over one hundred women through the government's program to provide school lunches to undernourished
children, and thirty-eight more for cooking demonstrators to teach
seventeen five-week courses in "cooking better cheap foods."[23]

Relief Society officers and county agencies continued to col-
laborate, as Almira's entry for October 8, 1935, indicates: "I had
a meeting here at home with County and City Welfare officers also
the Stake Relief Society presidents to consider distributing centers
for Government welfare." According to President Robison, "In
many stakes the County Commissioners have asked our stake [Re-
lief Society] presidents to meet with them, and help them plan
their work for the Winter."[24] The federal government had also
designated the Relief Society Welfare Department a public agency
for distributing state and federal relief, first under the Reconstruction Finance Corporation and then under the Federal Emergency
Relief Administration.[25] Sister Robison herself was the only woman
on the Utah State Board of Public Welfare.

The practical-minded general board's cooperation with county
relief agencies readily expanded to include support for the new
federal programs. General board minutes record counselor Kate
M. Barker's favorable report on WPA adult classes, followed by
President Robison's suggestion that board members support and
publicize the classes, which, she explained, "open fine opportunities for the membership of the Relief Society." The board even
expressed hope that WPA funds might help to build a new detention home for boys.[26] The general board also supported the National Youth Administration, a part of the WPA that supplied
scholarship funds and part-time jobs; Relief Society officers were
alerted in the "Notes to the Field" that needy Latter-day Saint
students could register with the National Re-employment Service
for such help.[27] Apparently the inevitable growth of the government
agencies into a vast bureaucracy and the astronomical multipli-
cation of the national debt were perceived, if at all, as lesser and
distant evils.

Amy Brown Lyman welcomed the new government programs
for her own reasons. "Today with the Government assuming the
great burden of unemployment relief we, with other private agen-

cies, have lightened loads and can therefore devote more time to preventive work," was her sanguine assessment in 1934.[28]

Sister Robison expressed a more cautious view to Relief Society officers gathered in the April 1935 conference. "For ninety-three years Relief Society has been saying that we take care of our needy ones," she said. She felt sure there were still some needy church members in every community who were trying to get along without federal aid, because they had "the spirit of the pioneers." "Encourage your Ward Presidents to see that these people are not allowed to suffer and are not forced to ask for Federal help if you can help them," she admonished the stake officers. Perhaps not wishing to seem unappreciative, she acknowledged, "The Government is now doing a wonderful thing . . . for those who are on relief," but, she added, "I wonder if we are leaving it too much to the Government now."[29] The question remained: how to balance accommodation with independence.

Genesis of the Church Welfare Plan

The government's emergency relief took a new turn in 1935. The Supreme Court struck down the sweeping National Recovery Act that year and cut off direct federal aid to the states for local welfare programs. Instead, a social security bill set up America's first comprehensive welfare system, a permanent federal program of jobs, unemployment insurance, and old-age pensions. It entrenched the federal government in roles that had traditionally been local or private and ended the close cooperation between public and private agencies that had characterized postwar welfare work. Relief Society officers undoubtedly welcomed at least some of these provisions. In place of the money once available through the defunct Sheppard-Towner Act, Title V gave the Children's Bureau a generous $5.82 million for maternal and child welfare, $3.87 million specifically for "crippled children" (a term broadly interpreted by Utah welfare agencies), and $24.75 million for aid to dependent children.

With the advent of a comprehensive social security system, professional social workers employed in newly established state departments of public welfare dispensed government relief funds, and private agencies ceased to function as administrators of public relief. The Relief Society Social Service Department, however, strengthened the direct services component of its work, maintained its employment, adoption, and foster care services, and continued to care for Latter-day Saint transients and cases referred by bishops.

Though fully cooperative with temporary government relief programs, the Church pulled away from the permanent federal system of aid. Instead, church leaders developed their own welfare program, first known as the Church Security Plan. The decision to establish a general church welfare system grew out of the Church's tradition of independence as well as from the depression crisis. The six Salt Lake City stakes had already begun pooling their welfare resources in 1932. Other stakes sponsored similar programs, but most of them relaxed their efforts when federal relief programs appeared. Salt Lake City's Pioneer Stake was still operating a successful welfare program in 1936 under the direction of Harold B. Lee, its dynamic stake president, when he was called that April "to head up the welfare movement to turn the tide from government relief, direct relief, and help to put the Church in a position where it could take care of its own needy."[30] The First Presidency described the philosophy of the new program: "Our primary purpose was to set up, in so far as it might be possible, a system under which the curse of idleness would be done away with, the evils of a dole abolished, and independence, industry, thrift and self respect be once more established amongst our people. The aim of the Church is to help the people to help themselves."[31]

Apparently few, if any, of the top Relief Society leaders realized in 1935 that the Church was about to draw up a grand welfare design that would bring both their social service and compassionate service into a much larger structure. The first mention of the new "Church Security Plan" appears in the general board minutes the week after the April 1936 conference: "President Robison called attention to the message of the First Presidency which had been given during the General Priesthood Meeting . . . [regarding] the Church policy in giving relief and aiding the people. The Relief Society will play a very important part in this work. Sister Robison felt that this was the beginning of a new epoch for Relief Society work."[32]

Relief Society was an integral part of the plan, if not of the advance planning. A member of the general presidency was to attend the weekly meetings of the new Church Security Committee, to "make it possible for the Relief Society Organization to work in the closest harmony and cooperation with the Stake Priesthood Presidents and Ward Bishops in carrying out the details of the program." Furthermore, a special committee of general board members would supervise the women's activities (through the stake Relief Society presidencies) "in such matters as family budgeting, the making of proper family analyses, investigating case problems, recommending assistance, . . . planning a safe canning program, considering ways and means of economical home cooking, sewing and home planning, standardizing women's work centers throughout the various church units, etc."[33]

For welfare purposes the Church organized its 117 stakes into regions, supervised by the General Welfare Committee. Relief Society served in key policy-making positions at this level also. The Salt Lake Region, for instance, formed six task committees in 1937, among them the Salt Lake Regional Relief Society Committee composed of four general board members and all the stake Relief Society presidents in the area. President Robison chaired this group, which formulated "all policies relating to the administration of relief, sewing centers, social welfare, family budgets, conservation of family resources, and contacts with other relief agencies." The committee also directed "all investigation work."[34] At the stake level, priesthood and Relief Society worked together to implement regional assignments. Marian M. Snow recalled that during the initial stages of the new program in the St. George Stake, "There was much trial and error, many long meetings, and many opinions and interpretations; but in it all, the women were loyal and willing."[35]

When the First Presidency presented the main features of the welfare plan at a special meeting for stake presidents and bishops during the April 1936 general conference, two items directly concerned Relief Society officers at the ward level: "Upon Ward teachers and the Relief Society must rest the prime responsibility for discovering and appraising the wants of the needy in the Ward,"[36] and "Every Bishop should aim to have accumulated by next October Conference sufficient food and clothes to provide for every needy family in his Ward during the coming winter. The Relief Society must cooperate in this work by directing and assisting the needy sisters of the Ward in drying and preserving fruits and vegetables, providing clothing and bedding, etc."[37]

While headquarters committees were still formulating policies, the sisters in the wards and stakes promptly began preserving food and providing clothing and bedding. The first summer after the program was announced, several stake Relief Societies cultivated

Sisters in St. George (Utah) Stake, using large metal tubs, can foods over open fire at the Brigham Jarvis home during 1930s. (Courtesy Utah State Historical Society)

city lots and canned their vegetable crops. A future general president of Relief Society, Belle Spafford, remembered picking up windfall peaches and apples with her ward sisters, which they then canned in their home pressure cookers. "We would can the fruits and vegetables working day after day after day," Sister Spafford recalled years later. "Almost before the bottles were cool, some of our finest people were standing in line to take the food. That's the kind of a situation we were up against."[38] Other sisters made quilts and articles of clothing. The Relief Society asked women who put up their own fruit to give every tenth jar to the Church Security Program.

In St. George the women's work director, Verda Seegmiller, oversaw the processing of 4,000 cans of meat and vegetables and 8,000 cans of peaches. She described their inventive method for canning peas: "We first dipped them in boiling water in cotton bags, then for shelling, we ran them through (stem end first) clothes wringers on brand new Speed Queen washing machines." As the pods squeezed through the wringer, the peas would pop out and fall into waiting tubs. "This surely speeded up operations," Sister Seegmiller concluded.[39]

The innovative St. George Stake Relief Society also started a burial clothing project on a ten-dollar shoestring from the stake welfare fund. With donated labor and a good location (the president's home was across the street from a mortuary), the sisters soon had a self-supporting cottage industry going.[40] They also collected used clothing and furnished sewing machines for a sewing center where mothers could come in the afternoon, select clothes to remodel, and receive help in tailoring them to fit family members. "Through this activity, young mothers received some splendid training, besides the lovely pieces they took home for their children to wear," remembered the stake Relief Society president.[41]

Although Sister Robison worried about their being overworked, some leaders bubbled with enthusiasm for welfare work. From Montclair, New Jersey, Leone Amott Rose wrote: "The women here are cheerful, hard working Holland and American converts, with a few of us from Utah. Many of them had never before canned anything—not even a bottle of jam. We have already filled over four hundred tin cans, and we have hardly begun peaches and tomatoes. We sliced our string beans and they are perfectly elegant. Most of the corn is whole kernel style, and, confidentially, it's plenty of work putting up corn, but my goodness it tastes good!" Besides food, the New Jersey sisters gathered "a big trunk full of clothing—mended, folded, listed as to size, etc., and de-mothed." President Rose sums up, "With such co-operation as all my officers are giving me, it is no wonder I am enthusiastic."[42]

Relief Society's energetic cooperation with priesthood officers was also essential to the welfare plan's success. Harold B. Lee explained that "the most important object that is to be achieved by the Church Security Program is the promoting of a spirit of cooperation and unity throughout the entire Church. . . . To the extent that Relief Society Organizations in Wards are operating in cooperation with Priesthood Quorums and Bishoprics just to that extent is there a security program in that Ward."[43]

The priesthood brethren were also admonished that "in this task of coordinating all the units of the Church, the Relief Society marches side by side with the Priesthood quorums. This worthy organization, more than any other, is in a position to render valuable service in the realm of welfare work."[44] Marion G. Romney, then assistant managing director of the welfare program, described the balance succinctly in 1941: "As the bishop is the 'father' of the ward, so the Relief Society may be described as the 'mother' of the ward."[45] Harold B. Lee, quoting J. Reuben Clark, Jr., had used

Ward Relief Society president Erma Clayton picks up food order from bishop's storehouse to deliver to needy ward members in 1938. (Courtesy LDS Church Archives)

the same comparison in 1939.[46] While policy had been set, offices and responsibilities clearly defined, this image of a familiar working relationship spoke eloquently to men and women alike.

The institution of the Church's welfare program would change Relief Society's traditional approach to charitable service in some far-reaching and dramatic ways. The sisters would do much of the work and the officers would be represented on the governing committees. But the society's own traditional charity work would increasingly find its place in the priesthood-directed system, which had been given responsibility for building and managing a vast new empire of farms, factories, and distribution centers. Through all the organizational juggling and individual stumbling that lay ahead, however, priesthood quorum brethren and Relief Society sisters would work together toward the vision of fostering both independence (work, thrift, and self-reliance) and a wholesome interdependence (cooperation, compassion, and responsibility for others). It was a significant step in working unitedly to maintain Zion.

The development of an effective system for administering welfare assistance was the most momentous outcome of the Great

Depression for Latter-day Saints. Other developments in the Church during the depression decade were less dramatic than the institution of the welfare plan but also served to intensify the Saints' sense of community and identity and to strengthen Relief Society. To be sure, missionary work had been scaled back (only 678 missionaries were called in 1939) and no new temples were built during the thirties. However, by the end of the decade a modest but steady increase had brought the membership from 630,000 to 803,000 and the number of stakes from 104 to 129. Relief Society proudly counted a membership of 62,902 in the United States, Canada, Europe, Hawaii, New Zealand, Australia, Tahiti, Tonga, South Africa, and Asia Minor.

Observing the Church's Centennial

The stock market crash of 1929 had little effect on the long-planned celebration of the Church's centennial on April 6, 1930. Though the future was dim, the occasion was too grand, the plans too well made to falter. A centennial pageant, "The Message of the Ages," drew crowds nightly to the Salt Lake Tabernacle for a month.[47] At the April general conference, President Heber J. Grant read a centennial message from the First Presidency "to the peoples of the world," solemnly affirming the gospel's restoration and the mission of the Church. He expressed particular gratitude for the comparatively new miracle of radio, already an important missionary tool.[48]

Other devices for amplifying the human voice perhaps facilitated another innovation: at the previous conference President Grant had called on the presidents of Relief Society (Louise Y. Robison), Young Ladies Mutual Improvement Association (Ruth May Fox), and Primary (May Anderson) to come to the stand and each "occupy a few moments of the time."[49] The three presidents spoke again in the 1930 general conferences.

Relief Society celebrated the centennial with articles in the *Relief Society Magazine* on fourteen outstanding women, symbolic of Latter-day Saint women's achievements during the hundred years. Some stakes prepared "jubilee" boxes and sealed them up as a fifty-year memorial, to be opened in 1980.[50] Other stakes opened jubilee boxes from 1880 in special ceremonies. One such box, containing "packages and mementos, pictures, newspapers and other matters of note of that time," had been placed in the care of the church historian by Sarah M. Kimball, who was serving in the 1880s as general secretary of the Relief Society. Its accompanying message was addressed to the general secretary of 1930: "Hon. Secretary: This is dedicated to you with the fond hope and firm belief you are enjoying many advantages and blessings that were not enjoyed by your predecessors. May God abundantly bless you and your labors." The message was signed by "Sarah M. Kimball, Sec. Relief Society, Salt Lake City, April 1st, 1881."

On April 1, 1930, in a ceremony attended by "a goodly company of Church officials, relatives, and friends or descendants of friends of Mrs. Kimball," Church Historian Joseph Fielding Smith presented the box. "This box has been safely guarded from that day until now," he said, "and my responsibility is at an end." With that he presented the box to Julia A. Lund, Sister Kimball's successor as general secretary of the Relief Society. President Heber J. Grant distributed the small packages of mementos to "those who had a right to claim them" and was pleased to find one from his own mother, Rachel Ivins Grant.[51]

Other historical events provided occasions to celebrate in this otherwise troubled decade. One of the most popular projects of Relief Societies in America in the early 1930s was tree planting in honor of the bicentennial of George Washington's birth.[52] On Arbor Day 1931, President Robison and members of her board joined Utah Secretary of State Milton H. Welling in planting a Norway maple on the State Capitol grounds. The tree also stood "in memory of the sacrifices they [the pioneers] made for us in appreciation for the trees they planted ... and in order that the women who will come after us may enjoy the protection and beauty of this stately Maple."[53] On March 17, 1932, the San Francisco Stake commemorated both the Washington bicentennial and the ninetieth anniversary of Relief Society by planting four pines, five redwoods, and five Japanese cherry trees in Golden Gate Park, where the little group of trees soon became known as "Mormon Grove." The park superintendent, J. W. McLaren, who had arranged for donation of the trees after being briefed on the history and purposes of Relief Society, also provided a flagpole and flag, tables, and benches for the ceremony.[54] In Canada the Taylor Stake adapted the tree-planting project to honor the Canadian Fathers of Confederation by planting 8,192 trees, mostly mountain ash, furnished by the Canadian government. The Alberta Stake Relief Societies chose five elm trees for their tribute.[55]

Another commemorative event was the erection of a Relief

Relief Society general officers — from left, counselors Amy Brown Lyman and Julie A. Child, President Louise Y. Robison, and magazine editor Mary C. Kimball — are photographed in 1933 in front of the new monument marking the site of the Nauvoo store where Relief Society was organized. (Courtesy LDS Church Archives)

Society monument in Nauvoo, the first effort to mark a historic LDS site in that city, in response to an address at a Relief Society general conference in 1932. In speaking to the sisters, Elder George Albert Smith said, "We have been marking the pioneer trails. I may get myself into difficulty by making a recommendation, but I think there is one thing lacking in the City of Nauvoo. There ought to be a monument to the Relief Society in that city."[56]

The proper site for the monument was a matter of debate, finally settled after research in church history showed that Joseph Smith had organized the Relief Society in the upper room of his red brick store, not in the Masonic Hall, as some believed. The site of the store belonged to the Reorganized Church of Jesus Christ of Latter Day Saints, whose president, Dr. Frederick M. Smith, graciously consented to the monument's placement. The foundation of the former building was cleared and landscaped, "giving the appearance of a sunken garden." The unveiling of the monument on July 25, 1933, was attended by many officers from both the LDS and RLDS churches.[57] Appropriately, a great-granddaughter of Emma Smith, Bertha A. Hulmes, unveiled the four-by-eight-foot monument of Tennessee quartzite.[58] On it was mounted a large bronze plaque showing the store in bas-relief and giving a brief history of the Relief Society. A smaller bronze plaque credited the donor of the site. The Reorganized Church later erected a replica of the Joseph Smith store on the original site. The 1933 marker eventually found an honored resting place in

1988 at the entrance to the Relief Society Monument to Women at Nauvoo. A new plaque recognized its historical significance.

The monument fostered new rapport between the Church and the citizens of Nauvoo, where some bitterness against the Church had persisted over the years. The women of the Reorganized Church hosted a luncheon for their Utah guests in the Nauvoo House on the bank of the Mississippi River, and the Unity Club of Nauvoo prepared a tour of Nauvoo and Carthage. It was reported that citizens of Nauvoo and neighboring towns were out "en masse" for the unveiling ceremony. The good feeling that prevailed was a step toward the future success of the Church in restoring the historic riverside area of Nauvoo.

Another significant commemorative event was the fiftieth anniversary of the first general (or "central") boards for the Relief Society, the Young Ladies Mutual Improvement Association, and the Primary Association. The organization of the first boards had taken place on June 19, 1880, at a day-long "sisters conference" in Salt Lake City.

The fiftieth birthday party on June 19, 1930, was only one of a number of cooperative efforts among the three auxiliaries. They had united at both the general and local levels to campaign against the repeal of the Eighteenth Amendment, the prohibition amendment. President Louise Y. Robison of the Relief Society and President Ruth May Fox of the Young Ladies Mutual Improvement Association spoke at mass meetings in Salt Lake City and Provo and also pled against repeal before the legislature's judiciary committee.Ward Relief Society and Mutual workers distributed anti-repeal literature. But President Roosevelt's election promise to repeal the generally unpopular amendment was immovable, and on December 5, 1933, Utah became the thirty-sixth state to adopt the Twenty-first Amendment, which repealed prohibition. An editorial in the *Relief Society Magazine* the following August branded repeal a mistake and the "control systems" a failure, but liquor was back to stay.

The Church subsequently mounted a strong campaign against the use of alcoholic beverages and tobacco. Visiting teachers distributed thousands of pamphlets. The general boards promoted and showed to "a vast number of people" an anti-alcohol film, *The Beneficent Reprobate,* which was purchased from the Young Men's Christian Association. In the April 1936 Relief Society conference, President Robison urged the sisters to work through the schools.

"I believe if the mothers of our communities were to ask that Alcohol Education be taught in the schools," she said, "it would be done."[59] For years the campaign was faithfully promoted in the *Relief Society Magazine* and other church publications. In 1938 the Church appointed a general committee to coordinate all anti-liquor and -tobacco committees at every level, including priesthood quorums and the Department of Education, as well as the auxiliaries that had led the way.[60]

The three auxiliaries cooperated on other projects. Relief Society, for instance, maintained a motherly interest in the children's hospital established by the Primary Association in 1922. Primary President May Anderson appealed to the Relief Society general board in 1936 for help in supplying toys for the children at both that facility and the LDS Hospital. "Sick children require many toys," she explained, and Primary leaders were hard pressed to keep up with the demand.[61]

In the mission field, Relief Society leaders often "mothered" the establishment of Primaries and Mutuals. In 1935, for example, the mission presidents in Europe officially commissioned the Relief Society sisters to organize home and neighborhood Primaries, which often attracted nonmember children and led their families to become interested in the Church.[62]

The European sisters also cooperated in welfare efforts. In Switzerland the eleven hundred Relief Society members in fifty-four branches not only held "successful, well attended bazaars, and branch conferences" but also sent clothing and food to needy Saints in Germany, where unemployment was severe.[63] The welfare of Latter-day Saints of all ages and nationalities was the common concern of the auxiliaries.

In Utah, Relief Society welfare concerns continued to include community service outside the Church Security Program. One community institution that benefited from Relief Society support was the State Training School for the mentally handicapped at American Fork, Utah, which opened on October 5, 1931. As a member of the Utah State Legislature in 1923, Amy Brown Lyman had worked diligently for the establishment of such a school, and she was later one of five members of the governor's commission that chose the American Fork site. Sister Lyman served on the school's board of trustees from its beginning. At Relief Society's general conference in April 1929, Louise Robison thanked the Utah sisters for their help. They had gathered a total of 25,065 signatures to be sent to the legislature. She quoted the Mental Hygiene Society, which said, "Had it not been for the Relief Society's efforts, this piece of work could not have been accomplished."[64]

Private agencies also received some qualified Relief Society support. When civic leaders asked the busy Mount Ogden Stake Relief Society president in January 1934 to serve on Ogden's newly formed Community Chest council, she traveled to Salt Lake to confer with President Robison and Sister Lyman. "They advised me by all means to accept," Almira Rich recorded, "as they considered it an honor to be asked." However, when she telephoned President Robison a week later "regarding our going into the [Community] Chest as a Relief Society," she received "no favorable answer."[65] The society intended to keep on collecting and disbursing its own charity funds.

In the stakes, community service continued side-by-side with traditional Relief Society welfare activities. The presidencies of the four Weber County stakes in Utah enjoyed working together in both areas. They took Christmas gifts to the "old people at the County Infirmary" and attended the church-sponsored Old Folks outing at Lorin Farr Park. They jointly accepted responsibility for distributing used clothing collected by the community welfare organization and unitedly supported the home-products campaign sponsored by the Ogden Chamber of Commerce. At a "home products dinner," awarded to the ward in each stake that had gathered the most labels from home products, Mayor Harmon Peery commented appreciatively, "I have always noticed that you can depend on the ladies of the Relief Societies to put over their work in a big way."[66]

The work of stake Relief Society officers was demanding, but it was sweetened by the sisterly association. Almira Rich's daughter Myrene, who was on her mother's stake board, often served as chauffeur since Almira did not drive. "That's when I learned to appreciate sisterhood," reflected Myrene in later years. "Those wonderful Relief Society sisters had such a good time together!"[67]

The most impressive stake project of these years was the Snowflake (Arizona) Stake's maternity hospital, which opened its doors to the small community on January 3, 1939. The need for a hospital had long been perceived, but the final impetus came at the presidents breakfast of the April 1937 Relief Society general conference, where "a special charge was given Stake Relief Society Presidents by General President Louise Y. Robison . . . to see that practical nurses were available in all the Stake communities; also to provide good maternity care for mothers and babies during confinement." The instructions were "in harmony with the ardent desires of our own Relief Society Stake Board," wrote Lenora S. Rogers, president of the Snowflake Stake Relief Society.[68]

After two years of "patience, perseverance, work, and faith to continue" as well as "the loyal support of the Stake Priesthood Presidency," the hospital began to take shape. The problem of finding a suitable location was solved when Marion Rogers, a stake high councilor and the husband.of Lenora, purchased the former Bank of Northern Arizona building and paid for the necessary remodeling and furnishings. After that, the community rallied behind the project. "Generous donations in the form of dishes, layettes, bed linen, canned fruits, vegetables, honey etc. were made by ward and stake Relief Society organizations, by the County Welfare Board, and by individuals," Sister Rogers reported. The Arizona State Board of Health paid the salaries of several nurses, and the National Youth Administration furnished young people to do the cooking, laundry, and janitorial work.

The stake Relief Society board then embarked on a speaking tour through the wards to convert expectant mothers to the advantages of hospital deliveries – not always an easy task. Sister Rogers remembered, "Our first patient, a stranger in town, needed us and we needed her. She was a good advertisement. She stayed ten days for $15.00, went home well and happy. That first year, 1939, we served 57 patients. . . . The second year, 1940, we served 82 patients, and so on up." For many years Sister Rogers was president of the hospital board, with her counselors as vice presidents. Their interest and influence kept the hospital alive during several funding crises. When a representative of the United States Children's Bureau visited the hospital, he wrote sympathetically in the guest book, "In the pain of constant limitations lies the power of continuous growth." At one point, the Children's Bureau helped fund the hospital's nursing staff of four.[69]

In July 1960 after twenty-two-and-a-half years of service, the hospital, by then under the direction of the Snowflake town council, lost its state license and was forced to close. Summarizing the hospital's accomplishments, Sister Rogers wrote, "More than 500 babies were born there, and the mothers declared they received the best care they had ever had during confinement." The hospital had served the community for long enough to bridge the gap between the time when home births were the norm and when hospital care was both popular and more readily available. As Sister Rogers noted, "The first baby born at the hospital was married and had a baby of her own before the hospital closed. Maybe it filled its mission." She added that when the hospital closed, "we were using our own L.D.S. Registered Nurses and the hospital was self-sustaining."[70]

Reports continued to appear in the *Relief Society Magazine* about community health clinics sponsored, medicine kits created, tonsillectomies arranged, eyeglasses provided, nursing and doctor care subsidized for the needy—but the reports grew fewer as the years went by. After 1939 they ceased almost entirely. Starting in that year, the Presiding Bishopric's office began mailing checks for interest on the wheat fund to the bishops instead of directly to Relief Society presidents. Almost in vain, Relief Society presidents were reminded in a magazine editorial to pick up the checks, made payable to them, and to use the money "as formerly in the interest of maternity and child welfare."[71] This minor inconvenience may have discouraged those welfare projects; use of the funds to buy wheat for church storage was undoubtedly another factor. But it is more likely that needs simply changed with the advent of the church welfare program and World War II. Much had been accomplished, however, in the years when child and maternal welfare was a major focus of the sisters. According to historian Thomas G. Alexander, "Cooperation between the Relief Society and public agencies produced in Utah the greatest reduction in the maternal death and infant mortality rates in the nation. By 1931 Utah ranked with five other states in the lowest group."[72]

New Emphases in Meeting Members' Needs

As work in health care waned, the Relief Society's energies turned to other needs. For women who needed or wanted to work outside the home, the Relief Society Employment Bureau continued to be of service. For a long time the society had sought good positions for women and girls, most often in domestic service as housekeepers, mothers' helpers, laundresses, nursemaids, tutors, and practical nurses. In 1939 the bureau placed an average of 250 such workers every month; 70 percent of them were under thirty years of age.

Few legal or government standards existed for domestic workers at that time, but Relief Society set its own, for both the employee and the employer. Personal interviews with applicants preceded recommendation, and references were checked. Vocational guidance, follow-up, and counseling were also part of the bureau's service.[73]

During the depression years, the society also perceived a need to provide a retail outlet for cottage industries. "In order to do all in our power to strengthen Church Security, an industry, under the name of Mormon Handicraft, has been established," reported President Robison at the April 1938 Relief Society conference. She added with pride, "Thousands of dollars have gone into homes from this enterprise."[74] Handmade items were sold on consignment so the sisters could supplement family income. This enterprise followed the pioneer pattern of women's cooperative stores that Relief Society had sponsored in the late 1800s. Contributors received 75 percent of the selling price and followed the quality standards set by the general board. Although the shop was intended for mature Latter-day Saint women, Mutual girls and Primary children were also eligible to take out memberships and to send their articles to the shop for sale. Later, men and non-Mormons would also become contributors.

Many women learned handwork skills at their ward Relief Society work days, guided by the general board's Work and Business Department. "The objectives of Work and Business are: to sew for the needy, to be thrifty and industrious, to help one another, to satisfy a social hunger, to magnify Relief Society values, to fill our homes with beauty, to increase attendance, to make everyone happy, and first and last to sew for the needy," Lotta Paul Baxter of the general board told stake leaders gathered for the Work and Business Department of the April 1932 Relief Society conference. The objectives were a mixture of the grand and the practical; their implementation was uneven. Stakes and wards were on their own in determining the work-day program, the general board acting as a clearinghouse for successful ideas and providing some guidelines. These stressed advance planning, variety ("so that all may participate"), informality, and sewing for the needy or for fundraising.[75] In the Liberty and Ensign stakes in Salt Lake City, for example, attendance was increased by "programs on Vocabulary Building and Correct Speech."

Sister Robison continued to emphasize the charitable aspect of the work meetings. Through the *Relief Society Magazine* she editorialized in 1936, "While we appreciate the excellent cultural departments which many of the organizations have inaugurated for their Work and Business periods, we call attention to the fact that the origin of Work and Business in our Relief Society was to care for those . . . in need." Gaining skill with one's hands was desirable; clothing the poor was essential. "Let us not in our joy in mental activities lose sight of these things," she pleaded.[76]

Others perceived a closer link between "mental activities" and charitable endeavors. "In addition to its welfare work," commented Amy Brown Lyman, "the Relief Society has a second well-established department which cooperates closely with the welfare department. It is the education department with a uniform course of study for the benefit of members. These two departments— education and welfare — react most favorably and beneficially upon each other."[77] A good example of how these two major aspects of Relief Society work benefited each other is the Amy Whipple Evans Fellowship established by Relief Society in 1937 at the University of Utah's new School of Social Work. The board's desire for a high level of scholarship is reflected in one of the grant's provisions: "Applicant's intention shall be to secure a Master's Degree in Social Work, research work to be available to the Relief Society General Board."[78]

As the press of immediate relief needs diminished after 1934, even work and business meetings sometimes took on an educational aspect, despite Sister Robison's warnings against replacing sewing with book reviews. When Relief Society produced its first official manual for "work day," *Handicrafts for Everywoman* by Glenn Johnson Beeley, its stated purpose was "to show how, in a simple way, and at little expense, the manual skill and the latent artistic tendencies of the average woman can be made to serve a beautiful purpose, not alone in her duties as a homemaker, but also in the development of her own personality."[79] The overarching purpose, even of handicrafts, was personal development.

With heavy emphasis on social service values, lesson writers continued to look for the best among secular authorities, as well as within the church. In the November 1937 conference, President Robison, who promoted learning from community agencies in addition to joining with them in relief work, specifically mentioned agricultural colleges, county agents and demonstrators, and state health departments as sources of "expert instruction," particularly in the homemaking arts. John Galsworthy's play *Justice* was selected for the literature course because "perhaps we have no other modern playwright who has given so much intelligent attention to social problems as has John Galsworthy."[80] *The Child: His Nature and His Needs*, published by the Children's Foundation, was used in Relief Society classes and found its way into many Latter-day Saint homes. Writers of the social science lessons also utilized booklets from the Third White House Conference on Children, convened by President Herbert Hoover in 1930.

But the use of secular texts posed a problem. "It is very difficult to find a scientific book which does not have statements or material which would conflict with the conception of the Latter-day Saints in reference to certain fundamental principles of faith," commented board member Inez K. Allen during a board discussion. She cautiously recommended Dr. Harry Overstreet's popular book *Influencing Human Behavior* as one that contained "less objectionable material . . . for the work of the Relief Society Social Service lessons."[81]

Even "less objectionable material" brought forth objections from the field, and the general board had to defend its policy in a bulletin to the missions, stating that "the General Board does not accept all opinions set forth in such books, and that they are used for the good which can be taken from them and which is beneficial and helpful."[82]

The board did not always try to avoid difficulties; sex education was recognized as an essential part of mothers' educational responsibilities. A child guidance course for the missions included a lesson on "Sex Education" in 1938, and the *Relief Society Magazine* recommended a book to help young mothers answer their children's questions "honestly and frankly." The book was *New Patterns in Sex Teaching* by Frances B. Strain, described as "a dignified volume that can be a lantern in the hand to every intelligent and progressive parent."[83] The magazine also published articles from time to time urging mothers to instruct their children adequately in what was considered a delicate subject.

Relief Society libraries were an educational project of the 1930s, when enforced leisure due to unemployment was considered a problem. Books of general interest were stocked, as well as those being studied in Relief Society. A 1934 conference report on a survey that revealed that over 80 percent of stakes had at least one ward with a Relief Society library concluded with this plea: "How about a resolution? 'Less time consumed in making pies, pickles and preserves, more time spent with poems, paragraphs and pages.' "[84]

President Robison also had a strong personal interest in the Burial Clothing Department. She listed this continuing Relief Society stewardship as one of the three main accomplishments of her decade in office, the other two being the *Relief Society Magazine* and the Mormon Handicraft Shop.[85]

The fifty-cent annual donation from each sister for temple work was discontinued in 1929. As an earlier correlation committee had suggested, such work was better left to the Genealogical Society. Still, local societies' enthusiasm for temple work burned as brightly as ever. Reports of temple activity abound in the *Relief Society Magazine*'s "Notes from the Field" during the 1930s, often revealing both social and spiritual reasons for the popularity of "temple excursions." Twenty-five sisters from the Eighth Ward Relief Society in Salt Lake City's Liberty Stake arrived at the Mesa Temple to be greeted by President Udall and "the temple workers . . . waiting for the sisters on the temple steps." After holding a testimony meeting and doing temple work "for the Lamanite sisters," the Salt Lake group toured the Indian reservation and returned home via Death Valley. "The whole excursion was wonderful," concluded the reporter.[86] Relief Society officers in St. George went regularly to the temple there and met after the session "in an upper room for a brief prayer meeting," noting "a great spiritual uplift and unity from these experiences."[87]

Support for temple work was not limited to temple trips. Sewing projects were also popular. Relief Society sisters in the St. Joseph (Arizona) Stake, for example, furnished the Arizona Temple with "a beautiful bridal outfit made for the brides of this stake to wear when they are married in the temple."[88]

Surprisingly, the depressed economy also prompted some temple work projects. In 1935 the general board joined with a stake Relief Society in Salt Lake City to contribute $350 for temple work by the unemployed. This project may have spurred a 1939 priesthood directive to stake presidents, bishops, Relief Society presidents, and genealogical committees: mission and "charity" names waiting for donated work were to be given to worthy members in every ward "who, because of physical handicap or age, are not laboring for the assistance their ward is now giving them." The Relief Society was singled out to "make a special effort to promote the project." And, significantly, the Relief Society was given the responsibility of finding and recommending the workers, with the bishops' approval. The Bishops' Executive Committee announced the appointment of Nettie F. Yates to supervise the temple-work project, which, in addition to providing useful work, was designed to "stimulate spirituality."[89]

Relief Society continued to foster other spiritual and social development. Music as a means to both was a special interest of President Robison. During her administration the world-famous "Relief Society Singing Mothers" choral groups were established.[90] In the depths of the Great Depression in 1931, Relief Society choristers were admonished: "Try to establish in the hearts of our sisters this idea, this desire—Hear Music, Make Music, Enjoy Music. Let us all remember there are no age limits to music—that music is the real fountain of youth. Music is a sacred, a divine thing that lifts us up to God. It helps us to feel His glory."[91]

That admonition could have come straight from President Robison, who particularly loved the music of the human voice. Her daughter recalled, "She would almost always sing or occasionally whistle while working." As she said many years later when the Singing Mothers were organized, "A singing Mother makes a happy home."[92] The exclusive nature of the name of the choruses did not seem a big problem, since most of the singers were indeed mothers. However, the Oslo Norway Relief Society, with many unmarried members, chose to call their choral group the "Singing Sisters." The original title designated not only the local groups but also a central chorus, which performed for several radio broadcasts and was made up of singers from Salt Lake City wards under the leadership of Charlotte O. Sackett.[93]

Successful stake music programs abounded. One stake in central Utah featured a chorus in every ward, all taking turns performing in stake-sponsored meetings of ward workers, which, it was reported, "creates a spirit of friendly rivalry." For special occasions the choruses united as "The Relief Society Singing Mothers of the South Sanpete Stake."[94] As an added incentive for young mothers to attend, a Sanpete ward "Junior Chorus" furnished music on the social service lesson day. When the Bear River Stake Relief Society in northern Utah sponsored a temple excursion, the Garland Ward brought along a "large and enthusiastic" group of Singing Mothers to furnish the music for the morning meeting.[95] For many years the standard Singing Mothers dress consisted of white blouses and dark skirts; President Robison felt that most women could afford such an outfit.

Singing Mothers groups were popular abroad. In Germany, the sisters memorized the words of all their songs and their singing was "much above the average chorus group," according to a report from the German-Austrian Mission. At the suggestion "that they work on a Relief Society Song," they responded, "We would like a song of our own."[96] The institution of Singing Mothers itself had become a song of their own that could be sung worldwide.

Twelve hundred Singing Mothers from ninety stakes and three missions sang at Relief Society general conference on September 20, 1937, to inaugurate the drive for 100,000 members by Relief Society's centennial year, 1942. At the end of 1937 membership stood at 75,064, over half of which was in Utah. The drive was launched with a slogan contest, with a ten-dollar prize awarded to the composer of the winning entry: "Members Old, Members New, One Hundred Thousand by '42."[97]

Another innovation, inaugurated in 1936, was an annual "Daughter's Day." Once a year mothers were to invite their daughters to a meeting "to see the possibilities and the beauty in Relief Society." The purpose was frankly recruitment of younger members; the slogan suggested by the general board was "Recruiting the Ranks." These Daughter's Days were enjoyed for a number of years.[98]

Daughter's Days, Singing Mothers, temple excursions — convivial activities such as these no doubt dispelled some of the worry of adverse economic circumstances. Yet even more compelling than the Great Depression, the threat of another world war haunted the 1930s. It lurked in every meeting agenda of the National and International Councils of Women and shadowed every hopeful view. The fiery old fighter for women's suffrage, Carrie Chapman Catt, put the question squarely to the 1933 Second International Congress of those councils: "Will your generation find how to abolish depressions? If you do, you will begin with the greatest cause of them, and the greatest cause of a depression is war." If the question was evaded, promised Mrs. Catt, "it will leave civilization hanging on a dead bough, over a fire of brimstone."[99]

Her message ended grimly: "We have not learned to keep the peace between individuals or between nations." Yet the hopeful and determined stance of the International Congress was that "these problems can and must be solved. . . . Women, as fully as men, are confronted with the task of shaping the institutions of social control."[100]

Louise Y. Robison attended the meetings, which were held in Chicago, along with other general board representatives of Relief Society, the Young Ladies Mutual Improvement, and the Primary associations. Such famous figures as Jane Addams of Hull House, Secretary of Labor Frances Perkins, and Mary R. Beard, world-renowned historian, were also present. President Robison counted it a signal honor that she was asked to conduct the morning session on July 18. She came away committed to the common cause of peace.

The ICW conference, held in conjunction with the Century of Progress Exposition in Chicago, had a large exhibit in the Hall of Social Science. A sixty-foot mural pictured one hundred years of "woman's march toward education, temperance, peace, and the entry of woman in business and professional fields." The activities of the Relief Society and Young Ladies Mutual Improvement Association appeared in three large books on women in education, social service, and recreation. In a poster display at the Palmer House, Relief Society showed its work in social welfare, education, health, and civic activity.

During one of the sessions, held in the Court of Honor at the Exposition's Hall of Science, the assembled congress listened to 250 Singing Mothers broadcasting from the Tabernacle in Salt Lake City. Announcing the concert, Richard L. Evans spoke eloquently of the progress made by women: "Woman has taken her rightful place. . . . The Century of Progress may claim forever one achievement of transcending greatness—a man's world has become a world for men and women!"[101]

Unlike the special International Congress in Chicago, the Tenth World Congress of Women held in Paris in 1934 was a regularly scheduled meeting of the ICW. President Robison was again a delegate. En route to France she visited Relief Societies in England—the first time British sisters had welcomed a general president of their society. The hopeful theme of the ICW meeting was "A better understanding among nations and outlawry of war."

But war was far from effectively outlawed when the ICW Golden Jubilee convened in 1938 in Edinburgh, Scotland. Peace was the chief concern of the nine hundred delegates, who included Amy Brown Lyman and Zina C. Brown. "There was probably not a single session where [peace] did not come up in one connection

Members of Prague Branch Relief Society were photographed with Amy Brown Lyman (seated center) during her visit to Czechoslovakian Mission, May 4, 1938. (Courtesy LDS Church Archives)

or another," reported Sister Lyman. "At the opening meeting there was a plea for peace in the various speeches. . . . At the last session there was expressed, in no uncertain terms, whole-hearted opposition to all war, and horror at modern methods of warfare of turning the heavens into hell."[102]

Thirty-one countries were represented at the ICW Golden Jubilee. Two were conspicuously absent: Germany and its conquered satellite Austria. The time was July 1938—less than one year and two months from Hitler's invasion of Poland and the start of World War II. The heavens were about to be turned into hell.

CHAPTER 9

SISTERHOOD AND SERVICE
IN A WORLD AT WAR
1940–1945

Amy Brown Lyman took office as the eighth general president of the Relief Society on January 1, 1940, three months after the start of World War II in Europe, and relinquished her position on April 6, 1945, just five months before the war's official end. Her entire administration was bounded by the restrictions, frustrations, and heartaches of that global conflict.[1] Sister Lyman's years as president, however, seem almost an epilogue to her monumental Relief Society service. For over thirty years she had served as general board member, assistant secretary, director of the Social Service Department, general secretary-treasurer, assistant business manager of the *Relief Society Magazine*, founder-teacher of Relief Society's social service training institutes, director of the women's auxiliaries in the European Mission, and first counselor in the general presidency. Her affiliation with professional and government organizations had expanded Relief Society's field of service. Her insistence on professional standards of social work had added a new dimension to Relief Society's concept of charity.

Sister Lyman's devotion to social work was part of her religious faith. Indeed, "religion and true social service" were to her "almost one and the same thing." Salvation was their common aim: "To save and rescue human beings is the strongest motive one can conceive, and this is a religious ideal. It is one of the ideals set up by the Prophet Joseph Smith for the Relief Society. It is also the chief object of social work."[2]

As the active director of the women's auxiliaries in the European Mission from 1936 to 1938, she had extended to her sisters there the vision of Relief Society. Thanks to her efforts, sisters

The newly sustained Relief Society general presidency sits for formal portrait: front, counselor Donna D. Sorenson, left, and President Amy Brown Lyman; back, general secretary Vera Pohlman, left, and counselor Marcia K. Howells. (Courtesy LDS Church Archives)

abroad as well as those at home were better prepared for the terrible challenges ahead. Her affection for them is evident in this tribute from her autobiography: "I have visited in their homes, slept in their beds, and eaten at their tables, and have thus learned of their beauty of character, their unselfishness, their understanding hearts, their faithfulness and their sacrifices. I honor beyond my power of expression this great sisterhood of service."[3] A world at war would greatly need both the sisterhood and the service.

Significantly, the last official act of Louise Y. Robison's retiring board had been to approve support for the Finnish Relief fund on December 27, 1939. The Soviet Union attacked Finland on November 30; desperately outnumbered, the Finns would surrender the following March. Meanwhile, their civilian population was suffering. A letter from the general board to Utah area Relief Society presidents explained the need and asked them "to be responsible for the collection of funds within your own groups" to be sent to Relief Society headquarters.[4] By January 11, 1940, Relief Society had collected $2,642.58 for the State Finnish Relief Committee.[5] This sad prelude to the fierce needs of global conflict presaged Relief Society's heartening response.

Adjusting to Troubled Times

World War II lasted officially from September 3, 1939, when France and England declared war on Germany following Hitler's invasion of Poland, to September 2, 1945, when Japan formally surrendered to the Allied Forces. For six years in more than seventy countries in every part of the globe, men, women, and children struggled, fought, and sacrificed in the most complex and devastating war the world has ever known. At its height in January 1944, a *Relief Society Magazine* message from the general board mirrored the anguish of those tormented years: "On the threshold of a New Year, Relief Society women, with the rest of mankind, face a troubled world — a world of turmoil, sorrow, and anxiety. War with all its attendant evils, horrors, and sacrifices is still raging; the innocent as well as the guilty are participating in it. Sorrow and death have entered many homes, and the end is not yet."[6]

After the swift subjugation of Poland in the fall of 1939 and a deceptive six-month pause, Hitler's *Wehrmacht* overran Denmark, Norway, Holland, Belgium, and France in the cataclysmic spring of 1940 and stood poised to invade England. "It is terrible to experience a war," wrote a Relief Society president in Holland to her brother in Salt Lake City after her country's surrender. "Any moment the sirens would scream when enemy aircraft approached. We had to find shelter in our homes or go to shelters, which have been built in large quantities in Holland." Perhaps tempering her opinions to avoid censorship, she continued, "We are now under German occupation. They are friendly to us Dutchmen and we adjust, because it is better this way than to have all that bloodshed."[7]

After war in Europe broke out, German submarines menaced American shipping, and most Americans sympathized with Great Britain and the subjugated countries. But in the United States the sentiment for neutrality was strong. "This government should hold aloof from any participation in wars on foreign soil," stated a Salt Lake *Tribune* editorial on August 29, 1939. The *Deseret News* was also judiciously isolationist. President J. Reuben Clark, Jr., first counselor in the First Presidency, denounced the growing conflict in Europe as "an unholy war . . . a war for empire."[8] He was not alone in this estimate of the situation. Yet many of the General Authorities also feared that Nazi domination of Europe was the "unholy" prospect.

As opinions differed even within the Church, the First Presidency prayed in October general conference for peace and brotherly love. When Amy Brown Lyman and her counselors, Marcia Knowlton Howells and Donna Durrant Sorensen, issued their first New Year's message as the Relief Society presidency in January 1940, they too included a plea for compassion: "To women elsewhere in the world has come this past year war and turbulence, death and sorrow, which are the aftermaths when the inhabitants of the earth take up arms one against the other. In our prayers that ascend daily let us not forget to remember womankind in foreign lands."[9]

The 1938 Relief Society statistics (the last available from Europe until after the war) had counted 2,230 members in Germany—more than in any single U.S. state except Utah, Idaho, Arizona, and California, more than in Canada, more than in Great Britain, more than in all of Mexico and Central and South America.[10] Impossible to dismiss as enemies, these German members posed a painful moral dilemma.

Then in 1941, with one lightning stroke, Japan unintentionally welded together all factions, forging the United States into a single national will—to win the war. Beginning at 7:55 A.M. on Sunday, December 7, 1941, Japanese planes bombed Pearl Harbor, destroying 347 planes and 18 ships, and killing 3,578 American military personnel. The next day President Franklin D. Roosevelt declared war on the Axis powers—Japan, Germany, and Italy.[11] The U.S. "arsenal of democracy," already in production, spun into high gear, and for the next four years the war would dominate every aspect of American life. Not, assuredly, as it did in the devastation on the war fronts in Europe and the Pacific, but inexorably and profoundly.

An immediate wave of alarm swept the Pacific Coast, which Japan was expected to invade. Enemy submarines were reported off the California coast—waiting, it was rumored, for signals from their countrymen on shore. To its later discomfiture, the government evacuated approximately 122,000 Japanese to "relocation camps" in the interior. Over half were American-born citizens. Canada also "relocated" about 23,000 Japanese from its west coast.[12]

What their European brothers and sisters had endured, and were still enduring, could await American families. California seemed the most vulnerable coastline. In an attempt to "prepare the sisters of the area for any eventuality," the Relief Society sent board member Leona Fetzer there to conduct two social service institutes. The head of the Red Cross in the Pacific area also came to assist at these two-week courses, held first in Oakland and then in San Francisco. Sister Fetzer reported that "the sisters of the wards and stakes were consistent in attendance in spite of the bitter, penetrating cold of that January." Her aim was to teach basic procedures for "rendering assistance . . . in urgent or other circumstances."[13]

After Pearl Harbor, most church programs took on a wartime emphasis. With the advent of food rationing, victory gardens became the preferred landscaping for the beautification program. The anti-liquor and anti-tobacco campaigns refocused on protecting the health of Latter-day Saints in military service. Full-time missionaries served only in North and South America, but young men and women in the armed services became unofficial ambassadors of the gospel, and in 1943 the Church organized the LDS Servicemen's Committee, headed by Elder Harold B. Lee.

Efforts to strengthen family life became more urgent as the war fragmented families and uprooted church members from familiar neighborhoods. Even in North and South America, where no battles raged and no bombs fell, family life was under attack. Millions of homesick men swarmed into military camps to be trained and shipped overseas. Many would never come back. It was patriotic to fill the absent men's places in the factories and offices. In the United States five million women were in the work force by 1943, some working up to eighty hours a week. It was also considered patriotic for women to entertain enlisted men at USO canteens, to give them one last fling. Some married in haste. Church officials worried about the increase in immorality. "Why should we fight against the tyranny and shackles of nations," asked Elder Spencer W. Kimball in a Brigham Young University baccalaureate address June 4, 1944, "and at the same time remain in bondage individually to sin?" He was disturbed by "the open lewdness of soldiers and girls" he had seen in his train travels.[14]

The war also accelerated the movement of young people from rural areas to cities, further contributing to the problem. Characteristically, the Church's women's organizations took a practical approach. In Salt Lake City, when by 1942 the Beehive House proved inadequate to the task of providing a suitable home for young LDS working women away from home, Salt Lake Relief

Societies conducted a house-to-house survey of their members, seeking accommodations for those arriving for defense work. The Young Women's Mutual Improvement Association then inspected and arranged placements in the hundreds of homes thus discovered. In December the Relief Society visiting teachers also delivered a "Message of Friendliness and Solicitation to the Mothers of the Church" in every LDS home with girls of MIA age; the message urged mothers to encourage their daughters away from home to attend MIA.

Elder Joseph F. Merrill of the Council of the Twelve chaired the Church No-Liquor–Tobacco Committee, consisting of representatives from the Presiding Bishopric, the Department of Education, and each of the auxiliary general boards. The Mutual Improvement Associations sponsored lively dramatic presentations designed to impress young people with the importance of a clean life.

"Cooperation Urged in Campaign for Non-Use of Liquor and Tobacco," instructed the August 1941 *Relief Society Magazine*. After detailing the efforts of the auxiliaries, the article reminded Relief Society members that the campaign merited "the heartiest cooperation of the mothers of the Church."[15] Visiting teachers were asked to distribute the thousands of pamphlets sent to the stakes. Relief Society members were advised "to take a personal interest in these splendid publications and to encourage all members of their families to read and discuss them." Two years later another magazine article expressed urgency: "The General Board urges mothers throughout the Church to place every possible safeguard about their children. An evil influence is abroad which threatens even the best homes. Social problems, greatly aggravated by the war, demand vigilance on the part of mothers."[16]

Relief Society also complied with requests from the General Authorities to simplify programs in behalf of strengthening families. The lesson courses were shortened to eight months, with opening and closing socials in September and June; union (leadership) meetings, bringing together officers from the wards and branches in each stake, were restricted to September through April, no oftener than monthly. When the First Presidency asked in 1940 for a further reduction in meetings so that parents could spend more time at home, Relief Society officers reduced their stake conference meetings from two days to one. Two years later, in early 1942, the general board discontinued "all institutes, conventions, and stake union meetings," and strictly limited general and stake board member visits to stakes and wards. Relief Society was assigned one evening meeting, the first Sunday in November, which it used for an annual ward Relief Society conference.[17]

In 1943–44, however, despite wartime travel restrictions to conserve fuel, first counselor Belle Spafford (appointed in 1942) and general secretary-treasurer Vera Pohlman were permitted to conduct regional discussion meetings with stake leaders who needed help. The two sisters traveled more than ten thousand miles in nine western states, holding forty-five meetings in 142 stakes and five missions. Some local stake boards found ingenious ways to circumvent travel restrictions in order to help new ward officers. "The board members traveled on school busses, milk trucks, commercial busses, poultry trucks and whatnot, to reach the small Societies, sometimes staying overnight until transportation home could be found," the Snowflake (Arizona) Stake reported.[18]

Observing the Centennial of Relief Society

One casualty of the war was the plan for a grand Relief Society centennial celebration in April 1942. The society's officers were understandably reluctant to abandon their long-cherished dream, even after the United States entered the war. A "great historic and symbolic pageant" titled "Woman's Century of Light" was scheduled for nine performances in the Tabernacle during March and April, and the usual two-day Relief Society conference was to be expanded to three days. In stakes and missions some 1500 Singing Mothers were practicing for a concert in the Tabernacle, and an international exhibit of handwork was announced. As a centennial gift from Relief Society, a bronze campanile, with art panels by Avard Fairbanks, was to be erected on Temple Square to house the Nauvoo Bell.

Following the First Presidency's request for curtailment of auxiliary activities requiring travel, members of the Relief Society general board voted on January 28, 1942, to postpone not only their grand celebration but also their regular general conference in April. They notified stake and mission Relief Society presidents of the change and also asked for postponement of stakewide centennial celebrations as well. Ward observances were permitted, however, and the board suggested that they take place on or near March 17, 1942. Even then, there was a pall over the celebrations. "Our president is very ill; my son was taken prisoner on Wake Island,

Lucile H. Ursenbach, president of the Calgary (Alberta) Ward Relief Society, wields a shovel to plant a centennial tree at the Crescent Road chapel while Bishop Morgan Pitcher steadies sapling. (Courtesy Maureen Ursenbach Beecher)

and it has been hard for me to be a cheerful leader," wrote one woman.[19] Although optimistically described as "postponed," the grand central celebration would never take place. The enormous "flame-proofed" cyclorama curtain, designed to close off the entire west end of the Tabernacle for the pageant, would be stored in the Tabernacle basement and later destroyed in a fire.[20] The campanile would languish unfinished for nearly a quarter century.

The centennial year did not pass entirely uncelebrated at headquarters, however. At eight o'clock on the morning of March 17, radio station KSL in Salt Lake City aired a half-hour "Relief Society Centennial Radio Broadcast," including a greeting from President Lyman.[21] A similar program was broadcast that evening. Just before noon a small group of board members, past and current, gathered in their winter coats and galoshes by the Temple Square greenhouse. There they watched a tree-planting ceremony, which would be repeated in many other places by local societies, repeating the tradition begun a decade earlier. The tree, an English elm selected by the Church Beautification Department, was identified by a round bronze marker reading "Relief Society Centennial Tree – 1942." Local Relief Societies in the United States and Canada planted 874 centennial trees in all, with 779 designated with a round bronze marker from headquarters.[22]

Perhaps the most touching ceremony was conducted by a lone sister in New Zealand whose Relief Society postponed its tree planting because of bad weather. Mission Relief Society president Elva T. Cowley reported that the sister "couldn't let the eventful day pass without planting a tree, so she went to the bush and dug up a young tree and planted it in her own garden, and conducted a simple ceremony by herself."[23]

The general board's tree planting was followed by an impromptu party in the Bishop's Building. Earlier that morning the Presiding Bishopric had presented the Relief Society presidency with a three-tiered birthday cake, crowned by a model of the proposed campanile and surrounded by a hundred candles. An accompanying letter, addressed to "President Amy Brown Lyman and Counselors and the Relief Societies all over the world," reflected the exuberance of Bishop LeGrand Richards and his counselors, Marvin O. Ashton and Joseph L. Wirthlin. "A million tongues today call your name blessed," they wrote. "More than a thousand bishops thank God for your organization. . . . You are angels of mercy to more than that many wards throughout the Church." His tribute concluded: "May we join the multitude this day in congratulating you from the bottom of our hearts for what this hundred years has stood for: — Kindness to the needy, Florence Nightingales to the sick, the essence of culture and champions of refinement in our Church. God bless you and all you stand for."[24]

Personal greetings also went out to the field from Relief Society headquarters. English-speaking societies in the continental United States, Canada, and Mexico received a phonograph record with a centennial greeting from President Amy Brown Lyman and a blessing from President Heber J. Grant. Although "uncertainties of shipping during the present war" prevented wider distribution, the records were a milestone. For the first time Church members could hear the voices of their prophet and the general president of Relief Society, preserved for replaying. A Relief Society counselor in Idaho poignantly expressed how much these centennial efforts strengthened a dispersed flock: "I have played the record a number of times already on my old Victrola, and each time I hear it, it gives me added encouragement. These are such trying days; we need all the inspiration and encouragement we can get."[25]

Far from being frivolous self-congratulation, the centennial record helped lift hearts and establish important historical links. A tiny group of sisters in Gainesville, Florida, reported: "On the night of March 17 we held a social at the home of one of the members. I carried a radio phonograph and the record, and I can't express in words the joy it was to us just to sit and listen to Sister Lyman and the voice of a Prophet of God. It was something we had never dreamed of. We only have six members in our Relief Society. We are very weak, as none of us had even attended a Relief Society meeting before, but we are trusting that we will grow stronger."[26]

Other souvenirs included a plate depicting the original organization meeting; a gold membership pin; a poetry anthology, *Our Legacy: Relief Society Centennial Anthology of Verse*; a Relief Society songbook; and a history prepared by members of the general board, *A Centenary of Relief Society*.[27] The board also published Sister Lyman's autobiography, *In Retrospect*, first in twelve installments in the 1942 *Relief Society Magazine* and then in book form in 1945. Eliza R. Snow's "Sketch of My Life," in eight installments, appeared in the 1944 issues of the magazine.[28] The 1942 covers of the magazine displayed scenes appropriate to the centennial; articles, stories, and poems featured centennial themes.

Although the centennial year did not lack reminders of its historical significance, because the large-scale social celebrations were muted, wards were left to devise their own observances. In the end the ward societies benefited from this cutback. Pageants, musical programs, tree plantings, and sacrament meeting speakers honored the centennial of Relief Society in an outpouring of recognition and involvement greater than any central celebration could have achieved. Significantly, 1942 was also the first year in which annual ward Relief Society conferences were held uniformly throughout the Church and ward Relief Society officers and teachers began to hold monthly preparation meetings.

In the Canadian Mission, wards sometimes combined anniversary celebrations with war work. Sister Johan Mark, whose mother had died in the bombing of Britain, sparked an enthusiastic missionwide project, "Bundles for Britain," in connection with the March celebrations. Twelve-pound bundles of clothing, "filled with warm, clean necessities for the newborn, and for children" were accompanied by postal notes of three dollars to pay for their delivery in Britain. The bundles went out regularly all during the war years.[29]

One part of the grand centennial plan not only reached but also surpassed its goal. The membership drive, under way since

Argentinian women created centennial banner depicting the sisterhood of women. The text under the logo reads, "We, the sisters of the Argentinian Mission, join hands with our sisters of the North in love and appreciation, to commemmorate the Centennial of our Ward Relief Society." (Courtesy Visual Resources Library)

1938, surpassed by 15,000 the 100,000 of its stated aim. The increase was steady: 6,000 new members the first year, 16,000 by 1940. Even so, the whole membership in 1940 of 91,064 represented just over 51 percent of the 177,000 women in the Church. Locally the growth manifest itself appreciably. Hurstville Branch in Australia recorded a "very satisfactory membership increase" from 17 to 24 members. Scipio (Utah) Ward reported that out of 135 families in the ward, 136 women were enrolled—the extra woman being a friendly non-member. In the main, however, the end goal was still afar. "Our task is not complete," said a sister in Ogden, citing remarks by Elder George Albert Smith at a stake conference, "until every woman in the ward is one of our number."[30] The final count, 115,015 at the beginning of 1942, gratifyingly surpassed the slogan goal of "members old and members new, one hundred thousand by '42."

Shifting Emphasis in Church Welfare

In Relief Society sisters' newer role as welfare companions to the priesthood, changes were taking place. One significant change was the demise of the Relief Society charity fund. To President Robison and her predecessors, the charity fund had been both a vehicle and a symbol of the society's commitment to care for the poor as the Prophet Joseph Smith had commissioned the women to do. Although their duty had altered with the advent of the Church Security Plan in 1936, the charity fund was a part of welfare's childhood that was not quickly outgrown. Small changes preceded its disappearance.

In a departure from Sister Robison's policies, the general board in October 1942 recommended that, in addition to maternal and child welfare and emergency relief, charity funds be available for Relief Society welfare projects. The projects, however, were to be service-oriented rather than production-related. Relief Society extended the use of charity funds to the production of quilts in 1943, and to clothing for welfare assignments in 1944.

Gradually President Lyman and the general board reached an inevitable conclusion. "We seriously question whether the Relief Society should continue to collect donations from ward members through the medium of visiting teachers, particularly in view of the apparent lack of need for these funds," stated an April 1944 memorandum from the general board to the Presiding Bishopric. The memo pointed out that the Church welfare program had modified Relief Society's century-old assignment from the Prophet Joseph Smith, and suggested that Relief Society continue to participate "as a service agency" in producing welfare commodities, particularly in sewing and food conservation, and in assisting the bishops "by helping to evaluate and determine family needs."[31]

During a later board discussion of this proposal, Sister Lyman noted the universal tendency "to adhere to established procedures and to accept proposed changes with reluctance." With her own characteristic blend of practicality and vision, she urged board members "to consider objectively any proposals made for changes in Relief Society procedure, saying that if any of the established practices were found to be outmoded, the board should be wise enough to recognize the condition and to plan new procedures."[32]

The collection of charity funds by visiting teachers was discontinued in October 1944. The change necessitated rewriting the directives to visiting teachers: by broadening their work to "a kindly personal friendly interest and responsibility toward the families," the sisters might continue to "give to 'charity never faileth' its true significance." As of January 1, 1945, the society combined the charity fund balance of $150,748.14 with its general fund. Relief Society was no longer to provide commodities or funds directly to needy families; however, its officers would still accept "free will offerings to the Society" and, under the bishop's direction, Relief Society would still provide services.[33]

The general board also pondered the effect of wartime and welfare changes on the visiting teaching program, noting that "visiting teaching has declined, that there is a shortage of women to serve as teachers . . . that a large proportion of women are found to be not at home. . . . Many of them do not want to receive the visiting teachers because they work nights and sleep during the day or are otherwise too busy"—and finally, the clinching problem: "Many teachers feel there is no purpose in the visiting since collections have been eliminated."[34] Giving the teachers a broader vision of their calling became a new priority.

The ward Relief Society president was recognized as the best one to evaluate family welfare needs. Presiding Bishop Joseph L. Wirthlin deferred to her judgment forthrightly: "To my way of thinking, there is only one individual who can go into a home, analyze its needs, and supply them wisely. That individual is one we may choose to call a home manager, a Relief Society president or her social aid. After all, these splendid women have homes of their own, have gone through the experiences related to motherhood and the management of homes."

To illustrate his point, Bishop Wirthlin recalled a personal experience from his days as a ward bishop during the Great Depression: "Some forty families during a week's time applied for assistance. In these families there were many small children. The bishopric concluded that if a few potatoes, a sack of flour, and some coal were sent to these families, their needs would be met adequately." They soon observed that their assessment of family needs fell far short of the mark. After calling in the Relief Society for assistance, the bishop noted, "It was not long before these forty needy families were receiving proper attention." He also recalled that the sisters had "contributed from Relief Society funds periodically in assisting the bishopric to meet the problem of finances." He cautioned, however, "No bishop should feel that he has the right to levy assessments upon our Relief Society sisters without their consent."[35]

Relief Society representatives served on general, stake, and ward welfare committees; in addition, the general presidency sat on some of the major subcommittees of the General Welfare Committee—President Lyman on the Grain Storage and Milling Committee, counselor Marcia K. Howells on the Clothing Committee, and secretary Vera W. Pohlman on the Deseret Industries Committee.[36] As members of these committees, the Relief Society officers not only influenced decisions but also joined the struggle to coordinate and centralize church welfare efforts. More and more the society regarded itself as part of a team effort.

The war also shifted welfare's focus. Both national and church leaders now emphasized unity of effort. No longer was the emphasis on putting the unemployed to work on welfare projects: unemployment had nearly disappeared and the projects were everyone's responsibility, as anyone might need them in an emergency. By 1944, of the 524,915 hours of welfare service given by Relief Society women, only 5 percent were from women whose families were being aided by the bishop.[37]

In a further shift of viewpoint, the employment of women outside their homes was sometimes accepted as necessary to the war effort. A *Relief Society Magazine* article titled "Relief Society at Work" proudly reported a training project in the operation of commercial power sewing machines, pointing out that "many women and girls, after a six-month training course on these machines, are placed in private industry."[38] In Utah the number of women employed in industry reached 60,000 by November 1943 — more than double the 1940 figure.[39]

Mothers with children at home, however, were encouraged to find other ways to help win the war. The Church knew from problems on its very doorstep about the impact of defense-industry employment of mothers. A new branch of over 3,000 Latter-day Saints sprang up in a government housing unit south of Ogden; many of the families consisted of two working parents and unsupervised younger children. One source estimated the number of children at 1,400. At first there was not even a school for them to attend. Complaints about their "getting into considerable trouble" led the First Presidency to call upon the Church Union Board of the Auxiliaries "to formulate plans for the recreational care of these children."[40] The proposals arrived at by the board, on which President Amy Brown Lyman represented the Relief Society, served chiefly to point up the difficulty of replacing the full-time mother as the caretaker of young children.

The *Relief Society Magazine* became a vehicle for encouraging sisters to help in the war effort as homemakers by cooperating with government programs. The magazine quoted extensively from bulletins from the U.S. Office of Price Administration and other agencies. One program, with the catchy label "Food Fights for Freedom," occupied a full page in the "Notes to the Field" section in February 1944. The program concerned the nationwide rationing of basic commodities such as butter, sugar, meat, canned goods, shoes, stockings, and gasoline. It was now patriotic to do without and to share. Frugality and communal effort had always been part of Relief Society's pioneer tradition.

The advent of rationing, travel restrictions, and the massive channeling of production toward the war effort forced the Church to alter its goals for the welfare plan. Even storing food and other commodities had to be justified as "conservation" and not overdone, lest it become "hoarding." One traditional food-storage project had already been successfully revived in Utah: the storage of Relief Society wheat. The general board confirmed on May 31, 1939, that a portion of the wheat fund would be used to purchase wheat, and a new grain elevator at 7th South and 7th West in Salt Lake City was dedicated by the Church on August 27, 1940. With the two smaller elevators in Idaho, the combined storage capacity was 400,000 bushels.[41]

Relief Society faithfully promoted the principles of thrift and storage, adapting applications to differing world circumstances. In Argentina, for instance, the sisters tried to store food and clothing, but reported "Prices are raising [sic] every day, and most of our Saints have but a meager living at best. There are no adequate facilities for bottling or canning foods."[42] The sisters devised a simpler form of welfare participation: each of the branch societies set up a welfare bank into which the sisters might donate a small amount of money, as often as they were able.

Although the welfare plan was not, at this time, considered exportable to missions overseas, Argentine Mission Relief Society president Lorraine S. Williams reported that the banked money was a donation to the welfare plan.[43] One small society of four members near Cape Town, South Africa, carried on its own charity work and contributed to the Mowbray Branch, keeping "a flock of ducks to help with their finances."[44] The ducks were also food storage; in future decades, as the Church spread to tropical developing areas, leaders would recognize the practicality of storage "on the hoof and in the ground."

Relief Society also promoted salvaging fats, tin cans, paper, and other materials for the defense effort. Making do became a

Longtime Relief Society teacher Floe Ellen Peterson Cutler of Snowville, Utah, proudly displays home-canned food storage for photographer Lee Russell in 1940. (Library of Congress)

patriotic effort instead of a depression necessity. Old-fashioned skills revived. "The sisters are keeping an old art alive," reported Orlene Henrie, president of the Gunnison (Utah) Stake Relief Society, "and this has proved very helpful during these many months of shortages. They not only carded all the wool for their welfare assignments, but have helped many families with their bedding problems."[45]

Wartime shortages spurred a resurgence of interest in the art of quilting. According to the 1943 annual report, "Although quilt-making has been traditional in the Relief Society for a hundred years, 1943 was doubtless the greatest quilt-making year in the history of the Society." That year the sisters supplied bishops' storehouses with 4,488 quilts, in addition to their usual activities for the Red Cross, ward first-aid supplies, and help-one-another family-preparedness projects. The quilts were part of the first uniform sewing assignment to all stake Relief Societies since the inception of the welfare plan in 1936. In many communities, quilts and warm clothing were important because of fuel shortages. "We have helped people to have warm bedding who have never had it before," reported one stake leader, "and we surely need it in Idaho."[46] Next to clothing for children, quilts were the biggest item in Relief Society sewing projects during most of the war years. The annual report of the Maricopa (Arizona) Stake listed an "incomplete count" of nearly 1,300 quilts made at "ward quilting, group quilting, and neighborhood quilting parties of all kinds."[47]

Members were advised to have a five-year supply of bedding and at least a year's supply of clothing on hand for their families, but the demands of an all-out war effort affected even the welfare clothing budget. It became apparent at the end of 1944 that the next year's clothing program could proceed only, as the Church Welfare Committee put it, "as materials become available to which we are properly entitled on a quota basis."[48] Those families with an active Relief Society mother were fortunate, as she could count on help in making over used clothing and on group participation in quilting.

Church welfare sewing produced clothing for men, women, and children, as well as bedding and household linens. The sisters were both economical and ingenious in their efforts. "One ward made most of their assignment from poultry feed-bags, which they collected from poultry men in their area, washed and bleached, and then made into slips and panties, pillowcases and dish towels," according to the organization's annual report. Some of the bags were "dyed in muted colors and made into dainty slips for the children."[49]

As in the first world war, Relief Society officially supported the Red Cross. The general board, for instance, recommended that, in addition to sewing for the needy, the sisters sew for the Red Cross in their regular monthly work meeting, keeping records of articles made. The response of the sisters in the Lyman (Idaho) Ward was typical: during 1943 and 1944 they spent an evening together every month folding bandages for the Red Cross for a total of 524 hours; in 1943 they sewed three quilts, sixteen blouses, twenty-two pairs of pajamas, and a temple robe for "the Welfare and Red Cross."[50] Evidently community service and church welfare meshed comfortably.

In February 1942, Relief Society headquarters issued a bulletin to all stake and mission societies outlining ways for the local societies to act as Red Cross units. That same year, 10,222 Relief Society sisters completed Red Cross courses, principally in home nursing, first aid, and nutrition. To the Red Cross, Relief Society donated that year alone 100,125 hours of volunteer sewing and 38,381 completed articles.[51] Many women also gave blood.

In February 1942 the general board began distributing to stake and ward societies a yearly "Survey of Registered and Practical Nurses." All United States and Canada societies copied off their local list before returning the survey to headquarters. For many years the lists proved to be invaluable in emergencies; they were eventually turned over to the Welfare Services Department.

By 1943 the war had imbued most traditional Relief Society activities with new meaning. In war-risk areas, certain women were called to become Red Cross first-aid instructors and to hold classes for women in their stakes. At this time Relief Society stressed health maintenance, in cooperation with war's first claim on doctors, nurses, and medical facilities. With renewed purpose, the society continued to urge women to take courses in home nursing and first aid and "to cooperate with their local Relief Societies in the establishment of home nursing supply chests." Visiting teachers distributed "a leaflet on these matters," bringing word directly from the general board to each individual woman.[52]

The sisters also served at USO and Red Cross canteens, and the societies enthusiastically purchased and promoted war bonds. Sisters in the South Los Angeles Stake held a welfare fair and demonstration for the public at which they sold $40,000 in bonds. Women in the Fountain Green (Utah) Ward made enough money at their fair to buy three $100 war bonds, one $50 bond, and one $25 bond; they reported confidently that after the war, the bonds would be cashed to help pay for a new chapel. Societies in Canada continued to send "bundles to Britain" of clothing, soap, safety pins, and other items scarce in the war-torn mother country. The sisters reported with pride: "A recent bundle came in from the Hamilton Branch in which were many children's sweaters made from ends of new material purchased from a knitwear factory by one of the employees who is an enthusiastic Relief Society worker. These ends were made into lovely sweaters, suits, garter waists and even underclothes. It was a beautiful bundle."[53]

The British Commonwealth nations were particularly zealous in war service. "Just now the feeling of patriotism is strong, and the sisters are offering their services, under the name of Relief Society, to help in any way they can," the supervisor of the women's organizations in New Zealand wrote. "I have suggested that they use part of their Work-and-Business Day and some of their evenings sewing for the soldiers. They are all enthusiastic, and I am sure that the country of New Zealand will know that there is a charitable organization in the Church of Jesus Christ of Latter-day Saints that responds to every call, no matter what creed or color, where human life is concerned."[54]

At Christmastime in 1942, Robert L. Simpson, serving with the African campaign in Egypt, was lonely and homesick. A non-Mormon friend he was visiting picked up a gaily wrapped package from a pile of Red Cross gifts and asked, "How would you like to have a bit of cheer from New Zealand?" Inside was a tasty fruitcake and a note that read, "To one of our valiant servicemen serving God and country—with our love and may the Lord bless you this holiday season especially. From the Takami Branch Relief Society of the Church of Jesus Christ of Latter-day Saints—Dannevirke New Zealand." Years later Elder Simpson remembered the joy he felt on reading that note, as he recognized "the very same sisters who had blessed me so abundantly as a New Zealand missionary just a couple of years before. . . . It was an answer to prayer."[55]

With such homey offerings, Relief Society sisters across the world reached out to comfort the "soldier boys" they rarely knew and responded to the special demands of wartime, both temporal and moral.

Changes in Curriculum and Correlation

The Relief Society educational curriculum also addressed special wartime needs. Although it rolled on in its accustomed main channels, its content was colored and shaped by the turbulent times. Patriotic themes such as "What America Means" and practical helps in "New Fashioned Thrift" were popular in the stakes. Even topics apparently irrelevant to the grim realities of world conflict were given a wartime rationale. The explanation for a 1941–42 course in "Humor in Life and Literature," for example, pointed out that "the tension and stress of the times through which we are passing is so great that we need to do all we can to keep ourselves from breaking under the strain of worry and dread. Humor should help to give the relief we so much need."[56]

However, this rationale was not stretched to apply to the situations of sisters in battlefield countries. Instead, the mission Relief Societies received an optional course on Latter-day Saint hymns—an appropriate choice, considering the probably more universal and elevated spiritual solace available through music. In introducing the course, the general board wrote: "We earnestly hope that any of our sisters who find themselves in distress will receive renewed faith and a determination to go ahead in the Lord's work through a heartfelt singing of the songs of Zion."[57] The first hymn to be studied was "The Morning Breaks, the Shadows Flee." In 1943 a churchwide promotion of hymn singing also testified to the intensified need for music in wartime.

The society was struggling to accommodate the needs of its worldwide sisterhood in other ways also. The previous year an optional course titled "Latter-day Saint Church History" had been available to missions in place of the literature lessons. Instead of the two-year social science course "What America Means," in 1942–43 and 1943–44 the society provided mission lessons on the general presidents of Relief Society and stories from the Book of Mormon.

In 1942 the "Home Topics" for work and business meeting changed from "Better Buymanship" to a course more appropriate for a wartime economy: thrift and conservation. Perhaps in reaction to the chaos of war, the following year the sisters took up the topic of "modern housekeeping methods." The text, *America's House-keeping Book*, a 576–page volume, contained considerable material that would soon be rendered obsolete by postwar technology and the disappearance of "household employees." The course was, however, timely, enjoining a patriotic practicality: "The objective of the course is to bring to the attention of homemakers new and approved methods of housekeeping which will enable them to perform the tasks of housekeeping efficiently with minimum effort, thereby releasing as much time as possible for other activities demanded of homemakers in these abnormal times."[58]

Citing time for "other activities" as reason for more efficient housekeeping was a sign of the abnormal times. Although home was still the heart of a Relief Society sister's stewardship, the patriotic fervor of World War II raised volunteer service and defense work to an unusually high priority.

The Relief Society curriculum reflected the changing times in other ways. The sisters' desire for lessons on work and business day led to a 1940–41 series of eight optional discussions on nutrition, to be conducted along with the sewing, even though the day was recognized chiefly as a day "for Church welfare sewing, regular Relief Society sewing, and to foster sewing skills and other handwork."[59] Women needed training in skills an earlier generation had learned at home. In 1944 the day was renamed work day—a name that would persist long after it had been retitled homemaking day.

Other changes in the Relief Society curriculum reflected shifts in perceived needs. In 1941 the title "social service" was changed to "social science" to indicate the wider range of subjects being studied. Education in its broader aspects was taking the place of paraprofessional training in social work. In a sense, Relief Society was now trying to train every woman to be a social worker in her own home.

The realities of war struck hard at the Latter-day Saint ideals of family life, among them the need for a full-time mother at home. The Church was not alone in its concern. "We've got to get over this idea that being a housewife and mother is not an important task in life," warned Hazel Corbin of the Maternity Center Association. "You see, it is financial pressure as well as the pressure of public opinion that forces many a mother with young children into industry and when that occurs the very foundations of her family, the very foundations of her children's security—the things her husband is fighting for—are destroyed." According to Corbin, war work, however patriotic, was undermining the family. "Does anyone think that a mother can hold a full-time job in a war factory, under the pressure of more, more, more, faster, faster, faster, and properly care for her family at the same time?" she demanded.[60]

The *Relief Society Magazine* championed the housewife's role with articles describing her contribution in the home as part of the larger war effort, featuring "Wartime Menus" for health (a patriotic duty) and articles such as "Unemployed Clothing Called into Service" ("vital to the war effort") and "Care of Children in Wartime" ("a war job of the highest priority"). The magazine also published an open letter from Katharine F. Lenroot, chief of the Children's Bureau, U.S. Department of Labor, stressing the nation's need for good parenting of its future citizens. Educating mothers to that end, Relief Society now considered not only a spiritual but also a patriotic duty.

The church correlation movement, out of sight for nearly twenty years, resurfaced with wartime interest in economy of effort. President J. Reuben Clark, Jr., first counselor to President Heber J. Grant, met with the heads of the Relief Society, Sunday School, Mutual Improvement Associations, Primary, and Genealogical Society on March 29, 1940, to consider a "Memorandum of Suggestions" proposing a reexamination of auxiliary programs and activities. This short but impressive document, destined to become a correlation cornerstone, presented four basic aims: to curtail the "evermounting burden" on members of sustaining church activities, to lessen the bishops' burdens, to cut programs that required large, expensive meetinghouses, and to keep the Church within its income. The auxiliaries were asked to "consolidate, cooperate, eliminate, simplify, and adjust their work so as to cooperate with the Presidency in reaching the aims above indicated."[61]

Proposals for the Relief Society included one that "the Relief Society go forward under the original mandate given to them by the Prophet Joseph," but that social service work be confined "as fully as possible" to assuming their role as "an integral part" of the welfare program. As for "their cultural work, they should seek primarily the promotion of faith and testimony."[62] The Relief Society presidency readily endorsed most of the memorandum; the society was already making efforts to strengthen the home, increase the spirituality of the lessons, and support the welfare program. Less predictable was the memorandum's encouragement to lessen dependence of local units on the general boards.

The general presidencies and superintendencies were called to serve as a new Executive Committee of the Church Union Board of the Auxiliaries, assigned to consider and respond to the memorandum. They met regularly—almost daily at first—until 1944, and at least once in 1949. Point by point they considered the memorandum's proposals. A proposal to combine the *Children's Friend* and the *Relief Society Magazine* into one publication and the *Instructor*, the *General Magazine for Week-day Religious Education*, and the *Improvement Era* into another also failed. The Relief Society's sure defense of its magazine won the board's support; the magazine was spared for nearly thirty more years.

A Committee on Publications was created in September 1944 "to pass upon and approve all materials, other than those that are purely secular, to be used by our Church Priesthood, Educational, Auxiliary, and Missionary organizations in their work of instructing members of the Church in the principles of the Gospel, and in leading others to a knowledge of the truth."[63] This decision was a benchmark in the correlation effort. The first committee consisted of Elders Joseph Fielding Smith, John A. Widtsoe, Harold B. Lee, and Marion G. Romney—a constellation of General Authorities whose visibility underscored the significance of their task. A prestigious reading committee assisted them. Subsequent correspondence indicates that both committees took their work seriously, even making small editorial changes in the lessons they reviewed.[64] Church lessons must be "fully consistent with the principles of the Restored Gospel . . . wholly free from any taint of sectarianism . . . filled with a spirit of deepest reverence," and, acknowledging the lay leadership of the Church, "so organized and written that the matter may be effectively taught by men and women untrained in teaching."[65] The committee was to approve writers as well as materials.

Perhaps in response to the memorandum's suggestion that local units function more independently, the central chorus of Relief Society Singing Mothers was released in 1940 "in order to strengthen Relief Society choruses in the wards and stakes of Salt Lake City" from which the singers had largely been drawn.[66] Local Singing Mothers continued to delight a variety of audiences. "Ranging in size from small ward choruses to large groups representing stakes and missions, they are singing at their regular Relief Society meetings, ward Sacrament meetings, ward, stake and mission Relief Society conferences, special concerts, radio broadcasts, and general community musicales and celebrations," reported an item in "Notes from the Field" in June 1940.

When "saints from all of Denmark" met in Copenhagen for a centennial memorial of the death of the Prophet Joseph Smith, their "new choir, the Singing Mothers" sang under the direction of Sister Valborg Johansen. The president of Relief Society in the Argentine Mission reported, "Our sisters had no opportunity to study music before being contacted by the elders. But in spite of this, we organized a group of Singing Mothers who furnished the music for our two semi-annual conferences in 1939; they had joy in singing."[67]

"With joy we sing the songs of Zion," wrote the president of the Stuttgart District Relief Society in the German Mission, "and put our trust in the Lord." Relief Society sisters in the war zones needed a particular trust in the Lord — and whatever joy they could find in singing. The Stuttgart sisters were fortunate in being able to hold their weekly meetings during the war, President Maria Speidel reported after the war's end. "The past five years have been difficult ones and we have become very humble. Our trust in the Lord and our testimony of his Church have been our pillar of strength." Her report was full of faith: "He has kept us mercifully, and although there was much to suffer, he has given to us a measure of his strength. Some of us have lost all our earthly possessions, every tangible thing ever dear to us, and when we say 'It is better to walk with God in the darkness than without him in the light,' we know whereof we speak."[68]

The Indomitable Faith of European Sisters

As the war progressed toward the death struggles of Hitler's *Reich*, other less fortunate German sisters clung to each other. "You can't imagine how alone we felt," said Sister Ruth Lippke years later, recalling those bleak days in Bernburg, Germany. "We had no communication with the Church—no transportation—no priesthood. Women laid hands on each other to pray for the sick. We used old lesson books when we met in each other's homes."[69] The sisters in Bernburg pooled their scanty food and fuel so they could meet together in the evenings in a warm room to study, sew for the needy, and eat a frugal meal. On one occasion they scraped together enough rations to make a birthday cake for a faithful elderly brother. "He cried, when he ate the first slice," wrote Sister Lippke.[70]

Beleaguered members in larger cities also helped each other. Latter-day Saint survivors in bombed-out Hamburg gathered in the rubble and shared their meager supplies with those who had lost everything. Funds were raised for the Relief Society to buy material for sewing, patching, and remodeling clothing to give to the destitute.[71]

Somehow, in the midst of chaos and fear, the sisters abroad carried on their work of charity, study, and care of their families. After the German invasion, the Netherlands Mission Relief Society president, Gertrude Zippro, wrote to her brother in Salt Lake City and described her efforts to get to devastated Rotterdam, where two sisters and a brother lived: "I left Amsterdam on Thursday morning, 16 May 1940, at about ten-thirty. Just then the German troops arrived, and I have never seen such an army." She had to travel the sixty miles by bicycle, through incredible scenes of devastation, because the rail lines had been destroyed and no cars or buses were available. She wrote: "It took me nine hours to go to Rotterdam, and that whole time the German army roared by me on motorcycles, tanks, tractors, etc. It was one long chain of materi[e]l they had. I could not believe my eyes. . . . I thought to myself, 'If mankind needs to be destroyed with that, God's judgement is really severe.' But immediately other thoughts took over—

'this is the work of Satan and of man himself.' " Nevertheless, she continued, "even though we know that these things will happen, our prayers still plead to God that it will end soon."[72]

The end was five long years away, and life had to go on. As the district Relief Society president in the mission, Sister Zippro was concerned not only about her family, whom she found safe, but about all the Saints in Holland. Her letter included a plea for her brother to ask Franklin J. Murdock, church mission secretary and former president of the Netherlands Mission, "about a collection for the members in Rotterdam who have lost everything." She added, "We will start a collection here also, and I will discuss it with the Mission President as well."[73]

Sister Zippro continued to visit the branches regularly, in spite of growing difficulties described by her son in his account of her life: "It became necessary for my mother to have identification in order for her to safely visit the various branches of the Relief Societies.... Curfew was imposed and many guards or sentries were posted on major thoroughfares. If you had no business in a particular area, you were stopped and searched, and many times your possessions were taken from you—such as bicycles." As the war continued, conditions deteriorated further. "It became increasingly dangerous to be out at night as the occupation continued for five years, and many women were molested or raped.... Can you imagine my mother braving those circumstances and going out at night on her bike many times, to visit another branch?" This Relief Society president's courage was astonishing. Her son John recalled that "no matter how she felt or what the circumstances, she would take care of her obligation. What a great woman and leader she was! There is no doubt in my mind now that she was hand-picked by the Lord to be the Relief Society President at that time."[74]

Train travel was hazardous after Allied planes began bombing German troop movements. One night as Sister Zippro was returning home by train, her son's account continues, "the shooting started. The train stopped immediately and the people jumped out, including mother. She crouched at the side of the tracks, making herself as small as possible, lying there in the cold, wet and muddy ditch, with bullets striking all around. One can imagine her fright." Trying to imagine what it must have been like for her, huddled and afraid as bullets strafed the area and bombs fell, John speculated: "I wonder if she even thought about what she [had] told us—'Do not worry. I'll be perfectly safe.' "[75]

The train was badly damaged, but Sister Zippro was unharmed. The next week she traveled again to visit her Relief Society sisters. "She must have had complete trust in the Lord," wrote her son, "to go time after time under those conditions, not knowing what problems she would encounter."[76] As the roads and trains became more dangerous, she often took the night boat on the inland canals to visit the little branches and "keep the work of the Relief Society moving along."[77] Despite difficulties, Sister Zippro completed the rigorous training program initiated by Brother Jan Copier for all the church leaders in Holland. "We will hold a leadership meeting in Utrecht next week for the Relief Society," she reported. "We hope and pray that it can take place undisturbed."[78]

Denmark was more fortunate; although occupied by Germany, its decision against armed resistance led to more humane treatment than other countries received. Food was available. "We have during the war taken up the work of helping our starving brother-land, Norway," wrote Eva M. Gregersen, president of the Danish Mission Relief Society board. "Together with the mission office, we have been giving money to this purpose and every month many nice packages with food have been sent to our brothers and sisters in Norway, who have been thankful beyond words." The Danish sisters were also able to maintain their own emergency stores and even to celebrate March 17, 1942, with a banquet.[79] The history of the Norway Mission described another banquet their generosity made possible—"a grand dinner to twenty-eight aged members of the [Oslo] branch, who accepted the invitation and enjoyed the sumptuous delicacies, which had been furnished by the Danish Mission."[80] Thus the European sisters shared with others their limited stores, kept up their visiting teaching—sometimes riding on bicycles with no tires—and prayed earnestly for better times.

Bombed by the *Luftwaffe* for three years and burdened with Allied forces readying the invasion of Europe, Great Britain had become an island fortress by the time a missionwide Relief Society convention was held in Birmingham on June 17 and 18, 1944. Although food in Britain was tightly rationed, Hugh B. Brown, president of the British Mission, reported that "these frugal sisters of the Relief Society had saved enough by a family rationing system within the national system to enable them to spread before the large numbers who were assembled a very palatable and refreshing meal and, in addition, to serve all the officers and teachers on the following day." He wrote of his admiration for those sisters: "There are hundreds of Relief Society women in the war zone who have been exposed to dangers, trials and hardships, comparable to that which our men undergo in the battle field. These brave women have carried on in the face of almost insuperable difficulties." He was especially impressed with their uncomplaining gratitude in the midst of great deprivations: "To kneel in prayer with these women and to hear them thank God for their simple blessings, for the preservation of their lives and the lives of their loved ones, and for their scanty provisions and their windowless homes is at once an inspiration and a reproof to many of us whose material blessings far exceed any enjoyed here, but who frequently complain at being deprived of a few luxuries."[81]

World War II ended for Europe with the surrender of German forces in Italy on May 2, 1945, and in Germany five days later. Japan surrendered in the Pacific on September 2, 1945, after the United States had unleashed the terrible power of the atom against Hiroshima and Nagasaki. Following the surrender ceremony, General Douglas MacArthur spoke by radio to the American people, assessing the prospects of future peace. "We have had our last chance," he warned solemnly. "If we do not devise some greater and more equitable system, Armageddon will be at our door."[82] An editorial in the October 1945 *Relief Society Magazine* shared that solemn apprehension: "The unleashing of a new force in the final phase of the war, whose future power either for good or evil seems to be incalculable, foreshadows the new world era."[83]

Relief Society sisters and their indomitable President Lyman had struggled to keep home hearths warm and clean while supporting the war effort, had multiplied their compassionate services, and had survived sorrow and death. They would now face the "new world era" with a tempered faith, under the leadership of a new president.

CHAPTER 10

A Companion Organization
to the Priesthood
1945–1974

When Belle Smith Spafford was called as general president of the Relief Society in April 1945, President J. Reuben Clark, Jr., of the First Presidency counseled her to "administer the affairs of the Relief Society . . . with the concept that the Relief Society is a companion organization to the priesthood." Over the years Sister Spafford adopted this view as her own. Years later she would state emphatically that the society is "without question, an essential part of the organization of the Church . . . more than just an organization for women. I think it's a companion to the priesthood in building the kingdom."[1] This broad vision fit her well to meet the challenges of growth and correlation that confronted her twenty-nine-year administration, the longest in the history of Relief Society. During her presidency, as the Relief Society expanded both internationally and internally, operations traditionally associated with Relief Society leadership changed dramatically.

Sister Spafford understood both the responsibilities and the doctrinal boundaries of that leadership. When a problem arose that needed to be discussed with priesthood leaders, she explained, a Relief Society president should first "carefully and prayerfully weigh it and discuss it" with her counselors, then "unitedly determine how they feel the matter might be most wisely dealt with." Then the president would be ready to present a recommendation, as well as the problem, to the priesthood leaders. She also had a responsibility "to call attention to any related established regulations that need to be considered." Sister Spafford's own faith in the ultimate source of church leadership shines through her firm statement of the final step: "Then, whatever counsel the priesthood presidency may give, the Relief Society presidency should accept and abide by it."[2] She herself set the example by accepting difficult correlation changes with grace and abiding by them with enthusiasm.

Sister Spafford learned the lesson of abiding by counsel early in her married life. The bishop of their new ward, becoming acquainted with the Spaffords, asked where she would like to serve. Sunday School or the Young Women's Mutual Improvement Association, responded Sister Spafford. The following Sunday the bishop called her as counselor in the Relief Society. "I couldn't believe it!" she later related. "I thought of all the places in the world for which I wasn't qualified it was to be in the Relief Society. And to me it was an older mothers' organization, and I just resisted, really resisted." She accepted the call, serving through the difficulties engendered by a cold church building, a new baby, and crying children. When continuing seemed impossible, her compassionate bishop blessed her to continue yet a while, and in so doing preserved for the Church one of its strongest Relief Society advocates and ablest leaders.[3]

Two qualities characterized Sister Spafford's leadership style: she was a teacher by training, and she was a firm, incisive administrator. Well might it be said of her that she was one to whom it was "given by the Holy Ghost to know the differences of administration."[4] A graduate of the University of Utah Normal School, she taught in Salt Lake City schools and the Brigham Young University Training School before her marriage to Willis Earl Spafford, an accountant who encouraged her interest in the intricacies of finance. She was also interested in good writing, and it was with her encouragement that the Relief Society short story contest was inaugurated in 1942 to improve the writing skills of the women of the Church. Her own literary style was carefully reasoned and didactic. She edited the history *A Centenary of Relief Society* and served as editor of the *Relief Society Magazine* from 1937 until her call to the presidency in 1945.

Her leadership skills benefited the wider community as well as the Church. As president of the National Council of Women and in other positions of public influence, Belle Spafford became known and respected worldwide.

The Postwar Years: Challenges and Opportunities

Belle Spafford's long presidency could be described as a drama in three acts: the postwar years in October 1945, the fearful yet hopeful 1950s, and the stormy years from the early 1960s to the mid-1970s.

The postwar years followed the end of World War II in 1945. The Allies had hammered through to hard-won agreement on a United Nations charter that same year, but their lack of true unity became apparent in the bitter peace that followed. Soviet armed forces in eastern Europe began to lengthen their line of communist satellites. In March 1946, addressing college students in Fulton, Missouri, England's Prime Minister Winston Churchill first used an expression that would become all too familiar in the years ahead: "An iron curtain has descended across the Continent." Another phrase, "the cold war," was coined by American businessman and statesman Bernard Baruch to describe the ongoing tension between Russia and the United States. The cold war fueled an arms buildup that continually threatened the fragile peace; the iron curtain cut off hundreds of Relief Society members from their sisters in the West.

"Over a year has passed since the great armies of the world laid down their arms," commented counselor Gertrude Garff in the 1946 Relief Society conference, "and most of the people on this earth rejoiced, expecting peace and security to prevail once again. As the months have passed, the quiet of peace and the sense of security have failed to materialize."[5] After the Soviets acquired the atomic bomb in 1949, with other countries soon to follow, a terrifying mushroom-shaped cloud shadowed all the hope for world peace.

Yet the postwar picture had its bright aspect. United States aid to Greece and Turkey and the spectacular Berlin airlift by British and American planes blocked the Soviet advance. The challenge of rebuilding destroyed cities and economies in Europe called forth an unprecedented generosity under the Marshall Plan. In an ironic reversal of roles, a revived West Germany and Japan became allies of the Western democracies against the Soviet Union and China. The North Atlantic Treaty Organization allied the United States with twelve European countries. The Nuremberg trials exposed the horrors of the Holocaust — impossible to redress yet chastening sensibilities in a way that impelled the United Nations to establish the state of Israel in 1948. Many European colonies in the Far East, Africa, and India gained their independence.

As soldiers came marching home to the United States from Europe and the Pacific, the specter of ten million unemployed melted away in the hot demand for consumer goods and housing. A significant number of the women in wartime jobs also returned home.[6] Nor were all the relinquished jobs in factories and offices. In a typical gesture, the former lieutenant commander of the U.S. Navy's WAVES, Dr. Mildred McAfee Horton, resigned her prestigious position as president of Wellesley College in favor of "being the kind of wife and home-maker she desired to be." The *Relief Society Magazine* reported her decision with obvious approval.[7]

The war's end coincided with new presidential eras in the Church and in Relief Society. President Heber J. Grant was ill and dying when Amy Brown Lyman and her counselors were released in general conference on April 6, 1945.[8] The newly appointed president, Belle Smith Spafford, and her counselors, Marianne Clark Sharp and Gertrude Ryberg Garff, were sustained at this wartime conference meeting attended only by a few priesthood leaders. George Albert Smith became president and prophet of the Church upon the death of Heber J. Grant in May, and the new Relief Society presidency and board were set apart in June, with an explicit charge "to spiritualize the homes of the Latter-day Saints."[9]

At the first postwar conference in October 1945, the sisters assembled in the Salt Lake Tabernacle received word of several other significant changes. "We begin the work of this new era with a new name," Sister Spafford announced. On June 27, 1945, the general board had changed the society's official designation from National Woman's Relief Society to Relief Society of The Church of Jesus Christ of Latter-day Saints.[10] Sister Spafford later explained motives for the change: "I had spoken at a meeting of the National Council of Women, giving a report on the work of the Relief Society organization. I was of the opinion that those in attendance didn't identify Relief Society with the Mormon Church. I felt it was extremely important that they know us as the women's auxiliary of The Church of Jesus Christ of Latter-day Saints."[11] The change was a harbinger of Relief Society's shift from a primarily national organization to an international sisterhood.

The sisters also heard that succeeding Relief Society conferences would be held annually, preceding the October general conference, instead of semiannually. Union meetings would be restored, although Sister Spafford cautioned stake leaders to do nothing that would hinder ward officers from "standing on their own feet," as they had done during the war. The forward-looking president saw a need to strengthen the ward organizations.

307

A postwar assessment of Relief Society revealed the effects of the war. Membership had dropped from over 115,000 in 1942 to fewer than 102,000 in 1945. Visiting teaching and attendance had declined because of gas rationing, shifts in population, and increased numbers of women working away from home. However, by 1946 the trend had already begun to reverse.[12]

Included in the 1946 annual report were statistics from the Danish, French, Swedish, and Swiss-Austrian missions, the first received from continental Europe since 1938. Not surprisingly, membership had declined in all four, but their mere survival was cause for gratitude. In 1947 the first reports came from the Czechoslovakian, East German, and Netherlands missions. Overall, the society was recovering from the war and preparing for future growth.

With the end of the war, the time seemed auspicious to renew the dream of a headquarters home for the growing society. At the first postwar conference in October 1945, President Spafford called for a vote on the proposal to erect a Relief Society building to "more adequately house the general offices, the Temple–Burial Clothes Department, the *Magazine*, the Welfare, and other departments. . . . Like one great wave," she remembered, "thousands of uplifted hands unanimously voted in the affirmative."[13] President George Albert Smith acknowledged, "I realize you have been disappointed in the past; you thought you had a house once before, but it turned out to be the Presiding Bishop's office also." He enthusiastically expressed support for the new plan, declaring, "I don't care how fine it is, how large it is, or how beautiful it is; it will not be better than you deserve."[14]

Raising money for the new building was an important step toward anticipated growth. The presidency wanted to begin work on their building "as soon as building restrictions are lifted." After seeking the First Presidency's approval, they promptly requested plans from architect George Cannon Young.[15]

The Presiding Bishopric also gave its support, sending all stake presidencies and ward bishoprics a copy of the Relief Society's letters announcing its fund-raising plans, "that you may be advised of their program and that you may do all you can to see that the suggestions they have made are enthusiastically and promptly carried out in your wards."[16]

A quota was set for each stake, based on an estimated five-dollar contribution from each sister. The missions were excepted —

"We sort of left it to the missions to do what they wanted," remembered counselor Marianne Sharp.[17] In some wards a sister who wished to earn her contribution could advertise her services through the society. Other wards chose to raise their quota with a banquet or other joint effort. Visiting teachers provided the vital communication system, publicizing the drive for funds, distributing supportive letters from bishops, and collecting donations. In many wards they distributed small containers, with the suggestion that they be left in a conspicuous place to encourage all family members to donate extra change. As their quotas were completed, wards and branches received recognition in the *Relief Society Magazine.*

Delores Torres, president of the Mexican Branch in Salt Lake's Temple View Stake, was seated in the Tabernacle when the fund-raising announcement was made. She thought, "We cannot do it. Our sisters are too poor. How can I ask such a sacrifice from them when there are already so many calls?" Then her eyes fell on President McKay seated on the stand behind Sister Spafford. She said to herself, "The First Presidency have permitted her to make this request and therefore it must be right, and *if it is right, we can do it.*"[18] Sister Torres and her officers decided to earn their contribution by giving a Mexican dinner. Every Relief Society member helped with the food, the girls in the YWMIA assisted with the serving and the program, and a big crowd came. The little society became the first in the Church to meet its quota.

In one year the 111,000 members raised $554,016, exceeding their goal of half a million dollars. The Primary and YWMIA presidencies also contributed generously, and an additional $8,000 that had been donated by 1906, when the sisters first contemplated a home of their own, now became part of the funds for the new building. In 1896 Sarah M. Kimball had said in general Relief Society conference that sisters had "contributed to all public places. Now we want to have a house, and we want land to build it on and it should be in the shadow of the temple." In a good-natured reference to the disappointing outcome of that first effort, the narrator at the 1948 conference explained: "We contributed $8,000 towards the construction of the Bishop's Building, as it came to be called, and moved into our offices there in December 1909. We've appreciated the offices, yes. But you know how you feel when you've been living with relatives and then get a chance to move into a home of your own."[19] However, in the postwar economy many others were waiting for the chance to move into homes of their own, including wards in need of new meetinghouses; nearly eight more years would pass before Relief Society could move into its new building.

Relieving the Suffering in Europe

An even more pressing need that claimed Relief Society's efforts was relief to Europe. When war ended in Europe on May 8, 1945, some 30,000 Latter-day Saints lived in England and on the Continent. Nearly half of these were in Germany, where the devastation was greatest and the distribution of relief supplies was the most difficult. In November 1945 President George Albert Smith headed a delegation to Washington to arrange transportation for relief supplies. President Harry S. Truman received them willingly. He asked how long it would take the Church to gather the supplies and was astonished to learn that food, clothes, and bedding were ready and waiting. "We have an organization in the Church that has over two thousand home-made quilts ready," President Smith told him, referring to the Relief Society.[20]

Shipments to the Saints in countries liberated by the Allies could be made immediately by parcel post in eleven-pound packages; the Church decided to send one package to each of the 7,245 members in those countries. Supplies available in bishops' storehouses included 175 blankets, 1,655 pairs of shoes, and over 3,300 quilts made by Relief Society sisters, who also made available over 6,600 quilts and nearly 2,000 blankets from their "war emergency kits." The immediate availability of these supplies made it possible for the Church to succor many of the European Saints during the unusually severe winter of 1945–46, when the need was greatest. "Destruction, hunger, and anxiety are on every hand," reported Elder Ezra Taft Benson, who supervised the distribution of the supplies. However, he added, "the faithful members of the Church . . . face the future with courage undaunted, in great contrast to the melancholy, suicides, and discouragement all around them."[21]

In November and early December of 1945, visiting teachers in every stake of the United States distributed a flyer to each member's home, requesting "for the suffering European saints, the good, clean clothing which has been accumulated in Latter-day Saint homes, available for this purpose."[22] On December 10 and 11, donations were collected in meetinghouses, where Relief Society workers sorted, sized, recorded, mended, and packed clothing

Copenhagen Branch Relief Society sisters distribute clothing and bedding sent to Denmark by American and Canadian Saints in 1946. (Courtesy Ane Andersen Asper)

for the ward welfare committees to transport to stake storehouses for shipment.[23] More than half a million articles of clothing were collected.

By the end of February in 1946, more than 8,000 quilts and blankets had been sent to European countries other than Germany, with another 1,000 reserved to be sent as soon as shipping to Germany was possible. In 1948, Relief Societies in the Northern States Mission sent the German Saints 1,020 children's dresses, 40 slips, and other articles of clothing—"all of them new and, for the most part, made by the sisters."[24] Layettes prepared by Salt Lake sisters for use by the Social Service Department were also shipped to Europe.

Soap, a wartime scarcity, was still rationed in the United States when President Spafford learned in December 1945 that the church welfare supply fell far short of immediate needs in Europe. With the First Presidency's permission, she requested a special collection "to secure enough soap to put in the packages being sent to Europe before Christmas." Relief Society presidents in ninety-one stakes were immediately notified by telephone of the need, and by the following Tuesday, December 18, Relief Society sisters were carrying to their meetings over 47,000 bars of the scarce commodity.[25]

The Saints in Europe were also reaching out to help each other. East Germany, under communist rule, was closed to outside church help, but it was reported that "a capable sister has been called on a mission to teach the sisters how to remodel clothing for those who are in urgent need." In the Netherlands and French missions, remodeling old clothing was also a high priority Relief Society activity, "as new purchases are impossible." Swedish sisters collected clothing for the less fortunate in Norway and Finland and also sewed baptism and burial clothes.[26] Sisters of the Norwegian Mission sent over one hundred packages of food to church members in Germany and Belgium.[27] Belgian members shared their precious welfare supplies with starving German Saints; the Swiss sent clothing and chocolate to Austria. Dutch Saints—men and women working together—planted potatoes in their devastated land and then sent most of the precious crop to members in Germany; the following year they sent another ninety tons of potatoes—along with eighty barrels of salted herring.[28]

Although the bulk of war relief went to Europe, Relief Society sisters in Hawaii—scene of Japan's 1941 attack on Pearl Harbor—reached out "to our saints and friends in stricken Japan." In cooperation with the local priesthood welfare committee, they collected food and clothing and mailed over seven hundred packages for "the relief of souls in Japan who need our help so desperately."[29]

The desolation of Europe, particularly of Germany, created a new wave of gathering to Zion, as church members fled the ruins to seek a better life in a new land of promise. The promise was not always fulfilled; prejudice against foreigners, especially from former enemy countries, sometimes cankered the dream. Members of the general Relief Society presidency were acutely aware of the need to teach tolerance and love as an antidote to the hatred generated by war. "Ours is a healing mission," they wrote in their 1947 New Year's greeting to the societies, "requiring the larger heart, the kindlier touch, the steadier will."[30] Lessons were prepared to address the new, yet age-old problems of attitude that surfaced in the wake of war.

Earlier, at the very end of the war in Europe, a Relief Society social science lesson on "Patterns of Prejudice and Persecution" made a strong and specific plea: "Jewish persecution, or anti-Semitism as it is called, has reached new peaks in ferocity and brutality during the last decade or so. Coming mainly from Germany, the movement has spread over practically all the world until now no place is entirely free from its vicious influence." Americans were not exempt. "Its spirit is one of hysterical bigotry as intense as the world has ever known. Already there are signs that anti-Semitism may be gaining momentum in America. May it never come!"[31] Appropriately, this lesson reached Relief Society sisters just a few weeks after Allied forces liberated the survivors of the Nazi camps in which over six million Jews had been slaughtered.

The 1948–50 social science course of study, titled "Latter-day Saint Political Thought," urged a heightened awareness of the impact of governments on the lives of individuals. The course was prepared by G. Homer Durham, then head of the Political Science Department of the University of Utah, who also contributed articles on government to the *Relief Society Magazine*. In 1949 he made a careful distinction that would prove useful in the future: "The Relief Society is not in politics and probably never will be. That is not its particular mission, as we understand things. But, if I may be permitted the thought, *more members* of the Relief Society, whether Republicans or Democrats, as well as other righteous women everywhere, should be in politics!"[32]

Getting the Spirit of Welfare and Service

The winding down of the war in 1945 brought a decided decrease in the Relief Society's welfare services. Comparative statistics for 1944 and 1945 show a 64 percent drop in hours spent on projects other than sewing, and fewer than half as many articles sewn. The number of articles sewn for the Red Cross dropped by more than 25 percent, and the number of sisters taking Red Cross courses decreased by more than half. The services given were still considerable, and accumulated surpluses made relief to the suffering Saints in Europe possible. However, the peak of wartime production fervor had passed.

By October 1947, when Elder Marion G. Romney addressed the general Relief Society conference, wartime exigencies had diluted basic welfare principles, such as Relief Society–priesthood partnership and self-help. Bishops could (and some did) raise cash to buy goods to meet their welfare quotas. Or they could buy materials—"and then," said Elder Romney, with some exasperation, "have the already overworked, faithful attenders at Relief Society meetings make them up on regular work and business days and on special work days." Although both methods provided clothing and bedding for the needy, he pointed out, neither was able "to help the families who will use the purchased and Relief Society made items avoid the curse of idleness, or abolish the evils of a dole, nor to develop within themselves independence, industry, thrift, or self-respect" — the original objectives of the welfare plan. Instead, he encouraged the sisters "to bring all women of the ward into the producing programs, whether they are active Relief Society members or not." Such an effort would "build unity among the sisters" and "give all an opportunity to get the spirit of Church Welfare and to be warmed up with the joy of service."[33]

Ward Relief Society presidents found it easier to enlist active members than to persuade inactive sisters to take part in welfare production; the "faithful, overworked" sisters continued to be the major producers. Nor did their work go unrecognized. Elder Mark E. Petersen, noting that "budgets worked out by the General Authorities to meet present emergencies, require a great deal of organized assistance from the women of the Church," succinctly summarized Relief Society welfare work: "Sewing, canning, nursing, directly assisting the poor with shelter, food, and raiment, make heavy demands upon the women of the Church. Organized activity is essential. The Relief Society provides it."[34]

The Emigration Stake Relief Society in Salt Lake City graphically exemplified such organized activity when its members responded in 1946 to a welfare assignment to weave 246 rugs, an assignment that President Lillie Adams later called "a rather difficult assignment." After locating a heavy wooden loom and a teacher, she sent out a call for rags — nearly a thousand pounds were needed to complete the assignment. Then, with the bishop's permission, the loom was set up in one ward's Relief Society room and instruction began. Each ward was asked to "select as many mechanically minded women as possible for the work of weaving," so both the labor and the learning might be shared. Though the work was hard and tedious, Sister Adams reported that after the assignments had been completed, the women wanted to weave rugs for themselves.[35] A similar assignment in San Francisco's Sunset Ward became a cooperative project, with the seventies quorum making the looms and high priests assisting their wives with the weaving.

Meanwhile, in the still-new church welfare program, some bishops needed reminding that Relief Society officers should be part of welfare planning as well as of production. "A wife in a home, a woman, is expected to be . . . an intelligent and inspired participant in the family partnership," observed Elder Harold B. Lee in a 1946 Relief Society conference address. "That is just where we think the place of the Relief Society is in the Welfare Program. . . . We expect that they shall be invited in as intelligent participants in the *planning* of the Welfare partnership."[36]

Noting the "extremely small number of family analyses" reported in the Relief Society annual report of 1946, Sister Spafford suggested to the General Church Welfare Committee that bishops might not be using the Relief Society presidents' expertise "in determining the needs of families receiving welfare assistance." At the suggestion of Presiding Bishop LeGrand Richards, she was invited to address the priesthood meeting of general conference, where thirty-five hundred bishops were present, to remind them of the partnership opportunities.[37] Although priesthood leaders in stakes and wards were slow to heed the admonition, and production continued to be the chief contribution of Relief Society to the welfare program, a standard had been established for the future.

By 1947, Latter-day Saints—now numbering over a million—were ready to celebrate the centennial of the pioneers' entrance into the Salt Lake Valley. Throughout the Church, parades and pageants honored the pioneers and lifted the spirits of a war-weary people now facing an uncertain future. An imposing monument by Mahonri M. Young was erected at the mouth of Salt Lake City's Emigration Canyon to mark the entrance of the Mormon pioneers and earlier Utah explorers, and a marble statue of Brigham Young was unveiled in the capitol building in Washington, D.C. The musical *Promised Valley,* commissioned for this occasion, was so popular in Salt Lake City that it was performed annually for many years. The *Relief Society Magazine* featured pioneer themes on its covers, with pioneer tales and historical sketches inside.[38]

Less memorable than the celebrations but more significant in the long run were the beginnings of microfilming vital genealogical records and the stirrings of a church-sponsored family hour. In 1947, at the request of the General Authorities, Relief Society visiting teachers took to every Latter-day Saint home an eight-page pamphlet of suggestions for a family hour. The next year an editorial in the *Relief Society Magazine* encouraged every Relief Society mother "to enlist the support of her husband in instituting such an observance in her own family."[39] The Council of the Twelve also asked the Relief Society to present in every ward a program on the family hour; the general board further recommended a poster "displayed in the Relief Society room or some other appropriate place . . . as a constant reminder of the Family Hour."[40] Not until 1964 would priesthood correlation put the full weight of the Church behind a family home evening. In the meantime, many a Relief Society mother and her supportive husband helped pave the way for the program to roll forth.

The 1950s: Refining Social Service and Homemaking Education

The 1950s began inauspiciously with the communist North Korean invasion of South Korea. The United Nations sent troops (mostly from the United States) to South Korea's aid. The 1953 armistice reestablishing the preinvasion boundaries between North and South Korea was hardly a victory; it did, however, bring relief from the fear that World War III was beginning.

America's participation in the Korean conflict did not delay its march toward remarkable prosperity. As historian T. H. White recalled, "America in the 1950s was about to erupt in a well-being utterly without precedent in history. . . . Drunk on cheap gasoline, lured by new roads, urged on by the butcher to upgrade from hamburger to steak, teased to new appetites by television, America was experiencing the Great Boom."[41] During these years of prosperity, Relief Society still emphasized good household management and thrift, though in the expansive 1950s a frugal Latter-day Saint housewife was clearly swimming against the tide.

One impetus for the consumer boom was the new crop of babies in cherished new homes. In the United States 3.7 was the birthrate for women of childbearing age. The typical American family (70 percent of all households) consisted of a working father, a stay-at-home mother, and one or more children.[42] Children were back in style, along with natural childbirth, breast feeding, and homemaking. Even the birth-control movement chose a more expansive name: Planned Parenthood. For a few years Mormon women with large families could enjoy swimming in the mainstream, before it shallowed and divided.[43]

At the end of the decade the world looked full of promise to the majority of Relief Society sisters. Automatic machines were taking much of the drudgery out of housework, employment was high, and house payments were low. Health care had improved, partly as a by-product of the war. The Primary's beautiful new hospital in Salt Lake City opened in 1952; the dreaded scourge of polio was conquered in 1954.[44] "We are living in a great, wide,

President Belle Spafford, wearing lei from Hawaiian sisters, addresses October 1959 Relief Society conference. Behind her are counselors Marianne Sharp and Louise Madsen and priesthood advisers Joseph Fielding Smith and Mark E. Petersen of the Council of the Twelve. (Courtesy Utah State Historical Society)

beautiful, wonderful world," exclaimed the general presidency in their New Year's greeting of 1960, "filled with endless resources for our well-being and happiness."[45]

When David O. McKay became president on April 9, 1951, the Church outside of North America had only one stake, one temple, and less than eight percent of its members. Military conscription in the United States and the Korean War had cut the number of missionaries in half. More widely traveled than any president before him, he increased the pace of internationalization of the Church. Over the next decade the number of stakes abroad would increase to five, and temples would be built in Switzerland, London, and New Zealand. He even explored the possibility of taking the Church to black Africa, sending Nathan Eldon Tanner, just released as president of the European Mission, and Sister Tanner to Nigeria in 1962 to talk with native religious leaders who had contacted the Church. The opportunity was real but the time was not ripe. Missionaries would not be able to get entry visas.

Latter-day Saint servicemen took the gospel to Korea, and the growth of the Church in the Pacific and Far East became one of the outstanding features of the decade. From 1950 to 1960, membership in the Orient increased from 439 to 7,400. The mission in

Japan reopened in 1948, and Relief Societies were organized there in 1949. With the help of Tomiko Shirota, a native sister missionary, Ethel L. Mauss, the mission Relief Society president, set up a Relief Society program in two branches in the Tokyo District.[46] By the end of 1950 the Relief Society annual report from the Japanese Mission showed sixty-seven sisters enrolled in the Ikebukuro and Meguro branches. Other groups of sisters in Japan were organized less formally as women's clubs. One such group in Juso, Osaka, sent a letter accompanied by an English translation to the general board. Dated April 20, 1950, the nine-foot scroll in Japanese characters expressed thanks for clothing sent from America and Hawaii and told of the group's activities.[47] A similar group in Nagoya began meeting officially as Relief Society in the fall of 1950. "We learned cooking, toured newspaper company, held bazaars, and distributed Relief Clothing and can goods sent from the church welfare, and the General Relief Society," wrote the president, Toshiko Yanagida. In 1951 the sisters in Nagoya conducted a successful "sidewalk bazaar" to which LDS servicemen contributed the main attraction — chocolate. Sister Yanagida, who served Relief Society in various offices through 1984, was characterized by one who knew her as "the Sister Spafford of Japan." Her organizational abilities and language skills helped her bridge the cultural gap between Western and Oriental sisters. She was also a link to the Church's past in the Orient: her father, Tomigoro Takagi, joined the Church in 1915 in Tokyo, and her uncle, editor of the Japanese *LDS Messenger,* was baptized in 1908.[48]

New Relief Societies appeared in Utah as well when branches and wards were organized at Brigham Young University. Relief Society met on Sunday, at the same time as priesthood meeting. Young women who had heretofore regarded Relief Society as an organization for their mothers and grandmothers became officers and teachers in their own societies. The regular program, with a few modifications, worked well for the students, and the first BYU student stake, organized in 1956, led the Church in most statistical measurements.[49]

While principles remained constant, procedures were changing. Together with priesthood leaders, Relief Society officers now received instructions in welfare principles and procedures at ward, stake, and regional welfare meetings.[50] The society no longer needed the social service classes initiated by Amy Brown Lyman, and institutes to train officers in principles of social welfare were discontinued. Instead, general board members—including President Spafford herself—were often invited to instruct Relief Society personnel at stake leadership and various welfare meetings, sometimes "about such things as the family visit [to determine welfare needs] and the next time about knowing what's in the storehouse," Sister Spafford commented in later years. "I can adjust to change. I've seen it and I've seen that with growth we have to change procedures," she said.[51]

Clear directives to bishops and Relief Society presidents spelled out their collaborative roles in welfare. Concerning the survey of needy individuals and families in the ward, the General Church Welfare Committee recommended, "It may be done by the bishop personally. In most cases, however, he will want it done by the ward Relief Society president, who will submit to the bishop her report and recommendation." As for the production budget, Elder Marion G. Romney, representing the committee, instructed: "What the ward undertakes to do is determined by the bishop and the ward Relief Society president in consultation with the stake Welfare Committee."[52] Collaboration appeared at higher administrative levels as well. All three members of the stake Relief Society presidency were members of the stake welfare committee, and the Relief Society general presidency members were designated as advisers to the general committee.

Relief Society also maintained some separate specialized welfare services under the direction of President Spafford and the general board. In the society's Social Service and Child Welfare Department, Sister Spafford carried forward the work begun under Amy Brown Lyman and sought professional quality in both department personnel and procedures, recruiting a director and caseworkers with master's degrees in social work. At her invitation the department began to train students from the University of Utah Graduate School of Social Work in social welfare field work, and the department's caseworkers also became active in community councils and professional conferences. In 1950 department services consisted of family welfare (as requested by bishops), employment for women, adoptions (including care of unwed mothers), and foster home care.[53]

During the 1950s, the number of adoption placements increased significantly; the department also enlarged its licensed services to include the Indian student placement program (1954) and the youth services program (1956), which included professional counseling, tutoring for disadvantaged children, and foster home placement. Offices and interview rooms in the new Relief Society Building were designed specifically for these services. In 1964, however, the Church established a separate Salt Lake City office at the former Veterans Hospital on Twelfth Avenue for youth services. Adoption, foster care, and Indian placements were all limited to Utah until 1962, when the Relief Society began to establish licensed agencies in other states. By 1965 such agencies were operating in Utah, Arizona, Nevada, and California.[54]

Developing a viable church program to aid the American Indians had been an ongoing project since the administration of President George Albert Smith. "We have started and stopped, but now this program must go on," Elder Delbert L. Stapley told the sisters in 1952. He defined the place of Relief Society in this program: to teach the Indian sisters the basics of cleanliness, nutrition, child health care, sewing, canning, and so on down the list of traditional Relief Society expertise; to invite "Indian brothers and sisters" to visit government-sponsored health clinics for examinations; and — most important — to include them in the societies as officers, musical performers, and leaders so they would have "a feeling of being wanted in this great Church program."[55]

Indian Relief Societies were already organized in various areas. The Seneca women on the Cattaraugus reservation in New York State had begun a Relief Society in 1950. According to a report from the group in the *Relief Society Magazine* in 1951, "All through the late winter and early spring the women prepared warm, nourishing meals for the men who, each Saturday, contributed their time to cutting logs and preparing them for the wood pulp mills, as their contribution to the building fund. When land and seed were needed for a branch welfare project, members of the Relief Society donated two and one half acres of land, with sufficient lima bean and corn seed to plant the entire plot."[56]

In the Southwest Indian Mission, Relief Society president Wilma Turley wrote, "The sisters make quilts, bake bread, and sew articles of clothing for themselves and to sell in bazaars."[57] Latter-day Saint Indian sisters outside North America included the first Cuna Indian Relief Society organized in 1966 in Cristobal, Panama, part of the Central American Mission. Two others, on adjoining islands, soon followed.[58]

President George Albert Smith had also wanted the Church to do something for Indian children. According to Sister Spafford,

Maricopa Indian children gaze at the camera while their mothers learn quilt making from supervising Relief Society sisters from Phoenix, Arizona, during 1950s. (Courtesy LDS Church Archives)

he believed that "if we could get the children young enough and get them active in the Church and in a good home environment, and give them a little education in the white man's world in which they had to live, work, and compete, that it would be a great thing for them." But he did not want the Indian children taken permanently from their parents and adopted into white families, as one national organization was promoting. "I want them kept for Father Lehi," he insisted.[59] The Indian student placement program evolved as the answer. It also answered the State of Utah's concern about informal placements that Church members had been arranging for about seven years.

The Indian Student Placement Committee was formed in 1954, with Elder Spencer W. Kimball, then an apostle, as the chairman. Because the Relief Society Social Service and Child Welfare Department was a licensed child-placing agency, it was assigned the placement of Indian students for the school year in white Latter-day Saint homes.[60] The staff of caseworkers found homes for the students, arranged their transportation, and provided for health clinics to test and treat the children as they arrived at reception centers. Local Relief Society sisters volunteered at the reception centers, preparing food, bathing the children, supplying towels and other materials. In 1964 the program's offices were moved from the Relief Society Building, although the program continued to operate under the license and direction of the society. By the end of 1966, the program was placing over 1,500 students a year. Relief Society sponsorship of the program continued until 1969, when it was transferred to the new Church Unified Social Services Department under the direction of the Presiding Bishopric. Relief Society women continued to serve, both as staff and as volunteers.

Active involvement of Relief Society in the community, so prominent in the preceding three decades, persisted in the 1950s in two other areas besides the professional services of the Social Service and Child Welfare Department: cooperation with the Red Cross and support for the fund-raising efforts of the March of Dimes and other health-related groups. The general board minutes of 1951 show a total of fifty-three community service organizations with which the society was cooperating in some way.

When development of the hydrogen bomb intensified fear of atomic war, the United States Federal Civil Defense Administration called for "a mighty force of housewives and mothers trained in home nursing" as an important part of homefront defense.[61] True to its traditions, Relief Society had already recruited volunteers to be trained as instructors for "lay classes in home nursing" under Red Cross auspices.[62] In 1956 the superintendent of the LDS Hospital in Salt Lake City asked Sister Spafford to recommend a woman to set up a program for volunteers at the hospital and to serve as an adviser. Sister Spafford recommended Rae B. Barker, a former member of the general board. Her highly successful "Pink Ladies" program soon spread to other hospitals.

President Spafford was circumspect, however. She counseled officers of local societies to support community programs as directed by their priesthood leaders. "Then we are not working at cross purposes nor under two directing heads," she said.[63] When the Red Cross requested Relief Society sisters to help feed and house victims of a Salt Lake City flood, Sister Spafford sent the representative first to the General Church Welfare Committee, which then made the request of Sister Spafford. The general board would keep in touch with—and sometimes support—a variety of public and private social agencies, but rarely with the direct and immediate involvement of the 1920s.

As for correcting community morals, in the absence of a clear call from church leaders to do so, Sister Spafford could say, "Ours is not necessarily the role of the campaigner against one or another of the existing community evils; ours is the role of the steady, consistent builder of men and women of integrity and moral fortitude who will uphold and promote virtuous community life."[64]

In addition to Relief Society's role as a service organization, leaders began expanding its role in educating its members, particularly with education for the homemaker. Two talks at the 1949 general Relief Society conference, one by Sister Spafford and the other by President J. Reuben Clark, Jr., of the First Presidency, emphasized women's divine — and endangered — calling as a homemaker. The General Authorities had just declared that the need for a family-hour program "was never greater in the history of the Church." Sister Spafford quoted the official publication of the National Family Life Association, voicing, albeit with exaggeration, a similar anxiety: "As the machine age spreads its patterns ever more widely, we have taken out of the home everything that has to do with living. You can't be born there, die there, be buried from there. . . . You can't work there, nor learn a skill. And entertainment must certainly be found elsewhere. What is there left but a lifeless dormitory where one changes one's clothes and where food, prepared elsewhere, is served?"[65] Although the description was overstated, it vividly expressed many people's fear that traditional values were being swept away in the onrushing flood of technology. In his talk the same afternoon President Clark commented that he had been "particularly struck" with what Sister Spafford had said. "We are," he feared, "losing the art of making homes."[66]

Sister Spafford had already quoted President Clark on woman's "high duty" as homemaker, and his earlier solemn warning: "You shall fail in your mission if you do not do it, and the world will be lost." Although she too felt it "a matter of deep concern," she was realistic, acknowledging that a woman might wish to combine another role with homemaking. This option was rarely available in earlier times, and she was, she said, "grateful for all that modern progress has done for woman — her liberation, her education, her opportunities."[67]

Both President Clark and Sister Spafford embraced a broad vision of homemaking. Although her talk recognized the importance of good housekeeping, that was not among the attributes of a good home that she listed in 1949. Those were: "a place of refuge . . . love and comradeship . . . family traditions, and ideals . . . culture and refinement . . . industry and thrift" — in sum, an environment "rich . . . in what President McKay has termed 'the great imponderables of life, such as serenity, faith, warm emotions, protectiveness, charity, affirmation, yes, and even common sense.' "[68]

This broad vision illumined, rather than limited, the Relief Society curriculum. After its core goal, "to develop within the members a firm and abiding testimony of the gospel," the further educational aim, "to make of them good mothers and homemakers," allowed for considerable variety. It also created a set of expectations that, while enlarging the sphere of many sisters, had repressive effects on others. The definition of homemaker was so broad that the curriculum could easily encompass the study of English and American literature (1949–1964), as well as of the Book of Mormon (1951–1957) and the Doctrine and Covenants (1957–1970). A good homemaker was expected to enrich her home, her children, and her own mind with the best in literature.

A homemaker was also expected to be a good manager, skilled in the arts of homemaking. Relief Society taught those specific skills monthly on work day, in both short lessons and workshop applications. Each woman was expected to give service to the needy as well as to her own family. The first year (1955–56) of the social science course, titled "Latter-day Saint Family Life," featured lessons that dealt with the individual Latter-day Saint woman, her society, and her service to others.

A homemaker was further expected to be a good citizen and knowledgeable about her government. Social science lessons were designed to teach her some basics. Following the 1948–50 course in "Latter-day Saint Political Thought," for three years (1950–53) Relief Society sisters studied lessons based on Joseph Fielding Smith's *The Progress of Man*, a gospel-oriented account of political and religious developments in the world. The United States Constitution itself was studied in detail from 1953 to 1956.[69]

The emphasis on an educated electorate received impetus from counselor Marianne Clark Sharp, who was in charge of curriculum. Even before her call to the general board, she had written in 1937, "Very often this summer I heard women close a political discussion half apologetically, — 'Well, I really don't know enough about the question to vote intelligently.' Our saying that 'it is impossible for a man to be saved in ignorance,' certainly includes the women."

St. George
Society of
front of th
Temple, c.
and Larso
Memories)

Sister Sharp did not excuse homemakers from the po
"Let us study not only the national problems, but
ones as well, as they affect us," she challenged women.
was implemented during the 1950s. Women who atte
Society classes and read the *Relief Society Magazine* c
exceptionally well informed about the United States
ernment and its relationship to international issues ar
day gospel. Political tensions of the times – the cold v
man doctrine of aid to foreign democracies, McCa
struggle of Third World countries for independence
1950s educational emphasis as pertinent to America
courses in the principles of social welfare had been
decades.

However, making the lessons pertinent to Relief S
worldwide was still an unsolved problem. Special stud
mission Relief Societies, published in the magazine
were discontinued in 1950, presumably because they ha
the problem. Societies outside the United States did t
could. "They'd take some of the same [theology] le
would," recalled Sister Sharp, "and then fill the rest c
with something else." Headquarters attempted to kee
trol of lesson content; according to Sister Sharp, "W

hem to prepare their own lessons, and then they'd send them in
o us, and then we'd keep them and could reissue them if we wanted
o. We were trying to get lessons to fit everybody."[71]

Besides liberal education, the society was, as ever, interested
n teaching homemaking skills, such as sewing, quilting, and other
ottage-industry crafts. Therefore, although welfare assignments
ad first claim on work-meeting time, the meeting's objective was
till to teach homemaking skills, particularly sewing. The postwar,
ong-skirted "new look," which quickly outdated whole wardrobes,
ueled the sewing program. Fashion shows, featuring models
lressed in clothing they had made themselves, followed in the wake
f sewing classes and were proudly reported in the magazine. As
he Great Depression and World War II faded into history, the
ewing became more oriented to clothing one's own family, beau-
ifying the home, and preparing for Relief Society–sponsored ba-
aars.

Bazaars were the sisters' chief method of raising funds to run
heir society, but money was not the only object. The primary
urpose, said Sister Spafford, was "developing and promoting the
reative arts of our sisters." Moreover, putting on a bazaar taught
omen useful principles of marketing—anticipating demand, con-
olling production, pricing, advertising, display techniques, and
ccounting.

Most of all, a bazaar was a social event and a tangible accom-
lishment. It could draw an inactive, lonely, or nonmember woman
to the circle of sisterhood. At a time when alienation was be-
oming a catchword for a modern malaise, the communal spirit of
Iormonism was flourishing in Relief Society bazaars and other
cial activities. Hundreds of pictures in the magazine's "Notes
om the Field" attested to their popularity. Even in countries
owly recovering from the war, the sisters found ways to mount a
azaar. "I admired their spirit to even try, with so little material
work with," wrote the Relief Society president about two bazaars
ld in the Finland Mission. She explained, "It is impossible to
y material or yarn of any kind here. The sisters unraveled old
eaters, socks, and shawls which had already been made over
veral times and remade them. They were happy with their efforts
d it was a goal for them to work toward."[72]

Most of the money earned from bazaars went to causes other
an the society budget or supplementing family incomes. The
ters in Turkey Creek, Louisiana, for instance, contributed hand-

Celebrating Relief Society: Left, presidency of Munich, Germany, branch Relief Society—Frauen-hilfsverein," or "FHV" on plate—are Ursula Kunids, secretary; Agnes S. Jacobs, president; and Ingeborg Gildner, counselor. (Courtesy LDS Church Archives) Right, sisters of Ogden (Utah) Eighteenth Ward present program in 1960. (Courtesy Eleanor Knowles)

somely to the construction of a new meetinghouse in 1953. "The Relief Society made so many quilts to sell for the building project that we could have wrapped the chapel three times around in quilts," said one contributor. She and the rest of the sisters had often worked late into the night making quilts and crocheting items to sell.[73] The money earned was theirs to spend, and they chose to donate it to the chapel.

Relief Society's New Home — "In the Shadow of the Temple"

In the 1950s, a decade of growth and prosperity, many new buildings were constructed. None was more important to the society than its own long-awaited home. The Relief Society Building benefited from the personal attention of Presiding Bishop LeGrand Richards, who, drawing on his long experience in real estate, gave wise counsel on the architect and the size and location of the building. When the First Presidency lagged in deciding on a site, Bishop Richards told President Spafford, "Now, if you will go to President McKay and tell him how embarrassed you are after hurrying the sisters to get their money in, and that the money is depreciating in value, and the cost of building is increasing every day, I believe he will give approval for you to commence construction. And if he asks you where you want to build, tell him that corner [where the building now stands], and if he asks for your

The Relief Society Building at 76 North Main Street in Salt Lake City was built with contributions from sisters around the world and dedicated in 1956. (Courtesy LDS Church Archives)

second choice, tell him that corner, and if he asks you for a third choice, tell him that same corner. It won't be any harder for them to decide where you can build it today than it will ten years from now." Sister Spafford followed his advice, and within ten days she received approval to go ahead.[74]

Ground was broken for the long-awaited Relief Society Building October 1, 1953, on the site Sarah M. Kimball had specified, "in the shadow of the temple," on the southeast corner of Main Street and North Temple in Salt Lake City. The following year a packet of items of historical interest, including the names of all contributors, was nested in the cornerstone.

Contributions had continued to come in since 1948, particularly from the European missions recovering from the war. The First Presidency matched not only the original half-million dollars but also the later donations of another hundred thousand dollars, which were spent in furnishing the building. Gifts arrived from sisters around the world, who expressed their desire to contribute to their society's home. Priceless Meissen porcelain from Germany and exquisite dolls from Japan confirmed that the sisterhood could heal old wounds. Some gifts were displayed in special built-in cases; all were carefully catalogued and acknowledged with individual letters from the general presidency.

The dedicatory services were held in the Salt Lake Tabernacle on October 3, 1956. At one point in the service, representatives of Relief Societies of thirty-two nations, dressed in their native costumes and carrying their national flags, marched down the aisles of the choir section and placed their flags, one by one, at each side of the rostrum. A large sphere symbolizing the world and bearing the words "World Sisterhood" further emphasized the international scope of Relief Society.[75]

In his dedicatory prayer, after quoting Paul's statement "Till we all come in the unity of the faith," President McKay added, "More potent for the good and happiness of the Church members than we realize are the Priesthood Quorums for the men, and the Auxiliary organizations for the women. These Thou hast placed in the Church for mutual service."[76] At the height of Relief Society's triumph as a unique organization with a home of its own, this was an important reminder of the interdependence of all the workers in the Lord's vineyard.

Priesthood Correlation: "A Program of Defense"

The halcyon years of the 1950s were followed by the stormy years, 1960–1974. Instead of the dreaded worldwide nuclear holocaust, however, the 1960s brought small-scale wars and small, savage acts of terrorism. In contrast to the yearning for stability that shaped the 1950s and early 1960s, discontent with the status quo plagued the succeeding decade. It was a time of ferment and dropouts, high ideals and bitter rebellion. The assassinations of President John F. Kennedy in 1963 and his brother Robert and the black leader Martin Luther King in 1968 seemed to brand the United States as a violent nation, but violence was worldwide—in Ireland with the Irish Republican Army, in Israel with that country's struggles with Arab neighbors and the Palestine Liberation Organization, at the infamous Berlin Wall, and in South Africa, South America, India, and China.

The long war in Vietnam evoked no rush of patriotism in the United States, only a longing for the war to end. "Letter to Viet Nam," first-prize winner in the 1965 Eliza R. Snow Poem Contest, closed with the couplet: "A wild goose honked, and in that spike of sound / I read 'Return' and felt my faith rebound."[77] Yet the national relief at the Vietnam pullout in 1973 immediately faded in the Watergate scandal that led to President Richard Nixon's resignation in 1974. The times were decidedly out of joint.

Sound and fury characterized America in the 1960s. Blacks and other minorities demanded their long-denied rights as citizens. The postwar "baby-boomers" became teenagers and demanded a louder voice in their schools or dropped out in "hippie" protests. Women demanded equal rights with men, especially their right to an equal slice of the economic pie. By 1960 the number of female workers was growing at a rate four times faster than that of males, and 40 percent of all women over sixteen were in the labor force, compared to 25 percent in 1940. But most of the women were in low-paying, low-status jobs, and voices raised in protest. Some of the voices were reasonable, some were strident. All were heard.

As a new president in 1961, John F. Kennedy created the first Presidential Commission on the Status of Women; the Civil Rights Act of 1964 included a ban on employment discrimination against women. The National Organization of Women (NOW) was founded in 1966. In 1972 the United States Congress finally passed a proposed Equal Rights Amendment to the Constitution, which then went to the states for ratification. In 1973 the United States Supreme Court opened the door to federally protected, welfare-funded abortions. Eventually a cigarette company would appeal to women with a series of ads headlined "You've Come a Long Way, Baby"—but where the way was leading was uncertain.

"We are in a program of defense," said Elder Harold B. Lee, speaking at the general conference priesthood session on September 30, 1961, and quoting from Doctrine and Covenants 115:6: "The Church of Jesus Christ was set upon the earth in this day . . . for a defense, and for a refuge from the storm, and from wrath when it should be poured out without mixture upon the whole earth." Elder Lee was chairman of the all-church coordinating council, newly organized by the First Presidency. In a carefully constructed address, he unfolded the plan for consolidating and simplifying priesthood and auxiliary curricula, programs, and activities.[78]

Successive efforts at church correlation in the twentieth century found fruition in this comprehensive plan for priesthood correlation. The new program began to spread its umbrella over every organization of the Church. If it cast a shadow over certain bright aspirations, that was the price of its protection. President David

O. McKay supported it, citing the need for unity in the Church. His successor, President Joseph Fielding Smith, approved the dramatic changes it brought during his administration, and President Harold B. Lee, who succeeded President Smith, was convinced of its necessity. Fear of threatening worldly forces hastened its growth.

By the 1970s the problems of church expansion also demanded the simplification promised by correlation. In the area of education alone, the writing, translating, printing, and distributing of manuals was becoming unmanageable. The simple, unmet needs of converts in distant lands seemed to reproach the elaborate programs designed for Utah's Wasatch Front. Even the conservation concerns of the times favored simplification.

In 1971 the Church commissioned several outside consultants to examine its administrative structure and make recommendations. These were helpful in the restructuring of church administration, further propelling many changes already begun and particularly affecting the auxiliaries.[79] Other changes were yet to come.

Some social analysts viewed the correlation movement as a successful attempt to deal with "organizational strains brought about by worldwide expansion and overwhelming growth." Some of the changes, however, unintentionally restricted the "responsibility, visibility and input" of Mormon women in their institutional roles.[80] Easily overlooked in any secular analysis, one strong intent of the correlation movement was to strengthen, not restrict, women's responsibility to teach and exemplify values deemed endangered in those troubled times. Relief Society's "institutional role" was to empower women as examples and teachers. Their administrative work in the Church was considered secondary.

"It is trite to say that foundations are crumbling under the home-life of the people," warned Elder Gordon B. Hinckley, speaking to Relief Society officers assembled in their 1966 conference. "This is evident not only in America. The bitter fruits of delinquency, hooliganism, and lawlessness are the subject of discussion and concern in England, in various parts of Europe, in Russia, in China, and in Japan." The influence of a good home was the answer, he continued, and the spirit of a home "generally is a reflection of the woman who stands as wife and mother." Relief Society could—and should—help her.[81]

Well aware of the Church's deepening concern, and in harmony with recommendations from the Church Correlation Committee, Relief Society had already begun teaching a series of lessons coordinated with Melchizedek Priesthood lessons and designed to help wives support their husbands in teaching the gospel in the home. So urgent was the need perceived that work meeting discussions made way for the new series from January through May of 1965, until the lessons could find their place in the social science time slot. Together with the priesthood lessons, they prepared the way for the new family home evening manual.

Pressed by the need, after fifty years of sporadic efforts the Church finally succeeded in promoting a family home evening that took root. Its success depended greatly on the sisters, who were encouraged by Relief Society and its "varied courses of study," nominally "under the direction of the Church Correlation Committee."[82] The direction of the committee was a light rein in 1967, when lessons were still initiated and the writers chosen by Relief Society. The courses of study were retitled in October 1966: theology became spiritual living, work meeting dressed up as homemaking meeting, social science was softened to social relations. Literature promised new dimensions as cultural refinement, though it continued the successful six-year course based on textbooks titled *Out of the Best Books*, compiled and edited by Bruce B. Clark and Robert K. Thomas of the Brigham Young University Department of English.

However, neither the board nor the correlation committees could solve the problem of fitting standard lessons to special needs. Mission leaders frequently made their own substitutions. In Japan, mission Relief Society president Toshiko Yanagida and her counselor Sister Yaginuma wrote courses of study (first obtaining permission from the mission president and sending the outlines to the general board), then had them printed and distributed. For the literature course in 1965–66, they reported, they "used Japanese poetry and encouraged sisters to write their own poetry and compiled their work into small books." Sister Yanagida commented with obvious satisfaction, "Thus it became a great stimulation."[83]

The general board produced two additional sets of lessons outside the standard curriculum. The first, a series of four volumes, was prepared for "possible use by the Lamanites and other special groups." The volumes included a four-year course in church history in place of the literature course, "Lessons from the Book of Mormon," by Kathryn S. Gilbert, and a short social science course titled "Essentials for Happy Family Living" by Camilla E. Kimball. Later, a separate set of manuals taught principles of sanitation and health. An inquiry into the use and value of these materials, sent to selected stake Relief Society presidents in May 1974, was inconclusive. Comments ranged from "In the branches where they are entirely Navajo . . . I would hate to see the Lamanite lessons discontinued," to "They resent having separate classes."[84] Nevertheless, the lessons were significant as precursors of the curriculum department's basic manuals for women and the welfare services training manuals, titled *Teaching Personal and Family Preparedness*, that would appear a decade later.

The second effort to provide special lessons targeted young women in campus Relief Societies. Reasoning that the younger sisters might need a choice of lessons, the general board developed a series of nine optional lesson booklets, designed primarily for young adults. For a while it seemed the lessons, which were well received, might be the vanguard of a trend toward diversification of lesson materials, but the trend toward simplification and consolidation was stronger. The optional lesson booklets were not republished after 1975.

In 1973 the three age-group committees relinquished their lesson-planning work to the new Curriculum Planning Committee. The following year a subcommittee, Instructional Development, was created as "an agent to ensure that all needed study materials are produced and correlated for adults, youth, and children."[85] The Relief Society general board would continue to submit course outlines and review lessons for another decade, but the Church was firmly committed to an integrated curriculum. The role of the auxiliaries was not to produce it, but to teach it — something the central committees could not do.

The teacher was the key, and in a lay church the teacher often needed training. In October 1970, an eleven-week, priesthood-sponsored teacher development program was announced. Offered at the ward and branch level, the popular course provided an impressive array of instructional materials and featured learning by group discussion and miniclass teaching experiences. Relief Society members were among the beneficiaries.

Correlation planners had defined welfare as one of four areas of priesthood responsibility. According to a 1966 training booklet, *The Church Correlation Program*, ward elders quorums had responsibility for the welfare program; seventies, for missionary work; and high priests, for genealogy.

The fourth correlation area, home teaching, came directly under the bishop; he was also chairman of the ward priesthood executive committee (composed of bishopric, Melchizedek Priesthood leaders, and Aaronic Priesthood general secretaries), which, with the addition of the Relief Society presidency, doubled as the ward welfare committee. The auxiliary presidents met monthly as part of the ward council, also chaired by the bishop; the priesthood executive committee and welfare committee met weekly.

At the general level, Relief Society involvement in welfare and social services altered significantly under correlation's administrative shifts. "In the employment service there were 34 countries and 47 states represented in the people who came for employment [in 1964]," reported Josephine Patterson, director of the Relief Society Social Service and Child Welfare Department, on March 3, 1965. "Our two employment counselors gave 11,385 interviews and placed 1,028 girls in jobs." It was her last report to the board about the employment arm of the department. The employment services — "both the clerical and the domestic service" — had been moved to the Church Welfare Department.[86] The rest of the Relief Society Social Service Department would soon follow.

At the general board meeting of October 8, 1969, President Spafford announced that the new Church Unified Social Services Department, chaired by a member of the Council of the Twelve, would take over Relief Society programs for unwed mothers and adoptions, as well as youth services, and Indian student placement.[87] Relief Society women would continue to serve as professional staff members and volunteers, thus assuring the continued success of social service programs the society had nurtured for half a century.

In 1973 the Health Services Corporation, Unified Social Services Department, and general church welfare program combined to become the Welfare Services Department, "bringing into full correlation the three welfare functions of the Church." Presiding Bishop Victor L. Brown chaired the new committee directing welfare services; President Spafford was on the committee.[88] She spoke in the first general welfare services meeting held in the Salt Lake Tabernacle on October 6, 1973, and at subsequent welfare sessions. Such continuing representation indicated that Relief Society had not been relieved of all responsibility in welfare services. President Kimball would later affirm with regard to the women, "There is partnership with the priesthood."[89]

"The Relief Society has been and still is the bishop's chief help in administering to those in need," Elder Henry D. Taylor, Assistant to the Council of the Twelve, assured the sisters gathered in Relief Society general conference in 1968.[90] Elder Harold B. Lee spoke of the relationship between Relief Society and the priesthood: "In their joint responsibility in rendering compassionate service, they present a sort of 'Father and Mother Image' in the Kingdom of God to look after the needy and the unfortunate."[91] Tradition and practicabilty favored the one-to-one relationship over the complexity of committees.

The society's emphasis now shifted to training the sisters to give more effective compassionate service as individuals rather than as part of a group. For three years (1973–1976) everyone who attended the social relations class received instruction in "the great opportunities for compassionate service available to each individual, as well as to the visiting teacher."[92] The social service institute courses of the 1920s and 1930s had focused on making Relief Society family welfare work more professional; although many of the same principles were taught in the new course, the emphasis now was on broadening the base of service. Every sister had a commission to serve.

The sisters also had new social projects to nourish. Among them was a health missionary program begun in February 1971, with forty-nine single women, all registered nurses, and three couples called to teach health principles and welfare concepts in disadvantaged areas of the Church. The society's long-standing promotion of nursing education had a new outlet.

In spite of the centripetal force of correlation, which on the whole drew the sisters' service inward to family and church, a centrifugal outreach into the community continued as a Relief Society goal during the 1960s. An editorial in the *Relief Society Magazine* in 1967 encouraged Latter-day Saint women to give volunteer service in such organizations as the Red Cross, Traveler's Aid, child-care clinics, and hospitals, and in "assistance to women while in prison and after release, youth guidance work, detention homes, parent-teacher associations, to name a few." Even a mother with children could "set aside time to engage as a volunteer, especially in programs which touch her children and community" — and then expand her services after her children were grown.[93]

Relief Society sponsored Red Cross home nursing projects again in 1968. In Arizona, two hundred women, including three Indian sisters, took the course to become certified instructors. They in turn taught several thousand women. According to the general board minutes, "It was the first time that the Red Cross has been able to have the nursing course taught in small communities."[94]

Relief Society units overseas also cooperated with the Red Cross. Mavis Cutts, president of the Melbourne Stake Relief Society in Australia, reported in 1962, "Recently we had shocking brush fires which encircled our city, and a national emergency was declared. After the fires had been raging for two days, the Red Cross society found that we keep a list of nursing sisters, and we were thrilled to be able to send some of our wonderful sisters to the rescue at very short notice. . . . We are prepared for any emergency."[95] Sister Cutts, an experienced social worker, also headed the Melbourne Stake Relief Society's licensed social service agency for unwed mothers and adoption placement. Five meetinghouses served as interviewing centers.[96]

"Mormon Women Have Something to Give"

Relief Society's membership in the National Council of Women (NCW) represented another long-standing commitment to community service. The society's eighty-year involvement with the NCW reached a new high under Sister Spafford. Yet she had not always favored that involvement. In fact, shortly after she became general president of Relief Society, she and her counselor Marianne Sharp felt that the society should discontinue its membership in NCW. Sister Spafford took their recommendation to President George Albert Smith, saying, "It's costly to go to New York, and really, President Smith, we don't get anything from that council." President Smith gently chastised, "Do you always think in terms of what you get? Don't you think it's well to think in terms of what you have to give?" He then urged her to a new perspective: "I think Mormon women have something to give to the women of the world and they may also learn from them. Rather than to terminate this membership, I suggest that you take two or three of your ablest board members and go to these meetings. . . . Go back and make your influence felt."[97]

In 1954 Sister Spafford had committed herself to the extent that she was chosen to head the NCW's ten-woman delegation to the International Council of Women's conference in Helsinki, Finland. At the official opening she was invited to lead the grand march of chairmen from the national delegations. As the chairmen stood before their national flags to be introduced, the Finnish NCW chairman announced that Mrs. Spafford represented "the oldest and most influential council in the world." At this moment, the honored delegate's thoughts leaped back in time: "As I looked out at the glittering audience made up of people of many nations and heard these words spoken, my mind suddenly flashed back to the words of our pioneer [Relief Society] leaders at which Sister Sharp and I had smiled . . . 'standing as we do at the head of the women of the world,' . . . [and on the masthead of the *Woman's Exponent*:] 'For the rights of the women of Zion and the rights of the women of all nations.' " These words no longer seemed high-blown, full of nineteenth-century fervor and hyperbole. "This night in that far-away northern country, I did not smile. I knew that our pioneer women leaders had been given by divine insight a knowledge of the destiny of Relief Society. . . . It is my conviction that the time had come for Relief Society's influence to be felt worldwide among womankind."[98]

Sister Spafford's influence reached even behind the iron curtain. In the course of her trip to Finland, she visited Berlin and taped greetings from "the women of America" to be broadcast over Radio Free Europe to women in Czechoslovakia, Poland, Bulgaria, and Romania. "In a world filled with sorrow and suffering, differing ideologies and political beliefs," she said, "there still remain constant a few virtues. One of these is the understanding of woman for woman."[99] In the NCW she actively sought to increase that understanding.

In 1967 Sister Spafford was nominated to serve as president of the NCW from 1968 to 1970. Though she was reluctant, President David O. McKay counseled her to accept the nomination. "We will help you," he assured her. "Come as often as you wish to the Presidency in your work." It was not what Sister Spafford wanted to hear and she started to cry, but once again she accepted counsel. Following her unanimous election, she requested a blessing from President N. Eldon Tanner. The problems would be great, he told her, but the light of the gospel would help her to see the way.[100]

Of her opportunities as president of the National Council, Belle Spafford said, "It will give me a chance to encourage ladies to achieve their full potentials. . . . Although I believe that a woman's primary place is in the home, I think that her world is expanding and changing. Today it is becoming more and more essential for her to be a contributing citizen in her community."[101] In her assessment of her term of office, she felt that she made three great contributions to the National Council of Women: she practiced principles of financial management that kept it solvent; she promoted good will among the member organizations; following her two-year term as president, she chaired the Constitutional Revision Committee that reviewed and rewrote the constitution and bylaws of the council.[102]

The outward thrust was, as usual, balanced by increased introspection and local activity, which could also affect the broader community. In 1966, the society finally succeeded in completing the bell tower for the Nauvoo bell on Temple Square. This long-postponed memorial to its past had been originally planned under President Amy Brown Lyman to honor the society's centennial in 1942. The bell was significant to the sisters in several ways. A gift from British converts, it had hung in the belfry of the Nauvoo Temple even before the building was completed. During the exodus from Nauvoo, Eliza R. Snow traveled in the same company as the bell and heard it call men and women to their daily prayers and duties. In the valley the bell was displayed in parades and celebrations; for a time it called the children to Brigham Young's schoolhouse.[103] Its significance extended into the future as well. General board member Mary Grant Judd wrote hopefully of the proposed campanile to house the 1,500-pound bell: "We believe that in the near future thousands of visitors who come to Temple Square will pause before this tie between the past and the present . . . as the guide recites the early history of the Church. . . . And, since the story of our organization will be included, our influence for good will extend on and on in ever-widening circles."[104]

Music was another display case for the society's widening spheres of influence. Relief Society choruses flourished during the 1960s, springing up even where none had been before. No society choruses existed in Austria when a separate mission was created there in 1960. The new mission president asked the Klagenfurt Branch Relief Society to present two choral numbers at the next district conference. "We can't sing," protested the Relief Society president, declaring they had "no solo voices or even good voices." "Sister, do you have faith?" asked the mission president. Yes, she had faith. "Then we will expect the Relief Society chorus of Klagenfurt to present two numbers in our next district conference," he concluded. As the eight members of the Klagenfurt Relief Society sang at the conference, amazement turned to appreciation.

Florence Jepperson Madsen rehearses local British sisters prior to their joining Singing Mothers from the United States for concerts in England and Ireland in 1961. (Courtesy Brigham Young University Photographic Archives)

Within the year nearly every branch in the mission had a Relief Society chorus.[105]

In 1961 the International Singing Mothers Chorus, made up of fifty-seven singers from Utah and two hundred from the British Isles, gave concerts in seven major British cities and at the dedication of the Hyde Park Chapel in London. By the end of 1962 there were over 2,700 Singing Mothers choruses and a new book, *Music Leadership in Relief Society*, by Florence Jepperson Madsen, was selling at Relief Society headquarters for ninety cents. In 1964 three hundred Singing Mothers from New York and adjacent stakes sang to thousands at the New York World's Fair and to many more on the National Broadcasting Corporation's radio series "Faith in Action." The 1967 Relief Society general conference featured four hundred Singing Mothers from Canada, celebrating their centennial that year, and NBC showcased another Singing Mothers chorus in a Christmas Eve Special.[106] The familiar white blouses, too bright for television, gave way to pastels in 1961, and the evocative but restrictive title Singing Mothers became Relief Society Chorus in 1971 and Relief Society Choir in 1974. As an incentive to women composers, the Relief Society began sponsoring a song contest in 1968, with prizes provided by general board member Cleone Rich Eccles, an accomplished violinist. Winning songs were performed at general Relief Society conference until 1976.

Consolidating and Simplifying Church Programs

The impact of continuing priesthood correlation, particularly on local Relief Societies, was felt most keenly at the end of the 1960s. Few changes in the traditional Relief Society structure could have been more trying to President Spafford than the loss of financial autonomy. She herself was an astute manager who had, for example, set up wage scales and job classifications for Relief Society employees at headquarters even before a church personnel department was established. In her 1963 official conference report she voiced the society's satisfaction with managing its own money. "Relief Society takes pride in the fact that it independently maintains itself financially," said Sister Spafford. "The judicious raising of funds and their wise disbursement are regarded as important in the training of Relief Society women."

Fund-raising activities were intended to "reflect the interests and regular work of the Society and, at the same time, develop the talents and abilities of the sisters."[107] Typical of the 1960s are these fund-raising activities of the Gooding (Idaho) Ward Relief Society: "We had cooked food sales and earned enough money to have three specially designed cribs made for the younger children and babies. . . . We also served a Democratic Rally Banquet and earned enough to purchase eight large folding tables for our work day activities and ward dinners."[108]

The presiding priesthood authorities, however, desired that the Relief Society sisters develop their abilities in other directions. On June 10, 1970, a letter from the First Presidency was posted to all stake, mission, branch, and district presidents and bishops announcing a change that would be a continuing challenge to both Relief Society and priesthood leaders: "It has been felt that in the past too much of the energy of the Relief Society has been diverted from its real purposes and channeled instead into money-raising activities. To remedy this situation, it has been decided that the Relief Society hereafter should be financed out of the budgets and thus be relieved of the burden of raising its operating funds by conducting bazaars or by other similar means." Justifying the move, the statement continued, "This change in policy will place the duty of fund raising properly where it belongs, on the Priesthood, leaving the sisters free to perform their specially assigned tasks."[109]

A follow-up letter dated July 17, 1970, specified that Relief Society dues were to be discontinued and all assets turned over to the appropriate priesthood officers. With the help of President Henry D. Moyle of the First Presidency, President Spafford had wisely invested Relief Society funds in bonds and securities. When the Relief Society headquarters assets were turned over to the Church, they amounted to over two million dollars.[110] One of the society's last expenditures from its own funds was for a gift to the Church Administration Building of a large oriental rug, "hand-woven originally for the Bulgarian Royal Palace."[111]

The First Presidency's initial letter had asked local priesthood leaders to "urge the sisters to concentrate their efforts now on their true purposes of rendering compassionate services, improving homemaking skills, and promoting the cultural and spiritual well being of the Relief Society's members." However, faced with the problem of providing money for the society from tight budgets, bishops and branch presidents frequently asked the sisters to help raise funds for the "over-all fund-raising program of the Church unit," as the second letter from the First Presidency permitted. Thus the original purpose of the change was somewhat diluted. Nonetheless, the principle had been stated: priesthood leaders were responsible for funding Relief Society.

Another adjustment that affected not only the Relief Society but all auxiliaries was the 1970 correlation of church publications. The little magazine that would fit in a woman's handbag had bloomed brightly during President Spafford's era. Sister Spafford saw the *Relief Society Magazine* as "a medium through which the literary aspirations of the sisters of the Church could find the light of day." Under her direction it had become more readable, with stories and poems appearing more frequently and artwork becoming more lavish. Conscious of the magazine's value as a historical repository, Sister Spafford thought that "everything of historical importance ought to be in that magazine . . . some of the great, great addresses by the Brethren and some of the great addresses by the women of the Church." Most of all, the magazine had offered "a means of teaching . . . not only to instruct the women in the principles of the gospel and the procedures of Relief Society, but in gracious womanhood."[112]

As both counselor in the presidency and editor of the magazine,

341

Marianne Clark Sharp had been well equipped to carry out President Spafford's desires. Her editorials were masterpieces of literary expression. Vesta Pierce Crawford, appointed associate editor in October 1947, was a frequent contributor and encouraged excellence. The poetry and short-story contests enticed good writers, not only with modest prizes but also with hopes of publication. "How-to-write" articles by recognized authors encouraged newcomers. Many a budding writer blossomed with the help of the magazine; it was an old-fashioned garden, where a variety of compositions bloomed in happy profusion, and its pages became the seedbed to such authors as Juanita Brooks, Rodello Hunter, and Emma Lou Thayne. Color arrived to stay in November 1958. After 1962 it was standard inside the magazine as well as on the covers. The periodical received two awards: one from the Simpson Lee Paper Company in 1959 for the Christmas cover, and the 1964 Mead Award of Merit "for excellence in editorial content, illustrations, color reproductions, and printing."[113]

The addition of color increased production costs and the society had to increase the subscription rate from one dollar a year to a dollar and a half, but the subscription list grew. By 1969 it had reached nearly 300,000—including 7,000 for a new Spanish edition. The first issue in Spanish, published in June 1966, featured on the cover a full-color picture of Machu Picchu in Peru. Translation, done in Salt Lake City with the encouragement and support of Mexico-born Elder Marion G. Romney, was well worth the extra effort. When President Spafford and her counselor Louise W. Madsen visited Mexico, the sisters showed them their magazines carefully protected with organdy covers. "They were so thrilled to know that they were getting just what the rest of the Church was getting," mused Sister Sharp in later years.[114]

A change affecting the Church's magazines was foreshadowed in 1961, when Elder Harold B. Lee said in his landmark correlation address to the priesthood session: "We may possibly and hopefully look forward to the consolidation and simplification of . . . church publications."[115] Two forces were at work: the desire for efficient use of financial resources and the push for unity in the priesthood-directed church. In 1968 a committee composed of Elders Spencer W. Kimball and Howard W. Hunter of the Council of the Twelve and Doyle L. Green, managing editor of the *Improvement Era,* was asked to make recommendations on consolidating the periodicals. Two years later a letter from the First Presidency, dated April 24,

1970, was sent to the heads of the auxiliaries and the Church School System, informing them that "for the overall good of the Church and in harmony with our correlation program," all Church magazines would be unified into three publications—one for adults, one for youth, and one for children—beginning in January 1971. The new magazines would be published under the direct supervision of the First Presidency and the Council of the Twelve, and the various organizations would have representation on advisory committees.[116]

When Sister Spafford read the letter to her general board, she reminded them that all the reasons against discontinuing the magazine had already been pointed out to the presiding authorities, and that the advantages of the new proposal outweighed the disadvantages. "Great blessings [will] come as the sisters of Relief Society adjust to the new program," she concluded. The board minutes recorded succinctly, "There was no discussion following this announcement."[117]

The *Relief Society Magazine* reached the end of its fruitful fifty-six-year career in distinguished company: the *Millennial Star*, which had been published in Great Britain since 1840; the Sunday School's *Instructor*, which had begun in 1866 as the *Juvenile Instructor*; the Mutual Improvement Associations' seventy-three-year-old *Improvement Era*; the Primary's *Children's Friend*, begun in 1902; and the seminaries' and institutes' more recent *Impact*.

The three new consolidated magazines—the *Ensign*, the *New Era*, and the *Friend*—would represent the Church, not its auxiliaries. Their main goal was "to strengthen the family, the basic unit of the Church. . . . The new magazines will be great aids to families in helping each member gain a testimony," wrote President Joseph Fielding Smith in the next-to-last issue of the *Improvement Era*, "for the gaining and the keeping of testimonies should be a family project."[118]

"Changing times bring changing conditions," began the editorial written by Marianne Clark Sharp in the final issue of the *Relief Society Magazine*, December 1970. It was the last of many she had written and, significantly, was titled "Facing Forward." After recalling some highlights of the magazine's fifty-six years and thanking those who had enriched its pages, Sister Sharp concluded, "We still, obedient to the priesthood and receiving direction from them, face forward in step with the new era of the 1970s with anticipation and a sense of dedication and support for the all-adult magazine. Moriturae te salutamus."

"We who are about to die salute thee." Thus, with characteristic dignity and good will, the former Latin teacher greeted the future on behalf of her beloved periodical as it passed into history. Perceptive readers, remembering that Roman gladiators saluted their emperor with the same words, might also have sensed the deep allegiance to leaders that had kept the Relief Society strong through the stormy years.

"Today is not an easy, comfortable period of time," admitted President Spafford in her 1969 conference address to the sisters. The problems of replacing the necessary functions of the magazine were not easily solved. The new *Ensign* tried to address the sisters' interests with a section titled "Today's Family," edited by Mabel Jones Gabbott, giving "special attention to the Mormon woman in her home, her community, her church, and her world today."[119] The *Ensign* also sponsored poetry and short-story contests open to all Latter-day Saints. The general board began communicating with the local Relief Society officers through a new quarterly leaflet with a familiar title: "Notes to the Field." New lesson manuals — still small enough to fit in a woman's handbag — were developed with the help of curriculum committees. And a new *Relief Society Handbook,* published in 1972, explained the many changes in policies and procedures.

Much of the impetus behind correlation changes was the Church's need to accommodate worldwide growth. The Relief Society had long been proud of its international membership, and now as the Church expanded rapidly following World War II, the number of societies grew also. Full-fledged stakes were springing up in Europe, South America, Asia, Africa, and elsewhere. At the same time, small groups of Latter-day Saints were meeting in homes or on military bases in Afghanistan, Guam, Libya, the Cook Islands, and other remote areas. Relief Societies were there, as well as in the burgeoning stakes, often headed by intrepid women like Maude Pearson of Beirut, Lebanon. Sister Pearson went to Beirut in 1950 on a three-year contract as nursing supervisor and instructor at the American University of Beirut and stayed for twenty-five years. As the third president of the Beirut Branch Relief Society, organized February 23, 1962, she found ample scope for her training as a nurse. "The Relief Society sisters were very busy assisting with compassionate services, health supervision and welfare among the refugee families who were rapidly taking up residency in Lebanon," reported her friend Rita Parker.[120] After Sister Pearson's retirement in 1975 and her return to Idaho, she received the Order of Health medal from the Lebanese government—a well-deserved honor in the tradition of Relief Society service.

Across a hostile border in Israel, another Latter-day Saint nurse, Margreta Spencer, was chief physiotherapist in the general hospital at Safed. Canadian-born, she chose to become an Israeli and was an active member of Relief Society when the Jerusalem Branch was organized in 1973. In the late 1980s she was a mainstay in the Galilee Branch in the Israel District.[121]

Once considered a sisterhood of older women, the society was still reaching out to different age groups as well as to far-off countries. Ward presidencies received instructions from the general board to conduct nurseries for the increasing numbers of young mothers attending. Under the supervision of counselor Louise Madsen, the board prepared a nursery kit and a booklet, *Our Relief Society Nursery,* followed in 1968 by a nursery manual compiled with the help of the Church Correlation Writing Committee. Older women were still a prominent age-group in Relief Society. In 1963 the society received a citation from the National Retired Teachers Association and the American Association of Retired Persons for "significant and valued contributions to the enrichment of retirement living."[122]

An announcement that would change Relief Society beyond all previous changes appeared in the second "Notes to the Field" in May 1971: "By directive of the First Presidency all Latter-day Saint women are to be enrolled as members of Relief Society effective September 1, 1971." No longer would Relief Society count only those women interested enough to pay dues. "Relief Society ward presidents are advised to welcome warmly [newly] enrolled members and to introduce them to the sisters at the first regular meeting of the Society which they attend," the directive continued. "Sisters will no longer be accepted by vote." Names of the too-busy, the inactive, and even the hostile would be on the rolls.

Some officers were shocked, foreseeing that their activity percentages would plummet. Others, more farsighted, gladly accepted the society's new responsibility for every Latter-day Saint woman. According to the general board minutes, the change was made "in recognition of the growth of the Church and the need to put much of what comes from records into computers."[123] Changing times—

and inspiration — had overruled tradition. The society had received a mandate to be responsible for enrolling all Latter-day Saint women. It would sponsor separate sessions for younger single women, with groupings flexible and responsive to personal interests.[124]

The general Relief Society conference of 1973 focused on the entrance of the younger women. The general board's youngest member, Kristin Theurer, twenty-one, said in an interview: "I think there will be a greater sisterhood among all the women in the Church. It's silly to talk about a generation gap in the gospel, because, basically, we're all working for the same end — eternal life."[125]

Of all the highlights of Belle Spafford's long administration — the aid to war victims, the Relief Society Building, the campanile, successful operation of social service agencies, the *Relief Society Magazine* in Spanish, the international recognition accorded the president — surely the enrollment of every Latter-day Saint woman in Relief Society was one of the most significant. Another was the loyal acceptance of correlation changes that brought the society under the umbrella of the priesthood.

"All working for the same end — eternal life." That was the key to understanding the changes that had taken place. Relief Society sisters had been released from responsibility for managing the social services of the Church, raising their own funds, and producing their own teaching materials and were being asked to achieve an even higher level of personal service to family and church. The new commandment to draw every Latter-day Saint sister into the Relief Society circle was an awesome responsibility. Imperfectly understood and impossible to fulfill completely, it was nonetheless the Lord's answer to the cries of alienation and despair during these stormy years — and to the hunger for love, the thirst for eternal values. The answer had been given; it needed only to be embraced.

CHAPTER 11

STARS TO STEER BY
1974–1984

On October 3, 1974, the customary crowd of stake Relief Society leaders filled the Tabernacle on Temple Square for the last session of the two-day Relief Society general conference. President N. Eldon Tanner had earlier paid special tribute to Belle S. Spafford, whose presidency of more than twenty-nine years, under six presidents of the Church, was already the longest in Relief Society history. Many of the sisters sitting in the Tabernacle had never served under another Relief Society general president — nor had the mothers of many.

When President Spencer W. Kimball announced at the last session of the conference that Sister Spafford was being released, gasps could be heard throughout the building. The whispered exclamations of "Oh, no!" were clearly heard by the new president, Barbara Bradshaw Smith, who sat among her fellow general board members. When she came to the podium to respond to her call, her voice quivered. "When you said, 'Oh, no,' " she acknowledged, "so did I. I have sat in this audience many times; when the conference was over, I have thanked my Heavenly Father that Sister Spafford was still our general president. And when President Kimball came to my home and called me to be the general president of Relief Society, I couldn't believe it could happen to me."[1]

Although she expressed feelings of inadequacy, Barbara Smith proved a capable leader through difficult times — a time when Latter-day Saint women's faith in divine authority would be scorned as submission to male domination. In every era the society had faced challenges to its cooperation with priesthood leaders and to its internal unity. Now correlation changes and increasing diversity among members would also strain the fabric of sisterhood.

Barbara Bradshaw Smith, an enthusiastic homemaker for

347

Relief Society president Barbara B. Smith, right, and predecessor Belle S. Spafford greet each other warmly at the 1980 women's meeting. (Courtesy LDS Church Archives)

whom rearing seven children and serving in the Church had been a full-time career, demonstrated the same understanding of priesthood authority as had Sister Spafford. At a time when many Latter-day Saint women were still unreconciled to the loss of their magazine and to other changes in Relief Society, Sister Smith insisted on willing cooperation. "All that the Brethren have taught me says that we have a companion relationship—not inferior or subordinate, but companion, side-by-side," she said. "Women need to know and feel the security of the priesthood direction and the joy of working in Relief Society as a companion organization to the priesthood."[2]

However, she did not turn a deaf ear to other views. One of her early projects was an ad hoc committee of key women in both the Church and community who met for several years on Sunday mornings to talk. Their discussions were spirited and sometimes critical of Relief Society and the Church, but Sister Smith listened and asked often, "What can we do about it?" Their concerns were not new, but they were growing: How could single sisters feel accepted in a marriage-minded church? Should mothers of young children work outside the home? Was abortion always wrong? or birth control? Should women join the military forces? How could a traditional Relief Society address the needs of all its diverse sisters? And what about the Equal Rights Amendment?

Sister Smith's search for answers led, among other things, to the establishment of the Women's Research Institute at the Brigham Young University in 1978. During its first five years, under the direction of Ida Smith, volunteers extracted information and catalogued topical files on women's issues, prepared reports, and assisted with the preparation of symposia. In addition to her administrative duties, Sister Smith prepared the documentation that brought a three-year grant from the National Science Foundation to sponsor Women in Science workshops at BYU, filled over one hundred speaking engagements, and counseled with both students and nonstudents. She and her counselors, Janath R. Cannon and Marian R. Boyer, consistently sought approaches that allow the fabric of sisterhood to stretch rather than unravel under stress.

Women's issues were, of course, only part of the challenge. Robert O'Brien, the senior editor of *Reader's Digest*, said of Americans in 1974, "Ironically, on the very eve of the nation's 200th birthday, many Americans feel bewildered, betrayed, and adrift. They seem to have lost their way. The thought of the manifest destiny of America no longer thrills them. They cannot bring themselves any longer really to believe in it."[3]

The United States Bicentennial celebration sparked a brief flare of patriotism in 1976, but the nation was still too shadowed by the memory of Watergate to be wholly proud. The controversial war in Vietnam finally drew to a close in 1974–75 after years of growing frustration. The unconditional surrender of South Vietnam to the communist forces of North Vietnam on April 10, 1975, following the earlier withdrawal of United States forces, set off a wave of refugees that swelled to a flood as guerrilla warfare and government oppression devastated Southeast Asia. In Utah alone, over six thousand refugees had arrived by 1981. Many of them were — or soon became — Latter-day Saints, bringing home to church headquarters the problems of language and culture barriers.[4]

Another challenge was the accelerating exodus of women from the home into the job market. By 1980 more American women were in the work force than at home; 47 percent of those mothers had children under six. In other Western nations the ratio was even higher; in Finland 73 percent of the women were employed in 1976.

The 1980 United States census also revealed that in one decade the ratio of divorced to married couples had doubled; the number living together without marriage had tripled; and the number of one-parent families (90 percent headed by women) had risen from

12 percent to 19 percent. Soaring inflation, a rising divorce rate, and vigorous demands by many women for a wage-earner's independence speeded a trend away from full-time homemaking and strengthened demands for ratification of the Equal Rights Amendment to the Constitution. The erosion of woman's traditional role as keeper of the hearth had great import not only for Relief Society but also for all other organizations dependent on women volunteers.

Changes in the Church during this decade would also affect Relief Society. Both the direction and the speed of church growth were set by a new prophet, seer, and revelator, President Spencer W. Kimball, who was ordained on December 30, 1973, after the sudden death of President Harold B. Lee. Perhaps the most dramatic change for the Church as a whole came on June 9, 1978, when the First Presidency announced that the Lord "has heard our prayers, and by revelation has confirmed that the long-promised day has come when every faithful, worthy man in the church may receive the holy priesthood . . . without regard for race or color."[5] A Relief Society president in New England remembers the excitement that greeted news of this change. "We were all thrilled with the announcement," she said. "We felt a great surge of love for President Kimball, especially when we read that he had spent so long praying about this question, sensing both his profound concern and his obedience. Quite a lesson as well as a reason for rejoicing!"[6]

Although theoretically race had never been a factor in Relief Society membership, a subtle barrier to universal sisterhood had been removed. As Elder Neal A. Maxwell observed, "The Church was first *local,* then moved westward to become *regional.* Later it became *national,* then *international.* With the priesthood revelation of June 1978, the Church received its authority to bestow *all* blessings on *all* of our Father's worthy children: its undertakings can be universal."[7]

Church membership from 1970 to 1980 increased by over a million, from 2,191,000 to 3,267,000. A burst of temple building accompanied the rise in membership. During President Spencer W. Kimball's administration, twenty-one temples were added to the previous total of fifteen, and ten more were announced. Relief Society temple clothing centers rose beside the new temples. By 1980 the missionary force had more than doubled, and the addition of older couples brought increased missionary involvement for women.

The number of new members living outside the United States increased dramatically. Hundreds of new church units headed by inexperienced officers needed simple, basic manuals and a manageable administrative structure. The influx of refugees from Southeast Asia and the increase in Hispanic immigration to the United States meant that even Utah had many "developing" groups.

By the time President Kimball presented a new basic-unit program in October 1980, the Relief Society general board was already debating proposals to have three levels of Relief Society. After much discussion a three-phase outline for beginning, interim, and full-scale Relief Society was approved by the Council of the Twelve on February 26, 1981. Simplicity was now available, though some small groups resisted adopting the simpler program, assuming it implied lesser status.[8]

Overall, in spite of the simplification ideal, church administration, in striving to accommodate growth, became more complex and professionalized as new levels of authority were added, departments multiplied, and priesthood direction was emphasized in all areas of activity. On occasion overzealous emphasis on priesthood leadership would need correction. In September 1978 the First Presidency and Council of the Twelve, for instance, clarified for Regional Representatives that "it is permissible for sisters to offer prayers in any meetings they attend, including sacrament meetings, Sunday School meetings, and stake conferences. Relief Society visiting teachers may offer prayers in homes that they enter in fulfilling visiting teaching assignments."[9]

At the general level, auxiliary presidencies accustomed to having members of the Quorum of the Twelve as advisers were assigned advisers from the newly strengthened First Quorum of Seventy. Some critics saw Latter-day Saint women as cut off from administrative power in this growth process; however, the Relief Society still had a certain partnership status in the church hierarchy. The general presidency still met regularly with the Presiding Bishopric. President Nathan Eldon Tanner explained to the Church Coordinating Council in January 1976 the concept that was later issued as policy to the Church at large: "The presidency of the Relief Society, having a specific responsibility placed upon them by the President of the Church at the time they were organized, should be considered as a partner with the Melchizedek Priesthood in somewhat the same manner as a wife would work with her husband in directing the affairs of the family."[10] The "father and mother" image, powerfully evoked in past welfare talks, had not disappeared.

New Responses to Welfare Needs

Welfare would remain a cooperative priesthood–Relief Society effort on many fronts. After divesting itself of fifteen hospitals in the western United States in 1974, the Church called more welfare missionaries to spread its new message of preventive health care. "The Church is not building hospitals and clinics throughout the world," Dr. James O. Mason, church commissioner of health services, explained. "They are not the most important health resource; the home is where good health begins."[11] The shift in health care emphasis had clear implications for Relief Society.

By 1974 Relief Society was increasingly involved in the total church response to welfare needs. Some of the needs were ongoing; others appeared suddenly in natural disasters. On June 5, 1976, the Teton Dam in eastern Idaho burst, sending a wall of water through ten communities and creating widespread destruction. As people fled, many took with them whatever came first to hand. One panic-stricken woman grabbed a pan of rising bread dough; another remembered counsel in a Relief Society lesson and rescued her genealogy and other important records. The safety of family members quickly became the major concern, and a death toll of only eleven was deemed miraculous.

The aftermath of the disaster provided a large-scale test of the Church's readiness to respond in such crises. In an area that was 95 percent Latter-day Saint, over eight hundred homes had been destroyed; thirty thousand acres of farmland were spoiled; and eleven church buildings were damaged. Everything in the path of the flood was covered with a thick layer of foul-smelling mud and debris.

Within hours of the first flood report, a truckload of supplies was on its way from church headquarters. Thousands of refugees from the flood were housed and fed at Ricks College in Rexburg, where a temporary bishops storehouse was established. In one day the college cafeteria served thirty thousand meals. Other help soon reached the stricken communities. As word of the flood damage spread, an estimated forty thousand volunteers, including many non-Mormons, arrived on buses, bringing their own tools and food, to shovel mud and clean what could be salvaged. Others, Relief

Society sisters among them, also ran the nurseries and dispensed the food. Prevention of disease from the contaminated mud and water was a serious concern, especially in dispensing food. Under priesthood direction, the Relief Society, with the Salvation Army and local health departments, coordinated and instructed volunteers in sanitary procedures.[12]

Some valuable lessons for the future came out of the Teton Dam disaster. After her visit to the flood area, Barbara Smith reported to the general board, "A disaster plan needs to be worked out on a family level and also on a stake and ward level."[13] Disaster planning thus received the impetus to become a major concern of Relief Society. A good communications system for emergencies became a high priority, as did a mobile unit to provide immediate aid. The Welfare Services Mobile Relief Unit was ready for evaluating in November 1979. A Relief Society general board member and nurse, Joy F. Evans, offered practical suggestions as one of nine initial observers from church headquarters; her ideas were incorporated, and she took part in testing the new mobile relief unit in a follow-up simulated disaster, "Operation Spearhead." The improved units, carrying everything needed to sustain life in a disaster, were soon available in bishops storehouses throughout the United States and Canada.

Relief Society also prepared its members. Classes, displays, and film presentations in the Relief Society Building regularly addressed home storage and disaster preparation. In 1976 Red Cross representatives Helen Gaborik, Jude Nicoletti, and Jesse Haws taught classes in basic disaster nursing techniques, assisted by a registered nurse from the general board. Twenty stake Relief Society presidents in the Salt Lake area each sent a registered or licensed practical nurse to take the course. Those who were trained trained others, and similar programs continued to be organized: a rigorous thirty-four-session course in 1979, and disaster preparation classes for sixteen hundred participants in 1980.

Local Relief Society officers often directed much of the neighborly help given during disasters. During the 1983 spring floods in Utah the Sevier River broke through a dam, flooding two small towns. A letter to President Smith from the Delta Utah West Stake marveled at the generosity of individual Relief Society sisters: "I have no idea how many hours of scrubbing and baby sitting, loads of laundry or dollars worth of food were donated by the sisters, but I know there are a lot of SAINTS in the Delta Area."[14] Before the flood, the local Relief Society had put together a booklet showing what to do, step by step, in such a disaster. "As a result," said the stake president later, "when the warning finally was sounded, we didn't have people running around in a panic. . . . The people were calm and organized."[15]

In disasters everywhere — earthquakes in Guatemala and California, floods in Hawaii and Utah, hurricanes in Texas, the eruption of Mount Saint Helens in Washington — Latter-day Saints received advance preparation and post-disaster help through the combined efforts of priesthood quorums and Relief Society.

In 1980, for the first time, the Welfare Services Department instructional handbook specified Relief Society participation at every level — ward, stake, region, multiregion, and area — as members of welfare services committees and councils. Weekly classes, titled "Relief Society Responsibilities on Priesthood Councils," were taught by general board members and drew hundreds of participants to Salt Lake City. Ward and stake Relief Society presidencies unable to attend could send for materials. On the ward and stake levels, Relief Society continued to provide volunteers for canning, sewing, and other projects; supported Deseret Industries; and implemented the homecraft program, which gave needy sisters the opportunity to market their handwork through Deseret Industries. At the general level, in 1976 Barbara Smith appointed Ruth Tanner Walker, a Brigham Young University professor with a Ph.D. in nutrition, to chair the general board's welfare committee and assist Welfare Services in developing handbooks, pamphlets, and other instructional materials.

Alarmed at the increase in crimes of personal assault against women and children, Relief Society headquarters sponsored classes in self-protection, taught by local law enforcement officers. An approved script, presentation outlines, and a rental film could be ordered from Relief Society headquarters. In the first three months, 588 persons attended the classes, including many non-members of the Church. Attendance at the ward and stake level was even higher — an average of 187 at each class during November 1979. Local priesthood leaders and law enforcement and church security officers supported this Relief Society project, often giving the lectures. One stake invited the entire town; the mayor came, and the local pharmacist passed out whistles at the door.[16] Young women's groups were often invited to the classes; with this age-group in mind, Relief Society produced a pamphlet, *Self-Protection for Baby-Sitters*, which was promoted by the Young Women.

Sometimes simply opening a door for communication solved problems. One woman expressed her gratitude for a self-protection program given for mothers and daughters in her stake: "It was only because of the sensitive manner in which it was conducted that one of the young girls told her mother afterwards of a man in their stake ... who had been regularly molesting the six-year-old girls in their ward and threatening them if they told anyone."[17] Knowledge led to immediate action against this unsuspected pederast. Relief Society produced another brochure, *Self-Protection for Women and Children*, in 1983. Welfare Services and Relief Society collaborated in 1976 on an anti-abortion film, *Very Much Alive*, scripted by Dr. Glen Griffin.

From 1973 to 1982, the Church's general conferences included early Saturday morning welfare meetings at which the Relief Society president always spoke. At the September 30, 1978, session, President Barbara B. Smith presented to the First Presidency a scroll symbolically decorated with stalks of wheat, representing 226,291 bushels of Relief Society wheat, with a net worth of $1,651,157, and also wheat fund assets of over three-quarters of a million dollars. The money had been considered "a sacred trust fund" for more than sixty years, carefully watched over by Relief Society officers.[18]

In her presentation Sister Smith briefly reviewed the long history of the wheat trust and concluded, "It is with great pride in the accomplishments of the past and with tenderness of heart that we, the women of Zion, place our wheat and wheat assets at your disposal, President Kimball, to be used for grain storage purposes under your administration, through the General Church Welfare Committee." Thus Relief Society relinquished the last of its private holdings, with this admonition: "We pray that the Relief Society wheat will continue to be considered as a sacred trust. May it bless the lives of all who are its recipients."[19]

Compassionate service by individual members had always been the backbone of Relief Society's welfare service and would remain so under the priesthood-directed welfare program. The 1980 *Welfare Services Resource Handbook* recognized this tradition, stating that "the Relief Society should train all sisters in compassionate service and emergency response, and should take initiative in helping the sick and afflicted."[20]

Relief Society's response to the influx of refugees from Southeast Asia was a good example of local and personal initiative in caring for the sick and afflicted. Stakes in California received the first wave of refugees following the surrender of South Vietnam in April 1975. The Newport Beach Stake Relief Society president, Dorothy Hurley, reported her stake's efforts: "Almost as the landing wheels of the aircraft touched down, Relief Society presidents were alerted; and before dawn a corps of women were there caring for the frightened infants—bathing, feeding, comforting. Hourly the sisters immersed their hands and arms in iodine solution to inhibit the spread of disease from infection many of the babies carried. One sister reported how she wept as she tried to bathe two little children that would not let go of each other's hands for fear of losing one another."[21] Other sisters supplied the refugees at Camp Pendleton with such necessities as first aid, clothing, soap, bedding, English lessons, and personal attention.[22]

In addition to the countless individual acts of compassion, in 1980 the Relief Society general board provided a different sort of aid to the refugees. While touring the camps in Southeast Asia where refugees awaited transportation to America, Elder Marion D. Hanks of the First Quorum of the Seventy had seen the need to prepare them for the culture shock ahead. At his request, Relief Society's welfare committee adapted the homemaking filmstrip *Everybody Needs a Home,* with audio tapes in Cambodian, Laotian, and Vietnamese, to show the future Americans what to expect. These adaptations proved useful in the United States as well.

After the refugees arrived in their new homes, stake and ward Relief Society presidents from California to New York accepted the challenge to help the refugee women adjust to a strange new life-style. The needs of Laotian and Hmong women in the Arvada Colorado Stake were typical. "We have special lessons for them in Relief Society. We teach them skills they need for everyday living; about foods, shopping, cooking. . . . Welfare missionaries are assigned to the Hmong Branch to teach such basic things as hygiene and the necessity of refrigerating food."[23]

This stake also mounted a quilting project to provide much-needed bedding. Working side-by-side as teachers and learners, the American and Asian sisters tied and stitched 120 quilts and learned to appreciate one another. "Quilting has been an excellent way to bring everyone together to work, eat and have a good time," said the stake Relief Society president.[24] Other stakes sponsored

In Arvada Colorado Stake, American and Asian sisters work side-by-side on quilting project. (Courtesy LDS Church Archives)

similar projects and cooperated with community agencies to help the refugees.

Quilting proved a popular way to give compassionate service. Relief Society sisters in Salt Lake City donated handmade quilts to the YWCA for their women's shelter and to the Salt Lake Children's Center for abused children. During the unusually cold winter of 1984, the general board sponsored the donation of several hundred lap robes to elderly patients in nursing homes.

Latter-day Saint women, trained by general board members, also served as full-time "missionaries with special assignments" in health and welfare. By 1982 more than 2,500 single sisters and couples had filled these missions, educating millions of people through demonstrations, clinics, workshops, seminars, and health fairs. Each prospective "health missionary" sister was instructed to meet with her Relief Society president before leaving home to learn about the operation and programs of Relief Society. They were then to "talk to or accompany an experienced visiting teacher in making visits," specifically noting "how visiting teachers can develop sensitivity to the needs of others." Part of their mission-field gear would be a *Relief Society Handbook* and lesson manual.[25] Preparation also included orientation sessions in the Relief Society Building (later at the Missionary Training Center in Provo, Utah). Cooperation with local leaders produced good results. For instance, during a pink-eye epidemic in the Philippines, health missionaries instructed Relief Society visiting teachers how to recognize symptoms, then asked them to visit all the members' homes and report back. "Because the local visiting teachers were known and trusted, the people were willing to cooperate."[26]

Such grass-roots networks grew increasingly important as the Church shifted its welfare focus from large-scale projects to personal and family self-reliance and to rendering service.[27] The kindness and commitment of faithful visiting teachers often met emotional needs that organized welfare efforts did not address, as excerpts from a series in the *Church News* entitled "The Visiting Teacher Who Made a Difference" indicate. From Washington a recently widowed convert wrote, "I was in desperate need of someone to whom I could reach out; someone who would listen to me.... And they listened. They comforted me. They wept with me. And they hugged me ... [and] helped me out of the deep despair and depression of those first months of loneliness."[28] The visiting teachers of a single mother of three took care of the children while the mother went to care for her own dying mother. Later they attended the eight-year-old's baptism. The four-year-old told her mother, "When I grow up, I want to be a visiting teacher."[29]

Another visiting teacher made salt-free bread and crackers for the special diet of the woman she visited in a nursing home almost every week. She wrote to the woman's daughter who lived far away, and when the woman died, her visiting teacher went to her funeral on a day so cold and wintry that few people came, and sang the woman's favorite hymn.[30] Among numerous accounts of help during crises or encouragements to renew church activity, one comment sums them all: "I knew that I was more than just a number on the record books for her to visit. I knew that she cared about me."[31]

In most areas of the Church, visiting teaching involves considerable travel. Furthermore, going unbidden to others' homes is sometimes awkward in cultures far removed from the neighborly traditions of Nauvoo and the American West. Yet sisters distant geographically had often developed supportive traditions that could be adapted to church assignments. New Relief Society sisters in the West African village of Umuelem Enyiogugu, Nigeria, reported, "We often visit the sick, pregnant women and old women who are in need of things as you have told us."[32] As the first black Relief Society president in Africa, Fidelia Obinna of the Aboh Branch had no church experience to guide her. Yet she and her sisters had been accustomed to visiting the sick in homes and hospitals,

Fidelia Obinna, right, Relief Society president of Aboh Branch in Nigeria, greets sisters arriving for meeting in 1979. (Courtesy Visual Resources Library)

often walking many miles, long before they joined the Church, so regular visiting was easy.

Whether visiting teaching was easy or hard, where the network was strong the sisters benefited. "I think visiting teaching is the most important work we do in the Church," said Sister Camilla Kimball after sixty years' experience. "I feel I really know a woman only when I enter her home. In this way I can serve her person-to-person. I have tried not to suppress any inclination to generous word or deed."[33]

A Monument to Latter-day Saint Women

Although welfare and charity work remained, as ever, the core of Relief Society, the society was forced now, perhaps more than in any previous era, to be conscious of itself less as a charitable organization than as a group representing church attitudes toward women. For many, the Relief Society Monument to Women at Nauvoo, Illinois, would express the eternal value and potential of women better than any conference address or press release. Women attending the June 1975 Relief Society conference heard this announcement: "We propose that we, as women of the church today, erect a fitting monument that will be symbolic of women of the past, women today, and women of the future. We propose that it be a monument of heroic proportions that would stand as a symbol of womanhood as conceived from a Latter-day Saint point of view."[34]

The commission to design the monument went to a young sculptor from Alpine, Utah, Dennis Smith, who proposed a daring concept: carefully modeled to scale in its garden setting—not one statue, as the presidency had envisioned, but twelve. A single statue could never adequately show the many facets of a woman's life, explained the artist. Florence Hansen was commissioned to create one of the twelve statues, "Teaching with Love," plus a thirteenth, "Joseph and Emma," suggested by Relief Society adviser Mark E. Petersen; it was a fitting symbol of the companion relationship of men and women, priesthood quorums and Relief Society. The site for the monument garden was a grassy expanse overlooked by the tall windows of the Nauvoo Visitors Center. Church architect Emil Fetzer and landscape gardener Durell Nelson amplified Dennis Smith's concept, transforming the flat, empty expanse of grass beside the Visitors Center into a vista of brick circles flowing through flowers and trees and enclosed within low, grassy hillocks.

Like the Relief Society Building, the monument was paid for by contributions from the sisters worldwide and would be a symbol of their unity. Husbands, fathers, children, and friends were also invited to donate money "as special gifts or memorials to Latter-day Saint women." Donations for the monument garden came from every continent, often accompanied by explanations of how the money had been raised. One popular way was through the traditional fair or bazaar; sisters in Zurich, Switzerland, made the equivalent of seventeen hundred dollars at a handicraft fair, where they also showed church films with help from the missionaries. Donations arrived from United States military and service groups in such remote areas as Iceland, Iran, and Saudi Arabia. President Kimball talked about the monument in his travels, and contributions came from over eighty-four branches, wards, stakes, and missions outside the United States and Canada. The wives of the General Authorities gave a significant sum. Many gifts memorialized loved ones who had died, and ten thousand dollars from the Relief Society wheat fund honored sisters of the past.

The thirteen statues and their garden setting took two-and-a-half years to complete. Long before the Monument to Women was finished, President Smith was planning the dedication. She wanted it to be a memorable event shared with as many Relief Society sisters as possible. Moreover, she saw the potential of the publicity such an event could generate. In 1978 the Church was under fire from pro-ERA forces, with charges of discrimination against women and neglect of their potential. The Monument to Women visibly demonstrated church appreciation for the contributions of Latter-day Saint women; that message needed to be heard. The hoped-for publicity was generated in newspapers, television, and radio with the help of Church Public Communications channels, and invitations were extended to stake and district Relief Society presidencies, General Authorities and their wives, a few prominent non-Mormon women, local dignitaries, and news media representatives to attend one of three dedication services on June 28, 29, and 30, 1978.

At this time Barbara Smith was a popular interview subject, partly because of her well-known stand against the controversial Equal Rights Amendment. In two whirlwind tours immediately preceding the dedication, she described the monument and its purpose in eighteen news interviews as well as eight meetings with Relief Society and priesthood leaders. Surprisingly, in view of the media's generally pro-ERA bias, the interviews were mostly favorable. One widely quoted report by Associated Press religion writer George W. Cornell rephrased her message in these words: "Hold your heads high, you wives, mothers, homemakers. You engender life and enrich it. Don't trade that pervasive force for fleeting, surface trinkets. Cherish it, enlarge it, magnify it. You hold a mighty office. That's the message of the leader of Mormon women, Barbara B. Smith." With no hint of detraction, he continued, "To honor that greatness of women and to proclaim it graphically, women of the Church of Jesus Christ of Latter-day Saints (Mormon) have joined in funding the erection in Nauvoo, Illinois, of an impressive array of monuments to women."[35]

The logistics of transporting, housing, and feeding some twenty thousand visitors over four days in the small town of Nauvoo required careful planning and the dedicated efforts of many people, including general board members and the stake Relief Society presidents in sixteen adjoining stakes. Belva B. Ashton, who chaired the planning committee, ensured that there was much for the visitors to see and do at the dedication festivities — sightseeing around

Two of the twelve statues that comprise the Nauvoo Monument to Women: "Teaching with Love" (left) by Florence Hansen, and "Woman and Her Talents" by Dennis Smith. (Courtesy Visual Resources Library)

Nauvoo, strolling groups of costumed musicians and dancers, reception lines in the visitors center, the dedication services, and an outdoor pageant in the evening. The pageant, *Because of Elizabeth*, was commissioned by Relief Society especially for the dedication. A collaboration of author and director Moana Bennett, composer Larry Bastian, lyricist Duane Hiatt, and producer Nathan B. Hale, it expressed the essence of the monument's message: the ever-widening circles of a faithful woman's influence.

In her speech at the banquet, Illana D. Rovner, officially representing the state of Illinois, referred to "the magnificent drama" she had seen the night before. Elizabeth of the pageant had been one of the persecuted Nauvoo Saints. "I think I ought to bring the Governor's apologies for what Illinois did 130 years ago!" the Governor's representative exclaimed. Laughter and applause greeted her rueful plea, "Please come back. We need you!"[36] Unlike most pageants, *Because of Elizabeth*, in a scaled-down version, later became a successful stage play as well, including performances during the Relief Society celebration of the Church's sesquicentennial in 1980.

President Spencer W. Kimball presided and gave the dedicatory prayer for the monument on three successive days at services in a big, brightly striped orange and red tent. It was significant that in Nauvoo, where Joseph Smith had first taught women regarding their divine potential and the purposes of Relief Society, General Authorities would give similar instruction. President Ezra Taft Benson of the Council of the Twelve called the assembled women "elect women of the kingdom of God," explaining that they had been elected by God to perform a unique and sacred work in the Lord's eternal plan. Elder Bruce R. McConkie of the Council of the Twelve spoke of great women in the scriptures and reminded the audience that Rebekah, wife of Isaac, went directly to the Lord for counsel and comfort — and received it, as was her right. "She did not say, 'Isaac, will you inquire of the Lord? You are the patriarch; you are the head of the house,' which he was. She went to inquire of the Lord, and she gained an answer."[37] Elder McConkie thus corrected a misconception then current that a woman could not receive counsel from the Lord except through a priesthood holder. It was a forum where, as with the original Relief Society meetings in Nauvoo, those gathered received spiritual guidance from key male and female leaders, including Elder L. Tom Perry of the Council of the Twelve, Relief Society president Barbara B. Smith and her counselors, Janath R. Cannon and Marian R. Boyer, and former Relief Society president Belle S. Spafford.

Another significant aspect of the dedication event was the support of non-Mormons in Nauvoo. Women of the Reorganized Church of Jesus Christ of Latter Day Saints made the fresh bread for the food carts, while Catholic sisters of St. Mary's Academy and priory housed the pageant cast and loaned their kitchen for food preparation. Sister Teresa Ann, the priory's Mother Superior, and Marjorie Troeh, director of Women's Ministry in the Reorganized Church, were among the honored guests at the banquet and dedication services.

Many non-Mormons who read the press reports of the dedication undoubtedly corrected their former misconceptions. As one Associated Press reporter commented, "All that I had read and all that I had been led to believe was that the Mormon woman was a slave to the home and her husband. But, since I have been here and witnessed these things and have listened to these remarks, I know now that the Mormon woman is committed to the home out of choice based on understanding that it is the place where she can be of greatest worth to humanity." She, like others, went home with a revised impression of Mormon women, commenting, "I'm glad that I came, for the false understanding I had of your people has been erased. All of you have a spirit that I wish I had in my life."[38]

Expressing, perhaps for many, the dedicatory service's effect on those who attended, an eighteen-year-old girl wrote to her grandmother: "Within seconds, it seemed that all that existed was me and the statues and the effect each one was having on me. There was something that took place within my soul that I can't even find words to describe—like a brand new awakening to a sense of my potential—my divine role as a seed of feminine deity." For this young woman, as for many others who were and will be visitors there, a moment of epiphany became a turning point. "I came away from that spot a different person, Grandma—basking in the glory of my womanhood. Never before have I felt such pride and blessedness in my holy calling as a daughter of God!"[39]

Not originally intended to be such, the Relief Society Building also became a significant showcase for the industry and activities of Mormon women, as Barbara Smith creatively envisioned the building's purpose in response to the Church's new administrative structure. In a few short years, she would transform it from an office building into an invaluable resource center. By October 1974, when she moved into the presidential office, many of the original functions of the building had moved elsewhere. Of the various departments once housed there, only the Temple and Burial Clothing Department and the general administrative offices remained. For the most part, the building in 1975 was quiet. The new president did not intend to let it remain so.

By general conference of April 1976, the Relief Society presidency was ready to announce the building's ambitious new look as a "major resource center" for women—"homemakers, Relief Society teachers, Relief Society presidents, and any other persons interested in improving their talents and skills in their homes or Church callings."[40] Relief Society sisters from local stakes helped plan and set up the exhibits, which were changed often; presented homemaking demonstrations, welfare-related classes, and workshops; staffed the resource library; and acted as hostesses at the building every weekday. Helen Jeppson, a member of the Relief Society general board, was the full-time hostess supervisor and building supervisor from 1976 to 1986. Her knowledge of the Spanish language was often an asset, and her calm, courteous manner set the tone for all the hostesses.

The gracious atmosphere of the building also made it attractive for socials, open houses, and receptions. In addition, orientations were held regularly in the building for new stake officers, welfare missionaries, International Mission representatives, and sisters from overseas. By March 1984, the visitors register and attendance rolls had recorded 612,420 names—a fraction of those who came to the building. Each general conference time, women from around the world thronged the building to meet friends and gather new ideas for their Relief Society work.

With the creation in 1984 of a historical time-line exhibit entitled "Strength and Honor: The Story of Latter-day Saint Women and Their Societies," Relief Society's headquarters had become a place to show what Mormon women could do, in both the present and the past.

Speaking Out on Community and National Issues

Increased emphasis on broader community involvement appeared early in Barbara Smith's administration. A 1975–76 social relations lesson stated: "Women in the Church should be knowledgeable and active in their own way in community affairs."[41] The 1977–78 social relations lessons were even more specific. "An important concept that should pervade the study and discussion of all these lessons," noted the teacher's supplement, "is that as Latter-day Saint women we have the ability, the opportunity, and the responsibility to improve the social order." The 1977 regional meeting theme, "Strengthening the Community," encouraged women to "become politically active."[42]

At general conference in October 1977, President Kimball spoke out vigorously: "Important as it is, building stronger homes is not enough in the fight against rising permissiveness. We therefore urge Church members as citizens to lift their voices, to join others in unceasingly combatting, in their communities and beyond, the inroads of pornography and the general flaunting of permissiveness." This plea reflected a decade of increasing concern over deteriorating moral standards, which was seen not as individual weakness but as a societal trend to be resisted. "Let us vigorously oppose the shocking developments which encourage the old sins of Sodom and Gomorrah, and which defile the human body as the temple of God," he implored.[43] On many occasions he had spoken bluntly against the evils of abortion, drug abuse, pornography, incest, and homosexuality. At a time when abortion was attractively labeled "reproductive freedom," and so-called "gay rights" were championed by civil liberties advocates, the threat to traditional moral values was real.

These two strong influences — an increased emphasis on community involvement and a call from church leaders to speak out against immorality — explain the vigorous Relief Society response to the Equal Rights Amendment. Although citizenship responsibility had been continuously promoted, institutional political action became a new Relief Society emphasis for sisters in the United States when ratification of the Equal Rights Amendment to the Constitution began its march through state legislatures in 1972. Popularly referred to as the ERA, the amendment stated, in total:

"Section 1: Equality of rights under the law shall not be denied or abridged by the United States or by any State on account of sex.

"Section 2: The Congress shall have the power to enforce, by appropriate legislation, the provisions of this article.

"Section 3: This amendment shall take effect two years after the date of ratification."

A more conservatively worded equal rights amendment had been promoted by the National Women's Party in the early 1920s, in the wake of the 19th Amendment, which gave women the vote.[44] The Women's Joint Congressional Committee and other advocates of protective social legislation for women vigorously opposed its passage, and the amendment failed to be ratified.[45]

By 1972, however, attitudes had changed. The ERA was generally perceived as the symbol of an equality no fair-minded American would wish to deny, or as the redresser of wrongs that could be righted no other way. Senator Sam Ervin proposed modification of the amendment to "allow," among other items: exemption of women from military service; laws to secure privacy to men and women; certain exemptions and protections to wives, mothers, or widows; and laws to punish sexual offenses.[46] All these proposed modifications were defeated. The defeat seemed to indicate congressional intent, to which future lawmakers might look for precedent: the amendment apparently forbade *any* distinctions or exceptions made on the basis of sex.

On March 22, 1972, the 92nd Congress passed the proposal to submit the amendment to the states for ratification. The first thirty of the required thirty-eight states ratified the amendment within a year. Then the momentum slowed as objections surfaced.

By the end of 1974, when the Utah legislature was preparing for its next session, some Latter-day Saints were asking, "What do leaders of the Church think of the ERA?" General Authorities were reluctant to commit the Church to a stand with political overtones, and particularly a stand against an amendment that was being promoted as pro-women. The first reply came appropriately from the president of Relief Society. Sister Smith had studied and discussed the amendment and decided that "the blanket approach of the Equal Rights Amendment" was "not the way" to deal with discrimination against women. After explaining her stand to her priesthood advisers and securing cooperation in arranging a forum for her to express her views,[47] she discussed the matter with her counselors and the general board. According to the December 12 board minutes, "Sister Smith said she would present an address tomorrow at a devotional at the University of Utah Institute of Religion to which the press had been invited." She then read her remarks and "requested by show of hands those of the board who could support her in the position taken in the address. There was unanimous approval."[48]

The thoughtfully composed talk was to become the most widely quoted of President Smith's addresses. "Women's rights are part of my heritage," she explained. Not only was her mother a teacher, but the doctor who delivered her was her own grandmother. "My grandmother sought her right to be . . . a professional woman, a practicing physician, in a time when it was not only very unusual here, but almost impossible for a woman to be so educated. She was, at the time she received her medical degree, a mother of three children."[49] Sister Smith honored the contributions of her predecessors and had always insisted that women earning a living be accorded equal pay and status among their male colleagues. However, after stating clearly her support for efforts to correct inequities in property rights, job benefits, credit, inheritance, and other grievances, she concluded: "It is my considered judgment that the Equal Rights Amendment is not the way. . . . Once it is passed, the enforcement will demand an undeviating approach which will create endless problems for an already troubled society."[50]

An editorial opposing the ERA appeared in the *Church News* of January 11, 1975, and quoted Sister Smith's talk with approval.

The Utah legislature decisively defeated the reintroduced ERA in February. Predictably, cries of Church interference in politics arose; but subsequent statements by the First Presidency (October 22, 1976; August 26, 1978; and October 12, 1978) identified ERA as a moral issue, "with many disturbing ramifications for women and for the family," on which the Church could appropriately take a stand. "Because of our serious concern, we urge our people to join actively with other citizens who share our concerns and who are engaged in working to reject this measure on the basis of its threat to the moral climate of the future," wrote the First Presidency.[51]

During the ratification process, the ERA became increasingly suspect in many religious circles because of the enthusiastic support of pro-abortion and homosexual-rights groups. In spite of most proponents' insistence that the amendment dealt only with discrimination based on gender, the wording "on account of sex," in a modern context, opened the door to broader interpretations by the courts in future litigation.

The opposition to ERA by Relief Society's president brought widespread media attention, resulting in a number of radio and television interviews. Her advice to general board members was to be "circumspect and non-aggressive."[52] The widest media coverage undoubtedly resulted from the appearance of Barbara Smith on the Phil Donahue television show, taped February 4, 1980. An earlier Donahue show had featured Sonia Johnson, an ERA supporter who had been excommunicated from the Church for attacking its leaders and hindering its missionary efforts. Sister Smith subsequently accepted an invitation to "explain the role of Mormon women in the Church"; appearing with her was Beverly Campbell, a member of the same Virginia stake as Sonia Johnson.[53] Sister Smith was at first disappointed that Mr. Donahue's questions had centered around ERA and gave her little chance to speak of Latter-day Saint women. Yet the show was well received. Many of the letters she subsequently received asked for more information about the Church and expressed appreciation for her honest answers to difficult questions.

The publicity also served to draw more Latter-day Saint women into political activity. When a state legislature's agenda included possible ratification of the ERA (or recision of an earlier ratification), Relief Society women became involved. Feelings ran high over the ERA, and media coverage was often critical of Mormon opposition. Yet the women learned some valuable lessons about organizing as concerned citizens and working with other groups. In answer to pleas for literature, Relief Society produced a pamphlet, *Why Mormon Women Oppose the ERA,* signed by the presidency. Its concluding counsel was far from inflammatory:

"1. Become well informed. . . . Then act and vote intelligently.

"2. Make our views known in every appropriate way.

"3. Form or join responsible citizens' groups.

"4. Actively support political candidates who are honest and trustworthy, and who oppose the Equal Rights Amendment.

"5. Vote and act as individual concerned citizens."

Clearly, a reasonable approach might have been possible had it not been for the complication of the International Women's Year (IWY) in 1975. The IWY, the state conferences it sponsored, and the final national conference in Houston, Texas, provided a battleground for the supporters and opponents of the Equal Rights Amendment. To nearly everyone's dismay, combatants frequently battled against each other rather than over the issues. The IWY format was also part of the problem. The recommendations coming out of the state meetings were supposed to influence the final resolutions drawn up at the National Conference to be held in Houston. The resolutions from the Houston meeting would then be considered a mandate from American women to the United States Congress. So it was hoped and planned.

However, deep-rooted seeds of conflict had already been sown. IWY organizers had proposed in advance fifteen basic recommendations to be considered as a "National Plan of Action." The officials and many of the participants in state conferences tended to see the state meetings as ratifying bodies for an already set plan. Other conference attendees expected to have a voice in *developing* the recommendations, as was indeed set forth in the original enabling act for the National Women's Conference.[54] Other problems included differing expectations about the meetings' overall purpose. Idealists hoped for a celebration of women's unity; however, special interest groups saw the conferences as opportunities to push for power, while traditionalists viewed them as battlefields between good and evil. The many divisive issues prevented women from uniting to address such universal problems as poverty and illiteracy. The stage was set for confrontation, and events moved forward with the inevitability of Greek tragedy.

Not originally conceived as a forum for the ERA, the IWY

and the proposed amendment soon became inextricable. As one Relief Society president in Washington, D.C., pinpointed it, many women felt unfairly railroaded by the commission's pre-set goals: "When two such inflammatory issues as abortion and ERA were established as major goals of the IWY commission—which was funded by $5 million of taxpayer money—citizens who value the sanctity of life or who feel there is a better and safer route than ERA to equal rights for women understandably were upset. Given these circumstances, how could IWY's leaders have expected all peace and love as they rolled toward Houston?"[55]

Utah's state conference was scheduled for June 24 and 25, 1977. The Utah State IWY Coordinating Committee, chaired by an active Latter-day Saint woman, asked for Relief Society help in publicizing the fifty-two preliminary mass meetings; but the turn-out was disappointing, despite phone calls from Relief Society headquarters asking local stake Relief Society presidents to encourage attendance. The IWY committee deplored this evidence of apathy. Shortly thereafter, Barbara Smith invited members of the committee to meet with the general presidency of Relief Society and better inform them about the upcoming state meeting.

At the end of the committee's visit, President Smith asked what she could do to be of help. The response was a request to invite Relief Society women to attend the IWY conference in the Salt Palace in Salt Lake City and to "give them a fact sheet with informative material, so they will come more informed." The presidency declined the fact sheet, feeling that it might be misunderstood, but agreed that Latter-day Saint women should be encouraged to take part, since the conference was supposed to represent all Utah women.[56] Thus began a chain of events that would lead to widespread misunderstanding.

The presidency then took the matter to their priesthood advisers in the Quorum of the Twelve with a proposal to officially encourage Relief Society women to attend the IWY conference. The advisers agreed to help, but they expressed concern over the wisdom of inviting large numbers of Relief Society sisters, most of whom were untrained in parliamentary procedures and debate tactics, into a political arena. The Relief Society presidency later explained why they had appealed to the brethren: "We realized that the results of our telephone calls for the mass meeting participation had not met IWY expectations, and so we used the priesthood channel of contacting our people." Their method this time was far more formal. First came "a priesthood telephone call" to the Utah regional representatives; then a follow-up letter was sent from Relief Society to the regional representatives and also to stake Relief Society presidents. Perhaps most important, the letter specifically requested ten volunteers from each ward, "since the general invitation had not been very effective."[57]

The fact that standard priesthood channels of communication were used for both the phone calls and the letters may have fueled a widely publicized charge that the Mormon male hierarchy had ordered Relief Society women to pack the Utah IWY conference. Ironically, the request had originated with the IWY Committee itself.

Instead of a fact sheet, the Relief Society letter encouraged Latter-day Saint women to read a forthcoming article in the *Deseret News* that would give information on conference procedures and the statements of recommendations as they would appear on the ballot.[58] The general board was also informed of the cooperation with IWY and the importance of intelligent participation. According to the general board minutes, "President Smith said Relief Society women are being urged to study the IWY issues and go as well informed as possible and then vote according to their personal convictions."[59]

In this instance and consistently throughout her administration, Barbara Smith always promoted thoughtful understanding of differing viewpoints and cautioned against divisive actions. To activists who came to see her, seeking Relief Society support, she responded that the society wanted its members "to have the opportunity to be impartial." However, hers was not the only influence at the IWY conference, and there were some unfortunate confrontations. In a postconference interview, she identified some precipitating causes: "fears generated by reports of biased meetings in other states" and "preconference sessions called by conservative political groups throughout Utah."[60] The presidency had not sanctioned the preconference sessions, but they were sometimes given an aura of authority by being identified with Relief Society. In retrospect, Sister Smith acknowledged that by trying to maintain impartiality, she had left the door open for "extremist groups and anybody who took the opportunity to use any method they wanted to get to the women."[61]

Not foreseeing the success of the Relief Society's letter of invitation, the IWY committee had planned for only twenty-five hundred participants—the average at state conferences already held. They were not prepared for the more than twelve thousand who registered. (The second largest attendance in the nation, at the California convention, was only half that number.) To alleviate the problem, and at the request of the IWY committee, the Church paid for Salt Palace space to make available a large enough hall for the general sessions.[62] Despite such help, tensions were heightened by a shortage of printed materials and overcrowding in halls, workshops, and voting areas. Many women came with apprehension fomented by preconference sessions and frightening reports from other states; they expected trouble and trickery. Women who were conducting certain workshops on controversial matters felt overwhelmed and defensive. The atmosphere was not conducive to reasonable dialogue on emotional issues.

Noncontroversial workshops fared better, and one noteworthy endeavor showed what cooperation could accomplish. At the request of the IWY's Women in Utah History Committee, the general board prepared a supportive exhibit in the Relief Society Building showing four historical eras of women in Utah. Jill Mulvay [Derr] and Susan Staker Oman, historians and members of the IWY History Committee, helped with the exhibit and also created a slide display that was shown in both the IWY workshop and the Relief Society Building.

Although the hectic two-day conference left little time for amenities, Barbara Smith personally escorted two important conference participants through the Relief Society Building: Helvi Sipila, a Finnish diplomat and United Nations official, and Mary Ann Krupsak, Lieutenant Governor of New York and a member of the National IWY Commission. Both were cordial, not only about the building but—surprisingly—about the conference, which Mrs. Krupsak described as the largest and most orderly state meeting she had attended.[63]

On the whole, however, it must be acknowledged that the conference generated more heat than light, with participants polarized into opposing camps. Fortunately the presiding officer was a highly respected and able local leader, Esther Landa, then president of the National Council of Jewish Women. Her parliamentary skill, composure, and good humor kept the proceedings moving forward without the serious disruptions that marred IWY conferences in some other states. She well deserved the applause and armful of roses that honored her at the conclusion. "As the marathon women's meeting closed 36 hours after it began," wrote one reporter, "women who had spent more than 30 hours of that time in the Salt Palace rose to their feet to applaud the woman, Esther Landa, who had spent most of that time on her feet before the vast crowd and maintained order, fairly and firmly. They credited her with the peaceful solution of volatile differences."[64]

Not all the participants in the "marathon women's meeting" agreed that the differences had been solved, and certainly not all was peaceful in the aftermath of the conference. Letters to the editors of local papers reflected hurt feelings and misunderstandings, as well as rejoicing. The conference had elected a slate of fourteen delegates to the national meeting in Houston, all of whom rejected the IWY "National Plan of Action," particularly such key proposals as the ERA, abortion on demand ("reproductive freedom"), and lesbian rights ("sexual preference"). Less controversial proposals involving increased federal funding for much-needed social programs were also rejected. Although conservatives had proposed alternative solutions for the problems dealt with in this last item, many of the more liberal participants indignantly condemned such apparent lack of caring, and some of the faithful Latter-day Saints among them felt betrayed.[65]

What was the overall impact of Relief Society participation in the Utah IWY Conference? Barbara Smith thought it was important to find out. Following the conference, she met at various times with the IWY executive committee, civic leaders, and seventy-five stake Relief Society presidents, whom she asked to send a summary of responses from women who had attended the conference. In her overall assessment, she noted that many Latter-day Saint women said they had been made aware of women's issues and of the need to learn more and be intelligently involved in community action. As a *Deseret News* editorial summarized: "This meeting was the first of its kind in Utah. Mistakes were made. Misunderstandings arose. But lessons were learned and communications established. As a result, Utah women will be better able to tackle such issues in the future."[66]

On the surface, participation in state IWY conferences seemed a wasted effort. A number of states besides Utah elected conservative delegates, but at the national conference at Houston, appointed at-large delegates diluted the influence of elected conservative delegates. The original recommendations of the "National Plan of Action" were passed with only minor changes.

ERA, free abortion, lesbian rights, and large increases in federal programs were declared to be the right and will of American women. However, that claim was challenged by minority reports, such as the one prepared and published by the Utah Association of Women, and by the publicity given to coalitions of religious and civic groups who opposed the IWY report. Legislators could not have failed to hear the voices of dissent.

Despite an unprecedented extension of time, boycotts against nonratifying states, and a door-to-door missionary effort, the ERA supporters came to the end of their rocky road on June 30, 1982. The amendment was still three states short of the necessary thirty-eight, not counting the five that had rescinded their earlier ratification, and went down in defeat. Yet supporters could take some consolation from the nation's heightened awareness of women's unique needs. Like the problems it purported to solve, the ERA — which was reintroduced in the 1983 Congress — demanded a thoughtful response from both women and men. Relief Society would continue to address social inequities and other problems through its traditional channels of compassionate service, cooperation with community agencies, and education.

"Much More Than Sunday Lessons"

"The purpose of the education program of Relief Society is to contribute to the spiritual, intellectual, and cultural development of the sisters of the Church," stated the 1976 *Relief Society Handbook*. During Barbara Smith's administration, the lessons encouraged that development through many changes in format, length, authorship, number, and supporting materials.

Some of the changes were cosmetic, such as the alteration in the size and shape of the lesson manual. Despite protests that an $8\frac{1}{2}$-by-11-inch size would not fit in a handbag, in 1976 manuals began to be printed in the larger size, with full-page illustrations in color and a professional design by the Graphics Department. Authors were anonymous, and supporting materials were put in a teachers' guide that was slim and simple.

Other changes were more substantive. As the Church continued to spread worldwide, the need for a twelve-month Relief Society became stronger. The society had long struggled with an awkward division between northern and southern hemispheres in the eight-month lesson schedule, to accommodate summer vacation months. Few countries outside the United States and Canada had

Sisters in Japan listen intently to Relief Society lesson. (Courtesy LDS Church Archives)

a three-month school vacation, so optional lessons were added gradually from 1974 to 1982, when the Church's change to a calendar year allowed the Relief Society curriculum to settle into a twelve-month time frame that was appropriate worldwide.

The society was also concerned about secular education for women, and actively encouraged them to regard education as more than a pastime. In a Mexico City stake, for instance, where sisters were handicapped by a tradition of limited schooling, stake Relief Society officers taught the sisters how to organize their home tasks so they would have time to take classes, provided them with lists of low-priced schools, arranged groups to attend the classes together, and provided transportation. When a group of sisters graduated from a course, they were honored at a special party.[67]

Relief Society encouraged women to take part in the "Pursuit of Excellence" program developed by the Church, and local groups often honored those who had completed the program. Education was clearly a goal to which the society was committed, a star to steer by.

Yet the dignity and worth of a woman's role in the home also needed affirmation in the seventies and early eighties. The social climate had changed since 1966, when Relief Society had replaced the term "work day" with "homemaking day," a title whose status had diminished in the wake of what a 1977 article in *Time* magazine termed "the 'just a housewife' syndrome." Ironically, the widening of women's options had radically devalued the choice to be a house-wife; homemaking had somehow become a nonchoice. As *Time* noted, "Today, when housewives are asked what they do, they tend to answer diffidently, 'Nothing really,' because they have been made to feel inferior."[68]

Almost overnight, it seemed, the Church's traditional emphasis on homemaking as a career for women had changed from a plat-itude to the defense of an endangered species. "Everybody needs a home, and every home needs a homemaker," was the message of a filmstrip produced in 1977. "You are a queen in your home," declared the first homemaking booklet produced by Barbara Smith's board, "a home where love abounds, where there is order, cleanliness and beauty. Such a home exemplifies the principles of provident living, artistic skills, and intellectual order." Such a home was within the grasp of every woman, married or single, employed or full-time homemaker. When Rhonda Joyner Smith, of Och-locknee, Georgia, was interviewed as Georgia Homemaker of the Year in 1980, she praised Relief Society as an institution that provided "a college education in the important things in life" since "everyone is a homemaker, whether we're nurses, doctors, teach-ers, secretaries, lawyers, students. Life centers around the home."[69]

The monthly homemaking day continued to provide opportun-ities for women to learn new skills and to develop and share their talents. An account of one successful homemaking program ap-peared in the *Church News* of May 23, 1981. When *Deseret News* editor William B. Smart visited the Dominican Republic, he found that two Latter-day Saint women were producing a local television program that had been a smash hit for fifteen months. The show, presented in a chatty, soft-sell approach, combined homemaking demonstrations with advice openly drawn from gospel principles. Provident living, the Word of Wisdom, observance of the Sabbath, and family home evening were blended with demonstrations of basic homemaking skills "familiar to any Relief Society sister," but "eye-opening to Dominicans." The sisters were not bashful about mentioning the Church. On several occasions they challenged fam-ilies to go to church together and then gave the addresses of the three Latter-day Saint branches in Santo Domingo. Editor Smart estimated that between them, the two women "have exposed more Dominicans to the Mormon Church than all the missionaries who have labored in the country and have been a major factor in making the land one of the most productive areas for missionary baptisms anywhere in the world during the past year."[70]

In less spectacular ways, the regular homemaking meeting was often an occasion for friendshiping and fellowshiping, a place to bring friends. In an increasingly impersonal world, many women were hungry for personal networks; the Relief Society homemaking program provided one.

And Relief Society did not cater just to those women who recognized their hunger. All Latter-day Saint women, totaling nearly a million, were now enrolled in Relief Society. But not all were active. Sensitive to some women's reluctance to participate in Relief Society, Sister Smith once acknowledged that "sometimes some sisters feel that there is too much perfection expected in Relief Society. My response is that we should recognize that ideals are stars to steer by; they are not a stick to beat ourselves with."[71] In 1975, early in Sister Smith's administration, the conference theme "Every Woman *in* Relief Society" reflected her determination to reach even the disinterested, the too-busy, the homebound, the single, and each sister with a special need. A new handbook set forth changes to implement that determination.

One change was greater emphasis on recreation as a means of encouraging sisterhood and physical fitness. A recreation leader, whose duties included planning and directing women's recreational activities, was added to stake and ward Relief Society personnel. The activities signaled a more youthful emphasis in the society.

The Church's program for single adults, which had begun in 1971, gradually worked its way through several name changes and organizational shuffles toward integration with the rest of the church organizations. The process was accompanied by an increase in the number of single adults, more attention to their needs, and an improved societal attitude toward singleness. By 1983 one-third of Relief Society's members were single—widowed, divorced, not-yet or not-to-be married.[72]

The desire to reach every sister motivated the establishment of special sessions of Relief Society for young adults, working women, women in nursing homes, and others who found the week-day sessions difficult to attend. The creation of a new set of officers for each special session gave young adults leadership opportunities in their own peer group. Relief Society further strengthened its ties to college women by officially sponsoring the LDS women's campus sorority, Lambda Delta Sigma, in 1977.

Changes in the visiting teaching program were also significant. "Not-at-home visits are no longer to be counted as visits," said President Smith, "as they do not fulfill the intent of visiting teaching."[73] To ease the burden of call-back visits, a "meaningful, prearranged visit at another place" could qualify as a monthly visit. The number of women to be visited by each pair of visiting teachers was reduced to "ideally . . . no more than five"—an ideal worth stating, even if it was not always achieved.

And finally, a new brochure, *Welcome to Relief Society*, was introduced at the last general Relief Society conference in 1975. The booklet underlined the desire to involve every sister in the society.

After the official demise of auxiliary general conferences in 1975, large gatherings of Relief Society women continued in other formats. The Church's area conferences often included women's meetings—sometimes called "mothers and daughters meetings"— from 1971 to 1980. These meetings were usually held at the same time as the priesthood sessions. In addition to the General Authorities, Sister Camilla Kimball, President Barbara Smith, and President Elaine Cannon of the Young Women frequently spoke at these conferences. Other meetings of women were sometimes held at the request of stake presidents, or at least with their blessing, but such gatherings were generally planned and organized by the women themselves. The planners had considerable latitude to reflect local concerns of Latter-day Saint women, a decided benefit. When general board members were invited as speakers, they and local leaders both benefited from question-and-answer sessions they often shared.

The most visible successors to the general auxiliary conferences were the general women's meetings held in the Salt Lake Tabernacle. The first such meeting, on September 16, 1978, was carried by closed-circuit audio facilities to more than fourteen hundred centers in the United States, Canada, Australia, and New Zealand. All adult women and girls over the age of twelve were invited. At this first meeting, President Kimball gave a directive that would suggest a new Relief Society emphasis: "We want our sisters to be scholars of the scriptures as well as our men."[74]

In 1980 and 1981, a "general Relief Society meeting" preceded the October general conference of the Church, but without organizational departments or instructions. The women's meeting in 1982 was part of a special "Tribute to Women" held in March to

Relief Society sisters in Mexico, assisted by children, pick beans. (Courtesy LDS Church Archives)

commemorate the 140th anniversary of the founding of Relief Society. In 1983 and 1984, the general women's meetings were, again, for all Latter-day Saint women and girls, with the age lowered to ten. As with the preceding women's meetings, these were broadcast to hundreds of centers. Even from places the broadcasts could not reach, women's voices were heard. At the 1980 meeting Elder Boyd K. Packer of the Council of the Twelve read greetings from twelve sisters he had recently visited in a tiny Relief Society "somewhere in Eastern Europe," carefully omitting the name of the country where such meetings might be suspect.[75]

The winds of change ruffled even the placid pool of the music program, long established and enjoyed. Standing Relief Society choirs were discontinued in 1976, as part of the encouragement to expand ward choirs. However, temporary Relief Society choirs continued to appear at general, stake, and ward conferences and at leadership meetings, socials, fairs, funerals, concerts, and other special occasions.

Emphasis also shifted from sponsoring concerts of large, well-trained choirs to encouraging every sister to make music part of her life. As one sister related, "I do not sing well. In fact, one of my teenage friends used to stop singing when we sat together in church so that everyone would know the musical mistakes were mine and not hers. But in one ward, I was really needed as part of a small group singing for stake [Relief Society] preparation meeting. While we sang that day, I realized for the first time what it means to sing praises to the Lord." This sister expressed her gratitude that, despite her lack of special ability, "Relief Society keeps me singing."[76]

Undoubtedly the most challenging change for auxiliaries in the 1980s came when the Church consolidated most weekly meetings in the United States and Canada into one three-hour time block on Sunday, a change soon implemented worldwide. Speaking of discussions that preceded the consolidated schedule, Elder Boyd K. Packer warned the sisters, "We had the concern that Relief Society might be regarded thereafter as little more than a Sunday class. . . . You must find ways to strengthen the charitable and the practical dimensions as well."[77]

One of those ways was to realign stake board duties and create counterpart ward positions. Each sister on a stake or ward board would now specialize in one of eight areas of Relief Society work; each stake board member would also serve as a liaison to her ward counterpart. Shirley Thomas, counselor to Barbara Smith, expressed the intent of the change: "Relief Society is much more than the Sunday lessons. The new structure helps us see that."[78] Although it ran counter to the push for simplification, the structure served its purpose for six years.

Relief Society sought to benefit the sisters in other practical ways as well. Prior to 1978, each organization had its own nursery program with many local variations. That year the Sunday School, Relief Society, and Primary united to devise a better nursery experience for small children during church meetings. A committee of representatives from the three organizations, chaired by Russell M. Nelson, then serving as general president of the Sunday School, soon completed the task. Under the consolidated schedule, responsibility for the Sunday nursery was given to the Primary. Relief Society, however, continued to have nurseries for monthly homemaking meetings, leadership meetings, and special events, especially when they were held in the daytime.

Another aspect of child care became a Relief Society concern when questions were referred to the general presidency about the propriety of mothers nursing their infants in church meetings. Since nursing in mixed groups was considered distracting in the Western culture, the Relief Society presidency recommended in "Notes to

A Relief Society nursery leader comforts a crying child. (Courtesy Visual Resources Library)

the Field" that "a comfortable room" with piped-in sound be reserved during meetings for mothers with infants.

A few bishops, schooled in church protocol, waited for a directive through priesthood channels. The First Presidency supported the Relief Society request with an official letter that brought better results.[79] Church architects soon incorporated a "mothers' room" in standard meetinghouse plans, and by 1985 some wards had both a room for nursing mothers and a "reverence room" for parents of small children.

"A Tribute to Women"

Another theme of Sister Smith's administration, begun with the Nauvoo Monument to Women, was the conscious public celebration of church values and accomplishments. The year 1980 was the third Jubilee Year for the Church—the 150th anniversary of its founding on April 6, 1830—which Relief Society commemorated with a handsome walnut Jubilee Box to be opened in the year 2030, full of messages and 1980 Relief Society memorabilia for sisters of the future.

In March 1982 Relief Society launched a month-long series of events to commemorate the 140th anniversary of its own founding. Built around the theme "Legacy, Remembered and Renewed," a potpourri of anniversary events was sponsored as "A Tribute to Women."

The celebration began with the dedication of the Sarah M. Kimball home in Nauvoo, restored with Relief Society's help under the direction of Elizabeth E. Simmons and Oma E. Wilcox. On March 11, 1982, it was filled with fresh flowers and the fragrance of homemade soup simmering in the fireplace kettle. On a bed lay a shirt based on the same pattern Sarah and her seamstress had used to make shirts for the temple workmen in 1842. A booklet, *Sarah Melissa Granger Kimball, Woman of Charity*, produced for the all-day dedication event, concluded with a quotation from George Q. Cannon's 1892 entry in Sarah's autograph book: "What an amount of interesting history you have helped to make.... Now you stand ... as a representative woman among your sex." Her history-making continued as women of the twentieth century honored her and her vision.

Fine arts exhibits, legacy lectures and concerts, singing and dancing groups, musical vignettes, walking tours of historic sites, a special *Ensign* issue by and about women, ward and stake celebrations, sacrament meetings honoring women, and a general women's meeting: all contributed to the anniversary celebration. Legacy lectures in the Relief Society Building were so popular that they continued for two more years, and several of the lectures were made available on cassette tapes and in a book, *A Woman's Choices*. The voices raised in praise of Latter-day Saint women would continue to be heard, for the "Tribute to Women" had accomplished its purpose: a statement to the public about the worth of Latter-day Saint women. The effort had also drawn women together churchwide. The success of the cooperative effort would strengthen the ties among all women—those who served in Relief Society and those Relief Society members who had callings to serve with the Primary and Young Women organizations.

Two years later those ties would again be made visible as the three auxiliary presidents—Barbara Smith of Relief Society, Elaine Cannon of the Young Women, and Dwan Young of the Primary— traveled together to South America, where they spoke at meetings directed by Elder Joseph B. Wirthlin. These women prepared the way for an even closer sisterhood in the future.

In analyzing the statistics she had carefully compiled during the fifteen years she served as Relief Society's general secretary-treasurer, Mayola R. Miltenberger showed that between 1974 and 1984, the years Barbara Smith served as general president, Relief Society membership doubled—ample cause for celebration. Located in eighty-nine countries and sixteen territories, speaking some eighty languages, the women of the Church numbered over 1.6 million in 1984.[80] Many of them were Primary and Young Women officers and teachers or held other temporary positions that kept them from full activity in Relief Society. Some were inactive because of too-busy lives or lack of understanding. A few had been alienated by the divisive forces of the times. All were Relief Society sisters; all were part of the vision spoken of by a general board member who said of Barbara Smith, "She has a vision of womanhood and of Relief Society and has brought a depth to LDS womanhood that she hasn't always gotten credit for. . . . I believe in years to come her administration will be marked by and remembered for her vision."[81]

Among the embodiments of that vision were the Relief Society Monument to Women at Nauvoo, the transformation of the Relief Society Building into a resource center for women, the "Tribute to Women," and this history, whose beginning was sponsored by President Barbara Smith.

CHAPTER 12

"STRIVING TOGETHER":
THE SISTER ORGANIZATIONS
1984–1990

"The young women, the intelligent women, women of faith, of courage and of purity [will] be associated with the Relief Societies." When President Belle Spafford quoted these words of President Joseph F. Smith in her 1973 Relief Society conference address, they seemed to her to be directly applicable to the society's new responsibility for "all women members 18 and over."[1] Eleven years later, in April 1984, the words took on another dimension when Barbara W. Winder succeeded Barbara B. Smith as general Relief Society president. One of the new president's outstanding assets was wide experience with youth. She had served as a Cub Scout den mother, ward Primary president, and ward Young Women president, and as a member of the Melchizedek Priesthood MIA general board. For nine years she was national president of the Church's sorority for college women, Lambda Delta Sigma. She was serving on the Relief Society general board when her husband was called to preside over the California San Diego Mission. That cherished experience with young missionaries was cut short by her call to be the eleventh president of Relief Society.

Barbara Woodhead Winder was born May 9, 1931, in the depths of the Great Depression when work was difficult to find and the future looked grim. Her sunny, optimistic disposition and successful life were a tribute to parents who were not afraid to invest faith in that future — as many feared to do in those traumatic years.

The year Sister Winder took office was symbolic of those fears. The futuristic novel *1984*, by British author George Orwell, had haunted readers ever since its publication in 1949. Compared to Orwell's world, which was divided into two repressive, war-scarred dictatorships, the real world in 1984 gave cause for both hope and gratitude. Spots of violent conflict still festered, economic recession still muted the relief of a cooling inflation, and nuclear extinction still waited in the wings. But though the Soviet athletes stayed home, the 1984 Olympics in Los Angeles radiated a spirit of co-operation and success, the American economy stayed afloat, and Israel's punitive expedition into Lebanon failed to trigger Armageddon. The earth still rolled in its orbit, thrilling astronauts with its airy grace and providing recalcitrant mankind with beauty, variety, and opportunities to progress.

Women found themselves with more opportunities than ever before, both at home and in the marketplace. In the United States the number of female engineers had tripled between 1970 and 1980; the number of female lawyers and judges had increased six times in that decade. President Ronald Reagan appointed the first woman judge to the Supreme Court; the Democratic party nominated the first female candidate for the U.S. vice-presidency. The alumni magazine of the Harvard Graduate School of Business regularly carried news of female graduates, and even advertisements for maternity business suits. Brigham Young University opened a "Women in Science Reading Room." The first Latter-day Saint delegate to the Interfaith Council in Richmond, Virginia, was a stake Relief Society president; a Relief Society president in California was an elected officer and fire engine driver in the local volunteer firefighters association.[2]

At the same time, full-time homemakers regained some of their lost status. According to an optimistic sociology professor at George Washington University, "There's definitely a trend toward women leaving their careers to be with their families. We're now seeing a general return to the traditional values and the family structure. The thrust of the seventies, where a woman placed her career ahead of her family, is definitely over."[3]

Women who had it all—both career and family—sometimes found a worm in the core of the coveted apple as they juggled competing demands, but their complaints were seldom militant. Pollster Daniel Yankelovich, updating a 1968 survey, found American women "less ideological" about feminism, "more strategic" in pursuing their goals.[4] With a few important exceptions, such as the emotional issue of abortion, women were learning to live with diversity. The battle lines drawn by the ERA faded perceptibly in a climate of growing acceptance in the United States.

Although its once-vigorous president, Spencer W. Kimball, had grown frail as he neared ninety, the Church was still strong in its forward thrust and increasingly international in its outlook. The fifteen hundredth stake was organized in Mexico on October 28, 1984, marking an increase of 870 stakes since 1974, nearly half of them outside the United States. Six temples were dedicated that year and fifteen more were begun. By 1985 the Church was established in over a hundred nations, territories, and colonies.

To relieve the burdens of central administration, the Church divided the world into thirteen areas and appointed thirteen presidencies from the First Quorum of the Seventy, six of whom would live in their areas outside the United States. The new presidencies would coordinate the work of mission and temple presidents through area councils, which would include regional representatives. It was the first large-scale effort to decentralize the day-to-day operations of the Church.

New positions were created for nine women from among the wives of the area presidencies. These women were called to serve as area general board representatives in Europe, South America, and the Pacific Islands. Each would represent the Primary, Young Women, and Relief Society general officers "in area council meetings and other settings" — a responsibility that would require broad knowledge and perspective. These first representatives were Velda G. Harris, Bea de Jager, Avanelle R. Osborn, Jelaire C. Simpson, Joyce D. Sonnenberg, Valoy A. Sonntag, Joyce E. Taylor, Marne W. Tuttle, and Elisa R. Wirthlin.[5] Soon representatives of the general boards would serve in all areas outside the United States and Canada. Eleven others were called in November 1985, and as area presidency assignments changed, so did the assignments of the wives. Although the general board representatives would have few direct ties to the general boards, the new positions fulfilled a desire long expressed by President Barbara B. Smith that the talents of General Authorities' wives be officially utilized in behalf of the sisters.

One of President Kimball's major contributions, made not long before his death, was a simple statement of the three main goals of all church activity: proclaim the gospel; perfect the Saints; redeem the dead. The clear and timely focus would hold long after his death on November 5, 1985. The new prophet-president, Ezra Taft Benson, reiterated President Kimball's goals and expressed his love for "all our Father's children" of every "color, creed, and political persuasion." He urged Latter-day Saints to respect the laws of their lands and strengthen their families, a continuing theme that Relief Society would be charged to implement. A strong emphasis on the Book of Mormon also characterized his "back to basics" administration.

Women's supportive role in the Church and family remained basically strong, but gender roles among younger members became surprisingly flexible. Men often helped with what had always been considered "women's work," doing such nontraditional things as serving dinner to the Relief Society sisters assembled for stake training meetings or washing the dishes after a ward dinner. Fathers were seen in greater numbers teaching in Primary and carrying crying babies out of church meetings. Meanwhile, many mothers followed the national trend toward breadwinning instead of bread baking. Relief Society, however, followed its traditional course of encouragement for those who chose homemaking as a full-time job. Talks by General Authorities still stressed the primary role of women, particularly mothers, as homemakers.

"That We Be Unified"

When Barbara Winder was sustained in the April 1984 general conference as the general Relief Society president, a new general president for Young Women was sustained at the same time—Ardeth G. Kapp, who replaced Elaine A. Cannon. Both the new and the former auxiliary presidents had the rare opportunity of addressing general sessions of the conference, as Presidents Louise Y. Robison, Ruth May Fox, and May Anderson had done in 1929 and 1930. "I love the sisters of the Church," said Sister Winder in the Sunday morning session. "I want so, and desire so, that we be unified, one together with the priesthood, serving and building the kingdom of God."[6]

Sister Winder's choice of counselors, secretary-treasurer, and board members demonstrated her desire for unity—first counselor Joy F. Evans from the former Relief Society board, second counselor Joanne B. Doxey from the Primary general board, and secretary-treasurer Joan B. Spencer from Lambda Delta Sigma; and four board members who had served on the general boards of all three women's auxiliaries. The goals of the three presidents—Relief Society, Young Women, and Primary—were clearly the same, as reported in the Church News of April 15, 1984: "Working through the priesthood, the women and young women of today can become a generation prepared for the Savior's commendation

387

General presidents of the women's organizations—Ardeth G. Kapp, Young Women, left; Barbara Winder, Relief Society; and Michaelene P. Grassli, Primary—visit President Ezra Taft Benson and his wife, Flora, on Sister Benson's birthday in July 1988. (Courtesy LDS Church Archives)

when He returns." The unity of the women's organizations would soon be visibly demonstrated, for they would share headquarters offices for the first time in over a quarter of a century.

The first months of President Winder's administration saw a dramatic change in the Relief Society Building. Walls and rooms were shifted to receive the officers and staff of the Young Women and Primary—Relief Society sisters all—in their new home. The historical time-line exhibit expanded to include historical highlights of the YWMIA and the Primary. Resource displays for Primary and Young Women joined Relief Society's, as did handout materials in the resource library. A new sign in front of the building announced: "General Offices of the Relief Society, Young Women, Primary." Two years later, the three women's organizations moved together to the Church Office Building while the Relief Society Building was completely renovated.

Sisters attending the general women's meeting on September 29, 1984, could see unification in action at the busy building. "Striving Together" was the theme of the meeting. "We are striving together with one heart and one mind to become that Zion society in which our beliefs are transformed into action," Sister Winder told the assembled sisters. She encouraged the same cooperation among the three organizations everywhere: "Sisters, we need to actively support each other as we teach and train. As sisters in the gospel, we are linked together by the service we render." The meeting was broadcast by satellite to stake centers in the United States and Canada and was videotaped for distribution later to other English-speaking countries.

The following May the three presidents traveled together to Brazil, Argentina, and Peru. It would be the first of other trio travels. Their purpose was to gain firsthand acquaintance with the auxiliaries' work in those areas and to confer with the new area general board representatives there. The presidents were also what Elder J. Thomas Fyans, their General Authority adviser, called "the best visual aid" for teaching the principles of unity and continuity among the three auxiliaries. "They would stand side by side in meetings, with their arms around each other," he explained. "I could point to them and say, 'Here we have someone who really cares for children, someone who really cares for young women, and someone who really cares for women. You can see there is no space between them, no place for the child to get lost between Primary and Young Women and no place for girls to get lost between Young Women and Relief Society.' "[7]

The three presidents had stood together the previous September to meet President Ronald Reagan. Their portraits hung together in the general board conference room, newly decorated with all the portraits of former Primary and Young Women presidents.

Another portrait was unveiled in March 1986, commissioned by Relief Society for a birthday commemoration. The artist, Nadine B. Barton, portrayed the first meeting of Relief Society, with Emma Smith rising from receiving her blessing as the first president of the Female Relief Society of Nauvoo, and Joseph Smith reading from the Book of Commandments to an audience that includes his wife Emma, Willard Richards, John Taylor, Bathsheba Smith, Desdemona Fullmer, Eliza R. Snow, Elizabeth Ann Whitney, Sarah M. Cleveland, and Sarah M. Kimball—all key figures in the establishment of the society. The painting was hung in the hall outside President Winder's office, the first work of art to be commissioned by her presidency.

389

Two other firsts took place in that first year. Barbara Winder and Ardeth Kapp were appointed to the board of trustees of Brigham Young University, the first time two women had served simultaneously on that board. And Relief Society counselor Joy F. Evans gave the keynote speech at the annual conference of the Association of Mormon Counselors and Psychotherapists, the first time anyone other than a General Authority had filled that role.

Administrative changes took place as the thrust of priesthood correlation and the internationalization of the Church continued. All general auxiliary and committee heads were reminded that they were not responsible for administering the programs of the Church in the wards, stakes, missions, and regions. Such administrative responsibility belonged to the new area presidencies "and those who serve under their leadership as directed by the First Presidency and the Twelve."[8] However, the auxiliaries and committees *were* charged to evaluate, advise, and train and to prepare handbooks and other materials as requested by the General Authorities. Relief Society sisters continued to serve on priesthood councils and committees at every administrative level.

From around the world, wards and branches pled for help in staffing their Relief Societies, citing the drain to stake positions as a major problem. In 1986 stake Relief Society boards were reduced to a president, two counselors, and a secretary-treasurer. They were responsible for visiting the wards and training ward presidencies — but not ward boards — at quarterly stake leadership meetings. The cutback also helped to solve the problems of time and transportation costs for women to and from meetings. Both stake officers and ward boards had considerable flexibility in meeting local needs with ad hoc service by specialists, as needed.

In order to give more opportunities for learning and sisterhood than the Sunday meetings could provide, optional enrichment meetings during the week could still be approved by the bishop and Relief Society presidency — a concession to the desire for diversity that would always resist simplification.

In 1984 the general presidency painstakingly worked out a new mission statement. Two years later, at the request of their advisers, it was made available in an attractive brochure to celebrate Relief Society's 144th anniversary. Its message:

"The mission of the Relief Society is to help women

"1. Have faith in God and build individual testimonies of the gospel of our Lord Jesus Christ.

"2. Strengthen the families of the Church.

"3. Render compassionate service.

"4. Sustain the priesthood."

"We see Relief Society blessing the lives of all women—young and old, married and single," said counselor Joanne Doxey. "Each sister should feel she can give, as well as receive, through Relief Society. I think the key is giving." President Winder concurred. "It truly is a blessing for every woman. As each woman comes to Relief Society with a mind open, a willingness to be taught, she will find solutions to her problems in the sisterhood and curriculum."9

Meeting Diverse Needs of the Saints

Problems for Relief Society sisters to address were not lacking in 1986. "We see sickness, tragedy and all the problems of the world," said counselor Joy Evans, in charge of welfare matters. "Yet, people experience those problems individually. And, individually, they can be helped." She added thoughtfully, "If we can prevent problems, as well as meet them when they come, it certainly strengthens families and builds the kingdom."10

The Relief Societies of Great Britain provided a good example. When a local couple returned to England from Ethiopia, where they had worked as volunteers to aid victims of a terrible famine there, the president of the Brighton Ward Relief Society invited them to show slides of their experience to ward members. Twenty-five of the sisters were moved to action. They not only collected cash donations of nearly one thousand pounds (approximately two thousand dollars), but also gathered 400 bars of soap, 100 blankets, 400 notebooks and pencils—and knitted more than 300 sweaters. The money was used to establish a medical clinic for Ethiopian refugees in the Sudan; the sisters also collected enough sewing machines, thread, and fabric for a sewing shop to be set up in the refugee camp. Word of their relief efforts inspired the rest of the stake to offer help. A stakewide fast brought additional contributions,11 and a local news story prompted others to offer help. "Seeing the Christian gospel of love in action" had a positive effect on nonmembers.12 The Church promoted the ideal of neighborly service to all, refuting the erroneous claim of some critics that The Church of Jesus Christ of Latter-day Saints was not "Christian" because it did not engage in "Christian service."

The tradition of neighborly service was alive and well in Scotland, where the Dundee Stake Relief Society participated in a civic

Women's Health Fair designed to promote better health habits. The sisters prepared food at their booth and served samples to more than seven hundred passersby, taking the opportunity to explain some of the church health standards as they served. Welfare instruction went hand in hand with missionary activity.

At Relief Society headquarters, a new welfare representative and board member, Ione J. Simpson, represented Relief Society on the Welfare Services Executive Committee, the Emergency Preparedness Committee, and the Coordinating Council for Members with Special Needs, and attended LDS Social Services staff meetings. One of the main projects she helped develop was a parenting resource manual.[13] She and other members of the general board welfare committee also met regularly with the Utah State Child Abuse and Neglect Advisory Council, the State Spouse Abuse Advisory Council, and the Red Cross. From time to time they attended meetings of the state councils on aging, drug and alcohol abuse, and dislocated workers, and of various community agencies, where they were "warmly welcomed."[14] Their function at these meetings was not, however, to take part in decision making or local activities, but to keep abreast of current problems and concerns in order to better serve the worldwide church.

Provident living, including food production and storage, continued to be a strong Relief Society emphasis. When the fifty-year anniversary of the welfare plan was observed in 1986, Presiding Bishop Robert D. Hales confirmed the family's primary place in that aspect of welfare. At general conference that April, he explained that "the Lord's real storehouse is indeed in the homes and hearts of His people."[15]

National trends in the United States prompted Relief Society to give increased attention to the welfare of single sisters who were heads of families through death or, increasingly, divorce. A steadily rising number of households were headed by women (in Utah, up from 6.5 percent in 1960 to 11.8 percent in 1984), paralleling the rising divorce rate. And of all Utah families living below the official poverty level in 1984, 96.1 percent were headed by women with children under eighteen.[16] A popular phrase, "the feminization of poverty," highlighted the difficulty of earning the living and rearing children at the same time. In 1985 the program for the Utah Valley area-wide LDS singles conference recognized the reality of single parenthood by including parent-child activities. A church-sponsored conference for single women in San Diego, Cal-

Younger women become visiting teachers and find common bonds of friendship and sisterhood in Relief Society worldwide. (Courtesy New Era)

ifornia, attended by six hundred, featured workshops on single parenting skills and reentering the work force.

Relief Society participation on stake and ward committees for single adults took on greater urgency, and the ward Relief Society president's responsibility for single adult sisters, particularly those needing welfare assistance, grew more complex. The responsibility was clearly stated in the *Single Adult Activities Guide,* published in April 1986: needs of single members were to be "served principally by the Melchizedek Priesthood quorums for the men and the Relief Society for the women."

Fortunately, there were examples of successful adjustment. In 1985 the only single-parent family ever to win the Great American Family Award, given by the American Family Society, was made up of Gladys Dickey of the Omaha Nebraska Third Ward and her four sons. Single women serving as Relief Society presidents (unusual in earlier generations) brought special insights to the singles dilemma. Aunts and grandmothers (many of whom could be classified as single) were included in a mother-daughter activity sponsored by the Blanding Utah Second Ward Relief Society in August 1985. Seventy percent of the ward's mothers and daughters came — plus the aunts and grandmothers.[17]

Women found comfort, inspiration, and instruction in other

gatherings. The annual women's conference at Brigham Young University attracted nearly three thousand women—and some men—in March 1986. They could choose from nearly forty workshops and eighty speakers to find answers to their questions. Some 725 women gathered from five Hawaiian islands for the women's conference at the BYU–Hawaii campus, where seventy workshops addressed concerns of women. In lesser numbers, but with the same spirit, 110 Dutch women attended a "sisters' conference" at the Hague; the theme: "A time to weep, and a time to laugh." And in Perth, Australia, the Southern River Stake Relief Society board invited all the sisters to a program titled "Woman—The Total You."

In the spring of 1986 the general presidents of the Relief Society, Young Women, and Primary traveled together to meet with sisters in Europe. Perhaps the gathering most indicative of the future was a Relief Society meeting attended by only a handful of sisters in the International Branch at Vienna. A young Iranian woman gave the mother education lesson. A Nigerian woman, one of three from Nigeria in attendance, had been baptized the night before the meeting, and a refugee from an Iron Curtain country was to be baptized that day. Two members from Ghana mingled with several sisters from the Philippines and one from South Africa. "There was a great deal of love and compassion," President Winder noted in her journal. "If I have ever seen the true love of Christ displayed, it was there seeing these inter-cultural [sisters] mixed together caring about one another."[18]

As the tour concluded, Sister Winder, accompanied by her husband, visited Czechoslovakia, where Brother Winder had previously served a mission. During their two-day visit, they met with faithful members and their friends in Prague and Brno. In Brno a young woman came running toward them with outstretched hand and offered her memorized greeting in English. "Hi! I am Olga," she exclaimed. "I am the Relief Society president!" Olga Kovarova was also a successful teacher of organizational management and an Olympic contender in track and field events. Baptized just three years earlier, she had been the first young woman convert in Czechoslovakia since 1951. Her contagious faith in the gospel had brought twenty people into the Church, including family members and several college students. During the visit, Elder Joseph B. Wirthlin of the Council of the Twelve set her apart as a district missionary, to continue the work she was already doing so successfully.[19]

New Options and Flexibility

Several long-contemplated changes in the Relief Society courses of study came to fruition in 1985 and appeared in the 1987 manual. The study of the cultural arts became optional in a week-day meeting, succumbing to the difficulties of translation and the emphasis on basic principles and programs in the worldwide church. In its place, a second spiritual living lesson was to be presented each month, increasing Relief Society's focus on spirituality. Compassionate service and social relations courses were combined, and mother education became home and family education, in recognition of the growing emphasis on the ongoing thrust of the Church to strengthen homes and families. Visiting teaching messages moved from the curriculum manual to the *Ensign* and the international church magazines, where they could more easily address current concerns. These changes allowed a return to a smaller manual; sisters who had complained that the larger one would not fit in a purse could now be satisfied.

A separate teacher's guide provided helps for all lessons. The introduction stressed the threefold mission of the Church (proclaiming the gospel, perfecting the Saints, redeeming the dead) and the new mission statement of Relief Society. Significantly, the manual was referred to as "a personal study guide" to the scriptures, which were the basic lesson materials for the whole church. Correlation principles were at work.

Even more innovative was new flexibility in choosing teachers for the Sunday classes. Local officers — bishops and Relief Society presidents together — had the option to call from one to five teachers, or even "a sister who is qualified in a certain subject . . . to teach a particular lesson without a formal call as a teacher."[20] Bishops and branch presidents with staffing problems welcomed the opportunity. The move to local options and controlled flexibility came in response to the Church's growing worldwide diversity and counterbalanced the increase in centralization.

Since effective teaching still depended more on the teachers than on the teaching materials, the Church sponsored ward and stake open-house events in 1985 and 1986 to promote better teaching methods. Relief Society sisters were proud to exhibit their visual aids, resource materials, and teaching techniques. Everyone benefited from seeing what the various organizations had to offer. Even nonmembers were attracted to the displays. "We'll try to make this a time when we can show people what we do, and at the same time, bear our testimonies," said Bishop Lamont Tingey of the Tooele Utah Twelfth Ward, as their openhouse was in preparation.[21]

Lessons in home management continued to be provided for the monthly weekday homemaking meeting. In 1987 the lessons were correlated with the six areas of personal and family preparedness, developed a decade before by the Welfare Department: literacy and education; career development; financial and resource management; home production and storage; physical health; and social, emotional, and spiritual strength. A new homemaking booklet, *Creative Homemaking for a Happy Life*, set forth a nourishing smorgasbord of ideas and recipes. Although full-time homemakers were an increasingly smaller minority in most countries, Relief Society continued to point out that everyone needed a home and every home needed a homemaker—whether full- or part-time. Wards might hold both daytime and evening homemaking sessions, so all sisters could participate. The timeless skills of homemaking and the socializing involved in practicing them together still attracted many women.

Still important was the sisters' love of music. During a period of neglect in most wards brought on by the consolidated Sunday schedule, Relief Society had kept singing alive in a five-minute practice period and occasional choral performances. When a new hymnbook was released in 1985, English-speaking Saints enjoyed a revival of interest in singing the songs of Zion. "We have tended to let condensed schedules crowd out the importance of music," admitted a *Church News* editorial on August 11, 1985. "We must awaken the sleeping giant of good music in the Church." The new hymnbook appeared exactly 150 years, to the month, from the publication of the first church hymnal prepared by Emma Smith, and translation into various languages was begun immediately.

Groups of Relief Society women also continued their tradition of singing together. The president of the Rexburg Idaho North Stake Relief Society, Mary B. Barfuss, proudly reported the success of a group called "The Golden Singers," made up of single and widowed sisters, ages sixty to eighty-seven. The singers had performed at a stake auxiliary training meeting and stake conference, "sharing their talents and gaining a real sense of fellowship in the process."[22]

The last years of the 1980s saw Relief Society engaged in supporting and meshing with the overall program of the Church. An emphasis on the Savior illuminated the 1988 and 1989 *Personal Study Guide,* and talks by the presidency and board centered on the mission of the Church to bring souls to Christ.

Reflecting an ongoing concern for minority groups, Relief Society general officers made a special effort to strengthen Lamanite sisters who lived on reservations in the United States and Canada. Led by counselor Joy F. Evans, herself a long-time participant in the Indian student placement program, they visited more than sixty small branches and wards during the 1986–89 years. In conferences for Lamanite women, they encouraged the sisters "to study and learn, teach their children, pray always and come unto Christ." The general board representatives also learned of needs and explained the resources available in Relief Society and other church programs for "job opportunities, education, and . . . being self-reliant." And they found time to make personal visits, such as one to Amy Kakaway, an elderly member living alone in the Carry the Kettle Branch of the Canada Winnipeg Mission. "When we got there," Sister Evans recalled, "she said, 'I have waited all day.' She cried a bit and didn't want us to leave." Sister Evans expressed the spirit that prompted the visits: "We are all children of God and need to work together."[23]

A revised *Relief Society Handbook* was adaptable worldwide, with a more flexible visiting teaching program. Where actual visits were too difficult, letters and telephone calls could provide the personal contact. Visiting teaching messages appeared in the *Ensign* and international magazines.

After two years in the Church Office Building, headquarters of the Primary, Young Women, and Relief Society moved back into the newly refurbished Relief Society Building in April 1988 amid general rejoicing to be "home" again. Once again the familiar building housed displays and resources to help teach and broaden the vision of local leaders. General officers and boards of the three organizations continued to meet together regularly to correlate their work of strengthening individuals and families.

As new aspects of the work of women were opening, two windows on the past also opened. A historical identification plaque was placed on the marble bust of Emmeline B. Wells in the rotunda of the Utah State Capitol, with the general Relief Society executive officers attending the ceremony in remembrance of the fifth president of the society. And in Nauvoo, cradle of the sisters' "charitable society," the original monument that had been erected in 1933, during Louise Y. Robison's presidency, was discovered in storage and installed at the entrance to the Monument to Women gardens. The weaving together of the society's history continued.

Special Blessings for a Worldwide Sisterhood

As in the beginning, temples and temple work continued to bless the lives and be a concern of Relief Society women. During Spencer W. Kimball's eleven years as president of the Church, twenty-one temples were built and dedicated; nine more were in the planning stage when he died. Only eighteen had been built in the entire preceding 138 years. Barbara Winder's board attended the Salt Lake Temple every month, reflecting an increased emphasis on personal spirituality among the leaders of the nearly two million Relief Society sisters.[24] Locally, women were active in temple work and genealogical research. Even the homebound could participate, using home computers in the name-extraction program of the Family History Department. Others traveled the distance to attend the nearest temple.

The building of smaller temples in countries throughout the world signaled a burst of activity for women who had never before had the opportunity to receive the special blessings found in the sacred houses of the Lord. When sisters in Brazil were asked to crochet seven altar cloths for the Buenos Aires Temple, they eagerly donated sixty-four. Hmong sisters in the Southeast Asia Branch of the San Diego North Stake raised money for the temple to be built in that area by selling their exquisite needlework, known as *pa dao*. The Relief Society president, May Yang, explained, "We give *pa dao* to sell and get money for our Church to build the temple," then added her testimony: "This Church helped us a lot, and we believe it is the only true Church of God."[25] Their traditional, treasured artwork was a fit offering for the highest expression of their new faith.

On the other side of the world, events in Eastern Europe dominated the headlines in the fall of 1989, with unexpected consequences for the Relief Society. Starting on Hungarian borders and reaching a grand climax at the infamous Berlin Wall, the iron curtain melted in a fiery demand for freedom. Repressive governments fell, and jubilant crowds flooded through newly opened gates. And through those gates the Church quietly entered lands long closed to the gospel's spread.

Representative of Latter-day Saints in the worldwide church are Alajosné Pekars, second from left, with son Alajos, left, and daughters Nicolett and Claudia, of Budapest, Hungary. (Courtesy Craig Dimond)

Poland and East Germany had already allowed the Church a cautious presence within their borders. There was even a temple in the latter country, permitted initially in order to discourage Latter-day Saints' requests for travel to western European temples. In February 1990 the newly elected government in Czechoslovakia granted the Church official recognition and permission to reopen a mission. The man called to preside was a former missionary to that land who had left in 1950 with the last group to be expelled by the Communist government, except for two elders later released from jail. In the April 1990 general conference, Richard K. Winder was announced as president of the revived Czechoslovakia Mission. His wife, Barbara W. Winder, was released as general president of the Relief Society to accompany him.

Six years earlier, Sister Winder had been released from a mission with her husband to accept a call to lead the women of the Church. Now her call would include not only missionary service but also an answer to a faith-filled plea from a tiny group of those sisters. Elder Boyd K. Packer had carried their letters from Czechoslovakia to the general women's meeting in October 1980: "A small circle of sisters send their own hearts and thoughts to all the sisters and beg the Lord to help us go forward."[26] Sister Winder, who had sympathetic ties with those sisters from her earlier visits, was ready in heart and thought to help them go forward, as she had been called to do.

During Sister Winder's presidency, the Relief Society had focused on basic principles: faith in God and his Son, Jesus Christ; cooperation with priesthood leaders; education; and compassionate service. Sisters worldwide, however diverse their cultures, could understand and practice those principles. The enriching aspects of the society, such as music, homemaking skills, and sociality, might vary among cultures, but the basics formed the common bond. In every ward and branch of the rapidly growing church, that bond would draw women together in the network of caring known as Relief Society.

comprise it were yet standing in the archway, looking at the new paths and fruitful fields that awaited them. President Jack came to feel that, as President Belle Spafford said in 1966, "Relief Society is only on the threshold of its divine mission."[4]

The New Presidency

Elaine Low Jack had roots sunk deep in the fertile soil of gospel truths and the Alberta prairie. Born March 22, 1928, in Cardston, Alberta, Canada, she grew up a half-block from the Alberta Temple. Her parents, Lovina Anderson Low and Sterling Oliver Low, were among the first couples to be sealed there. Her grandfather, John F. Anderson, a skilled stonedresser, had laid the first stone of the Alberta Temple, labored throughout the temple construction, and acted as master mason in laying the cornerstone in 1915.

Elaine remembers a childhood of roller skating around the temple block, playing on the well-tended lawns, performing baptisms for the dead, and in her high school years transcribing patriarchal blessings in a quiet, secluded room in the temple for her grandfather Anderson, then a patriarch.[5] She later received her own endowment, and on September 16, 1948, she was married to Joseph E. Jack, a young doctor, in the same temple.

Living so close to the temple made a profound difference in Elaine's life because she was surrounded by people who took advantage of its blessings and were completely dedicated to their covenants. The temple was a pervasive part of what went on in Cardston; it was the main focus of life. The Saints didn't discuss the temple much; rather, they busied themselves in living worthily the commitments they made there. These examples of faithful living stayed with her long after she left Cardston.

Elaine made the transition from life in a small LDS community to life as an English major at the University of Utah. Here she met her future husband during his senior year of medical school. After one spring quarter of dating and a summer of letters between Salt Lake City and Cardston, they became engaged. Elaine then returned to her studies in Salt Lake City while Joe began his internship at Staten Island Hospital in New York. Another year of letters was to follow before their marriage the following September. Joe's residency training in surgery kept them in New York, and his military obligations with the United States Public Health Service took them to Boston. Their first son was born in Massachusetts, where Elaine served in the Relief Society presidency of the Cambridge Branch. The Jacks moved back to New York for additional surgical training, and that is where their second son was born. Finally the Public Health Service transferred them to Sitka, Alaska, where they lived two years before settling in Salt Lake City in 1958. Two more sons were born in Utah.

The years of church service as a young mother living far from family both stretched and strengthened Elaine Jack. She became aware of her own abilities and her personal testimony. One Sunday after a ninety-minute commute to church, she sat in fast and testimony meeting, thinking, *You do believe in the gospel of Jesus Christ. You believe what you are hearing or you wouldn't make all the effort to go to church.* "It was," she said, "a moment of realization that made all the difference to me."[6] This quiet moment was like most other life passages for Elaine, a time of calm realization. She developed habits of doing what she could do—what she had to do—in the best way she could. Even momentous transitions—marriage, motherhood, becoming Relief Society general president—were times when she tackled the tasks at hand with a pragmatic, positive attitude. She learned how to marshal the resources around her and saw her personal relationships as the best resource of all.

Her attitudes and faith led to a lifetime of extraordinary church service that included various ward and stake positions. In 1972 she was called to the Relief Society general board, a position she held under Presidents Belle Spafford and Barbara Smith. When Barbara Smith was released in 1984, so was Elaine. She returned to ward service for three years. During that time, among other assignments she supported her husband, Joe, in his calling as bishop of a singles ward. She was then called to be second counselor to Ardeth G. Kapp in the Young Women general presidency, where she served for three years until she returned to Relief Society in 1990, this time as general president. The Relief Society she was called to head had three million members in 135 countries and territories.

To help her lead a worldwide organization of such magnitude, Sister Jack needed spiritual, strong, capable women by her side. She chose Chieko N. Okazaki to be first counselor and Aileen H. Clyde to be second counselor. In both women President Jack found the depth of testimony and experience sorely needed in this new era. Sister Okazaki, a Hawaii native and convert to the Church, came to Relief Society from the Primary general board, where her quick, resourceful mind and vast educational experience as a

Elaine L. Jack, center, is flanked by her counselors, Chieko N. Okazaki, left, and Aileen H. Clyde. (Courtesy Visual Resources Library)

teacher and principal had proved to be a great asset. Sister Clyde was chairing the Utah Task Force on Gender and Justice and had served broadly in the community and in the Church, including on the Young Women general board. Carol L. Clark, who had served with President Jack on the Relief Society general board previously, was asked to serve as administrative assistant, leaving her position as founder and director of Utah's Women's Business Development Office.

As they met with Relief Society members worldwide, both counselors drew from their rich personal experiences. Sister Okazaki spoke to women in New Zealand, Samoa, and throughout the United States of her roots as "the child of poor Japanese laborers on a plantation on the big island of Hawaii." She joined the Church at age fifteen, a convert from the Buddhist faith. She supported herself through high school by working as a maid, and paid for her college education with the help of her mother, who made and sold slippers. She married Edward Okazaki, a fine man who was not then a member of the Church. He later joined the Church, serving in many remarkable ways. Her personal experiences taught Sister Okazaki the differences between local cultures and a Christ-centered way of life, and she often explained these differences to sisters she visited. She encouraged women to "lighten up" and enjoy life, and she bore fervent testimony of the truthfulness of the gospel of Jesus Christ.[7]

Aileen Clyde, a native of Springville, Utah, told sisters of her parents' insistence that she gain her own testimony rather than rely solely on theirs, of the many blessings her disabled brother brought into the family, of the dangers of stereotyping others and ourselves, and of the importance of each woman's abilities and contributions. Throughout the Caribbean and the USA, she bore her strong testimony while encouraging Relief Society leaders to think, to work together, and to rely on the Spirit of the Lord. In the October 1991 general conference, she discussed charity and, reflecting her awareness of an increasing problem, told the Saints, "It is not charity or kindness to endure any type of abuse or un-righteousness that may be inflicted on us by others."[8]

Women of great diversity, the Relief Society general presidency brought to their callings many years' experience as wives, mothers, church and community workers, and educators. They also brought zeal, tenacity, courage, and commitment to the Lord and his church. They determined to make a difference for good and to share generously their testimonies as well as their vision of the grandeur of Latter-day Saint women and their organization, Relief Society.

President Jack found it hard to comprehend that Relief Society was an organization of three million women. To do so, she said, could be overwhelming. She preferred to think of Relief Society as a series of individual faces, the beautiful faces of Relief Society women she met around the world. It was easy for her to think in terms of individuals because she related to so many of the women she met. She spoke of herself as "a very ordinary woman who has spent much of my life dealing with the day-to-day complications and joys of being a wife and a mother of four sons. Complications like keeping enough milk in the refrigerator; joys like having an even number of socks come out of the dryer."[9]

President Jack felt one with her sisters in Relief Society, what-ever their individual circumstances, and she prayerfully sought to understand them. She knew of their individual and collective worth, and in her first public remarks when she was called in April 1990, she spoke of her belief that "the women of the Church have a unique contribution to make."[10] Humility, candor, a sense of hu-mor, and personal warmth — these qualities in their new president appealed to sisters who saw in her a woman who could understand and care about their needs and aspirations.

Unified Sisterhood

The presidency nominated eleven diverse women to the Relief Society general board. In the fall of 1990, as their first work together, the presidency and board studied the compelling discussion of charity in Moroni 7. During their weekly board meetings, each board member took a turn sharing her perspectives about a few verses. The entire group then discussed the scriptures, in order that they all might be spiritually enriched and better prepared to understand charity and faith, the underpinnings of Relief Society.

The presidency felt that the microcosm of the general board with its diverse makeup would be the ideal place to learn how women can become unified in purpose, yet feel valued for their individuality. President Jack reminded the board often that their experience with sisterhood should happen in every Relief Society. As board members gained confidence in their assignments, she told them, "It's exciting to see your already bright and sensitive minds expand."[11] Board members resonated to such praise and rallied to the presidency. Carma M. Hales, the twelfth board member, was added in January 1992. Together, the fifteen members of the presidency and general board became sisters "knit together in unity and love one towards another." (Mosiah 18:21.)

Speaking to the women of the Church in her first address at the September 29, 1990, general women's meeting, Sister Jack established herself as someone real who wanted to talk heart to heart with the women of the Church, whom she felt to be her sisters. She said, "We want you to live lives of spiritual maturity and fulfillment. . . . Some of you may say, 'I'm just average. There's nothing special about me or my life.' And yet what is manifested plainly to me is that you are extraordinary, you whose average day is lived in accordance with our Heavenly Father's laws." She concluded, "Our goal is that each of you enjoys the process of life. . . . These things are real—testimony, individuality, charity, families, sisterhood. . . . And so are you. . . . I pay tribute to you."[12]

With this talk she set the tone for her presidency—straight talk, friend to friend, sister to sister, about women's major concerns, always with a vision of the glorious reality of being daughters of God. It was a vision Relief Society shared with the other women's organizations in the Church.

From the outset the presidency put major emphasis upon establishing warm working relationships with their sisters in the Primary and Young Women. The members of the Relief Society presidency strongly believed that in order to build the kingdom of God, men and women must live the Savior's teaching, "If ye are not one, ye are not mine." (D&C 38:27.) As a counselor in Young Women, Elaine had participated in the literal moving together of the three women's organizations when the Relief Society Building was remodeled between 1986 and 1988 to accommodate offices for all three groups under the same roof. She recalled the moment when the presidencies and administrative assistants met in the building's large reception room, which was still devoid of furniture: "The twelve of us, sitting together there on the floor, compiled statements of our unified purpose — how we would work together, how we saw each other — and then we all signed it. It was a very comfortable, unified, loving situation."[13]

Existing friendships were the foundation of closer organizational relationships. Elaine Jack had served for three years with Ardeth Kapp in Young Women, Chieko Okazaki had worked with Primary general president Michaelene Grassli, and Aileen Clyde was a personal friend of many members of the Young Women presidency and board. The three organizations joined together for combined training of the area general board representatives, wives of area presidency members serving outside the United States and Canada and thus the women responsible for the Relief Society, Young Women, and Primary in their respective area assignments. In addition, in the fall of 1990, before each president's message to women leaders at the semiannual open houses, the three presidents linked arms and taught the sisters that unity, identity, equity, and continuity were the four concepts that governed the working relationships of the women's presidencies at headquarters. They spoke of their support for their priesthood leaders. They invited leaders to work together and to support local priesthood leaders. The presidency rejoiced in a letter that had been forwarded by the general board representatives in the Africa area. It began: "Your letter reached us and lit a candle of joy in our minds." Love Nwokoro, N. Okwandu, and P. Ekeinde, presidents of the Aba Nigeria Stake Relief Society, Primary, and Young Women, continued, "We are mothering the first Stake in Nigeria." They testified, "We sustain the living Prophet and the Powers of the Priesthood," and asked, "We would wish you pray for us."[14] Such messages heartened the general presidency and fueled their efforts to work as sisters with their counterparts.

Early in 1991 the Relief Society general board committee on transition, chaired by Bonnie Parkin, invited the Primary and Young Women to discuss shared concerns, not only the major transition from Young Women to Relief Society, but also the other adjustments girls and women make from one organization and from one stage of life to another.

A culminating symbol of the quality of the auxiliary relationships was a gift from Young Women to Relief Society in November 1991, in acknowledgment of the Relief Society sesquicentennial. The Young Women integrated the Young Women values and the Relief Society purposes into one statement. Over the torch in the Relief Society logo on the sesquicentennial poster, they superimposed the Young Women torch, symbolizing both auxiliaries' single-minded allegiance to the light of Christ. It was a moment when the Relief Society presidency and board felt they were indeed enjoying a unified sisterhood.

Gathering and Sharing Information

As a new presidency, Elaine Jack and her counselors keenly felt the need for increased communication with the local Relief Society officers and members. They thought of invitations to visit individual local units as precious opportunities to learn and teach together. To capitalize on these visits, they planned carefully.

As part of each training and speaking assignment, general board and presidency members held "focus groups" in which local Relief Society leaders were invited to ask eight to ten women to spend approximately an hour sharing their concerns, joys, and feelings with the Relief Society representative from headquarters. Focus groups were generally held prior to training sessions and other meetings. These groups accurately conveyed to sisters in local units the presidency's interest in what women were experiencing. Visiting presidency and board members did not comment in focus groups; they listened. And they learned much. The information they received proved invaluable. It was used in presentations to the Brethren, as the basis for additional research, and in the creation of policy statements.

Relief Society leaders were not surprised that women around the Church faced similar issues: How do I apply the gospel in my daily life? How can I overcome economic pressures? How do I resolve family problems? How can I overcome my high level of stress? As the presidency and board listened, they could understand these sisters' life challenges with greater appreciation and love. In the training sessions and talks that followed, the general board members could offer encouragement from their personal experiences, guided by principles of the restored gospel. They were to teach women the value of receiving personal spiritual direction. Sister Jack emphasized that the presidency and board cannot solve each woman's problems, but they can remind each one that she has access to the Lord and his teachings. Remind them, she stressed, that what matters most is not what they do but who they are and what type of relationships they create with the Lord and with each other.

In their efforts to know their sisters, the presidency consulted with the Church's Research Information Division. Division employees Linda Charney and Perry Cunningham taught board members how to listen more effectively and how to gather information about women's experiences in the field. At Relief Society's request, they and Margie Holmes orchestrated a small study at the fall 1991 open house leaders' training sessions about the effectiveness of the materials presented. In-depth research aided the presidency's work, clarifying and enriching their perceptions from their visits with sisters at headquarters and in the field.

Based on experience with focus groups and other contacts with women in the field, the presidency felt that LDS women were an untapped trove of spiritual riches. Under the direction of board member Cherry Silver, they issued this request in the *Ensign*, *Church News,* and international magazines in February 1991 under the heading "Women's Voices": "In conjunction with the Relief Society's 1992 sesquicentennial celebration, the General Relief Society Presidency would like to hear from you. Write your feelings about being a woman and a member of the Church, your conversion story, your struggles, or your hopes and dreams."[15] These two sentences elicited three hundred responses in the first four months, as women shared conversion stories, testimonies, family anecdotes, and spiritual experiences.

The presidency loved each contact with women and sought to make sisters' visits to Relief Society's home in Salt Lake City equally meaningful. Before the presidency was called, plans were underway to turn the ground floor of the Relief Society Building into a resource center for the entire Priesthood Department. Sunday School, LDS Student Association, Military Relations, and others would join the auxiliaries in providing educational and informational displays for visiting members and nonmembers.

Board members Anne Pingree and MarJean Wilcox redesigned the Relief Society corner of the center, creating a hands-on educational area. Monthly training sessions for Relief Society leaders were held there; posters presented ideas from local units; trained stake Relief Society president volunteers served as docents to help visitors use the center; and wall panels explained how the mission of Relief Society could be used to bless individuals. The resource center became an inviting repository of ideas and suggestions.

Sister Jack brought to Relief Society a belief that women can provide much-needed support of each other, of the families of Zion, and of priesthood leaders. She taught that Relief Society is a means of generating close alliances among Latter-day Saint sisters, and that when women live righteously and develop their potential, they have a common ground. She has taught Relief Society leaders, "You are the harbor pilots. We are bringing you the ship of Relief Society, and we know that you have the ability and you have the inspiration to take the program of Relief Society to your sisters because you know the local conditions, you know their special needs."[16] This statement of belief in the inspired leadership of local sisters was echoed during the first months of her administration in remarks she gave in Australia, Tahiti, Ghana, South Africa, Canada, Ivory Coast, and the United States.

Before six months of their presidency had passed, Elaine, Chieko, and Aileen had studied the Relief Society program carefully. They wanted to help sisters in the field use the program in meaningful ways, best suited for their individual circumstances. Visitors to headquarters from Poland, Yugoslavia, and other areas of the developing church helped them understand how basic and clear instruction must be.

The presidency talked about Relief Society in terms of its four components: Sunday lessons, welfare, homemaking, and visiting teaching. They decided to develop training materials to teach leaders how to use these components to help bless the individual sister and to present these clear and consistent messages:

1. We have confidence in you.
2. You have all you need to aid you in your calling.
3. You are called of the Lord to be a leader at this time.
4. You must spiritually prepare and rely on the Lord.

5. Value each other and work well with priesthood and women leaders.

6. Plan so that you can help meet individual needs.

7. Act as a resource to priesthood leaders and think of them as a resource to you. President Jack taught that "women serve as indispensable partners with priesthood leaders."[17]

The workshops used in local wards and branches were crafted to deliver these messages well. Board members worked with Chieko Okazaki to develop workshops that would help women understand how they could plan more effectively to use Relief Society as a means to help sisters. A workshop where leaders could learn techniques to help them in their callings was premiered every six months at the open houses held before general conference. The workshops emphasized such topics as planning with a purpose, strengthening families, building sisterhood, learning together, and welfare. All workshops included a teaching component about developing effective partnerships with priesthood leaders.

Increasingly sensing the importance of training, the presidency folded the visiting teaching and leadership training committees into a curriculum/leadership/visiting teaching committee. In 1992 this committee began coordinating all visiting teaching and training messages.

Notes from the Field

Through conversations and correspondence, the Relief Society general presidency and board members learned about the challenges facing women throughout the world. Representative of the diversity of women were three who visited the Relief Society offices: Hattie Soil, a sharecropper's daughter who earned a college degree while mothering her children in the inner city of Chicago; Edith Krause, a native of Dresden, Germany, who helped the Church survive through the fire bombing of World War II; and Priscilla Sampson-Davis, a native of Ghana, who taught a sister to read as she served her as a visiting teacher.

From Russia came a letter reporting, "We are taking our first steps in the formation and work of the Moscow Relief Society." President Nina Leont'eva and her counselors, Evgeniya Korosteleva and Tat'yana Petrova, sent "sincerest wishes of health, well-being, happiness, prosperity and success." They assured the presidency, "In spite of the enormous distance and oceans separating us geographically, our hearts beat in unison, united by the love of truth, God, and Jesus Christ, and by charity for those who are suffering in the world." Asking that "our womanly solidarity be strengthened," they explained that March 17, "the traditional celebration of the Relief Society . . . is becoming our celebration also."[18]

Julie Ellis, president of the Chalan Lau Branch Relief Society in Saipan, described a membership of sisters from the Philippines, Truk, India, the United States, China, Korea, and Samoa. With thirteen languages spoken among them, teaching was a major challenge. Their solution: they took turns in presenting the material in short segments so each active sister now understood at least five minutes of the lesson, since she prepared it herself.[19]

The president of the Parramatta Australia Stake Relief Society, Leigh Stachowski, expressed her desire to meld into a loving sisterhood "many different cultures, a large proportion of single sisters," wage-earning mothers, and women who were "married and home with children." She spoke of the "marathon of caring, ministering, listening [to] and teaching" officers of the thirteen units of the stake, six of which consisted of non-English-speaking sisters.[20]

Reports of charitable service contained happy messages. Sisters in Grants Pass, Oregon, completed fifty-two single and thirty-five baby quilts, which they distributed to several local agencies — "blanketing the area," as one recipient put it.[21] At the same time members of the Sunnyside Ward in Arcadia, Pretoria, South Africa, knit squares for lap rugs for the aged. The compassionate service leader reported that "one blind soul of 86 years made me tell her all the colours in her rug and had me run her fingers over it again and again to get the feel of it."[22]

The presidency welcomed the invitation in 1991 to co-sponsor the women's conference held each spring for two days at Brigham Young University. The April 1991 conference drew over five thousand participants. The conference committee, chaired by general board member Carol Lee Hawkins, assembled a commanding program featuring approximately one hundred presenters. For the first time, excerpts from several presentations were made available on videocassette at Church Distribution Centers. Plans were made to produce a similar program of excerpts from the May 1992 conference. Many of the talks were also selected for publication in a book titled *Women Steadfast in Christ.*[23]

One Hundred and Fifty Years of Relief Society

Nothing pleased Elaine Jack, Chieko Okazaki, and Aileen Clyde more than the chance to serve during the planning and celebration of the Relief Society sesquicentennial in 1992. They saw 150 years of Relief Society as a time to reemphasize the truths that had strengthened Relief Society throughout its history. They wrote to the sisters of the Church, "We rejoice in the opportunity to celebrate through service in 1992, as we rededicate our efforts to furthering the work of our Heavenly Father. When the Relief Society was founded, Emma Smith, the first Relief Society General President, said, 'We are going to do something extraordinary.' Because our sisters are extraordinary, so are the accomplishments of Relief Society throughout its history."[24]

The First Presidency sent priesthood leaders a letter that was read in sacrament meeting to all members of the Church. In part they wrote: "The celebration of the Relief Society sesquicentennial during 1992 is an event of great importance in the Church. . . . We are grateful for our sisters who play a vital role in building the kingdom of God throughout the earth. We rejoice in the organization of Relief Society, in its mission, and in the good that comes to the entire world because of the women who are its members."[25]

The sesquicentennial celebration guidelines, distributed in English and seventeen other languages in the fall of 1991, explained that the Relief Society motto, "Charity Never Faileth," was to be the theme of the celebration. The guidelines outlined a celebration based primarily at the ward or branch level, with an international satellite broadcast to "celebrate our worldwide sisterhood."[26]

In preparation for the celebration, five stake Relief Society leaders from Mexico, Germany, Zimbabwe, Korea, and Australia were invited to headquarters to tape statements on the five parts of the Relief Society mission statement. These words were later broadcast on the satellite program in their native languages. They attended the general women's meeting on September 28, 1991, and sessions of general conference the following week. Their time together at headquarters represented the breadth and extent of the worldwide sisterhood of Relief Society. For the presidency as well as the visitors, it was a glorious time. To bond with five women from diverse cultures — and to see them bond with each other — was an experience that transcended language barriers and nationalities.

The symbolism of this visit was never more evident than at an open house held in their honor October 2, 1991. President Thomas S. Monson of the First Presidency, general presidencies of the three women's organizations, Sister Marjorie Hinckley, wife of President Gordon B. Hinckley, area presidencies and their wives, and other Relief Society leaders and guests joined in an evening of multi-lingual conversation punctuated by many embraces and some tears. If any present had ever doubted the ability of women to unite in a common cause, despite geographic, educational, and cultural differences, being with Relief Society leaders from every populated continent would have erased all question. The evident and abundant feelings of sisterhood energized the presidency and board, reaffirming their desire to share with others the reality of what Relief Society had become.

The March 14, 1992, satellite broadcast was an event unprecedented in the Church. The Relief Society's original request for a satellite downlink of five continents, to literally connect women in a worldwide sisterhood, was expanded to ten downlink cities at the initiative of Elder James M. Paramore, executive director of the Church's Audiovisual Department. Members of the First Presidency and Quorum of the Twelve welcomed the suggestion and urged the presidency to proceed. In an international hookup involving eight international and one domestic satellite, pretaped and live talks and music, and translation into fourteen languages, the Church undertook a technical feat never before tried. Margaret Smoot, the broadcast's producer, devoted her superb skills and talents to working with the Church's audiovisual team. Even with such expertise, Relief Society leaders and those working with them understood that innumerable things could go wrong in such a technically sophisticated work. President Jack and her counselors invited all involved in the broadcast to participate in a day of fasting on March 5 to seek the Lord's blessing upon their efforts.

On March 14 at 10:00 A.M. Mountain Standard Time, Sister Jack welcomed ward Relief Society presidencies assembled in the Tabernacle and sisters throughout the United States, Canada, and the Caribbean; and in Frankfurt, Germany; Huddersfield, England; Paris, France; Seoul, Korea; Taipei, Taiwan; Tokyo, Japan; Johannesburg, South Africa; Sydney, Australia; Auckland, New Zealand; and Manila, Philippines. "This is truly a remarkable gathering of sisters," she told the worldwide audience. "Never before have so many women in the world sat down together to pray, sing, and

Elaine L. Jack addresses Relief Society sisters from the Salt Lake Tabernacle pulpit during the 1992 sesquicentennial satellite worldwide broadcast. (Courtesy Visual Resources Library)

speak to each other the feelings of our hearts, to share in the ways the Lord has blessed us as women and members of his Church."[27] Messages from five international Relief Society leaders, the members of the Relief Society general presidency, and President Thomas S. Monson emphasized the significance of individual faith in the Lord and his gospel, adherence to holy covenants, each woman's divine nature and remarkable accomplishments, the sacred nature of family responsibilities, the support women can experience as they strive to love each other, and the glories of membership in an international church with its worldwide sisterhood of righteous women.

Response to the broadcast moved all who were involved with it. A mission president in Taiwan said, "A special spirit flooded the chapel as the opening prayer was given in Mandarin [Chinese], the native language of the sisters present. . . . Eyes were damp as each of our Relief Society sisters realized that [she] played an important role in an international sisterhood that has no ethnic or language barriers."[28] From Paris: "Perhaps the most important thing is that [the broadcast] was received in France live from the Tabernacle across 6,000 miles of ocean and continent. There is a significant difference, being this far away, between a live broadcast from Temple Square and a delayed showing of the same program by video tape 30 or 60 days after the fact. The Relief Society sisters in Paris were extremely pleased to be part of this historic occasion, even as it was happening."[29]

Dozens of sisters sent responses. From Utah: "Since hearing your powerful messages I have resolved to do what I can within the circle of my influence to serve unstintingly, even though it might be in small acts, and to develop greater charity in thought, attitude and action."[30] From New Zealand: "Never before have we felt so much a part of a world-wide sisterhood. Never before have we had such a desire to make a difference."[31] From Brigham Young University: "Every one of us must come away from the Sesquicentennial Celebration knowing that we are loved, knowing that we are daughters of God, knowing that we have power to do good, and having greater courage in serving and living as covenant women."[32] From Tennessee: "Thank you for a clearer vision of my role as a blessed daughter of God."[33]

Comments like these gratified and humbled all at Relief Society headquarters. Board members, staff, and the presidency knew the Lord had answered their many prayers for the success of the satellite broadcast. All felt that Margaret Smoot spoke the truth when she said at the program's conclusion, "We won't know for a long time all the ways the Lord has blessed us with this broadcast."[34] The reaction of sisters in the field capped the sesquicentennial in an unforgettable and unique manner.

While the satellite broadcast, the only major sesquicentennial event at headquarters, provided an opportunity for linking sisters together, the heart of each local celebration was a "celebrate through service" project. The idea was to "plan and carry out one or more local service projects that will bless people living in the community." Guidelines counseled, "Plan all socializing as part of the service project, not as a separate event. The service project *is* your celebration." The overview added, "Plan all your Relief Society activities so that service is the focus throughout 1992."[35] The presidency hoped that this emphasis on service would enliven the sisterhood of Relief Society, enrich each woman's life, and expand the sisters' vision of what a society devoted to relief might add to the world.

As the sesquicentennial service projects began to develop, reports came to the general offices from the field. A Relief Society president in California told of inviting a local community service worker to homemaking meeting to share ideas the sisters might consider for their project. When the community worker learned that every Relief Society unit in the Church was doing a project, she said, "Then we can solve all the problems of the world."[36] The general presidency wanted all sisters in a ward to be part of the planning and implementation of the project, believing that service would broaden the views of many women, deepen their feelings of compassion, and do much good in their local communities. They emphasized that sisters should not feel burdened by this service: "Do what you can, and do it lovingly. The Lord asks this of you, and we ask nothing more."[37]

Another sesquicentennial activity was the presentation of "A Society of Sisters," a theatrical production. The author, Frances Smeath, wrote a narration to introduce the production, which was then left open for inclusion of local stories and histories, with the hope that it would "create a spiritual sharing that truly reflects the diversity of your Relief Society membership."[38] Each unit was also asked to prepare "a record of the history of its Relief Society, including a record of its presentation of 'A Society of Sisters' and its service project,"[39] and to send a synopsis of its history to headquarters.

As a permanent reminder of what the sesquicentennial represented, Deseret Book published a book of photographs of contemporary LDS women. *Something Extraordinary: Celebrating Our Relief Society Sisterhood,* featuring pictures of LDS women throughout the world and a message from the general presidency, showed the diversity and unity of women who are members of Relief Society. A sesquicentennial poster, using a border from a 1923 *Relief Society Magazine,* and the Relief Society logo as it appears on the 1942 *Centenary of Relief Society*, proclaimed the sesquicentennial.

At the Museum of Church History and Art in Salt Lake City, Marjorie Conder mounted a year-long exhibit about Relief Society, entitled "Come Let Us Rejoice." The exhibit, scheduled to run from March 1992 to February 1993, was designed to illustrate how the ideas of faith in Christ, nurturing, sisterhood, compassion, community betterment, and development of individual gifts and talents have been part of Relief Society for 150 years. The March 1992 *Ensign* celebrated Relief Society in most of its articles.

The sesquicentennial was the ideal moment to reemphasize individual covenants and the cardinal principles of Relief Society. During several meetings in 1991 the presidency explained to members of the Church's Priesthood Executive Council, and later to the General Authorities assembled in leadership training sessions, that nothing mattered more to them than to open the way for women. They wanted their sisters to learn the skills that would allow them to participate fully in the gospel and bless their families. Sharing their vision of what the women of Zion are and can be, they described the many ways women could make a difference.

A significant emphasis of the sesquicentennial was "a focus on literacy," based on the tenet that "all women should possess basic literacy skills so they are able to learn the gospel, teach their families, and improve their circumstances."[40] Two pilot literacy projects were initiated in late 1991, and the presidency planned to send guidelines to the field in early 1993 so that literacy projects could be implemented worldwide.

President Jack and her counselors hoped the literacy effort would be the most significant contribution of their administration. The enthusiastic support of priesthood leaders at Church headquarters encouraged them to move forward vigorously on this program. In an article in the March 1992 *Ensign,* the issue that commemorated Relief Society, President Gordon B. Hinckley stated: "Now a great new project is to be undertaken. It is a practical and much-needed part of this 150th anniversary celebration. But its consequences will go on and on and be felt in the lives of generations yet to come. It is a program to teach those who suffer from functional illiteracy. It is designed to bring light into the lives of those who can neither read nor write. . . . Imagine, if you can, the potential of this inspired program. Who dare dream of its consequences?"[41] President Monson continued this theme in his remarks at the Relief Society sesquicentennial satellite when he said, "I compliment you sisters of Relief Society on your carefully chosen theme to eliminate illiteracy. . . . Sisters of Relief Society, you can lift [the] cloud of despair and welcome heaven's divine light as it shines upon your sisters."[42]

The Vision of Relief Society

Elaine Jack began her tenure as the twelfth general president of Relief Society by proclaiming, "This is a joyous gospel! I know that in the strength of the Lord we can do all things required of us."[43] In her many talks she often shared her vision of who Relief Society women are and what they can accomplish. She asked her sisters to maintain their hope. She talked of "a perfect brightness of hope" as a "light, ebullient phrase. . . . [As] I've stood on a mountaintop at sunrise and thought of that phrase, it moves and warms me so."[44] She spoke of the good that comes as all "value the diversity of women."[45] She explained in talks to the Church Welfare Department, to Regional Representatives, and to Relief Society leaders that "Relief Society women live true to the purposes of our organization. . . . When we say our motto, 'Charity Never Faileth,' we speak of our methods and our message."[46] She emphasized the importance of developing good family relationships,[47] and invited visiting teachers to create meaningful relationships with the sisters they were assigned to visit.[48]

At the dedication of the Toronto Temple and the rededication of the Alberta Temple, she reminded sisters, "What a blessing it is . . . to consider that each time we enter the temple, we have the opportunity to purify our hearts and rededicate ourselves to righteous living."[49]

Sister Jack has based her presidency on love of, respect for, and confidence in the sisters of Zion. In her message at the worldwide sesquicentennial satellite broadcast, she spoke with urgency and possibility to these women: "I ask you to undertake with me a spiritual journey worthy of our best efforts. I ask you to press forward with me in the quest for unparalleled levels of personal spirituality. Let us seek keener vision and stronger hearts. Let us make 'charity never faileth' a motto of such personal significance that the whole world will be blessed by us, the daughters of God who are the sisters of Relief Society."[50]

The message in *Something Extraordinary*, the sesquicentennial photo book, captured the spirit of Elaine Jack's administration:

"In the 150 years since Relief Society began, the women of Zion have done many things extraordinary, and done them extraordinarily well. Relief Society has grown steadily in numbers and influence. This is because Relief Society is the sum of the righteousness of each sister. This is because your life is a testament to your testimony of our Savior, Jesus Christ. This is because you are something extraordinary."[51]

This belief in the extraordinary nature of each Relief Society member has been extolled by Elaine Jack, self-defined as "a very ordinary woman," her counselors, and members of her board. To this they added their testimonies, their best efforts, and their faith that a brilliant future awaits their sisters, the women of Relief Society.

"The Same God . . . Worketh All in All"

"As has been said of our Relief Societies," observed President Zina D. H. Young in 1891, "we commenced with a handful of patches to make quilts."[1] With that homely metaphor is suggested the piecemeal development of Relief Society from 1842 to the present. "Line upon line, precept upon precept," the Lord promised the faithful,[2] and so has been the unfolding of Relief Society, transforming and innovating as needed in its mission to the world as part of The Church of Jesus Christ of Latter-day Saints. "We have had to grow a little by little," Aunt Zina continued. "For one thing is true: you cannot put a quart into a pint cup."[3]

From the handful of sisters who with their brethren heard the gospel message, experienced the witness of the Spirit, centered the covenant, and became Saints of the latter days, to the present time, the basic pattern has never varied in its essential components. Olga Kovorova in Czechoslovakia in 1983 traced the same path to membership in the Church, and in Relief Society, as did Zina Huntington in New York in 1835: they heard, they prayed, they received witness, they were baptized into the Church of Jesus Christ, and they received the Holy Ghost. Thereafter they took whatever steps opened to them: they learned the doctrines; they bore testimony; they participated in projects and programs; they blessed the lives of others and were blessed in turn. Available to them, as the gospel spread abroad, were and are the blessings of the Spirit, of sisterhood, of priesthood direction, and of the temple. As Zina Huntington Young witnessed America's western movement, the struggle for suffrage, and the compromises toward statehood, so Olga Kovarova experienced the dissolution of the communist eastern bloc and her country's adaptation to free-market economy. But above the maelstrom of world affairs, observed Sister Zina, "is the grandeur of the spirit of God that quickens our souls, that causes love to happily live, and imparts knowledge of the life to come. What greater things, what nobler aspirations can we desire?"[4]

Venerable Elizabeth Ann Whitney, who had been a counselor in the Female Relief Society of Nauvoo, looked back from 1878 to the 1842 beginning: "The Relief Society then was small compared to its numbers now, but the Prophet foretold great things concerning the future of this organization, many of which I have lived to see fulfilled."[5] By the time of her writing, Mother Whitney had witnessed some of those "great things": the Relief Society in Nauvoo had grown from twenty to thirteen hundred in two years; the women had felt the strength of the Spirit, had grown in sisterhood as they crossed the plains together, had rebuilt their society in Utah wards, and, with priesthood blessing, had extended it churchwide. Relief Society had mothered the Young Ladies and Primary associations, had sponsored home industries, had improved community health care, had established and maintained connections with women worldwide, had made strong beginnings to women's political enfranchisement and in all these endeavors received support from priesthood leaders.

In Mother Whitney's understanding, surely the blessings of the temple were preeminent. In those holy houses, sisters ministered to sisters, and they received, as faithful women still receive, the "knowledge and intelligence" that the Prophet Joseph Smith promised. In temples, through the highest ordinances of the Melchizedek Priesthood, women entered the new and everlasting covenants sealing in union wives and husbands, children and parents. Still, Sister Whitney continued, "there are many things which yet remain to be fulfilled in the future of which [Joseph Smith] prophesied, that are great and glorious; and I rejoice in the contemplation of these things daily."[6] Surely she would have observed with satisfaction the shipment of Relief Society wheat to ameliorate catastrophe; the creation of facilities for improving maternity care; the establishment of communitywide social service programs; the projects to relieve wartime sufferers. And along with that, the spiritual advancement of women as they strengthened families, served missions, created courses of study, taught one another, and entered the temples in ever greater numbers and with increasing frequency.

The twentieth century saw Relief Society and the Church as a whole adapt progressive principles and new technology to their purposes. Geometrically increasing membership demanded systematization, which threatened to replace with mechanization the familiarity that had warmed the women's meetings. "All organiz'd bodies have their peculiar evils, weaknesses and difficulties," Joseph Smith had told the Nauvoo Relief Society;[7] they too must learn to adapt to circumstances. With church growth, the whole must be divided into manageable parts, hierarchical relationships emphasized, priesthood correlation strengthened, and programs and lessons standardized.

Two world wars and a worldwide economic depression forced the reach of the women beyond their own narrow borders. Where the Prophet Joseph had told the few in Nauvoo, "Let your labors be confin'd mostly to those around you in your own circle,"[8] the new challenge voiced by succeeding prophets encouraged the sisters to reach beyond their early confines. President Spencer W. Kimball wrote in 1979 that "much of the major growth that is coming to the Church in the last days will come because many of the good women of the world . . . will be drawn to the Church in large numbers." In both numerical and the spiritual growth, he said, the "female exemplars of the Church will be a significant force." In them, he observed, "there is often such an inner sense of spirituality."[9] Recent years have seen marked increase not only in the numbers of sister missionaries, but also in the community activities of Latter-day Saint women at home and business and professional women in their communities at large.

Relief Society is a worldwide sisterhood, not, as earlier, in the organizational sense of holding corporate membership in international councils, but in the immediacy made possible by the technology of air travel and instant communication. The "small circle of sisters" in Czechoslovakia who sent, through Elder Boyd K. Packer, their "hearts and thoughts" to all the Relief Societies, are encircled into the larger sisterhood of the Church. "Each sister, no matter where in that circle she stands, can look to either side and feel the spirit of inspiration coming back as she extends the gentle hand of charity to those on either side," Elder Packer explained.[10]

The in-gathering to a geographical Zion, which marked early Mormonism, pivoted at the meridian of this dispensation into a worldwide diaspora. Women who clustered for safety in the sheltered valleys of the Great Basin mothered granddaughters and great-granddaughters who now make their homes in the far reaches of the globe, where they strengthen and are strengthened by local

convert members. Together they build and are building Relief Society. Five generations of one family illustrate:

In 1837 Elizabeth Haven [Barlow], a twenty-six-year-old convert, left her Massachusetts home and joined with the Saints in
Missouri. Driven with them to Illinois, she found solace among her
sisters in Nauvoo, and on April 28, 1842, she was accepted into
the Female Relief Society there. She delivered her fifth child en
route to the Valley. There she and her husband made their home
in Bountiful, just north of Salt Lake City. In 1857 she was called
to preside over the Relief Society in Bountiful. Despite the inter-
ruption of the move south during the Utah War, she continued as
presidentess into her seventies, being released just three years
before her death.

Elizabeth's daughter Pamela, meanwhile, married and was sent
with her husband, David Thompson, to colonize in Panaca, Nevada.
There she was called as Relief Society president. Widowed in Nevada, she returned with her children to Utah. Theresa, Pamela's
daughter, just ten years old when her father was killed, married at
seventeen and joined the Saints who moved to Mexico's northern
provinces. She served there as counselor in the Relief Society. Most
of those Saints returned to Utah after the 1910 Mexican revolution.
Theresa's daughter, Athelia Call Sears, served as Relief Society
president in Ogden, Utah, during the years when money-making
projects demanded much of the women. Despite her seventy years,
Sister Sears led her women in a catering contract that enabled
them not only to finance their own Relief Society, but also to equip
the ward kitchen and hand the bishop a check for a thousand dollars
for other ward uses.

By now Relief Societies were being organized in student
branches at universities in the United States and Canada, and
Athelia Sears's namesake daughter, Athelia Tanner, was one of
the first to serve at the University of Utah branch in Salt Lake
City. Sister Tanner settled finally in Pasadena, California, where
she served in a Relief Society. Her daughter followed suit as a
Relief Society president in a student ward at Brigham Young University and later in a family ward in Texas.[11] Change of circumstances and continuity of spirit pervade the history of this one family
of Relief Society workers.[11]

Still other Latter-day Saint women in their moves find themselves totally isolated from the Church. Cherry Bushman Silver,
who was called to the Relief Society's general board in 1991, was

in the mid-1970s the lone Latter-day Saint woman on an Ivory Coast plantation, where her husband managed a sugar operation. "Everything but a common humanity separated us from our African neighbors," she wrote. "Thinking of the satisfactions of Relief Society," Cherry invited the wives of eighty company workers—Vietnamese, Mauritian, British, American, French, and Malagasy, as well as African—to inaugurate a monthly gathering. Over the more than two years the Silvers were there, the quasi-Relief Society put on a Christmas party for the children and established and staffed a lending library for the workers' families. "Given a goal, some handicrafts, and a chance to sit down and work together," Cherry became convinced, "women worldwide could weld bonds across cultural barriers and reduce their feelings of difference."[12] Quoting from the Indian prophet of peace, Mahatma Gandhi, an Idaho Relief Society member wrote, "I do not want my house to be walled in on all sides and my windows to be stuffed. I want the culture of all the lands to be blown about my house as freely as possible."[13]

Relief Society women find much that is familiar in the account of Relief Society activities in the Oslo Norway Third Ward. To her friend Marian Johnson in Utah, Alshield Morteng typed a newsy letter about their mutual friends. Sister Vigdis Johansen, ill since before the birth of her last child, is in the hospital, Alshield reported. In socialist Norway, there would be government support for the family of seven children; even so, she wrote, "this is a great challenge to the women in R. S. We try to bring dinner for the family at least 2 or 3 times a week." Most of the women in her Relief Society are employed full time, she had said earlier, adding a dimension to her comment now that "the sisters are wonderful in doing this beside all the other things they do."

In her gentle observation that "we have lately had several difficult situations to be organized in R. S., situations as I never have experienc[e]d before," Oslo's Sister Morteng touched the most universal challenge of Relief Societies worldwide: the multiplicity of differences apparent between earlier Relief Societies and contemporary ones, and among Relief Societies in the hundred-plus nations where they are organized.[14]

"To Relieve the Poor"

Remote from the basically homogeneous Relief Societies of the Utah church in past years are tiny circles of Eastern European or African women, rural societies of central Mexico, affluent societies of southern California, or central-city societies of, say, Chicago. Statistics of the Hyde Park Ward in Chicago evidence the church of the nineties in ways no Relief Society presidency had dealt with until recently. The ward boundaries encompass the southern half of Chicago, with a population of over 1.5 million, in a basically middle-class, racially integrated community that encompasses both the University of Chicago and some of the nation's poorest ghetto neighborhoods. High convert baptism rates (during 1990 there were 140 baptisms, half of them adult women) and the transience inherent in university wards keep the ward leadership in flux. Economically the picture is mixed. Several Relief Society members, highly educated, earn over $100,000 yearly. Several others are students, both single and married, living frugally on loans and part-time work. Twenty-five percent of the society members are single parents. Low-paying jobs, unemployment, and lack of vocational skills are the most serious problems for many, and state welfare remains the only option for several. Even though most are high school graduates, many are functionally illiterate.

Supporting these sisters in their family responsibilities demands innovation and imagination on the part of ward priesthood and Relief Society leaders. Catherine Stokes, a health services administrator, had been a member of the Church just four years when she was called as Relief Society president in Hyde Park in 1983. She learned quickly that the visiting teaching coordinator was in fact her most important "counselor." She got "the best woman in the ward" for the job, and "spent as much time with her" as she did with her counselors, she later reflected.[15] Communication among the diverse women of her ward was not easy, and she lightheartedly defined her mission as "helping you white folks understand us black folks."

Temporal responsibilities weigh heavily on twentieth century Latter-day Saint women as they did on their foremothers. Wars, depressions, and natural catastrophes have taught contemporary women the lessons that taming a wilderness and building communities taught their ancestors: the virtues of diligence, hard work, and self reliance. In that tradition many Latter-day Saints, especially those without financially supportive husbands, have had to take on the responsibility of supporting themselves and their families. Camilla Eyring Kimball advised sisters in Europe to "qualify in two vocations—that of homemaking, and that of preparing to earn a living outside the home, if and when the occasion requires."[16] Relief Society, she urged, would assist women in achieving their temporal objectives as well as the spiritual ones.

Nevertheless, the consistent message of the Church to women, in particular those who are parents, has set the priorities in order: "No career approaches in importance that of wife, homemaker, mother," reiterated President Ezra Taft Benson in 1987, citing his predecessor, Spencer W. Kimball.[17] "Mothers," President Benson stressed, "teach your children the gospel in your own home, at your own fireside." Echoing scriptural precedent he promised, "Your children will remember your teachings forever, and when they are old, they will not depart from them. They will call you blessed."[18]

Traditionally Relief Society has strongly supported women in their important work as nurturers, in their own homes and within the broader community of Saints. Providing quilts for immigrants arriving in the valley of the Great Salt Lake or for Cambodian refugees arriving in California, taking classes in midwifery and obstetrics to save mothers or serve as health missionaries, visiting teaching in the homes of their sisters, or tutoring homeless children, Relief Society sisters nurture with skill and with love.

Single or partnered, Relief Society women have been taught an outreach beyond their own intimate circle as an essential element in gospel living. For many, as for board member Cherry Silver, "loneliness dissolves when I have someone with whom to share and someone to care for, when I have work that is important to do, and when I confide in our Heavenly Father and feel his assuring care."[19] As President Amy Brown Lyman observed, "Relief Society women have never been satisfied with mere self improvement." They "have had a feeling that life was incomplete unless through their work and themselves they were able to make a contribution toward the welfare of others."[20]

Including successive generations of women in the work of Relief Society has been a challenge since the 1890s. President Joseph F. Smith's 1907 invitation remains current: "We want the young women, the women of faith, of courage, of purity . . . to take hold of this work with vigor, with intelligence and unitedly, for the building up of Zion and the instruction of women in their duties — domestic duties, public duties, and every duty that may devolve upon them."[21]

In admonishing women to work "unitedly, for the building up

of Zion," President Smith reiterated a core Relief Society principle. Sarah Kimball, in the 1870s, attributed the remarkable success of her ward society to the willingness of the sisters to work "in unison." Working in unison with their brethren and under priesthood authority, as she and other sisters learned, was just as imperative. The partnership of women and men in building the kingdom was the natural extension of the partnership of parents in the family. "Neither the man without the woman, nor the woman without the man, in the Lord," was applicable to the larger body as to the intimate family.

"In the Lord" — or in other words, under the holy priesthood direction — men and women covenant together to serve God, whose kingdom they are building. The presence of Relief Society in the ecclesiastical organization reflected this divine pattern. Speaking, as a contemporary scholar has expressed it, "in a different voice,"[22] women help move both the family and the community of Saints toward wholeness, completeness, eventual perfection. Relief Society's fruitful history has affirmed the importance of balance of male and female, the pattern of partnership established in Nauvoo by the Prophet Joseph Smith.

Seen in the eternal setting, men's and women's interests are not separate. Nor is the well-being of individuals separable from the well-being of the community, in the Lord. The body of the Church is one whole; likewise the temporal and the spiritual merge in divine oneness.

"To Save Souls"

Relief Society's vision of its sacred purpose has from its inception set the Mormon sisterhood apart from other social or charitable women's groups. Its members were to be "a select Society separate from all the evils of the world, choice, virtuous and holy."[23] They were women of covenant, endowed with knowledge from on high. To foster the spiritual growth of individual members, to prepare them to receive and to honor the saving ordinances of the priesthood, remains the highest aspiration of the Relief Society.

It is difficult to assess, or even describe, the spiritual dimension of women's lives. Following the Doctrine and Covenants injunction not to "boast themselves of these things," Latter-day Saint women speak quietly and reverently, if at all, of the sacred moments in their lives, "given unto you," the scripture continues, "for your profit and for salvation."[24] Like their sisters of the past, however, contemporary women do experience the gifts of the Holy Ghost, to whose power they testify.

The gift of tongues, Joseph Smith taught, was solely for the comfort and assurance of the Saints, and so was it received in the early days of the restoration.[25] With the extension of the Church into areas where other languages are spoken, however, the original gift has been expressed anew to a new dimension: as on the day of Pentecost, when people needed to hear the word in their own tongues, so the gift has been experienced in the twentieth century.

Relief Society in the Hauula Hawaii First Ward in the early 1970s was composed of Tahitian, Tongan, and Samoan speakers as well as those whose native tongue is English. After opening exercises, the Polynesian sisters and those who spoke English would separate for their lessons, to return for the closing hymn and prayer. Wrote Marvelee Soon Tahauri of the Polynesian sisters, "I always stayed in the English session, watching those women come and go, never knowing their names, where they lived, or what they discussed." Then, in August 1977, stake leaders challenged the Relief Societies to dissolve the language sessions in order to unify the sisters, and Sister Tahauri, who was called as spiritual living teacher, adopted "occasionally unusual" methods toward the objective of mutual growth, understanding, and appreciation. English speakers self-consciously mouthed scriptures in halting Tahitian or Tongan, the Polynesian women nodding encouragement; a Samoan sister read in English, "By this shall all men know that ye are my disciples, if ye have love one to another."[26]

"Then one day," recalled Sister Tahauri, "after I had presented a lesson on turning our weaknesses into strengths, a sister stood, weeping while bearing testimony in her native tongue. Suddenly she rushed over to where I sat and embraced me, kissing me time and time again. 'Thank you, thank you!' she sobbed. I should have been prepared to experience this realm of the Spirit," reflected Sister Tahauri, "yet I was trembling, and the tears flowed unrestrained."[27] It was the same gift, surely, as that which blessed the Nauvoo sisters, the gift of tongues "for your comfort." "Who can interpret my tears?" queried a young women in a Nauvoo testimony meeting in 1982.

Healing the sick as a gift of the spirit has not left the women of the restoration, although its forms have changed. Men, women, and children join in fasting and prayer, individually as well as in families and wards, on behalf of the sick. Holders of the Melchizedek Priesthood administer to those in need, and all members of the Church may add to their faith, as they ask the Lord to bless an individual.

A Latter-day Saint woman serving a mission with her husband in Coalinga, California, heard the prompting of the Spirit to her and applied her faith in the healing of a sister. In her July 13, 1942, report to their mission president, she wrote of meeting the woman, who was afflicted with cancer, outside the sick woman's home. "She was feeling so bad and tired," the missionary wrote, "that my husband said to me, 'Take her in the house and get her to lie down.' This I did, and feeling so sorry for her, I drew up my chair close to the bed." Reaching out to touch the woman, she said, " 'Now go to sleep.' She seemed to be comforted and soon began to doze, when a still small voice said to me, 'Why don't you pray?' " Silently and humbly, the missionary prayed, asking not only that the woman's pain would cease but also that she would be blessed "that the cancer would die and even go out of the bone and that she would be healed from the crown of her head to the soles of her feet." When the woman awoke, the missionary said, she reported that the pain had gone, and she "got up and went about her work." Some time later the missionaries received word through the woman's daughter that her mother was well and strong. "Through her faith she was healed," reported the missionary.[28]

Woman participate in the gift of healing by being themselves as well as by applying their faith to others' needs. A Delaware mother, called as president of the stake Relief Society, found her negative attitude affecting her service. "One day," she wrote, "as I drove the 75 miles to the stake center alone, I began to pray aloud in the car. I realized I needed a healing of my mind.... Weeping and praying, I asked the Lord to either heal me or release me so that the work would not suffer further. Suddenly the Spirit touched my mind, gently and lovingly, and smoothed away that wrinkle of confusion." From that affirmation came her testimony that "God can heal anything—our prejudices, our bad habits, and our minds, bodies, and spirits."[29]

"If you live up to your privileges," Joseph Smith promised the women in Nauvoo's Relief Society, "the angels cannot be restrain'd from being your associates."[30] Such was the experience when, awaiting the dedication of the Manti Temple in 1888, Mary Ann Burnham Freeze heard angelic voices. Such experiences recur among contemporary sisters. One young woman, having spent much of her life practicing piano and organ, felt strongly the potential of music to infuse the congregation with the Lord's spirit, to bring the worshipers closer to the Lord. Called as choir director, she felt on one occasion a commitment to making a particular anthem a gift to the congregation, an affirmation of her testimony and the testimonies of the choir members that the Savior lives and loves them. Together they prepared well and prayed. Sunday arrived, and they stood to perform their offering. As she conducted the choir, the young woman "felt light coming forth from them, and mingled with their voices she heard the voices of angels." Never had she heard sounds so beautiful; others in the congregation shared the experience.[31] Women of the twentieth century, like their sisters of the nineteenth, have learned to reach for and receive the assurances of the Spirit that their service is accepted.

A contemporary mother told her friend of her benefaction in the time of her need. The new school term was about to begin, and the children were to receive blessings from their father. The living room was tidied, the children settled, their father ready in suit and tie. The Spirit was present, the mother said, as the father pronounced the blessings. The baby in her lap began to fuss, so she carried him to the bedroom. She looked about that cluttered room in the dim light. Clothes, papers, books were everywhere, chaotic in dark contrast to the order and light of the room she had left. It seemed to her that she was part of the dimness, the disarray — that she was not worthy to be in the happy circle of peace and light in the living room. As she prayed for help, she had the impression of light descending, encircling her and her baby. With the light came peace and confirmation; the Lord loved her and accepted her offerings.[32] The gift was as sure as had she received it, as her predecessors sometimes had, in more dramatic and more public manifestation.

The assurances of the Spirit, as the Prophet Joseph reminded the sisters in Nauvoo, are "for your comfort." Now, 150 years later, those sweet outpourings are as needed as ever. But for contemporary women, as for the Nauvoo sisters, the manifestations of the Spirit are not sufficient for salvation. Now, as earlier, their faith, thus reinforced by the Spirit, brings Latter-day Saint women to the doors of the holy temple. There, under authority of the Melchizedek Priesthood, they receive endowments from on high. There they augment their baptismal covenants and partake of the "knowledge and intelligence" promised to them. There they cement their bonds with husbands under the new and everlasting covenant of marriage, and begin to learn the meaning of divine daughterhood and sonship. Under priesthood authority are sealed the blessings of which the Spirit bore witness, the blessings through which the men and women are taught, tested, redeemed, eventually to be exalted.

"God Hath Tempered the Body Together"

It is significant that Joseph Smith based his spiritually moving and doctrinally significant April 28, 1842, address on the epistles of Paul as recorded in 1 Corinthians 12 and 13. He began, as the apostle did, by identifying many gifts—tongues, prophecy, healing, knowledge, and faith among them—as being possessed by individual members, but all as necessary to the Church as eyes, ears, and hands are to the body. These diverse gifts, Paul explained, are from the same source, of the same Spirit.[33]

As each individual member of the body of Christ, the Church, possesses his or her own gifts, so each epoch of the Church and each entity of its organization has its own purposes. "There are differences of administrations," Paul wrote, "but the same Lord. And there are diversities of operations, but it is the same God which worketh all in all."[34]

So it is that the Nauvoo Relief Society sisters sent petitions to their governor and administered to the sick; that the first Utah societies sewed clothes for Lamanite women and children; that the 1870s Relief Society gathered wheat and built halls; that in the 1920s the Relief Society administered social services for state and local governments; that during World War II they operated an employment agency; and that in the 1970s they built statues honoring women's lives. Differences of administrations, Paul observed, and diversities of operations, but "the same God which worketh in all."

Having thus justified the uses of those spiritual and administrative gifts, however, the apostle Paul extended his vision to one that transcended them all. "But whether there be prophecies," he writes, "they shall fail; whether there be tongues, they shall cease; whether there be knowledge, it shall vanish away."[35] They are the lesser gifts, "for your comfort," but impotent to save. Only charity, "the pure love of Christ," has the power to redeem mankind. "Charity never faileth," promised Paul. In its choice of motto, Relief Society chose the better part.

The temporal obligations of Relief Society are but schoolmaster to its spiritual responsibility: to bring souls to Christ. In concert with their brethren, women of the Church reach toward that perfection which comes as the grace of God "after all we can do." "For we know in part, and we prophesy in part. But when that which is perfect is come, then that which is in part shall be done away."[36] All the lesser gifts, partial blessings, are circumscribed in that vast and all-encompassing love. That charity which is "the pure love of Christ" is the lodestar of Relief Society. "And now abideth faith, hope, charity, these three; but the greatest of these is charity."[37]

GENERAL RELIEF SOCIETY
PRESIDENCIES AND OFFICIALS
1842–1992

GENERAL PRESIDENCIES

President Emma Hale Smith, March 17, 1842–March 16, 1844
First Counselor Sarah M. Cleveland, March 17, 1842–March 16, 1844
Second Counselor Elizabeth Ann Whitney, March 17, 1842–March 16, 1844
Secretary Eliza R. Snow, March 17, 1842–March 16, 1844
Assistant Secretary Phebe J. Wheeler, 1842–1844
Treasurer Elvira A. Cowles (Holmes), 1842–1844

President Eliza Roxcy Snow, 1866–December 5, 1887
First Counselor Zina D. H. Young, June 19, 1880–April 1888
Second Counselor Elizabeth Ann Whitney, June 19, 1880–February 15, 1882
Secretary Sarah M. Kimball, 1880–1887
Treasurer Mary Isabella Horne, 1880–1887

President Zina D. H. Young, April 8, 1888–August 28, 1901
First Counselor Jane S. Richards, October 11, 1888–November 10, 1901
Second Counselor Bathsheba W. Smith, October 11, 1888–November 10, 1901
Third Counselor Sarah M. Kimball, 1892–1898
Third Counselor Sarah Jenne Cannon, 1898–1901
Secretary Sarah M. Kimball, 1888–1892
Assistant Secretary Romania B. Pratt (Penrose), 1888–1892
Corresponding Secretary Emmeline B. Wells, 1888–1892
General Secretary Emmeline B. Wells, 1892–1901
General Treasurer Mary Isabella Horne, 1888–1901

President Bathsheba W. Smith, November 10, 1901–September 20,1910
First Counselor Annie Taylor Hyde, November 10, 1901–March 2, 1909
Second Counselor Ida Smoot Dusenberry, November 10, 1901–September 20, 1910
General Secretary Emmeline B. Wells, 1901–1910
General Treasurer Clarissa Smith Williams, 1901–1910

President Emmeline B. Wells, October 3, 1910–April 2, 1921
First Counselor Clarissa Smith Williams, October 3, 1910–April 2, 1921
Second Counselor Julina L. Smith, October 3, 1910–April 2, 1921
General Secretary Olive D. Christensen, 1910–1913
Assistant Secretary Amy Brown Lyman, 1910–1913
General Secretary Amy Brown Lyman, 1913–1921
Corresponding Secretary Susa Young Gates, 1913–1921
General Treasurer Emma A. Empey, 1911–1921

President Clarissa Smith Williams, April 2, 1921–October 7, 1928
First Counselor Jennie B. Knight, April 2, 1921–October 7, 1928
Second Counselor Louise Y. Robison, April 2, 1921–October 7, 1928
General Secretary-Treasurer Amy Brown Lyman, 1921–October 7, 1928

President Louise Y. Robison, October 7, 1928–December 1939
First Counselor Amy Brown Lyman, October 7, 1928–December 1939
Second Counselor Julia A. Child, October 7, 1928–January 23, 1935
Second Counselor Kate M. Barker, April 3, 1935–December 1939
General Secretary-Treasurer Julia A. F. Lund, 1928–1939

President Amy Brown Lyman, January 1, 1940–April 6, 1945
First Counselor Marcia K. Howells, April 1940–April 6, 1945
Second Counselor Donna D. Sorensen, April 1940–October 12, 1942
Second Counselor Belle S. Spafford, October 1942–April 1945
General Secretary-Treasurer Vera W. Pohlman, 1940–1945

President Belle S. Spafford, April 6, 1945–October 3, 1974
First Counselor, Marianne C. Sharp, April 6, 1945–October 3, 1974
Second Counselor, Gertrude R. Garff, April 6, 1945–September 30, 1947
Second Counselor, Velma N. Simonsen, October 3, 1947–December 17, 1956
Second Counselor, Helen W. Anderson, January 1957–August 1958
Second Counselor, Louise W. Madsen, August 1958–October 3, 1974
General Secretary-Treasurer, Blanche B. Stoddard, April–October 1945
General Secretary-Treasurer, Margaret C. Pickering, 1945–1957
General Secretary-Treasurer, Hulda Parker Young, 1957–1969
General Secretary-Treasurer, Mayola R. Miltenberger, 1969–1974

President Barbara B. Smith, October 3, 1974–April 7, 1984
First Counselor Janath R. Cannon, October 3, 1974–November 1978
First Counselor Marian R. Boyer, November 1978–April 7, 1984
Second Counselor Marian R. Boyer, October 3, 1974–November 1978
Second Counselor Shirley W. Thomas, November 28, 1978–June 24, 1983
Second Counselor Ann S. Reese, October 1, 1983–April 7, 1984
General Secretary-Treasurer Mayola R. Miltenberger, 1974–1984

President Barbara W. Winder, April 7, 1984–March 31, 1990
First Counselor Joy F. Evans, May 21, 1984–March 31, 1990
Second Counselor Joanne B. Doxey, May 21, 1984–March 31, 1990
Secretary-Treasurer Joan B. Spencer, 1984–1990

President Elaine L. Jack, March 31, 1990–

First Counselor Chieko N. Okazaki, March 31, 1990–
Second Counselor Aileen H. Clyde, March 31, 1990–
Administrative Assistant Carol L. Clark, 1990–

GENERAL BOARD MEMBERS 1880–1992

Note: In the following lists, dates after names indicate total years of service on the general board. Those immediately recalled to the board when a new president begins serving are not listed twice.

1880–1887: Eliza R. Snow, president; 1888–1892: Zina D. H. Young, president. The central board organized in 1880 consisted of the executive officers: Eliza R. Snow, Zina D. H. Young, Elizabeth Ann Whitney, Sarah M. Kimball, and Mary Isabella Horne. New officers in 1888 were Jane S. Richards, Bathsheba W. Smith, Romania B. Pratt Penrose, and Emmeline B. Wells.

1892–1901: Zina D. H. Young, president. General board members called: Zina D. H. Young, 1892–1901. Sarah M. Kimball, 1892–1898. Mary Isabella Horne, 1892–1905. Jane S. Richards, 1892–1910. Bathsheba W. Smith, 1892–1910. Romania B. Pratt Penrose, 1892–1921. Emmeline B. Wells, 1892–1921. Laura M. Miner, 1892–1898. Emilia D. Madsen, 1892–1902. Lucy S. Cardon, 1892–1902. Susan Grant, 1892–1914. Mary M. Pitchforth, 1892–1901. Harriet D. Bunting, 1892–1893. Martha Tonks, 1892–1900. Helena E. Madsen, 1892–1902. Elizabeth Howard, 1892–1893. Aurilla Hatch, 1892–1900. Hattie C. Brown, 1892–1901. Martha B. Cannon, 1892–1907. Emma S. Woodruff, 1892–1910. Julina L. Smith, 1892–1921. Emily S. Richards, 1892–1921. Minerva W. Snow, 1892–1896. Adeline H. Barber, 1893–1898. Harriet C. Brown, 1893–1902. Rebecca E. Sandring, 1896–1902. Sarah Jenne Cannon, 1898–1921. Ellis R. Shipp, 1898–1907. Julia P. M. Farnsworth, 1899–1921. Elizabeth J. Stevenson, 1900–1906. Annie Taylor Hyde, 1900–1909.

1901–1910: Bathsheba W. Smith, president. New members called: Phebe Y. Beattie, 1901–1921. Ida Smoot Dusenberry, 1901–1921. Clarissa Smith Williams, 1901–1928. Carrie S. Thomas, 1902–1921. Alice Merrill Horne, 1902–1916. Annie Wells Cannon, 1902–1910. Priscilla P. Jennings, 1902–1918. Margaret A. Caine, 1902–1907. Rebecca E. Little, 1905–1909. Elizabeth S. Wilcox, 1906–1921. Harriet B. Harker, 1907–1910. Minnie H. James, 1907–1910. Rebecca N. Nibley, 1907–1921. Amy Brown Lyman, 1909–1945. Annie K. Hardy, 1909–1910.

1910–1921: Emmeline B. Wells, president. New members called: Olive D. Christensen, 1911–1913. Emma A. Empey, 1911–1939. Elizabeth C. McCune, 1911–1921. Edna May Davis, 1911–1919. Susa Young Gates, 1911–1922. Sarah M. McLelland, 1911–1935. Elizabeth C. Crismon, 1911–1921. Jeanette A. Hyde, 1913–1929. Sarah Eddington, 1914–1921. Lillian Cameron (Roberts), 1916–1923. Donette S. Kesler, 1918–1921. Annie Wells Cannon, 1919–1939.

1921–1928: Clarissa Smith Williams, president. New members called: Jennie B. Knight, 1921–1939. Louise Y. Robison, 1921–1939. Lalene H.

Hart, 1921–1939. Lotta Paul Baxter, 1921–1938. Julia A. Child, 1921–1935. Cora L. Bennion, 1921–1939. Julia A. F. Lund, 1921–1939. Amy W. Evans, 1921–1939. Ethel R. Smith, 1921–1935. Barbara H. Richards, 1921–1929. Rosannah C. Irvine, 1921–1939. Alice L. Reynolds, 1923–1930. Nettie D. Bradford, 1925–1939. Elise B. Alder, 1925–1937. Inez Knight Allen, 1927–1937. Ida Peterson Beal, 1927–1939.

1928–1939: Louise Y. Robison, president. New members called:
Kate M. Barker, 1929–1939. Marcia K. Howells, 1929–1945. Hazel H. Greenwood, 1929–1936. Emeline Y. Nebeker, 1929–1939. Mary Connelly Kimball, 1930–1937. Janet M. Thompson, 1935–1939. Belle S. Spafford, 1935–1974. Donna D. Sorensen, 1935–1945. Vivian R. McConkie, 1937–1945. Leda T. Jensen, 1937–1945. Beatrice F. Stevens, 1937–1941. Rae B. Barker, 1937–1945. Nellie O. Parker, 1937–1945. Anne S. Barlow, 1938–1945.

1940–1945: Amy Brown Lyman, president. New members called:
Vera W. Pohlman, 1940–1945. Achsa E. Paxman, 1940–1953. Mary Grant Judd, 1940–1955. Luella N. Adams, 1940–1947. Marianne C. Sharp, 1940–1974. Anna B. Hart, 1940–1969. Ethel B. Andrew, 1940–1942. Gertrude R. Garff, 1940–1947. Leona Fetzer (Wintch), 1940–1945. Edith Smith Elliott, 1940–1969. Pauline T. Pingree, 1940–1945. Alice B. Castleton, 1940–1945. Priscilla L. Evans, 1941–1948. Florence Jepperson Madsen, 1941–1969. Ann Parkinson Nibley, 1941–1947. Agnes M. Bolto, 1943–1945. Leone G. Layton, 1944–1972.

1945–1974: Belle S. Spafford, president. New members called:
Blanche B. Stoddard, 1945–1969. Evon W. Peterson, 1945–1969. Leone O. Jacobs, 1945–1956. Velma N. Simonsen, 1945–1958. Margaret C. Pickering, 1945–1956. Isabel B. Callister, 1946–1947. Mary J. Wilson, 1946–1954. Florence G. Smith, 1946–1948. Lillie C. Adams, 1946–1953. Ethel C. Smith, 1947–1950. Louise W. Madsen, 1947–1974. Aliene M. Young, 1947–1972. Josie B. Bay, 1948–1967. Alta J. Vance, 1948–1953. Christine H. Robinson, 1948–1962. Alberta H. Christensen, 1948–1974. Nellie W. Neal, 1949–1954. Mildred B. Eyring, 1950–1969. Helen W. Anderson, 1950–1958. Gladys S. Boyer, 1953–1958. Charlotte A. Larson, 1953–1964. Edith P. Backman, 1953–1969. Winniefred S. Manwaring, 1953–1974. Elna P. Haymond, 1953–1969. Annie M. Ellsworth, 1955–1962. Mary R. Young, 1955–1972. Hulda Parker (Young), 1957–1967. Mary V. Cameron, 1957–1968. Afton W. Hunt, 1957–1969. Wealtha S. Mendenhall, 1957–1966. Pearle M. Olsen, 1958–1964. Elsa T. Peterson, 1958–1969. Irene B. Woodford, 1958–1962. Fanny S. Kienitz, 1959–1972. Elizabeth B. Winters, 1959–1971. LaRue H. Rosell, 1950–1966. Jennie R. Scott, 1959–1970. Alice L. Wilkinson, 1960–1974. LaPriel S. Bunker, 1960–1964. Marie C. Richards, 1960–1961. Irene W. Buehner, 1960–1973. Irene C. Lloyd, 1961–1969. Hazel S. Cannon, 1962–1964. Hazel S. Love, 1962–1972. Fawn H. Sharp, 1962–1974. Celestia J. Taylor, 1962–1974. Anne R. Gledhill, 1962–1969. Belva Barlow (Ashton), 1962–1978. Zola J. McGhie, 1962–1969. Oa J. Cannon, 1963–1972. Lila B. Walch, 1963–1971. Lenore C. Gunderson, 1963–1974. Marjorie C. Pingree,

1964–1974. Darlene C. Dedekind, 1964–1974. Cleone R. Eccles, 1964–1968. Edythe K. Watson, 1964–1978. Ellen N. Barnes, 1964–1976. Kathryn S. Gilbert, 1964–1972. Verda F. Burton, 1964–1972. Myrtle R. Olson, 1964–1976. Alice C. Smith, 1964–1978. Lucile P. Peterson, 1965–1970. Elaine B. Curtis, 1965–1976. Zelma R. West, 1966–1976. Leanor J. Brown, 1967–1978. Reba Carling (Aldous), 1967–1976. Luella W. Finlinson, 1968–1976. Norma B. Ashton, 1968–1974. Mayola R. Miltenberger, 1968–1984. Maurine M. Haycock, 1968–1974. Amy Y. Valentine, 1969–1982. Marian R. Boyer, 1969–1984. Orlene J. Poulsen, 1969–1972. Marjorie M. Reeve (Emery), 1969–1976. Ada J. Jones, 1969–1972. Helen G. Lach, 1969–1976. Aline R. Pettit, 1969–1978. Johna de St. Jeor, 1969–1976. Beverly J. Pond, 1969–1984. Inez T. Waldron, 1969–1976. Anna Jean B. Skidmore, 1969–1978. Helen W. Jeppson, 1970–1984. Arlene S. Kirton, 1970–1984. Barbara B. Smith, 1971–1984. Sarah M. Grow, 1971–1978. Ann S. Reese, 1971–1984. Judy N. Komatsu, 1971–1974. Carol T. Hansen, 1972–1980 and 1983–1984. Shirley W. Thomas, 1972–1983. Marjorie Y. Nelson, 1972–1984. Clara L. Boren, 1972–1977. Ruth T. Walker (Doxey), 1972–1984. Elaine L. Jack, 1972–1984. Josette B. Ashford, 1972–1978. Bonna A. Brinton, 1972–1984. LaVon P. Smith, 1973–1974. Arlene J. Flanders, 1973–1984. Kristin Ruth Theurer (Stone), 1973–1980. Carol L. Clark, 1973–1984.

1974–1984: Barbara B. Smith, president. New members called:
Janath R. Cannon, 1974–1978 and 1980–1984. Helen L. Goates, 1974–1975 and 1978–1984. Ramona H. Barker, 1974–1982. Marian R. Johnson, 1974–1984. Miriam B. Milne, 1974–1984. Junko I. Shimizu, 1974–1984. Joy F. Evans, 1975–1984. Barbara W. Winder, 1977–1982. Helen B. Gibbons, 1977–1984. Addie Fuhriman, 1977–1984. Margaret Smoot, 1977–1984. Judith H. Steenblik, 1977–1977. Mary Frances Watson (Rich), 1977–1980. Mary F. Foulger, 1977–1984. Jewel J. Cutler, 1978–1984. Anne G. Osborn (Poelman), 1980–1982. Christine L. Barnhurst, 1982–1986. Shirley A. Cazier, 1982–1984. Jeanne B. Inouye, 1982–1984. Carol T. Hansen, 1983–1984. Francine R. Bennion, 1983–1984. Janice J. Anderson, 1983–1989. Shirley J. Thomas, 1983–1984. Barbara D. Hatch, 1983–1987. Barbara C. Gibbs, 1983–1984.

Acting general board members / national officers of Lambda Delta Sigma:
Arlyne C. Briggs, 1982–1984. Joan B. Spencer, 1982–84. Patricia P. Romney, 1982–1984. Jeanne M. Hughes, 1982–1984. Marilyn P. Adams, 1982–1984. Jayne B. Malan, 1982–1984. (Note: Under Barbara W. Winder's presidency, Lambda Delta Sigma officers no longer served as acting members of the Relief Society general board, although they met with the board in an associate capacity. Names of acting general board members who were later called as general board members are repeated.)

1984–1990: Barbara W. Winder, president. New members called:
Barbara W. Winder, 1984–1990. Joanne B. Doxey, 1984–1990. Joan B. Spencer, 1984–1990. Jeanne L. Nibley, 1984–1989. Jackie A. Smith, 1984–1989. Wylene H. Fotheringham, 1984–1989. Joan H. Child, 1984–

1990. Marilyn C. Barker, 1984–1989. Ione J. Simpson, 1985–1990. Jayne B. Malan, 1985–1986. Mary Ellen Edmunds, 1986–. Mila M. Mitchell, (Clark) 1986–1990. Brenda L. Hales, 1986–1990. Colleen Y. Staker, 1987–1990. Sheri Dew, 1989–1990. Carol B. Cooper, 1989–1990. Evelyn T. Marshall, 1989–1990. Julie A. Anderson, 1989–1990. Berylene C. Frampton, 1989–1990.

1990– : Elaine L. Jack, president. New members called:
Chieko N. Okazaki, 1990–. Aileen H. Clyde, 1990–. Carol L. Clark, 1990–. Mercedes T. Harding, 1990–. Carol Lee S. Hawkins, 1990–. Kate L. Kirkham, 1990–. Bonnie D. Parkin, 1990–. Anne C. Pingree, 1990–. Cherry B. Silver, 1990–. Carol B. Thomas, 1990–. Barbara Thompson, 1990–. MarJean C. Wilcox, 1990–. Carma M. Hales, 1992–.

Magazine Editors

Woman's Exponent Editors: Lula Greene Richards, 1872–1877. Emmeline B. Wells, 1877–1914.

Relief Society Magazine Editors: Susa Young Gates, 1914–1922. Alice L. Reynolds, 1923–1930. Mary Connelly Kimball, 1930–1937. Belle S. Spafford, 1937–1945. Marianne C. Sharp, 1945–1970.

Directors of Social Services Department, 1919–1969

Utah Agency (Salt Lake City): Amy Brown Lyman, 1919–1934. Amy W. Evans, 1934–1939. Ora W. Chipman, 1939–1943. Eva W. Darger (acting director), 1943–1944. Ruth Lohmoelder, 1944–1946. Marie H. Tanner, 1946–1948. Mary L. Dillman, 1948–1949. Lauramay Nebeker, 1949–1956. Margaret M. Keller, 1956–1961. Josephine Scott Patterson, 1961–1969. Mayola R. Miltenberger, 1969. Helena H. Evans (acting director), 1969.

Ogden, Utah, Office: Leona Fetzer, 1940–1941. Louise Call, 1941–1942. Elva H. Kunz, 1943–1949.

Arizona Agency: Mayola R. Miltenberger (caseworker–case supervisior), 1962–1969. LaMar Odgen, 1969.

Nevada Agency: Vivian Griffin, 1965–1966. Mayola R. Miltenberger (acting director), 1966 (one month). Regenia Chadwick (resident assistant), 1966–1967. Victor L. Brown, Jr., 1967–1969.

Idaho Agency: Rollin Davis, 1967–1969.

California Agency: Alice H. Osborn (social worker), 1934. George J. Wollaston (youth guidance director), 1966. Glen Van Wagenen, 1967.

Australia (Melborne) Agency: Mavis Cutts, caseworker–director, 1966.

For more information, see Miltenberger, *Fifty Years of Relief Society Social Services.*

NOTES

Unless otherwise indicated, all general, stake, mission, ward, and branch Relief Society minutes cited in the notes are located in the Archives of the Historical Department of The Church of Jesus Christ of Latter-day Saints, Salt Lake City, cited herein as Church Archives. References to "A Record of the Organization, and Proceedings of the Female Relief Society of Nauvoo" are cited as "Nauvoo Minutes." Full references to works cited in the notes are found in the Bibliography.

PROLOGUE: WOMEN OF THE RESTORATION, 1830–1842

1. Nauvoo Minutes, April 28, 1842.

2. Lucy Mack Smith, in Nauvoo Minutes, March 24, 1842.

3. Nauvoo Minutes, April 28, 1842.

4. Joseph Smith, quoted in Sarah Kimball, "Auto-biography," *Woman's Exponent* 12 (September 1, 1883): 51.

5. Elizabeth Haven to Elizabeth Howe Bullard, February 24, 1839, as quoted in Godfrey et al., *Women's Voices*, 111.

6. D&C 128:18.

7. See Joseph Smith, "History [1832]," in Jessee, ed., *The Papers of Joseph Smith* 1:3–6. For the full account of the first years, see Bushman, *Joseph Smith and the Beginnings of Mormonism*.

8. Lucy Mack Smith, *Biographical Sketches of Joseph Smith the Prophet*, 37, 54–56.

9. Ibid., 69.

10. See Ahlstrom, *A Religious History of the American People;* Cross, *The Burned-Over District;* Backman, *The Heavens Resound;* Backman, *American Religions and the Rise of Mormonism.*

11. Hill, "The Role of Christian Primitivism in the Origin and Development of the Mormon Kingdom, 1830–1844," Ph.D. dissertation.

12. Desdemona Wadsworth Fullmer, Autobiography, holograph, Church Archives. Phonetic spelling is hers.

13. Sarah Studevant Leavitt, Autobiography, in Godfrey et al., *Women's Voices*, 27–29.

14. Drusilla Dorris Hendricks, "Historical Sketch of James Hendricks and Drusilla Dorris Hendricks," in *Henry Hendricks Genealogy*, 10.

15. Tullidge, *Women of Mormondom* 41.

16. Eliza R. Snow, "Sketch of My Life," holograph, Bancroft Library.

17. Snow, Journal, as quoted in Beecher, "The Eliza Enigma: The Life and Legend of Eliza R. Snow," in Burgess-Olson, ed., *Sister Saints*, 8. The poem was first printed in *Western Courier* (Ravenna, Ohio), February 14, 1829.

18. Smith, *Biographical Sketches of Joseph Smith*, 169. See also Newell and Avery, *Mormon Enigma: Emma Hale Smith*, 217.

19. Joseph Smith III, "Last Testimony of Emma Smith," *The Saints' Herald* 26 (October 1, 1879): 289–90.

20. D&C 3:1.

21. Interview of David Whitmer with Orson Pratt and Joseph F. Smith, *Deseret Evening News*, November 16, 1878.

22. Tullidge, *Women of Mormondom*, 162–63.

23. Zina D. H. Young, "How I Gained My Testimony of the Truth," *Young Woman's Journal* 4 (April 1893): 318.

24. Leavitt, Autobiography, in Godfrey et al., *Women's Voices*, 30.

25. "Autobiographic Sketch of Phebe W. Woodruff," Bancroft Library.

26. Caroline Barnes Crosby, Autobiography, microfilm of holograph, Church Archives.

27. Mosiah 18:8–9.

28. Nauvoo Minutes, March 17, 1842.

29. Patriarchal Blessings of Leonora Cannon Taylor, July 23, 1843; Rebecca Harriet Doolan, April 24, 1869; Martha A. Riggs, November 11, 1876; Louise Yates Robison, n.d.; Susanah Bigler, January 1844; Bathsheba W. Smith, April 20, 1856; Abigail Mead McBride, June 8, 1836; Margaret M. Martin, July 7, 1843; Lydia Savage, September 26, 1860. From the files of Carol Cornwall Madsen, Joseph Fielding Smith Institute for Church History, Brigham Young University, Provo, Utah. All quotations from patriarchal blessings in subsequent paragraphs are taken from these same blessings.

30. Hendricks, "Historical Sketch."

31. Nancy Naomi Alexander Tracy, "Life History of Nancy Naomi Alexander Tracy, Written by Herself," typescript, Church Archives.

32. Crosby, Autobiography.

33. Joel 2:28–29.

34. *History of the Church* 1:101.

35. Hartley, *"They Are My Friends" . . . the Joseph Knight Family*, 55.

36. Zina D. H. Young, "How I Gained My Testimony."

37. D&C 37:3.

38. Smith, *Biographical Sketches of Joseph Smith*, 173, 176–77, 178–81.

39. D&C 43:2.

40. D&C 88:119.

41. D&C 95:8.

42. Snow, "Sketch of My Life." The bread she here "cast upon the waters" returned to her "one of the little hinges on which events of immense weight occasionally turn." The Building Committee, she recounts, insisted on giving her in return for her gift a duplex on a Kirtland lot. This allowed her to send

for her sister, a single parent, and her daughters to gather with the Saints, and to rent the other part to support them all.

43. "Extracts from H. C. Kimball's Journal," *Times and Seasons* 6 (April 15, 1845): 867.

44. Sarah M. Kimball, in "Relief Society Reports," *Woman's Exponent* 5 (September 1, 1876): 50.

45. Tullidge, *Women of Mormondom*, 76. Tradition has it that when the exterior was nearly finished, women sacrificed their finest china and glassware to be crushed and mixed with stucco to give sparkle to the outer walls of the sandstone temple. There is no evidence, either documentary or archaeological, to support this oft-told tale.

46. D&C 109:12–13.

47. *History of the Church* 2:427–28.

48. Tracy, "Life History," 9.

49. Tullidge, *Women of Mormondom*, 207–8.

50. Mary Fielding to Mercy [Fielding] Thompson, July 8, 1837, in Godfrey et al., *Women's Voices*, 61.

51. Tracy, "Life History," 9.

52. Crosby, Autobiography; also in Godfrey et al., *Women's Voices*, 56.

53. D&C 90:28, 30.

54. Joseph Smith to Vienna Jacques, September 4, 1833, in Jessee, ed., *The Personal Writings of Joseph Smith*, 294.

55. Patience Palmer reminiscence, *Utah Magazine*, February 1892, p. 195.

56. Eliza R. Snow, "Though Deepening Trials," *Hymns*, 1985, 122–23.

57. Elizabeth Haven to Elizabeth Bullard, February 24, 1839, as quoted in Godfrey et al., *Women's Voices*, 107–8.

58. Emma Smith to Joseph Smith, March 7, 1839, manuscript, Joseph Smith Letterbooks, Church Archives.

59. *History of the Church* 4:390.

60. D&C 118:4.

61. Vilate Kimball to Heber C. Kimball, September 21, 1839, holograph, Heber C. Kimball Papers, Church Archives, also quoted in Ronald K. Esplin, "The Emergence of Brigham Young and the Twelve to Mormon Leadership, 1830–1841" (Ph.D. dissertation), 407.

62. Hannah Pitt Kington's house in Dymock, "which was hers before her marriage, was often used by the apostles and missionaries as a home and meeting place." Bloxham, et al., eds., *Truth Will Prevail: The Rise of the Church of Jesus Christ of Latter-day Saints in the British Isles, 1837–1987*, 143–44. *The Manuscript History of Brigham Young*, ed. Elden Jay Watson, May 20, 1840, lists the Benbows' contribution as 250 pounds.

63. Brigham Young to Mary Ann Young, October 16, 1840, Luna Eunice Caroline Young Thatcher Collection, Church Archives; also quoted in Esplin, "Emergence of Brigham Young," 408.

CHAPTER 1: THE TURNING OF THE KEY, 1842–1844

1. Ellen Douglas [Parker] to "Father and Mother," June 2, 1842, typescript, Church Archives.

2. Ibid.

3. Maureen Ursenbach Beecher, "Letters from the Frontier: Commerce, Nauvoo, and Salt Lake City," *Journal of Mormon History* 2 (1975): 35–47.

4. Autobiography of Bathsheba W. Smith, 8–9, microfilm of manuscript, Church Archives.

5. Bathsheba W. Smith to George A. Smith, June 15, 1844, Family Correspondence, George Albert Smith (1817–1875) Papers, 1834–1875, Church Archives; also quoted in Godfrey et al., *Women's Voices*, 130.

6. Sally Randall to Friends, October 6, 1843, typescript, Church Archives. Spelling has been standardized.

7. Bathsheba W. Smith to George A. Smith, October 2, 1842, George Albert Smith (1817–1875) Papers.

8. See Allen and Leonard, *The Story of the Latter-day Saints*, 1976, 156–60. The several lodges eventually established in Nauvoo became more numerous than all other Illinois lodges combined. Within the year of their charter, the Nauvoo lodges began building their Masonic temple, but before its dedication in April 1844, state officers had withdrawn their recognition.

9. Melder, *Beginnings of Sisterhood,* 39.

10. Ibid., 42.

11. Sarah M. Kimball, "Auto-biography," *Woman's Exponent* 12 (September 1, 1883): 51. Her miscalculation here dated the event as summer 1843, which date she cites more accurately in "Record of the Relief Society from First Organization to Conference Apr 5, 1892, Book II," Church Archives, catalogued as "Relief Society Record, 1880–1892," 29, 30.

12. See Ann Firor Scott, "On Seeing and Not Seeing: A Case of Historical Invisibility," *Journal of American History* 71 (June 1984): 7–21.

13. Kimball, "Autobiography," 51.

14. Nauvoo Minutes, March 17, 1842.

15. Nauvoo Minutes, March 17, 1842. The names of Athalia Robinson and her sister Nancy Rigdon, daughters of Sidney Rigdon, were later crossed out, presumably because of their subsequent dissent and departure from Nauvoo. Thereafter most published accounts of the charter meeting counted eighteen rather than twenty women in actual attendance.

16. See Maureen Ursenbach Beecher and James L. Kimball, Jr., "The First Relief Society: A Diversity of Women," *Ensign* 9 (March 1979): 25–29.

17. Nauvoo Minutes, March 17, 1842.

18. Nauvoo Minutes, March 17, 1842.

19. Emma Hale Smith, Blessing [1844], photocopy of typescript, Church Archives; also quoted in Jill Mulvay Derr and Susan Oman, "The Nauvoo Generation: Our First Five Relief Society Presidents," *Ensign* 7 (December 1977): 36.

20. Nauvoo Minutes, March 17, 1842.

21. Ibid. The distinction between "ordain," as the conferral of priesthood, and "set apart," as the delegation of authority in the Church, would not be made until the Utah period, sometime before 1880.

22. *Woman's Exponent* 9 (September 1, 1880): 53–54.

23. Eliza R. Snow, Nauvoo Journal, August 3, 1842, holograph, Church Archives.

24. "Ladies Relief Society," *Times and Seasons* 3 (April 1, 1842): 743.

25. Nauvoo Minutes, March 17, 1842.

26. Ibid.

27. Ibid.

28. Ibid., April 28, 1842.

29. Ibid., July 28, 1843.

30. Nauvoo Minutes, July 28, 1843.

31. Ibid., August 13, 1843.

32. Ibid., June 9, 1842. The Prophet donated a lot and "the frame of a house," but the project was "blasted in the bud" by persecution, according to Eliza R. Snow, "The Female Relief Society: A Brief Sketch . . . ," *Woman's Exponent* 1 (June 1, 1872): 2.

33. Ibid., July 28, 1843.

34. *Relief Society Magazine* 23 (June 1936): 36.

35. Nauvoo Minutes, May 27, 1842.

36. Ibid., July 7, 1843.

37. Eliza R. Snow, "Female Relief Society," *Times and Seasons* 4 (August 1, 1843): 287.

38. Nauvoo Minutes, October 14, 1842.

39. Ellen Douglas [Parker] to "Father and Mother," April 14, 1844.

40. Nauvoo Minutes, undated, between June 16 and July 7, 1843.

41. Ibid., July 15, 1843.

42. Ibid., April 19, 1842.

43. Ibid., March 24, 1842.

44. Ibid., April 28, 1842.

45. Ibid., June 9, 1842.

46. Ibid.

47. Ibid.

48. Moroni 7:47.

49. Nauvoo Minutes, March 30, 1842.

50. Ibid., April 28, 1842.

51. Ibid., August 31, 1842.

52. Eliza R. Snow, Nauvoo Journal, July 29, August 9, 1842; Eliza R. Snow, "Sketch of My Life," holograph, Bancroft Library; Roberts, *A Comprehensive History of the Church* 2:28, 78, 148–55.

53. Emma Smith to His Excellency Governor Carlin, August 17, 1842, *History of the Church* 5:116.

54. Nauvoo Minutes, August 13, 1843.

55. William G. Hartley, "'Upon You My Fellow Servants': Restoration of the Priesthood," in Porter and Black, eds., *The Prophet Joseph: Essays on the Life and Mission of Joseph Smith,* 49.

56. D&C 84:110.

57. D&C 2.

58. D&C 110:1; Malachi 4:6.

59. Ronald K. Esplin, "Joseph Smith's Mission and Timetable: 'God Will Protect Me Until My Work is Done,' " in Porter and Black, eds., *The Prophet Joseph Smith*, 282, 288.

60. D&C 124:28, 41–42.

61. "Relief Society Record, 1880–1892," 29, 30. An autobiographical ac-

count written by Sarah M. Kimball and published in the *Woman's Exponent* quoted the Prophet Joseph Smith's response differently: "'Tell the sisters their offering is accepted of the Lord, and he has something better for them than a written Constitution. I invite them all to meet with me and a few of the brethren in the Masonic Hall over my store next Thursday afternoon, and I will organize the women under the priesthood, after the pattern of the priesthood.' He further said, 'The Church was never perfectly organized until the women were thus organized.' " *Woman's Exponent* 12 (September 1, 1883): 51.

62. Nauvoo Minutes, March 17, 1842.

63. Ibid.

64. Maureen Ursenbach Beecher, "The Female Relief Society of Nauvoo," 8, typescript, in authors' files.

65. Nauvoo Minutes, March 17, 1842. In the original minutes, the sentence reads in full: "If any Officers are wanted to carry out the designs of the Institution, let them be appointed and set apart, as Deacons, Teachers &c. are among us." The Prophet thus emphasized that the organization of women should, following the pattern of priesthood organization, appoint different officers to perform various functions. There is no indication from Joseph Smith's subsequent actions or from subsequent actions by the women present on this occasion that the Prophet's comparison—"as Deacons, Teachers &c. are among us"—implied that women should be ordained to priesthood offices. The Relief Society teachers appinted in July 1843 were not ordained to the office of teacher in the Aaronic Priesthood. The ward Relief Society organization set up by Sarah M. Kimball in Utah in 1868 included "deaconesses" and a "quorum of teachers," but nowhere in the detailed Fifteenth Ward minutes is there any indication that women were ordained or claim to have been ordained to offices in either the Aaronic or the Melchizedek Priesthood. See pp. 98–99 in the present volume.

66. D&C 84:29.

67. Ephesians 4:16.

68. D&C 84:110.

69. Nauvoo Minutes, March 30, 1842.

70. Ibid., April 28 and March 30, 1842.

71. D&C 84:109.

72. Minutes for the previous meeting contain the testimony of a Sister Durfee who had earlier received the sisters' healing administration, and also indicate that after the close of the meeting, "Mrs. Leonard was administered to for the restoration of health, by Councillors Cleveland and Whitney." Nauvoo Minutes, April 19, 1842.

73. Franklin D. Richards, in "Report of the Relief Society Meeting held in the Ogden Tabernacle, July 19th, 1888 . . . ," *Woman's Exponent* 17 (September 1, 1888): 53–54.

74. *History of the Church* 1:368.

75. D&C 84:73.

76. D&C 121:35–41.

77. D&C 84:23.

78. Mercy R. Thompson, in "Recollections of Joseph Smith," *Juvenile Instructor* 27 (July 1, 1892): 398.

79. Nauvoo Minutes, June 9, 1842.

80. See Matt. 16:19; D&C 27:12–13; 81:2. In D&C 128:14, the term "keys of the kingdom" is associated with both "the sealing and binding power" and knowledge. Whether, on this occasion, the Prophet was referring to Relief Society or priesthood leaders "placed at the head to lead" is not clear from Eliza R. Snow's April 28, 1842, minutes.

81. This summary of the importance of Joseph Smith's authority as prophet and head of the Church in organizing the Relief Society and turning the key to women has been drawn largely from Bruce R. McConkie, "The Relief Society and the Keys of the Kingdom," *Relief Society Magazine* 37 (March 1950): 148–51. Though this article provides manuy useful insights into the Prophet Joseph Smith's important declaration, it should be noted that the First Presidency and the Council of the Twelve, as confirmed in more recent writings of Elder McConkie himself, currently use the terms "keys of the kingdom" and "keys of the presidency" in a more restricted sense than Elder McConkie used them in his 1950 article. He himself refined his use of the phrase "keys of the kingdom" in his book *A New Witness for the Articles of Faith*, 209–10. "The keys of the kingdom are the power, right, and authority to preside over the kingdom of God on earth, which is the Church, and to direct all of its affairs," he explains. Enlarging the concept of keys, he continues: "The keys of any particular ministerial service authorize the use of the priesthood for that purpose." The phrase "keys of the priesthood" he describes thus: "The keys of the priesthood are the right and power of presidency. They are the directing, controlling, and governing power. Those who hold them are empowered to direct the manner in which others use their priesthood" (pp. 320–23).

82. Nauvoo Minutes, March 17, 1842, and June 9, 1842; Joseph F. Smith, *Gospel Doctrine*, 385.

83. McConkie, "The Relief Society and the Keys of the Kingdom," 151.

84. Relief Society Minutes, April 28, 1842.

85. Joseph Fielding Smith, "Relief Society—An Aid to the Priesthood," *Relief Society Magazine* 46 (January 1959): 4.

86. Nauvoo Minutes, April 28, 1842; *History of the Church* 4:604–7.

87. "R.S. Reports," *Woman's Exponent* 9 (September 1, 1880): 53.

88. A statement entitled "Correction" in the *Woman's Exponent* 34 (January 1906): 44 reads: "In the Woman's Exponent, November number, 1905, [p. 36,] in the article republished from the Jubilee report given March 17, 1892, we find an error which we feel should be corrected. The paragraph alluded to reads thus: 'President Smith stated that the meeting was called for the purpose of making more complete the organization of the Church by organizing the women in the order of the Priesthood.' We find by comparing it with the original record no such statement was made. [signed] Bathsheba W. Smith, President [and] Emmeline B. Wells, secretary." The historical account prepared by Sarah M. Kimball and read at the Jubilee celebration appears in "Relief Society Jubilee," *Woman's Exponent* 20 (April 1, 1892): 141. The search of the Nauvoo Minutes is reported in Relief Society Minutes,

1892–1911, January 19, 1906, and Emmeline B. Wells, Diaries, December 30, 1905.

The correction had broader implications. Bathsheba W. Smith, like her predecessor Zina D. H. Young, affirmed with her counselors as they undertook their work as the general presidency of Relief Society in 1901: "We have not taken these responsibilities upon ourselves, but have been called in the order of the holy Priesthood." *Woman's Exponent* 30 (January 1902): 68. Emmeline B. Wells and her counselors, in assuming the presidency in 1910, used the different words, declaring: "We have not taken this responsibility upon ourselves, but have been called by the Holy Priesthood." "Official Announcement," *Woman's Exponent* 39 (January 1911): 44.

89. McConkie, *A New Witness for the Articles of Faith,* 309–10.

90. See, for example, *Encyclopedia of Mormonism,* s.v. "Keys of the Priesthood."

91. Joseph Fielding Smith, "The Relief Society Organized by Revelation," *Relief Society Magazine* 52 (January 1965): 4–6.

92. Nauvoo Minutes, April 28, 1842.

93. See Carol Cornwall Madsen, "Mormon Women and the Temple: Toward a New Understanding," in Beecher and Anderson, eds., *Sisters in Spirit: Mormon Women in Historical and Cultural Perspective,* 83.

94. Nauvoo Minutes, June 16, 1843.

95. Ibid., June 16 and July 28, 1843.

96. Ibid., October 14, 1843.

97. D&C 124:30.

98. Madsen, "Mormon Women and the Temple," 81.

99. Sally Randall to Friends, April 21, 1844, and November 12, 1843, in Godfrey et al., *Women's Voices,* 136, 138–39.

100. Joseph Smith, in "The King Follett Discourse: A Newly Amalgamated Text," ed. Stan Larson, *BYU Studies* 18 (Winter 1978): 198–99, 205, 207.

101. D&C 84:19–20.

102. D&C 84:22; 76:62.

103. 2 Peter 1:4; Romans 8:17. While in his epistle to the Romans Paul is speaking to his "brethren" as "sons of God," the Book of Mormon affirms that those "spiritually begotten" of Christ are "his sons and his daughters." (Mosiah 5:7.) Joseph Smith indicated that those who die worthily – "husband, father, wife, mother, child" – "will be heirs of God and joint-heirs with Jesus Christ." See "The King Follett Discourse," 201.

104. *History of the Church* 4:492–93.

105. 1 Peter 2:9; Exodus 19:6.

106. Nauvoo Minutes, March 30, 1842.

107. Bathsheba W. Smith, in Clara L. Clawson, "R.S. Reports: Pioneer Stake," *Woman's Exponent* 34 (July–August 1905): 14.

108. *History of the Church* 5:2.

109. Madsen, "Mormon Women and the Temple," 83.

110. Nauvoo Minutes, May 27, 1842.

111. That she received her endowment on or before this date is evident from Joseph Smith Journal, July 15, 1843–February 29, 1844, manuscript, Church Archives.

112. Thompson, in "Recollections of the Prophet Joseph Smith," 400.

113. D&C 132:18.

114. Madsen, "Mormon Women and the Temple," 86.

115. D&C 132:30.

116. D&C 132:16, 19.

117. D&C 132:20, 22, 31.

118. D&C 131:2.

119. E[liza] R. S[now], "Position and Duties," *Woman's Exponent* 3 (July 15, 1874): 28.

120. Madsen, "Mormon Women and the Temple," 102–3.

121. 1 Corinthians 11:11.

122. "A Brief Biographical Sketch of the Life & Labors of Lucy Walker Kimball Smith," holograph, Church Archives.

123. D&C 132:37, 40, 44–45.

124. A more extensive discussion of the introduction of the practice of plural marriage and its relationship to the Female Relief Society of Nauvoo is found in chapter two. See also Ronald K. Esplin and Danel Bachman, "Plural Marriage," *Encyclopedia of Mormonism* 3:1091–95.

125. Moses 7:18.

126. D&C 105:4.

127. D&C 35:2.

128. D&C 132:19–20.

129. President Wilford Woodruff ascribed to Eliza R. Snow the initial conceptualization of the doctrine as "a revelation . . . given to us by a woman." "Discourse," *Millennial Star* 56 (April 9, 1894): 229. President Joseph F. Smith said, "God revealed that principle to Joseph Smith; Joseph Smith revealed it to Eliza Snow Smith, his wife; and Eliza Snow was inspired, being a poet, to put it into verse." *Deseret News* 9 (February 1895). For Eliza Snow's statement, see David McKay to Mrs. James Hood, March 16, 1916, photocopy of holograph, Church Archives.

130. *Times and Seasons* 6 (November 15, 1845), 1039. The poem is dated "City of Joseph, Oct. 1845." See also Eliza R. Snow, *Poems, Religious, Historical, and Political* 1:1–2.

131. Affirming her existence, yet acknowledging a lack of specific knowledge of the Mother in Heaven, President Gordon B. Hinckley said in 1991: "[N]one of us can add to or diminish the glory of her of whom we have no revealed knowledge," *Ensign,* 21 (November 1991): 100. See also Joseph F. Smith, John R. Winder, and Anthon H. Lund, First Presidency of the Church, "The Origin of Man," *Improvement Era* 13 (November 1909): 78: "All men and women are in the similitude of the universal Father and Mother, and are literally the sons and daughters of Deity"; Spencer W. Kimball, *Conference Report,* April 1978, 7: "[W]hen we sing that doctrinal hymn and anthem of affection, 'O My Father,' we get a sense of the ultimate in maternal modesty, of the restrained, queenly elegance of our Heavenly Mother."

CHAPTER 2: "TRIBULATION WORKETH PATIENCE," 1844–1866

1. Rich, *Autobiography of Mary Ann Phelps Rich,* 16, copy in the authors' files.

2. Zina Diantha Huntington Young, Diaries, 1844–1845, 1886, 1889, June 17–20, 1844, holograph, Church Archives; also published in Maureen Ursenbach Beecher, ed., " 'All Things Move in Order in the City': The Nauvoo Diary of Zina Diantha Huntington Jacobs," *BYU Studies* 19 (Spring 1979): 292.

3. Ibid.

4. V[ilate] K[imball] to [Heber C. Kimball], June 9, 1844, Kimball Family Correspondence, 1838–71, Church Archives; also published in Ronald K. Esplin, ed., "Life in Nauvoo, June, 1844: Vilate Kimball's Martyrdom Letters," *BYU Studies* 19 (Winter 1979): 234–35.

5. Rich, *Autobiography*, 16.

6. Nauvoo Minutes, April 28, 1842.

7. Parley P. Pratt, "Proclamation," *Millennial Star* 5 (March 1845): 151; also in Esplin, "Joseph Smith's Mission and Timetable," in Porter and Black, eds., *The Prophet Joseph Smith*, 309. Esplin here provides meticulous documentation for the momentous spiritual and theological developments that occurred simultaneously with the growing threats to the Prophet's life and the well-being of the Saints.

8. Maureen Ursenbach Beecher, "The 'Leading Sisters': A Female Hierarchy in Nineteenth Century Mormon Society," *Journal of Mormon History* 9 (1982): 30–31.

9. Bostwick was fined $50 and costs on February 26, 1844; Phelps first read his defense, "Voice of Innocence," to a "general meeting in the interest of the temple" on March 7. *History of the Church* 6:225, 240–41. Since that meeting would have consisted of men, it was logical that meetings would be called the following two Saturdays for the women to hear the defense. One copy of the text is in the hand of Thomas Bullock, signed by Emma Smith, and another in Phelps's own hand; both are in Church Archives. That Phelps actually composed the piece is consistent with his role in Joseph Smith's service and with his prose style at the time. The piece was published over Emma Smith's name in *Nauvoo Neighbor* 1 (March 20, 1844): 187. Bruce A. VanOrden, "Return of the Prodigal: W. W. Phelps' Service as Joseph Smith's Political Clerk in Nauvoo," paper presented at the Nauvoo Symposium, Brigham Young University, September 21, 1989. Copy in the authors' files.

10. Nauvoo Minutes following September 28, 1842. See also *History of the Church* 5:4–12 passim.

11. Nauvoo Minutes, March 16, 1844.

12. Zina Young, Diary, November 10, 1844. The text quoted continues: "and when we become sufficiently united our enemies would have no more power, nether shall we see such maraculous displays of the Power of God as some antisipate until after the Thousand years reign. Union will cause the Menlenean [Millennium]. It is not a momentary work."

13. *Woman's Exponent* 8 (November 1, 1879): 85.

14. West Jordan Ward, Salt Lake Stake, Relief Society Minutes, September 7, 1868.

15. *Woman's Exponent* 9 (September 1, 1880): 53–54. President Taylor is here addressing the general meeting of the Relief Society held July 17, 1880.

16. *The Prophet* 1 (August 17, 1844): n.p. See also September 14, 1844,

when, in response to queries, it was announced a pamphlet on the group's constitution had been made available.

17. Hosea Stout, *On the Mormon Frontier: The Diary of Hosea Stout 1844–1861,* 1:27. In his entry for March 13, 1845, Stout describes the Evans Ward meeting as being "got up for the purpose of organizing the Sisters into an Association according to their several occupations" to promote home industry. "When we came there we found the house crowded full waiting for us." Brother Rich explained the benefits of such an organization, and "the order which was instituted in Nauvoo." That the group is not called a Relief Society and has a very different agendum suggests that the 1844 cessation had been firm; however, his mention of "the order . . . in Nauvoo" indicates that the precedent is not fully out of mind.

18. First Council of the Seventy Minutes and Early Records, Book B, 1844–48 (March 9, 1845), 78, Church Archives. The complete text reveals an intensity of feeling unusual for Brigham Young and is indicative of the degree to which he considered the Church had been harmed by the women's actions.

19. West Jordan Ward Relief Society Minutes, September 7, 1868.

20. Senior and Junior Cooperative Retrenchment Association Minutes, March 28, 1873, Church Archives.

21. Eleventh Ward, Salt Lake Stake, Relief Society Minutes, March 3, 1869.

22. "Relief Society Reports, Alpine Stake," *Woman's Exponent* 40 (October 1911): 24.

23. Seventies Quorum Records, Second Quorum, 1844–1894, February 5 and 12, 1845, Church Archives.

24. Ibid.

25. Allen and Leonard, *The Story of the Latter-day Saints,* 1976, 210.

26. These first women temple workers were among the few who, with their husbands, received their endowments under Joseph Smith's direction in 1843–44, before the temple was dedicated in 1845. Once the temple opened, they would be charged with presiding over the women's work. See D. Michael Quinn, "Latter-day Saint Prayer Circles," *BYU Studies* 19 (Fall 1978): 79–87; Heber C. Kimball Journal, November 29 and December 6, 1845, holograph, Church Archives; Heber C. Kimball, *On the Potter's Wheel: The Diaries of Heber C. Kimball,* 153, 159, 163.

27. Bathsheba Wilson Bigler Smith, Autobiography, microfilm of manuscript, Church Archives.

28. The idea is expanded in Rex Eugene Cooper, "The Promises Made to the Fathers: A Diachronic Analysis of Mormon Covenant Organization with Reference to Puritan Federal Theology" (Ph.D. dissertation), passim.

29. Eliza R. Snow, Diaries, 1845–1849, January 1, 1847, holograph, Huntington Library, San Marino, California.

30. Hendricks, "Historical Sketch," 28.

31. Louisa Barnes Pratt, Journal, in Carter, comp., *Heart Throbs of the West* 8:240–41. That the medication was to be so precisely administered "in a glass tumbler with a silver teaspoon," and that the sister was willing to comply, suggests not so much petulance on Louisa's part as recognition by

both women that despite their rude conditions they were, after all, gentle ladies.

32. "A Venerable Woman: Presendia Lathrop Kimball," *Woman's Exponent* 12 (June 1, 1883): 2.

33. The figures are Rebecca Cornwall's, cited in Maureen Ursenbach Beecher, "Women at Winter Quarters," *Sunstone* 8 (July-August 1983): 16.

34. Eliza Maria Partridge Lyman, Journal, June 1–2, 1847, holograph, Church Archives. Elvira Holmes is the "Elvira Coles" of the founding Relief Society meeting.

35. Nauvoo Minutes, April 28, 1842.

36. Helen Mar [Kimball] Whitney, "Scenes and Incidents at Winter Quarters," *Woman's Exponent* 14 (December 15, 1885): 106.

37. "A Venerable Woman: Presendia Lathrop Kimball," *Woman's Exponent* 12 (July 15, 1883): 27.

38. Helen Mar Whitney, "Scenes and Incidents at Winter Quarters," *Woman's Exponent* 14 (December 1, 1885): 98.

39. Emmeline B. Wells, "History of the Relief Society," *Woman's Exponent* 32 (June 1903): 6.

40. D&C 136, received January 14, 1847.

41. Maureen Ursenbach Beecher, "Women's Work on the Mormon Frontier," *Utah Historical Quarterly* 49 (Summer 1981): 276–90.

42. "Biographical Sketch: Relief Cram Atwood," *Woman's Exponent* 33 (March 1905): 66.

43. Mary Jane Lambson to Bathsheba W. Smith, Family Correspondence, George Albert Smith 1817–1875 Papers, September 6, 1847.

44. Jane Snyder Richards, Reminiscence, holograph, Church Archives.

45. Eliza M. Partridge Lyman, Journal 1846–85, April 25, 1849, holograph, Church Archives; "Life Sketch of Elizabeth Manning James," typescript by Henry J. Wolfinger, Wilford Woodruff Papers, Church Archives.

46. Richard L. Jensen, "Forgotten Relief Societies, 1844–67," *Dialogue* 16 (Spring 1983): 107. This is the most thorough study of the Relief Society during what the earlier histories call its "interim." Jensen's findings inform much of what is contained in the treatment of the period here, and we are grateful for his work.

47. Patty Sessions, Diary, April 24, 1852, holograph, Church Archives. The dress reform movement was deemed significant enough to be included in a report of George A. Smith to his fellow apostle Franklin D. Richards in England, August 31, 1855, Church Archives. A photo of the costume, mistakenly called the "Retrenchment dress," is in *A Century of Sisterhood: Chronological Collage, 1869–1969*, 13. It can be compared with the Bloomer costume as pictured in Mary Curtis, "Amelia Bloomer's Curious Costume," *American History Illustrated*, June 1978, 12, 13.

48. Zina Young, Diary, August 26, 1855.

49. Beecher, "Women's Work on the Mormon Frontier," 286.

50. As quoted in William L. O'Neill, *Everyone Was Brave: The Rise and Fall of Feminism in America*, 8–9.

51. *Journal of Discourses* 10 (July 31, 1864): 320.

52. *Journal of Discourses* 1 (April 9, 1852): 48; *Journal of Discourses* 12 (January 12, 1868): 153.

53. Eliza R. Snow, "The New Year, 1852," *Deseret News*, January 19, 1852.

54. Eliza R. Snow, "Woman," *The Mormon,* December 27, 1856; reprinted in *Poems Religious, Historical and Political* 2:173.

55. *Journal of Discourses* 9 (June 15, 1862): 308.

56. *Journal of Discourses* 4 (September 21, 1856): 55; *Journal of Discourses* 14 (August 8, 1869): 106.

57. Eliza R. Snow, "Woman." Emphasis is Snow's.

58. Ibid.

59. *History of the Church* 4:604, 607.

60. Historian's Office Journal, August 8, 1855, Church Archives.

61. "Record of the Female Relief Society Organized on the 9th of Feby in the City of Great Salt Lake 1854," holograph, Louisa R. Taylor Papers, Special Collections, Harold B. Lee Library, BYU. Also Jensen, "Forgotten Relief Societies," 109.

62. Minutes of Meeting, Parowan, May 21, 1854, Thomas Bullock Minutes Collection, Church Archives, as quoted in Jensen, "Forgotten Relief Societies," 111.

63. J. H. M[artineau] to G. A. Smith, May 30, 1855, *Deseret News*, July 11, 1855, as quoted in Jensen, "Forgotten Relief Societies," 111.

64. Lucy Meserve Smith, "Historical Sketches of My Great Grandfathers," holograph, Special Collections, Marriott Library, University of Utah, Salt Lake City, Utah. Her autobiographical account is published in Godfrey et al., *Women's Voices*, 261–71.

65. "Autobiography of Priscilla Merriman Evans," typescript, pp. 7, 8, Utah State Historical Society, Salt Lake City, Utah.

66. Wilford Woodruff, Diaries, June 17, 1857, Church Archives. Punctuation added. On September 16, 1856, Woodruff records the founding meeting, and on February 11, 1857, he attends with Bishop Hoagland and other priesthood leaders a meeting where "we laid hands upon them [the presidency] and ordained them & set them apart to their office and calling." There is no explanation given for the gap between the September organization and the February setting apart.

67. "Relief Society in the Early Days," *Woman's Exponent* 24 (July 1, 1895): 21.

68. Seventh Ward, Salt Lake Stake, Relief Society Minutes, March 21, 1857.

69. "The Relief Society," Carter, comp., *Our Pioneer Heritage* 14:15; Seventh Ward, Salt Lake Stake, Relief Society Minutes, March 21, 1857; Thirteenth Ward, Salt Lake Stake, Minutes, as quoted in Arrington, *From Quaker to Latter-day Saint: Bishop Edwin D. Woolley* 337–38.

70. Eighteenth Ward, Salt Lake Stake, General Minutes, 1854–57, September 6, 1855, p. 9.

71. Susa Young Gates, "Relief Society Beginnings in Utah," *Relief Society Magazine* 9 (April 1922): 195. Gates, born in 1856, was too young to have remembered these societies, but she could well have heard accounts from her

mother's contemporaries. It is doubtful if she had access to any more contemporary records than are now available to us.

72. Brigham Young, September 13, 1857, *Journal of Discourses* 5:232, as quoted in Richard D. Poll, "The Move South," *BYU Studies* 29 (Fall 1989): 66. Much of the background for this section is from Poll's excellent discussion of the move.

73. Poll, "The Move South," 82.

74. "The Relief Society," Carter, comp., *Our Pioneer Heritage* 14:75.

75. "Journal of Mary Ann Weston Maughan," Carter, comp., *Our Pioneer Heritage* 2:387.

76. Martin Luther Ensign, Autobiography, microfilm of typescript, Church Archives. As quoted in Poll, "The Move South," 83.

77. As cited in Poll, "The Move South," 88 n.81.

Chapter 3: Wise Stewards, 1866–1887

1. Leslie, *A Pleasure Trip from Gotham to the Golden Gate*, 78.

2. Estelle Friedman, "Separatism as Strategy: Female Institution Building and American Feminism, 1870–1930," *Feminist Studies* 5 (Fall 1979): 522. See also Judith Paine, "The Women's Pavillion of 1876," *The Feminist Art Journal* 4 (Winter 1975–76): 5–12.

3. Eliza R. Snow, "Women's Centennial Territorial Fair," *Woman's Exponent* 4 (February 15, 1876): 141.

4. "The Ladies' Centennial Fair," *Deseret News* 25 (July 12, 1876): 369.

5. Eliza Snow herself had been both prizewinner (needlework bedspread, 1858; woolen carpet, 1861; and embroidered veil and carpet, 1862), and later committee member and head of the women's department of the Deseret Agricultural and Manufacturing Society fair.

6. Eliza R. Snow to Marinda Johnson Hyde, June 25, 1876, holograph, Church Archives. She describes also the original plan to set the fair in the Social Hall, two blocks away, scuttled at President Young's request that they use instead the smaller space in the Old Constitution Building. Despite an explosion in the latter facility, which necessitated repairs, the change proved fortuitous, for the fair lasted two months instead of one and could remain on the same premises when the women turned the fair into a retail outlet.

7. Brigham Young Letterbook 14:533–34, October 4, 1876, Church Archives. The President offered support, even to the point that "if you can not be satisfied with the selection of Sisters from among yourselves to take charge, we will render you assistance by furnishing a competent man for the transaction of the financial matters of this Establishment." The offer was never accepted.

8. Mary Ann Maughan, quoting Eliza R. Snow, Wellsville Ward, Cache Stake, Relief Society Minutes, 1868–1916, July 11, 1868.

9. Brigham Young, Unpublished Sermons, [St. George, 1877,] Church Archives. That the president's words were heeded is confirmed in Third Ward, Salt Lake Stake, Relief Society Minutes, 1868–1884, January 4, 1877. President Elizabeth Weiler there applauded her members for joining other sisters who go to the Woman's Store "and spend their time there for nothing," i.e., for no salary.

10. Eliza R. Snow, Nauvoo Journal, holograph, Church Archives, October 5, 1843. The journal, as edited by Maureen Ursenbach [Beecher], is published in *BYU Studies* 15 (Summer 1975): 391–416.

11. Eliza R. Snow to Mary [Elizabeth Lightner], April 3, 1865, typescript in the authors' files, courtesy of Norlyn Snow Torres.

12. Wilford Woodruff, Diaries, December 26, 1866, Church Archives. Spelling and capitalization have been modernized.

13. Brigham Young, April 8, 1868, *Journal of Discourses* 12:201.

14. Brigham Young, December 8, 1867, *Journal of Discourses* 12:115.

15. Ibid.

16. *Deseret News*, August 11, 1869.

17. Richard O. Cowan, "The 'Reformation' of the 1860s: A Remarkable Period of Ecclesiastical Expansion," typescript in the authors' files.

18. Eliza R. Snow to "My Dear Sister [Augusta] Smith," May 7, 1868, in "The Relief Society," in Carter, comp., *Our Pioneer Heritage* 14:110.

19. Snow, "Sketch of My Life," holograph, Mormon Collection, Bancroft Library, University of California, Berkeley.

20. First Ward, Salt Lake Stake, Relief Society Minutes, 1870–1893, March 24, 1870.

21. Eighth Ward, Salt Lake Stake, Relief Society Minutes, 1867–1877, December 16, 1867.

22. Third Ward, Salt Lake Stake, Relief Society Minutes, 1868–1884, September 30, 1868. Punctuation has been emended.

23. Jordan Ward, Salt Lake Stake, Relief Society Minutes, September 7, 1868. Capitalization has been modernized.

24. St. George Stake Relief Society Minute Book, 1868–1892, undated.

25. Snow to Smith, 108–10. Emphasis is hers. Nauvoo Minutes, March 17, 1842.

26. Snow to Smith, 110.

27. Ibid.

28. Eleventh Ward, Salt Lake Stake, Relief Society Minutes, March 3, 1869. Spelling and capitalization have been modernized.

29. Eliza R. Snow Smith to [Willmirth] East, April 23, 1883, holograph, Church Archives. Emphasis hers.

30. Sixth Ward, Salt Lake Stake, Relief Society Minutes, 1867–1883, August 16, 1868.

31. Eliza R. Snow to Mary Elizabeth Lightner, May 27, 1869, photocopy of holograph, Special Collections, Harold B. Lee Library, Brigham Young University, Provo, Utah.

32. Mount Pleasant North Ward, Sanpete Stake, Relief Society Minutes, 1878–1889, August 7, 1880. Spelling and capitalization have been modernized.

33. Third Ward, Salt Lake Stake, Relief Society Minutes, 1868–1884, September 23, 1868; June 29, 1870.

34. Ibid., May 4, 1882.

35. Tenth Ward, Salt Lake Stake, Relief Society Minutes, 1873–1910, January 22, 1874.

36. Snow, "Sketch of My Life." D&C 25:7–9.

37. The entire speech is found in *Woman's Exponent* 17 (February 15,

1889): 137–38. The quotations are from "Emily S. Richards," *Dedication Program*, BYU Heritage Halls, n.d.

38. Eliza R. Snow, "Female Relief Society," *Deseret News*, April 22, 1868.

39. [Emmeline B. Wells], "Chronicle of the Relief Society," *Woman's Exponent* 38 (September 1909): 21.

40. Third Ward, Salt Lake Stake, Relief Society Minutes, June 29, 1870.

41. Pinto Ward, St. George Stake, Relief Society Minutes, 1869–1904, November 31, 1878.

42. Snow, "The Relief Society."

43. Emmeline B. Wells, Diaries, August 10, 1874, Harold B. Lee Library, Brigham Young University, Provo, Utah.

44. *Deseret News*, July 26, 1882.

45. D[aniel] H. Wells, in "Report of the Dedication of the Kaysville Relief Society House," November 12, 1876, as reported in *Woman's Exponent* 5 (March 1, 1877): 149. The concept is more broadly developed in Shipps, *Mormonism: The Story of a New Religious Tradition*, 121–27.

46. For a full discussion of the economics of the time, see Arrington, *Great Basin Kingdom*, especially chapters 7–10.

47. Leonard J. Arrington, "The Economic Role of Pioneer Mormon Women," *Western Humanities Review* 9 (Spring 1955): 150–52.

48. Presiding Bishopric, Minutes of Bishops Meetings 1851–1884, February 18, 1869, manuscript, Church Archives.

49. Eliza R. Snow, August 14, 1873, "An Address," *Woman's Exponent* 2 (September 15, 1873): 63; *Latter-day Saints' Millennial Star* 34 (January 13, 1874): 20.

50. Not only have the economic enterprises been treated in earlier histories of the Relief Society, they have also been the subjects of scholarly articles and theses. Leonard J. Arrington's "Economic Role" in 1955 was followed by Chris Rigby Arrington's "The Finest of Fabrics: Mormon Women and the Silk Industry in Early Utah," *Utah Historical Quarterly* 46 (Fall 1978): 376–96; Sherilyn Cox Bennion, "Enterprising Ladies: Utah's Nineteenth-Century Women Editors," *Utah Historical Quarterly* 49 (Summer 1981): 291–304, and "Lula Greene Richards: Utah's First Woman Editor," *BYU Studies* 21 (Spring 1981): 155–74; Jessie L. Embry, "Relief Society Grain Storage Program, 1876–1940" (master's thesis). Papers dealing with women's involvement in business, medicine, and education, presented at a 1982 conference of the Utah Women's History Association, were published as Sillito, ed., *From Cottage to Market: The Professionalization of Women's Sphere*.

51. [Sarah M. Kimball], "Duty of Officers of F[emale] R[elief] Society," Fifteenth Ward, Salt Lake Stake, Relief Society Minutes, 1868–1873. The holograph document consists of four loose pages found inside the minute book. For more on Sarah Kimball see Jill C. Mulvay [Derr], "The Liberal Shall Be Blessed: Sarah M. Kimball," *Utah Historical Quarterly* 44 (Summer 1976): 204–21; also in Burgess-Olson, ed., *Sister Saints*, 21–40.

52. *Woman's Exponent* 14 (June 15, 1885): 14.

53. Fifteenth Ward Relief Society Minutes 1868–1873, November 12, 1868.

54. Ibid., May 28, 1868; June 11, 1868; February 25, 1869; and August 12, 1869.

55. Ibid., January 8, 1878.

56. *Woman's Exponent* 27 (December 15, 1898): 78; Seegmiller, *Robert Taylor Burton*, 1.

57. Sarah M. Kimball, "Our Sixth Sense, or the Sense of Spiritual Understanding," *Woman's Exponent* 23 (April 15, 1895): 251.

58. Fifteenth Ward Relief Society Minutes, January 6, 1876. It speaks well for President Burton's regard for the women's contribution to the ward that during his 1873–75 mission to England he organized the first British Relief Society in Whitechapel in the London Conference. *Woman's Exponent* 35 (September 1906): 22.

59. Fifteenth Ward Relief Society Minutes, October 12, 1871.

60. Ibid., passim.

61. Wells, in "Report of the Dedication of the Kaysville Relief Society House," *Woman's Exponent* 5 (March 1, 1877): 149.

62. "General Meeting of Central and Ward Committees, on the Grain Movement," *Woman's Exponent* 5 (December 1, 1876): 99.

63. Ibid.

64. Fifteenth Ward Relief Society Minutes, 1876; *Woman's Exponent* 6 (October 1, 1877): 69.

65. John Taylor, March 2, 1879, *Journal of Discourses* 20:169.

66. Louisa W. Jones and Mary E. White, "Biographical Sketch — Sister Lucinda Houd," *Woman's Exponent* 31 (August 1 and 15, 1902): 23.

67. Susa Young Gates Papers, typescript, Utah State Historical Society, Salt Lake City, Utah.

68. "The Saving of Grain," *Woman's Exponent* 22 (September 15, 1893): 36.

69. John Taylor, George Q. Cannon, and Joseph F. Smith, "To the Bishops of the Various Wards," *Woman's Exponent* 12 (July 15, 1883): 28.

70. M[ary] A[nn] Hyde to "My dear Sister Peterson," January 23, 1883, typescript, Peterson Family Papers 1844–1957, Church Archives.

71. The best study of the grain project to date is Embry, "Relief Society Grain Storage Program, 1876–1940" (master's thesis).

72. Brigham Young, St. George, April 6, 1877, *Journal of Discourses* 18:355; Eliza R. Snow, *Woman's Exponent* 5 (April 15, 1877): 173; Brigham Young, in "General Conference at St. George," *Woman's Exponent* 5 (April 15, 1877): 172.

73. Arrington, "The Finest of Fabrics: Mormon Women and the Silk Industry in Early Utah," is the most complete account of the venture.

74. "Journal of Mary Ann Weston Maughan," Carter, comp., *Our Pioneer Heritage* 2:397.

75. Brigham Young to Nicoline Olsen, August 15, 1867, Brigham Young Letterbooks, Church Archives; Mrs. M. J. Coray to Brigham Young, July 18, 1872, Brigham Young Incoming Correspondence, Church Archives.

76. *Woman's Exponent* 2 (July 15, 1873): 27; 2 (August 1, 1873): 35. The Amanda Smith quoted is the same whose son was cured by her inspired

ministrations when his hip was shot away at Haun's Mill in 1838. Her account is in Tullidge, *Women of Mormondom,* 121–32.

77. Ibid., 2 (September 15, 1873): 63. The "Mrs. Barker" is Dr. Mary H. Barker, graduate physician from the eastern United States. She remained in Salt Lake City only three years.

78. *Woman's Exponent* 4 (October 15, 1875): 75.

79. [Romania B. Pratt] to Presidents of Relief Societies, April 21, 1878, Peterson Family Papers 1844–1957, Church Archives.

80. Besides Dr. Ferguson, staff physicians included Dr. Martha (Mattie) Paul Hughes [Cannon] and Dr. Pratt. It is significant that two daughters of William Anderson, one of the male physicians, became doctors themselves.

81. Hannah Adeline Hatch Savage, Autobiography, holograph, Church Archives.

82. Susa Young Gates to Lucy Bigelow Young, April 18, 1879, as quoted in Godfrey et al., *Woman's Voices,* 334.

83. Edward Tullidge, "Emmeline B. Wells," *Tullidge's Quarterly Magazine* 1 (January 1881): 252, as quoted in Sherilyn Cox Bennion, "The *Woman's Exponent*: Forty-two Years of Speaking for Women," *Utah Historical Quarterly* 44 (Summer 1976): 231.

84. Maureen Ursenbach Beecher, "A Decade of Mormon Women—The 1870s," *New Era* 8 (April 1978): 34–39 provides examples of the commercial and professional activities of individual women.

85. That by 1870 an estimated 40 percent of Utah married women were or had been married polygamously can be extrapolated from Bean, Mineau, and Anderton, *Fertility Change on the American Frontier,* 94. For those women, as for others not personally involved in the practice, the principle remained a sacred privilege, one they considered protected by the constitutional freedom of religion.

86. Fifteenth Ward Relief Society Minutes, 1868–1873, January 6, 1870. We are grateful for the recent work of Lola Van Wagenen in tracing the politicizing of Utah Mormon women. She demonstrates clearly that the achievement of suffrage did not come about solely because, as has been believed, "the progressive Mormon hierarchy . . . obliged Utah territory in 1870," but by the women's own demonstrated ability to act appropriately and effectively in the public sphere. " 'A Matter for Astonishment': Woman Suffrage in Territorial Utah," and "In Their Own Behalf: The Politicization of Mormon Women and the 1870 Franchise." The latter paper was presented at the Mormon History Association annual meeting, Quincy, Illinois, May 1989, and later published in *Dialogue* 24 (Winter 1991): 31–43. The traditional view is represented in Buhle and Buhle, *The Concise History of Woman Suffrage,* 25.

87. "Minutes of a Ladies' Mass Meeting," *Deseret News,* January 11, 1870.

88. Van Wagenen, " 'A Matter for Astonishment,' " 35–38. *New York Times,* February 8, 1870; other Eastern newspapers are quoted in *Deseret News,* February 16, 1870. All are as quoted in Van Wagenen, " 'A Matter for Astonishment.' "

89. "The Woman Suffrage Bill," *Deseret News,* February 12, 1870.

90. Ibid., February 23, 1870.

91. Fifteenth Ward Relief Society Minutes, February 19, 1870.

92. Ibid., February 19, 1870.

93. Ibid., July 20, 1871.

94. Brigham Young to Heber Young, February 16, 1870, in Jessee, ed., *Brigham Young's Letters to His Sons,* 140. Thus Utah women became the first women to vote in a general election in the United States.

95. Lee, *A Mormon Chronicle: The Diaries of John D. Lee, 1848–1876,* ed. Cleland and Brooks, 2:114.

96. Ibid.

97. Brigham Young, November 14, 1869, *Journal of Discourses* 13:153.

98. Ibid.

99. Ibid., 13:155.

100. Gordon B. Hinckley, "Ten Gifts from the Lord," *Ensign* 15 (November 1985): 87; James 5:14–15.

101. Augusta Joyce Crocheron, comp., *Representative Women of Deseret,* 21.

102. That history is recounted in detail in Gates, *History of the YLMIA,* and later in *A Century of Sisterhood.*

103. Mary Isabella Horne, Senior and Junior Cooperative Retrenchment Association Minutes, October 11, 1873, typescript, Church Archives.

104. Retrenchment Association Minutes, July 10, 1875.

105. Ibid.

106. Ibid.

107. Ibid., September 15, 1872. "How is it with a great many of our young people?" she asked an audience in Ogden, Utah, in 1873. "Do they know what the Holy Ghost is? Do they ever minister in the Holy Ghost? Have they ever had the gifts of the Gospel? Look around you and think how many there are, children of the Latter-day Saints, who know no more of the Gospel of Jesus Christ than the heathens do." Eliza R. Snow, "An Address," *Woman's Exponent* 2 (September 15, 1873): 62.

108. Retrenchment Association Minutes, August 30, 1873; May 1, 1875.

109. Junius F. Wells, as quoted in Gates, *History of the YLMIA,* 80–82.

110. Retrenchment Association Minutes, February 20, 1875.

111. Gates, *History of the YLMIA,* 9–10.

112. *Woman's Exponent* 33 (July 1904): 15.

113. Emmeline B. Wells, Diaries, July 10, 1878.

114. *Woman's Exponent* 7 (October 1, 1878): 66.

115. Jill Mulvay Derr, "Sisters and Little Saints: One Hundred Years of Mormon Primaries," in Alexander, ed., *The Mormon People: Their Character and Traditions,* 75–102. For a full treatment of the history, see Madsen and Oman, *Sisters and Little Saints: One Hundred Years of Primary.*

116. Eliza R. Snow to Aurelia S. Rogers, August 4, 1878; Rogers, *Life Sketches of Orson Spencer and Others, and History of Primary Work,* 212, both as cited in Madsen and Oman, *Sisters and Little Saints,* 5–6.

117. William G. Hartley, "The Priesthood Reorganization of 1877: Brigham Young's Last Achievement," *BYU Studies* 20 (Fall 1979): 3–36.

118. *Woman's Exponent* 35 (September 1906): 21.

119. Elmina S. Taylor, Diary, June 30, 1879, Church Archives.

459

NOTES TO PAGES 120–128

120. *Woman's Exponent* 6 (December 15, 1877): 108.

121. Ibid., 9 (July 1, 1880): 21–22.

122. Nauvoo Minutes, March 17, 1842; Sarah M. Kimball, "Autobiography," *Woman's Exponent* 12 (September 1883): 51.

123. *Woman's Exponent* 9 (September 1, 1880): 53–54.

124. Mary Ann Burnham Freeze, Diary, March 9, 1883, Special Collections, Harold B. Lee Library, Brigham Young University, Provo, Utah.

125. Gates, *History of the YLMIA*, 71. Eliza Snow's 1880 "Brief Sketch of the Organizations Conducted by the Latter-day Saint Women," holograph, written for Bancroft's *History of Utah*, is found in the Bancroft Library, University of California at Berkeley.

126. Hartley, "Priesthood Reorganization," 27; *Woman's Exponent* 35 (July 1906): 13–14 lists all the stakes with their dates of organization and initial presidencies.

127. Carol Cornwall Madsen, "Mormon Missionary Wives in Nineteenth Century Polynesia," *Journal of Mormon History* 13 (1986–87): 76, 62; M. Mitchell, "From the Sandwich Islands," *Woman's Exponent* 3 (June 1, 1874): 3; Jane E. Molen, "Extracts from a Letter," *Woman's Exponent* 5 (February 15, 1877): 139; Jane E. Molen, "Extracts of Letters from Hawaiian Islands," *Woman's Exponent* 6 (June 15, 1877): 13; Jane E. Molen, "Correspondence," *Woman's Exponent* 6 (May 15, 1878): 187; J. E. Molen, "Visit of the Queen to the Relief Society," *Woman's Exponent* 7 (August 15, 1878): 43; [Emmeline B. Wells], "Chronicle of the Relief Society," 35 (September 1906): 22.

128. [Emmeline B. Wells], "Visit to Sanpete—Notes by the Way," *Woman's Exponent* 9 (August 15, 1880): 44; M. Elizabeth Little, "A Welcome," *Woman's Exponent* 9 (September 1, 1880): 52. Punctuation emended.

129. Mount Pleasant North Ward Relief Society Minutes, 1878–1889, August 20, 1880. Spelling has been corrected.

130. "Relief Society Beginnings in Foreign Lands," *Relief Society Magazine* 9 (March 1922): 120–22.

131. *Woman's Exponent* 6 (January 1, 1878): 114.

132. Snow, "Sketch of My Life."

133. *Woman's Exponent* 2 (September 15, 1873): 63.

CHAPTER 4: IN BONDS OF SISTERHOOD, 1888–1901

1. *Woman's Exponent* 9 (April 1, 1881): 165.

2. Ibid. Zina Huntington Jacobs was sealed to Joseph Smith October 27, 1841; Eliza Roxcy Snow, on June 29, 1842.

3. Emmeline B. Wells, Diaries, December 5 and 6, 1887, Harold B. Lee Library, Brigham Young University, Provo, Utah. Although the date of Eliza R. Snow's death is inscribed on her grave as December 4, 1887, the most immediate contemporary accounts indicate the later date.

4. In Lelia, "No Black for Me," *Woman's Exponent* 10 (15 November 1881): 91.

5. Weber Stake Relief Society Conference Minute Book, 1855–1899, December 8, 1887, Church Archives. Threat of prosecution for "illegal cohabitation" under the laws that the women had protested so long kept the church presidency from attending. Eliza's brother Lorenzo himself could be present

only because he had already served his eleven months for his obedience to the principle of plural marriage.

6. Wells, Diaries, March 26, 1900.

7. Zina Young Card to Zina D. H. Young, May 25, 1889, holograph, courtesy Mary Brown Woodward.

8. Emmeline B. Wells, "Zina D. H. Young: A Character Sketch," *Improvement Era* 5 (November 1901): 45–46.

9. E. S. Wilcox, "Mrs. Zina D. H. Young and the Relief Society," *Woman's Exponent* 28 (April 15 and May 1, 1900): 121.

10. Wells, "Zina D. H. Young," 47.

11. "R. S. Reports," *Woman's Exponent* 3 (September 15, 1875): 58.

12. Wells, Diaries, June 12, 1888.

13. "Minutes of a special general conference of the Relief Societies and Young Ladies Associations of Weber Stake," July 19, 1877, typescript, insert in holograph volume, Weber Stake Relief Society Conference Minute Book, 1855–1899. Brigham Young considered the women's direction so significant that when he reorganized the Box Elder Stake the next week, he required Sister Richards to leave the sickbed of her child to accompany him there. "They continued in close conversation during the trip," reads the account, "he instructing her in the varied duties of her presidency."

14. Wells, Diaries, April 7, 1891.

15. "The Women of Utah Represented at the International Council of Women, at Washington, D.C.," *Woman's Exponent* 16 (April 1, 1888): 164–65.

16. "General Relief Society Conference," *Woman's Exponent* 28 (November 15 and December 1, 1899): 77–78.

17. C.B.P., "In Memoriam: Sketch of Sister Mary John," *Woman's Exponent* 34 (February 1906): 55.

18. Mary L. Ransom and Sarah Webb, "Biography and Resolution," *Woman's Exponent* 30 (May 15, 1902): 111; W. East, "Reports: St. Joseph Stake, Arizona," *Woman's Exponent* 12 (January 15, 1884): 128.

19. "Sketch of Julia P. Lindsay," *Woman's Exponent* 39 (January 1911): 47; 39 (March 1911): 63–64; 39 (May 1911): 71–72.

20. "Relief Society Conference," *Woman's Exponent* 22 (December 15, 1893, and January 1, 1894): 77–78.

21. See Kimberly Jensen James, " 'Between Two Fires': Women on the 'Underground' of Mormon Polygamy," *Journal of Mormon History* 8 (1981): 49–61, and master's thesis.

22. For a fuller account of LDS women's involvement with the NWSA, see Madsen, "A Mormon Woman in Victorian America" (Ph.D. dissertation). Both Emmeline and Zina were appointed to committees at this first conference, and Emmeline later became vice president of the association for Utah. For a brief discussion of the federal antipolygamy crusade, see Gustive O. Larson, "The Crusade and the Manifesto," in *Utah's History*, ed. Richard D. Poll, 257–74.

23. *Woman's Exponent* 14 (March 1 and 15 and April 1, 1886) features the LDS women's mass meeting and resolutions. Ibid. (April 15, 1886): 169–70

provides Wells's brief account of the Washington visit. See also Madsen, "A Mormon Woman in Victorian America," 220–22.

24. Peggy Pascoe deals with the Industrial Christian Home in the context of her insightful *Relations of Rescue: The Search for Female Moral Authority in the American West, 1874–1939,* 20–31ff., on which this account is based. After 1893 the building served federal and local governments as office space, although, in an ironic twist, the board of the Deseret Hospital, by then in dire financial straits, made a last-ditch application to move its operation there. The building stood at its Fifth East location until 1989. See also Gustive O. Larson, "An Industrial Home for Polygamous Wives," *Utah Historical Quarterly* 38 (Summer 1970): 263–75.

25. In his diary, then apostle Heber J. Grant, on hearing the arguments describing government threats to escheat the Saints of their properties, clarified: "If it had not been for the Manifesto, all the work for the living and the dead in our temples would have had to stop." The ordinances of the temple were the more fundamental and essential covenants. Heber J. Grant, Diary, April 2, 1891, as quoted in Edward Leo Lyman, *Political Deliverance: The Mormon Quest for Statehood,* 147.

26. Wells, Diaries, October 6, 1890.

27. Zina D. H. Young, Diary, October 6, 1890.

28. As quoted in Ann Vest Lobb and Jill Mulvay Derr, "Women in Early Utah," in Poll et al., *Utah's History,* 349. Annie Clark Tanner's autobiography is *A Mormon Mother.*

29. Zina D. H. Young, Diary, October 6, 1890.

30. Lawrence Foster, "From Frontier Activism to Neo-Victorian Domesticity: Mormon Women in the Nineteenth and Twentieth Centuries," *Journal of Mormon History* 6 (1979): 10.

31. To underline their opposition to polygamy, the more "respectable" wing, the American Woman Suffrage Association, declined at first to admit the Mormons as affiliates.

32. Minutes of Relief Society Conference, April 5, 1894, in Relief Society Minutes 1892–1911, April 5, 1894; also quoted in Jill Mulvay Derr, "'Strength in Our Union': The Making of Mormon Sisterhood," in Beecher and Anderson, *Sisters in Spirit,* 181.

33. Carol Cornwall Madsen, "The Mormon–Gentile Female Relationship in Nineteenth Century Utah," unpublished paper in authors' files; Madsen, "A Mormon Woman in Victorian America," 248–49. Eventually several leading Gentile women would become active members of the association.

34. Kathleen Marquis, "'Diamond Cut Diamond': Mormon Women and the Cult of Domesticity in the Nineteenth Century," University of Michigan Papers in Women's Studies 2.2 (1974): 105–23.

35. Etta L. Gilchrist, "The World's Fair," *Woman's Exponent* 21 (June 15, 1893): 178. We appreciate Harriet Arrington for calling this to our attention.

36. Weber Stake Relief Society Conference Minute Book, 1855–1899, June 8, 1886.

37. "Women and the World's Fair," *Woman's Exponent* 21 (December 1, 1892): 84.

38. Zina D. H. Young, Jane S. Richards, and Bathsheba W. Smith, "Letter

of Greeting," January 21, 1892, facsimile, in *History of Relief Society 1842–1966*, 118.

39. Almo Ward, Cassia Stake, Relief Society Minutes 1884–1908, March 17, 1892.

40. Franklin D. Richards, Diaries, March 17, 1892, Church Archives.

41. Ibid., March 15, 1892. President Zina Young requested each society to submit, "for future use and reference," its own history, together with the minutes of its Jubilee celebrations. "Important to the Relief Society," *Woman's Exponent* 20 (April 1, 1892): 139.

42. "Relief Society Jubilee," *Woman's Exponent* 20 (April 1, 1892): 143.

43. Ibid., 137.

44. Ibid., 139.

45. Ibid., 143.

46. Relief Society Minutes, 1892–1896, April 5, 1893; also quoted in Madsen, "A Mormon Woman in Victorian America," 356.

47. Mary Ann Burnham Freeze, Diary, Harold B. Lee Library, Brigham Young University, Provo, Utah. April 6, 1893; May 21, 1888.

48. Ibid., May 8, 1893.

49. Relief Society Minutes 1892–1911, April 6, 1893; April 5, 1894. Courtesy Carol Cornwall Madsen.

50. Wells, Diaries, March 21, 1892. The concept was not new to Wells, who, in company with M. Isabella Horne, had met with the counselors in the First Presidency, and again with Franklin D. Richards and others, as early as July 1891. Ibid., July 7, 1891.

51. Ibid., October 2 and 3, 1892.

52. Madsen, "A Mormon Woman in Victorian America," 351.

53. Fifteenth Ward Relief Society Minutes, 1893–1899.

54. Relief Society Minutes 1892–1911, April 8, 1895.

55. *Woman's Exponent* 20 (April 1, 1892): 140.

56. Zina D. H. Young, Weber Stake Relief Society Conference Minute Book, 1855–1899, June 16, 1887.

57. Belva A. Lockwood, "The Mormon Question," broadside, 1888, Church Archives.

58. L. L. Greene Richards, "Woman, 'Rise," *Young Woman's Journal* 6 (February 1893): 201; also in *Utah Woman Suffrage Song Book*, 5–6.

59. For full discussion of the process see Beverly Beeton, *Women Vote in the West: The Woman Suffrage Movement 1869–1896*, 82–101.

60. "Susan B. Anthony's Letter," *Woman's Exponent* 23 (August 1 and 15, 1894): 169; also cited in Jean Bickmore White, "Woman's Place Is in the Constitution: The Struggle for Equal Rights in Utah in 1895," *Utah Historical Quarterly* 42 (Fall 1974): 44–69. Information for this and the following paragraph is from this source.

61. Ruth May Fox, Diaries, February 22–25, 1895, holograph, Utah State Historical Society. Typescript in authors' files. See also Linda Thatcher, " 'I Care Nothing for Politics': Ruth May Fox, Forgotten Suffragist," *Utah Historical Quarterly* 49 (Summer 1981): 239–53.

62. Ibid., April 1, 1895.

Chapter 5: Peaceable Mothers in Zion, 1901–1910

1. *Woman's Exponent* 30 (December 1901): 50.

2. Relief Society Minutes 1892–1911, October 1, 1901; *Woman's Exponent* 30 (Christmas 1901): 62.

3. *Woman's Exponent* 30 (December 1901): 52.

4. "Official Announcement," *Woman's Exponent* 30 (January 1, 1902): 68.

5. The most comprehensive discussion of this period of transition is Thomas G. Alexander, *Mormonism in Transition,* 94. See especially chapter 6, "Administrative Modernization."

6. Ibid., 241.

7. Ibid., 107.

8. "Dedication of Huntsville Relief Society Hall," *Woman's Exponent* 31 (August 1 and 15, 1902): 20.

9. "Relief Society Reports: Snowflake," *Woman's Exponent* 31 (May 1903): 96.

10. Relief Society Minutes 1892–1911, August 7, 1903.

11. See Jill Mulvay Derr, "'Strength in Our Union: The Making of Mormon Sisterhood,'" in Beecher and Anderson, *Sisters in Spirit,* 182–83.

12. "Reception and Banquet," *Woman's Exponent* 31 (July 1 and 15, 1902): 14–15.

13. *Woman's Exponent* 31 (March 1903): 77; 34 (October 1905): 31; 35 (November 1906): 37.

14. "Beware of Evil Influences," *Woman's Exponent* 31 (February 1903): 68.

15. As quoted in Carol Lois Clark, "The Effect of Secular Education upon Relief Society Curriculum" (Ph.D. dissertation), 66.

16. Ibid., 68.

17. As quoted in ibid., 63.

18. "Relief Society General Conference," *Woman's Exponent* 31 (June 1 and 15, 1902): 6

19. "Relief Society Reports, Alpine Stake," *Woman's Exponent* 38 (November 1909): 34.

20. See chapter 6 of this volume; also Clark, "Relief Society Curriculum," 70.

21. President Roosevelt, "Extracts," *Woman's Exponent* 33 (April 1905): 79–80.

22. "Mother's [*sic*] Work," *Woman's Exponent* 34 (June 1905): 2.

23. Ibid., 3.

24. *Woman's Exponent* 34 (November 1905): 39; 34 (January 1906): 47; 35 (January 1907): 45; 35 (February 1907): 49.

25. Ibid., 35 (May 1907): 68.

26. Emmeline B. Wells to E. L. S. Udall, August 19, 1906, St. Johns Stake Correspondence, Relief Society Headquarters Historical Files.

27. The Relief Society missionaries, part of the system of "home missions" to the Saints as distinguished from proselyting assignments abroad, were not members of the board, though they were invited to attend the last board meeting each month. Their removal from full involvement created some dis-

crepancy in their message, a problem addressed by providing them with written instructions from the president prior to their visits. A set of such instructions would typically include organizational matters, such as a directive that the nurse class and mothers' work were to be supervised by the Relief Society president, not by independent officers; or a listing of the duties of the various society officers.

28. "Report of the National Woman's Relief Society . . . ," *Woman's Exponent* 32 (February 1904): 69.

29. Emmeline B. Wells to E. L. S. Udall, August 28, 1906, St. Johns Stake Correspondence, Relief Society Headquarters Historical Files.

30. Fay Tarlock, "The Visitors," *Relief Society Magazine* 35 (March 1948): 166–67. We appreciate Helen Stark's calling this gem to our attention.

31. "General Conference Relief Society," *Woman's Exponent* 32 (May 1904): 94.

32. *Woman's Exponent* 37 (June 1908): 4.

33. Ibid., 38 (September 1909): 24.

34. Ibid., 30 (March 1902): 8.

35. Ibid., 37 (August 1908): 14.

36. Emma N. Huff, comp., *Memories That Live: Utah County Centennial History* ([Provo, Utah:] Daughters of Utah Pioneers of Utah County, 1947), 138. As quoted in Chris Rigby Arrington, "The Finest of Fabrics: Mormon Women and the Silk Industry in Early Utah," *Utah Historical Quarterly* 46 (Fall 1978): 395.

37. "The New Year 1908," *Woman's Exponent* 36 (January 1908): 44.

38. Arrington, "The Finest of Fabrics," 396.

39. Relief Society Minutes 1892–1911, April 18, 1906; Jessie L. Embry, "Relief Society Grain Storage Program, 1876–1940" (master's thesis), 25.

40. "Relief Society Reports, Uintah Stake," *Woman's Exponent* 38 (September 1909): 27; 34 (May 1906): 71.

41. *Woman's Exponent* 30 (January 1, 1902): 66; 30 (March 1902): 86; 35 (June 1906): 5; 35 (October 1906): 31; 36 (September 1907): 23; 31 (November 1 and 15, 1902): 46.

42. "General Conference Relief Society," *Woman's Exponent* 32 (May 1904): 94.

43. "Report of the National Women's Relief Society," *Woman's Exponent* 32 (February 1904): 69; "Relief Society Nurse Class," ibid., 70; Relief Society Minutes 1892–1911, November 1, 1907.

44. Susa Young Gates, "L.D.S. Relief Society Class for Training Nurses' Aids," *Relief Society Magazine* 7 (July 1920): 382–85.

45. Relief Society Minutes 1892–1911, September 4 and 11, 1908.

46. "R. S. Reports: Alpine Stake," *Woman's Exponent* 33 (August 1904): 21.

47. "Relief Society Work Abroad," *Woman's Exponent* 36 (October 1907): 29; "A Very Interesting Letter," *Woman's Exponent* 38 (January 1910): 41–42.

48. Richard L. Jensen, "Mother Tongue: Use of Non-English Languages in the Church of Jesus Christ of Latter-day Saints in the United States, 1850–1983," in *New Views of Mormon History*, ed. Bitton and Beecher, 279. Public

opinion at the onset of World War I would force the closure of some of the buildings and cause church authorities to rethink the question.

49. "General Relief Society Conference," *Woman's Exponent* 32 (October 1903): 38.

50. "General Relief Society Conference," *Woman's Exponent* 35 (July 1906): 10.

51. Ibid.

52. "Peace Meetings," *Woman's Exponent* 32 (August 1903): 19.

53. "Peace Demonstration," *Woman's Exponent* 33 (November 1904): 36.

54. Ellis R. Shipp, "Prohibition," *Woman's Exponent* 37 (March 1909): 41.

55. "The Berlin Meetings," *Woman's Exponent* 33 (June 1904): 7–8.

56. Maureen Ursenbach Beecher and Kathryn L. MacKay, "Women in Twentieth Century Utah," in *Utah's History*, ed. Richard Poll et al., 564.

57. Relief Society Minutes 1892–1911, November 10, 1902.

58. "Alpine Stake," *Woman's Exponent* 30 (January 24, 1902): 86.

59. "Fulfillment of Prophecy," *Woman's Exponent* 36 (July 1907): 13.

60. Relief Society Minutes 1892–1911, November 10, 1902. The Cardston Ward in Alberta found an answer to that charge. Zina Y. Card, YLMIA president there, reported that they had organized a "new society . . . composed principally of young married sisters, who do themselves the favor of being active members in both Relief Society and Improvement Associations." "Letter from Canada," *Woman's Exponent* 26 (July 15 and August 1, 1897): 170.

61. "General Conference of Relief Society," *Woman's Exponent* 31 (May 1903): 93.

62. Orson F. Whitney, "Woman's Work and 'Mormonism,' " *Young Woman's Journal* 17 (July 1906): 295.

63. *Woman's Exponent* 34 (July–August 1905): 9.

64. "R. S. Reports, Beaver Stake," *Woman's Exponent* 38 (June 1909): 2.

65. "Alpine Stake," *Woman's Exponent* 31 (November 1 and 15, 1902): 47.

66. "General Relief Society Conference," *Woman's Exponent* 32 (October 1903): 38.

67. "Snowflake Stake," *Woman's Exponent* 34 (October 1905): 31.

68. "Weber Stake," *Woman's Exponent* 36 (July 1907): 14.

69. "Relief Society Report: Sevier Stake," *Woman's Exponent* 36 (December 1907): 38; *Woman's Exponent* 35 (July 1906): 6.

70. "A Few Stray Thoughts," *Woman's Exponent* 34 (February 1906): 52. In 1909 church attorneys examined titles to local Relief Society property and found that in many cases, due to changes in local leadership, the titles were "in a deplorable condition and getting worse." After study and discussion, the First Presidency, the Presiding Bishopric, and the Relief Society general board agreed that "all Relief Society property should be held by the bishops of the different wards, in trust as a corporate sole." This provided a means of properly maintaining the titles, since they would be vested in the presiding officer of each corporation sole (the bishop) "and would pass to his successor upon his death or release." Relief Society Minutes 1892–1911, May 1, 1908; citations from the Presiding Bishopric Office Journals, 1901–1946, April 29, May 12 and 15, and June 8, 1908, provided by the Church Archives staff; Alexander, *Mormonism in Transition,* 106.

71. Relief Society Minutes 1892–1911, October 3, 1896; also cited in Jill Mulvay Derr and C. Brooklyn Derr, "Outside the Mormon Hierarchy: Alternative Aspects of Institutional Power," *Dialogue* 15 (Winter 1982): 21.

72. Relief Society Minutes 1892–1911, March 26, 1901.

73. Zina D. H. Young et al. to Mrs. E. L. S. Udall, November 2, 1900, St. Johns Stake Correspondence, Relief Society Headquarters Historical Files.

74. "General Conference Relief Society," *Woman's Exponent* 30 (December 1901): 55–56.

75. "R. S. Reports," *Woman's Exponent* 30 (January 1, 1902): 70–71.

76. Bathsheba W. Smith, Martha H. Tingey, and Louie B. Felt, to the Presidency of the Church . . . , January 23, 1907, First Presidency, General Administration Correspondence, Church Archives.

77. Relief Society Minutes 1892–1911, February 1 and 15, 1907.

78. Nauvoo Minutes, April 28 and March 30, 1842.

79. "Relief Society Reports, Bannock Stake," *Woman's Exponent* 36 (October 1907): 30; 36 (December 1907): 39.

80. Belle S. Spafford Oral History, interviews by Jill Mulvay Derr, 1975–1976, typescript, 108–9, James H. Moyle Oral History Program, Church Archives.

81. "Relief Society Headquarters," *Woman's Exponent* 38 (January 1910): 45.

82. "Eliza R. Snow," *Woman's Exponent* 38 (February 1910): 52; Snow, "Evening Thoughts," *Poems* 1:4.

83. Lydia D. Alder, "Thoughts on Missionary Work," *Woman's Exponent* 30 (August 1, 1901): 21.

84. Emmeline B. Wells, "L.D.S. Women of the Past: Personal Impressions," *Woman's Exponent* 37 (August 1908): 10.

85. "Some Things Our Girls Should Know, Lesson XI," *Young Woman's Journal* 13 (June 1902): 288.

86. Emmeline B. Wells, "Why a Woman Should Desire to Be a Mormon," *Woman's Exponent* 36 (December 1907): 39 [emphasis hers]; "The Age We Live In," *Woman's Exponent* 30 (April 1902): 89–90.

87. Bathsheba W. Smith, "Greeting and Congratulations," *Woman's Exponent* 38 (January 1910): 41.

CHAPTER 6: HOLDING FAST THE COVENANT, 1910–1921

1. Willard Ward, Box Elder Stake, Relief Society Minutes, Officers Meetings, June 8, November 16, December 7, 1911, and January 7, 1912.

2. The women had struggled steadily against weevils and spoilage. They made sure their wheat was harvested during the dry period and then kept their bins dry. Those with cement granaries added slacked lime to prevent fermentation. Some began to rotate their wheat more often or switched to a better strain, heeding the counsel to buy the "best Turkey wheat." Others built steel tanks and added carbonic acid gas to the grain. Despite these efforts to improve preservation, an increasing number of societies concluded that the granaries of which they had once been so proud were now inadequate. See Jessie L. Embry's excellent study, "Relief Society Grain Storage Program, 1876–1940" (master's thesis).

3. Emmeline B. Wells and Olive D. Christensen to President of Relief Society, November 20, 1911, Relief Society Circular Letters, 1914–1922, Church Archives.

4. Willard Ward, Box Elder Stake, Relief Society Minutes, November 7, 1912.

5. See Madsen, "A Mormon Woman in Victorian America" (Ph.D. dissertation), 335. This is the most comprehensive biographical study of Emmeline B. Wells to date. A short introduction to Wells's life is Patricia Rasmussen Eaton-Gadsby and Judith Rasmussen Dushku, "Emmeline B. W. Wells," in Burgess-Olson, *Sister Saints*, 457–78. For Wells's involvement in grain storage, see "The Mission of Saving Grain," *Relief Society Magazine* 2 (February 1915): 47–49.

6. "Emmeline B. Wells, Lit. D.," *Woman's Exponent* 40 (March 1912): 50.

7. "President of Relief Society," *Deseret News*, October 8, 1910; Annie Wells Cannon, "Mothers in Israel," *Relief Society Magazine* 3 (February 1916): 68.

8. "Birthday of President Emmeline B. Wells," *Relief Society Magazine* 8 (February 1921): 113.

9. Following the death of Bathsheba W. Smith, on October 1, 1910, the First Presidency called a meeting of the general board and "told all present to write on a slip of paper two names to be first and second choice for president of Relief Society." The ballots indicated that Emmeline B. Wells, "who was also the unanimous choice of the First Presidency," should be president. Relief Society Minutes 1892–1911, October 1 and 3, 1910. Madsen, "A Mormon Woman in Victorian America," draws from Wells's diaries to describe the call and indicates that Wells, Williams, and Smith "had the highest number of votes of the sisters" (373–75).

10. Six board members had been released in October 1910, when the new presidency was announced. At that time, the First Presidency had made changes in several general boards in connection with a new policy that church members should not hold concurrent major church positions. When the Relief Society general board reconvened in May 1911, President Wells formally announced that six former board members had been released – Emma Smith Woodruff, Annie Wells Cannon, Harriet Harker, Minnie Horne James, Annie K. Hardy, and Jane S. Richards, all stake Relief Society presidents. Seven women had been appointed as new members of the board: Olive D. Christensen, secretary; Amy Brown Lyman, assistant secretary; Emma A. Empey, treasurer; Elizabeth Claridge McCune, Susa Young Gates, Edna May Davis, Sarah M. McLelland, and Elizabeth Caine Crismon. Carol Cornwall Madsen observed: "Two of Emmeline's original appointments were single women; two other unmarried women joined the board in 1914 and 1916. The appointment of the youngest, a single woman, twenty-eight-year-old Edna May Davis, created much comment. The choice of these four women was a dramatic departure from the past, and, generally, Emmeline was commended for her initiative" ("A Mormon Woman in Victorian America," 377).

11. Grun, *The Timetables of History*, sv. 1910ff.

12. Thomas G. Alexander observed that it is difficult if not impossible

to document the influence of progressive ideas in these changes, though important and useful comparisons can be drawn. *Mormonism in Transition,* 126.

13. Aileen S. Kraditor, *The Ideas of the Woman Suffrage Movement, 1890–1920,* 67–68.

14. Mariam Adams Gudmunsen, "Past and Future," *Woman's Exponent* 39 (November 1910): 40. Stanley J. Lemons indicates that "long before masses of women were deeply concerned with suffrage, they were working to make their communities more 'homelike'" (*The Woman Citizen,* 234). Women's work in the community "to redeem the world as love and work only can" is described in Karen J. Blair, *The Clubwoman as Feminist,* 48.

15. Relief Society Minutes 1892–1911, October 4, 1911.

16. Relief Society General Board Minutes 1842–1990, April 22, 1913.

17. "R. S. Reports: Portland Oregon Branch," *Woman's Exponent* 40 (November 1911): 31; "Do We Want Prohibition?" *Woman's Exponent* 39 (May 1911): 67; Relief Society Minutes 1892–1911, April 8, 1911. An enlightening discussion of church leaders' involvement in the prohibition movement is found in Alexander, *Mormonism in Transition,* 258–71.

18. Relief Society General Board Minutes, February 6, 1913.

19. Relief Society General Board Minutes, July 25 and August 18, 1913; June 18, 1914. The First Presidency and Presiding Bishopric contributed to Salt Lake City milk stations in 1916. Ibid., April 13, May 18, and June 13 and 24, 1916; Priscilla P. Jennings et al. to the First Presidency, April 14, 1916, First Presidency General Administration Correspondence, Church Archives.

20. Relief Society General Board Minutes, February 3 and 10, 1916.

21. Concerned that emigrants arriving at the train depot in Salt Lake City were being met by non-Mormon women, the Relief Society general board appointed sisters from Salt Lake stakes to meet the trains, but decided that the work of helping new arrivals "could not be done satisfactorily without a home as these people must be taken care of." Relief Society Minutes 1892–1911, June 15, 1911. The Relief Society made a written request to the First Presidency for help with the project. Emmeline B. Wells and Amy Brown Lyman to President Joseph F. Smith, March 3, 1912, First Presidency, General Administration Correspondence, Church Archives.

22. "Relief Society Home for Women and Girls," *Relief Society Bulletin* 1 (February 1914): 16–17.

23. Relief Society General Board Minutes, October 26, 1916; also May 15, 1913; June 19, 23, and 30, 1913; September 4, 11, and 25, 1913; October 3 and 16, 1913; December 4 and 19, 1913; February 26, 1914; January 25, 1917; February 8, 1917.

24. "Resolutions passed by the Officers and Members of the Relief Society of the Church of Jesus Christ of Latter-day Saints, October 7, 1912," broadsheet, Relief Society Headquarters Historical Files.

25. Joseph F. Smith, Anthon H. Lund, and Charles W. Penrose to "Sisters," September 22, 1916, circular letter. Reprinted as "A Call to the Women of the Church," *Relief Society Magazine* 4 (January 1917): 36.

26. Emmeline B. Wells et al. to "Dear Sister," and "Resolution on Dress," both January 1917; Amy Brown Lyman to "Dear Sister," March 30, 1917" (ca. 1917), all included in Women's Committee on Dancing and Dress

Report, Church Archives. The three members from each of the three women's general boards met during November 1916 and proposed to discourage extreme styles of dress and dancing and encourage strict chaperonage of young girls at parties. Social Advisory Committee Minutes, 1916–1922, November 1, 2, and 8, 1916, Church Archives.

27. Joseph F. Smith, "Dress and Social Practices," *Improvement Era* 20 (December 1916): 173.

28. "The Relief Society in Its Attitude to Dress and Social Customs," *Relief Society Magazine* 4 (February 1917): 101–3; "Social Work: Dress," *Relief Society Magazine* 4 (April 1917): 224. Punctuation emended.

29. Counselor Julina Lambson Smith echoed the sentiments of her prophet-husband in declaring that "if girls do not desire to take up the burden of motherhood they should not marry," and that "the lack of wealth is no excuse for limiting the family" ("General Conference of the Relief Society," *Relief Society Magazine* 4 [June 1917]: 313).

30. Social Advisory Committee Minutes, December 4, 11, and 18, 1916.

31. Address by Stephen L. Richards, "General Conference of Relief Society," *Relief Society Magazine* 6 (December 1919): 699.

32. Alexander, *Mormonism in Transition*, 153.

33. Relief Society General Board Minutes, January 16, 1913. A member of the Relief Society general board was to team up with a member of the Primary Association board, and these teams of two would visit conferences convened during May, June, and July.

34. Letter to Stake Relief Society Presidents, May 12, 1914, as recorded in Relief Society General Board Minutes, April 10, 1914, indicated that "some stakes might not receive visitors."

35. Relief Society Minutes 1892–1911, October 19 and November 2, 1906; December 6, 1907; December 7, 1911; January 18, 1912. A comprehensive discussion of the educational program of Relief Society is Carol Lois Clark, "The Effect of Secular Education upon Relief Society Curriculum" (Ph.D. dissertation).

36. "General Relief Society Conference," *Woman's Exponent* 39 (June 1910): 6.

37. For example, the Benson (Utah) Stake's 1912 outline contained individual authors' lessons on home and mother, on finance in the home, on moral, social, and civil laws and the benefits of the emerging juvenile courts, and on temple attendance and genealogy. *Outlines of the Mothers' Work of the Relief Society of the Benson Stake for the Year 1912* (n.p., n.d.), copy from library of Janath R. Cannon, Salt Lake City, Utah.

38. Autobiography of Alice Merrill Horne, ed. Zorah Horne Jeppson and children, typescript, chapter entitled "Relief Society Study Lessons," p. 1, courtesy Zorah Horne Jeppson, Salt Lake City, Utah.

39. Relief Society Minutes 1892–1911, October 19, 1911.

40. "Suggestions for the Relief Society," *Woman's Exponent* 40 (April 1912): 60.

41. Relief Society General Board Minutes, January 16, 1913.

42. Ibid., March 27, 1913. Italics added.

43. *Relief Society Guide*, 7.

44. Ibid., 8.

45. "Address to Be Read at Work and Business Meeting," *Relief Society Bulletin* 1 (January 1914): 1–3.

46. Relief Society General Board Minutes, December 10, 1913.

47. Ibid., June 4 and July 23, 1914.

48. "Volume Forty-one," *Woman's Exponent* 41 (September 1912): 4.

49. Madsen, "A Mormon Woman in Victorian America," 384.

50. "Volume Forty-one," *Woman's Exponent* 41 (September 1912): 4; Relief Society General Board Minutes, January 13, 1914. Details concerning the difficulty of the decision are presented by Madsen, "A Mormon Woman in Victorian America," 384–86.

51. "The Fortieth Volume," *Woman's Exponent* 40 (July 1911): 4. See also Sherilyn Cox Bennion, "The Woman's Exponent: Forty-two Years of Speaking for Women," *Utah Historical Quarterly* 44 (Summer 1976): 222–39. The use of the *Exponent* by modern scholars is evident in works cited in Carol Cornwall Madsen and David J. Whittaker, "History's Sequel: A Source Essay on Women in Mormon History," *Journal of Mormon History* 6 (1979): 123–45.

52. Relief Society General Board Minutes, September 24 and October 1 and 8, 1914. The first volume of the *Relief Society Magazine* was actually labeled volume 2, since the board had decided to label the twelve issues of the *Bulletin* as volume 1.

53. Relief Society General Board Minutes, October 1 and 2, 1915; January 6, 1916.

54. Joseph F. Smith, "Peace on Earth, Good Will to Men," *Relief Society Magazine* 2 (January 1915): 18.

55. "General Conference of the Relief Society," *Relief Society Magazine* 4 (June 1917): 305–30; "General Conference of Relief Society," Statistics, *Relief Society Magazine* 5 (June 1918): 310.

56. In this regard Relief Society played a role similar to that of numerous secular women's clubs and associations, sometimes disparagingly referred to as "middle-aged women's universities," which served "the cause of cultural enlightenment for masses of women" (Blair, *The Clubwoman as Feminist*, 58).

57. Eagar Ward Relief Society to Dear Sisters, n.d., typescript, Relief Society Headquarters Historical Files; "Notes from the Field," *Relief Society Magazine* 2 (October 1915): 453.

58. "Efficiency," *Relief Society Magazine* 3 (February 1916): 109; Janette A. Hyde, "Home Science Department," *Relief Society Magazine* 3 (March 1916): 158. Leah D. Widtsoe, who assisted Hyde, had graduated from the Pratt Institute in 1896.

59. Autobiography of Alice Merrill Horne, chapter entitled "Relief Society Study Lessons," pp. 6–7. Sister Horne compiled a textbook for use in connection with the art and architecture lessons, *Devotees and Their Shrines*.

60. Rose Ellen B. Valentine, "A Hidden Opportunity," *Relief Society Magazine* 18 January 1931): 37–41.

61. Susa Young Gates, ed. and comp., *Surname Book and Racial History*, published in 1917, proved to be a significant help to those engaged in genealogical study for religious or for secular reasons.

62. "October Conference," *Relief Society Bulletin* 1 (November 1914): 11; "The April Conference," *Relief Society Magazine* 3 (May 1916): 315.

63. "General Conference of the Relief Society," *Relief Society Magazine* 2 (December 1915): 529.

64. Relief Society General Board Minutes, November 11, 1915.

65. "The April Conference," *Relief Society Magazine* 3 (May 1916): 314.

66. "R. S. Reports," Bear Lake Stake, *Woman's Exponent* 36 (September 1907): 24.

67. [Susa Young Gates], "The Scope of the Relief Society," *Relief Society Magazine* 2 (April 1915): 198–99.

68. "General Relief Society Conference" and "Resolutions of Relief Society," *Woman's Exponent* 41 (November 1913): 78–79.

69. "Circular of Instructions to Officers and Members of the Relief Society," *Relief Society Magazine* 2 (March 1915): 111–41.

70. Relief Society General Board Minutes, May 14, 1914, and September 2, 1915.

71. Ibid., March 13 and 26 and July 30, 1914.

72. "Amy Brown Lyman," Amy Lyman Engar's personal recollections of her grandmother, oral presentation to Institute of Religion, University of Utah, February 26, 1987, in Engar's possession.

73. Relief Society General Board Minutes, March 31 and April 5, 1913.

74. Ibid., January 14, 1915.

75. The Church began exercising careful budgetary control in 1899, opening a new set of books in 1902, the same year the Presiding Bishopric initiated a new system for more accurate and effective ward accounts. See Alexander, *Mormonism in Transition*, 99, 106.

76. "Notes from the Field," *Relief Society Magazine* 4 (May 1917): 275; "General Conference of Relief Society," *Relief Society Magazine* 5 (June 1918): 309; "Relief Society Annual Report for 1920," *Relief Society Magazine* 8 (June 1921): 362. Figures rounded to nearest dollar.

77. The board decided that the staff at headquarters should receive some remuneration for their office work. Aging Emmeline B. Wells, who had previously received pay as secretary, continued to receive a salary. Salaries were also paid to Emma Empey, general treasurer; to the editor, the business manager, and the assistant editor of the magazine; and to Julina L. Smith, who worked full time in the temple clothing department. Relief Society General Board Minutes, January 25, 1917.

78. Relief Society General Board Minutes, December 10, 1914.

79. Joseph F. Smith, Anthon H. Lund, and Charles W. Penrose to "Dear Sister," undated, as reproduced in Relief Society General Board Minutes November 7, 1912. *History of Relief Society, 1842–1966*, 90, indicates that two stores in turn "established by Relief Society" had sold the clothing, but when the second "was being discontinued in 1912, an appeal was made to the General Board to take over this part of the business." See Alexander, *Mormonism in Transition*, 242.

80. "The Historical Office of the First Presidency: And the New Relief Society Department Headquarters," *Relief Society Magazine* 4 (November 1917): 608.

81. The eight-month nursing course, opened to women ages eighteen to forty-five, met five days a week in the Bishop's Building. It was taught, as previously, by Dr. Margaret C. Roberts, who taught an additional course in obstetrics for nurse-midwives. She proudly told the graduating class of 1915 that she had helped graduate a total of 320 Relief Society nurses, students from Arizona, Colorado, Canada, Idaho, Mexico, Nevada, Utah, and Wyoming. "Reasons for a Relief Society Nurse School," *Relief Society Magazine* 2 (July 1915): 318.

82. Relief Society General Board Minutes, May 15, July 25, August 18, and September 11, 1913. "Nursing in the Relief Society," *Relief Society Magazine* 2 (July 1915): 317; "Notes from the Field," *Relief Society Magazine* 3 (January 1916): 35; "The April Conference," *Relief Society Magazine* 3 (May 1916): 316–17.

83. *Latter-day Saints' Relief Society Class for Training Nurses Aid . . . ,"* pamphlet (n.p., 1920), Church Archives. This course was discontinued in 1924 due to objections of the National Hospital School Rating Bureau. See *History of Relief Society 1842–1966*, 87–88.

84. "Autobiography of Maydell Cazier Palmer, Lethbridge, Alberta, 1980," mimeograph, in the authors' files.

85. In 1920 the board considered sponsoring only one official conference each year at which each stake would be represented. The board deferred to Emmeline B. Wells's objection to such a change, though it was implemented in 1945. Relief Society General Board Minutes, September 2, 1920.

86. Gates and Parry, eds., *Relief Society Song Book,* . no. 127. Relief Society songbooks are discussed in *History of Relief Society, 1842–1966,* 100.

87. "Important Step in Relief Society Organization," *Woman's Exponent* 41 (November 1912): 20; Relief Society General Board Minutes, October 29, November 5, and December 17, 1914.

88. "Notes from the Field," *Relief Society Magazine* 3 (May 1916): 271.

89. Report by Mary J. Miller in Susa Young Gates, "Relief Society Work in the Missions," *Relief Society Magazine* 5 (July 1918): 380–81.

90. "Notes from the Field," *Relief Society Magazine* 4 (May 1917): 277–78.

91. "Notes from the Field," *Relief Society Magazine* 2 (November 1915): 505–6.

92. Amy Brown Lyman, "General Relief Society Conference," General Officers' Meetings, *Relief Society Magazine* 4 (December 1917): 667.

93. "Notes from the Field," *Relief Society Magazine* 5 (November 1918): 640.

94. "October Conference," *Relief Society Bulletin* 1 (November 1914): 11.

95. "General Relief Society Conference," General Officers' Meetings, *Relief Society Magazine* 4 (December 1917): 667.

96. "General Conference of the Relief Society," *Relief Society Magazine* 2 (December 1915): 527.

97. "Notes from the Field," *Relief Society Magazine* 8 (May 1921): 298.

98. "Notes from the Field," *Relief Society Magazine* 2 (October 1915): 453; "General Relief Society Conference," General Officers' Meetings, *Relief Society Magazine* 4 (December 1917): 667–68.

99. Relief Society Minutes 1892–1911, October 9, 1911; Relief Society General Board Minutes, August 15, 1912.

100. "Notes from the Field," *Relief Society Magazine* 4 (May 1917): 283.

101. Amy Brown Lyman, "General Conference of the Relief Society," *Relief Society Magazine* 4 (December 1917): 670; 5 (June 1918): 310. Figure rounded to nearest dollar.

102. Susa Young Gates, "Relief Society Work in the Missions," *Relief Society Magazine* 5 (July 1918): 379.

103. Ibid., 385.

104. Mary Smith Ellsworth, "Relief Society Reports: Milwaukee Relief Society," *Woman's Exponent* 39 (February 1911): 56.

105. "Notes from the Field," *Relief Society Magazine* 5 (March 1918): 156.

106. "Notes from the Field," *Relief Society Magazine* 8 (March 1921): 167.

107. "Notes from the Field," *Relief Society Magazine* 4 (April 1917): 218.

108. Relief Society Minutes 1892–1911, October 9, 1911; "Notes from the Field," *Relief Society Magazine* 2 (January 1915): 76.

109. "Correspondence," *Woman's Exponent* 40 (May 1912): 71.

110. "The April Conference," *Relief Society Magazine* 3 (May 1916): 314.

111. Relief Society General Board Minutes, October 7, 1912.

112. "Notes from the Field," *Relief Society Magazine* 3 (March 1916): 161.

113. Susa Young Gates, "Relief Society Work in the Missions," *Relief Society Magazine* 5 (July 1918): 380.

114. "Organized Charity," *Woman's Exponent* 40 (February 1912): 45–46. The request brought accountings of the Christmastime charity work of Granite, Ensign, Liberty, Pioneer, and Salt Lake stakes, including the number of families supplied with Christmas dinner and the money and provisions distributed by Relief Society.

115. Relief Society General Board Minutes, October 7, 1913.

116. Norena B. Robbins to Mrs. Amy Brown Lyman, November 16, 1915, in Susa Young Gates, research notes for Relief Society history, Susa Young Gates Papers.

117. "Notes from the Field," *Relief Society Magazine* 3 (July 1916): 406.

118. Amy Brown Lyman, "General Conference of the Relief Society," *Relief Society Magazine* 5 (June 1918): 309–10.

119. Relief Society General Board Minutes, November 5, 1914.

120. "Notes from the Field," *Relief Society Magazine* 2 (November 1915): 505.

121. Between 1911 and the outbreak of the war in 1914, the number of branches of the Relief Society in the Swiss-German Mission increased from two to seventeen. "General Conference of Relief Society," *Relief Society Magazine* 4 (June 1917): 309–10. "Notes from the Field," *Relief Society Magazine* 4 (March 1917): 154–55; "General Conference of Relief Society," *Relief Society Magazine* 4 (June 1917): 310.

122. Susa Young Gates, "Relief Society Work in the Missions," *Relief Society Magazine* 5 (July 1918): 366–67; "Notes from the Field," *Relief Society Magazine* 4 (March 1917): 154.

123. "Epistle to the Relief Society Concerning These War Times," *Relief Society Magazine* 4 (July 1917): 364.

124. As quoted in Noble Warrum, *Utah in the World War*, 84.

125. "Epistle to the Relief Society," *Relief Society Magazine* 4 (July 1917): 365.

126. Warrum, *Utah in the World War*, 133–34.

127. "Are You Conserving Yourself?" *Relief Society Magazine* 4 (October 1917): 580. Punctuation modified. Similarly Amy Brown Lyman urged women to watch out for "three signals of overwork—worry, nagging, and bossing." "General Conference of the Relief Society," *Relief Society Magazine* 4 (December 1917): 673.

128. Amy Brown Lyman, "General Conference of the Relief Society," *Relief Society Magazine* 5 (June 1918): 312.

129. "Notes from the Field," *Relief Society Magazine* 5 (January 1918): 27.

130. Alpine Ward, Alpine Stake, Relief Society Minutes, October 25, 1917, microfilm, Church Archives.

131. "Patriotic Department: Red Cross," *Relief Society Magazine* 5 (June 1918): 346–50.

132. Relief Society General Board Minutes, May 31, 1917.

133. Emmeline B. Wells et al. to Stake Presidents of the Relief Society, *Relief Society Magazine* 4 (September 1917): 510–11.

134. "History of Portland Central R. Society," microfilm of holograph, Church Archives.

135. "Notes from the Field," *Relief Society Magazine* 4 (September 1917): 512.

136. "Notes from the Field," *Relief Society Magazine* 3 (March 1916): 160.

137. "Notes from the Field," *Relief Society Magazine* 2 (January 1915): 76.

138. Susa Young Gates, "Relief Society Work in the Missions," *Relief Society Magazine* 5 (July 1918): 386.

139. Ibid., 381.

140. "The New Year Relief Society Prayer," *Relief Society Magazine* 5 (January 1918): 45.

141. Emmeline B. Wells, "The Grain Question," *Relief Society Bulletin* 1 (September 1914): 1.

142. Emmeline B. Wells, "The Mission of Saving Grain," *Relief Society Magazine* 2 (February 1915): 49. See also Emmeline B. Wells, "Sisters Be in Earnest," *Woman's Exponent* 15 (October 1876): 76.

143. Relief Society General Board Minutes, October 9, 1911.

144. Emmeline B. Wells and Olive D. Christensen to President of Relief Society, November 20, 1911, Relief Society Circular Letters, 1914–1922, Church Archives.

145. Relief Society General Board Minutes, February 4, 1915.

146. *Relief Society Bulletin* 1 (October 1914): 2.

147. Relief Society Wheat Letters, Susa Young Gates Papers; "Church Wheat to Be Turned Over to Government," *Deseret News*, May 20, 1918; Embry, "Relief Society Grain Storage Program," 52. Ibid., 55, discusses the varying quality of the wheat.

148. Box Elder Stake Relief Society Minutes 1918–1919, 25, Church Archives; Embry, "Relief Society Grain Storage Program," 53.

149. First Presidency and Presiding Bishopric to Stake Presidents, August

26, 1918; John Wells to "Brother," no date, Relief Society Wheat Letters, Susa Young Gates Papers.

150. Emmeline B. Wells, Clarissa S. Williams, Julina L. Smith to "Sister," October 15, 1918, Relief Society Executive Files, 1911–1959; "Relief Society Funds" ca. 1919, Relief Society Circular Letters, Church Archives.

151. Relief Society General Board Minutes, May 23, 1918.

152. Ibid.

153. Presiding Bishopric to "Brethren," June 29, 1918, Relief Society Wheat Letters, Susa Young Gates Papers.

154. Relief Society General Board Minutes, July 11, 1918. A published account of government officials' response is in Milton H. Welling, "Relief Society Wheat," speech, June 7, 1918, broadsheet, Government Printing Office, Church Archives.

155. "Official Roundtable," *Relief Society Magazine* 6 (November 1919): 656.

156. D&C 121:41–42.

157. Relief Society Minutes 1892–1911, September 7, 1911.

158. See Amy Brown Lyman, "Social Service Work in the Relief Society, 1917–1928," typescript, Church Archives; also in Relief Society General Board Minutes, April 1928. Loretta L. Hefner, "This Decade Was Different: Relief Society's Social Services Department, 1919–1929," *Dialogue* 15 (August 1982): 64–73.

159. Relief Society General Board Minutes, October 23, 1919.

160. Lena Andreason, [History of] Relief Society Vineyard Ward, Orem South Stake, Church Archives.

161. Susa Young Gates to the Presidency and Board of the Relief Society, November 4, 1919, typescript, Susa Young Gates Papers. The disagreement among board members is discussed in Janath R. Cannon and Jill Mulvay Derr, "Resolving Differences/Achieving Unity: Lessons from the History of Relief Society," in Stovall and Madsen, eds., *As Women of Faith: Talks Selected from the BYU Women's Conferences,* 126–32.

162. Relief Society Minutes 1892–1911, October 8, 1910; Relief Society General Board Minutes, October 26, 1916.

163. Understanding that some women had affiliated with Lodges and Hives in order to receive insurance benefits, the general board decided in 1914 to work in connection with Beneficial Life Insurance Company to offer its members life and burial insurance. By carrying such policies, the board also procured for itself a small income. *Relief Society Bulletin* 1 (March 1914): 13–15; (June 1914): 1–4. Madsen provides some discussion of the relationship with Utah State Agricultural College in "A Mormon Woman in Victorian America," 393.

164. Relief Society General Board Minutes, May 21, 1915.

165. Ibid., April 10 and 17 and September 4, 1913.

166. "Joseph F. Smith, Anthon H. Lund, and Charles W. Penrose to Pres. E. B. Wells and Counselors of the Relief Society," February 6, 1914, as reproduced in Relief Society General Board Minutes, February 13, 1914.

167. Address by Joseph F. Smith, Relief Society 72nd Anniversary, Relief Society General Board Minutes, March 17, 1914.

168. Relief Society General Board Minutes, August 19, 1920.

169. Ibid., October 21, 1920.

170. Ibid., April 2, 1915.

171. "R.S. Reports: Alberta Stake," *Woman's Exponent* 39 (January 1911): 48.

172. Relief Society General Board Minutes, October 7, 1913.

173. Joseph F. Smith, Anthon H. Lund, and Charles W. Penrose, "To the Presidents of Stakes and Bishops of Wards, 3 October 1914," First Presidency Circular Letters, 1899–1990, Church Archives.

174. General President of the Relief Society, "Answers to Questions," mimeograph, and "Dear Sister," typescript, ca. 1903, Relief Society Headquarters Historical Files.

175. Smith, Lund, and Penrose, "To the Presidents of Stakes and Bishops of Wards, 3 October 1913."

176. Joseph Fielding Smith to General Relief Society Presidency, July 19, 1946, in Clark, ed., *Messages of the First Presidency* 4:314.

177. Louise Y. Robison to Bishop Wm. Albert McClellan, March 31, 1936, Relief Society Headquarters Historical Files.

178. The announcement of the First Presidency and Council of the Twelve decision "that all special circles would hereafter be discontinued" is found in James E. Talmage Prayer Circle Minutes, 1912–1929, March 29, 1929, as cited in D. Michael Quinn, "Latter-day Saint Prayer Circles," *BYU Studies* 19 (Fall 1978): 99–100.

179. Alexander, *Mormonism in Transition,* 296. An excellent discussion of the changing emphasis is found on pages 290–98.

180. Susa Young Gates, "Our Testimony Meetings," *Relief Society Mgazine* 5 (June 1918): 359–60.

181. For a more complete tracing of women's use of spiritual gifts and a different interpretation of changes over time, see Linda King Newell, "Gifts of the Spirit: Women's Share," in Beecher and Anderson, *Sisters in Spirit,* 111–50.

182. Susa Young Gates to Mrs. A. W. McCune, October 18, 1919, Susa Young Gates Papers.

183. Nauvoo Minutes, March 17, 1842.

184. Relief Society General Board Minutes, April 2, 1921.

185. Emmeline B. Wells, "The Age We Live In," address read February 20, 1902, at the National Council of Women, Washington, D.C., *Woman's Exponent* 30 (April 1902): 89.

CHAPTER 7: "RELIEF" BECOMES "SOCIAL SERVICES," 1921–1928

1. Amy Brown Lyman, "General Conference of Relief Society," *Relief Society Magazine* 8 (December 1921): 693.

2. Emily M. Carlisle, "Cottonwood Stake Maternity Hospital," *Relief Society Magazine* 18 (July 1931): 415–16.

3. In 1951 Relief Society relinquished its responsibility for the Cottonwood Maternity Hospital to the LDS Hospital. Unlike the pioneer Deseret Hospital, however, the Cottonwood facility continued to flourish after it left the nurturing arms of Relief Society. The hospital continued its service in a

new location until the Church divested itself of its hospitals in 1974 to a non-church corporation, Intermountain Health Care. When the Cottonwood Hospital Medical Center established a Center for Women's Health in 1984, it was proudly advertised as the descendant of the original Cottonwood Maternity Hospital, and pictures of Amanda Bagley and her counselors Mary Cornwall and Rena Wheeler were displayed in the foyer. *The Cottonwood Health Care Foundation*, 1. See also Relief Society General Board Minutes, August 29, 1951.

4. Jill Mulvay Derr and Susan Oman, "These Three Women," *Ensign* 8 (February 1978): 67. This article places the incident too late, since Clarissa Williams was sixty-two years old when she was called as president in 1921 and her youngest son, Lyman, born in 1899, was then twenty-two years old.

5. A detailed treatment of the Sheppard-Towner Act is Loretta L. Hefner, "The National Women's Relief Society and the U.S. Sheppard-Towner Act," *Utah Historical Quarterly* 50 (Summer 1982): 255–67. An explanation of Relief Society's support of the act is in *Handbook of the Relief Society*, 1931, 62–64.

6. Relief Society General Board Minutes, April 4, 1922.

7. Amy Brown Lyman, "Conference Minutes," *Relief Society Magazine* 10 (December 1923): 623, 607. That Sister Williams received support from the Presiding Bishopric concerning the society's exclusive use of its funds is evident in the instructions given to priesthood leaders at general conference in April 1925 "that the funds in the Relief Society treasury had been collected for the work of the organization, and that the stake presidency and bishops should not call upon them to take funds from their treasury for general stake and ward purposes" (Relief Society General Board Minutes, April 22, 1925). See also *Handbook of Instructions for Bishops*, no. 14, 1928, p. 37.

8. Journal History of the Church, December 20, 1924.

9. Relief Society General Board Minutes, April 1924.

10. Amy Brown Lyman, "General Conference of Relief Society," *Relief Society Magazine* 8 (December 1921): 707. Sister Smith described conditions in England at this time: strikes, unemployment, and fuel shortages were widespread; Americans, particularly Mormon missionaries, were unwelcome; churches were almost empty, as "people seem to have really deserted the Lord." Conditions were even worse on the Continent, where World War I had caused greater devastation.

11. "Notes from the Field," *Relief Society Magazine* 12 (September 1925): 490–91.

12. [Amy Brown Lyman,] "Social Service Work in the Relief Society, 1917–1928," typescript, 23, Church Archives. See also Clarissa S. Williams, "Special Instructions," in "Relief Society Conference," *Relief Society Magazine* 14 (June 1927): 275.

13. Relief Society General Board Minutes, April 1, 1927.

14. The general board reported with satisfaction that these businesses "felt that the Relief Society was so well organized and was doing such good work that it was more able to give proper assistance to those in need than any other agency." Relief Society General Board Minutes, July 28, 1921.

15. Amy Brown Lyman, *National Woman's Relief Society . . . : Historical Sketch, 1842–1931*, 48.

16. Relief Society Annual Reports, 1921, Church Archives.

17. *Relief Society Magazine* 8 (May 1921): 302; 12 (April 1925): 203.

18. Relief Society General Board Minutes, June 15, 1921.

19. Ibid., May 10, 1922; May 17, 1922.

20. Lauritz G. Petersen, Office of the Church Historian, to Elder Ezra Taft Benson, September 9, 1966, 2, concerning a brief history of the Palestine-Syrian Mission. Photocopy in authors' possession. Rao Humphreys Lindsay, "A History of the Missionary Activities of the Church of Jesus Christ of Latter-day Saints in the Near East, 1884–1929" (master's thesis), 161. See also "Notes from the Field," *Relief Society Magazine* 10 (July 1923): 357.

21. Amy Brown Lyman, *In Retrospect,* 64. Lyman added, possibly with some personal pride, that the work continued to be "under the direction and supervision of the general secretary, who for sixteen years (1918–1934) directed the work." For a firsthand report, see [Lyman,] "Social Service Work."

22. See Bruce D. Blumell, "Welfare Before Welfare: Twentieth Century LDS Church Charity Before the Great Depression," *Journal of Mormon History* 6 (1979): 98–99, which summarizes some of Lyman's detailed history.

23. [Lyman,] "Social Service Work," 2.

24. Cora Kasius, "The Relief Society Social Service Institute," *Relief Society Magazine* 12 (July 1925): 345–49.

25. Relief Society General Board Minutes, January 21, 1925. [Lyman,] "Social Service Work," includes a detailed history of locations, topics, and participants in the Relief Society social service institutes, 1919–1928, 29ff.

26. [Lyman,] "Social Service Work," 4–5.

27. *History of Relief Society 1842–1966,* 94.

28. A distinction was later made between the "untrained" ward social service aides and stake aides who had been trained in Relief Society institutes. The real problem was their lack of a recognized place in the organizational structure. The aides were totally dependent on the Relief Society president's perception of their usefulness, which only time and need could establish. Relief Society General Board Minutes, September 2, 1925. Presiding Bishop Sylvester Q. Cannon praised the institutes and the aides in October 1925 in his address to the Relief Society conference, *Relief Society Magazine* 12 (December 1915): 646–49. Specific duties for aides were outlined in 1930.

29. Lyman, *In Retrospect,* 66; Relief Society General Board Minutes, April 4, 1922.

30. This action followed a fund-raising drive by the Home Finding Association of Utah, to which the Presiding Bishopric responded that "the Church is able to take care of its own children and child-placing. The brethren feel that the duty of child-placing in the Church should be done by the Relief Society." The Relief Society had previously contributed to such drives. Relief Society General Board Minutes, June 22, 1921. Early plans called for such an agency to be affiliated with a proposed maternity home under the direction of the Relief Society general board. Ibid., July 28, 1921.

31. Relief Society General Board Minutes, October 14, 1925.

32. Although the society supported the Community Chest, the central agency for private charities after 1926, it received no money from that organization.

33. "History of Gooding Ward Relief Society Presidents, 1917 to 1971, followed by Gooding Ward History by May G. Nielson," typescript, 1, 10, Church Archives.

34. Ibid., 1, 9, 10.

35. Ibid., 3.

36. *Relief Society Magazine* 8 (June 1921): 347.

37. J. S. May, "Relief Society Day in Far-Away Tonga," Journal History of the Church, July 16, 1921.

38. *Relief Society Magazine* 12 (June 1925): 313; 12 (October 1925): 546.

39. Relief Society General Board Minutes, January 26, 1927.

40. *Relief Society Magazine* 15 (December 1928): 667.

41. *History of the Relief Society 1842–1966*, 81.

42. First Presidency to Chairman of the Committee on Priesthood Outlines and Courses of Study and General Superintendencies and Presidencies of Auxiliary Associations, October 5, 1922; recorded in Relief Society General Board Minutes, December 13, 1922.

43. "The New Circular Issued by the Presiding Bishopric," *Relief Society Magazine* 8 (October 1921): 577–78.

44. [Lyman,] "Social Service Work," 15.

45. Ibid.

46. "The New Circular Issued by the Presiding Bishopric," 578.

47. History of the Vernal Second Ward Relief Society, Church Archives.

48. Dewsnup and Larson, *Relief Society Memories — A History of Relief Society in St. George Stake*, 77–78, 99–101.

49. Anderson, Shawcroft, and Compton, *The Mormons, 100 Years in the San Luis Valley of Colorado*, 129.

50. "The New Circular Issued by the Presiding Bishopric," 578.

51. Ibid., 579, 576.

52. Relief Society General Board Minutes, May 9, 1923. Similarly, when the three stake Relief Societies in Ogden turned over $3,000 of their "charity money" to help build the Ogden gymnasium, "upon a request from the Priesthood," President Williams took the matter to the Presiding Bishop, who disapproved. Relief Society General Board Minutes, December 21, 1921.

53. Jensen, *Relief Society Memories of Rexburg*, 12.

54. "Notes from the Field," *Relief Society Magazine* 12 (September 1925): 492.

55. "Guide Lessons for January," *Relief Society Magazine* 15 (November 1928): 616.

56. Clark, "Relief Society Curriculum," 111.

57. "Teachers' Training Course," *Relief Society Magazine* 6 (July 1919): 426.

58. *Relief Society Magazine* 8 (April 1921): 249.

59. A new class began twice yearly on February 15 and August 15.

60. Relief Society General Board Minutes, May 17, 1922. The story of the establishment of the home that eventually became the Primary Children's Hospital is found in Madsen and Oman, *Sisters and Little Saints*, 67–71.

61. Pohlman, *[In Memoriam] Amy Brown Lyman, 1872–1959*, 13.

62. Clarissa Williams to Amy Brown Lyman, August 1928, Amy Brown Lyman Papers.

63. Relief Society General Board Minutes, October 4, 1928.

64. Report by Utah State Board of Health, *Handbook of the Relief Society,* 1931, 64.

CHAPTER 8: DARK DAYS—THE GREAT DEPRESSION, 1928–1940

1. Jill Mulvay Derr and Susan Oman, "These Three Women," *Ensign* 8 (February 1978): 68.

2. Belle S. Spafford, Oral History, 40.

3. Adelia Busch, "First Bishop's Storehouse, Ogden, Utah," October 1936, 15, bound typescript in Relief Society Headquarters Library, Salt Lake City, Utah.

4. Louise Y. Robison, address given at Sunset Ward, San Francisco Stake, November 1944, 1, in Gladys Robison Winter Collection, Church Archives.

5. "The Children's Vacation Hours," *Relief Society Magazine* 16 (August 1929): 417.

6. Pruette, *Women Workers through the Depression,* 5.

7. John F. Bluth and Wayne K. Hinton, "The Great Depression," in Poll et al., *Utah's History,* 482–88.

8. John Hart, "1936 'Security Plan' Built on Experience of Previous Century," *Church News,* April 6, 1986, 7.

9. Leuchtenburg, *The Life History of the United States, Vol. 11: 1933–1945,* 8.

10. Poulsen, *Life of Emily Almira Cozzens Rich,* 68.

11. Almira Cozzens Rich, Journals, March 7, 1932, Weber State University Library, Ogden, Utah.

12. Relief Society General Board Minutes, July 21 and October 8, 1930.

13. Amy Brown Lyman, "Relief Society Conference," *Relief Society Magazine* 19 (May 1932): 283. This comment accompanied Sister Lyman's regrets that "in many instances the workers have not been used" after they returned home from the training institute, "probably because the Relief Society has not understood exactly the training that the workers have had."

14. See Jill Mulvay Derr, "Changing Relief Society Charity to Make Way for Welfare, 1930–1944," in Bitton and Beecher, *New Views of Mormon History,* 247.

15. Relief Society General Board Minutes, September 14, 1932.

16. See Loretta L. Hefner, "This Decade Was Different: Relief Society's Social Services Department, 1919–1929," *Dialogue: A Journal of Mormon Thought* 15 (Autumn 1982): 64–73.

17. Lewis, Oral History, 3, 6.

18. Annie D. Palmer, "The Social Worker in the Unemployment Emergency," *Relief Society Magazine* 19 (January 1932): 17.

19. Pohlman, Oral History, 9.

20. *Relief Society Magazine* 19 (November 1932): 648; 18 (January 1931): 8.

21. Maureen Ursenbach Beecher and Kathryn L. MacKay, "Women in 20th Century Utah," in Poll et al., *Utah's History*, 580.

22. William H. Chafe in Friedman and Shade, *Our American Sisters*, 386–87.

23. Rich, Journals, January 6, 1934. "Have spent most of the day soliciting food for cooking school (obtained 78 cans of Morning Milk from a Salt Lake Firm, also 48 cans of tomato Jinco here & 10# of butter from Mr. Robinson for our classes tomorrow.)"

24. Louise Y. Robison, "Official Instructions," *Relief Society Magazine* 19 (November 1932): 652. She quoted from a note one commissioner had written to a president: "We would like you to meet with us all the time, we know your help."

25. The department served as District 7 of the Salt Lake County Department of Public Welfare during 1933–34. See Derr, "Changing Relief Society Charity," 252, 255.

26. Relief Society General Board Minutes, October 28, 1936.

27. *Relief Society Magazine* 23 (April 1936): 266.

28. Amy Brown Lyman, "R. S. Conference," *Relief Society Magazine* 21 (November 1934): 685.

29. *Relief Society Magazine* 22 (May 1935): 272.

30. *My Kingdom Shall Roll Forth*, 99.

31. Heber J. Grant, in Conference Report, October 1936, 3.

32. Relief Society General Board Minutes, April 15, 1936.

33. "Bulletin Describing Relationship of Relief Society Organization to Women's Activities throughout the Regions and Stakes in Connection with the Church Security Program," undated, Church Archives. The bulletin, which went out over the signatures of Melvin J. Ballard, chairman of the Church Security Program's General Committee, and President Louise Y. Robison, detailed the responsibilities of Relief Society officers in regional and stake committees.

34. Joseph L. Wirthlin, "Spirit of '37," *Relief Society Magazine* 25 (March 1938): 158.

35. Dewsnup and Larson, *Relief Society Memories*, 34.

36. However, Relief Society was mentioned first, instead of second, in J. Reuben Clark, Jr., *Suggestive Directions for Church Relief Activities*, pamphlet, 1933, 15, 17. In the precursor pamphlet, the society heads every list of helps to the bishop "in all his relief activities." President Clark's estimate of Relief Society's place in the relief structure reflected the common understanding in 1933. By 1936 a significant shift had taken place.

37. Heber J. Grant, J. Reuben Clark, Jr., and David O. McKay, "An Important Message from the First Presidency," Journal History of the Church, April 7, 1936; also quoted in *Improvement Era* 39 (May 1936): 305; and in Henry D. Taylor, *The Church Welfare Plan* (1984), bound typescript, 21, Church Library.

38. Spafford, Oral History, 14, 57, 58.

39. Dewsnup and Larson, *Relief Society Memories*, 28.

40. Ibid., 29, 30.

41. Juanita Brooks in ibid., 22.

42. "Notes from the Field," *Relief Society Magazine* 23 (December 1936): 775.

43. Harold B. Lee, "Place of the Relief Society in the Church Security Plan," *Relief Society Magazine* 24 (March 1937): 143.

44. George Stewart, Dilworth Walker, and E. Cecil McGavin, *Priesthood and Church Welfare*, 30.

45. Marion G. Romney, "The Church Welfare Program for 1942," *Relief Society Magazine* 28 (December 1941): 844.

46. "The bishop is the father of his ward; the Relief Society is the mother": Harold B. Lee, "The Relief Society in the Welfare Plan," *Relief Society Magazine* 26 (August 1939): 526.

47. Rehearsals for the pageant preempted the Relief Society general conference. The sisters had hoped to continue the practice begun in April 1929 of holding general Relief Society conference sessions in the Tabernacle. Instead the pageant forced them into the smaller Assembly Hall. Participants repeated their remarks fifteen minutes after they had spoken in the Assembly Hall to overflow crowds in the auditorium of the Bishop's Building. The divided meeting was a modest historic first and sign of growth.

48. *My Kingdom Shall Roll Forth*, 94.

49. "President Louise Y. Robison Speaks at General Conference," *Relief Society Magazine* 17 (January 1930): 28. This was "the first time in the history of the Church that the heads of these three important organizations affecting so vitally the work of women and children in the Church have been called on to speak in a general conference."

50. For an elegant example of Jubilee boxes, see "Box Elder Stakes (Utah) Place Chest in Civic Center for Display," *Relief Society Magazine* 57 (June 1970): 454.

51. Annie Wells Cannon, "Jubilee Boxes," *Relief Society Magazine* 17 (July 1930): 366–69.

52. Relief Society General Board Minutes, April 2, 1931. The Norway maple was selected as the official Relief Society tree after general board member Inez K. Allen's "rather extensive survey" showed this tree "to be best suited to this climate."

53. *Relief Society Magazine* 18 (April 1931): 368.

54. *Relief Society Magazine* 19 (June 1932): 375; Esther D. Stephens, "Relief Society Scores," *Relief Society Magazine* 25 (October 1938): 582. Six years later the stake added an identifying copper plaque, donated by the Utah Copper Company, set in a large granite boulder. One of the speakers at the installation ceremony was Stephen L. Winter, president of the San Francisco Stake and a son-in-law of Louise Y. Robison. He commented that "with the placing of this plaque on the Pacific Coast a chain of markers had now been placed by the Latter-day Saints from the Atlantic to the Pacific, a lasting monument to their part in the building of our great country."

55. *Relief Society Magazine*, 18 (July 1931): 461.

56. George Albert Smith, "To the Relief Society," *Relief Society Magazine* 19 (December 1932): 703.

57. The upper room of the store had sometimes been used as a meeting place by members of the Masonic Lodge of Nauvoo before their hall was

97. "Music Department," *Relief Society Magazine* 24 (November 1937): 704. In April 1938 "a massed chorus of Singing Mothers" from various stakes joined the Relief Society Singing Mothers of Salt Lake City to sing for the society's conference. For this occasion white blouses were to be uniform, and directions for making the approved style were included in the magazine.

98. "Notes to the Field," *Relief Society Magazine* 24 (March 1937): 170.

99. *Our Common Cause Civilization,* 240.

100. "The International Congress of Women," *Relief Society Magazine* 20 (September 1933): 525.

101. May Anderson, "Greetings on Wings of Song," *Relief Society Magazine* 20 (September 1933): 519–21.

102. Amy Brown Lyman, "World Parliament of Women," *Relief Society Magazine* 25 (September 1938): 577–78.

CHAPTER 9: SISTERHOOD AND SERVICE IN A WORLD AT WAR

1. Tragedy also disrupted Sister Lyman's home life. On November 12, 1943, her husband was excommunicated. She stood by him with quiet dignity and faith, and his membership was later restored.

2. Amy Brown Lyman, "The Development of Spirituality Through the Social Service Department," *Relief Society Magazine* 23 (November 1936): 700.

3. Lyman, *In Retrospect,* 160–61.

4. Relief Society General Board Minutes, December 27, 1939.

5. Ibid., January 17, 1940.

6. "Message," *Relief Society Magazine* 31 (January 1944): 1.

7. Gertrude Zippro to Pieter Lodder, May 31, 1940, photocopy typescript of English translation in authors' files.

8. In Quinn, *J. Reuben Clark: The Church Years,* 203.

9. Amy Brown Lyman, Marcia Knowlton Howells, and Donna Durrant Sorensen, "New Year's Thoughts," *Relief Society Magazine* 27 (January 1940): 1.

10. Julia A. F. Lund, "Annual Report," *Relief Society Magazine* 26 (May 1939): 33; Margaret C. Pickering, "Annual Report—1946," *Relief Society Magazine* 34 (September 1947): 612–13.

11. The lone dissenting vote in the U.S. Congress was cast by a woman—Jeannette Rankin, who had also voted against the 1917 resolution for war with Germany during her earlier term as the first United States congresswoman. See Jensen, *The Revolt of American Women,* 62.

12. *The World Book Encyclopedia,* 1985, 21:408.

13. Leona Fetzer Wintch to Janath R. Cannon, February 8, 1983, in authors' files.

14. Spencer W. Kimball, "The Peace Which Passeth Understanding," *Church News,* June 10, 1944, 13; Kimball and Kimball, *Spencer W. Kimball,* 218.

15. "Notes to the Field," *Relief Society Magazine* 28 (August 1941): 542–43.

16. "Care of Children in Wartime," *Relief Society Magazine* 30 (May 1943): 332.

17. Lyman, *In Retrospect,* 149–50.

18. Vera White Pohlman, "Annual Report–1942" *Relief Society Magazine* 30 (June-July 1943): 415.

19. Ibid., 414; Vera White Pohlman, "Relief Society Celebrates Its Centennial," *Relief Society Magazine* 29 (April 1942): 230. The twenty-page article thoroughly describes the multifaceted celebration, 225–44.

20. Vera W. Pohlman, Oral History, 15.

21. "The Relief Society Centennial Radio Broadcast," *Relief Society Magazine* 29 (April 1942): 245–51.

22. Pohlman, "Annual Report–1942, 414. An official bulletin of August 20, 1941, which detailed centennial plans for 1942, described the symbolism of tree planting: "Not only will these trees add to the beauty of Church grounds, wherever planted, but they will be a living monument to Relief Society throughout the years. A majestic tree slowly but surely growing with its roots firmly planted in the earth and its branches ever reaching heavenward is typical of our great organization and its century of service" (*Relief Society Magazine* 29 [April 1942]: 226). Relief Society sisters planted many varieties of trees to honor the centennial – blue spruce in Utah, magnolias in the South, oak trees in England, the breadfruit tree in Hawaii, a native maple at the Hill Cumorah. The tree on Temple Square was removed, along with the greenhouse, during a later remodeling of the north gate area.

23. "Notes from the Field," *Relief Society Magazine* 30 (June-July 1943): 407.

24. Pohlman, "Relief Society Celebrates Its Centennial," 235, 237–38. The cake called for an impromptu reception, to which General Authorities, other auxiliary leaders, and general board members, past and present, were quickly invited. The general boards of the YWMIA and Primary Association brought a gift of blue and gold flowers arranged in a copper bowl; gleaming in the water were a hundred silver dollars, a donation to the campanile fund.

25. Ibid., 230.

26. Ibid.

27. The history was prepared with the help of Amy Brown Lyman and others by a committee headed by Belle S. Spafford and Marianne C. Sharp, and was published by the general board.

28. For this publication a photostatic copy of Eliza R. Snow's sketch was procured from the Bancroft Library of the University of California at Berkeley.

29. "Notes from the Field," *Relief Society Magazine* 31 (November 1944): 650.

30. Ibid., 29 (May 1942): 347.

31. Relief Society General Board Minutes, April 19, 1944.

32. Ibid., May 24, 1944.

33. Ibid., June 7, 1944.

34. Ibid., February 28, 1945.

35. Joseph L. Wirthlin, "Relief Society – An Aid to the Bishops," *Relief Society Magazine* 28 (June 1941): 417.

36. Relief Society General Board Minutes, November 29, 1944.

37. Vera White Pohlman, "Annual Report–1944," *Relief Society Magazine* 32 (August 1945): 482.

38. *Relief Society Magazine* 28 (May 1941): 311.

39. Cited in Edith Berghout, "The Effect of War upon the Employment of Women" (Master's thesis), 60. Berghout's graduate work was made possible by Relief Society's Amy Whipple Evans fellowship.

40. John A. Widtsoe to George Q. Morris, July 28, 1943; Church Union Board Executive Committee Minutes, August 3 and 5, 1943, Relief Society Union Board files, Church Archives.

41. At the October 1940 general conference, President J. Reuben Clark reported on the wheat storage program. "The Relief Society Wheat Fund will be used by the Relief Society to fill the elevators with wheat," he said. "Thus we return to its original form the donations of wheat, made by the people to the sisters, and by the Relief Society sisters themselves, beginning back in the time of Brigham Young" (Conference Report, October 1940, 10). Wheat was purchased by using one-fourth of the funds invested from the sale of wheat to the United States government in 1918. See Donna D. Sorensen, "Church Grain Elevator Dedication," *Relief Society Magazine* 27 (October 1940): 653–57.

42. "Notes from the Field," *Relief Society Magazine* 27 (September 1940): 633.

43. Ibid., 29 (March 1942): 199.

44. Ibid., 27 (April 1940): 279.

45. Ibid., 33 (May 1946): 347.

46. Ibid., 30 (October 1943): 629. See Vera White Pohlman, "Annual Report–1943," *Relief Society Magazine* 31 (July 1944): 370.

47. "Notes from the Field," *Relief Society Magazine* 30 (November 1943): 691.

48. "Notes to the Field," *Relief Society Magazine* 32 (March 1945): 161.

49. Annual Report, Relief Society General Board Minutes, December 1944.

50. Jensen, *Relief Society Memories of Rexburg*, 49.

51. Amy Brown Lyman, "Relief Society in Action Today," *Relief Society Magazine* 31 (March 1944): 138.

52. "Notes to the Field," *Relief Society Magazine* 30 (January 1943): 36.

53. Annual Report, Relief Society General Board Minutes, December 1944.

54. "Notes from the Field," *Relief Society Magazine* 27 (September 1940): 629.

55. Robert L. Simpson to Janath Cannon, in authors' files; and Robert L. Simpson, "Relief Society: Arm in Arm with the Priesthood," *Relief Society Magazine* 55 (March 1968): 165.

56. "Literature: Humor in Life and Literature," *Relief Society Magazine* 28 (July 1941): 496, 497.

57. "Lesson Preview—1941–42," *Relief Society Magazine* 28 (June 1941): 410.

58. *Relief Society Magazine* 30 (June-July 1943): 436–37.

59. Relief Society General Board Minutes, May 3, 1944.

60. *The Child*, monthly bulletin of the Children's Bureau, U.S. Department of Labor, May 1943, 165, quoted in *Relief Society Magazine* 30 (June-July 1943): 458.

61. "Memo of Suggestions," 1–6, Church Union Board Executive Committee Minutes, Church Archives.

62. Ibid., 6.

63. First Presidency to Elders Joseph Fielding Smith, John A. Widtsoe, Harold B. Lee, and Marion G. Romney, August 9, 1944, copy in Relief Society Executive Files, Church Archives.

64. A relaxation of the assignment to screen reference books (and possibly some differences of opinion among committee members) appears in a 1946 comment by John A. Widtsoe about Joseph Fielding Smith: "He feels, as I told the committee he generally feels, that we do not examine books of reference." John A. Widtsoe to Bishop Roy A. West regarding use by Relief Society of West's book *Family Eternal*, August 19, 1946; original letter in authors' files.

65. First Presidency to Elders Joseph Fielding Smith, John A. Widtsoe, Harold B. Lee, and Marion G. Romney, August 9, 1944, 1, 2, as found in Relief Society General Board Minutes, September 13, 1944.

66. *History of Relief Society 1842–1966*, 83–84.

67. "Notes from the Field," *Relief Society Magazine* 27 (September 1940): 632.

68. Ibid., 33 (February 1946): 123.

69. Conversation between Ruth Lippke and Janath R. Cannon, November 21, 1982, Albuquerque, New Mexico; notes in authors' files.

70. Ruth Lippke to Janath R. Cannon, March 2, 1983, in authors' files.

71. Babbel, *On Wings of Faith*, 111.

72. Gertrude Zippro to Pieter Lodder, May 31, 1940. News from Sister Zippro's letter was reported by the church mission secretary in "Notes from the Field," *Relief Society Magazine* 27 (September 1940): 626. It was the first news to church headquarters from the Netherlands following the invasion.

73. Gertrude Zippro to Pieter Lodder, May 31, 1940. In the May invasion, over seven hundred people were killed in Rotterdam and seventy-eight thousand people were left wounded and homeless; the entire center of the city was flattened. See Collins and Pierre, *Is Paris Burning?* The meetinghouse on the St. Jansstraat was completely destroyed.

74. "Life Story of John Zippro," unpaged ms. in authors' files.

75. Ibid.

76. Ibid.

77. Conversation between Corry Zippro DeMille, daughter, and Janath R. Cannon, December 1984, Salt Lake City.

78. Gertrude Zippro to Pieter Lodder, May 31. 1940.

79. "Notes from the Field," *Relief Society Magazine* 33 (February 1946): 118–19.

80. Ibid., 31 (April 1944): 237.

81. Ibid., 31 (October 1944): 591–92.

82. Leuchtenburg, *Life History of the United States* 11:153.

83. "Comfort Ye My People," *Relief Society Magazine* 32 (October 1945): 602.

CHAPTER 10: A COMPANION ORGANIZATION TO THE PRIESTHOOD

1. Belle S. Spafford, Oral History, 80, 238.

2. Spafford, *A Woman's Reach*, 111.

3. Spafford, Oral History, 11.

4. D&C 46:15.

5. Gertrude R. Garff, "The Value of Relief Society Membership," *Relief Society Magazine* 34 (March 1947): 153.

6. Between 1940 and 1945 the percentage of women in the workforce had increased from 25 to 36 percent; between 1945 and 1947 it dropped from 36 to 28 percent. *The Good Housekeeping Women's Almanac*, 554.

7. Ramona W. Cannon, "Woman's Sphere," *Relief Society Magazine* 36 (May 1949): 309.

8. Sister Lyman had requested her release on September 12, 1944. Relief Society General Board Minutes, April 4, 1945.

9. Relief Society General Board Minutes, June 13, 1945.

10. The former name had been adopted following affiliation with the National Council of Women in 1891, and Relief Society incorporated under that title on October 10, 1892. See pp. 144–46 in the present work. On October 10, 1942, the fifty-year charter of the National Woman's Relief Society had expired.

11. Spafford, Oral History, 198. On January 9, 1946, in accordance with counsel from the First Presidency, Relief Society was also incorporated for one hundred years as the Relief Society General Board Association, thus enabling it to carry out its business and specialized social services in accordance with Utah state law. The Utah state charter was granted on January 12, 1946. *History of the Relief Society, 1842–1966*, 48; Minutes of the Relief Society General Board, January 9, 1946.

12. The 1946 Annual Report showed membership gradually increasing and 121 new societies organized in 38 missions and 42 organized in seven new stakes. Inspiring conventions had been held that year in many stakes. In addition, the general board, visiting every stake, had conducted two full-day conferences for Relief Societies, with local officers involved to develop leadership skills. Of the societies—now organized in every state of the United States—all but one stake and 17 missions were represented at Relief Society conference in October 1946.

13. Belle S. Spafford, "Plan for Financing a Relief Society Building," *Relief Society Magazine* 34 (December 1947): 797.

14. "Address to the Members of the Relief Society," *Relief Society Magazine* 32 (December 1945): 715.

15. Relief Society General Presidency to the First Presidency, August 6, 1945, and First Presidency reply; see Relief Society General Board Minutes, August 22, 1945.

16. "Relief Society Building News," *Relief Society Magazine* 35 (January 1948): 24.

17. Marianne Clark Sharp, Oral History, 56.

18. *Builders for Eternity*, pamphlet, 12, 13, See also Spafford, Oral History, 116.

19. Relief Society Minutes 1892–1911, October 3, 1896; Vera Mae Fuller, "The Symbol of a Dream," *Relief Society Magazine* 36 (February 1949): 88–89.

20. George Albert Smith, in Conference Report, October 1947, 6. Pres-

ident Smith called the attention of the White House to the Relief Society again the following year. At his suggestion a group of delegates from the society, headed by President Spafford, visited Mrs. Truman and presented her with a handmade lace tablecloth from the Mormon Handicraft Shop and a copy of *A Centenary of Relief Society*. A note accompanying the cloth concluded with "We hope you will enjoy using it, and that it will serve to remind you that rare handwork skills are being perpetuated by our Society." See Belle S. Spafford, "Relief Society Women Received at the White House," *Relief Society Magazine* 33 (November 1946): 723–28.

21. Conference Report, April 5, 1946, 176. See also Ramona W. Cannon, "Woman's Sphere," *Relief Society Magazine* 33 (April 1946): 249.

22. Relief Society General Board Minutes, November 28, 1945.

23. Counselor Marianne C. Sharp noted sadly that eight stakes had failed to store bedding or had disposed of it too hastily and so could not help. She hoped this experience would "teach the stakes to follow counsel." See Relief Society General Board Minutes, December 5, 1945.

24. "Notes from the Field," *Relief Society Magazine* 36 (January 1949): 41.

25. *History of the Relief Society 1842–1966*, 71.

26. "Notes from the Field," *Relief Society Magazine* 35 (February 1948): 121.

27. Ibid., 35 (August 1948): 546.

28. William G. Hartley, "War and Peace and Dutch Potatoes," *Ensign* 8 (July 1978): 23.

29. Georgia H. Weenig, in "Notes from the Field," *Relief Society Magazine* 34 (July 1947): 477.

30. Belle S. Spafford, Marianne C. Sharp, and Gertrude R. Garff, "The New Year," *Relief Society Magazine* 34 (January 1947): 3.

31. Harold T. Christensen, "Patterns of Prejudice and Persecution," *Relief Society Magazine* 32 (July 1945): 445, 446.

32. G. Homer Durham, "The Tasks of Modern Citizenship," *Relief Society Magazine* 36 (August 1949): 510.

33. Marion G. Romney, "The Joys of Welfare Service," *Relief Society Magazine* 34 (November 1947): 728. The other women's organizations were also part of the cooperative effort. Speaking of the ward sewing budget, Elder Romney told the Primary workers that although "the Relief Society president, being in a sense the mother of the ward, has the responsibility to get it done," Primary workers could also help with production — and so could the children. See Relief Society General Board Minutes, April 30, 1947.

34. Mark E. Petersen, "The Mission of the Relief Society," *Relief Society Magazine* 35 (March 1948): 149.

35. Lillie C. Adams, "Rag Rug Weaving in Emigration Stake, Salt Lake City," *Relief Society Magazine* 33 (July 1946): 457–59.

36. Harold B. Lee, "The Place of Relief Society in the Welfare Plan," *Relief Society Magazine* 33 (December 1946): 814. Emphasis added.

37. Relief Society General Board Minutes, April 9, 1947.

38. Individual societies made a special effort to recognize the pioneer centennial. The sisters of the Northern States Mission gave President George

Albert Smith a bronze statue of Joseph Smith kneeling in prayer, sculptured by Avard Fairbanks. The statue was an especially appropriate gift, said Relief Society president Elna Haymond, "since the Prophet was guided by inspiration to organize the Relief Society and thus set in motion the special work of Latter-day Saint women." She added, "We have tried hard to make prayer a part of all Relief Society work." "Notes from the Field," *Relief Society Magazine* 34 (July 1947): 475.

39. M[arianne] C. S[harp], "Editorial: The Family Hour," *Relief Society Magazine* 35 (September 1948): 594–95.

40. Bulletin issued November 20, 1950, in Relief Society General Board Minutes, January 31, 1951.

41. White, *In Search of History,* 369–70.

42. See "New Rules – Old Rules," *BYU Today* 36 (June 1982): 29.

43. Utahns could also boast that by 1961 Utah had the lowest infant death rate in the United States (20.3 per thousand live births), partially a credit to Relief Society's long emphasis on maternal and child health. Katherine B. Oettinger, chief of the Children's Bureau, in Ramona W. Cannon, "Woman's Sphere," *Relief Society Magazine* 50 (December 1963): 906.

44. The polio epidemics of 1948, 1949, and 1950 left 100,000 victims in the United States alone. Money from the March of Dimes paid for hospitalization, emergency nurse service, iron lungs, wheelchairs, crutches, and physical therapy. Relief Society vigorously supported the drive for donations with editorials in the *Relief Society Magazine* and announcements in meetings. After the discovery of the Salk vaccine in 1954, Relief Society continued its loyal support as the March of Dimes transferred its work to other crippling diseases and birth defects.

45. Belle S. Spafford, Marianne C. Sharp, and Louise W. Madsen, "New Year's Greetings," *Relief Society Magazine* 47 (January 1960): 1.

46. Relief Society General Board Minutes, April 26, 1950.

47. Of Sisters Needham and Okimota, who taught them from the Bible and Book of Mormon, the Japanese sisters wrote this touching tribute: "By teaching from two sisters who have always humble and faithful spirits in God, we are very glad to learn that by being good and noble, we can become the children of God." See Relief Society General Board Minutes, April 26, 1950.

48. Conversations with and documents in possession of Junko Shimizu, Salt Lake City, former member of Relief Society general board, English translation by Junko Shimizu, notes in authors' files. Hereafter cited as Shimizu Collection.

49. Allen and Leonard, *The Story of the Latter-day Saints,* 1976, 587.

50. The revised *Handbook of Instructions of the Relief Society of The Church of Jesus Christ of Latter-day Saints,* issued in 1949, shows the change that had come to "charity work" since the handbook of 1931. Under "Welfare Activities," the work was newly divided into "Compassionate Services," "Place of Relief Society in the Church Welfare Plan," and "Specialized Welfare Services." Compassionate service was formally defined as care of the sick, visits to the sick and homebound, and service at time of death – all to be recorded and reported by the sisters. Relief Society's place in the welfare plan was explained with quotes from the General Church Welfare Committee and an

address by Marion G. Romney, then assistant managing director of the committee. Both emphasized the companion role of the bishop and ward Relief Society president. See pp. 82–88.

51. Spafford, Oral History, 53.

52. Quoted in *Handbook of the Relief Society,* 1949, 87–88.

53. The local presidents' need in "dealing with individuals receiving help" led Marion G. Romney to suggest in a Relief Society conference address that "the social service department of the General Relief Society organization is bulging with rich information in this field." He advised local leaders: "Call upon the General Relief Society Presidency for it" ("Relief Society and the Church Welfare Program," *Relief Society Magazine* 38 [December 1951]: 813).

54. The development and expansion of Relief Society social services are thoroughly discussed by Mayola R. Miltenberger, *Fifty Years of Relief Society Social Services* (Salt Lake City: The Church of Jesus Christ of Latter-day Saints, 1987), a mimeograhed document of 305 pages. Sister Miltenberger directed the Arizona agency (1962–1969) and then the Utah agency (1969) until she was appointed by Sister Spafford as Relief Society general secretary-treasurer, a position she maintained under President Barbara Smith.

55. Delbert L. Stapley, "The Place of Relief Society in the Indian Program," *Relief Society Magazine* 39 (February 1952): 79–81.

56. "Notes from the Field," *Relief Society Magazine* 38 (January 1951): 49.

57. Ibid., 47 (January 1960): 45.

58. Dorothy H. Brewerton, "Cuna Indian Relief Society," Central American Mission, *Relief Society Magazine* 54 (December 1967): 932–33.

59. Spafford, Oral History, 220.

60. John Farr Larson, director of the Bureau of Services for Children in the Utah State Department of Public Welfare, wrote to Sister Spafford on April 16, 1954, suggesting the LDS Relief Society Social Service and Child Welfare Department as an appropriate agency for Indian student placement. He also met with President Stephen L. Richards of the First Presidency, Elder Spencer W. Kimball, and attorney T. Quentin Cannon to work out details of the "Boarding Care Program," as it was known at first. Further information is given in Clarence R. Bishop, "A History of the Indian Student Placement Program," (Master's thesis, University of Utah, 1967). Bishop was an active participant in and later director of the Indian student placement program.

61. "Needed . . . home nursing for civil defense," Program Guide [FCDA, 1955], 14, in authors' files.

62. Relief Society General Board Minutes, August 4, 1954.

63. Spafford, Oral History, 65.

64. B[elle] S. S[pafford], "Editorial: Strengthening Community Virtues," *Relief Society Magazine* 46 (January 1959): 33.

65. Belle S. Spafford, "Woman's Role as Homemaker," *Relief Society Magazine* 36 (November 1949): 725.

66. J. Reuben Clark, Jr., "The Prophet's Sailing Orders to Relief Society," *Relief Society Magazine* 36 (December 1949): 797.

67. Spafford, "Woman's Role as Homemaker," 724–25.

68. Ibid., 726.

69. Writing lessons to fit everybody was not easy. What did the United States Constitution mean to a sister in Korea? In his preface to the study of the Constitution, Albert R. Bowen attempted a justification: "Its influence and scope go far beyond the shores of our great and wonderful Nation. . . . What happens to the United States and her free institutions will determine the fate of men everywhere." See Albert R. Bowen, "The Constitution of the United States," *Relief Society Magazine* 42 (June 1955): 412.

70. Marianne Clark Sharp, "A Present Day Challenge," *Relief Society Magazine* 24 (January 1937): 7.

71. Sharp, Oral History, 62.

72. "Notes from the Field," *Relief Society Magazine* 35 (April 1948): 277.

73. "Aunt Susan Is the Mainstay of the Branch," *Church News*, October 4, 1980, 12.

74. Quoted in Tate, *LeGrand Richards, Beloved Apostle*, 220.

75. Description drawn from *History of the Relief Society, 1842–1966*, 131–32.

76. "Dedicatory Prayer of the Relief Society Building," *Relief Society Magazine* 43 (December 1956): 788. The quotation is from Ephesians 4:13.

77. Eva Willes Wangsgaard, "Letter to Viet Nam," *Relief Society Magazine* 53 (January 1966): 10.

78. Harold B. Lee, Conference Report, September–October 1961, 91. Members of three new age-group correlation committees – child, youth, and adult – were assigned to recommend curricula and other specifics of the overall plan. Some of the women who served on these committees were later called to the general presidencies of the auxiliaries they had helped to alter. Among them were Ruth H. Funk, Young Women president, 1973–1978; Hortense Child Smith, Young Women first counselor, 1973–1978; Ardeth G. Kapp, Young Women second counselor, 1973–1978, and president, 1984–1992; Elaine A. Cannon, Young Women president, 1978–1985; and Janath R. Cannon, Relief Society first counselor, 1974–1978.

79. See Allen and Leonard, *The Story of the Latter-day Saints*, 1976, 606.

80. Marie Cornwall, "Women and the Church: An Organizational Analysis," 1, typescript, in Relief Society Headquarters Files 1958–1984, Salt Lake City. Dr. Cornwall's paper analyzes the effect of correlation changes on the women's auxiliaries up to 1982. A summarizing statement on page 10 is particularly worth noting: "Scriptural mandates placed the responsibility for administering the programs of the church on the priesthood organization, not on the auxiliaries. But, it was never very clear exactly what the organizational implications would be of 'putting the priesthood at the center.' One thing can be said for certain, the intention, stated or unstated, was never to limit or weaken the role of women in the organization. Rather the intention was to structure the organization in such a way as to utilize priesthood authority and give greater emphasis to the work of the priesthood quorums."

81. Gordon B. Hinckley, "Personal Development through Relief Society," *Relief Society Magazine* 53 (March 1967): 165, 166.

82. Hulda P. Young, "1966 Annual Report," *Relief Society Magazine* 54 (June 1967): 451.

83. Shimizu Collection, in authors' files.

84. Letter of February 5, 1975, and summary of responses, copies in authors' files.

85. "News of the Church: Instructional Development Coordinator Named," *Ensign* 4 (March 1974): 74.

86. Relief Society General Board Minutes, March 3, 1965.

87. Elder Marion G. Romney of the Council of the Twelve was named chairman of the new department, and Elder Marvin J. Ashton, the general manager.

88. "Three Welfare Units Joined," *Church News*, April 7, 1973, 4.

89. "Principles of Welfare Service Emphasized by Church Leaders,' *Church News*, April 13, 1974, 17; Spencer W. Kimball address, *Conference Report*, April 1, 1978, 6.

90. Henry D. Taylor, "Relief Society in the Welfare Plan," *Relief Society Magazine* 56 (March 1969): 167.

91. Harold B. Lee, "Obligations of Membership in Relief Society," *Relief Society Magazine* 56 (January 1969): 12.

92. *1973–74 Relief Society Courses of Study,* 189–90.

93. M[arianne] C. S[harp], "The Joy of Volunteer Service," *Relief Society Magazine* 54 (January 1967): 35.

94. Relief Society General Board Minutes, April 24, 1968.

95. "From Near and Far," *Relief Society Magazine* 49 (May 1962): 314.

96. Relief Society General Board Minutes, February 16, 1966.

97. Spafford, Oral History, 89.

98. Spafford, *A Woman's Reach*, 97–98.

99. Relief Society General Board Minutes, September 1, 1954.

100. Belle S. Spafford, "Report on the National Council of Women," 2; Relief Society General Board Minutes, October 21, 1970.

101. Rose Mary Pedersen, "The Role of Women," *Deseret News*, November 5, 1968, A-7.

102. Spafford, Oral History, 135, 136.

103. For more on the Nauvoo bell, see Gertrude R. Lobrot, "Bell, Boat, and Cannons Trekked West Together," *Church News*, July 14, 1985, 5, 13.

104. Mary Grant Judd, "A Monument with a Message," *Relief Society Magazine* 29 (January 1942): 12. See also Belle S. Spafford, "Relief Society Centennial Memorial" address, cited in *History of Relief Society 1842–1966*, 138, 139. Vera W. Pohlman, Oral History, 17–18, indicated that Howard Barker located misplaced parts of the tower, facilitating its completion.

105. *1973–74 Relief Society Courses of Study,*, 282–83.

106. General board member Ellen N. Barnes was usually the director on these occasions. See Belle S. Spafford, "International Singing Mothers Concert Tour," *Relief Society Magazine* 48 (May 1961): 290–91.

107. Belle S. Spafford, "Report and Official Instructions," *Relief Society Magazine* 50 (November 1963): 821, 822.

108. "History of Gooding Ward Relief Society Presidents, 1917 to 1971, followed by Gooding Ward History by May G. Nelson," typescript, Church Archives.

109. First Presidency to Priesthood Leaders, June 10, 1970, in Relief Society General Board Minutes, August 5, 1970.

110. Belle S. Spafford to J. Alan Blodgett, Comptroller, February 25, 1971, as reproduced in Relief Society General Board Minutes, following February 24, 1971. The released assets did not include the wheat, which would be held "in trust" by Relief Society for another seven years. Some six thousand dollars in special trust funds also remained with Relief Society headquarters to be administered in accordance with the donors' wishes.

111. Relief Society General Board Minutes, January 27, 1971.

112. Spafford, Oral History, 34–35.

113. "Relief Society Magazine Receives Outstanding Award," *Relief Society Magazine* 51 (September 1964): 666. See also Mann, "A History of the *Relief Society Magazine* 1914–1970" (master's thesis), 106.

114. Sharp, Oral History, 58.

115. Conference Report, October 1961, 81.

116. The First Presidency to heads of organizations, April 24, 1970, in Relief Society General Board Minutes, May 13, 1970.

117. Relief Society General Board Minutes, May 13, 1970.

118. Joseph Fielding Smith, "The Old and the New Magazines," *Improvement Era* 73 (November 1970): 10–11.

119. Mabel Jones Gabbott, "Today's Family," *Ensign* 1 (January 1971): 91.

120. Document in possession of Janath R. Cannon, Salt Lake City.

121. Baldridge, *Grafting In,* 111–15.

122. See also M[arianne] C. S[harp], "The Worth of a Grandmother," *Relief Society Magazine* 54 (August 1967): 584–85.

123. Relief Society General Board Minutes, February 10, 1971. A new correlated reporting system that went into effect September 1, 1973, for all auxiliaries and quorums superseded all previous Relief Society report forms and discontinued the practice of sending reports from the stakes to the society headquarters. Hereafter, ward Relief Society secretaries were to mark attendance of women at Relief Society, sacrament, and Sunday school meetings for the ward correlated report.

124. "Relief Society Views Priesthood MIA Role," *Church News*, June 30, 1973, 5.

125. "Relief Society Serves Entire Womanhood," *Church News*, September 29, 1973, 14.

CHAPTER 11: STARS TO STEER BY

1. *Selected Addresses from the 1974 Relief Society General Conference,* 55.

2. "A Conversation with Sister Barbara B. Smith, Relief Society General President," *Ensign* 6 (March 1976): 11–12.

3. Quoted in "LDS Scene: Former Tabernacle Choir Director Honored," *Ensign* 5 (February 1975): 86.

4. JoAnn Jolley, "Splitting the Bamboo Curtain," *Ensign* 11 (September 1981): 76.

5. "LDS Church Extends Priesthood to All Worthy Male Members," *Deseret News*, June 9, 1978, A–1.

6. Helen Claire Sievers to Janath R. Cannon, June 16, 1978, in authors' files.

7. Elder Neal A. Maxwell, "The Church Can Be Universal with Priesthood Revelation of 1978," *Church News*, January 5, 1980, 20.

8. Relief Society's special lessons for Lamanite sisters foreshadowed two basic Church manuals for women, *The Latter-day Saint Woman, Part A* and *Part B,* published in 1979. These manuals, designed by the Instructional Development Department as a two-year course for convert women, contained lessons in gospel principles, women's church duties, homemaking, and personal and family development – all in a simple format.

9. Marvin K. Gardner, "Report of the Seminar for Regional Representatives," *Ensign* 8 (November 1978): 100.

10. Minutes of Coordinating Council Meetings, Correlation Department, January 28, 1976, Church Archives; "4 New Committees Formed," *Church News*, June 5, 1976, 3.

11. "News of the Church: Relief Society Conference Emphasizes Spirit of Compassion," *Ensign* 4 (January 1974): 133.

12. Thomas, *That Day in June,* 222. Profits from the sale of this compilation were donated to the Relief Society Monument to Women at Nauvoo.

13. Relief Society General Board Minutes, June 10, 1976.

14. Marilyn I. Tenney, Delta Utah Stake Relief Society president, to Barbara B. Smith, August 15, 1983, copy in authors' files.

15. Glen W. Swalberg as quoted in Gerry Avant, "River Turns to Monster: Readiness Lessens Disaster," *Church News*, July 3, 1983, 8.

16. "Report of Rape Protection Training in Relief Society Building, September through November 1979," and memos from Kevin Richardson to Ruth Walker during 1980, copies of typescripts in authors' files.

17. Ruth Walker to Barbara B. Smith, October 6, 1980, copy in authors' files.

18. *A Centenary of Relief Society, 1842–1942,* 73; Mayola R. Miltenberger, *A Decade of Relief Society 1974–1984* (Relief Society General Board, 1984), 3. The transfer was preceded by a sustaining vote of the women seated in the Tabernacle, representing the body of Relief Society. Earlier that year letters had been sent to the 169 stakes that still held Relief Society wheat deposit certificates as of July 1, 1957, together with consent forms that would release their claim on the wheat.

19. "The Fruit of Welfare Services Labors," *Ensign* 8 (November 1978): 77.

20. *Welfare Services Resource Handbook,* 41.

21. Barbara B. Smith, "The Relief Society Story," Legacy Lecture, March 16, 1983, Collected Talks, Vol. 1, 2c, "Anniversary"; Relief Society Headquarters Library, Salt Lake City, Utah.

22. See Relief Society General Board Minutes, June 10, 1976.

23. Rosalie Hill as quoted in Gerry Avant, "Quilts Bring Warmth, Bind Friendships," *Church News*, December 18, 1982, 6.

24. Ibid.

25. *Notes to the Field* 6 (June-October 1976).

26. Relief Society General Board Minutes, June 10, 1976.

27. "News of the Church: Individual and Family Self-reliance Featured in Leadership Session," *Ensign* 13 (May 1983): 84.

28. Vivien D. Okon, "The Visiting Teacher Who Made a Difference," *Church News*, May 15, 1983, 2.

29. Elena Lenz, ibid., April 24, 1982, 2.

30. Nancy M. Hoch, ibid., April 3, 1983, 2.

31. Hope Connell Vernon, ibid., June 12, 1982, 2.

32. Fidelia Obinna to Janath R. Cannon, October 6, 1980, copy in authors' files.

33. Miner and Kimball, *Camilla,* 175. In recognition of Sister Kimball's generous words and deeds in her Relief Society callings, the society donated $300,000 to the Brigham Young University in 1984 in support of the Camilla Eyring Kimball Chair of Home and Family Living.

34. Report of Relief Society General Conference 1975, 8, typescript in authors' files; hereafter cited as Relief Society Conference Report 1975. The next year all auxiliary general conferences were to be replaced by expanded regional meetings.

35. "Homemakers Get a Boost," *Fresno [California] Bee*, April 5, 1978, C-5.

36. "Illinois State Official Hails Achievements of Mormons," *Church News*, July 8, 1978, 3.

37. Bruce R. McConkie, "Our Sisters from the Beginning," address at the Monument to Women Dedication, June 29, 1978, typescript in Relief Society Headquarters Files.

38. Margaret McCay, Associated Press, quoted in a memorandum to Heber Wolsey from Charles Graves, dated July 14, 1978, in "Nauvoo Monument to Women," Scrapbook III, comp. Wanda W. Badger, p. 74, Relief Society Headquarters Historical Files.

39. Heather Nelson to Marian R. Boyer, typed copy in authors' files.

40. "News of the Church: Relief Society Building to Become Major Resource Center," *Ensign* 6 (March 1976): 77.

41. *1975–76 Relief Society Courses of Study,* 164.

42. *1977–78 Relief Society Teachers Supplement, Social Relations,* 1; Relief Society Discussion Leaders Material, Regional Meeting 1977, 3, Relief Society Headquarters Files.

43. Spencer W. Kimball, "The Foundations of Righteousness," *Ensign* 7 (November 1977): 5.

44. The amendment approved by the National Women's Party at the Seneca Falls (New York) convention in 1923 read: "*Men and Women* shall have equal rights throughout the United States and every place subject to its jurisdiction." Until 1970, Section Two read: "The Congress *and the States* shall have the power to enforce . . . the provisions of this article" (emphasis added). Thus two key objections to the later version were not present: (1) the term "men and women" clearly identified gender as the sole subject of the amendment, which the broader category of "sex" did not; (2) inclusion of the states in the enforcement clause avoided the states' rights issue.

45. See Lemons, *The Woman Citizen,* 191.

46. *Congressional Record*, 92d Cong., 2d sess., 1972, 118, pt. 2:1ff.

47. Barbara B. Smith, Oral History, 66–67.

48. Relief Society General Board Minutes, December 12, 1974.

49. Barbara B. Smith, "The Equal Rights Amendment," copy in authors' files.

50. Gerry Avant, "Equal Rights Amendment Is Opposed by R.S. President," *Church News*, December 21, 1974, 7.

51. Quoted in *The Church and the Proposed Equal Rights Amendment: A Moral Issue* (Salt Lake City: The Church of Jesus Christ of Latter-day Saints, 1980), 21, 23. The 23-page pamphlet was an insert in *Ensign* 10 (March 1980).

52. Relief Society General Board Minutes, January 23, 1975.

53. Information regarding Sonia Johnson's excommunition is from "Church Court Action Clarified," *Ensign* 10 (March 1980): 79–80. The circumstances preceding the appearance of Sisters Smith and Campbell on the Donahue show reveal the complex nature of the ERA controversy. Barbara Smith was first asked by the show's program director to appear opposite Sonia Johnson. She later explained her refusal: "It seemed as if Sonia Johnson was being made a media martyr, and I didn't want to contend with her on the air." See Janet Thomas, "Barbara B. Smith, Woman for the World," *This People*, Summer 1980, 13. Asked to recommend someone else, Sister Smith suggested Beverly Campbell. Donahue agreed and Beverly Campbell accepted, but after Sonia Johnson refused to appear on the show with Sister Campbell, the show aired with Sonia Johnson alone. During the show with Sonia Johnson, Phil Donahue wrongly commented that no Mormon woman would agree to appear. When the show was flooded with protests, a second invitation was made to Sister Smith, this time to appear with Beverly Campbell.

54. U.S. Public Law 94–167, Sec. 3, (a), (5).

55. Ellie Colton, "A Mormon Woman Looks at the ERA," *Washington Post*, November 21, 1977.

56. Letter from the General Presidency of Relief Society, prepared in 1977 in answer to inquiries about the Church's participation in the Utah IWY Conference, p. 1, copy in Church Archives. Hereafter cited as Relief Society Presidency: IWY. See also Smith, Oral History, 75.

57. Relief Society Presidency: IWY, 1, 2.

58. Rosemary Pederson, "Utah Women Plan for Their First Statewide Meeting," *Deseret News*, June 15, 1977, C-1; "How to Get Involved in the Issues at Women's Meeting," *Deseret News*, June 16, 1977, C-2.

59. Relief Society General Board Minutes, June 23, 1977.

60. Angelyn Nelson, "Relief Society Head Sensitive to Women," *Salt Lake Tribune*, August 14, 1977, W-1.

61. Smith, Oral History, 75.

62. Ibid., 71.

63. Ibid.

64. Jennie L. Hansen, "Women Defeat National Issues," *Valley View News*, Salt Lake City, June 30, 1977, 1.

65. See, for example, Aileen H. Clyde, "Other Voices," *Exponent II* 4 (Fall 1977): 5.

66. *Deseret News*, June 30, 1977.

67. Janice Smith, "Relief Society: Mukluks in Alaska, Night School in Mexico, Canned Bananas in Missouri," *Ensign* 6 (March 1976): 13.

68. "The New Housewife Blues," *Time*, March 14, 1977, 68.

69. Gerry Avant, "Georgia Chooses LDS Woman as Year's Homemaker," *Church News,* January 3, 1981, 7.

70. William B. Smart, "LDS women Are a TV Hit in Caribbean," *Church News*, May 23, 1981, 5.

71. "A Conversation with Barbara B. Smith, Relief Society General President," *Ensign* 6 (March 1976): 8.

72. Addie Fuhriman, "Singles Statistics," Relief Society General Board Minutes, November 17, 1983.

73. Barbara B. Smith, "Report and Official Instructions," Relief Society Conference Report 1975, 2.

74. Lynn Hollstein, "Women Urged to 'Reach for Stars,'" *Church News*, September 23, 1978, 3.

75. Boyd K. Packer, "The Circle of Sisters," *Ensign* 10 (November 1980): 109.

76. Patricia W. Higbee, "Relief Society Keeps Me Singing," *Ensign* 8 (October 1978): 24.

77. Packer, "The Circle of Sisters," 110.

78. "A Conversation with the General Relief Society Presidency," *Ensign* 12 (March 1982): 27.

79. See "The First Presidency to All Stake, Mission, and District Presidents, Bishops and Branch Presidents in the United States and Canada," September 21, 1977, First Presidency Circular Letters, Church Archives.

80. Miltenberger, *A Decade of Relief Society 1974–1984,* 2.

81. Sheri L. Dew as quoted in Carol Clark, "A Woman for Her Time," *This People* 5 (June/July 1984): 21.

CHAPTER 12: "STRIVING TOGETHER": THE SISTER ORGANIZATIONS

1. "Relief Society Conference Emphasizes Spirit of Compassion," *Ensign* 4 (January 1974): 130.

2. "Relief Society President Fights Fires . . . ," *Church News*, August 24, 1986, 7.

3. Barbara Wagner and Roberta Grant, "The New One-paycheck Family," *Ladies Home Journal*, September 1984, 88.

4. "Today's Americans," *Deseret News*, December 4, 1983, A-21. For a less sanguine assessment, see "Feminism's Identity Crisis," *Newsweek*, March 31, 1986, 58–59: "Old-line feminism has encountered a backlash from women who take the gains for granted—but resent the sacrifices."

5. "New Church Era Begins," *Church News*, July 7, 1985, 16. Also "Representatives Named for Boards," *Church News*, May 5, 1985, 10.

6. Barbara W. Winder, "I Love the Sisters of the Church," *Ensign* 14 (May 1984): 59.

7. "South America Visit Launches 'New Beginnings,'" *Church News*, May 19, 1985.

8. Relief Society Annual Report, April 1984–April 1985, 4. Copy in Relief Society Headquarters Files.

9. Gerry Avant, "Relief Society Emphasizes Basics on 144th Birthday," *Church News*, February 23, 1986, 7.

10. Ibid.

11. Patricia M. Grant, "British Women's 'Love in Action' Aids Ethiopians," *Church News*, May 11, 1986, 10.

12. The contribution was not limited to this stake: a churchwide fast for the African famine victims, requested by the First Presidency, brought donations of six million dollars. See "First Presidency Calls Special Fast Day," *Church News*, January 20, 1985; also Gordon B. Hinckley, "The Victory over Death," *Ensign* 15 (May 1985): 53–54.

13. The manual was prepared and intended for publication by the Relief Society. However, publication was delayed for several years. Eventually the book was released by Deseret Book Company in 1990 under the title *Parenting from A to Z: An Encyclopedia for LDS Families.*

14. Wylene Fotheringham, Report on Community Welfare Meetings, in Relief Society Headquarters Files.

15. Robert D. Hales, "Welfare Principles to Guide Our Lives: An Eternal Plan for the Welfare of Men's Souls," *Ensign* 16 (May 1986): 29.

16. "The Feminization of Poverty," *Deseret News Magazine*, June 15, 1986, 6.

17. "From Around the World," *Church News*, August 11, 1985, 11.

18. Journal of Barbara W. Winder, April 14, 1986, typescript in Relief Society Headquarters Files.

19. *Church News*, April 20, 1991, 13.

20. Stake Auxiliary Training Meeting, Relief Society Department, 1986 material, unpaged, copy in authors' files.

21. *Church News*, December 22, 1985, 10.

22. "Happenings," *Deseret News*, June 9, 1985, 12.

23. Kellene Ricks, "Message of Love Taken to Lamanites," *Church News*, February 10, 1990, 3.

24. Responsibility for managing distribution centers for temple and burial clothing was transferred from Relief Society to the Presiding Bishopric April 8, 1981. The Relief Society had continued to establish temple clothing and garment centers in various world locations until this time, and had consolidated 277 stake and mission temple clothing and garment outlets into a mail-order department. Mayola R. Miltenberger, *A Decade of Relief Society 1974–1984,* 4.

25. *Church News*, August 4, 1985, 6.

26. Boyd K. Packer, "The Circle of Sisters," *Ensign* 10 (November 1980): 109.

CHAPTER 13: THE ROOTS AND THE VISION, 1990 –

1. *Ensign* 21 (January 1991): 74.

2. Elaine L. Jack, "The Mission of Relief Society," Relief Society open house talk, September 27, 1990, copy in Relief Society Headquarters.

3. Clark, et al., *Knit Together in Love: A Focus for LDS Women in the 1990s.*

4. "Relief Society–Yesterday, Today, and Tomorrow," *History of Relief Society 1842–1966,* 140.

5. Elaine L. Jack, interview by Dawn Hall Anderson, June 25, 1990,

transcript in Relief Society Headquarters; hereafter referred to as Jack, Oral Interview.

6. Ibid.

7. Chieko N. Okazaki, "Surrounded by Samaritans," photocopy of typescript in authors' files. Used with permission.

8. Aileen H. Clyde, "Charity Suffereth Long," *Ensign* 21 (November 1991): 77.

9. Elaine L. Jack, "Stability in Our Times," in Cornwall and Howe, *Women of Wisdom and Knowledge*, 34.

10. Elaine L. Jack, "I Will Go and Do," *Ensign* 20 (May 1990): 78.

11. Notes in the possession of Carol L. Clark, September 1991.

12. Elaine L. Jack, "These Things Are Manifested unto Us Plainly," general women's meeting, September 29, 1990.

13. Jack, Oral Interview.

14. Love Nwokoro, N. Okwandu, and P. Ekeinde to Area General Board Representatives of Relief Society, Primary, and Young Women, British Isles/ Africa Area, August 24, 1988, Jack files, Relief Society Headquarters.

15. "Women's Voices," *Ensign* 21 (February 1991): 80.

16. Jack, "The Mission of Relief Society."

17. Elaine L. Jack, "Welfare and Relief Society," Regional Representatives seminar, October 16, 1990, manuscript in Relief Society Headquarters Files.

18. Nina Leont'eva, Evgeniya Korosteleva, and Tat'yana Petrova to Elaine L. Jack, ca. April 1991, Jack files.

19. Julie Ellis to Chieko Okazaki, May 29, 1991, Jack files.

20. Leigh Stachowski to Elaine L. Jack, June 20, 1991, Jack files.

21. Louise W. Champneys to Elaine L. Jack, November 10, 1990, Jack files.

22. Veronica Dallender to Elaine L. Jack, November 30, 1990, Jack files.

23. Dawn Hall Anderson and Marie Cornwall, eds., *Women Steadfast in Christ*.

24. Letter to the field from Relief Society General Presidency, August 1, 1991, copy in Relief Society Headquarters Files.

25. First Presidency to Priesthood Leaders, August 1, 1991, copy in Relief Society Headquarters Files.

26. "Relief Society Sesquicentennial Celebration," guidelines sent to local units, August 1991.

27. Sesquicentennial satellite broadcast conducting notes, p. 1, copy in Relief Society Headquarters Files.

28. Fax from Kent D. Watson, Taiwan Taichung Mission president, to Relief Society Presidency, March 16, 1992; original in Relief Society Headquarters Files.

29. Fax from Charles E. Jones, France Paris Mission president, to Relief Society General Presidency, March 16, 1992; original in Relief Society Headquarters Files.

30. Mayola Miltenberger to Relief Society General Presidency, March 19, 1992; original in Relief Society Headquarters Files.

31. Jan Malloy to Relief Society General Presidency, undated; original in Relief Society Headquarters Files.

32. Barbara D. Lockhart, Provo, Utah, to Relief Society General Presidency, March 16, 1992; original in Relief Society Headquarters Files.

33. Marilyn Woodruff, Franklin, Tennessee, to Relief Society General Presidency, March 14, 1992; original in Relief Society Headquarters Files.

34. Notes in the possession of Carol Clark, dated March 16, 1992.

35. Ibid.

36. Notes in the possession of Elaine L. Jack, December 15, 1991.

37. *Something Extraordinary: Celebrating Our Relief Society Sisterhood* (Salt Lake City: Deseret Book, 1992), 90.

38. Relief Society Sesquicentennial Celebration Guidelines.

39. Ibid.

40. Ibid.

41. Gordon B. Hinckley, "Ambitious to Do Good," *Ensign* 22 (March 1992), 6.

42. " 'Move with Vision, Fueled by Faith,' into Next 150 Years," *Church News,* March 21, 1992, 7.

43. Jack, "I Will Go and Do," 78.

44. Elaine L. Jack, "A Perfect Brightness of Hope," in Anderson and Cornwall, *Women Steadfast in Christ,* 6.

45. Jack, "The Mission of Relief Society," 2.

46. Jack, "Welfare and Relief Society," 1.

47. Elaine L. Jack, "Strengthening Families," openhouse talk, fall 1991, copy in Relief Society Headquarters Files.

48. Elaine L. Jack, "The Principles of Visiting Teaching," openhouse talk, April 1991, copy in Relief Society Headquarters Files.

49. Elaine L. Jack, "Temple Blessings," Alberta Temple rededication, June 2–24, 1991, copy in Relief Society Headquarters Files.

50. Elaine L. Jack, "Look Up and Press On," *Ensign* 22 (May 1992): 98.

51. *Something Extraordinary,* 6–8, 11–12.

Epilogue: "The Same God . . . Worketh All in All"

1. Weber Stake Relief Society Conference Minute Book 1877 [1855]–1899, December 10, 1891, 291.

2. D&C 98:12.

3. Weber Stake Relief Society Conference Minute Book, December 10, 1891.

4. Ibid.

5. Elizabeth Ann Whitney, *Woman's Exponent* 7 (August 15, 1878): 91.

6. Ibid.

7. Nauvoo Minutes, May 26, 1842.

8. Nauvoo Minutes, April 28, 1842.

9. Spencer W. Kimball, "The Role of Righteous Women," *Ensign* 9 (November 1979): 103–4.

10. Boyd K. Packer, "The Circle of Sisters," *Ensign* 10 (November 1980): 109.

11. Athelia T. Woolley and Athelia S. Tanner, "Our Five-Generation Love Affair with Relief Society," *Ensign* 8 (June 1978): 38–39.

12. Cherry Silver, "When a Woman Is Alone," *Ensign* 8 (June 1978): 40–43.

13. Dianne Dibb Forbis, " 'Gifts of Bright': Relief Society Strengthens My Family," *Ensign* 17 (March 1987): 11.

14. Alshield Morteng to Marian Johnson, January 15, 1992, typewritten, copy in authors' files.

15. Catherine M. Stokes, " 'Plenty Good Room' in Relief Society," *Dialogue* 21 (Winter 1988): 85.

16. Camilla Kimball, "A Woman's Preparation," *Ensign* 7 (March 1977): 59.

17. *To the Mothers in Zion: An Address Given at a Fireside for Parents by President Ezra Taft Benson ... 22 February 1987* (Salt Lake City: The Church of Jesus Christ of Latter-day Saints, 1987), 5.

18. D&C 83:2.

19. Silver, "When a Woman Is Alone," 43.

20. Amy Brown Lyman, "Remarks, Welfare Session of General Conference ... October 4, 1941," *Relief Society Magazine* 28 (November 1941): 727.

21. Joseph F. Smith, *Conference Report*, April 1907, as quoted in Janath R. Cannon, "I Have a Question," *Ensign* 7 (August 1977): 40.

22. Carol Gilligan, *In a Different Voice.*

23. Nauvoo Minutes, March 30, 1842.

24. D&C 84:73.

25. Nauvoo Minutes, April 28, 1942.

26. John 13:35.

27. Marvelee Soon Tahauri, "Dissolving Language Barriers in Hauula," *Ensign* 12 (March 1982): 55–57.

28. Fanny A. Oleson to Pres. and Sister Ellsworth, July 13, 1942, original, typewritten and signed, in possession of Ray A. Field, Laramie, Wyoming. Copy in authors' files. Internal quotation marks have been added for clarity.

29. Louanne Brown Barrett, "Healing Attitudes," *Ensign* 14 (March 1984): 32.

30. Nauvoo Minutes, April 28, 1842.

31. JoEllen Mulvay Anderson, as reported to Jill Mulvay Derr, text in authors' files.

32. Neill Foote Marriott, as reported to Jill Mulvay Derr, text in authors' files.

33. 1 Corinthians 12:7–11, 20, 27.

34. 1 Corinthians 12:4–6.

35. 1 Corinthians 13:8.

36. 1 Corinthians 13:9–10.

37. 1 Corinthians 13:13.

SELECTED BIBLIOGRAPHY

CHURCH RECORDS AND ADMINISTRATIVE FILES

During the time the authors researched these materials, some were moved from the Relief Society Headquarters to the Archives of the Historical Department of The Church of Jesus Christ of Latter-day Saints, Salt Lake City, Utah, cited as Church Archives. Archives staff members have inventoried most of the Relief Society's historical materials, and it should be noted that the Church Archives will most likely be the eventual repository for all Relief Society records and files.

General Manuscript Records

Auxiliary Executive Files, 1923–1938. Church Archives.

Bancroft, H. H. Mormon Collection. Bancroft Library, University of California at Berkeley.

Church Union Board Executive Committee Minutes and Church Union Board Minutes. Church Archives.

First Council of Seventy Minutes and Early Records, 1844–1848. Church Archives.

First Presidency General Administration Correspondence. Church Archives.

Historian's Office Journal. Church Archives.

Journal History of the Church of Jesus Christ of Latter-day Saints. This scrapbook chronicle of events in LDS Church history was maintained by Church historians to represent the years 1830–1972. The original is in Church Archives, with microform copy at Harold B. Lee Libraries, Brigham Young University, and elsewhere.

Moyle, James. Oral History Collection. Church Archives.

Presiding Bishopric Bishops Meeting Minutes. Church Archives.

Presiding Bishopric Office Journals, 1901–1946. Church Archives.

Seventies Quorum Records, Second Quorum, 1844–1894. Church Archives.

Senior and Junior Cooperative Retrenchment Association Minutes. Church Archives.

Smith, Joseph. Diaries, 1832–1844. Church Archives.

———. Letterbooks. Church Archives.

Social Advisory Committee Minutes, 1916–1922. Church Archives.

Special Collections, Harold B. Lee Library. Brigham Young University, Provo, Utah.

Women's Committee on Dancing and Dress Report. Church Archives.

Young, Brigham. Incoming Correspondence. Church Archives.

———. Letterbooks. Church Archives.

———. Unpublished Sermons. Church Archives.

Relief Society Manuscript Records

RELIEF SOCIETY GENERAL RECORDS

"A Record of the Organization, and Proceedings of the Female Relief Society of Nauvoo," 1842–1844. Holograph. Church Archives.

"Record of the Relief Society from First Organization to Conference Apr 5, 1892, Book II." Catalogued as Relief Society Record, 1880–1892. Holograph volume kept by general secretary Sarah M. Kimball, including retrospective accounts.

Relief Society [General Board] Minutes, 1892–1911. Three holograph volumes of general board meeting and conference minutes were kept by general secretary Emmeline B. Wells. Vol. 1, October 10, 1892, to April 8, 1901; vol. 2, June 22, 1901, to April 13, 1906; vol. 3, May 1906 to April 8, 1911. A fourth volume, apparently used for drafting minutes, covers October 10, 1892, to October 3, 1896. Church Archives.

Relief Society General Board Minutes, typescript, 1842–1990. The record includes excerpts from the Nauvoo Minutes and the *Woman's Exponent;* 1842–1892, a brief synopsis of Emmeline B. Wells's Relief Society minutes, 1892–1911; and a continuing record of general board meetings, Relief Society conferences, and other Relief Society concerns and affiliations, 1911–1990. Church Archives.

Relief Society Annual Reports, 1913–1973. Church Archives.

Relief Society Circular Letters. Church Archives.

Relief Society Executive Files, 1911–1959. Church Archives.

Relief Society, "Social Service Work in the Relief Society, 1917–1928," by Amy Brown Lyman. Typescript. Church Archives. Also in Relief Society General Board Minutes, April 1928.

Snow, Eliza R. "Brief Sketch of the Organizations Conducted by the Latter-day Saint Women." Holograph. Mormon Collection. Bancroft Library, University of California, Berkeley.

RELIEF SOCIETY LOCAL RECORDS

The Church Archives maintains a splendid collection of local Relief Society minutes and histories, catalogued under names of ward and stake or branch and mission.

Relief Society Headquarters Files

Housed in the Relief Society Headquarters, Salt Lake City, Utah, are the files of current presidencies, including at this printing the files of Elaine L. Jack, Barbara W. Winder, and Barbara B. Smith. Also in the Relief Society offices vault is a valuable collection of Historical Files. These are generally arranged by topic, though historical materials from some local units are included.

Authors' Files

In the course of the research, many documents came to the attention of the authors from individuals who permitted copies to be made. The authors also had in their own possession publications from which they drew information. These materials, identified simply as "in the authors' files," will, after a reasonable period, be transferred to the Special Collections section of the Harold B. Lee Library at Brigham Young University, where they will be available to researchers.

PERSONAL ACCOUNTS, MANUSCRIPT AND PUBLISHED

Atwood, Relief Cram. "Biographical Sketch." *Woman's Exponent* 33 (March 1905): 65–66.

Boyer, Marian R. Oral History. Interview by Jessie L. Embry, 1977. Typescript. James Moyle Oral History Program. Church Archives.

Crosby, Caroline Barnes. Autobiography. Microfilm of holograph. Church Archives.

DeMille, Corry Zippro. Interview by Janath R. Cannon. December 1984, Salt Lake City.

Douglas, Ellen [Parker]. Letters. Typescript. Church Archives.

Engar, Amy Lyman. "[Personal Recollections of] Amy Brown Lyman." Typescript of oral presentation to Institute of Religion, University of Utah, February 26, 1987. In possession of Amy Lyman Engar, Salt Lake City.

Evans, Priscilla. "Autobiography of Priscilla Merriman Evans." Typescript. Utah State Historical Society, Salt Lake City, Utah.

Fox, Ruth May. Diaries. Holograph. Utah State Historical Society. The 1894–95 diary is also published in Linda Thatcher, " 'I Care Nothing for Politics': Ruth May Fox, Forgotten Suffragist." *Utah State Historical Quarterly* 49 (Summer 1981): 239–53.

Freeze, Mary Ann Burnham. Diary. Special Collections, Harold B. Lee Library, Brigham Young University, Provo, Utah.

Fullmer, Desdemona Wadsworth. Autobiography. Holograph. Church Archives.

Gates, Susa Young. Papers. Utah State Historical Society, Salt Lake City, Utah. Microfilm. Church Archives.

Hendricks, Drusilla Dorris. "Historical Sketch of James Hendricks and Drusilla Dorris Hendricks." In *Henry Hendricks Genealogy*. Compiled by Marguerite Allen. Salt Lake City: Hendricks Family Organization, 1963.

Higbee, Patricia W. "Relief Society Keeps Me Singing." *Ensign* 8 (October 1978): 22–24.

Horne, Alice Merrill. "Autobiography of Alice Merrill Horne." Edited by Zorah Horne Jeppson and children. Typescript. In possession of Zorah Horne Jeppson, Salt Lake City.

Huntington, William. Diary. Typescript. Harold B. Lee Library, Brigham Young University, Provo, Utah.

James, Jane. Autobiography. Church Archives.

Kimball, Heber C. Diary. Church Archives. Also published in *On the Potter's Wheel: The Diaries of Heber C. Kimball.* Edited by Stanley B. Kimball. Salt Lake City: Signature Books, 1987.

Kimball, Lucy Walker Smith. "A Brief Biographical Sketch of the Life & Labors of Lucy Walker Kimball Smith." Holograph. Church Archives.

Lee, John D. *A Mormon Chronicle: The Diaries of John D. Lee, 1848–1876.* Edited by Robert G. Cleland and Juanita Brooks. 2 vols. Salt Lake City: University of Utah Press, 1983.

Lewis, Evelyn Hodges. Oral History. Interviews by Loretta L. Hefner, 1979. Typescript. James Moyle Oral History Program. Church Archives.

Lyman, Amy Brown. *In Retrospect: Autobiography of Amy Brown Lyman.* Salt Lake City: Relief Society General Board, 1945.

———. Papers. Special Collections, Harold B. Lee Library, Brigham Young University, Provo, Utah.

Lyman, Eliza Maria Partridge. Diary. Holograph. Church Archives.

Maughan, Mary Ann Weston. Autobiography. Holograph. Church Archives. Also published in Carter, comp., *Our Pioneer Heritage* 2:346–417.

Miltenberger, Mayola R. Oral History. Interviews by Jessie L. Embry, 1977. Typescript. James Moyle Oral History Program. Church Archives.

Munk, Margaret Rampton. "Service Under Stress: Two Years as a Relief Society President." *Dialogue* 19 (Summer 1986): 127–45.

Palmer, Maydell C. "Autobiography of Maydell Cazier Palmer, Lethbridge, Alberta, 1980." Mimeograph, in the authors' files. Also in Special Collections, Harold B. Lee Library, Brigham Young University, Provo, Utah.

Palmer, Patience. Reminiscence. *Utah Magazine*, February 1892.

Peterson Family Letter Collection, Church Archives.

Pohlman, Vera White. *In Memoriam: Amy Brown Lyman, 1872–1959.* In the authors' files. Privately printed, 1960.

———. Oral History. Interviews by Loretta L. Hefner, 1980–81. Typescript. James Moyle Oral History Program. Church Archives.

Poulsen, Ezra J. *The Life of Emily Almira Cozzens Rich.* 1871. Reprint, Salt Lake City: Granite Publishing Company, 1954.

Pratt, Louisa Barnes. Autobiography and Journal. In Carter, comp., *Heart Throbs of the West* 8:189–398.

Randall, Sally Carlisle. Papers. Church Archives.

Rich, Almira Cozzens. Journals. Weber State University Library, Ogden, Utah.

Rich, Mary Ann Phelps. *Autobiography of Mary Ann Phelps Rich*. Pamphlet prepared by family members. N.p., n.d.

Richards, Franklin D. Diaries. Church Archives.

Richards, Jane Snyder. Reminiscence. Holograph. Church Archives.

Richards, Mary Haskin Parker. Diary. Church Archives.

Savage, Hannah Adeline Hatch. Autobiography. Holograph. Church Archives.

Sessions, Patty. Diaries. Holograph. Church Archives.

Sharp, Marianne Clark. Oral History. Interview by Jessie L. Embry, 1977. Typescript. James Moyle Oral History Program. Church Archives.

Shimizu, Junko. Collection. Papers in possession of Junko Shimizu. Notes in the authors' files.

Smith, Barbara B. *A Fruitful Season: Reflections on the Challenging Years of the Relief Society 1974–1984*. Salt Lake City: Bookcraft, 1988.

——. Oral History. Interviews by Jessie L. Embry, 1977. Typescript. James Moyle Oral History Program. Church Archives.

Smith, Bathsheba Wilson Bigler. Autobiography. Microfilm of manuscript; typescript. Church Archives.

Smith, Lucy Meserve. "Historical Sketches of My Great Grandfathers." Holograph. Special Collections, Marriott Library, University of Utah, Salt Lake City.

Snow, Eliza R. Diaries, 1845–1849. Holograph. Huntington Library, San Marino, Calif.

——. Nauvoo Journal and Notebook. Holograph. Church Archives. The journal, as edited by Maureen Ursenbach [Beecher], is published in *BYU Studies* 15 (Summer 1975): 391–416.

——. "Sketch of My Life." Holograph. Mormon Collection, Bancroft Library, University of California, Berkeley.

Spafford, Belle S. Oral History. Interviews by Jill Mulvay Derr, November 1975–March 1976. Typescript. James H. Moyle Oral History Program. Church Archives.

Stokes, Catherine M. " 'Plenty Good Room' in Relief Society." Included in "How Do You Spell Relief? A Panel of Relief Society Presidents," with Maureen Ursenbach Beecher, K. Carpenter, and Sharon Lee Swenson. *Dialogue* 21 (Winter 1988): 75–101.

Stout, Hosea. *On the Mormon Frontier: The Diary of Hosea Stout 1844–1861*. Edited by Juanita Brooks. 2 vols. 1964. Reprint. Salt Lake City: University of Utah Press, 1982.

Tanner, Annie Clark. *A Mormon Mother: An Autobiography by Annie Clark Tanner*. 1969. Rev. ed., Salt Lake City: Tanner Trust Fund, University of Utah Library, 1973.

Tarlock, Fay. "The Visitors." *Relief Society Magazine* 35 (March 1948): 164–69.

Taylor, Elmina S. Diary. Church Archives.

Taylor, Louise R. Papers. Special Collections, Harold B. Lee Library, Brigham Young University, Provo, Utah.

Tracy, Nancy Naomi Alexander. "Life History of Nancy Naomi Alexander Tracy, Written by Herself." Typescript. Church Archives.

Wells, Emmeline B. Diaries. Harold B. Lee Library, Brigham Young University, Provo, Utah.

Whitney, Elizabeth Ann. "A Leaf from an Autobiography." *Woman's Exponent* 7 (August 1878–February 1879), passim.

Whitney, Helen Mar Kimball. "Scenes and Incidents at Winter Quarters." *Woman's Exponent*, vols. 13 and 14 passim.

Winter, Gladys Robison. Collection. Church Archives.

Woodruff, Phebe. "Autobiographic Sketch of Phebe W. Woodruff." Holograph. Mormon Collection, Bancroft Library, University of California, Berkeley. Also microfilm of holograph, Marriott Library, University of Utah, Salt Lake City.

Woodruff, Wilford. Diary. Church Archives. Also published as *Wilford Woodruff's Journal.* Edited by Scott G. Kenney. 9 vols. Midvale, Utah: Signature Books, 1983.

Woolley, Athelia T., and Athelia S. Tanner. "Our Five-Generation Love Affair with Relief Society." *Ensign* 8 (June 1978): 38–39.

Young, Zina Diantha Huntington. Diaries. Holograph. Church Archives.

———. "How I Gained My Testimony of the Truth." *Young Woman's Journal* 4 (April 1893): 317–19.

"Life Story of John Zippro." Unpaged ms. in the authors' files.

MISCELLANEOUS CHURCH PUBLICATIONS

The Book of Mormon, Doctrine and Covenants, and Pearl of Great Price join with the Holy Bible as scriptural texts for the Latter-day Saints.

Builders for Eternity. Salt Lake City: General Board of the Relief Society, 1948.

A Centenary of Relief Society. [Edited by Belle S. Spafford and Marianne C. Sharp.] Salt Lake City: General Board of the Relief Society, 1942.

A Century of Sisterhood: Chronological Collage, 1869–1969. [Salt Lake City:] Young Women's Mutual Improvement Association, [1969].

The Church and the Proposed Equal Rights Amendment, A Moral Issue. Pamphlet. Salt Lake City: The Church of Jesus Christ of Latter-day Saints, 1980. Bound in *Ensign,* March 1980.

Conference Report of The Church of Jesus Christ of Latter-day Saints. Salt Lake City: The Church of Jesus Christ of Latter-day Saints, 1880–present.

Gates, B. Cecil, and Edwin Parry, Jr., comps. *Relief Society Song Book.* Salt Lake City: Relief Society General Board, 1919.

General Handbook of Instructions. Salt Lake City: The Church of Jesus Christ of Latter-day Saints, 1899–1989 passim.

The General Relief Society: Officers, Objects, and Status. Salt Lake City: [Relief Society] General Officers, 1902.

History of Relief Society 1842–1966. [Edited by Marianne C. Sharp and Irene B. Woodward.] Salt Lake City: The General Board of Relief Society, 1966.

Hymns of The Church of Jesus Christ of Latter-day Saints. Salt Lake City: Church of Jesus Christ of Latter-day Saints, 1985.

Instructions for Making Temple Clothing and Clothing the Dead. Salt Lake City: The Church of Jesus Christ of Latter-day Saints, 1961, 1979.

Lambda Delta Sigma Handbook. Salt Lake City: The Church of Jesus Christ of Latter-day Saints, 1960–1992.

Latter-day Saints' Relief Society Class for Training Nurses Aid. N.p., 1920.

The Latter-day Saint Woman, Part A, and *The Latter-day Saint Woman, Part B*. Salt Lake City: The Church of Jesus Christ of Latter-day Saints, 1979.

Lyman, Amy Brown. *National Woman's Relief Society, Historical Sketch, 1842–1931*. Salt Lake City: Relief Society General Board, 1931.

Madsen, Florence Jepperson, and Grace Hildy Croft. *Music Leadership in the Relief Society*. Salt Lake City: Relief Society General Board Association, 1963.

Miltenberger, Mayola R. *A Decade of Relief Society 1974–1984*. Salt Lake City: Relief Society General Board, 1984.

———. *Fifty Years of Relief Society Social Services*. Salt Lake City: The Church of Jesus Christ of Latter-day Saints, 1987.

My Kingdom Shall Roll Forth. Sunday School manual. Salt Lake City: The Church of Jesus Christ of Latter-day Saints, 1979.

Outlines of the Mothers' Work of the Relief Society of the Benson Stake for the Year 1912. N.p., n.d.

Priesthood and Church Welfare. Melchizedek Priesthood study guide. Salt Lake City: The Church of Jesus Christ of Latter-day Saints, 1939.

Relief Society Courses of Study. Salt Lake City: The Church of Jesus Christ of Latter-day Saints, 1971–present, published annually.

Relief Society Guide. [Salt Lake City: General Board of Relief Society, 1914.]

Relief Society Handbook. Salt Lake City: General Board of Relief Society, 1931, 1949, 1954, 1962, 1964, 1966, 1967, 1968, 1972, 1975, 1976, 1983, 1988, 1991.

Selected Addresses from the 1974 Relief Society General Conference. Salt Lake City: The Church of Jesus Christ of Latter-day Saints, 1975.

Single Adult Activities Guide. Salt Lake City: The Church of Jesus Christ of Latter-day Saints, 1986.

To the Mothers in Zion: An Address Given at a Fireside for Parents by President Ezra Taft Benson . . . 22 February 1987. Salt Lake City: The Church of Jesus Christ of Latter-day Saints, 1987.

Welfare Services Resource Handbook. Salt Lake City: The Church of Jesus Christ of Latter-day Saints, 1980.

NEWSPAPERS AND PERIODICALS

Brigham Young University Studies (Provo, Utah). 1959–present.

BYU Women's Research Institute Newsletter (Provo, Utah). 1986–present.

Church News, weekly section of *Deseret News* (Salt Lake City, Utah). 1931–present.

Deseret News (Salt Lake City, Utah). 1850–present.

Dialogue: A Journal of Mormon Thought (Palo Alto and Los Angeles, Calif.; Washington, D.C.; Salt Lake City and Logan, Utah). 1966–present.

Ensign (Salt Lake City, Utah). 1971–present.

Exponent II (Arlington, Mass.). 1972–present.

Improvement Era (Salt Lake City, Utah). 1897–1970.

Journal of Mormon History (Provo, Utah). 1974–present.

Juvenile Instructor (Salt Lake City, Utah). 1866–1919.

Latter-day Saints' Millennial Star (Liverpool, England). 1840–present.

The Mormon (New York, N.Y.). 1855–1857.

New Era (Salt Lake City, Utah). 1971–present.

Relief Society Magazine (Salt Lake City, Utah). 1914–1970.

Saints' Herald [RLDS] (Independence, Missouri).

Salt Lake Tribune (Salt Lake City, Utah). 1871–present.

Sunstone (Salt Lake City, Utah). 1975–present.

This People (Salt Lake City, Utah). 1979–present.

Times and Seasons (Nauvoo, Ill.). 1839–1846.

Utah Historical Quarterly (Salt Lake City, Utah). 1928–1934; 1938–present.

Utah Magazine (Salt Lake City, Utah). 1868–1869.

Washington Post (Washington, D.C.). 1877–present.

Western Humanities Review (Salt Lake City, Utah). 1947–present.

Woman's Exponent (Salt Lake City, Utah). 1872–1914.

Young Woman's Journal (Salt Lake City, Utah). 1872–1914.

ARTICLES

Alder, Lydia D. "Thoughts on Missionary Work." *Woman's Exponent* 30 (August 1, 1901): 21.

Anderson, Lavina Fielding. "Relief Society Presidents Prove the Second Mile Is Paved with Innovation." Part 1, *Ensign* (June 1978): 30–35. Part 2, *Ensign* 8 (July 1978): 50–55.

———. "Mormon Women and the Struggle for Definition: Contemporary Women." *Sunstone* 6 (November–December 1981): 12–16.

Arrington, Chris Rigby. "The Finest Fabrics: Mormon Women and the Silk Industry in Early Utah." *Utah Historical Quarterly* 46 (Fall 1978): 376–96.

Arrington, Leonard J. "Modern Lysistratas: Mormon Women in the International Peace Movement, 1899–1939." *Journal of Mormon History* 15 (1989): 89–104.

———. "The Economic Role of Pioneer Mormon Women." *Western Humanities Review* 9 (Spring 1955): 150–52.

Avant, Gerry. "Equal Rights Amendment Is Opposed by R.S. President." *Church News,* December 21, 1974, 7.

———. "Relief Society Emphasizes Basics on 144th Birthday." *Church News,* February 23, 1986, 7.

Beecher, Maureen Ursenbach. "A Decade of Mormon Women—the 1870s." *New Era* 8 (April 1978): 34–39.

———. "The 'Leading Sisters': A Female Hierarchy in Nineteenth Century Mormon Society." *Journal of Mormon History* 9 (1982): 25–39.

———. "Women at Winter Quarters." *Sunstone* 8 (July-August 19830): 11–19.

———. "Women's Work on the Mormon Frontier." *Utah Historical Quarterly* 49 (Summer 1981): 276–90.

———, ed. " 'All Things Move in Order in the City': The Nauvoo Diary of Zina Diantha Huntington Jacobs." *BYU Studies* 19 (Spring 1979): 285–320.

Beecher, Maureen Ursenbach, and James L. Kimball, Jr. "The First Relief Society: A Diversity of Women." *Ensign* 9 (March 1979): 25–29.

Beecher, Maureen Ursenbach, and Patricia Lyn Scott. "Mormon Women: A Bibliography in Process, 1977–1985." *Journal of Mormon History* 12 (1985): 113–28.

Bennion, Francine Russell. "Mormon Women and the Struggle for Definition: What Is the Church?" *Sunstone* 6 (November–December 1981): 17–20.

Bennion, Sherilyn Cox. "Enterprising Ladies: Utah's Nineteenth-Century Women Editors." *Utah Historical Quarterly* 49 (Summer 1981): 291–304.

———. "Lula Greene Richards: Utah's First Woman Editor." *BYU Studies* 21 (Summer 1977): 155–74.

———. "The Woman's Exponent: Forty-two Years of Speaking for Women." *Utah Historical Quarterly* 44 (Summer 1976): 222–39.

Benson, Ezra Taft. "The Honored Place of Women." *Ensign* 11 (November 1981): 104–7.

Blumell, Bruce D. "Welfare Before Welfare." *Journal of Mormon History* 6 (1979): 89–106.

Cannon, Annie Wells. "Jubilee Boxes." *Relief Society Magazine* 117 (July 1930): 366–69.

Cannon, Annie Wells, et al. "Grain Saving in the Relief Society." *Relief Society Magazine* 2 (February 1915): 50–58.

Cannon, Janath R. "Priorities and the Pursuit of Excellence." *Ensign* 6 (April 1976): 70.

Carlisle, Emily M. "Report on Cottonwood Stake Maternity Hospital." *Relief Society Magazine* 18 (July 1931): 415–16.

Carter, Kate B., comp. "The Relief Society." In Carter, comp., *Our Pioneer Heritage* 14 (1970–71): 61–124.

Clyde, Aileen. "Other Voices." *Exponent II* 4 (Fall 1977): 5.

Colton, Ellie. "A Mormon Woman Looks at the ERA." *The Washington Post*, November 21, 1977.

"A Conversation with Barbara B. Smith, Relief Society General President." *Ensign* 6 (March 1976): 11–12.

Curtis, Mary. "Amelia Bloomer's Curious Costume." *American History Illustrated*, June 1978, 12–13.

Darger, Eva W. "The Relief Society and the Welfare Plan." *Relief Society Magazine* 26 (December 1939): 827–28.

[Derr], Jill C. Mulvay. "Eliza R. Snow and the Woman Question." *BYU Studies* 16 (Winter 1976): 29–39.

Derr, Jill Mulvay. "Woman's Place in Brigham Young's World." *BYU Studies* 18 (Spring 1978):377–95.

Derr, Jill Mulvay, and C. Brooklyn Derr. "Outside the Mormon Hierarchy: Alternative Aspects of Institutional Power." *Dialogue* 15 (Winter 1982): 21–43.

Derr, Jill Mulvay, and Susan Oman. "The Nauvoo Generation: Our First Five Relief Society Presidents." *Ensign* 7 (December 1977): 36–43.

———. "These Three Women." *Ensign* 8 (February 1978): 66–70.

Dew, Sheri L. "[Barbara B. Smith:] A Woman for Her Time." *This People* 5 (June/July 1984): 21.

Embry, Jessie L. "Grain Storage: The Balance of Power Between Priesthood Authority and Relief Society Autonomy." *Dialogue* 15 (Winter 1982): 59–66.

Esplin, Ronald K., ed. "Life in Nauvoo, June, 1844: Vilate Kimball's Martyrdom Letters." *BYU Studies* 19 (Winter 1979): 231–40.

Evans, Joy S. "Overcoming Challenges Along Life's Way." *Ensign* 17 (November 1987): 92–94.

Foster, Lawrence. "From Frontier Activism to Neo-Victorian Domesticity: Mormon Women in the Nineteenth and Twentieth Centuries." *Journal of Mormon History* 6 (1979): 3–21.

Friedman, Estelle. "Separatism as Strategy: Female Institution Building and American Feminism, 1870–1930." *Feminist Studies* 5 (Fall 1979): 512–29.

Garff, Gertrude R. "The Value of Relief Society Membership." *Relief Society Magazine* 34 (March 1947): 153.

Gates, Susa Young. "L.D.S. Relief Society Class for Training Nurses' Aids." *Relief Society Magazine* 7 (July 1920): 382–85.

———. "Relief Society Beginnings in Utah." *Relief Society Magazine* 9 (April 1922): 184–96.

———. "Relief Society Work in the Missions." *Relief Society Magazine* 5 (July 1918): 365–88.

[———.] "The Scope of the Relief Society." *Relief Society Magazine* 2 (April 1915): 198–99.

Grant, Patricia M. "British Women's 'Love in Action' Aids Ethiopians." *Church News*, May 11, 1986, 10.

Hafen, Marie K. "Sustaining—and Being Sustained by—the Priesthood." *Ensign* 17 (March 1987): 6–8.

Hartley, William G. "The Priesthood Reorganization of 1877: Brigham Young's Last Achievement." *BYU Studies* 20 (Fall 1979): 3–36.

———. "War and Peace and Dutch Potatoes." *Ensign* 8 (July 1978): 19–23.

Hefner, Loretta L. "The National Women's Relief Society and the U.S. Sheppard-Towner Act." *Utah Historical Quarterly* 50 (Summer 1982): 255–67.

———. "This Decade Was Different: Relief Society's Social Services Department, 1919–1929." *Dialogue* 15 (August 1982): 64–73.

Hinckley, Gordon B. "Ten Gifts from the Lord." *Ensign* 15 (November 1985): 86–89.

Huefner, Dixie Snow. "Church and Politics at the Utah IWY Conference." *Dialogue* 11 (Spring 1978): 58–75.

Jack, Elaine L. "I Will Go and Do." *Ensign* 20 (May 1990): 78.

———. "These Things Are Manifested unto Us Plainly." *Ensign* 20 (November 1990): 88–90.

Jensen, Richard L. "Forgotten Relief Societies, 1844–67." *Dialogue* 16 (Spring 1983): 105–25.

Jolley, JoAnn. "Splitting the Bamboo Curtain." *Ensign* 1 (September 1981): 76–79.

Kasius, Cora. "The Relief Society Social Service Institute." *Relief Society Magazine* 12 (July 1925): 345–49.

Kimball, Sarah M. "Auto-biography." *Woman's Exponent* 12 (September 1, 1883): 51.

———. "Our Sixth Sense, or the Sense of Spiritual Understanding." *Woman's Exponent* 23 (April 15, 1895): 251.

Kimball, Spencer W. "Privileges and Responsibilities of Sisters." *Ensign* 8 (November 1978): 102–4.

———. "The Role of Righteous Women." *Ensign* 9 (November 1979): 102–4.

Knight, Jennie B. "Relief Society Libraries." *Relief Society Magazine* 21 (April 1934): 265–67.

"Ladies Mass Meeting." *Woman's Exponent* 14 (March 1 to April 1, 1886): 148–49, 157–60, 166–67.

Larson, Gustive O. "An Industrial Home for Polygamous Wives." *Utah Historical Quarterly* 38 (Summer 1970): 163–75.

"LDS Church Extends Priesthood to All Worthy Male Members." *Deseret News*, June 9, 1978.

Lee, Harold B. "Obligations of Membership in Relief Society." *Relief Society Magazine* 56 (January 1969): 8–15.

———. "Place of the Relief Society in the Church Security Plan." *Relief Society Magazine* 24 (March 1937): 140–43.

Lyman, Amy Brown. "Relief Society in Action Today." *Relief Society Magazine* 31 (March 1944): 137–39.

———. "The Development of Spirituality Through the Social Service Department." *Relief Society Magazine* 23 (November 1936): 699–701.

———. "World Parliament of Women." *Relief Society Magazine* 25 (September 1938): 577–80.

Madsen, Carol Cornwall. "Mormon Missionary Wives in Nineteenth Century Polynesia." *Journal of Mormon History* 13 (1986–87): 62–76.

———. "Mormon Women and the Struggle for Definition: The Nineteenth Century Church." *Sunstone* 6 (November–December 1981): 7–11.

Madsen, Carol Cornwall, and David J. Whittaker. "History's Sequel: A Source Essay on Women in Mormon History." *Journal of Mormon History* 6 (1979): 123–45.

McConkie, Bruce R. "The Relief Society and the Keys of the Kingdom." *Relief Society Magazine* 37 (March 1950): 149.

Packer, Boyd K. "The Circle of Sisters." *Ensign* 10 (November 1980): 109–11.

Paine, Judith. "The Women's Pavillion of 1876." *The Feminist Art Journal* 4 (Winter 1975–76): 5–12.

Petersen, Mark E. "The Mission of the Relief Society." *Relief Society Magazine* 35 (March 1948): 149.

Pohlman, Vera White. "Relief Society Celebrates Its Centennial." *Relief Society Magazine* 9 (March 1922): 120–25.

Poll, Richard D. "The Move South." *BYU Studies* 29 (Fall 1989): 65–88.

Quinn, D. Michael. "Latter-day Saint Prayer Circles." *BYU Studies* 19 (Fall 1978): 79–87.

"Reaching Every Facet of a Woman's Life: Relief Society: A Conversation with Belle S. Spafford." *Ensign* 4 (June 1974): 14–18.

"Relief Society Beginnings in Foreign Lands." *Relief Society Magazine* 9 (March 1922): 120–25.

"Relief Society Conference Emphasizes Spirit of Compassion." *Ensign* 4 (January 1974): 130–35.

Richards, L. L. Greene. "Woman, 'Rise'." *Young Woman's Journal* 6 (February 1893): 201.

Robison, Louise Y. Conference Address. *Relief Society Magazine* 23 (May 1936): 332.

Romney, Marion G. "The Church Welfare Program for 1942." *Relief Society Magazine* 28 (December 1941): 844.

———. "The Joys of Welfare Service." *Relief Society Magazine* 34 (November 1947): 723–31.

Scott, Anne Firor. "On Seeing and Not Seeing: A Case of Historical Invisibility." *Journal of American History* 71 (June 1984): 7–21.

Sharp, Marianne C. "A Present Day Challenge." *Relief Society Magazine* 24 (January 1937): 7.

———. "Facing Forward." *Relief Society Magazine* 57 (December 1970): 894–95.

Simpson, Robert L. "Relief Society: Arm in Arm with the Priesthood." *Relief Society Magazine* 55 (March 1968): 165.

Smith, Barbara B. "The Relief Society Role in Priesthood Councils." *Ensign* 9 (November 1979): 83–85.

Smith, Bathsheba W. "Greeting and Congratulations." *Woman's Exponent* 38 (January 1910): 41.

Smith, George Albert. "To the Relief Society." *Relief Society Magazine* 19 (December 1932): 703–10.

Smith, Janice. "Relief Society: Mukluks in Alaska, Night School in Mexico, Canned Bananas in Missouri." *Ensign* 6 (March 1976): 13–15.

Smith, Joseph F. "Dress and Social Practices." *Improvement Era* 20 (January 1917): 173.

——. "Peace on Earth, Good Will to Men." *Relief Society Magazine* 2 (January 1915): 13–20.

Smith, Joseph Fielding. "Relief Society—An Aid to the Priesthood." *Relief Society Magazine* 46 (January 1959): 4–6.

——. "The Relief Society Organized by Revelation." *Relief Society Magazine* 52 (January 1965): 4–6.

Snow, Eliza R. "Female Relief Society." *Deseret News Weekly*, April 22, 1868.

——. "The New Year, 1852." *Deseret News*, January 19, 1852.

——. "The Female Relief Society." *Woman's Exponent* 1 (June 1 and 15, 1872): 2, 10.

——. "Position and Duties." *Woman's Exponent* 3 (July 15, 1874): 28.

——. "Woman." *The Mormon*, December 27, 1856; reprinted in *Poems Religious, Historical and Political.* 2 vols. Salt Lake City: Deseret Steam Press, 1877.

——. August 14, 1873, *Latter-day Saints' Millennial Star* 34 (January 13, 1874): 20.

Spafford, Belle S. "International Singing Mothers Concert Tour." *Relief Society Magazine* 48 (May 1961): 284–92.

——. "Plan for Financing a Relief Society Building." *Relief Society Magazine* 34 (December 1947): 795–99.

——. "Strengthening Community Virtues." *Relief Society Magazine* 46 (January 1959): 33.

——. "Woman's Role as Homemaker." *Relief Society Magazine* 36 (November 1949): 724–27.

Stapley, Delbert L. "The Place of Relief Society in the Indian Program." *Relief Society Magazine* 39 (February 1952): 76–82.

Taylor, Henry D. "Relief Society in the Welfare Plan." *Relief Society Magazine* 56 (March 1969): 164–69.

Thornton, Genevieve. "The Relief Society Social Service Department." *Relief Society Magazine* 18 (January 1931): 14–17.

"Three Welfare Units Joined." *Church News*, April 7, 1973, 4.

Van Wagenen, Lola. "In Their Own Behalf: The Politicization of Mormon Women and the 1870 Franchise." *Dialogue* 24 (Winter 1991): 31–43. A copy of a longer version, entitled " 'A Matter for Astonishment': Woman Suffrage in Territorial Utah," is in the authors' files.

Wagner, Barbara, and Roberta Grant. "The New One-paycheck Family." *Ladies Home Journal*, September 1984, 88.

Weenig, Georgia H. "Central Pacific Mission Relief Society Sends Food and Clothing to Saints in Japan." *Relief Society Magazine* 34 (July 1947): 477.

[Wells, Emmeline B.] "Chronicle of the Relief Society." *Woman's Exponent* 35 (July to November 1906): passim, and 38 (September 1909): 21.

Wells, Emmeline B. "History of the Relief Society." *Woman's Exponent* 31 (February to May 1903): passim; 32 (June 1903): 6–7.

——. "L.D.S. Women of the Past: Personal Impressions." *Woman's Exponent* 36 (February to May 1908), and 37 (June to October 1908): passim.

———. "Why a Woman Should Desire to Be a Mormon." *Woman's Exponent* 36 (December 1907): 39.

Wells, Emmeline B., et al. "Epistle to the Relief Society Concerning These War Times." *Relief Society Magazine* 4 (July 1917): 363–66.

White, Jean Bickmore. "Woman's Place Is in the Constitution: The Struggle for Equal Rights in Utah in 1895." *Utah Historical Quarterly* 42 (Fall 1974): 345.

Whitney, Orson F. "Woman's Work and 'Mormonism'." *Young Woman's Journal* 17 (July 1906): 293.

Williams, Clarissa S. Address. "Relief Society Conference Minutes." *Relief Society Magazine* 10 (December 1923): 621–24.

Winder, Barbara W. "I Love the Sisters of the Church." *Ensign* 14 (May 1984): 54, 59.

———. "Instruments to Accomplish His Purposes." *Ensign* 20 (May 1990): 76–77.

Wirthlin, Joseph L. "Relief Society—An Aid to the Bishops." *Relief Society Magazine* 28 (June 1941): 415–20.

Woodruff, Wilford. "Discourse." *Millennial Star* 56 (April 9, 1894): 225–29.

BOOKS

The Relief Society Magazine: A Legacy Remembered, 1914–1970. Salt Lake City: Deseret Book, 1982.

A Woman's Choices: The Relief Society Legacy Lectures. Salt Lake City: Deseret Book, 1984.

Ahlstrom, Sydney E. *A Religious History of the American People.* New Haven: Yale University Press, 1972.

Alexander, Thomas G. *Mormonism in Transition: A History of the Latter-day Saints, 1890–1930.* Urbana: University of Illinois Press, 1986.

———, ed. *The Mormon People: Their Character and Traditions.* Provo, Utah: Brigham Young University Press, 1980.

Allen, James B., and Glen M. Leonard. *The Story of the Latter-day Saints.* Salt Lake City: Deseret Book, 1976.

Anderson, Carleton Q., Betty Shawcroft, and Robert Compton, eds. and comps. *The Mormons, 100 Years in the San Luis Valley of Colorado.* Albuquerque, N.M.: Adobe Press, 1982.

Anderson, Dawn Hall, and Marie Cornwall, eds. *Women and the Power Within: To See Life Steadily and See It Whole.* Salt Lake City: Deseret Book, 1991.

———. *Women Steadfast in Christ: Talks Selected from the 1991 Women's Conference Co-sponsored by Brigham Young University and the Relief Society.* Salt Lake City: Deseret Book, 1992.

Arrington, Leonard J. *From Quaker to Latter-day Saint: Bishop Edwin D. Woolley.* Salt Lake City: Deseret Book, 1976.

———. *Great Basin Kingdom: An Economic History of the Latter-day Saints 1830–1900.* Cambridge: Harvard University Press, 1958.

Arrington, Leonard J., and Davis Bitton. *The Mormon Experience: A History of the Latter-day Saints*. New York: Alfred A. Knopf, 1979. See esp. chapter 12.

Babbel, Frederick W. *On Wings of Faith*. Salt Lake City: Bookcraft, 1972.

Backman, Milton V., Jr. *American Religions and the Rise of Mormonism*. Salt Lake City: Deseret Book, 1970.

———. *The Heavens Resound*. Salt Lake City: Deseret Book, 1983.

Baldridge, Steven W., comp. *Grafting In*. Jerusalem: Jerusalem Branch, 1989.

Bean, Lee L., Geradine P. Mineau, and Douglas L. Anderson. *Fertility Change on the American Frontier*. Berkeley: University of California Press, 1990.

Beecher, Maureen Ursenbach, and Lavina Fielding Anderson, eds. *Sisters in Spirit: Mormon Women in Historical and Cultural Perspective*. Urbana: University of Illinois Press, 1987.

Beeley, Glenn J. *Handicrafts for Everywoman*. Salt Lake City: Deseret News Press, 1935.

Beeton, Beverly. *Women Vote in the West: The Woman Suffrage Movement 1869–1896*. New York: Garland Publishing, 1986.

Bitton, Davis, and Maureen Ursenbach Beecher, eds. *New Views of Mormon History*. Salt Lake City: University of Utah, 1987.

Blair, Karen J. *The Clubwoman as Feminist: True Womanhood Redefined, 1868–1914*. New York: Holmes and Meier Publishers, 1980.

Bloxham, V. Ben, James R. Moss, and Larry C. Porter. *Truth Will Prevail: The Rise of The Church of Jesus Christ of Latter-day Saints in the British Isles, 1837–1987*. Solihull, England: The Church of Jesus Christ of Latter-day Saints, 1987.

Buhle, Mari Jo, and Paul Buhle. *The Concise History of Woman Suffrage*. Urbana: University of Illinois Press, 1978.

Burgess-Olson, Vicky. *Sister Saints*. Provo, Utah: Brigham Young University Press, 1976.

Bushman, Claudia, ed. *Mormon Sisters*. Cambridge, Mass.: Emmeline Press Limited, 1976.

Bushman, Richard L. *Joseph Smith and the Beginnings of Mormonism*. Urbana: University of Illinois Press, 1984.

Carter, Kate B., ed. *Heart Throbs of the West*. 12 vols. Salt Lake City: Daughters of Utah Pioneers, 1947.

———. *Our Pioneer Heritage*. 15 vols. Salt Lake City: Daughters of Utah Pioneers, 1971.

Clark, Bruce B., and Robert K. Thomas, eds. *Out of the Best Books: An Anthology of Literature*. 5 vols. Salt Lake City: Deseret Book, 1964–1968.

Clark, Carol L., et al. *Knit Together in Love: A Focus for LDS Women in the 1990s*. Salt Lake City: Deseret Book, 1991.

Clark, James R., ed. *Messages of the First Presidency*. 6 vols. Salt Lake City: Bookcraft, 1965–1975.

Collins, Larry, and Dominique Pierre. *Is Paris Burning?* New York: Simon & Schuster, 1965.

Cornwall, Marie, and Susan Howe, eds. *Women of Wisdom and Knowledge: Talks Selected from the BYU Conferences*. Salt Lake City: Deseret Book, 1990.

The Cottonwood Health Care Foundation. [Salt Lake City:] Cottonwood Health Care Foundation, n.d.

Crocheron, Augusta Joyce, comp. *Representative Women of Deseret*. Salt Lake City: J. C. Graham and Co., 1884.

Cross, Whitney R. *The Burned-Over District: The Social and Intellectual History of Enthusiastic Religion in Western New York, 1800–1850*. New York: Cornell University, 1950.

Dewsnup, Verna L., and Katharine M. Larson, comps. *Relief Society Memories: A History of Relief Society in St. George Stake*. Springville, Utah: Art City Publishing Co., 1956.

Ehat, Andrew F., and Lyndon W. Cook, eds. *The Words of Joseph Smith*. Provo, Utah: Brigham Young University, Religious Studies Center, 1980, 347.

Friedman, Jean E., and William G. Shade. *Our American Sisters*. Boston, Mass.: Allen and Bacon, Inc., 1976.

Froiseth, Jennie Anderson, ed. *The Women of Mormonism; or The Story of Polygamy As Told by the Victims Themselves*. Detroit: C. G. G. Paine, 1881.

Gates, Susa Young. *History of the Young Ladies' Mutual Improvement Association*. Salt Lake City: Deseret News, 1911.

———. *Surname Book and Racial History*. Salt Lake City: n.p., 1917.

Godfrey, Kenneth, Audrey M. Godfrey, and Jill Mulvay Derr, eds. *Women's Voices: An Untold History of the Latter-day Saints*. Salt Lake City: Deseret Book, 1982.

The Good Housekeeping Women's Almanac. Editors of *The World Almanac*. New York: Newspaper Enterprise Association, 1977.

Grun, Bernard. *The Timetables of History: A Horizontal Linkage of People and Events*. New York: Simon and Schuster, 1979.

Hartley, William G. *"They Are My Friends": A History of the Joseph Knight Family*. Provo, Utah: Grandin Books, 1986.

Horne, Alice Merrill. *Devotees and Their Shrines: A Handbook of Utah Art*. Salt Lake City: Deseret News, 1914.

Jensen, Elsie K. *Relief Society Memories of Rexburg and North Rexburg Stakes, 1883–1945*. Rexburg, Idaho: The Rexburg Journal, 1949.

Jensen, Oliver. *The Revolt of American Women*. New York: Harcourt, Brace & Co., 1952.

Jessee, Dean C., ed. *Brigham Young's Letters to His Sons*. Salt Lake City: Deseret Book, 1974.

———. *The Papers of Joseph Smith*, Vol. 1. Salt Lake City: Deseret Book, 1989.

———. *The Personal Writings of Joseph Smith*. Salt Lake City: Deseret Book, 1984.

Journal of Discourses. 26 vols. Liverpool and London: Latter-day Saints' Book Depot, 1855–1886; reprint, Salt Lake City, 1967.

Kimball, Camilla Eyring, et al. *Women to Woman: Selected Talks from the BYU Women's Conferences.* Salt Lake City: Deseret Book, 1986.

Kimball, Edward L., and Andrew E. Kimball, Jr. *Spencer W. Kimball.* Salt Lake City: Bookcraft, 1977.

Kimball, Spencer W., et al. *Woman.* Salt Lake City: Deseret Book, 1979.

Kraditor, Aileen S. *The Ideas of the Woman Suffrage Movement, 1890–1920.* New York: Columbia University Press, 1967.

Lemons, Stanley J. *The Woman Citizen: Social Feminism in the 1920s.* [Urbana: University of Illinois Press, 1973.]

Leslie, Mrs. Frank. *A Pleasure Trip from Gotham to the Golden Gate.* New York: G. W. Carleton & Co., 1877.

Leuchtenburg, William E. *The Life History of the United States, Vol. 11: 1933–1945.* Edited by Henry F. Graff. New York: Time, Inc., 1964.

Ludlow, Daniel H., et al. *Encyclopedia of Mormonism.* 4 vols. New York: Macmillan, 1991.

Lyman, Amy Brown. *A Lighter of Lamps: The Life Story of Alice Louise Reynolds.* Provo, Utah: Alice Louise Reynolds Club, 1947.

Lyman, Edward Leo. *Political Deliverance: The Mormon Quest for Statehood.* Urbana and Chicago: University of Illinois Press, 1986.

Madsen, Carol Cornwall, and Susan Staker Oman. *Sisters and Little Saints: One Hundred Years of Primary.* Salt Lake City: Deseret Book, 1979.

McConkie, Bruce R. *A New Witness for the Articles of Faith.* Salt Lake City: Deseret Book, 1985.

Melder, Keith E. *Beginnings of Sisterhood: The American Woman's Rights Movement, 1800–1850.* New York: Schocken Books, 1977.

Miner, Caroline Eyring, and Edward L. Kimball. *Camilla.* Salt Lake City: Deseret Book, 1980.

Newell, Linda King, and Valeen Tippets Avery. *Mormon Enigma: Emma Hale Smith.* Garden City, N.Y.: Doubleday, 1984.

O'Neill, William L. *Everyone Was Brave: The Rise and Fall of Feminism in America.* Chicago: Quadrangle Books, 1969.

Our Common Cause Civilization, Report of the International Congress of Women. New York: National Council of Women of the United States, 1933.

Pascoe, Peggy. *Relations of Rescue: The Search for Female Moral Authority in the American West, 1874–1939.* New York: Oxford University Press, 1990.

Poll, Richard D., et al., eds. *Utah's History.* Provo, Utah: Brigham Young University Press, 1978.

Porter, Larry C., and Susan Easton Black, eds. *The Prophet Joseph Smith: Essays on the Life and Mission of Joseph Smith.* Salt Lake City: Deseret Book, 1988.

Pruette, Lorene, ed. *Women Workers through the Depression.* New York: Macmillan, 1934.

Quinn, D. Michael. *J. Reuben Clark, The Church Years.* Provo, Utah: Brigham Young University Press, 1983.

Roberts, B. H. *A Comprehensive History of The Church of Jesus Christ of Latter-day Saints*. 6 vols. Reprint. Provo, Utah: Brigham Young University Press, 1965.

Seegmiller, Janet Burton. *The Life Story of Robert Taylor Burton*. Robert Taylor Burton Family Organization, 1988.

Shipps, Jan. *Mormonism: The Story of a New Religious Tradition*. Urbana: University of Illinois Press, 1985.

Sillito, John R., ed. *From Cottage to Market: The Professionalization of Women's Sphere*. Salt Lake City: Utah Women's History Association, 1983.

Smith, Joseph, Jr. *History of the Church of Jesus Christ of Latter-day Saints*. 7 vols., 2d ed. rev. Edited by B. H. Roberts. Salt Lake City: The Church of Jesus Christ of Latter-day Saints, Deseret Book, 1971.

Smith, Joseph F. *Gospel Doctrine*. Salt Lake City: Deseret Book, 1939, 1986.

Smith, Lucy [Mack]. *Biographical Sketches of Joseph Smith the Prophet and His Progenitors for Many Generations*. Lamoni, Iowa: Reorganized Church of Jesus Christ of Latter Day Saints, 1912. Also published as *History of Joseph Smith by His Mother, Lucy Mack Smith*. Salt Lake City: Bookcraft, 1979.

Snow, Eliza Roxcy. *Poems Religious, Historical and Political*. 2 vols. Liverpool: S. Richards, 1856, and Salt Lake City: Deseret Steam Press, 1877.

Something Extraordinary: Celebrating Our Relief Society Sisterhood. Salt Lake City: Deseret Book, 1992.

Spafford, Belle S. *A Woman's Reach*. Salt Lake City: Deseret Book, 1974.

Stovall, Mary E., and Carol Cornwall Madsen. *A Heritage of Faith: Talks Selected from the BYU Women's Conferences*. Salt Lake City: Deseret Book, 1988.

———. *As Women of Faith: Talks Selected from the BYU Women's Conferences*. Salt Lake City: Deseret Book, 1989.

Tate, Lucile C. *LeGrand Richards: Beloved Apostle*. Salt Lake City: Bookcraft, 1982.

Thomas, Janet, et al., eds. *That Day in June*. Rexburg, Idaho: Ricks College Press, 1977.

Tullidge, Edward. *The Women of Mormondom*. New York: Tullidge & Crandall, 1877.

Utah Women Suffrage Song Book. Salt Lake City: Woman's Exponent, n.d.

Warenski, Marilyn. *Patriarchs and Politics: The Plights of Mormon Women*. New York: McGraw-Hill, 1978.

Warrum, Noble. *Utah in the World War*. Salt Lake City: Utah State Council of Defense, January 1924.

Watson, Elden Jay, ed. *Manuscript History of Brigham Young*. Salt Lake City: privately published, 1968.

White, Theodore H. *In Search of History*. New York: Warner Books, 1979.

DISSERTATIONS, THESES, AND UNPUBLISHED SCHOLARLY PAPERS

Beecher, Maureen Ursenbach. "The Female Relief Society of Nauvoo." Typescript in the authors' files.

Beecher, Maureen Ursenbach, Carol Cornwall Madsen, and Jill Mulvay Derr. "The Latter-day Saints and Women's Rights, 1870–1920: A Brief Survey." Task Papers in LDS History, no. 29. Salt Lake City: Historical Department of The Church of Jesus Christ of Latter-day Saints, 1979.

Berghout, Edith. "The Effect of War upon the Employment of Women, with Special Reference to Utah." Master's thesis, University of Utah, 1944.

Bishop, Clarence R. "A History of the Indian Student Placement Program." Master's thesis, University of Utah, 1967.

Clark, Carol Lois. "The Effect of Secular Education upon Relief Society Curriculum." Ph.D. diss., University of Utah, 1979.

Conder, Marjorie Draper. "Constancy and Change: Role Prescriptions for Mormon Women as Seen Through Selected Mormon Periodicals, 1883–1984. Master's thesis, University of Utah, 1985.

Cooper, Rex Eugene. "The Promises Made to the Fathers: A Diachronic Analysis of Mormon Covenant Organization with Reference to Puritan Federal Theology." 2 vols. Ph.D. diss., University of Chicago, 1985.

Cornwall, Marie. "Women and the Church: An Organizational Analysis." Typescript. Relief Society Headquarters Files.

Cowan, Richard O. "The 'Reformation' of the 1860s: A Remarkable Period of Ecclesiastical Expansion." Typescript in the authors' files.

Derr, Jill Mulvay. "A History of Social Services in The Church of Jesus Christ of Latter-day Saints, 1916–1984." Typescript in authors' Files

Embry, Jessie L. "Relief Society Grain Storage Program, 1876–1940." Master's thesis, Brigham Young University, 1974.

Esplin, Ronald K. "The Emergence of Brigham Young and the Twelve to Mormon Leadership, 1830–1841." Ph.D. diss., Brigham Young University, 1981.

Evans, Vella Neil. "Woman's Image in Authoritative Discourse: A Rhetorical Analysis." Ph.D. diss., University of Utah, 1985.

Godfrey, Audrey M. "Starting from Scraps: The Mormon Village Relief Society." Paper presented at the 1980 Sperry Symposium, Brigham Young University.

Hayward, Barbara. "Utah's Anti-Polygamy Society, 1878–1884." Master's thesis, Brigham Young University, 1980.

Hill, Marvin S. "The Role of Christian Primitivism in the Origin and Development of the Mormon Kingdom, 1830–1844." Ph.D. diss., University of Chicago, 1968.

James, Kimberly Jensen. "Between Two Fires: Women on the 'Underground' of Mormon Polygamy." Master's thesis, Brigham Young University, 1981.

Lindsay, Rao Humphreys. "A History of the Missionary Activities of the Church of Jesus Christ of Latter-day Saints in the Near East, 1884–1929." Master's thesis, Brigham Young University, 1958.

Madsen, Carol Cornwall. "A Mormon Woman in Victorian America." Ph.D. diss., University of Utah, 1985.

———. "Remember the Women of Zion: A Study of the Editorial Content of the Woman's Exponent, a Mormon Woman's Journal." Master's thesis, University of Utah, 1977.

———. "The Mormon–Gentile Female Relationship in Nineteenth Century Utah." Copy in the authors' files.

Mann, Patricia Ann. "A History of the *Relief Society Magazine* 1914–1970." Master's thesis, Brigham Young University, 1971.

Marquis, Kathleen. " 'Diamond Cut Diamond': Mormon Women and the Cult of Domesticity in the Nineteenth Century." University of Michigan Papers in Women's Studies 2.2 (1974): 105–23.

Porter, Larry C. "A Study of the Origins of the Church of Jesus Christ of Latter-day Saints in the States of New York and Pennsylvania, 1816–1831." Ph.D. diss., Brigham Young University, 1971.

Stovall, Mary E., and Carol Cornwall Madsen. "Accomplishments of the Women's Research Institute, 1983–1988." Copy in files of Women's Research Institute.

VanOrden, Bruce A. "Return of the Prodigal: W. W. Phelps' Service as Joseph Smith's Political Clerk in Nauvoo." Paper presented at the Nauvoo Symposium, Brigham Young University, September 21, 1989. Copy in the authors' files.

INDEX

Single adults, 377, 392–93
Sipila, Helvi, 372
Sloan, Edward, 109
Smart, William B., 376–77
Smeath, Frances, 418
Smith, Amanda, 38, 75, 106, 457n.76
Smith, Barbara Bradshaw: becomes R.S. president, 347; photo of, 348; on priesthood and R.S., 348; on disaster plan need, 353; turns wheat funds over, 355; and Monument to Women, 361, 363; opposes to ERA, 367; on Donahue show, 368, 499n.53; assesses IWY conference responses, 373; on ideals, 377; speaks to women, 378; travels to South America, 382; vision of, 382–83
Smith, Bathsheba W., 49; homes of, in Nauvoo, 23–24; child of, falls ill, 25; attends first R.S. meeting, 27; on Prophet's teachings, 53–54; helps prepare Nauvoo Temple, 64; describes preparations for exodus, 64; on women studying medicine, 106; moves to demand franchise, 111; counselor to Zina Young, 128; on Relief Society Building, 142–43; R.S. president, 151; description of, 152; observes 84th birthday, 156; on R.S. study topics, 161; decries changed building plans, 175; photo of, 176; last message and death of, 179; on worthiness to perform sacred functions, 220; on R.S. and priesthood, 447–48n.89; temple grant established in honor of, 485n.88
Smith, David A., 237
Smith, David Hiram, 39 (photo)
Smith, Dennis, 360; statue by, 362 (photo)
Smith, Emma Hale: supports husband, 6; is baptized, 8;

revelation (D&C 25) addressed to, 9–10; as "elect lady," 10, 28; flees Missouri with family, 19; writes to husband in Liberty Jail, 19; at first R.S. meeting, 27; first R.S. president, 28–29; looks for for "extraordinary occasions," 31; recommends needy sister's needlework, 31; urges overcoming evil feelings, 36; petitions Governor Carlin, 38–39; picture of, 39; receives endowment, 55; opposes plural marriage, 60–63
Smith, Emma S., 156, 173
Smith, Frederick M., 263, 483n.57
Smith, George A., 23–24, 152, 452n.47
Smith, George Albert, 215, 263, 287, 307, 308, 310, 321, 336, 483n.57
Smith, Hortense Child, 494n.78
Smith, Hyrum, 60
Smith, Ida B., 200, 206, 349
Smith, Joseph, Jr.: turns key to women, 1; first vision of, 3; on fullness of times, 3; translates and publishes Book of Mormon, 5–7; on Kirtland temple, 15; at temple dedication, 16; on women's organization, 27, 41, 445–46n.61; directs first R.S. meeting, 28; on purpose of R.S., 30; donates five dollars to R.S., 31; on women's charitable feelings, 31–32; on being long-suffering, 36; on treatment of husbands, 37; on charity toward sinners, 37; on praying for leaders, 38; writs for arrest of, 38; on R.S. officers, 42, 43; on record keeping, 42; on body's need for every member, 43, 432; April 28 discourse of, 43–47; on salvation for dead, 52; on endowment, 54; and plural marriage, 56; leaves Nauvoo but returns, 59–60; foreshadows end